BEGINNINGS & BEYOND

5th Edition

Guest Editors

Edith M. Dowley
Olivia N. Saracho
Elizabeth Jones
Jim Greenman
Louise Derman-Sparks
Jonah Edelman

Ann Miles Gordon
Consultant

Kathryn Williams Browne
Cañada College
Redwood City, California
DeAnza College
Cupertino, California

Delmar
Thomson Learning™

Africa • Australia • Canada • Denmark • Japan • Mexico • New Zealand • Philippines
Puerto Rico • Singapore • Spain • United Kingdom • United States

NOTICE TO THE READER

Publisher does not warrant or guarantee any of the products described herein or perform any independent analysis in connection with any of the product information contained herein. Publisher does not assume, and expressly disclaims, any obligation to obtain and include information other than that provided to it by the manufacturer.

The reader is expressly warned to consider and adopt all safety precautions that might be indicated by the activities herein and to avoid all potential hazards. By following the instructions contained herein, the reader willingly assumes all risks in connection with such instructions.

The Publisher makes no representation or warranties of any kind, including but not limited to, the warranties of fitness for particular purpose or merchantability, nor are any such representations implied with respect to the material set forth herein, and the publisher takes no responsibility with respect to such material. The publisher shall not be liable for any special, consequential, or exemplary damages resulting, in whole or part, from the readers' use of, or reliance upon, this material.

Delmar Staff

Business Unit Director: Susan Simpfenderfer
Executive Editor: Marlene McHugh Pratt
Acquisitions Editor: Erin O'Connor Traylor
Editorial Assistant: Alexis Ferraro
Executive Marketing Manager: Donna Lewis

Executive Production Manager: Wendy Troeger
Project Editor: Christopher Leonard
Production Editor: Sandra Woods
Cover Design: Timothy J. Conners

Printed in the United States of America
5 6 7 8 9 10 XXX 05 04 03 02

For more information, contact Delmar, 3 Columbia Circle, PO Box 15015, Albany, NY 12212-0515; or find us on the World Wide Web at http://www.delmar.com

Library of Congress Cataloging-in-Publication Data
Gordon, Ann Miles.
    Beginnings & beyond / Ann Miles Gordon, Kathryn
Williams Browne; guest editors, Edith Dowley…[et al.].—5th ed.
        p.   cm.
    Includes bibliographical references and index.
    ISBN 0-8273-8420-3
    1. Early childhood education. 2. Early childhood education—
Curricula. 3. Child development. I. Browne, Kathryn Williams. II. Dowley, Edith.
III. Title. IV. Title: Beginnings and beyond.
    LB1139.23.G663   2000
    372.21—dc21   99-21476
                                                    CIP

Contents

What Is the Field of Early Childhood Education?   1

Guest Editorial: Early Childhood Education in the Shipyards by Edith M. Dowley

Chapter 1   History of Early Childhood Education   3

Chapter 2   Types of Programs   40

Guest Editorial: The Essence of Our Mission
by Louise Derman-Sparks

Section Six

How Do We Teach for Tomorrow? 550

Guest Editorial: Take a Stand For Children
by Jonah Edelman

Chapter 15 Issues and Trends in Early Childhood Education 552

Foreword by Carol Brunson Phillips

Whenever a book has enough lasting power to reach its fifth edition, we can safely assume there must be something unusual about it. In the case of *Beginnings and Beyond*, it is the way Ann Gordon and Kate Browne respond to the human development diversity issues.

As child development textbooks go, many have taken on the challenge to be sensitive and respectful of diversity, particularly cultural diversity. But they often pursue that challenge by making mention of cultural differences in random places in the text, or in some cases, devoting a chapter to the topic. What we read in these pages is quite different.

To make genuine progress in how we address human diversity, we need to find strategies that will take our thinking beyond the superficial approaches that often stem from the desire to "respect" culture and cultural differences. Rather than learning merely to reserve judgment about cultural habits, we want to break the habit of thinking about children of white European ancestry as having *human* qualities while thinking about children of black African ancestry as having *cultural* qualities. We want to fundamentally change our subconscious responses, so that western Eurocentric values no longer serve as the standard against which everything is judged or measured. Instead, we would learn to see them as one among many cultural takes on the world.

This kind of shift in perspective might well be transformational in that it could free us to create the kind of new knowledge in human development that our science strives for—knowledge upon which to craft program practices that are liberating for children's growth and development in ways we never thought possible.

Though no textbook alone can transform our thinking in this way, the textbooks of our discipline can and must engage us in this change process. By providing us with some enabling experiences through what we read and are asked to think about, writers can engage us in the work it will take to get western Europe out of the center of our thought universe. But perhaps more important, they can cast us—the readers—into the role of change agents. Each of us consequently can become active in reconstructing what we know about children and families.

Toward this end, various strategies are useful. First, new facts must be added to our child development database, facts that expand our knowledge beyond the limits of its traditional core. In this text for example, the fact that the history of early childhood goes back to a time *before* European thinkers, to the Nile Valley civilization, is important. Furthermore, we are pointed to obscure citations and sources of information and are introduced to researchers and theorists from a wide variety of cultural backgrounds whose views are often neglected elsewhere. Through this practice of juxtaposing new material against the traditional, an important message comes through: our perspective on human development is dynamic and changing, and what we do "know" today is limited, incomplete, unfinished work.

Second, we must be reminded of our ethnocentrism and helped to be reflective about it. Up-front and straightforward statements punctuating this theme can be found throughout this text—for example statements such as "these things are true for one cultural group but not another." These messages are important in situating western European ancestry, general dialect, standard-English-speaking white children as a cultural group, and they serve as reminders to help us break the habit of thinking of them just as human children. Further, as we are told that the earliest theories were based on observations of male or white subjects and are admonished to not use one standard for "normal," we are encouraged to question the generalizeability of our knowledge. Thus we are challenged to become and remain conscious of the risk of distortion in how we view developing children and their families.

Third, we must consciously shift our goal from an emphasis on multiculturalism to an emphasis on pluralism. As the melting pot/tossed salad debate is unveiled in the text, the opposing and contrasting views among various ethnic and cultural groups are presented. Rising from these are important developmental topics, such as group identity and bicultural development, posed and effectively discussed without falling into the traps of the either/or mentality of traditional melting pot multiculturalism. Thus a potential new frontier looms as an ideal, where the preservation of home culture is an important developmental goal for children and families without having to be viewed as a threat to maintaining a common civilization.

Fourth, bias must be identified as a contributor to underdevelopment and discussed in its broadest sense. Topics such as biracial identity development and homophobia, not raised as a matter of course in child development texts, are discussed here in the search for ways to make practices appropriate to development. We are given permission to address such topics as a matter of course and a vocabulary to use when addressing them. Bringing these topics to the discussion table adds to our ability to directly address bias and stereotypes—what they look like in children's behavior and what teachers and other adults ought to do to prevent them from being obstacles to development.

Fifth and finally, we must promote activism among child development professionals in direct and indirect ways. Our texts must tell us, as this one does, that eliminating inequality in our society will require a national reform agenda. Topics such as children's rights and strategies for social action must be discussed in our child development courses, and we must give students an abundance of examples to guide their thinking to new places. Further, as we do here, we must hear from an assemblage of the best voices in the field to lead us in this view—Louise Derman-Sparks, Frances Wardle, and Jonah Edelman. In so doing, a dynamic quality to the discipline will be assured.

It is very encouraging to have a view of our field that expects it to do better than it already has done. And it is empowering to know that the change requires each of us to participate. So insofar as this fifth edition of *Beginnings and Beyond* is full of the action and energy one would expect in the place where change happens, it only awaits you to jump in and get busy.

Preface

The new century is here, bringing with it continuing challenges for those who work with young children. One of the most significant tasks is responding to the call for culturally and ethnically sensitive teaching practices in all early childhood settings and programs, creating an atmosphere for teaching tolerance and appreciating diversity. We must teach children to respond positively to the full range of human differences. This responsibility is the dominant focus for the fifth edition of *Beginnings and Beyond*.

If a textbook reflects the authors' viewpoint, this edition is a witness to our belief that the issues of diversity must be a major theme for the early childhood community in the new millennium. Creating classrooms and early childhood settings that reflect diversity and equality is no longer an option but a mandate based on the multicultural character of the world in which we live in the year 2000 and beyond. Although recent demographic changes in the United States first prompted our interest, our concern stems from the belief that every child and family is unique and that they deserve the respect and affirmation of their cultural identity. Therefore, this edition is *infused* with a multicultural approach to teaching and learning to reflect more accurately the wide diversity found in today's children, families, teachers, and caregivers and to help prospective teachers and caregivers increase

their sensitivity to different cultural practices and values.

Early childhood professionals who are preparing to work with young children must understand two separate and distinct aspects of diversity. They must prepare children to live in a world of differences and to live with diversity. At the same time, teachers and caregivers must attend to their own learning as persons who live and work in a diverse society. Each adult needs to understand that we all operate out of a cultural context and that our own family background and life experiences influence what we do with young children. Our approach to the issues of diversity in this edition emphasizes this twofold outlook on multiculturalism.

The process of *infusion* means integrating multicultrual awareness into the learning environment, incorporating relevant cultural perspectives and frames of reference appropriate to each setting. Concepts of diversity are elaborated and expanded *within the context* of the current curriculum and teaching practices. We used this same strategy to incorporate diverse cultural, ethnic, and racial perspectives and viewpoints into the existing content of *Beginnings and Beyond*. Our goal is to have a positive awareness of equity and cultural sensitivity permeate teachers' thinking, the programs they plan, and the people they serve.

Beginnings and Beyond has always been known for its inclusive nature and multicultural focus, yet for this edition we felt it needed expansion and enhancement. Therefore, we had the previous edition analyzed by reviewers with expertise in and awareness of issues of diversity in early childhood settings. To raise our own level of consciousness, throughout the revision we worked closely with a diversity consultant who critiqued the content of each chapter to enhance the overall multicultural early childhood focus of the book. Through her insights, we looked at each chapter and made appropriate changes that reflect the ethnic and cultural diversity in today's world. Our goal was to infuse this edition of *Beginnings and Beyond* with diverse perspectives.

Fifteen years ago, our initial purpose in writing this book was "to promote the competence and effectiveness of new teachers through a presentation of basic knowledge, skills, attitudes, and philosophies . . . based on the premise that new teachers must have opportunities to learn fundamental skills as they begin their teaching experience." In the Preface to the first edition, we wrote "We believe that weaving a multicultural perspective and consciousness throughout the text will emphasize it as an overriding issue more clearly than treating it separately." That commitment has been strengthened by the inclusion of material that will enrich the reader's understanding of diversity and equity issues in the early childhood field today.

OTHER NEW AND REVISED FEATURES OF THE FIFTH EDITION

- *Our Diverse World*, which first appeared in the fourth edition, has been expanded and refreshed throughout each chapter. Content in the text that is related to cultural diversity, anti-bias curricula, and children with special needs is highlighted by this icon.

- A footnote at the bottom of the pages provides additional information that will enrich the student's understanding of the issues related to cultural pluralism and inclusion. A primary function of Our Diverse World is to help students learn that the children they teach will have to interact in new and different ways with others in a world grown small.

- *Developmentally Appropriate Practice (DAP)* is clearly the subtheme of *Beginnings and Beyond*. From its inception 15 years ago, we stressed the importance of creating programs and building curriculum based on an understanding of the nature of the child and the factors affecting a child's growth and development. We have maintained the feature "Word Pictures" in Chapter 3, which describe the major characteristics of children from infancy and have expanded those charts through age 8 years. As these are applied throughout the text, students become familiar with expected behaviors in young children as a frame of reference for creating programs and curriculum, which respond to children's interests as well as their needs. NAEYC's decade of experience in the definition and application of *developmentally appropriate practice* has given us further insights, which are reflected throughout the book, but particularly in Chapters 2, 7, 9, 10, and 11. Below we note how some of the specific Guest Editorials and Focus Boxes complement and inform DAP.

- *Guest Editorials and Focus Boxes* continue to lend other experienced voices to the text. Nationally renowned leaders in the field of early childhood education address relevant and important issues within each chapter and at the beginning of each section of the book. In this millennium anniversary edition, we include both new and old editorials and focus boxes. In response to suggestions that more persons of color or people who would underscore our multicultural viewpoint participate, we reprised some contributions from previous editions and then added a fresh emphasis from new contributors.

New Guest Editorials from *Olivia Saracho* and *Jonah Edelman* challenge us in two different arenas. Saracho reminds us of the importance of using a child's family language and culture as a foundation for learning, and Edelman propels us out of the classroom and into the role of child advocacy. It seemed obvious and appropriate that *Louise Derman-Sparks*'s previous Guest Editorial on freeing us and our children from bias and stereotypes be included in this edition.

Focus Boxes in this edition, which specifically address multiculturalism, are eclectic in their themes:

● *Frances Wardle* speaks to the unique needs of multiracial and multiethnic children and families, and *Hedy Nai-Lin Chang* encourages us to look at the beneficial aspects of bilingualism.

● *Janice Hale*'s article, reprinted from a previous edition, outlines some of the critical issues she believes affect the achievement of African American students, and *Stacey York* explores the teacher's role in culturally relevant education.

● *Janet Gonzalez-Meña* combines a previous article with new insights on how our observations of children are influenced by our own culture.

● In a touching and hopeful reprint, *Gretchen Buchenholz* describes early childhood programs, which include homeless, disabled children, as well as those children who face terminal illness.

The theme of developmentally appropriate practice (DAP) is reinforced in a significant way by new Guest Editorials and Focus Boxes and several that appeared in previous editions. *Larry Schweinhart* makes a strong case for child-initiated learning, and *Nancy Barbour's* article on child assessment outlines a holistic, integrated process of documenting children's growth and development. Both are new to this edition. From past editions, we brought back those that have particular relevance to developmentally appropriate practice:

● In her introduction to Section 3, *Elizabeth Jones* defines the developmentally appropriate teacher at the same time that she reinforces the process of play as the primary foundation for learning. *Ron Lally*, in his article on play, notes the many purposes of play, depending on the individual child and the observer's interpretation.

● Echoing Jones's emphasis on play, *Jim Greenman*, introducing the section on environments, speaks of play spaces designed for individual children who learn through interactions with people and play materials. *Paula Carreiro*'s view of outdoor space reflects the belief that all aspects of development—physical, social, and cognitive—are integrated into the program, indoors and out of doors. *Rebecca New*'s discussion of the total environment of the Reggio Emilia schools highlights a developmentally appropriate school system in Italy, which has attained international prominence.

- *Elizabeth Crary* and *Cary Buzzelli* both apply sound developmental principles in their articles. Both writings suggest ways in which teachers can use what they know about each child and a variety of strategies to help them solve problems.

- There is no one name more associated with DAP than *Sue Bredekamp*. In Chapter 10, Bredekamp spells out the benefits of accreditation as a way to improve program quality, and in Chapter 11 she articulates some of the basic components that go into a high-quality experience for young children.

The remainder of the book includes a variety of articles by guest authors that speak to a number of issues. Two women provide moving and graphic portraits of historical importance. From the first edition of *Beginning and Beyond*, we replay the late *Edith Dowley*'s fascinating account of the Kaiser Shipyard child care centers during World War II. *Elizabeth Bradburn* provides us with a deeper sense of one of the field's greater pioneers. *Jackie McCormick* gives a personal account of family child care, and *John Chattin-McNichols* highlights Montessori programs. Developmentalists *Laura Berk* and *Helen Bee* provide thoughtful articles, respectively, on Vygotsky's contribution to the field and a critique of Piaget's work. *Yvonne Ricketts* shares a parent's view of child care, which appeared in a previous edition, and *Carol Sharpe*, a new contributor, describes an exciting professional development project, the California Child Development Permit Matrix.

We believe that the Guest Editorials and Focus Boxes in this edition bring you "The Best of *Beginnings and Beyond*."

- *Photographs and Graphics* communicate an immediacy about children and their environments. All photographs are new and demonstrate a wide variety of age groups, representing many cultures, and early childhood settings. Additional charts, plus a new layout, will appeal to instructors and students by making the information more accessible.

- *The Last Chapter*, "Issues and Trends in Early Childhood Education," has been modified to reflect social and political realities of the day, with particular emphasis on demographics and changing populations. With Chapter 1, the last chapter serves as a bookend for the text, reflecting the continuum from past to future.

- *The Appendixes* have been changed to enhance the stronger emphasis on supporting material for diversity and pluralism issues. The *Timeline for Early Childhood Education* continues to serves as a historical record of the field and will add to classroom discussions throughout the semester. NAEYC's Statement of Commitment serves as a constant reminder of the moral guidelines adopted by the early childhood profession. New to this edition is an excerpt from NAEYC position statement *Responding to Linguistic and Cultural Diversity—Recommendations for Effective Early Childhood Education*, which underscores the text's emphasis on culturally sensitive teaching by focusing on the issue of language diversity. Also new are Appendix D, a list of organizations that serve the early childhood community as resources and advocates, and additions to the glossary.

ABOUT THE AUTHORS

Ann Gordon has been in the field of early childhood for more than 40 years as a teacher of young children, a teacher of parents, and a teacher of college students. She has taught in laboratory schools, church-related centers, and private and public preschool and kindergarten programs. While at Stanford, Ann was at the Bing Nursery School for 11 years and was a lecturer in the Psychology Department. For 10 years she also served as an adjunct faculty member in four colleges, teaching the full gamut of early childhood courses. Ann served as executive director of the National Association of Episcopal Schools for 14 years, where more than 1100 early childhood programs were a part of her network. She is now consulting in the areas of early childhood curriculum governance and professional development. Ann is the mother of two grown children. As a doting first-time grandmother, Ann now brings an enhanced perspective on infants and toddlers to *Beginnings and Beyond*, as well as up-to-date experience with center-based child care. She is delighted that her granddaughter is enrolled in an NAEYC-accredited center!

Kathryn Williams Browne has been a teacher most of her adult life: a teacher of young children for nearly 20 years, a guide for parents of the families she served, and, more recently, a parent educator since 1990, and an instructor of college students for more than 15 years. Her work with children includes nursery school, parent cooperatives, full-day child care, prekindergarten and bilingual preschools, and kindergarten and first grade. Kate's background in child development research led her to choose early childhood education, for to truly understand child development one needs to *be* with children. While a Head Teacher at Bing Nursery School and a lecturer with Stanford University, Kate developed a professional relationship with Ann, which blossomed into work in teacher and parent education. Moreover, *Beginnings and Beyond* has been influenced by Kate's role as a parent; her two children were born during the first two editions, so the book grew along with them. Recent work as a consultant and public elementary School Board Trustee has offered Kate new perspectives into schools, reform, and collaboration. Perhaps most important, Kate has been teaching in two community colleges over the last decade. Working closely with her students, she has been given constructive insights that inform this text in every revision. The balance of career and family, of work *with* children and *for* children, and of the special challenges of early childhood as a professional field guide her work.

Ann and Kate are also co-authors of *Guiding Young Children in a Diverse Society* (Allyn & Bacon, 1996).

ACKNOWLEDGMENTS

By the fifth edition, a book takes on a life of its own, transcending its original vision by integrating valuable information from many sources. First and foremost, we are grateful to *Ruth Robinson Saxton* from Georgia State University for her ongoing guidance as our diversity consultant. She led us into a greater awareness of our own limitations and enriched our own understanding of culturally inclusive practices in early childhood programs.

Of immeasurable help with this edition were the reviewers who challenged us with their questions, questioned our assumptions, and in so many ways, assisted us in clarifying our intent and focusing our content. We gratefully acknowledge the contributions of:

Linda Aiken
Southwestern Community College
Sylva, NC

Alice Beyrent
Hesser College
Manchester, NH

Martha Dever
Utah State University
Logan, UT

Judith Lindman
Rochester Community and Technical
  College
Rochester, MN

Colleen Olsen
Cuyahoga Community College
Cleveland, OH

Ruth Saxton
Georgia State University
Atlanta, GA

Stacey York
Minneapolis Community and Technical
  College
Minneapolis, MN

Fresh insights, new voices, and added perspectives are the gifts of our Guest Editors and Focus Box article individuals. To past and present authors, we thank you for your unique contribution to this edition: the late Edith Dowley, Olivia Saracho, Elizabeth Jones, Jim Greenman, Louise Derman-Sparks, Jonah Edelman, Elizabeth Bradburn, Jackie McCormick, John Chattin-McNichols, Frances Wardle, Janice Hale, Laura Berk, Helen Bee, Stacey York, Janet Gonzalez-Meña, Elizabeth Crary, Yvonne Ricketts, Rebecca New, Nancy Barbour, Sue Bredekamp, Ron Lally, Paula Carreiro, Larry Schweinhart, Hedy Chang, Cary Buzzelli, Gretchen Buchenholz, and Carol Sharpe.

Thanks, too, to Jim Gordon and Barbara Glendenning for their research efforts, to Mara Berman of Delmar for her able assistance, and, always, to Karen McLaughlin for too many things to name.

We appreciate the patience and forbearance throughout this project of our families: David Gordon and Marty, Julia, and Campbell Browne. Their willingness to put up with another year of manuscript deadlines made a significant contribution.

Finally, we acknowledge the continuing pleasure our collaboration on this book brings to us both personally and professionally. "The Book" reflects over 15 years of working together on a project that grows and changes with each new edition. Each of us receives from the other a depth of support, humor, and affection that enhances the written words, the philosophy, and the finished product. This collaboration has deepened over the life of *Beginnings and Beyond* to one of mutual respect and admiration—a bonus to a friendship begun long ago.

Beginnings and Beyond expresses our professional outlook but also carries our indelible personal stamp. Photos of our children have adorned many pages of past editions, particularly those of Julia and Campbell Browne. With this edition we introduce Ann Gordon's granddaughter Abra, who begins a new generation of family involvement with this book.

We are most appreciative of our many loyal readers who chose *Beginnings and Beyond* for their classes.

Dedication

To Abra, my delightful granddaughter. May you grow to love all that is good and just and kind and come to know the joy of living in a world of many peoples, many cultures, many voices.—*AMG*

To those who have opened my eyes—
Students of Cañada College's Early Childhood Education classes
Parents of DeAnza College's "Parenting by Heart" classes
Colleagues Dianne Eyer, Kathleen Burson, Marsha Howard, and Ruth Saxton.—*KWB*

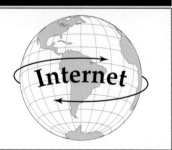 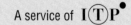

What Is the Field of Early Childhood Education?

Guest Editorial

EARLY CHILDHOOD EDUCATION IN THE SHIPYARDS

Edith M. Dowley

If you are thinking about working with young children as a career, perhaps you are wondering how early childhood education compares in prestige and importance with elementary or secondary education. Does it have a background of tradition? Is it truly a profession with the potential for growth and change? Can a student preparing to work with young children today look forward to a challenging, intellectually stimulating, and rewarding future in an early childhood profession?

My career with young children began during the Great Depression, a time of arrested economic growth and widespread unemployment. My undergraduate major and minors were in fields where job opportunities were, at the time, apparently hopeless. However, with the help of wise

counselors and some very good luck, I spent two years in graduate study with outstanding professors of child development and worked as an assistant with nursery school teachers chosen as models of artistic technique and effective nurturers of young children. I found working with children so challenging and rewarding, I made it my life's work! Forty years later, when I "retired," I could truthfully say I was never disappointed.

All but two of those years were spent in university settings where research and theory questioned, modified, and sometimes changed our attitudes, interpretations, and reactions to child growth and behavior. They were years of growing and learning, of planning, struggling, and some accomplishments. No two years— actually no two days—were ever the same.

But this editorial is about a different, unforgettable experience I had with young children, far removed from a university setting, in a period of national crisis. It occurred during World War II, in an innovative project that not only was a remarkable solution to a problem for those times, but that also has special relevance and appropriateness, I believe, for the present.

In early 1943, the Kaiser Shipbuilding Corporation was faced with the necessity of employing more women to meet the stepped-up schedule for producing warships in their two shipyards in Portland, Oregon. Of the 12,000 women already employed, one third of them were mothers who had no place to leave their preschool children while they worked. Absenteeism among women was running

50 percent higher than among men and was contributing to slow-downs in production that seriously affected the war effort. The reasons most women gave for being late or for missing work were that the baby-sitter did not show up or a child was ill and could not be left at home until seen by a doctor. Henry Kaiser, reportedly in typical fashion, responded to the dilemma by saying that if mothers were worried about leaving their children, he would provide them with nurseries. He resolved to build the finest child care centers in the country.

Within a few weeks, architects were drawing plans for two child service centers to be placed at the entrances to the shipyards—one at Swan Island and the other at Oregon Yard. Paid for by the United States Maritime Commission and absorbed as part of the cost of building ships, these centers turned out to be not only very fine centers, but also the largest child care centers in the world.

Dr. Lois Meek Stolz, a well-known leader in the fields of child development and early childhood education, was chosen by Edgar Kaiser to direct the two child service centers. She planned the entire children's program and made provisions for staffing the centers. She brought James L. Hymes, Jr., former editor of *Progressive Education*, to the program as Manager of the Child Service Centers, and she recruited Dr. Miriam Lowenberg,

a well-known nutritionist, to be responsible for the children's nutritional needs.

The Staff

Each center had a supervisor who was responsible for the total operation over all three shifts— day, swing, and graveyard. There were group supervisors, head teachers, assistant teachers, dieticians, and nurses under her direction. In addition, each center had a social worker who served as a liaison between the teachers in the centers and the parents in the shipyard. All of the staff members were recruited from nursery school training centers throughout the United States. All of the teachers had college degrees, and the supervisors and most of the head teachers had master's degrees and years of experience with children. They were young, energetic women "chosen for their comfortable qualities as well as for their scientific knowledge" (Jean Muir, from an article she wrote for the *Oregon Journal*, Sunday, December 12, 1943).

The Setting

The teaching staff began arriving in late October as the finishing touches were being made on the buildings. They found, to their delight, that the centers, although temporary, were beautifully and functionally designed. Each center was built around a large, octagonally shaped courtyard with four

wading pools where children could play away from the hazards of traffic. The courtyard itself was grass-covered, with a hard-surfaced area designed for wheel toys that extended around the perimeter. Because of the long rainy season in Portland, covered porches, equipped with jungle gyms, climbing boxes, slides, and large, hollow blocks, connected the interior rooms to the grassy areas. Children could thus enjoy vigorous outdoor play every day of the year, regardless of the weather.

A cog-wheel plan of architecture provided for 15 rectangular playrooms (26′ by 49′) extending out from a central circular corridor. Between and opposite every two playrooms were smaller rooms for teachers' meetings, special play, or story times. Each of the 15 playrooms had windows on two sides to provide light and interesting views of the outside world. Window seats, low enough for children to sit on, were built so that the children could curl up on them and watch the ships, cars, trucks, and cranes in the busy shipyard below where their parents were working. This proved to be a special delight as darkness came and the yards were lighted, showing the outlines of the ships and their reflections in the water.

The interior colors were soft pastel shades of blue, yellow, and apricot, depending on the exposure of the individual room. Adult-height counterspace covered the expansive shelving where children could readily reach the many unit blocks, toys, games, books, and puzzles that were neatly and meaningfully stored there. Children's lockers, arranged like a dressing room unit, provided hooks for coats and jackets, a shelf for caps, mittens, and art work to take home, and a place for safekeeping of special possessions. Each room had its own toilet room with toilets and wash basins scaled to child size. Wash cloths and towels provided by the center were hung on hooks within the children's reach and marked with individual symbols matching the ones on their lockers.

There was a large room in each center, separated from the playrooms, where children could be cared for when they were ill. Comfortable cribs, like those used in children's hospitals, were placed in glass-sided cubicles that allowed children quiet places to sleep, eat, or sit up and play while recovering from colds, coughs, earaches, or upset tummies. A registered nurse was on duty at all times in the infirmary, and teachers planned and provided the play materials and projects for both the bed patients and those who were up and about.

Each center had a fully equipped, large, modern kitchen that was adequate for serving meals and snacks, over a 24-hour day, to some 400 children and their teachers. Large, heated rolling carts were available to deliver the china, silverware, and food to each room, where children were served at small, low tables.

Usually, five children and a teacher dined together each day as a "family."

The architects thoughtfully included one additional feature: several large, square bath tubs raised two steps above the floor. These tubs allowed teachers, when necessary or desirable, to bathe a child without bending over. These tubs also provided safe places for children to "swim" and splash and engage in relaxing water play.

Opening Days

The teaching staff, of which I was a part, arrived in Portland about two weeks before the centers opened. Until we found more permanent places to live, we were housed in a dormitory for female workers at the Swan Island shipyard. Each evening, we met with Dr. Hymes and the supervisors, building a common but shared philosophy about child care and our roles as educators. During the days, we prepared the playrooms in anticipation of the day when the children would arrive.

Oregon Center, where I was a group supervisor, opened its doors on November 8, 1943, to children, age 18 months to six years, of parents working on the day and swing shifts. On that day, a total of 67 children came to the center. We were, of course, very disappointed in this turnout. We realized, however, that the majority of people in the area had never even heard of a nursery school and were not able to

imagine a children's center that would stay open twelve months a year, six days a week, and twenty-four hours a day! So we planned "open house" on Sundays and invited the public to tour the centers. We went down into the shipyards to talk to the workers about the child services available. Feature articles with many photographs appeared in the local newspapers. Gradually, more children were enrolled. By Christmas of that year, there were over 100 children being cared for in the center. In January, the graveyard shift was started, as was a Saturday and after-school program for older children. By August 27th, when Oregon Shipyard went on a seven-day work week, the Center was operating seven days a week, with an average daily attendance of 370 children.

Everything possible was done to keep workers on the job of building ships. Parents paid only nominal fees for child service: 75 cents a day for one child in a family and 50 cents for each additional child, paid by the week. If a child came seven days a week, parents were only charged for six days.

The Children

The children we worked with in the Center were much the same as the children most of us had worked with before. Each was a unique individual, with distinctive characteristics and special needs. They had strong ties to their parents and families and depended on them for love, approval, and support. Mothers or fathers brought the children to their rooms at the Center each day before their shifts began, and picked them up after the shift ended. Day-shift children often spent nine or more hours in the Center as that was the longest shift. Day-shift parents were always in a hurry, it seemed, and were less able to spend time helping their children make the transition from home to school. Separating from their mothers and fathers was painful for some children at first. It was probably hardest of all for the 18-month-olds and two-year-olds to adjust to being left with strangers in a strange place for such long hours. Some of these little ones, most of whom had not yet begun to talk, cried for long periods and were difficult to comfort. Some refused to let anyone remove their coats, snowsuits, or hats all day, clinging to them as perhaps the last link with home and mother. They would stay on their feet, apart from the others even during snacks or meal times, unwilling to sit or to accept food from a strange table. Eventually, hunger would overcome this reluctance, and when teachers wisely left finger foods within their sight and reach, they devoured them quickly and covertly. Sleep, too, overcame them, even though they steadfastly resisted lying on a nursery school cot when invited to nap. Still in their heavy outdoor clothing, they would drop to the

floor, asleep. Then, a teacher would carefully place the child on a cot close to an open window. The child would waken hours later, refreshed and on the way to trusting a smiling, loving teacher and the safety of the nursery school environment.

After working out in the cold and rain for long hours at a stretch, day-shift parents were very tired and in a hurry at the end of the day when they came to pick up their children. Some were cross and impatient as they hurried their preschoolers to avoid missing the bus or car-pool ride. There was no time to talk over their child's day with the teacher. So, teachers communicated with parents about their children by writing brief comments next to a child's name on a chart hung outside the playroom door. These comments had to be worded with great tact, we discovered. Even such comments as "John didn't finish his lunch" or "Betsy didn't take a nap today" could result in angry scolding or slapping of the child. We tried to emphasize the positive behaviors in our messages in order to make each child appear more lovable and interesting to parents.

For the children on the swing shift, life was quite different. They usually arrived early after a leisurely day at home or out shopping with their parents. Mothers and fathers on their way to work often stayed for a while at the center, reading stories or looking at toys or interesting things the children described to

them the night before. There was a more relaxed atmosphere in the playrooms during the swing shift than during the day shift. This was evident in the conversations between children, and especially in their dramatic play. In contrast to the day-shift children, who rarely used the doll corner to "keep house," swing-shift children meticulously swept the floor, made the doll beds, set the table, bathed and dressed the dolls, and sat down quietly for pretend tea parties. In contrast, day-shift children, especially the four-year-olds, turned the sink and stove upside down in the doll corner and "launched them" in noisy excitement. They were more aggressive in their play and more destructive of play materials. They probably had fewer occasions to observe their mothers making beds, preparing meals, or enjoying homemaking tasks.

Swing-shift children were served supper as a group, after which they had time to play, listen to stories, enjoy music and play games, paint pictures and, in summertime, play outside until dark. They then undressed and went to bed. The children were then awakened and dressed before their tired parents arrived.

Additional Services

The Center also tried to provide time-saving services to parents that might relieve some of the stresses under which they worked. Home Service Foods began in January of 1944.

Precooked meals, planned by Dr. Lowenberg, were prepared in the centers' kitchens. Priced at fifty cents each, one order was ample for a working man or woman, and a single portion would serve two preschool children. These ready-packaged meals were ordered two or more days in advance and contained the main course and dessert, the foods that usually required the most preparation time. Directions were included for heating and serving, and suggestions for additional foods to round out the meal were offered.

In time, other services were added, such as mending children's clothes, buying their shoelaces, and haircutting. In February, a program of immunizations was begun. Children whose parents had not been able to arrange for the necessary shots required for nursery school attendance were able to receive their shots at the Center. Teachers, in the absence of parents, brought children in turn to the Center's physician, holding them on their laps to reassure and comfort them while they got their shots.

Parent–Teacher Interactions

Parent–teacher conferences were usually difficult to arrange. We found ways to talk briefly with a mother by walking with her to a waiting bus or car. Teachers invited parents into the playrooms to see the art work of their children or to view special block buildings preserved for their admiration.

Parent meetings took place occasionally when dinner was served to the mothers and fathers in one room while their children had dinner in another. Group supervisors went down into the shipyard to talk to a parent when it seemed necessary. On these occasions, I found myself surrounded by fathers and mothers who eagerly asked "What was my child doing when you left?" As parents realized how much teachers knew and cared about their children, they made time for interviews and shared their problems and pleasures with them.

Program Results

One of the most gratifying aspects of the Kaiser experience was the steady growth and change we observed in the children. The outdoor play, regular sleep and rest, and especially the excellent nutrition wrought dramatic improvements in the health and appearance of many of the children. Before the centers opened, some of the children had no regular meal times but ate whatever "handouts" (usually bread) were made available to them by neighbors or caretakers. When they first came to the centers, bread was the only food some children would eat. After the children seemed comfortable with the nursery school routines, Dr. Lowenberg omitted bread from the meals entirely. The hungry children began to taste and enjoy a wide variety of unfamiliar flavors and textures. Later on, when bread was again included in the form of small sandwiches, they were accepted as just another food.

Patience and planning reduced aggression and destructive behavior and, as children were convinced that their teachers really liked them and cared what happened to them, they confided in them their fears and worries and sought comfort and assurance from them. An emerging sense of trust freed the children to develop confidence in their bodies. Their motor skills increased, their self-esteem was enhanced, and they grew more friendly, more tolerant of one another, and more giving.

We also saw measurable growth in language development. Opportunities to develop the ability to listen to a teacher's direction, to enjoy longer and more complex stories, and to verbalize shared experiences with pets or on walks was part of the program planning.

Many good things happened in the Child Service Centers in the Kaiser Shipyards—for children, for parents, for the industry, for all of us. We all had a part in winning the war as "champion shipbuilders," as we were told, and for that we were proud. The head of the Maritime Commission told the teachers that, without their help, it would have been impossible to keep the shipyards in production seven days a week. Parents told us that when they were tired and tempted to sleep late on Sunday morning, their children would awaken them, saying "Get up, get up. If you don't go to work, we don't get to go to school." When the centers were closed in 1945 at the end of the war, records showed that "3,811 children were taken care of—a total of 250,000 child care days—which freed almost 2 million working hours for the women" (Stanford University Campus Report, Interview with Lois Stolz, March 30, 1983).

But I think the most remarkable, the best thing that happened was that, in a time of war, when mothers of preschool children worked eight and nine hours a day, six or seven days a week, the lives of almost 4,000 children were made happy, healthy, and in some ways, better than they ever were before. This could only happen as a combination of skillful professional planning, strong professional leadership, and some of the best teachers the nursery school profession has ever prepared. I believe that all children deserve to benefit from that combination, especially in their early years.

You who are beginning the study of early childhood education have many career paths open to you. Ours is a profession that is constantly growing, branching out in many directions and ready to meet emerging challenges in flexible, innovative ways. At present, employment prospects may look discouraging and preschool teachers' salaries substandard, but these conditions must change. In a society where 50 percent of women work for a living, we can no longer function without a nationwide, high-quality program for the care and education of children under six years of age.

When this happens, we must wonder whether there will be enough professionally prepared specialists in the field to provide leadership. Will there be enough teachers who are knowledgeable about the nature and development of infants and young children and sensitive to their individual needs? Will there be enough enlightened and caring personnel to license and monitor (with in-service education) facilities and programs for an entire nation's children? You—and those who follow in your footsteps—hold the answers to these questions.

EDITH M. DOWLEY was involved in early childhood education for 50 years. She was a student at the Merrill-Palmer Institute in 1933 and 1934, and a faculty member from 1945 through 1948. Dr. Dowley received her master's degree in Child Development in 1935, and taught for 9 years at the University Elementary School at the University of Michigan. She was a group supervisor in the Kaiser Child Service Centers, and later became the first director of Stanford University's Bing Nursey School, a position she retained until 1975. She served as a national consultant to Project Head Start from 1965 to 1968, and from 1971 to 1972 she was a member of the California Task Force on Early Childhood Education.

Dr. Dowley was a visiting instructor at the University of Victoria (British Columbia, Canada) and the University of Hawaii and conducted summer workshops in Santa Barbara and Berkeley, California. The late Dr. Dowley was most recently Professor Emerita of Psychology and Education at Stanford University.

CHAPTER 1

History of Early Childhood Education

Questions for Thought

What distinguishes early childhood education from other levels of education?

Why is it important to know about the history of early childhood education?

How has our field been influenced from abroad?

What are the major American influences to our field?

What other fields have influenced the development of the early childhood philosophy? What has been their impact?

What have been the basic themes in early education throughout history?

How do current events—political, social, and economic—affect the direction of education?

INTRODUCTION TO THE FIELD

Early childhood education has a rich and exciting history. The story of its development is the chronicle of people who took bold steps toward improving children's lives. Critical events have had a hand in shaping the history of early childhood education. As the images of the child change through the centuries, so, too, does the education of the young child and the educators themselves.

For the moment, imagine yourself as a time traveler. As you go back in time, you span the centuries and meet the people whose vision helped to shape our profession. You learn how Froebel's own unhappy childhood inspired a new way of teaching called the kindergarten. You see the passion and struggle of Montessori as she convinces the world that "slum children" can learn and succeed. In the 1960s, you witness the dedication of America to create a program for preschoolers known as "Head Start."

New models are forged through necessity and innovation, thus changing what we know about children and their care and education. The energies of so many on behalf of children have produced bold ideas, creative models, even contrary beliefs and practices. Across the globe and through the centuries, the education of young children has evolved.

Why History?

Most early childhood students and many educators know little about the origins of their chosen profession. The names of Rousseau, Froebel, Montessori, and Dewey may not seem to have much significance at this time (although many teachers are familiar with some of their techniques), but knowing something about the roots of this profession is important.

First of all, there is a sense of *support* that comes from knowing that history. Contemporary education has its roots in the past; finding a suitable beginning point for that past helps provide an educator with perspective. New insights blend with ideas from past traditions, as the history of early childhood education is truly a history of rediscovery.

Think about this, then: the "education" of the 21st century actually stems from children's schooling thousands of years ago.

For instance, works of Socrates, Plato, and Aristotle are part of the philosophical foundation on which educational practices are built. Schools in ancient Greece and Rome taught literature, the arts, and science. Unfortunately, many historical documents are works of Western Europe. A search for historical records from diverse cultures would be beneficial to understanding American experience. For instance, Hilliard (1997) points out

> Abundant oral and written records exist to describe the history of education on the African continent, especially in its ancient and indigenous forms. The best recorded ancient tradition of primary, secondary, and higher education in the entire world is found in the Nile valley complex of cultures.

Educators would have a broader foundation of education's roots with this kind of historical perspective.

Knowing that early childhood *philosophy* has deep roots can be an *inspiration* and helps teachers develop *professional expression*. As early childhood educators, we must learn to express our ideas, finding our own voice. Professionalism in education "relates to doing things well, at the right time, and for the right reason" (Spodek, Saracho, & Peters, 1988). The past as well as the present and future must be considered when developing sound educational programs for young children. The *tenets* expressed by past educators help develop better methods of teaching. Looking at history gives an overview of how various ages looked at children and their learning, based on the religious, political, and economic pressures of the time. Reviewing the professional record demonstrates how the needs of society affect education. Perhaps some of the mistakes of the past can be avoided if history is remembered.

Drawing upon knowledge of the past creates *an awareness and understanding* of changes in education. Into the fabric of early childhood education are woven many threads of influence that are responsible for current philosophies. By understanding and telling the story of the past, we are better equipped to interpret our own history, to have a sense of mission and purpose. "Doing history" is a good idea for early childhood educators, for Spodek tells us

> When we [become] early childhood educators, each of us accepts as our own, either deliberately or implicitly, the mission that is central to our field: We are committed to enhancing the education, development, and well-being of young chil-

dren. Our saga helps renew our sense of identity and commitment to our profession (Spodek in Bauch, 1988).

In this chapter, the people, the ideas, and the circumstances that have influenced early childhood are introduced by examining historical forces that have affected educational trends. *It is important to note that the historical resources available are dominated by works from Europe and America, and schools of the past were overwhelmingly created for boys and men.* This gender bias added to the underdevelopment of girls and women, as a Eurocentric standard contributed to a biased habit of thinking. However, educational programs that included girls and the role of people of color in the early childhood movement are documented. After all, every culture has had and still does have the task of socializing and educating their young. So although the written record may document a part of educational philosophy and teaching, there is no single monopoly on ideas about raising and educating children. Educational changes of a more recent nature follow. The impact of other disciplines, such as medicine and psychology, and the recurrent themes of early childhood education are also explored.

Defining the Terms

The term **early childhood education** refers to group settings deliberately intended to effect developmental changes in children from birth to the age of entering first grade. More recent definitions include the elementary years as well. For our purposes, we shall define early childhood as from infancy through third grade. In terms of a child's life, that is roughly from birth to 8 years of age. In school terms, it includes group settings for infants through the primary years of elementary school, grades one through three. In programmatic terms, the education of young children includes formal and informal group settings regardless of their initial purpose. For instance, after-school programs for kindergarten and first-graders are included, as are their formal academic sessions.

Early childhood educators thus build bridges between a child's two worlds, school (or group experi-

ence) and home. It is during these years that the foundation for future learning is set; these are the building block years, during which a child learns to walk, talk, establish an identity, print, and count. In later years, that same child builds on these skills to be able to climb mountains, speak a foreign language, learn to express and negotiate, learn cursive writing, and understand multiplication.

INFLUENCES FROM ABROAD

When did early childhood education first begin? *A Timeline for Early Childhood Education* can be found in Appendix A. It is impossible to pin-point the origins of humankind because there are few records from millions of years ago. Some preparation for adult life was done informally, mostly through imitation. As language developed, communication occurred. Children learned dances, rituals, and ceremonies, and both boys and girls were taught skills or their respective roles in the tribe. Ancient historical documents seem to indicate that child-rearing practices were somewhat crude; DeMause (1974) even suggests that the further one goes back in history, the more likely the case of abandonment and brutality.

In Ancient Times

The definition of childhood has varied greatly throughout history. For example, in ancient times children were considered adults by age 7. A society's definition of childhood influences how it educates its children.

Many of our own practices are founded on those developed in Greece and Rome. Greek education—and virtually all classical European schooling—was provided for the boys of wealthy families, while girls and working-class children received training for domestic work or a trade.[1,2] Education began by age 6 or 7, although Plato and Aristotle both spoke of the need to educate the younger child. Some ancient Romans felt that education should begin at home as soon as a child began to talk, and highlighted the use of

[1] Early childhood professionals need to keep in mind the heavy influence of Western European thought in the philosophy that dictates our teaching practice, especially when working with children from families of non-Western European cultures.

[2] Keep in mind how much of the research and history in our field has a race, class, and gender bias (i.e., the tendency to be based on the experiences of and research on white, middle-upper class males).

rewards and ineffectiveness of corporal punishment (Hewes, 1993).

Through medieval times (approximately the 5th through the 13th centuries), childhood hardly lasted beyond infancy. This period was largely an era of ignorance. Faced with the fall of the Roman Empire and the beginning of lawlessness and anarchy, people left villages and towns for the safety of a local baron or king, and schools ceased to exist. Few members of the ruling class could read or write their names, and the monastery schools were for priests and religious instruction only. The education of children was fairly simple before the 15th century; there was no educational system, and the way of life was uncomplicated as well. The church control of school in the medieval period meant that education projected a view of children as basically evil in their natural state. The value of education was in preparation for an afterlife. Children learned mostly through their parents or by apprenticeship outside the family. The child was expected and encouraged to move into adulthood as fast as possible. Survival was the primary goal in life. Because the common religious belief was that people were naturally evil, children had to be directed, punished, and corrected constantly.

What little we know of systematic learning developed during the Dark Ages through the policies of Charlemagne—who proclaimed that the nobility should know their letters—and from those monastery schools that maintained libraries. A new social class in the form of craft guilds began to grow as apprenticeships expanded. Although education was sparse, the seeds of learning were planted, including the introduction of the concepts of equality and brotherhood, a continuing concern of educators today.

The Renaissance and the Reformation

With the Renaissance (late 1300s and early 1400s) and the Reformation (14th through 16th centuries), society gradually became more enlightened. Society's notion of childhood as abandonment or ambivalence was giving way to the sense that childhood was a legitimate period of life. Several political, social, economic, and religious movements combined. The first humanist educators began to advocate a basic education for all children, including girls and the poor. The call for a *universal education* and *literacy* are two fundamental effects of this period on education as we know it today. Concern for the common man was on the rise, as skilled craftsmen formed a kind of middle

class. By the 1500s, schools that taught subjects such as reading, writing, arithmetic, and bookkeeping were fairly common throughout Europe.

The German school system had its beginnings established at this time and would continue to influence education in all parts of Europe. People changed the way they looked at children and their education. Towns grew and expanded, and there was an opportunity to move to new lands. Living conditions improved and infant mortality waned. Children were living longer. The acquisition of knowledge and skills at an earlier age became important. If educated, children could be expected to help their family improve its situation. Parents found they needed help in teaching their children.

Into Modern Times

Comenius

John Amos Comenius (1592–1670), a Czech educator, wrote the first picture books for children. Called *Orbis Pictus (The World of Pictures, 1658)*, it was a guide for teachers that included training of the senses and the study of nature. Comenius fostered the belief that education should follow the natural order of things. His ideas included the "school of the mother's lap," where children's development follows a timetable of its own and their education should reflect that fact. Comenius advocated approaching learning based on the principles of nature. He believed that "in all the operations of nature development is from within," so children should be allowed to learn at their own pace. He also proposed that teachers should work with children's own inclinations, for "what is natural takes place without compulsion." Teachers must observe and work with this natural order, the timetable, to ensure successful learning. This idea was later reflected in Montessori's sensitive periods and Piaget's stages of development. Today it is recognized as the issue of school **readiness**.

Comenius also stressed a basic concept that is now taken for granted: learning by doing. He encouraged parents to let their children play with other children of the same age. Rather than pushing a standard curriculum, Comenius said that "the desire to know and to learn should be excited . . . in every possible manner" (Keatinge, 1896). He also reflected the growing social reform that would educate the poor as well as the rich. In summary, probably the three most significant contributions of Comenius are *books with*

Cornix cornicatur,   à à A a
The *Crow* crieth.

Agnus balat,   b è è è B b
The *Lamb* blaiteth.

Cicàda stridet,   cì cì C c
The *Grasshopper* chirpeth.

Upupa dicit,   du du D d
The *Whooppoo* saith.

Infans ejulat,   è è è E e
The *Infant* crieth.

Ventus flat,   fi fi F f
The *Wind* bloweth.

Anser gingrit,   ga ga G g
The *Goose* gagleth.

Os halat,   hà'h hà'h H h
The *Mouth* breatheth out.

Mus mintrit,   ì ì ì I i
The *Mouse* chirpeth.

Anas tetrinnit, kha, kha K k
The *Duck* quaketh.

Lupus ululat,   lu ulu L
The *Wolf* howleth.
   [mum
Ursus murmurat, mum- M m
The *Bear* grumbleth.

Figure 1.1 ● *Orbis Pictus,* by John Comenius, is considered the first picture book written for children.

illustrations, an emphasis on *education with the senses*, and the *social reform* of education.

Locke

An English philosopher of the 1600s, John Locke (1632–1714) is considered to be the founder of modern educational philosophy. He based his theory of education on the scientific method and the study of the mind and learning. Locke theorized the concept of **tabula rasa**, the belief that the child is born neutral, rather than evil, and is a "clean slate" on which the experiences of parents, society, education, and the world are written. He based his theory on the scientific method and approached a child as a doctor would examine a patient. He was one of the first European educators to discuss the idea of individual differences gleaned from observing one child rather than simply teaching a group. Education needed to take the individual learner into account.

The purpose of education, he claimed, is to make man a reasoning creature. A working knowledge of the Bible and a counting ability sufficient to conduct business was the fundamental education required of adults, so children were taught those basics. Locke suggested that such instruction should be pleasant, with playful activities as well as drills. Locke's influence on education was not felt strongly at the time. Later, however, his best ideas were popularized by Rousseau, such as the notion that the teacher must work through the senses to help children reach understanding. Today, teachers still emphasize a sensory approach to learning.

In summary, Locke's contribution is felt most in our acceptance of *individual differences*, in *giving children reasons* as the basis for helping children to learn, and in his theory of a "clean slate" that points to the effect of the environment on learning.

Rousseau

After Comenius, new thoughts were everywhere in Europe. Locke offered some educational challenges, and Darwin brought a change to science. The time was ripe for new ideas about childhood. Jean Jacques Rousseau (1712–1778), a writer and philosopher of the middle 1700s, brought forth the idea that children were not inherently evil, but naturally good. He is best known for his book *Emile* (1761) in which he raised a hypothetical child to adulthood. He reasoned that education should reflect this goodness and allow spontaneous interests and activities of the children. "Let us lay it down as an incontrovertible rule that the first impulses of nature are always right; there is no original sin in the human heart . . . the only natural passion is self-love or selfishness taken in a wider sense."

Rousseau's ideas on education in and of themselves were nothing short of revolutionary. According to Boyd (1997), these included such radical ideas for the times as:

- The true object of education should not be primarily a vocational one.

- Children only really learn from first-hand information.

- Children's view of the external world is quite different from that of adults.

- There are distinct phases of development of a child's mind and these should coincide with the various stages of education.

- Teachers must be aware of these phases and coordinate their instruction appropriately.

Although he was not an educator, Rousseau offered insights that were valuable. He suggested that

school atmosphere should be less restrained and more flexible to meet the needs of the children. He insisted on using concrete teaching materials, leaving the abstract and symbolism for later years. His call to *naturalism* transformed education in such a way that led educators to eventually focus more on the early years. For instance, he extolled others to "sacrifice a little time in early childhood, and it will be repaid to you with usury when your scholar is older" (*Emile*, 1761). Pestalozzi, Froebel, and Montessori were greatly influenced by him. The theories of developmental stages, such as of Jean Piaget and Arnold Gesell (see Chapter 4), support Rousseau's idea of natural development. In Europe, his ideas had a ripple effect that sent waves across the Atlantic Ocean.

Rousseau's ideas are still followed today in early childhood classes. Free play is based on Rousseau's belief in children's inherent goodness and ability to choose what they need to learn. Environments that stress autonomy and self-regulation have their roots in Rousseau's philosophy. Using concrete rather than abstract materials for young children is still one of the cornerstones of developmentally appropriate curriculum in the early years.

Pestalozzi

Johann Heinrich Pestalozzi (1746–1827) was a Swiss educator whose theories on education and caring have formed the basis of many common teaching practices of early childhood education. Like Rousseau, he used nature study as part of the curriculum and believed that good education meant the development of the senses. Rather than simply glorify nature, however, Pestalozzi became more pragmatic, including principles on how to teach basic skills and the idea of "caring" as well as "educating" the child. Pestalozzi stressed the idea of the **integrated curriculum** that would develop the whole child. He wanted education to be of the hand, the head, and the heart of the child. Teachers were to guide self-activity through intuition, exercise, and the senses. Along with intellectual content, he proposed that practical skills be taught in the schools. He differed from Rousseau in that he proposed teaching children in groups rather than using a tutor with an individual child. Pestalozzi's works *How Gertrude Teaches Her Children* and *Book for Mothers* detailed some procedures for mothers to use at home with their children. Probably his greatest contribution is the blending of Rousseau's strong romantic ideals with his own egalitarian attitude that built skills and independence in a school atmosphere that paralleled that of a firm and loving home.

Froebel

Friedrich Wilhelm Froebel (1782–1852) is one of the major contributors to early childhood education, particularly in his organization of educational thought and ideas about learning, curriculum, and teacher training. He is known to us as the "father of the kindergarten," not only for giving it a name, but for devoting his life to the development of a system of education for young children. The German word **kindergarten** means "children's garden," and that is what Froebel felt best expressed what he wanted for children under 6 years of age. Because his own childhood had been unhappy, he resolved that early education should be pleasant. He advocated the radical thought that children should be able to play, to have toys, and to be with trained teachers, so he started the first training school. Early childhood historian Dorothy Hewes (1993) notes:

> Froebel started his kindergarten in 1836, for children aged about two to six, after he had studied with Pestalozzi in Switzerland and had read the philosophy promoted by Comenius two hundred years earlier. His system was centered around self-activity and the development of children's self-esteem and self-confidence. In his *Education of Man*, he wrote that "Play is the highest phase of child development—the representation of the inner necessity and impulse." He had the radical idea that both men and women should teach young children and that they should be friendly facilitators rather than stern disciplinarians.

Over 100 years ago, Froebel's kindergartens included blocks, pets, and fingerplays. Froebel observed children and came to understand how they learned and what they liked to do. He developed the first educational toys, which he termed "gifts." These materials were to be manipulated for children to learn about themselves, life, and civilization. As Froebel himself put it:

> The life of the boy . . . is, in truth, but an external representation of his inner being, of his power, particularly in and through (plastic) material . . .

Figure 1.2 ● Finger plays, which are common activities in today's early childhood programs, were also a part of Froebel's kindergarten programs. (From Wiggins and Smith, 1895.)

even in its external form the laws and conditions of inner development—it must be rectangular, cubical, beam-shaped, and brick-shaped. The formations made with this material are either external aggregations—*constructive*—or developments from within—*formative*.

> When the children are just making friends with the teacher and with each other, it is very interesting and profitable for them to formulate their mite of knowledge into a sentence, each one holding his ball high in the air with the right hand, and saying:
>
> My ball is red like a cherry.
> My ball is yellow like a lemon.
> My ball is blue like the sky.
> My ball is orange like a marigold.
> My ball is green like the grass.
> My ball is violet like a plum.

Margaret McMillan 1860–1931

Dr. E. Bradburn

Born in Westchester, New York, Margaret McMillan—a pioneer of open-air nursery schools—spent most of her life in Britain where she profoundly changed the provision and content of early childhood education. Believing that through education a better and more caring society could be built, she waged a relentless battle against the widespread dirt and disease that impeded children's all-round growth.

On becoming a manager of three elementary schools in 1904 in Deptford, one of London's problem-saturated slum areas, she met children in schools who were so dirty, sick, and hungry as to be unable to benefit from the schooling offered. Thus Margaret saw the importance of promoting healthy bodies before attempting to instruct the mind.

Later, this realization informed all the working models she established in Deptford, including their buildings. Her clinics, night camps, camp school, baby camp, open-air nursery school, and training college all reflected her conviction that health was the hand-maiden of education. This idea was one of her main contributions to the education of young children.

Her many views on the intellectual, social, and emotional development of children were both revolutionary and seminal. For instance, she maintained that children under age 5 would benefit from appropriate intellectual stimulation, and that well-trained teachers, not just motherly women, should be employed for this purpose in nursery schools. Furthermore, she saw parents and teachers as partners in the educative process. These and other ideas, combined with her intense love of children, undergirded all her practical experiments and helped her move toward her long-term goal—the creation of "a nobler human race in a new and nobler social order."

Dr. E. Bradburn, M.Ed., Ph.D.
Previously National Vice-President of the British Association for Early Childhood Education and the National Vice-President of Britain's Preschool Play Groups Association

14

Angeline Brooks (1886), a teacher in an American Froebelian kindergarten in the late 1800s, described the gifts this way:

> Froebel regarded the whole of life as a school, and the whole word as a school-room for the education of the [human] race. The external things of nature he regarded as a means to making the race acquainted with the invisible things of the minds, as God's *gifts* for use in accomplishing the purpose of this temporal life. Regarding the child as the race in miniature, he selected a few objects which should epitomize the world of matter in its most salient attributes, and arranged them in an order which should assist the child's development at successive stages of growth.

Some of his theories about children and their education later influenced Montessori and were reflected in the educational materials she developed.

Every day, teachers in centers and homes across the country practice the Froebelian belief that a child's first educational experiences should be a garden: full of pleasant discoveries and delightful adventure, where the adults' role is to plant ideas and materials for children to use as they grow at their own pace.

Montessori

At the turn of the century, Maria Montessori (1870–1952), became the first female physician in Italy. She worked in the slums of Rome with poor children and with mentally retarded children. Sensing that what they lacked was proper motivation and environment, she opened a preschool, *Casa di Bambini*, in 1907. Her first class was 50 children from 2 to 5 years of age. The children were at the center all day while their parents worked. They were fed two meals a day, given a bath, and provided with medical attention. Montessori designed materials, classrooms, and a teaching procedure that proved her point to the astonishment of people all over Europe and America.

Before her, no one with medical or psychiatric training had articulated so clearly the needs of the growing child. Her medical background added credibility to her findings and helped her ideas gain recognition in this country. The Montessori concept is both a philosophy of child development and a plan for guiding growth, believing that education begins at birth and the early years are of the utmost importance. During

Figure 1.3 ● Maria Montessori designed materials, classrooms, and learning methods for young children. (Photo courtesy of American Montessori Society, New York, NY.)

this time, children pass through "sensitive periods," in which their curiosity makes them ready for acquiring certain skills and knowledge.

Dr. Montessori was an especially observant person and used her observations to develop her program and philosophy. For instance, the manipulative materials she used were expensive, so were always kept in a locked cabinet. One day the cabinet was left unlocked and the children took out the materials themselves and worked with them quietly and carefully. Afterward, Montessori removed the cabinet and replaced it with low, open shelves. She noticed that children liked to sit on the floor so she bought little rugs to define the work areas. She designed the school around the size of the children. Through her enlightenment, child-sized furniture and materials are now used in classrooms. By focusing on the *sequential steps of learning*, Montessori developed a set of learning materials still used widely today. One of her most valuable contributions was a theory of how children learn. She believed that any task could be reduced to a series of small steps. By using this process, children could learn to sweep a floor, dress themselves, or multiply numbers.

Montessori materials are graded in difficulty and emphasize her interest in self-help skills. To foster this, she developed frames with buttons and laces so children could learn to be responsible for themselves when dressing. The layout of the room and the distribution and presentation of materials furthered this concept. Montessori placed great emphasis on the environment—the "prepared environment," as she called it. A sense of order, a place for everything, and a clear rationale are hallmarks of the Montessori influence.

Her procedures as well as her materials contain **self-correcting** features. Nesting cylinders, for example, fit together only one way and are to be used that way. Montessori supported earlier educational ideas of sensory developments; she felt that cognitive abilities stem from sensory discrimination. Thus, most of her equipment was **tactile** and enhanced the senses as well as the mind. In the Montessori method, the role of the teacher is primarily one of observer and facilitator. Teachers demonstrate proper use of materials and communicate as needed, avoiding any acts that might cause a child to become dependent on them for help or approval. At the same time, Montessori saw the goal of education as the formation of the child and development of character. After Montessori was introduced in the United States in 1909, her methods received poor reception and were often misunderstood. Chattin-McNichols (1993) notes that "adaptation of her methods in a variety of ways, a focus on academics by demanding middle class parents, and a flood of 'trainers' and authors eager to capitalize on Montessori contributed to a rapid downfall of Montessori schools in the U.S. by 1925 or so." A second American Montessori movement began in the late 1950s and early 1960s. Differences between Europeans and Americans generated the American Montessori Society, founded by Dr. Nancy McCormick Rambusch. According to Chattin-McNichols (1993):

> Today with a much wider range of children than ever before, the majority of Montessori schools are private preschools and child care centers, serving 3- to 6-year-old children. But there are many which also serve elementary students, and a small (but growing) number of programs for infants, toddlers, and middle-school students. . . . The word *Montessori*, however, remains in the public domain, so that Montessori in the name of

a school or teacher education program does not guarantee any adherence to Montessori's original ideas.

(See Chapter 2 for more information on Montessori programs.)

Rudolf Steiner

Rudolf Steiner (1861–1925) was a German educator whose method of education is known today as the Waldorf School of Education. This sytem has influenced mainstream education in Europe and its international reputation is being felt in American early childhood programs today. Steiner theorized that childhood is a phase of life important in its own right. It has three periods: that of the "will" (0–7 years), the "heart" or feelings (7–14 years), and the "head" or a fusion of the spirit and the body (14 years on). Early childhood is the period of "willing," and the environment must be carefully planned to protect and nurture the child.

As did Froebel and Montessori, Steiner emphasized the whole child and believed that different areas of development and learning were connected into a kind of unity. The role of the teacher is that of a mother-figure, and her goal is to allow the child's innate self-motivation to predominate. The teacher is to understand the temperament of each child, and to go with it; thus, play has a large place in Waldorf classrooms.

Self-discipline will emerge from the child's natural willingness to learn and initiate, and the classroom needs to support this self-regulation process. Yet, while the child's inner life is deeply valued by Steiner, experiences in early childhood must be carefully selected. For instance, fairy stories help children acquire time-honored wisdom; modern Waldorf followers insist television be eliminated. For Steiner, the people with whom the child interacts are of central importance. Waldorf schools are discussed later in this chapter and in Chapter 2.

AMERICAN INFLUENCES

Colonial Days

The American educational system began in the colonies. When thinking of Colonial America, people often envision the one-room schoolhouse. Indeed, this was the mainstay of education in the New England colonies. Although home teaching of the Bible was common, children were sent to school primarily for religious reasons. Everyone needed to be able to read the Bible, the Puritan fathers reasoned. All children were sent to study, though historically boys were educated before girls.[1] Not only the Bible was used in school, however; new materials like the New England Primer and the Horn Book were also used.

Early life in the New England colonies was difficult, and estimates run as high as 60% to 70% of children under age 4 dying in colonial towns during the "starving season." Discipline was harsh and children were expected to obey immediately and without question. Parents may have loved their children, but Puritan families showed little overt affection. Children were important as economic tools, and they worked the land and were apprenticed into trades early.

In the South, it was a different story. Plantation owners imported tutors from England or opened small private schools to teach just their sons to read and write.[2] Although the reasons were different, the results were similar: a very high percentage of adult readers. From these came the leaders of the American Revolution and the new nation.

The Revolutionary War brought the establishment of both the Union and religious freedom. By affirming fundamental principles of democratic liberty, the Founding Fathers paved the way for a system of free, common, public school systems, the first the world had seen (Cubberly, 1920). However, after the Revolutionary War, there were no significant advances in education until the late 1800s. Leaders like Thomas Jefferson felt that knowledge ought to be available to all, but that opinion was not widely shared. Most of the post-Revolutionary period focused on growing crops and pioneering the frontier, not teaching and educating children. Even by the 1820s, education for the common man was not readily available. Industrialization in both the North and South did little to encourage reading and writing skills. Manual labor and machine-operating skills were more important. Although public schools were accepted in principle, in reality no tax basis was established to support them.

Children in Enslavement

The first African Americans were not slaves but indentured servants, whose debts repaid by their labor would buy them their freedom. However, by 1620 Africans were being brought to the New World as slaves. In many states, children of slaves were not seen as human beings but rather as property of the owner. During the Revolutionary War, many Americans turned against slavery because of the principles of the natural rights of the individual, as embodied in the Declaration of Independence and the U.S. Constitution. By the early 1800s, most northern owners had freed their slaves, although living conditions for them were generally poor.

Because of the high economic value of children as future laborers, there was a certain level of care given to pregnant women and babies. Osborn (1991) tells of a nursery on a South Carolina plantation (around 1850) in which

> infants and small children were left in a small cabin while the mothers worked in the fields nearby. An older woman was left in charge and assisted by several girls 8–10 years of age. The infants, for the most part, lay on the cabin floor or the porch—and once or twice daily, the mother would come in from the field to nurse the baby. Children of toddler age played on the porch or in the yard and, at times, the older girls might lead the group in singing and dancing.

Prior to the Civil War, education was severely limited for African Americans. Formal schools were scarce, and most education came through the establishment of "Sabbath schools."[3] As part of religious instruction, slaves were often provided literary training. However, many plantation owners found these schools threatening, and banned them by making laws

OUR DIVERSE WORLD OUR DIVERSE WORLD OUR DIVERSE WORLD OUR DIVERSE WORLD OUR DIVERSE WORLD OUR DIVERSE WORLD OUR DIVERSE WORLD OUR DIVERSE WORLD

[1] History can provide us with reminders of the strides that have been made in American society in providing equal educational experiences for both boys and girls—the challenge continues.

[2] We need to remember that the challenge of equity in education for girls and boys remains; early childhood educators must stay alert to the biases that still exist in society and are replayed in the classroom.

[3] See footnote on page 9. Although great strides have been made in providing public education for all children in America, remember inequities based on color, linguistic ability, and social class continue to exist.

prohibiting the teaching of slaves. Another facility then developed, that of the clandestine, or midnight school. Because of its necessary secretive existence, few records are available, although it is reasonable to conclude that the curriculum was similar to that of the prohibited Sabbath schools.

After the Civil War, private and public schools were opened for African Americans. Major colleges and universities were founded by the end of the 1800s. Booker T. Washington, born into slavery, founded the Tuskegee Normal & Industrial Institute in Alabama in 1881, and emphasized practical education and intercultural understanding between the two races as a path to liberation. Many former slaves and graduates established schools for younger children. Of integrated schools, Osborn (1991) reports

> Generally, however, if the schools accepted Blacks at all, it was on a strictly quota basis . . . Blacks were often excluded from kindergartens. Thus, as the early childhood education movement began to grow and expand in the years following the Civil War, it grew along separate color lines.

Hampton Institute of Virginia established a laboratory kindergarten for African Americans in 1873, and by 1893 the Institute offered a kindergarten training school and courses in child care.[1] The graduates of Hampton Institute became the teachers at the laboratory school because, in the words of its principal "[the] students know the children and the influences surrounding them. . . . Their people are proud to see them teaching. They furnish what has always been a missing link between me and the parents" (Pleasant, 1992).

John Dewey

By the end of the 1800s, however, a nationwide reform movement had begun. In education, the *Progressive Movement*, as it was called, received its direction primarily through one individual, John Dewey (1858–1952).

Dewey was the first real American influence on American education. Raised in Vermont, he became a professor of philosophy at both the University of Chicago and Columbia University. In the years that

Figure 1.4 ● Hampton Institute.

OUR DIVERSE WORLD OUR DIVERSE WORLD OUR DIVERSE WORLD OUR DIVERSE WORLD OUR DIVERSE WORLD OUR DIVERSE WORLD OUR DIVERSE WORLD OUR DIVERSE WORLD
[1] It would be worth investigating if all the laboratory schools for African Americans copied European models, as did those of most American universities, or reflected some African influences.

followed, Dewey would be responsible for one of the greatest impacts on American education of all time.

Dewey believed that children were valuable and that childhood was an important part of their lives. Like Froebel, he felt that education should be integrated with life and should provide a training ground for cooperative living. As did Pestalozzi and Rousseau, Dewey felt that schools should focus on the nature of the child. Until this time, children were considered of little consequence. Childhood was rushed. Children as young as 7 were a regular part of the work force—on the farms, in the mines, and in the factories. Dewey's beliefs about children and learning are summarized in Figure 1.5.

Dewey's ideas of schooling emerged from his own childhood and his family life as a parent. Jane Dewey, his sixth child, offered that "his own schooling had bored John; he'd disliked the rigid, passive way of learning forced on children by the pervasive lecture-recitation method of that time" (Walker, 1997). Furthermore, the Deweys' parenting style caused a stir among friends and neighbors; the children were allowed to play actively in the same room as adult guests, to ignore wearing shoes and stockings, and even to "stand by during the birth [of brother Morris] while Mrs. Dewey explained the process" (Walker, 1997). His passionate belief in the innate goodness of children, and encouragement of their experimentation, shaped John Dewey's ideals.

A new kind of school emerged from these ideals. Even the buildings began to take on a different look. Movable furniture replaced rows of benches. Children's projects, some still under construction, were found everywhere. The curriculum of the school began to focus on all of the basics, not just a few of the academics. If a group of 6-year-olds decided to make a woodworking table, they would first have to learn to read to understand the directions. After calculating the

My Pedagogic Creed—John Dewey	What It Means Today
1. "... I believe that only true education comes through the stimulation of the child's powers by the demands of the social situations in which he finds himself."	This tells us that children learn to manage themselves in groups, to make and share friendship, to solve problems, and to cooperate.
2. "... The child's own instinct and powers furnish the material and give the starting point for all education."	We need to create a place that is child-centered, a place that values the skills and interests of each child and each group.
3. "... I believe that education, therefore, is a process of living and not a preparation for future living."	Prepare the child for what is to come by enriching and interpreting the present to him. Find educational implications in everyday experiences.
4. "... I believe that ... the school life should grow gradually out of the home life ... it is the business of the school to deepen and extend ... the child's sense of the values bound up in his home life."	This sets the rationale for a relationship between teachers and parents. Values established and created in the home should be enhanced by teaching in the schools.
5. "... I believe, finally, that the teacher is engaged, not simply in the training of individuals, but in the formation of a proper social life. I believe that every teacher should realize the dignity of his calling."	This says that the work teachers do is important and valuable. They teach more than academic content; they teach how to live.

Figure 1.5 ● John Dewey expressed his ideas about education in an important document titled *My Pedagogic Creed* (Washington, DC: The Progressive Education Association, 1897).

cost, they would purchase the materials. In building the table, geometry, physics, and math were learned along the way. This was a group effort that encouraged children to work together in teams and so school became a society in miniature. Children's social skills were developed along with reading, science, and math. The teacher's role in the process was one of ongoing support, involvement, and encouragement.

The contribution of John Dewey to American education cannot be underestimated. As described in Figure 1.5, Dewey's ideas are part of today's classrooms in several ways. His child-oriented schools are a model of child care centers and family child care homes, as learning and living are inseparable. As the following sections on kindergarten and nursery schools illustrate, John Dewey had a vision that is still alive today.

KINDERGARTEN

The word *kindergarten*—which is German for "children's garden"—is a delightful term. It brings to mind the image of young seedlings on the verge of blossoming. The similarity between caring for young plants and young children is not accidental. Froebel, the man who coined the word *kindergarten*, meant for that association to be made. As a flower opens from a bud, so too does a child go through a natural unfolding process. This idea—and ideal—are part of the kindergarten story.

The first kindergarten was a German school started by Froebel in 1837. Over a dozen years later, in 1856, Margaretha Schurz, a student of Froebel, opened the first kindergarten in the United States. It was for German-speaking children and held in her home in Wisconsin. Schurz inspired Elizabeth Peabody (1804–1894) of Boston, who opened the first English-speaking kindergarten there in 1860. Peabody, in turn, after studying kindergartens in Germany, influenced William Harris, superintendent of schools in St. Louis, Missouri. In 1873, Harris allowed Susan Blow (1843–1916) to open the first kindergarten in the United States that was associated with the public schools. By the 1880s kindergarten teachers such as Eudora Hailmann were hard at work inventing wooden beads, paper weaving mats, and songbooks to use with active 5-year-old children (Hewes, 1993).

Looking at the kindergarten in historical perspective, it is interesting to trace the various purposes of this specialized educational experience. During the ini-

tial period in this country (1856–1890), Froebel's philosophy (see section on Froebel earlier in this chapter) remained the mainstay of kindergarten education. At the same time, kindergartens began to become an instrument of social reform; since these included a "day care" function, they were called charity kindergartens. For instance, "in the early kindergartens, teachers conducted a morning class for about 15 children and made social calls on families during the afternoon. The children were taught to address the teachers as 'Auntie' to emphasize her sisterly relationship with their mothers" (Hewes, 1995).

Moreover by early 1900, the voices of dissent were being heard. Traditional kindergarten ideas had come under the scrutiny of G. Stanley Hall and others, who were interested in a scientific approach to education, and of Dewey, who also advocated a community-like (rather than garden-style) classroom. A classic clash of ideals developed between followers of Froebel (conservatives) and those of Dewey's new educational viewpoint (progressives). Support for the latter came from those who saw kindergartens as a social service. Many of the kindergartens started in the late 1800s were established by churches and other agencies that worked with the poor. It was an era of rising social conscience, and the reasons for helping the less fortunate were not unlike the rationale that led to the creation of Head Start and Follow-Through 60 years later.

Critics of Froebel took exception to his seemingly rigid approach. The emphasis in a Froebelian kindergarten was on teacher-directed learning. Dewey's followers preferred a more child-centered approach, with teachers serving as facilitators of children's learning. It is the same tension that exists today between the "back to basic" movement and the supporters of open education. The progressives found fault with the "gifts" of Froebel's curriculum. Those who followed Dewey believed that "real objects and real situations within the child's own social setting' should be used (Read and Patterson, 1980). Froebel was viewed as too structured and too symbolic; Dewey was perceived as child-oriented and child-involved. Even the processes they used were different. Froebel believed in allowing the unfolding of the child's mind and learning, whereas Dewey stressed adult intervention in social interaction.

The debate raged on. The progressives succeeded in influencing the content of kindergarten programs, retaining some of Froebel's basic concepts. The reform of kindergarten education continued through the 1920s and 1930s and led to the creation of the modern American kindergarten. By the 1970s, a trend was

Figure 1.6 ● John Dewey's lab school involved children in activities of a practical, real-life nature, such as weaving small rugs to use in the classroom. (Special thanks to Sheila Roper of MacClintock Photo Collection, Special Collections, Morris Library, Southern Illinois University at Carbondale.)

developing for the kindergarten to focus on the intellectual development of the child; thus, a programmatic shift placed more emphasis on academic goals for the 5-year-old. By the late 1990s, the concept of developmentally appropriate practices advocated a shift toward more holistic, broad planning for kindergarten, although worksheets and large group, teacher-directed instruction still abounds. Moreover, the schedule for kindergarteners themselves seems to favor a time of longer than half a day in school.

Patty Smith Hill

Patty Smith Hill (1868–1946) of Teacher's College, Columbia University, was an outstanding innovator of the time and one of the Progressive Movement's most able leaders. It was she who wrote the song "Happy Birthday" and founded the National Association for Nursery Education (NANE). Now the largest association of early childhood educators, it is known today as the National Association for the Education of Young Children (NAEYC). Trained originally in the Froebelian tradition, she worked closely with G. Stanley Hall and later with John Dewey. Thus,

her philosophy of classroom teaching was a blended one. She believed strongly in basing curricula and programs on the nature and needs of the children, and she was one of the major education experimenters of her day. She was

> . . . guided by principles of democracy and respect for individuals. She argued for freedom and initiative for children, as well as a curriculum relevant to children's lives. It was she who originated large-muscle equipment and materials suitable for climbing and construction, a departure from the prescribed small-muscle activities of the Froebelians. Patty Hill also urged unification of kindergarten and first grade work, but her objective was not to start 5 year olds on first grade work, as we today might readily assume. Rather, emphasis was on giving six year olds the opportunity for independent, creative activities before embarking on the three R's (Cohen and Randolph, 1977).

These ideas became the backbone of kindergarten practice. Moreover, Hill did not work for kindergarten alone. In fact, during the 1920s Hill rekindled Froebel's early ideas to promote nursery schools for children too young to attend kindergarten. Regardless of controversy within, kindergartens were still on the fringes of the educational establishments as a whole. In fact, Hill (1941) herself commented that "adjustment to public-school conditions came slowly . . . [and] until this happy adjustment took place, the promotion of the self-active kindergarten children into the grades has made it possible for the poorest and most formal first-grade teacher to criticize and condemn the work of the best kindergarten teacher as well as the kindergarten cause, because of the wide gap that existed between kindergarten and primary ideals at that time. . . ."

As Hill and others prevailed and made continual improvements in teaching methods, materials, guidance, and curriculum, the interests of kindergarten and primary education could be seen as more unified.

When the 1960s highlighted the problems of the poor and their failure in schools and society, kindergarten and the early years were brought back into the spotlight. Today, although there are still "gaps" between kindergarten and primary schooling, the kindergarten is found in some form in nearly every country of the world. Although the content of the program and the length of the day vary widely in the United States, kindergarten is available in every one of the states.

The stability of both the Froebelian and the Dewey kindergartens has been challenged in the latter part of this century, as the "basic skills" curriculum is moved down to the kindergarten classroom. The problems in this shift from developmentally appropriate practices to more academic material is not new. Educators have been discussing various curriculum content and teaching approaches for years. Chapter 2 will discuss the issue of programs, as we continue to decide "how the best ideas of the past can be integrated with the best practices of today and transformed into the best programs for the future" (Himitz in Bauch, 1988).

Nursery Schools

Establishment in America

The very phrase "nursery school" conjures up images of a child's nursery, of a carefully tended garden, of a gentle place of play and growing. In fact, the name was coined to describe a place where children were nurtured (see the section on the McMillan sisters). Nursery schools have always been a place of "care," of physical needs, intellectual stimulation, and the socioemotional aspects of young children's lives.

Early childhood educators took Dewey's philosophy to heart. Their schools reflected the principles of a **child-centered approach**, active learning, and social cooperation. By the 1920s and 1930s, early childhood education had reached a professional status in the United States. Nursery schools and day nurseries went beyond custodial health care. They fostered the child's total development. The children were enrolled from middle- and upper-class homes as well as from working families. However, until the 1960s, nursery schools served few poor families.[1]

Parent education was acknowledged as a vital function of the school and led to the establishment of **parent cooperative schools**. Brook Farm, a utopian cooperative community in the 1840s, had "the equivalent of an on-site child care center 'for the use of parents doing industrial work' or for mothers to use 'as a kindly relief to themselves when fatigued by the care of children'" (Hewes, 1993). The first of these parent participation schools was developed in 1915 at the University of Chicago. A group of faculty wives started the Chicago Cooperative Nursery School. Chapter 2 describes the parent cooperative model in detail.

Research centers and child development laboratories were started in many colleges and universities from about 1915 to 1930. As Stolz (1978) describes it, "the [preschool] movement from the beginning was integrated with the movement for child development research. The purpose . . . was to improve nursery schools, and, therefore, we brought in the people who were studying children, who were learning more about them, so we could do a better job." It is noteworthy that professionals such as Hill, Stolz, Dowley, and others encouraged researchers to share their findings with classroom teachers to integrate these discoveries right into the daily programs of children.

These schools followed one of two basic models. One model, patterned after the first psychological laboratory in Leipzig, Germany, in 1879, was formed to train psychologists in the systematic training of child study. This model adopted a scientific approach to the

[1] A challenge in our profession is to create funding mechanisms to provide an early childhood education experience for all children and families—regardless of income.

Figure 1.7 ● American nursery schools, from the turn of the century through the present day, have included time for the group to be together. (Photo from Golden Gate Kindergarten Association, San Francisco, Calif.)

study of human beings, as the field of psychology itself attempted to become more like the biologic sciences. The second approach, like the Butler School of Hampton Institute and later at Spelman College, was established primarily for training teachers. The latter model took its influence almost exclusively from educational leaders. The nursery school laboratory schools attempted a multidisciplinary approach, blending the voices from psychology and education with those of home economics, nursing, social work, and medicine. By 1950, when Katherine Read (Baker) first published *The Nursery School: A Human Relationships Laboratory* (now in its 9th printing and in seven languages), the emphasis of the nursery school was on understanding human behavior, then building programs, guidance techniques, and relationships accordingly. In her estimate (1950),

> the nursery school is a place where young children learn as they play and as they share experiences with other children. . . . It is also a place where adults learn about child development and human relationships as they observe and participate in the program of the school. . . . Anyone working in an educational program for children, even the most experienced person, needs to be learning as well as teaching. The two processes, learning and teaching, are inseparable.

These laboratory schools were active in expanding the knowledge of how important a child's early years are.

Lucy Sprague Mitchell

Early childhood education in the United States grew out of John Dewey's progressive movement largely because of Lucy Sprague Mitchell (1878–1967) and her contemporaries. Raised in an environment of educational and social reform, Mitchell developed the idea of schools as community centers as well as places for children to learn to think. As Greenberg (1987) explained, she gathered together, in a democratic, cooperative venture, many talented people to brainstorm, mastermind, and sponsor:

● A remarkable Bureau of Educational Experiments

● A school to implement and experiment with these principles

● A laboratory to record and analyze how and why they function as she knew they did (and as we know they do!)

● A teachers' college to promote them

● A workshop for writers of children's literature (a new genre—a number of currently famous authors of juvenile books attended)

● A bulletin to disseminate it all, as well as disseminating what a plethora of progressive educators were up to elsewhere, *beginning in 1916!*

Strongly influenced by John Dewey, she became a major contributor to the idea of "educational experiments," that is, trying to plan with teachers curriculum experiences that would then be observed and analyzed "for children's reactions to the various learning situations [and] the new teaching techniques" (Mitchell, 1951). For instance, Mitchell suggested that teachers expand on what they knew of children's "here-and-now" thinking:

> So our trips with kindergarteners were to see how work was done—work that was closely tied up with their personal lives. . . . the growth in thinking and attitudes of the teachers had moved far . . . toward the conception of their role as a guide as differentiated from a dispenser of information.

By establishing Bank Street College of Education (and its laboratory school), Lucy Sprague Mitchell emphasized the link between theory and practice, namely, that the education of young children and the study of how children learn are intrinsically tied together.

Abigail Eliot

The nursery school movement was pioneered by Abigail Eliot (1892–1992). A graduate of Radcliffe College and Harvard University, Eliot had worked with the McMillan sisters (see section in this chapter) in the slums of London. A social worker by training, she became interested in children and their relationships with their parents. Eliot had a lively and clear view of what good schools for children could be. She is generally credited with bringing the nursery school movement to the United States. She founded the Ruggles Street Nursery School in the Roxbury section of Boston, teaching children and providing teacher training, and was its director from 1922 to 1952, when it was incorporated into Tufts University and today is alive as the Eliot-Pearson Department of Child Study.

Eliot became the first woman to receive a doctoral degree from Harvard University's Graduate School of Education, and after retiring from Tufts moved to California, where she helped establish Pacific Oaks College. In all her work, she integrated Froebel's gifts, Montessori's equipment, McMillan's fresh air, as well as her own ideas. As she put it (Hymes, 1978):

> . . . the new idea—was program. I had visited many day nurseries in Boston as a social worker. I can remember them even now: dull green walls,

no light colors, nothing pretty—spotlessly clean places, with rows of white-faced listless little children sitting, doing nothing. In the new nursery school, the children were active, alive, choosing.

Midcentury Developments

While the economic crisis of the Depression and the political turmoil of World War II diverted attention from children's needs, both gave focus to adult needs for work. Out of this necessity came the Works Progress Administration (WPA) nurseries of the 1930s and the Lanham Act nurseries of the 1940s. The most renowned program of the midcentury was the Kaiser Child Care Center.

Kaiser Child Care Centers

During World War II, funds were provided to deal with the common situation of mothers working in war-related industries. Further support came from industry during World War II. An excellent model for child care operated from 1943 to 1945 in Portland, Oregon. It was the Kaiser Child Care Centers. Kaiser became the world's largest such center and functioned "round the clock" all year long. A number of services were made available on site. An infirmary was located nearby for both mothers and children. Hot meals were made available for mothers to take home when they picked up their children. Lois Meek Stolz was the director of the centers, and James L. Hymes, Jr., the manager. In her Guest Editorial, Edith Dowley, who was one of the teachers, describes in detail the environment and experiences of this remarkable project.

Stolz and Hymes describe the centers this way:

> . . . The centers were to have three distinctive qualities. One, they were to be located not out in the community but right at the entrance to the two shipyards, convenient to mothers on their way to and from work. They were to be industry-based, not neighborhood-centered. Two, the centers were to be operated by the shipyards, not by the public schools and not by community agencies. They were to be industrial child care centers, with the cost borne by the Kaiser company and by parents using the service. Three, they were to be large centers, big enough to meet the

need. In the original plan each center was to serve a thousand preschool children on three shifts (Hymes, 1978).

These centers served 3811 children. As Hymes points out, they provided 249,268 child care days. They had freed 1,931,827 woman work-hours.

Once the war had ended, though, the workers left. Child care was no longer needed, and the centers closed. The Kaiser experience has never been equaled, either in the universal quality of care or in the variety of services. However, it left us a legacy, which Hymes has stressed ever since (in Dickerson, 1992):

> It is no great trick to have an excellent child care program. It only requires a lot of money with most of it spent on *trained* staff.

The model they provide for child care remains exemplary.

Chances to Learn

The Depression was a particularly difficult time for African Americans, as the living standards for those Americans in poverty plummeted. Roosevelt's administration and the emerging industrial union movement gave impetus to blacks looking for both employment and political change. World War II continued the process of transformation for many adults, but for children the situation was still bleak. As DuBois (1903) wrote

> the majority of Negro children in the United States, from 6 to 18, do not have the opportunity to read and write. . . . even in the towns and cities of the South, the Negro schools are so crowded and ill-equipped that no thorough teaching is possible.

In fact, the legal challenge to segregation offered new focus, struggle, and ultimately improvement for black children. As Weinberg (1977) states:

> Midcentury marked a turning point in the history of black America. The movement for equality came under black leadership, embraced unprecedented numbers of Negroes, and became national in scope. A persistent black initiative forced a reformulation of public policies in education.

The attack against the segregation system had begun. As seen in the historic cases of *McLaurin* (1950) and *Brown v. Board of Education* of Topeka (1954 [see Weinberg, 1977]), the concept of "separate but equal" was overturned. Furthermore, the Civil Rights Act of 1964 continued the struggle for equality of opportunity and education, one that persists today in our schools and society.

The "Free School" Movement

A.S. Neill (1883–1973) was the most famous proponent of the "free/natural school" movement of the midcentury. His book *Summerhill* describes 40 years of that educational program, of which he was headmaster. Neill claimed that most education was defective because it arose from the model of original sin. Assuming children were inherently evil caused educators to force children into doing what was contrary to their nature. Neill shared Rousseau's belief in noninterference, as he states: "I believe that a child is innately wise and realistic. If left to himself without adult suggestion of any kind, he will develop as far as he is capable of developing" (Neill, 1960).

Neill's belief in freedom was practiced in his school, where children governed themselves and worked toward equal rights with adults. The benefits from such liberties were touted as highly therapeutic and natural, an escape from repression and guilt. Several influences are clear in these educational programs: Rousseau's belief in the child's innate goodness, Freud's idea of the dangerous effects of guilt, and some of the social idealism of Dewey and the Progressives.

Head Start

After the war, few innovations took place until a small piece of metal made its worldwide debut. Sputnik, the Soviet satellite, was successfully launched in 1957 and caused an upheaval in educational circles. Two questions were uppermost in the minds of most Americans: Why weren't we first in space? What is wrong with our schools? The emphasis in education quickly settled on engineering, science, and math in the hope of catching up with Soviet technology.

The civil rights struggle in the early 1960s soon followed. In pointing out the plight of the poor, education was highlighted as a major stumbling block toward equality of all people. It was time to act, and Project

Head Start was conceived as education's place to fight the "war on poverty." The same goals of Froebel and Montessori formed the basis of Head Start: helping disadvantaged preschool children.

Project Head Start began in 1965 as a demonstration program aimed at providing educational, social, medical, dental, nutritional, and mental health services to preschool children from a diverse population of low-income families. In 1972, it was transformed into a predominantly part-day, full-year program. Key features included offering health services, small groups, parent-teacher collaboration, and the thrill of communities getting involved with children in new ways. Osborn (1965) tells us:

> I wish I knew how to tell this part of the story . . . the bus driver in West Virginia who took time off from his regular job and went to the Center to have juice and crackers with "his" children because they asked him to. . . . The farmer who lived near an Indian Reservation and who each morning saddled his horse, forded a river and picked up an Indian child—who would not have attended a Center otherwise. . . . they represent the true flavor of Head Start.

Over the years, Head Start has provided comprehensive developmental services to more than 10 million children and their families.

This was an exciting time—a national recognition of the needs of young children and a hope for a better quality of life. Three major points included in the Head Start program are noteworthy:

● *Compensatory education*—programs that compensate for inadequate early life experiences.

● *Parental involvement*—inclusion of parents in planning, teaching, and decision making.

● *Community control*—local support and participation.

These three objectives combined to reinforce the goals of the program in real and concrete ways. Head Start was an attempt to make amends, to compensate

Figure 1.8 ● Head Start is the largest publicly funded education program for young children in the United States.

poor children by preparing them for school and educational experiences. Parents, by being required to participate at all levels, were educated along with their children. The purpose of the community-based governing boards was to allow the program to reflect local values and concerns. Concurrently, underprivileged, poor people were being encouraged to take part in solving some of their own problems.

The spirit of Head Start was infectious. As a result of community interest in Head Start, there was a burst of enthusiasm for many programs for the young child. Because of Head Start's publicity, there has been an expanding enrollment in nursery school, kindergarten, and day care programs. Thanks to Head Start, there is national attention to the need for providing good care and educational experiences for young children. The Head Start program is alive and well today and is nationally recognized as an effective means of providing comprehensive services to children and families, serving as a model for the development of the ABC Child Care Act of 1990. We will discuss it further in Chapter 2.

INTERDISCIPLINARY INFLUENCES

Several professions enrich the heritage of early childhood. This diversity was apparent from the beginning; the first nursery schools drew from six different professions: social work, home economics, nursing, psychology, education, and medicine. Three of the most consistent and influential of those disciplines were medicine, education, and child psychology.

Medicine

The medical field has contributed to the study of child growth through the work of several physicians. These doctors became interested in child development and extended their knowledge to the areas of child rearing and education.

Maria Montessori

Maria Montessori (1870–1952) was the first woman in Italy ever granted a medical degree. She began studying children's diseases, and through her work with mentally defective children found education more appealing. Her philosophy is discussed earlier in

this chapter and will be part of Chapter 2 on educational programs.

Sigmund Freud

Sigmund Freud (1856–1939) made important contributions to all modern thinking. The father of personality theory, he drastically changed how we look at childhood. Freud reinforced two specific ideas: (1) a person is influenced by his early life in fundamental and dramatic ways; and (2) early experiences shape the way people live and behave as adults. Thus, psychoanalytic theory is mostly about personality development and emotional problems. Freud's work set into motion one of the three major strands of psychological theory that influence the developmental and learning theories of early childhood today. Although the impact of psychoanalysis on child psychology is not as great as it was 25 years ago, it still contributes significantly to the study of early childhood. Though he was not involved directly in education, Freud influenced its development. Freud and psychoanalytic theory influenced education greatly. Chapter 4 will enlarge on the theory and its application in early childhood education.

Arnold Gesell

Arnold Gesell (1880–1961) was a physician who was concerned with growth from a medical point of view. Gesell began studying child development when he was a student of G. Stanley Hall, an early advocate of child study. He later established the Clinic of Child Development at Yale University, where the data he collected with his colleagues became the basis of the recognized norms of how children grow and develop. He was also instrumental in encouraging Abigail Eliot to study with the McMillan sisters in England and influenced Edna Noble White to open the Merrill-Palmer School.

Gesell's greatest contribution was in the area of child growth. He saw maturation as an innate and powerful force in development. "The total plan of growth," he said, "is beyond your control. It is too complex and mysterious to be altogether entrusted to human hands. So nature takes over most of the task, and simply invites your assistance" (Gesell, Ames, & Ilg, 1977). This belief became known in psychological circles as the **maturation theory** and will be discussed at length in Chapter 4.

Through the Gesell Institute, guides were published using this theory. With such experts as

Dr. Frances Ilg and Dr. Louise Bates Ames, Gesell wrote articles that realistically portrayed the child's growth from birth to adolescence. These guides have sharp critics regarding their overuse and inappropriate application to children of cultures other than those studied.[1] Still, the "ages and stages" material is used widely as a yardstick of normal development.

Benjamin Spock

Benjamin Spock's book *Baby and Child Care* was a mainstay for parents in the 1940s and 1950s. In a detailed "how-to" format Dr. Spock (1903–1998) preached a common-sense approach that helped shape the childhood of many of today's adults. By his death in 1998, the book had sold almost 50 million copies around the world and had been translated into 42 languages.

Spock saw himself as giving practical application to the theories of John Dewey (see this chapter) and Sigmund Freud (see Chapters 1 and 4), particularly in the ideas that children can learn to direct themselves, rather than needing to be constantly disciplined.

Spock suggested that mothers use the playpen less and allow children freedom to explore the world firsthand. To that end, he asked parents to "child proof" their homes—a radical thought at the time. The word *permissiveness*, as it relates to child rearing, became associated with Dr. Spock's methods, although Spock himself described his advice as relaxed and sensible, while still advocating for firm parental leadership.

Dr. Spock became an outspoken advocate for causes that extend his ideas. He was an active critic of those forces, be they economic, social, or political, that destroy people's healthy development. In his own words:

> I'll summarize my thoughts this way: Child care and home care, if well done, can be more creative, make a greater contribution to the world, bring more pleasure to family members, than 9 out of 10 outside jobs. It is only our mixed-up, materialistic values that make so many of us think the other way around (Spock, 1976).

T. Berry Brazelton

Dr. T. Berry Brazelton (1918–) is a well-known pediatrician who supports and understands the development of infants and toddlers. He developed an evaluation tool called the Neonatal Behavior Assessment Scale (also known as "the Brazelton") to assess newborns. Cofounder of the Children's Hospital Unit in Boston and professor emeritus of pediatrics at Harvard Medical School, he is also a well-known author. His pediatric guides to parents deals with both physical and emotional growth. His writings speak to the parents' side of child raising, such as setting limits, or listening to what children say and observing what they do. Brazelton (1974) discussed the 2-year-old and sharing this way:

> Understanding such concepts as fair and unfair, of giving and receiving and the process of sharing, all demands a kind of self-awareness. If a child is not sure of his own limits and of his own strengths, he cannot afford to allow his toys, equivalent to parts of himself, to be passed out to someone else, trusting that they will come back. At the same time, the ability to do so is evidence of an awareness of behavior in others comparable to his own and denotes the beginning of an awareness of non-self.

More recently Brazelton has advocated a national parental leave standard and is involved in a federal lobbying group known as "Parent Action." He is also a popular TV personality, hosting the nationally syndicated show entitled *What Every Baby Knows.*

Education

Early childhood is one part of the larger professional field known as education. This includes elementary, secondary, and college or postsecondary schools.

OUR DIVERSE WORLD OUR DIVERSE WORLD OUR DIVERSE WORLD OUR DIVERSE WORLD OUR DIVERSE WORLD OUR DIVERSE WORLD OUR DIVERSE WORLD OUR DIVERSE WORLD

[1] This is another reminder of the importance of being able to notice the sociocultural bias in the research in our field, keeping the information that is supportive to sound practice, and to expand or disregard what does not support good practice with children in a multicultural society.

Along with John Dewey and Abigail Eliot, several other influences from this field bear attention.

The McMillan Sisters

In the first three decades of this century, these two sisters pioneered in early education. Nursery schools in Britain and America probably were developed because of the drive and dedication of the McMillan sisters.

Both women had broad international backgrounds. They grew up in North America and Scotland. Margaret studied music and language in Europe. She was well read in philosophy, politics, and medicine. Rachel studied to become a health inspector in England.

Health studies of 1908–1910 showed that 80% of children were born in good health, but that by the time they entered school, only 20% could be classified that way. Noticing the deplorable conditions for children under age 5, the McMillan sisters began a crusade for the slum children in England. Their concern extended beyond education to medical and dental care for young children. In 1910 they set up a clinic in Deptford, a London slum area, which became an open-air nursery a year later. The McMillans called it a "nurture school." Later, a training college nearby was named for Rachel. With no private financial resources, these two women faced tremendous hardships in keeping their school open. It is to their credit that Deptford still exists today.

The McMillan theory of fresh air, sleep, and bathing proved successful. "When over seven hundred children between one and five died of measles, there was not one fatal case at Deptford School" (Deasey, 1978). From the school's inception, a primary function was to research the effects of poverty on children.

Of the two sisters, Margaret had the greatest influence at the school at Deptford. In fact, it was Margaret who continued to champion early education issues beyond Deptford, as described in Dr. Bradburn's Focus Box earlier in this chapter. Abigail Eliot writes of her:

Miss McMillan invented the name [nursery school]. She paid great attention to health: a daily inspection, the outdoor program, play, good food—what she called "nurture." But she saw that an educational problem was also involved and she set to work to establish her own method of education for young children. This was why she called it a "school" (Hymes, 1978).

Figure 1.9 ● Margaret McMillan, along with her sister Rachel, developed the "open-air" nursery school and training schools in England. (Reproduced from *Margaret McMillan: Framework and Expansion of Nursery Education* by Dr. Elizabeth Bradburn with permission of the National Christian Education Council.)

Susan Isaacs

Susan Isaacs (1885–1948) was an educator of the early 20th century whose influence on nursery and progressive schools of the day was substantial. In 1929 she published *The Nursery Years*, which emphasized a different point of view than that of the behaviorist psychologists of the times. She interpreted Freudian theory for teachers and provided guidance for how schools could apply this new knowledge of the unconscious to the education of children. She proposed

the opportunity for free unhindered imaginative play not only as a means to discover the world but also as a way to reach the psychic equilibrium, in working through wishes, fears, and fantasies so as to integrate them into a living personality (Biber, 1984).

The teacher's role was different from that of a therapist, she asserted, in that teachers were "to attract mainly the forces of love, to be the good but regulating parent, to give opportunity to express aggression but in modified form, and not to attract herself to the negative explosive reactions of hatred and oppression" (Biber, 1984).

Isaacs' influence is felt today in schools whose philosophy emphasizes the child's point of view and the notion of play as the child's work.

The Progressive Education Movement

As indicated earlier in the sections on John Dewey and Patty Smith Hill, it was the Progressive Movement of the late 1800s and first half of the 20th century that changed the course of education in both elementary and nursery schools in America. Coinciding with the political progressivism in this country, this philosophy emphasized a child-centered approach that gained advocates from both the scientific viewpoint, such as G. Stanley Hall and John Dewey, and those of a psychoanalytic bent, such as Susan Isaacs and Patty Smith Hill.

Some of the major features of the educational progressive philosophy were:

1. Recognizing individual needs and individual differences in children

2. Teachers [must be] more attentive to the needs of children.

3. Children learn best when they are highly motivated and have a genuine interest in the material.

4. Learning via rote memory is useless to children.

5. The teacher should be aware of the child's total development—social, physical, intellectual, and emotional.

6. Children learn best when they have direct contact with the material (Osborn, 1991).

These beliefs were instrumental in changing the old traditional schools from a strict and subject-based curriculum to one that centered on children's interests as the foundation for curriculum development. Creating mass education during the Progressive era was a struggle between the values of efficiency and those of individual development. The Progressives, under the leadership of Dewey and others, believed that public school should nurture individual differences, while at the same time encourage problem solving and teamwork. In his own words, Dewey wanted educators to work on "how a school could become a cooperative community while developing in individuals their own capacities and satisfying their own needs" (1916). Although Dewey and others did not reject the teaching of basic skills, the shift was away from such subject matter education. Therefore, it is no surprise that progressive education had many critics among those interested in schooling for academic preparation. Still, most early childhood centers can thank the progressives for much of their philosophy and techniques for developing curriculum for their children today.

The Waldorf School

The first Waldorf School was established in Stuttgart, Germany, in 1919, by Rudolf Steiner, who is described earlier in this chapter. Patterned after his educational philosophy and personal beliefs, it was based on the premise that education's aim is to help all people find their right place in life and thus fulfill their destiny. There is close personal attention to the child's developing temperament, and self-directed activity is valued. Children must be protected as they develop, so the teacher and parents must adhere to specific actions to protect the child from the noise of the modern world and technology.

Steiner agreed with Froebel and others that education should begin where the learner is. Whatever the child brings to the educational experience is to be worked with, not against. The curriculum of Waldorf schools is, therefore, both interdisciplinary and multisensory, with an emphasis on the arts, on tales of wisdom, and the concepts of community and respect for a person's individual needs. Often a teacher stays with the same group of children for 8 years.

Although this movement is essentially an elementary and secondary one, it is noteworthy as one of the largest nonsectarian, independent school movements in the world. Waldorf has more than 640 schools, 1087 kindergartens, 300 curative (special needs) centers, and 60 teacher education institutes worldwide; moreover, it is the model of choice for the changing Soviet and Eastern European school systems (Caniff, 1990). It is one of the fastest growing movements in America today. With its foundations in Froebelian tradition, and elements of Montessori and progressive education, the Waldorf school has a contribution to make to our knowledge of children and educational practices.

The Child Study Movement

A survey of education influences is incomplete without mentioning the child study movement in the 1920s and 1930s. It was through the child study movement that education and psychology began to have a common focus on children. Besides the Gesell Institute, many research centers and child development laboratories were established at colleges and universities around the country. Their inception reflects the interest of several disciplines in the growth of the young child. Schools of psychology looked for children to observe and study; schools of education wanted demonstration schools for their teachers-in-training and for student-teacher placement. Schools of home economics wanted their students to have firsthand experiences with children. These on-campus schools provided a place to gather information about child development and child psychology.

This period of educational experiment and child study led to an impressive collection of normative data by which we still measure ranges of ordinary development. Broman (1978) sums up the influence of the movement this way:

> From the beginning of the child study movement in the 1920s ... early childhood was not a major emphasis in education until after the War on Poverty and the establishment of Head Start in 1965. The child study movement, however, was the impetus that began the search for the most appropriate means of educating young children.

The British Infant School

Developed by Robert Owen in the early 19th century, the British infant schools had a strong commitment to social reform (Spodek et al., 1988). In England, the term *infant school* refers to the kindergarten and primary grades. Then in 1967, the Plowden Report proposed a series of reforms for the schools. These changes paralleled those of American early childhood education. As a result, many American teachers in both the preschool and primary grades adapted the British infant school approach to their own classrooms.

Figure 1.10 ● The history of early childhood education includes contributions from many ethnic groups. San Francisco's Golden Gate Kindergarten Association has provided nursery education for the city's various neighborhoods from the turn of the century to the present.

Three aspects of this **open school** style that received the most attention were:

1. **Vertical, or family, groupings.** Children from 5 to 8 years of age are placed in the same classroom. Several teachers may combine their classes and work together in teaching teams. Children may be taught by the same teachers for 2 or 3 years.

2. **Integrated day.** The classroom is organized into various centers, for math, science, and the arts. The teacher moves from one child or center to another as needed. Play is often the central activity, with an emphasis on follow-through with children's ideas and interests as they arise.

3. **Underlying concept.** There is a fundamental belief that the process of thinking takes precedence over the accumulation of facts. Learning how to think rather than stockpiling data is encouraged. How to identify and solve problems is valued more than having a finished product. Teachers focus on the child's current learning rather than on the future.

Just as Owen's ideas took hold in America in the 19th century, so, too, did the 20th-century version of the infant school fire the imaginations of teachers in the United States. Their tenets of open education are developmentally appropriate for both preschool and primary schools (Bredekamp, 1988).

Reggio Emilia

In the last part of this century, yet another educator and educational system have influenced early childhood thinking. Loris Malaguzzi (1920–1994) developed his theory of early childhood education from his work with infants, toddlers, and preschoolers while working as the founder and director of Early Education in the town of Reggio Emilia, Italy. His philosophy includes creating "an amiable school" (Malaguzzi, 1993) that welcomes families and the community and invites relationships among teachers, children, and parents to intensify and deepen to strengthen a child's sense of identity. Malaguzzi continually asked teachers to question their own practices and listen to the children, as we can hear in his letter (Gandini, 1994) excerpted below:

> My thesis is that if we do not learn to listen to children, it will be difficult to learn the art of staying and conversing with them. . . . It will also be difficult, perhaps impossible, to understand how and why children think and speak; to understand what they do, ask, plan, theorize or desire. . . . Furthermore, what are the consequences of not listening? . . . We adults lose the capacity to marvel, to be surprised, to reflect, to be merry, and to take pleasure in children's words and actions.

Reggio Emilia has attracted the attention and interest of American educators because of its respect for children's work and creativity, its project approach, and its total community support. Reggio Emilia serves as a model of early childhood practices. This high-quality program is also discussed in Chapters 2, 9, 11, and 14.

Psychology

The roots of early childhood education are wonderfully diverse, but one tap root is especially deep: the connection with the field of psychology. In this century particularly, the study of people and their behavior is linked with the study of children and their growth.

Initially, child development was mostly confined to the study of trends and descriptions of changes. Then the scope and definition of child development began to change. Developmental psychologists now study the processes associated with those changes. Specifically, child development focuses on language acquisition, the effect of early experiences on intellectual development, and the process of attachment to others. Such is the world of early childhood—it is no wonder that we are so closely tied to the world of psychology.

There is no one theory or name that encompasses all of developmental psychology. Indeed, there are many. The major theories, their creators, and their influence on early education will be discussed in depth in Chapter 4.

THEMES IN EARLY CHILDHOOD EDUCATION

When we review the colorful and rich history of early childhood education, three major themes emerge. These same themes reappear and are reflected in the ensuing thought and theory of each age.

Ethic of Social Reform

The first theme is that of the ethic of social reform. Early childhood education programs often have had the expectation that schooling for the young will lead to social change and improvement. Montessori, the McMillans, Patty Smith Hill, Abigail Eliot, and Head Start all tried to improve children's health and physical well-being by attending first to the physical and social welfare aspects of children's lives. Other more recent examples illustrate how important this theme is to our work. Marian Wright Edelman (see Guest Editorial in Section 6) is an outstanding children's advocate. A graduate of Spelman college and Yale Law School, Edelman began her career as a civil rights lawyer (the first black woman to be admitted to the Mississippi state bar). By the 1960s she had dedicated herself to the battle against poverty, moving to Washington, DC, and founded a public interest law firm that eventually became the Children's Defense Fund. The ABC Act of 1990, spawned by her tireless work with the Children's Defense Fund, received much of its impetus from the impoverished state of so many children in America. The author of several books, including *Families in Peril, The Measure of Our*

Success, and *Guide My Feet*, Edelman also writes regular newspaper columns ("A Voice for Children" and "Child Watch"). Her work is being carried on by her son, Jonah (see Guest Editorial in Section 6), who helped her organize the Washington, DC, rally "Stand for Children," which attracted over 200,000 people and 3700 organizations in June 1996. Edelman herself articulates the ethic of social reform when she says, "CDF seeks to ensure that no child is left behind and that every child has a Healthy Start, a Head Start, a Fair Start, a Safe Start, and a Moral Start in life with the support of caring parents and communities" (Edelman, 1998).

In the 1980s, Dr. Louise Derman Sparks (see Guest Editorial in Section 5), in collaboration with Betty Jones (see Guest Editorial in Section 3) and colleagues from Pacific Oaks College, published *Anti-Bias Curriculum: Tools for Empowering Young Children* (1989). This book outlined several areas in which children's behavior was influenced by biases in our society and suggested a host of ways that teachers (and parents) could begin addressing these issues. These professionals have added an important dimension to the notion of social reform, for they focus our attention on ourselves, the school environment, children's interactions, and the community of parents and colleagues in educational settings.

Finally, social reform in the latter part of this century has been championed by educators and citizens beyond early childhood education. Robert Coles, a psychiatrist and educator, has written and lectured extensively about his observations and work with children of poverty and is best known for *Children of Crisis: A Study of Courage and Fear* (1971). Additionally, Jonothan Kozol has spoken extensively about segregation in the schools, most notably in his book *Savage Inequalities: Children in America's Schools* (1991), where he writes:

> Surely there is enough for everyone in this country. It is a tragedy that these good things are not more widely shared. All our children ought to be allowed a stake in the enormous richness of America. Whether they were born to poor white Appalachians or to wealthy Texans, to poor black people in the Bronx or to rich people in Manhasset or Winnetka, they are all quite wonderful and innocent when they are small. We soil them needlessly.

Educators today still assert that tired, undernourished children are not ready to learn or to be educated. Social reform can go a step further, such as with Head Start, improving the whole family situation and involving the community in its efforts.

Importance of Childhood

The second theme is the importance and uniqueness of childhood. In fact, the entire notion of the importance of childhood rests on the concept of the child as a special part of human existence and, therefore, a valuable part of the life cycle. Before 1700 or so, Western society showed little concern for children. Infanticide was pervasive, if not actually accepted. Once families and society began to value children, life changed dramatically for the young. The saying "As the twig is bent, so grows the tree" could apply to all children and their early childhood learning experiences as well as to an individual child. When people accepted the importance of childhood, they began to take responsibility for a quality life for children. From Comenius, Rousseau, and Froebel of earlier centuries to Neill, Russell, and the Child Study Movement of more recent times, society has begun to provide for the health and physical welfare of children and come to understand the necessity to care for their minds.

Modern early childhood teachers believe the early years form the foundation for later development, physically, intellectually, socially, and emotionally. David Elkind wrote in the 1980s of a "hurried child" syndrome, in which children were pushed unnecessarily out of a relaxed childhood by a fast-paced society whose pressure to succeed and move fast put children of all ages at risk. As he put it (1982):

Figure 1.11 ● Childhood is a special time of life.

We should appreciate the value of childhood with its special joys, sorrows, worries, and concerns. Valuing childhood does not mean seeing it as a happy, innocent period but rather as an important period of life to which children are entitled. They have a right to be children, to enjoy the pleasures and to suffer the trials of childhood that are infringed upon by hurrying. Childhood is the most basic human right of children.

Children need special attention during these years. Childhood is fundamentally different from adulthood; it needs to be understood and respected as such. Children's styles of learning, of letting the child "learn by doing" and "learn by discovery" are part of the essential respect for children and childhood. Public recognition of that need has created a wealth of programs for the young not dreamed of at any other time in history.

Transmitting Values

The third recurrent theme in our educational heritage is that of transmitting values. What children should ultimately *do* and *be* is at the core of all child-rearing practices, whether in the home or the school. Values—be they social, cultural, moral, or religious—have been the essence of education for centuries. For example, the Puritan fathers valued biblical theology. Therefore, schools of their time taught children to read in order to learn the Bible. Rousseau and Froebel valued childhood, and so created special places for children to express their innate goodness and uniqueness. The works of Montessori, Dewey, and Steiner reflected a belief in the worth and dignity of childhood. They transmitted these values into the educational practices we have inherited. Finally, the initiators of Head Start (see Chapter 2) and the Anti-bias Curriculum (see Chapter 9) realized the child's self-worth would be enhanced by valuing one's culture or origin. An awareness and an appreciation of ethnic heritage is becoming an integral part of the early childhood curriculum.[1]

Since the early 1900s, the group of early childhood educators has begun to develop a sense of professionalism, in the realm of identity as well as mission and purpose. Professional organizations such as the National Association for the Education of Young Children (NAEYC) and the Association for Childhood Education International (ACEI) have been advocating for the concerns of children, families, and educators for the better part of a century. Both groups have worked to develop standards for working with children. These efforts have resulted in important improvements in the status of children in group care and have begun to establish appropriate practices (NAEYC's Academy standards will be discussed in Chapters 9 and 10), pay and working standards for teachers (quality-compensation-affordability studies will be discussed in Chapter 15), and a Code of Ethics for early childhood educators (Code of Ethical Conduct will be discussed in Chapter 5).

Teaching children to live in a democratic society has always been valued in the United States. In the curriculum from kindergarten through college, this belief is reflected as we educate our children for citizenship.[2] It is how we define these values and how we teach them that are the critical issues in education.

These three themes have been at the center of early education for centuries. Occassionally, one theme dominates, as it did in the 1960s when the desire for social reform led to the creation of Head Start. At other times they seem indistinguishable from one another. Together, they have shaped the direction of early childhood education as we know it today. As we learn more about children, society, and ourselves, the next millenium will be a time to reconsider and redefine our aims and directions. It is a formidable challenge—and a worthy one.

INTEGRATING HISTORY WITH EARLY CHILDHOOD EDUCATION

The history of early childhood education is like a tapestry—woven of many influences. A broad field such as medicine is a thread in this cloth, as is the passion of a Patty Smith Hill or a Lucy Sprague Mitchell.

OUR DIVERSE WORLD OUR DIVERSE WORLD OUR DIVERSE WORLD OUR DIVERSE WORLD OUR DIVERSE WORLD OUR DIVERSE WORLD OUR DIVERSE WORLD OUR DIVERSE WORLD

[1] Informed early childhod educators really are leading the way in educational practice in terms of *celebrating* the diversity of the families!

[2] The early childhood profession provides the opportunity for one to be an agent for social change—to actually translate the values of democracy into practice.

The history forms the theory on which we base our teaching, and every child, every class, every experience translates our history into educational practice and makes another thread in this grand cloth.

Events of history have had a hand in shaping early childhood education. Forces such as war (which produced the Kaiser Shipyards project), political movements (such as progressivism), and the state of the economy (which brought the War on Poverty and Head Start) bring about change and development in how children are cared for in this country. The ingredients that early childhood educators consider essential today—that care and education are inseparable, that teaching practices are developmentally appropriate, and that adequate funding is critical for success—all stem from historical events and people.

Several fields of study and a number of professions have added to our knowledge of children and, therefore, have affected educational theory. From the professions of education, medicine, and psychology, early childhood education has developed a theory of what is best for children. The medical model offered a view of childhood that is both maturational and environmental. Psychology confirmed this blending of nature and nurture and offered observational study as a basis for educational practice. As a result, early childhood theory includes both an attention to physical growth and developmental stages and a respect for personal experience in learning. The field of education brought to early childhood theory the components of a holistic approach to child and family, variable grouping of children and activities, and a sensitivity to the social and reform possibilities of educating our young. These influences will be described at length in Chapter 4.

The individuals who created our history have had a profound effect on early childhood theory and practices. Their strong and passionate beliefs have captured our imaginations and fueled our commitment to enhancing the well-being of children. What John Dewey, Lucy Sprague Mitchell, and Susan Isaacs all had in common was a drive to extend themselves on behalf of young children. Thus, early childhood theory has a *personal* component, an emotional investment that gives each early childhood teacher and caregiver a sense of belonging to a larger cause. The work that has gone before goes on through us and extends beyond us—to children of all ages and any era.

From this blending of professional discoveries and personal commitment comes a challenge. Early childhood history calls on teachers to learn from the past and to know the theories on which the profession is based. These theories must be continually tested in the classroom and refined as they apply to children every day. In this way, the profession stays relevant and legitimate. Finally, early childhood education history affirms the value of being connected with others and remaining steadfastly committed to the common cause of young children (see Chapter 5 and Appendix B). As the NAEYC Code of Ethics states:

> I will know about, abide by, and advocate for laws and regulations that enhance the quality of life for young children.
>
> I will support the rights of children to live and learn in environments that are responsive to their developmental needs.
>
> I will improve my competencies in providing for children's needs.
>
> I will appreciate each child's uniqueness, thus enhancing the child's self-respect.

Summary

This chapter traces the roots of early childhood education from ancient times. Knowing this history gives teachers a sense of support and inspiration. A historical overview offers insights that illuminate present program and societal needs and prevent future mistakes. It helps us appreciate the legacy left by others.

Early childhood education involves children from infancy through the primary years. The term itself offers its own professional challenges:

EARLY: How do YOUNG children grow and learn best?
CHILDHOOD: How do CHILDREN think, feel, learn?
EDUCATION: How can children LEARN and be TAUGHT?

These questions have been addressed by educators in Europe and America throughout history, and, no doubt, in other parts of the world, though we in America have less documentation. Their answers have influenced educational philosophy and practice and, in turn, have been affected by the social and political forces of the day. The most notable modern developments in this country have been the advent of nursery schools and kindergartens, the Kaiser Child Care Center in World War II as a day care model, and Head Start.

Early childhood education itself is an interdisciplinary field. Important contributions have come from medicine, education, and psychology.

Certain themes emerge in early childhood education with a study of its history. The ethic of social reform, the importance of childhood, and the transmission of values have been at the core of this field throughout history.

The contributions of many pioneers leave us dreams for the young children of our society. This can give meaning to our lives as teachers as we continue to create a climate for the child who will make history tomorrow.

Review Questions

1. Identify and describe five key people who influenced the field of early childhood education. With whom would you like to have studied or worked? Why?

2. Match the name with the appropriate phrase. Put them in the order that best matches your own theory of early childhood education. State your reasons.

Rousseau	"prepared environment"
Montessori	"nurture" school
Froebel	children are naturally good
Malaguzzi	father of kindergarten
Dewey	common-sense approach
Spock	first picture book for children
McMillan sisters	Progressive Movement
Comenius	Reggio Emilia

3. Define early childhood education in your own words. Include age ranges and what you believe to be its purpose. Contrast this to the text definition and defend your position.

4. Name three institutions or living persons who are influencing the history of early childhood today. Describe your reactions to each and how they have influenced your educational philosophy.

5. Maria Montessori made several contributions to education. What are some of her theories, and how did she adapt them for classroom use? How are Montessori materials or teaching methods used in your classroom?

6. "Who Said It?" Match the historical figures with their quotations:

"[T]he nursery school is a place where young children learn as they play and . . . where adults learn about child development and human relationships."	Jean Jacques Rousseau
"What is natural takes place without compulsion."	Katherine Read Baker
"Play is the purest, most spiritual activity of man. . . . It gives, therefore, joy, freedom, contentment."	Loris Malaguzzi

"My thesis is that if we do not learn to listen to children . . . it will also be difficult, perhaps impossible, to understand how and why children think and speak."

Marian Wright Edelman

"[N]o child is left behind and . . . every child has a Healthy Start, a Head Start, a Fair Start, a Safe Start, and a Moral Start in life with the support of caring parents and communities."

John Amos Comenius

Learning Activities

1. Find out when and by whom the school or center in which you are teaching was started. What were some of the social, economic, and political issues of those times? How might they have affected the philosophy of the school?

2. Write your own pedagogic creed. List five of what you consider to be the most important beliefs you hold about educating young children. How do you see those beliefs expressed in school today?

3. Make a list of the values you think are important to teach children. In an adjoining column, add the ways in which you would help children learn those values. In other words, list the materials and curriculum you would use.

Bibliography

Aries, P. (1962). *Centuries of childhood.* New York: Knopf.

Bain, W. E. (1967). *75 years of concern for children.* Washington, DC: Association for Childhood Education International.

Bauch, J. P. (Ed.). (1988). *Early childhood education in the schools.* Washington, DC: National Education Association.

Biber, B. (1984). *Early education and psychological development.* New Haven, CT: Yale University Press.

Boyd, D. (1997). *Jean Jacques Rousseau.* Unpublished paper. Redwood City, CA: Canada College.

Bradburn, E. (1976). *Margaret McMillan: Framework and expansion of nursery education.* Surrey, England: Denholmouse Press.

Bradburn, E. (1989). *Margaret McMillan: Portrait of a pioneer.* London: Routledge.

Brazelton, T. B. (1974). *Toddlers and parents.* Reading, MA: Addison-Wesley.

Brazelton, T. B. (1992). *Touchpoints.* Reading, MA: Addison-Wesley.

Bredekamp, S. (Ed.). (1988, January). NAEYC position statement on developmentally appropriate practice in the primary grades, serving 5- through 8-year olds. Washington, DC: NAEYC. *Young Children, 3*(2).

Broman, B. L. (1978). *The early years in childhood education.* Chicago: Rand McNally College Publishing.

Brooks, A. (1886). *Four active workers.* Springfield, MA: Milton Bradley.

Caniff, D. I. (1990, November 28). Why the 'Waldorf' movement is thriving in Eastern Europe. *Education Week, X*(13).

Chattin-McNichols, J. (1993). In A. Gordon & K. W. Browne (Eds.), *Beginnings and beyond* (3rd ed., p.). Albany, NY: Delmar.

Cleverley, J., & Phillips, D.C. (1986). *Visions of childhood: Influential models from Locke to Spock* (Rev. ed.). New York: Teachers College.

Cohen, D. H., & Randolph, M. (1977). Kindergarten and early schooling. Englewood Cliffs, NJ: Prentice-Hall.

Coles, R. (1971). *Children of crisis: A Study of courage and fear.* New York, NY: Houghton Mifflin.

Cubberly, E. P. (1920). *A brief history of education.* Boston: Houghtin.

Deasey, D. (1978). *Education under six.* New York: St. Martin's Press.

DeMause, L. (1974). *The history of childhood.* New York: Psychohistory Press.

Dewey, J. (1897, 1916). *My pedagogic creed.* Washington, DC: The Progressive Education Association and Democracy and Education.

Dickerson, M. (1992, Spring). James L. Hymes, Jr: Advocate for young children. *Childhood Education.*

DuBois, W. E. B. (1995). The talented tenth. Published in *The Negro Problem* (1903), excerpted in F. Schultz (Ed.), *Sources: Notable selection in education.* Guilford, CT: Dushkin Publishing Group.

Edelman, M. W. (1998). *The state of America's children.* Washington, DC: Children's Defense Fund.

Elkind, D. (1982). The hurried child. *Young Children.*

Elkind, D. (1987, May). The child yesterday, today, and tomorrow. *Young Children, 42*(4).

Froebel, F. (1887). *The education of man* (M. W. Hailman, Trans.). New York: D. Appleton.

Gandini, L. (1994, July). Tribute to Loris Malaguzzi. *Young Children, 49*(5).

Gesell, A. L., Ames, L. A. & Ilg, F. L. (1977). *The child from five to ten.* New York: Harper & Row.

Giles, M. S. (1996). A letter to students in early childhood education. In A. Gordon & K. W. Browne (Eds.), *Beginnings and beyond* (4th ed. p.). Albany, NY: Delmar.

Greenberg, P. (1987, July). Lucy Sprague Mitchell: A major missing link between early childhood education in the 1980s and progressive education in the 1890s–1930s. *Young Children, 42*(5).

Greenberg, P. (1996, November). Approaching the new millennium: Lessons from NAEYC's first 70 years. *Young children, 52*(1).

Hainstock, E. G. (1971). *Montessori in the home: The school years.* New York: Random House.

Hewes, D. (1993). On doing history. In A. Gordon & K. W. Browne (Eds.), *Beginnings and beyond* (3rd ed., p.). Albany, NY: Delmar.

Hewes, D. (1995, November). *Sisterhood and sentimentality — America's earliest preschool centers.* Redmond, WA: Childcare Information Exchange.

Hill, P. S. (1996). Kindergarten. From the *American Educator Encyclopedia* (1941). In Paciorek & Munro. *Sources: Notable selections in early childhood education.* Guildford, CT: Dushkin Publishing Group.

Hilliard, A. G., III. (1997, September). Teacher education from an African American perspective. In J. Irvine (Ed.), *Critical knowledge for diverse teachers and learners.* Washington, DC: AACTE.

Hymes, J. L., Jr. (1978–79). *Living history interviews* (Books 1–3). Carmel, CA: Hacienda Press.

Keatinge, M. W. (1896). *The great didactic of John Amos Comenius* (Trans. and with introductions). London: Adams and Charles Black.

Kozol, J. (1991). *Savage inequalities: Children in America's schools.* New York: Crown Publishers.

Malaguzzi, L. (1993, November). For an education based on relationships. *Young Children.*

McMillan, M. (1919). *The nursery school.* London and Toronto: J. M. Dent & Sons; New York: E. P. Dutton.

Mitchell, L. S. (1951). *Our children and our schools.* New York: Simon & Schuster.

Montessori, M. (1967). *The Montessori method* (Trans. A. E. George). Cambridge, MA:

Neill, A. S. (1960). *Summerhill: A radical approach to child rearing.* New York: Hart Publishing.

Osborn, D. K. (1991). *Early childhood education in historical perspective* (3rd ed.). Athens, GA: Education Associates.

Osborn, D. K. (1996). Project Head Start: An assessment (1965). Excerpted in Paciorek & Munro. *Sources: Notable selections in education.* Guildford, CT: Dushkin Publishing Group.

Pleasant, M. B. B. (1992). *Hampton University: Our home by the sea.* Virginia Beach, VA: Donning.

Read, K. B. (1950). *The nursery school: A human relationships laboratory.* New York: Saunders.

Read, K., & Patterson, J. (1980). *The nursery school and kindergarten.* New York: Holt, Rinehart & Winston.

Rousseau, J. J. (1961). *Emile* (Trans. by B. Foxley). London and Toronto: J. M. Dent & Sons.

Sparks, L. D. (1989). *Anti-bias curriculum: Tools for empowering young children.* Washington DC: National Association for the Education of Young Children.

Spock, B. (1947). *The common sense book of baby and child care.* New York: Duell, Sloan & Pierce.

Spock, B. (1976, April). Taking care of a child and a home: An honorable profession for men and women. *Redbook Magazine.*

Spodek, B., Saracho, O. N., & Peters, D. L. (Eds.). (1988). *Professionalism and the early childhood practitioner.* New York: Teacher College.

Standing, E. M. (1957). *Maria Montessori: Her life and work.* Fresno, CA: Sierra Printing and Lithography.

Steiner, R. (1926). *The essentials of education.* London: Anthroposophical Publishing Company.

Stolz, L. M. (1978). In Hymes, J. *Living history interviews.* Carmel, CA: Hacienda Press.

Walker, L. R. (1997, Fall). John Dewey at Michigan. *Michigan Today.*

Washington, B. T. (1995). The Atlantic Exposition address (1895). In F. Schultz, F. (Ed.), *Sources: notable selections in education.* Guildford, CT: Dushkin Publishing Group.

Weinberg, M. (1977). *A chance to learn: The history of race and education in the United States.* Cambridge, MA: Cambridge University Press.

Wiggins & Smith. (1895). *Froebel's gifts.* Boston: Houghton Mifflin.

Types of Programs

CHAPTER 2

Questions for Thought

What are some of the different types of early childhood programs?

What are the indicators of quality in group programs for young children?

What is the range of early childhood education, and which programs correspond to the various age levels?

What are the major issues facing kindergartens today?

Around which programs are there controversies — and why?

How does the role of the teacher differ in each of the early childhood settings?

How are programs structured to meet specific needs of children and families?

How does Head Start differ from other early childhood programs?

How do infant/toddler programs differ from preschool programs, and how do they differ from one another?

DIVERSITY OF PROGRAMS

From the types available, to the numbers of children who attend these schools, the name of the game in early childhood programs is diversity. Early childhood programs abound; every community has some type of schooling for the young child. The range can encompass a morning nursery school for toddlers, a primary school classroom, an infant–parent stimulation program, or a full child care service for 3- to 6-year-olds. Some programs run for only a half-day; others are open from 6:00 AM until 7:00 PM. Still other centers, such as hospitals, accept children on a drop-in basis or for 24-hour care. Child care arrangements can range from informal home-based care to more formal school or center settings. Churches, school districts, community-action groups, parents, governments, private social agencies, and businesses may run schools.

Schools exist to serve a number of needs, which often overlap. Some of these are:

1. Caring for children while parents work (e.g., family child care homes or child care center)

2. Enrichment programs for children (e.g., half-day nursery school or laboratory school)

3. Educational programs for parent and child (e.g., parent cooperatives, parent–child public school programs, or high school parent classes)

4. An activity arena for children (e.g., most early childhood programs)

5. Academic instruction (e.g., kindergarten or many early childhood programs)

Programs generally reflect the needs of society as a whole. Millions of mothers of children under age 6 are in the labor force as never before. Early childhood schools provide a wide range of services for children from infancy through 8 of age to meet some of that need. According to the Children's Defense Fund (1998), only 30% of mothers with children under age 6 were in the work force in 1973; by 1997, that percentage had increased to 65%. For school-age children, the rate of increase rose from 50% in 1973 to 77% in 1997.

In the human life cycle, early childhood is a period of maximum dependency. The various programs available reflect this in a number of ways. The teacher-child ratio varies in relation to the child's age; infants, at the higher end of the dependency scale, require more teachers per child in a classroom than do 6-year-olds. The program itself reflects the age group it serves. The size of the group, the length of the program, and the equipment used are related to the enrolled children's capabilities and needs. Even the daily schedule mirrors the dependent relationship between the child and the teacher. Bathrooming, snack and meal routines, as well as clothing needs, call for longer periods of time in a toddler group than in a class of 4-year-olds.

Diversity is apparent, too, in the philosophy expressed by the specific program.[1] Some schools, such as Montessori programs, follow a very clear, precise outline based on a philosophical approach developed by Maria Montessori nearly 100 years ago. Other schools are more eclectic; they draw from a number of theories, choosing those methods and ideas that best suit their needs.

Indicators of Quality

Early childhood programs vary greatly in their educational goals and practices, their methods of instruction, and even in the kind of social "mood" or atmosphere they create. Yet, varied as they are, most early childhood programs share some common principles. The quality of these programs is based on three essential factors: (1) the teacher-child ratio, that is, the number of children cared for by each staff member; (2) the total size of the group or class; and (3) the education, experience, and training of the staff. The importance of these three factors cannot be underestimated and they underline each of the principles that follow.

The National Association for the Education of Young Children (NAEYC), the largest professional organization for early childhood educators and caregivers, has established a list of criteria for high-quality early childhood programs, based on a consensus of thousands of early childhood professionals. NAEYC (1998) defines "high quality" as a program that "meets the needs of and promotes the physical, social, emo-

---

 OUR DIVERSE WORLD OUR DIVERSE WORLD OUR DIVERSE WORLD OUR DIVERSE WORLD OUR DIVERSE WORLD OUR DIVERSE WORLD OUR DIVERSE WORLD OUR DIVERSE WORLD

[1] In observing programs for young children, consider the influences on the teachers' philosophy and practice; in many cases it is eclectic, a little bit of this and a little bit of that. It is another indication of how practice is influenced by life in a democratic and multicultural society.

tional, and cognitive development of the children and adults—parents, staff, and administrators—who are involved in the program." The following 10 criteria serve as a standard of excellence for any group program for young children. After each one is a reference to the chapter(s) in this text where the topic is more fully developed.

1. *Interactions between children and staff* provide opportunities for children to develop an understanding of self and others and are characterized by warmth, personal respect, individuality, positive support, and responsiveness. (Chapters 3, 5, 7, and 14)

2. *The curriculum* encourages children to be actively involved in the learning process, to experience a variety of developmentally appropriate activities and materials, and to pursue their own interests in the context of life in the community and the world. The program is inclusive of all children, including those with identified disabilities and special learning and developmental needs.[1] (Chapters 11, 12, 13, and 14)

3. *Relationships among teachers and families* are based on a partnership to ensure high-quality care and education, and parents feel supported and welcomed as observers and contributors to the program. (Chapter 8)

4. *The program is staffed by adults who are trained in child and family development* and who recognize and meet the developmental and learning needs of children and families. They recognize that the quality and competence of the staff are the most important determinants of the quality of an early childhood program. (Chapters 3, 5, and 15)

5. The quality of the early childhood experience for children is affected by the efficiency and stability of the program's administration. *Effective administration* includes good communication, positive community relationships, fiscal stability, and attention to the needs and working conditions of staff members. (Chapters 10 and 15)

6. *The staffing structure of the program is organized* to ensure that the needs of individual children are met, and it facilitates individualized, responsive care and supports learning. Smaller group size and high staff-child ratios are related to positive outcomes for children. (Chapters 3 and 5)

7. *The indoor and outdoor physical environments* should be designed to promote optimal growth and development through opportunities for exploration and learning. The quality of physical space and materials affects the levels of involvement of the children and the quality of interaction between adults and children. (Chapter 10)

8. *The health and safety of children and adults* are protected and enhanced. Good programs act to prevent illness and accidents, are prepared to deal with emergencies should they occur, and also educate children concerning safe and healthy practices. (Chapter 9)

9. *Children are provided with adequate nutrition* and are taught good eating habits. (Chapter 9)

10. *Ongoing and systematic evaluation* is essential to improving and maintaining the quality of an early childhood program. Evaluation should focus on the program's effectiveness in meeting the needs of children, families, and staff. (Chapters 2 and 10) (NAEYC, 1998)

These are the 10 essential components on which a program is judged for accreditation through NAEYC's Academy of Early Childhood Programs.

Developmentally Appropriate Practice (DAP)

Throughout this text and whenever NAEYC principles are discussed, we use the term *developmentally appropriate practice*. These core principles are reflected in the components for high-quality program we just discussed. What exactly is *developmentally appropriate practice*, or DAP, as it is more familiarly known?

In the late 1980s, the NAEYC published a position paper, "Developmentally Appropriate Practice in Early Childhood Programs Serving Children from Birth to Age 8," which articulated standards for high-quality care and education for young children. The guidelines were issued in response to the need for a set of unified standards for accreditation through

[1] Young children with special needs should have opportunities to engage in the normal activities of early childhood.

NAEYC's newly established National Academy of Early Childhood Programs and to the growing trend toward formal academic instruction in the early years (Bredekamp & Copple, 1997). They had great impact and influence in the early childhood field, and "DAP" became common terminology in early childhood circles. A DAP approach stressed the need for programs based on what we know about children through years of child development research and what we observe of their interests, abilities, and needs and called for an activity-based learning environment. These guidelines provided a necessary antidote to the more teacher-directed, academic preparation and skills-teaching approach, which was encroaching on many early childhood programs.

 Although embraced in many quarters, DAP was not without controversy. Many felt that NAEYC's position was too rigid, did not apply to all children at all times, and did not consider family background or the cultural context of children's lives.[1] There was concern that "good" practice meant only one definition of "good," rather than "many best ways" to support a child's growth and development (Hyun, 1998). Further, some critics felt that the definitions of DAP did not leave enough leeway for teachers to make decisions that were culturally congruent *and* developmentally appropriate (Bredekamp, in Bredekamp & Copple, 1997). Others considered the age-appropriate expectations questionable because they are usually based on data from the majority culture (Bredekamp, in Bredekamp & Copple, 1997).

The position paper was revised and adopted by NAEYC in 1996, following an extensive review by early childhood professionals over a 2-year period. That position statement of "Developmentally Appropriate Practice in Early Childhood Programs Serving Children from Birth through Age 8" (NAEYC, 1997) cites three criteria on which teachers and caregivers should base their decisions about young children's growth and development:

1. *What is known about child development and learning*—knowledge of age-related characteristics that permit general predictions within an age range about what activities, materials, interactions, or experiences will be safe, healthy, interesting, achievable, and also challenging to children.

2. *What is known about the strengths, interests, and needs of each individual child*—to be able to adapt and respond to individual variation.

3. *Knowledge of the social and cultural contexts in which children live*—to ensure that learning experiences are meaningful, relevant, and respectful for the children and their families (NAEYC, 1988).

The early childhood professional should address all three principles when designing good programs for young children, keeping in mind that each is connected to the other two in significant ways. Together, they influence the way teachers and caregivers plan and prepare high-quality experiences for young children.

How does this work? Let's look at what might happen when planning for a toddler program.

What does child development tell us about toddlers? We know that they want to do everything by themselves, usually more than they can actually achieve. We know they like to feel independent and learn quickly if given a little help and then encouraged to do what they can for themselves.

What do we know about each individual child in the group? Many of these toddlers rely on their parents to do things for them, such as helping them put on coats or shoes, feeding them, or putting their toys away. Others are being encouraged to try these activities by themselves, and some of them are being taught step by step at home. Most children come to a teacher for assistance, and a few call for help. On the other hand, one child will stay at a dressing task for nearly 5 minutes, while another will throw shoes across the floor if they don't slip on easily the first time she tries.

What do we know about the social and cultural context of their homes? Most of the children in this group come from homes where help is readily available through siblings and extended family members. The dominant cultural values and child-rearing practices reinforce dependence and community, although there is a smaller group of families that want their children to become independent as soon as possible.

By looking at all three criteria in conjunction with one another, we have some decisions to make about how or whether to go forward in setting goals for the toddlers, which would help them achieve greater independence. Respecting cultural diversity means we

 OUR DIVERSE WORLD OUR DIVERSE WORLD OUR DIVERSE WORLD OUR DIVERSE WORLD OUR DIVERSE WORLD OUR DIVERSE WORLD OUR DIVERSE WORLD OUR DIVERSE WORLD

[1] Many thought that the developmental norms reflected primarily Euro-American culture.

begin by talking to parents, perhaps at a parent meeting, where families are invited to share their child-rearing practices from their cultural viewpoints. Once we have an understanding of what families expect and want, we have an opportunity to work together to find a solution that would be good for the toddler and good for the parents as well.[1] This is what Hyun (1998) refers to as "'negotiable curriculum,' where teachers are no longer the ultimate power holders in any decision making." According to Hyun, the diverse voices of children and their parents are the "main agent in teacher's appropriate approach," creating a sense of shared power.

Let's look at another example of using the criteria to make planning decisions.

What does child development tell us about 4- and 5-year-olds? We know that they are great talkers; they like to play with language, making up stories, songs, and poems. They love being read to, and they enjoy dictating stories of their experiences and ideas. We know that children this age need increasing experiences in using oral language to connect those experiences with words and letters to begin to understand the use of the written word in their daily lives. We know that children learn to read by spending time reading and writing about what interests them.

What do we know about each individual child in the group? We have observed that a few of the children are creating more elaborate stories, complete with drawings. At the same time, there are several children who rarely participate in any of the art or story activities.

What do we know about the social and cultural context of their homes? We know that all of the parents have expressed interest, if not concern, that their children learn to read to do well when they get to kindergarten. Many of the children come from homes where reading is highly valued and where all members of the family enjoy books. Many come from family backgrounds where storytelling is a primary method of transmitting culture, history, and values. Most of the children are encouraged by their families to draw "stories" about their experiences.

There appears to be a common interest among the parents about reinforcing the concept of reading. The task becomes one of helping parents understand the meaning of literacy in the early years and developing an activity area that engages the preschoolers in meaningful activities that support the program's goals for literacy development. The daily schedule is adjusted to allow for small group times when the children tell stories to one another or dictate them to a teacher. Areas of the classroom are modified for literacy-rich experiences: picture books about building are added to the block corner; children are encouraged to write or draw notes to one another, recipes with drawings instead of words are used in cooking activities; paper and crayons are placed in the dramatic play area to encourage the writing of grocery lists and telephone numbers. Long-term projects involving children writing stories together or writing stories of their lives can be integrated into the planning as well.

Developmentally appropriate principles are reflected when:

● Programs and curriculum respond to the children's interests as well as their needs.

● Children are actively involved in their own learning, choosing from a variety of materials and equipment.

● Play is the primary context in which young children learn and grow.

● Teachers apply what they know about each child and use a variety of strategies, materials, and learning experiences to be responsive to individual children.

● Teachers consider widely held expectations about each age group and temper that with challenging yet achievable learning goals.

● Teachers understand that any activity has the potential for different children to realize different learning from the same experience.

● All aspects of development—physical, social/emotional, cognitive, and language—are integrated in the activities and opportunities of the program.

One of the important aspects of the creation and revision of DAP is that it reflects a consensus among early childhood professionals. These guidelines grew out of the profession's need to establish standards for

OUR DIVERSE WORLD OUR DIVERSE WORLD OUR DIVERSE WORLD OUR DIVERSE WORLD OUR DIVERSE WORLD OUR DIVERSE WORLD OUR DIVERSE WORLD OUR DIVERSE WORLD

[1] Although DAP stresses the importance of self-help skills, this may need to be examined as a culturally sensitive teaching practice for all children.

accreditation and to have some general agreement on what constitutes "best practice." It demonstrates clearly that the field of early education is inherently dynamic, growing, and changing to improve the way we support and encourage young children's learning.

In a variety of ways, DAP is integrated into other sections of the text. The Word Pictures in Chapter 3 offer a view of some general characteristics of children at various age levels, which can inform a teacher's decision-making process about developmentally appropriate practices. In Chapter 6, observations that focus on individual children are discussed and related to DAP. Chapter 9 outlines DAP daily schedules and environments for young children. Chapter 10 discusses developmentally appropriate evaluation of children, and, in Chapter 11, curriculum approaches that meet DAP criteria are discussed. A reading of NAEYC's position paper (see Appendix B) provides a more in-depth rationale for the various components of DAP, its philosophical foundation, and examples of appropriate practice for infants and children through age 8.

Developmentally and Culturally Appropriate Practice (DCAP)

Culturally appropriate practice is the ability to go beyond one's own sociocultural background to ensure equal and fair teaching and learning experiences for all. This concept, developed by Hyun, expands DAP to address cultural influences that emphasize the adult's ability to develop a "multiple/multiethnic perspective" (Hyun, 1998). Preparing teachers and caregivers for multiculturalism is not just about becoming sensitive to race, gender, ethnicity, religion, socioeconomic status, or sexual orientation, according to Hyun. It is also related to an understanding of the way individual histories, families of origin, and ethnic family cultures make us similar to and yet different from others. Through such insights, teachers will be able to respond positively to the individual child's unique expressions of growth, change, learning styles, culture, language, problem-solving skills, feelings, and communication styles (Hyun, 1998).

Hyun stresses the need for "cultural congruency"[1] between a child's home and school experience and suggests the following questions as a way to begin addressing the issue:

1. What relationships do children see between the activity and work they do in class and the lives they lead outside of school?

2. Is it possible to incorporate aspects of children's culture into the work of schooling without simply confirming what they already know?

3. Can this incorporation be practiced without devaluing the objects or relationships important to the children?

4. Can this practice succeed without ignoring particular groups of people as "other" within a "dominant" culture? (Hyun, 1998)

According to Hyun, a consistency between home and school would "allow for children to express and show the importance of their own family culture and identity" by "using children's personal experience, family culture, and diverse language expressions as important sources of learning and teaching." A culturally congruent approach to DAP would respect the variances in children's perceiving and understanding, and teaching practices would be based on children's different decision-making styles and social interaction abilities (Hyun, 1998). NAEYC's criteria for respecting cultural diversity, in Table 2.1, provide examples of ways in which to connect a child's sense of cultural continuity between home and school.

THE CORE OF EARLY CHILDHOOD EDUCATION

What do programs for the young child look like? How are the similarities and differences expressed in school settings? What marks a program as unique? The answers to these questions can be found by looking at some of the most common programs in early childhood education.

 OUR DIVERSE WORLD OUR DIVERSE WORLD OUR DIVERSE WORLD OUR DIVERSE WORLD OUR DIVERSE WORLD OUR DIVERSE WORLD OUR DIVERSE WORLD OUR DIVERSE WORLD
[1] Children's growth and development can be understood only within their cultural context.

DAP In Action — Respect For Cultural Diversity

Using NAEYC's criteria for cultural diversity, these examples demonstrate how DAP supports greater consistency between home and school cultures when you:

● Build a sense of the group as a community, bringing each child's home culture and language into the shared culture of the school so each child feels accepted and gains a sense of belonging

● Provide books, materials, images, and experiences that reflect diverse cultures that children may not likely see, as well as those that represent their family life and cultural group

● Initiate discussions and activities to teach respect and appreciation for similarities and differences among people

● Talk positively about each child's physical characteristics, family, and cultural heritage

● Avoid stereotyping of any group through materials, objects, language

● Invite families' participation in all aspects of the program

● Take trips to museums and cultural resources of the community

● Infuse all curriculum topics with diverse cultural perspectives, avoiding a "tourist" approach

(NAEYC, 1998)

Table 2.1 ● All children and their families deserve to be in programs where their lives are respected and where they can be proud of their cultural heritage.

The Traditional Nursery School

The traditional nursery school exemplifies a developmental approach to learning. Nursery schools, child care centers, laboratory schools, and parent cooperatives have been modeled after these programs, in which children actively explore materials and where activity or learning centers are organized to meet the developing skills and interests of the child. Most of these programs serve children from 2½ to 5 years of age.

The philosophy of these schools is best described by Katherine Read Baker in her now classic book *The Nursery School: A Human Relationships Laboratory.* First published over 50 years ago, this book serves as an encyclopedia of the traditional nursery school, its methods, and its philosophy, reflecting the influence of Comenius, Locke, Rousseau, Pestalozzi, Froebel, and Montessori.

The idea of a school as a place of human activity mirrors the thoughts of Dewey, Piaget, Erikson, and others. Read Baker develops this philosophy fully, with an educational model that emphasizes the human needs, growth patterns, and relationships in a young child's life. Developmentally, a traditional nursery school focuses on social competence and emotional well-being. The curriculum encourages self-expression through language, creativity, intellectual skill, and physical activity. The basic underlying belief is the importance of interpersonal connections children make with themselves, each other, and adults.

In theory, the objectives of traditional nursery schools are prescribed. The schools have some general characteristics in common, such as the daily schedule. The schedule reflects the values of the school. For example, large blocks of time are devoted to free play, a time when children are free to initiate their own activities and become deeply involved without interrup-

9:00	Children arrive at school
9:00–9:45	Free play (indoors)
9:45	Cleanup
10:00	Singing time (large group)
10:15–10:30	Toileting/snack time (small groups)
10:30–11:30	Free play (outdoors)
11:30	Cleanup
11:45	Story time
12:00	Children leave for home

Figure 2.1 ● A sample schedule for traditional half-day nursery schools is the core of early education programs.

tions, emphasizing the importance of play. In this way, children learn to make their own choices, select their own playmates, and work on their interests and issues at their own rate. A dominant belief is that children learn best in an atmosphere free from excessive restraint and direction.[1]

A typical daily schedule also indicates an awareness of the developing child's characteristics and needs. Programs attend to the physical and health needs (toileting, snacks, fresh air). There is a balance of activities (indoors and out, free choice, and teacher-directed times). Closer inspection of the environment reveals a wide variety of activities (large- and small-muscle games, intellectual choices, creative arts, social play opportunities).

Then, too, there is the clear acknowledgment of change and the time it takes children to make and adjust to changes. Children must have plenty of time for arrival and departure from school, greetings, cleanup, and transition times between activities. The amount of time given to any one part of the day's activities directly reflects the values the school endorses.

There are also aspects of the traditional model that are not immediately evident by looking at a daily schedule. The role of the teacher and methods of teaching are important. Nursery schools assume that young children need individual attention and should have personal, warm relationships with important adults. Therefore, the groups of children are generally small,

often fewer than 20 in a class. The teacher-child ratio is low, as few as 6 to 10 children for each teacher. Teachers learn about children's development and needs by observation and direct interaction, rather than from formalized testing. They work with children individually and in small groups and often teach through conversation and materials. Always, the teacher encourages the children to express themselves, their feelings, and their thinking. Such rapport between teacher and pupil fosters self-confidence, security, and belonging. Proponents of the traditional nursery school believe that these feelings promote positive self-image, healthy relationships, and an encouraging learning environment.

There are several programs within the traditional preschool framework. Three important variations on the theme are public school preschools, child care centers, laboratory schools, and parent cooperative nursery schools.

Public School Prekindergarten

In a growing number of states, many school districts offer prekindergarten programs for 4-year-olds, although some include 3-year-olds as well. Depending on their goal, these programs fall somewhere between traditional nursery schools and not quite full-day care. For some, the focus is on school readiness; others give priority to children at risk for school failure, children who come from families where English is not spoken, or low-income families. In states where early education has achieved a level of support, all 4-year-olds are eligible for enrollment, regardless of income.

Child Care Centers

Some of the first nursery schools in England operated from 8:00 AM until 4:00 or 5:00 PM. It was only later in America that the nursery school evolved into a part- or half-day program. Child care, then, is not a modern phenomenon. Child care center patterns differ from those of half-day nursery schools. By definition, a **child care center** is a place for children who need care for a greater portion of the day. The school schedule is extended to fit the hours of working parents. The program roughly models what ordinarily

OUR DIVERSE WORLD OUR DIVERSE WORLD OUR DIVERSE WORLD OUR DIVERSE WORLD OUR DIVERSE WORLD OUR DIVERSE WORLD OUR DIVERSE WORLD OUR DIVERSE WORLD

[1] This is not true for all cultures.

Figure 2.2 ● Individual attention and warm relationships—essential components in every program.

happens in the routines of a child's play at home. Therefore, the adults who work in a child care center have somewhat different responsibilities and training. Child care centers are for infants and toddlers, as well as for the 2½- to 5-year-old range. In this section, the focus is on those centers for the nursery school age range.

Child care has a number of unique qualities.

Scheduling. Compare the nursery school schedule with the child care schedule. The morning starts slowly. Children arrive early because their parents must go to work. The center will usually supply breakfast; mid-morning and midafternoon snacks supplement a noon lunch. A nap period for 1 to 2 hours for all the children gives a needed rest and balances their active, social day with quiet, solitary time. The program also includes extended experiences outside the school—field trips, library story hour, or swimming lessons—because children spend the major portion of their waking hours

on-site. As the day draws to a close, children gather together quietly, with less energy and activity.

Licensing. Licensing is the process of fulfilling the legal requirements, standards, and regulations for operating child care facilities. There are no national standards or policies regarding licensing of child care facilities in the United States. Many local and state governments, however, do require licensing of child care centers and family day care homes. Nor is there one central licensing agency in each state. Depending on the state, a license may be issued by the Department of Health, Department of Education, or Department of Social Welfare. Certification of child care workers is again left to local options.

Early childhood professional groups are calling for increased standardization of licensing procedures to ensure that children are receiving the best possible care in safe and healthy environments. The primary concern is to establish effective licensing policies that

7:00–8:30	Arrival/breakfast; limited indoor play
8:30	Large group meeting
8:45–9:45	Free play (inside)
9:45	Cleanup/toileting
10:00	Snack time (small groups)
10:15–11:30	Free play (outside)
11:30	Cleanup/handwashing
12:00	Lunch
12:30	Toothbrushing/toileting
1:00–2:00	Nap time
2:00–3:00	Free play (outside)
3:00	Group time
3:15	Snack time (small groups)
3:30–5:00	Inside and outside free play/library hour
5:00	Cleanup
5:15–5:30	Departure

Figure 2.3 ● A typical full-day care schedule. Most child care programs combine education and caring for basic needs.

are reinforced and will ensure that all programs will provide adequate care to meet the basic developmental needs of children. Standardized licensing regulations will protect children at all economic levels. All children will be treated equally whether they attend a family day care home in Houston, a Head Start classroom in Jacksonville, a child care center in Harlem, or a public school extended day program in Sacramento. The same minimum standards will apply to adult-child ratios, suitable safety precautions, health and nutrition needs, and the amount of training and preparation required of caregivers.

The need for standards arises out of recent changes in early childhood. The number of children in out-of-home care settings has increased. Many are infants and toddlers, a younger population than previously served. Children are spending longer hours in child care, and there are more programs sponsored by a variety of agencies such as churches, public schools, and private for-profit firms. With this diverse mix, a common set of standards for licensing is imperative to ensure the best possible care for all children who need these services. (See Chapters 3, 9, 10, and 15 for

further discussion of licensing, regulations, and standards for early childhood programs.)

In 1997, NAEYC issued a position statement in support of licensing and regulation of early care and education programs by the states (NAEYC, 1998). Although licensing needs to provide basic protection for children, NAEYC makes further recommendations for an effective regulatory system, including the provisos that:

● All programs providing care and education for two or more unrelated families should be regulated and that there be no exception or exemptions from this requirement.

● All centers or schools serving 10 or more children that provide services to the public should be licensed.

● States should establish licenses for individuals, such as teachers, caregivers, and program administrators.

● Licensing regulations should address health and safety, group size, adult-child ratios, and preservice and inservice standards.

NAEYC links the success of such a regulating system with the success of the whole field of early child care and education. Setting high standards and creating guidelines require an integrated approach of issues that affect the whole system of child care and education in this country. These include addressing child care, health, employment, and social services as a whole, and they call for an understanding of the meaning of quality, professional development, career advancement opportunities, equitable financing to ensure access for all children, and active involvement of all the stakeholders. Unless these factors are included, licensing and regulation will have little impact.

Staffing. What does child care mean for teachers? First, they must be aware of and trained to deal with the parenting side of teaching. The children may need more nurturing, clearer consistency in limits, and established routines. At the same time, they need individual flexibility and understanding and regular private time with caring adults.

Parents' needs also may be greater and require more of the teachers' time. Teachers should communicate with and support parents effectively. Parents want to trust their children's teachers and be relaxed with them. Teachers in a child care center find it valuable to take the time to be good listeners and clear communicators with parents about their child; this builds the trust and support that are so vital when working with young children. Child care parents may require extra effort; they have full-time jobs as well as child-rearing responsibilities draining their energies. It takes a strong team effort on the part of the teacher and the parent to make sure the lines of communication stay open.

The teaching staff undoubtedly has staggered schedules, perhaps a morning and an afternoon shift. Administration of this type of program is therefore more complex. An effort must be made to ensure that all teachers get together on a regular basis to share the information and details about the children in their care. Both shifts must be aware of what happens when they are not on site to run the program consistently.

See Chapter 15 for further discussion on child care issues.

Need for Child Care

Child care in the United States used to be primarily custodial, providing basic health and physical care. But times have changed. Full-day care is an American way of life, providing enriched programs for total development. Thousands of families rely on child care centers. Each day, 13 million preschoolers, including 6 million infants and toddlers (Children's Defense Fund, 1998), spend time in early care and education settings. As noted previously, the percentage of children attending nonparental child care and early education programs rose from 30% to 65% between 1973 and 1997. When significantly more than half the new mothers in the United States are in the workplace, a new pattern of family life is established.

The rising divorce rate, single-parent families, the women's movement, and the economy have all contributed to a greater need than ever for child care.

Quality early care and education contribute to the healthy cognitive, social, and emotional development of all children, but particularly those from low-income families[1] (Cost, Quality, and Child Outcomes Study Team, 1995). Yet data from the Children's Defense Fund (1998) paint a bleak picture for those who might benefit the most. The cost of child care, which may range from $4000 to $10,000 a year, is disproportionately high for poor parents. Half of American families with young children earn less than $35,000 a year. Nearly half of all children in families headed by single mothers were below the poverty line as of 1996, and the number of single-parent households has increased.

Good, affordable, accessible child care that will meet the increasing needs of American families is one of today's most crucial issues. The distinction between day care (stressing the protective, custodial services) and early education (emphasizing schooling) has appropriately blurred. Today, child care professionals recognize the concept of child care inherent in all programs for young children and the concept of education as an integral part of caring for young children.

This desire to link child care services with educating the young child is best expressed by the trend toward labeling many early childhood programs "child care" rather than the traditional "day care."

This term implies that child care is a permanent part of American life, including both teaching and nurturing functions. It removes some of the stigma previously attached to day care as primarily a babysitting, custodial function.

Child Care Issues

Millions of children are in child care settings every day. The questions and concerns, the issues, and the controversies center around the effects on children who spend so much of their early years in group care and the quality of that care.

Every day, scores of parents search for affordable programs and reliable providers. A Carnegie Corporation study (1996) confirmed that the quality of child care has a lasting impact on children's well-being and ability to learn and that too many 3- to 5-year olds are in substandard programs. They also reported that children in poor-quality child care have been found to be delayed in language and reading skills and display more aggression. Bredekamp and Glowacki (1996) succinctly summarize the primary issues in child care today. "The economics of child care continue to create a trilemma—quality for children, affordability for parents, and adequate compensation for staff." Even

OUR DIVERSE WORLD OUR DIVERSE WORLD OUR DIVERSE WORLD OUR DIVERSE WORLD OUR DIVERSE WORLD OUR DIVERSE WORLD OUR DIVERSE WORLD OUR DIVERSE WORLD

[1] There is a critical need for early childhood advocates to be the voice for poor and minority children.

though the past decade has brought about greater awareness of what quality means and what it costs, the solutions remain elusive.

A recent study (Cost, Quality, and Child Outcomes Study Team, 1995) reported finding that the average child care is mediocre in quality and identified certain characteristics of a high-quality educational experience for children in child care settings:

● Cognitive and social development are positively related to the quality of the child care experience.

● Children benefit emotionally, socially, and cognitively when child care centers have a high staff-child ratio, small group sizes, low staff turnover, and higher levels of staff compensation and training.

The focus of the child care issues centers on a few core problems that threaten the *quality* of child care throughout the country. A few statistics highlight the issues:

● The annual turnover rate for child care staff is over 30% (Whitebrook, Howes and Phillips, 1997).

● Thirty-two states do not require prior training to teach in child care centers, and 39 and the District of Columbia do not require training of family child care providers (Children's Defense Fund, 1998).

● A study of child-staff ratios (Snow Teleki, & Reguero-de-Atiles, 1996) found that fewer states met NAEYC-recommended standards for 4-year-olds in 1995 than in 1981.

● Snow and coworkers (1996) also found that only 18 states met the NAEYC recommendations for group size for infants.

Each of the four indicators of quality programs for young children is being undermined. Low salaries contribute to high staff turnover. The quality of child care is further jeopardized when increasingly more children are being served by fewer adults.

Fees for parents have remained relatively unchanged over the last 15 years, however. Child care costs for families, according to the U.S. Bureau of the Census (1996), seem unevenly distributed. Families earning $14,000 pay 25% of their monthly income on

child care (Children's Defense Fund, 1998). Obtaining affordable child care for those for whom it is a financial burden is a major concern that must be resolved.

Despite these threats to quality child care, there are a few encouraging signs. A U.S. Department of Education study, (1990), for instance notes that the number of licensed child care centers tripled between 1976 and 1990 and that early childhood providers significantly increased their levels of education and training.

The National Academy of Early Childhood Programs reports that as of June 1998, 6038 early childhood programs have been accredited and that 11,913 are in the process of self-study. Eighty-five percent of those who begin the self-study go on to be accredited.

The Child Care and Development Block Grant Act was passed by Congress in 1990, the most comprehensive child care bill to date. A landmark piece of legislation, this bill includes a program of direct aid to lower-income parents through child care certificates that can be used to purchase services from child care providers. It will surely be tested in the courts because it allows parents vouchers to pay for child care in church-based centers. The bill further provides for expansion of Head Start services to full-day and full-year care, for before-school and after-school care programs, and an "earned income tax credit" for low-income families. Improving the standards for child care and incentives for businesses to provide child care are also included in this legislation.

Where are the children who are in child care? What types of settings do parents commonly choose? A 30-year pattern has been dramatically altered: in the early 1960s only one out of every three preschool children of a working mother was enrolled in a child care center. By 1996, nearly half were being cared for in child care centers or family child care homes, and most of the remainder are in the care of family or relatives[1] (U.S. Bureau of the Census, 1996).

Work in child care is long and intense and coupled with undesirable wages. This creates high staff turnover and low morale. Full-time child care is expensive. Sometimes it is too costly for poorly paid or underemployed parents to pay for quality child care. Occasionally, a center will cut corners to keep

OUR DIVERSE WORLD OUR DIVERSE WORLD OUR DIVERSE WORLD OUR DIVERSE WORLD OUR DIVERSE WORLD OUR DIVERSE WORLD OUR DIVERSE WORLD OUR DIVERSE WORLD

[1] An ethnic breakdown of who uses child care shows that 46% of Hispanics, 62% of Euro-Americans, and 66% of African Americans are likely to receive supplemental child care from persons other than the child's parents (U.S. Department of Education, 1995).

tuition reasonable, but these shortcuts are usually detrimental to children.

The issues can be reduced to their core: how to expand affordable quality child care and at the same time address the lack of salary compensation and benefits so urgently due the early childhood professionals who subsidize the enterprise. Chapter 15 discusses the issue of child care in greater depth.

Family Child Care

Family child care is a type of service that cares for children in ways reminiscent of an extended family grouping. The child care provider takes in small numbers of children in the family residence. The group size can range from 2 to 12, but most homes keep a low adult-child ratio, enrolling fewer than 6 children. Seventeen percent of the mothers of children under age 5 select family child care, and, when combined with the 25% who have relatives taking care of their children (U.S. Bureau of Census, 1996), this becomes one of the most popular options.

The home setting, sometimes right within the child's own neighborhood, offers a more intimate, flexible, convenient, and possibly less expensive service for working parents. The children in a family child care home can range from infants to school-age children who are cared for after regular school hours.

Trawick-Smith and Lambert (1995) have noted four distinct differences between family child care providers and those who work in child care centers. Because they often care for infants, preschoolers, and after-schoolers, the developmental ranges that family child care providers must meet may span up to 12 years. That poses a challenge to develop experiences and activities for a mixed-age group of children. Family child care providers work and live in the same environment posing logistical problems of storage, space definition, and activity space. Often, family child care providers care for their own children within their programs, leading to problems with separation and autonomy of their children and providing enough time to the child as a parent. Family child care providers are administrators and managers as well as teachers and caregivers, faced with budgets and fee collections.

Advantages. Family child care has many advantages. It is especially good for children who do well in small groups or whose parents prefer them in a family-style setting. This is especially appropriate care for infants and toddlers. Family child care homes often schedule flexible hours to meet the needs of parents who work. The wide age range can be advantageous as well. Consistency and stability from a single caregiver throughout the child's early years and a family grouping of children provide a homelike atmosphere that is especially appropriate for infants and toddlers.

Family child care providers own and operate their own small business in their homes. Providing child care is a way for women who want to remain at home with their children to contribute to the family income. Meeting the requirements for licensing, fulfilling all the administrative tasks of a business and an educational program, and keeping current with the local, state, and federal tax requirements are part of the professionalism required for this type of child care arrangement.

Challenges. Family child care has its disadvantages, too. Many homes are unregulated; that is, they are not under any sponsorship or agency that enforces quality care, and many are exempt from state licensing.

Accountability to a licensing agency and training in child development are the two major factors affecting the quality of family child care programs. According to the Child Care Action Campaign of New York, there are at least 1.5 million family child care providers, only 20% of which are regulated. Training on an annual basis is mandated for family child care providers in only 13 states (Children's Defense Fund, 1998).

Family child care providers can feel isolated from others in the child care field. A hopeful sign, however, is that more articles on family child care are being included in professional publications, and early childhood conferences and workshops are now including issues related to the family child care provider. The National Association for Family Child Care, a network of family child care providers, has been established and publishes a quarterly publication of interest to its members.

The "Study of Children in Family Child Care and Relative Care" conducted by the Families and Work Institute (Galinsky, Howes, Kontos, & Shinn, 1994) made a number of important observations regarding in-home care. They found that:

● Families select providers who are similar to themselves in race and income.

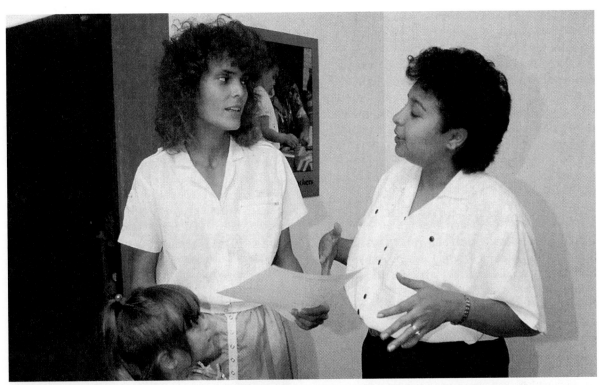

Figure 2.4 ● The family child care provider runs a small business in her home. She is flexible enough to adapt to changing work schedules and children's needs.

● Ethnic background and economics aside, parents and providers agreed that the following were characteristics of quality care: (1) the child's safety; (2) communication between parent and provider about the child; and (3) warm and attentive relationships between provider and child.

● Characteristics of providers that affect the quality of child care were: (1) they had a commitment to taking care of children and felt the work was important; (2) they took part in family child care training and sought to learn more about child development and planned experiences for the children in their care; (3) they networked with other providers and participated in their state's regulation process; (4) they cared for slightly larger groups and had higher adult-child ratios; and (5) they charged higher rates and followed standard business and safety practices.

The study also identified concerns, most notably that only half the children they observed in homes were securely attached to their providers and that only 9% of the homes studied were of good quality. They also found that children from low-income families are in lower quality care than children from higher income families and that children from minority families are in somewhat lower quality care than nonminority children.[1] These last two issues may be related to the fact that child care centers for low-income families have historically been subsidized by the government but those funds are not yet available for in-home providers.

This type of care could be a star in the galaxy of child care options. Small and personalized, it offers parents an appealing choice of home-based care. It is obvious, though, that further regulation of standards, availability of training for providers, and an awareness of the advantages of family child care need to be addressed. For those who need child care, this should

OUR DIVERSE WORLD OUR DIVERSE WORLD OUR DIVERSE WORLD OUR DIVERSE WORLD OUR DIVERSE WORLD OUR DIVERSE WORLD OUR DIVERSE WORLD OUR DIVERSE WORLD

[1] Responsibility for meeting the child care needs of all families should be shared more equitably by employers and governments, as well as families.

be a viable alternative; for those who want to work at home, this type of career should be given serious consideration.

Two Focus Box articles help enlarge our understanding of family child care. In this chapter, Jackie McCormick, a long-time family child care provider, gives insights into this special type of care. In Chapter 8, Yvonne Rickets speaks to the issues from a parent's viewpoint.

Children in the Workplace

Employer-Sponsored Child Care

Employer-sponsored child care refers to child care facilities on or near the job site and supported by the business or industry. Hospitals, factories, colleges, and military bases often provide this service.

The role of industry and business in group child care has an outstanding, if brief, history. The most notable example in this country is the Kaiser Shipyard Centers during World War II (see the Guest Editorial on pages 1–6 on these centers). When child care was equated with a national cause—winning the war—government and industry joined forces to provide quality child care in industrial settings. Recently this model has been examined as one way businesses can support working parents' efforts to find quality child care.

The number of women working outside the home and the increase in single-parent families encourage us to look at the workplace as a logical solution for child care needs. Employers who have implemented child care claim that the benefits are increased employee morale and better recruitment and retention of employees. For parents, there is the added appeal of having their children close by and being part of their educational process.

Industry has begun to respond to the need to create a supportive structure for women who combine work and family. Child care has rapidly become a corporate issue, leading one trendwatcher to observe that employer child care is "the hottest growth niche in the child care arena" (Neugebauer, 1998), with both large and small corporations participating. In 1990, 64% of private employers with more than 2000 employees offered some form of child care assistance. By 1995, that number had risen to 85%. Neugebauer (1998) defines this growth another way. Over an 8-year period, from 1989 to 1996, the largest management organizations operating employer child care centers increased the amount of child care by 750% at the same time the child care market as a whole increased by about 50%.

Government agencies are among the largest employers offering child care options. The federal government has over 1000 centers and sponsors nearly 10,000 family child care providers for use by military personnel (Neugebauer, 1998).

Several trends are notable. More companies are hiring management organizations to operate their child care facilities rather than maintaining them themselves. Employers are also insisting on quality, and centers are being accredited through NAEYC. The Cost, Quality, and Child Outcomes Study (1995) revealed that work-site centers receiving employer subsidies ranked among the highest in quality.

Benefits to employees may include the option for one or more of the following: parental leave, flexible hours, corporate group discounts at local centers or

Figure 2.5 ● More and more corporations and businesses, including hospitals, help parents by offering on-the-job child care facilities.

Family Child Care

Jackie McCormick

It is early on a Monday morning in July. The sun is streaming through the playroom windows even though it is only a little past 7 AM. Already my house is alive with the sounds of blocks tumbling, die-cast trucks rumbling down the hallway, and the shrieks and squeals of children at play. A mother drops off her 2-year-old in his pajamas with his pacifier and blankie firmly in hand. Carson and his mother have been locked in a battle of wills for a number of weeks because Carson refuses to get dressed first thing in the morning. So I take this "slow starter" from his mom for a few minutes of cuddling. We have breakfast, talk about his new Ninja Turtles, and soon join the other children in the playroom. Before we go outside to play, I dress him in play clothes and stow his pacifier and blankie safely away in his basket until naptime. For Carson and his stressed-out mother, a little flexibility in the morning routine goes a long way toward eliminating a potentially messy battle and allows a late riser to adjust more comfortably to the morning.

Indeed, flexibility is the cornerstone of successful home child care and an essential building block in provider–child relationships. Flexibility allows me to adapt to parents' changing work schedules, children's changing sleep patterns, and even to alter the days activities with the changing weather. By remaining flexible, especially to the children's needs, I have built a deep, personal relationship with each of the children I care for. I find ways to adapt to their schedules as much as possible instead of forcing them into a routine of the center.

That is not to say that our days are not structured, however. But the day's activities are closer to those of a well-planned family life rather than nursery school. Their play is supervised rather than directed. The basic life lessons are reinforced in a home atmosphere—eat healthy meals, get plenty of rest, take turns, ask questions, create freely, express yourself. In fact, my philosophy is to treat each child as if he were my own and build the same kinds of bonds that families build. Although I will never take the place of mom and dad, I can at least provide a safe haven where the children can play, and learn, and grow.

If there is a down side to family child care, it is the intrusion of the business on my own family life—the blurring of the boundaries between my two careers. It is not easy for my children to have the other children spend long hours in our home, to invade their territory, and to have a strong attachment to their mom. Most afternoons they clamor for my attention, bursting with news of their day and impatient for my undivided time. I find it difficult (as any working parent does) to be energetic, enthusiastic, or patient with my own family after my surrogate family has gone for the day. I feel frustrated, too, at not having much quality time for myself, or even much adult conversation beyond the pleasantries exchanged with my clients.

Despite these drawbacks, I feel that family child care is a most enriching profession! The satisfaction I get from each hug, from every brightly crayoned picture, from each wobbly first step or gurgled first word is a reward for a job well done. My extended family keeps me challenged and very, very busy, but they also keep me eternally young.

Jackie McCormick is a family child care provider.

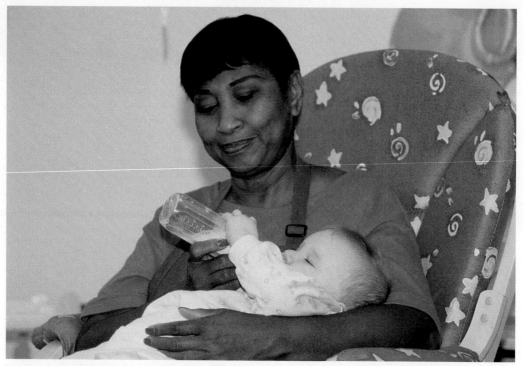

Figure 2.6 ● Routines, such as feeding, provide a balance to an active and busy day at the child care center.

family child care homes, resource and referral services, pretax salary reductions for child care, vouchers to purchase child care, reserved spaces in specific child care settings supported by the company. Companies located near each other may collaborate on the costs of these benefits.

These signs of growth are positive and likely to continue. Despite the movement, however, employer-supported child care still reaches less than 1% of all employees (Neugebauer, 1998).

Workplace Schools

A recent spinoff of employer-supported child care has emerged in an unusual collaboration between businesses and public school districts. In Florida and Minnesota, kindergartens have been established in rent-free corporate space while the school district supplies the staff and materials. Children ride to work with their parents, attend school, and stay on for a child care program until their parents are ready to go home. This innovative program, which is open to employees of other local businesses, hopes to include first and other elementary grades in the future and is a way for businesses to become more sensitive to families. It is a movement that bears watching.

Laboratory Schools

The college and university laboratory schools were among the first preschools established in the United States. They usually focus on teacher training, research, and innovative education. These schools serve as standards for model programs in early childhood education. They add to our knowledge of children, child development, and teaching methods. An important part of education in the United States, they are often supported or subsidized by the college.

As part of the child study movement, laboratory schools gathered information previously unknown about children and child development. Early ones include Hampton Institute in 1873, the University of Chicago, founded by John Dewey in 1896, Bank Street School in 1919, begun by Harriet Johnson, and the laboratory nursery school at Columbia Teacher's College, started in 1921 by Patty Smith Hill. In the late 1920s, Vassar, Smith, and Mills colleges all opened laboratory schools. Shortly after World War II, the Bing Nursery

School at Stanford University opened. Much more recently, community-college campuses have followed the lead of these pioneers. Campus child care centers have begun to combine child care services with the laboratory function of teacher training in one setting. The types and roles of the schools vary, depending on the educational philosophy and needs of the college and its students.

Regardless of their specific purposes, laboratory schools enlarge our understanding of children. They are often excellent places for beginning teachers to learn ways of teaching children. They encourage the joining of psychology, medicine, and other related fields to early education, and they serve as professional models for the public at large for what is good in child care and education.

The isolation of college campuses sometimes restricts the number and type of children who enroll. The program itself is tailored to meet the needs of student teachers who, under the guidance of skilled people, do much of the teaching. College calendars may be unable to accommodate the needs of children for full-time and year-round care. In addition, teachers trained in a laboratory school atmosphere will have to adjust to the realities of subsequent school settings, with typically fewer resources and large staff-child ratios.

Parent Cooperatives

Parent cooperatives schools are organized and run by parents. This type of early childhood setting offers a unique opportunity for parents to be involved in the education of their child. The very first parent cooperative, the Chicago Co-operative Nursery School, was started in 1915 by faculty wives at the University of Chicago.

Parent cooperative schools may offer half-day or full-day child care programs and are usually nonprofit organizations. They are similar to other nursery schools, with two notable exceptions. First, parents organize and maintain the school: they hire the teachers, buy supplies and equipment, recruit members, raise funds, influence school philosophy, and manage the budget. Second, traditionally, parents or their substitutes were required to participate in the classroom on a regular basis. In light of current family work patterns and the unavailability of many parents, this requirement has been modified in most programs. More professional teachers are hired, or other parents who are available are paid to substitute for parents who cannot work at the center.

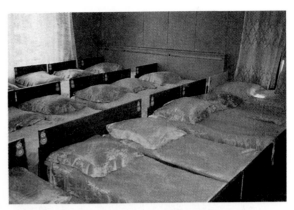

Figure 2.7 ● Child care around the world: a nap room in a Russian child care center.

Cooperative schools work well for many reasons. Popular with young families, they have low operating costs, the appeal of being with parents in similar circumstances, and the mutual support that is generated among members of a co-op. Friendships grow among parents who share child rearing as participants in their own and in their child's education. But what a co-op does not cost in dollars, it may cost in time. By their very nature, cooperatives can exclude working parents unless another adult is able to substitute for them in classroom participation. Maintenance is very much the parents' responsibility; they must regularly schedule work parties to refurbish the facility.

Depending on the size of the school, parents hire one or more professional teachers. These teachers must be able to work well with adults, have curriculum-building skills, and model good guidance and discipline techniques. Because many parent cooperatives require a weekly or monthly parent meeting, the teaching staff must also be competent in parent education. Child development and child-rearing topics are part of almost any cooperative nursery school discussion and require a practiced teacher to lead. The role of the teacher in this setting, then, is twofold: to provide for a sound educational experience for young children and to guide and direct parents in their own learning.

Church-Based Programs

Church-related schools are those owned or operated by an individual congregation or other recognized church organization. They are considered part of that congregation's community service or outreach and

Figure 2.8 ● There are similarities among all programs, but the relationship among parents, children, and caregiver is the universal consideration.

represent the church's intentional ministry to families. Two thirds of church-based programs are owned and operated by the local church; the remaining third are operated by other parties who rent space from the church but are not an integral part of the church's program. Many different denominations house a variety of educational and child care programs.

Throughout this nation's history, churches have demonstrated their concern for the welfare of children and their families. It was the churches that established many of the early schools, advocating the education of children. At the turn of the last century, church day nurseries and settlement houses cared for children of immigrants and poor working mothers. Later, hospitals and orphanages were founded, and churches spoke out for children's rights and the creation of child labor laws. In each era, depending on social and economic conditions, the churches have responded to the needs of children.

Role in Child Care

It is no surprise, then, to find that churches are deeply involved in child care today; there are over 20,000 child care programs housed in churches throughout the country, and more than 75% operate on a full-day basis, supporting the claim that churches are the largest single provider of child care in the United States (Lindner, Mattis, & Rogers, 1983).

Church-housed programs are broad-based. Toddler groups, full- and part-time nursery classes, all-day care, and after-school care are typical. Some churches sponsor programs for children with special needs and children of migrant farm workers. They serve the community at large and rarely restrict participation to their own congregations or denominations.[1]

Religious or spiritual development is not the explicit aim of the majority of programs for preschoolers. Churches are committed to caring for children of

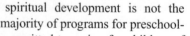

OUR DIVERSE WORLD OUR DIVERSE WORLD OUR DIVERSE WORLD OUR DIVERSE WORLD OUR DIVERSE WORLD OUR DIVERSE WORLD OUR DIVERSE WORLD OUR DIVERSE WORLD

[1] Churches and synagogues have been forerunners in providing comprehensive early care and education to the underserved populations of children and families in the United States, adding to the diversity of program options for all families.

working parents, providing a warm and loving environment to help children develop positive self-esteem (Lindner et al., 1983). The teaching of religious values to children in this age group is not common practice in most child care settings. The policy will vary, however, with each individual setting.

Church support of child care programs is primarily in the use of space. Known as "benign landlords" (Lindner et al., 1983), churches typically offer free or reduced-cost rent and may subsidize utilities, maintenance services, repairs, and some insurance. The church's nonprofit tax-exempt status is usually applied to child care programs that exist as part of the congregation's ministry. Programs housed in churches, however, suffer the same indignities as other child care facilities, such as low staff wages and poor or nonexistent benefits.

Common problems that arise in church-housed settings include sharing space with other church programs, frequent changes in leadership in the church's governing body, unclear policies and procedures regarding decision-making groups within the church, and inappropriate church governance structures regulating the operation of the child care program.

Academic Church Schools. For those parents who seek alternative education in a religious context, church schools fill the need. Many denominations serve children from early childhood through senior high. The relationship with the individual church organizations and the academic philosophy will vary from setting to setting.

Church and State Controversy. Two issues that cause controversy regarding church-housed programs are licensing and government funding. The landmark federal Child Care and Development Block grant passed by Congress in 1990 presently allows for parents to use the funds in programs that they choose, even those that are religiously based. This is sure to be tested in the courts at the first opportunity. Supporters of this issue cite parents' right to choose their own child care and the fact that nine of the ten organizations with the most child care centers in the country are religious organizations. Those who oppose use of public funds in any church-housed center argue that the First Amendment prohibits such use of government monies.

Most religious groups support the need for regulations and abide by licensing procedures even if their state exempts them.

Early childhood professionals, joined by many church leaders, are deeply concerned that exemption from even the most minimal standards not only undermines the national effort to create uniform standards for child care but also threatens the safety and welfare of children.

For-Profit Child Care

Sometimes called "proprietary child care," the for-profit establishments comprise over one third of all child care centers. A number of national chains of child care centers developed rapidly over the last 20 years, with some controlling anywhere from 100 to 1000 centers. For-profit child care was seen as a good investment opportunity, so businesses flourished and grew. A few very large companies dominate the scene, creating child care chains across the country, primarily as managers of employer-sponsored programs or franchisors of centers.

For-profit centers offer a variety of programs to meet parents' needs. Infant and toddler programs, preschools, kindergartens, before-school and after-school care, as well as summer sessions accommodate working parents. Many programs are expanding into kindergarten and primary grades, and some are opening charter schools (Neugebauer, 1998). Originally criticized for minimal salaries, lack of benefits, and a less educated staff (Meisels & Sternberg, 1989), the quality of for-profit child care has improved; yet the major concern of 80% of the chief executives of the nation's for-profit child care organizations is the shortage of qualified teachers (Neugebauer, 1997, 1998). One of the four largest for-profit child care chains has set as a corporate goal of accreditation of its 500 centers and is well on its way to achieving that goal (Neugebauer, 1997).

Many for-profit owners are providing on-site child care in industrial parks or focusing on employer-based child care. Future directions for the for-profit child care sector may lie in the area of elder care[1] and may provide the growth opportunity for child care organizations in the near future (Neugebauer, 1997).

OUR DIVERSE WORLD OUR DIVERSE WORLD OUR DIVERSE WORLD OUR DIVERSE WORLD OUR DIVERSE WORLD OUR DIVERSE WORLD OUR DIVERSE WORLD OUR DIVERSE WORLD
[1] Many facilities already exist where an intergenerational approach to child care includes young children and senior citizens.

Nannies

Originating in England, the nanny movement became popular during the 1980s as a child care option for parents who could afford to have child care in their homes. Nanny training programs can be found in community colleges and vocational schools, where their training may include child development, nutrition, and family relationships. Living arrangements vary; nannies may or may not live in the child's home and they may or may not be responsible for housekeeping or meal preparation. *Au pairs* differ from nannies in that they are allowed to spend only 1 year in the United States and do not receive any special training for their child care role.

Home Schooling

Traditionally, parents who chose not to enroll their children in school but to teach them at home did so for religious reasons. A growing number of the estimated 1.23 million home-schooled children (Viadero, 1997), however, are learning at home because of their parents' dissatisfaction with public schools, reflecting their concerns about school violence, poor academic quality, and peer pressure (Schnaiberg, 1996). Although home schooling is legal in all 50 states and the District of Columbia, regulations vary widely regarding teaching qualifications, evaluations, and accountability. Both the National Association of Elementary School Principals and the National Education Association have criticized home schooling, in part because of the lack of quality control. Studies show that most home-schoolers come from two-parent, middle-class families[1] (Schnaiberg, 1996).

A national study (Vaidero, 1997) found that students who are schooled at home outperformed public school pupils on most standardized tests, regardless of whether their parents had teaching credentials. The study also indicated that home-schooled children are not isolated socially and participate in any number of activities in the community, from sports to 4-H clubs (Viadero, 1997). It will be interesting to see if, as the result of these data, home schooling gains further endorsement as a viable educational option.

Teen Parent Programs

To serve the scope of human needs today, some early childhood programs focus on caring for children in a very specific context. Many high schools now have on-campus child care programs. Some serve as laboratory facilities to introduce adolescents to child care principles and practices before they become parents.

Others are part of a growing trend to provide support services to teenage parents. Young mothers are encouraged to complete their high school education by returning to campus with their young children. In addition to their regular academic classes, parents are required to participate in parent education classes, where they discuss child-rearing policies and parenting concerns. They also spend time in the children's classroom, applying their skills under the supervision of professional child care workers.

The aim of these programs is to help meet the long-term needs of adolescent parents by providing educational skills necessary to secure a job. At the same time, valuable support and training for parenthood help teenagers deal with the reality of the young children in their lives.

Other Programs

Hospitals also provide group settings for children who are confined for a period of time. Schools for children with special needs[2] address the needs of specific disabilities, offering a combination of educational, medical, and therapeutic services. Children who attend these schools may or may not be integrated part-time into other school settings.

Homeless Children

The plight of homeless children raises questions about program needs for this new and tragic phenomenon. Families with children now represent more than one third of the homeless population (Children's Defense Fund, 1998). These children attend schools closest to the shelter in which they stay for a brief time, then change schools when their parents move to another shelter. Many times these are children who

---

OUR DIVERSE WORLD OUR DIVERSE WORLD OUR DIVERSE WORLD OUR DIVERSE WORLD OUR DIVERSE WORLD OUR DIVERSE WORLD OUR DIVERSE WORLD OUR DIVERSE WORLD

[1] In class discussion it would be interesting to speculate why this is so.

[2] In the study of child development one needs to be aware of the full range of development and not focus on only typically developing children. Many programs are attempting to integrate 75% typically developing children along with 25% children having been recognized as having a special need.

already experience problems and failures in school. State and federal legislation is now being enacted to ensure full and equal educational opportunities for homeless children.[1]

Note: A discussion of children at risk from abuse and neglect is found in Chapter 15 under "Endangered Childhood." A discussion of children with special needs and programmatic implications follows in Chapter 3.

SCHOOLS WITH A MESSAGE

Head Start

Beginnings

In 1965, the federal government created the largest publicly funded education program for young children ever (Greenberg, 1990). (See also WPA nursery schools and the Lanham Act in Chapter 1.) Head Start began as part of this country's social action in the War on Poverty, and the implications of the program were clear: if underprivileged, disadvantaged, poverty-stricken children could be exposed to a program that enhanced their schooling, their intellectual functions might increase, and these gains would help break the poverty cycle.

In over 30 years, Head Start has served more than 16 million children and their families (U.S. Department of Health and Human Services, 1998). The success of Head Start can be attributed to its guiding objectives and principles, most notably expressed through:

● *Its comprehensive nature:* The child was seen as a whole, requiring medical, dental, and nutritional assessment, as well as intellectual growth. Extensive health, education, and social services were offered to children and their families. Today, Head Start is "the leading health care system for low-income children in the country" (Greenberg, 1990), providing health and medical screening and treatment for thousands of youngsters.

● *Parent participation and involvement:* Head Start redefined the role of parents by expecting parents to serve as active participants. Head Start parents were involved in the program at all levels: in the classroom as teacher aides, on governing boards making decisions about the program, and as bus drivers and cooks. The success of that approach is apparent. By 1998 Head Start reported that 30% of the staff were parents of current or former Head Start students (U.S. Department of Health and Human Services, 1998).

● *Services to families:* Many of the comprehensive services offered to children were extended to parents as well to assist them in their fight against poverty. Paid jobs in the program, on-the-job training, continuing education and training to prepare for some jobs, and health care are some of the support services families received. Parent education took on new meaning for low-income families with children in Head Start.

● *Community collaboration:* Interest and support from the local community helped Head Start respond to the needs of the children and families it served. Public schools, churches, libraries, service clubs, and local industry and businesses were included as partners in this war on poverty. These contacts throughout the community supported the underlying concepts of Head Start. Fostering responsible attitudes toward society and providing opportunities for the poor to work with members of the community in solving problems were fundamental Head Start goals.

● *Multicultural/multiracial education:* Since its inception, Head Start has sought to provide a curriculum that reflects the culture, language, and values of the children in the program.[2] Head Start efforts in this regard have been the models for other early childhood programs.

● *Inclusion of children with special needs:* Since 1972, Head Start has pioneered the inclusion of children with disabilities in its classrooms.[3] Head Start has the distinction of being the first and largest fed-

 OUR DIVERSE WORLD OUR DIVERSE WORLD OUR DIVERSE WORLD OUR DIVERSE WORLD OUR DIVERSE WORLD OUR DIVERSE WORLD OUR DIVERSE WORLD OUR DIVERSE WORLD

[1] Early childhood educators should advocate for consistent and quality care and education for all children whether their challenge is economic, social, or physical.

[2,3] See footnote 2 on p. 60. Head Start created a model for providing services that are *inclusive* (i.e., race, ethnicity, language, and physical ability) of all children.

erally funded program for children with special needs (Greenberg, 1990).

● *Ecology of the family:* Head Start programs looked at children within the context of the family in which they lived and viewed the family in the context of the neighborhood and community. This concept of taking the many forces that work against low-income families and viewing them as interrelated was a key factor in Head Start's success (See also "Ecology of the Family," Chapter 15).

The success of Head Start led to the creation of three specific programs that furthered the goals of Head Start: Parent and Child Centers, which served infants and toddlers and their families; the Child and Family Resource Programs, which provided family support services; and the Child Development Associate credential, which provided early childhood training and education for Head Start teachers.

The objectives outlined above could apply to any good nursery or kindergarten class. They take on an added dimension, though, when viewed as part of the total effort of Project Head Start, which was designed to be comprehensive enough to ensure appropriate programs for children and flexible enough to meet individual needs within the family and community.

It should be noted that at its inception, one aim of Head Start was to change the language and behavior patterns of the low-income children served, many of whom came from minority groups, and to resocialize them into cultural patterns and values of the mainstream, middle class. Head Start was a "compensatory" program, and the implications were that children from poor or minority families were unprepared for the demands of school in terms of language and cognitive skills, achievement, and motivation. To "compensate" for the presumed lack of appropriate school readiness, Head Start came into being. Although well-meaning, this attitude represents the prevailing perspective during the early efforts of the War on Poverty. Of course, Head Start was not the only program that held this view. The academic literature named this widely held perspective of the 1960s the "cultural disadvantage" model, which suggests that any language, cognitive, or relational style that differs from the Anglo, mainstream, middle-class style is necessarily detrimental rather than supportive to the educational process. Contrast this view with the more recent, pluralistic perspective, called the "cultural difference" model, which affirms that no one way of "behaving and believing" should be required for successful participation in school or society. Current "Multicultural Policies" of Head Start reflect this pluralistic view.

Head Start Today

Head Start has had a rocky history, its contributions notwithstanding. Struggling against budget cuts and controversy over its effectiveness, Head Start has undergone program improvements and expansions.

A national panel of early childhood experts, federal officials, and Head Start administrators formed an Advisory Committee on Head Start Quality and Expansion prior to Head Start's reauthorization by Congress in 1994. Although noting Head Start's effective combination of parent involvement in education and health and social services, the panel criticized the uneven quality and management of some Head Start centers. When passed, the bill supported the panel's recommendations for improving the quality and expansion of existing services, as well as for refocusing on the needs of today's families (Head Start, 1998). The key components of the bill are: (1) high-quality, comprehensive services with trained and qualified staff; (2) a program serving every eligible child; (3) responsiveness to community needs, including full-day, full-year services for children of families who are employed or in job-training programs; and (4) a program that is fully integrated into the community.

Two significant small grant programs are included in the reauthorization. One creates a group to explore ways to serve children from birth to 3 years of age, and the other is a transition grant that fosters Head Start–type services into elementary grades. Stressing accountability, the bill also allows the withdrawal of funds from programs that do not improve quality within a year's time. It is the first time that a Head Start center's past performance has been factored into its funding (Cohen, 1994b).

The recommendations and subsequent funding indicate the high esteem in which Head Start is held throughout the country. The original vision of Head Start was improved and expanded for the 1990s as a model that challenges the effects of poverty and promotes physically and mentally healthy families. Head Start has a formidable challenge ahead as it protects the high quality of its original charter while expanding and increasing services (Table 2.2).

A Picture of Head Start

Children

Enrollment	Approximately 800,000 children	
Ages enrolled	5-year-olds	6%
	4-year-olds	60%
	3-year-olds	30%
	Under 3	4%
Racial/ethnic composition		
	Native American	4%
	Hispanic	26%
	African American	36%
	Euro-American	31%
	Asian/Pacific Islander	3%
Children with disabilities		13%

Staff

Percentage of staff with degrees in early childhood education or CDA	90%
Percentage of staff who are parents of current or former Head Start students	30%

Programs

Percentage of programs that were home-based	57%
Percentage of programs that provide some full-day services	50%

Funding

Percentage of funding from the federal government[1]	80%
Percentage of funding from the local community	20%

Table 2.2 ● Head Start continues to be a vital program that serves the needs of a diverse population. (U.S. Department of Health and Human Services, 1998.)

Head Start and Multiculturalism

Head Start Program Performance Standards (1998) reflect a strong commitment to multicultural principles, with explicit references to the importance of respecting cultural diversity, language differences, and cultural backgrounds. An example is:

● *Performance Standard:* Provide an environment of acceptance that supports and respects gender, culture, language, ethnicity, and family composition.

● *Rationale:* Encouraging an understanding of human diversity helps children to grow up confident of their identity and to be respectful of the identity of others.

The Performance Standard guidelines define diversity as "a key element to consider in organizing and planning the use of materials," in designing space, the aesthetic environment, and teaching styles, and they state that environments "reflect the community and the culture, language, and ethnicity of the children

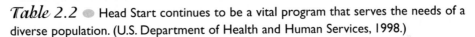

OUR DIVERSE WORLD OUR DIVERSE WORLD OUR DIVERSE WORLD OUR DIVERSE WORLD OUR DIVERSE WORLD OUR DIVERSE WORLD OUR DIVERSE WORLD OUR DIVERSE WORLD

[1] A good example of government support for early childhood programs.

and families" (Head Start Program and Performance Standards, 1998). The Performance Standards define an "environment of respect" as provided by adults who:

● Demonstrate through actions a genuine respect for each child's family, culture, and life-style

● Provide an environment that reflects the cultures of all children in the program in an integrated, natural way

● Foster children's primary language while supporting the continued development of English

● Avoid activities and materials that stereotype or limit children according to their gender, age, disability, race, ethnicity, or family composition

● Model respect and help children demonstrate appreciation of others (Head Start Program Performance Standards, 1998)

Other Performance Standards under the rubric "Cultural Background" address equipment, toys, and materials; home language and ethnic background; interactions with families, staff, and consultants familiar with families culture; and staff–parent relationships. Under the title "Cultural Diversity," the areas of bilingual communications in the classroom, family involvement, and parent involvement in program planning are articulated.

Evaluating Head Start's Effectiveness

Two studies have helped highlight Head Start's impact over the years. One, the Consortium for Longitudinal Studies, pooled data from a number of smaller studies in the hopes that clear trends regarding early intervention could be identified. Brown (1985) noted two significant findings: (1) that Head Start children were less likely to be placed in special education classes, and (2) that early intervention programs were associated with a significant increase in IQ and school achievement. The second study, the Perry Preschool Project, was not of a Head Start program but had an enormous impact on policy makers and government officials and affected Head Start funding in significant ways.

The High/Scope Perry Preschool Study. This study, though not a Head Start program, presented the most convincing evidence to date of the effectiveness of early intervention programs for low-income children.

Begun in the 1960s, it is the first longitudinal study to measure the effects of preschool education and to track the children from preschool years through age 27.

One hundred twenty-three African American children from poor families, with IQs ranging from 60 to 90, were randomly assigned to two groups. Children from the first group were placed in high-quality early childhood programs at age 3; the other group did not attend preschool. The results showed great differences between the children who had the advantage of a high-quality program and those who did not. Low-income children who had attended preschool significantly outperformed those who had not.

The latest round of data cite the most dramatic benefits to date. The children attending the preschool program were better educated, spent fewer than half as many years in special education programs, had higher earnings, were less likely to receive welfare, and were five times less likely to be arrested (Schweinhart & Weikart, 1993). Gender differences were also noted: preschool program girls had a significantly higher rate of graduation than did the girls who did not attend preschool, whereas, in comparison, preschool program boys completed slightly less schooling than non-preschool boys (Cohen, 1993b).

Not only does this study underscore the need for high-quality preschool programs for children who live in poverty, but it also demonstrates the potential impact that Head Start has on the country's future.

It is the first study of its kind to suggest the economic impact of early intervention. Because most of the children in the high-quality early childhood program required less remedial education, had better earning prospects, and were less costly to the welfare and justice systems, early intervention in education was shown to be cost-effective. The estimated value gained over the lifetime of the students in the preschool program "may be more than seven times the cost of one year's operation of the program." (Berrueta-Clement, Schweinhart, Barnett, Epstein, & Weikart, 1984). That assessment still holds true today.

The High/Scope Perry Preschool Study reinforces the focus of Head Start's vision for the future and has served the early childhood community well by demonstrating that high-quality programs for young children can have a permanent and significant impact on children at risk.

Follow-Through. In 1968, to build on the gains children developed in Head Start, Follow-Through provided funds for programs for children in kindergarten through third grade. Using many different educational models and approaches, Follow-Through was the beginning of a collective effort to see that the impact of Head Start was not lost and that gains could be strengthened by developmentally appropriate curricula as well as health and social services up to age 8. It is a unique model that calls for the collaboration between Head Start and public school leadership. Whereas there are relatively few programs in the country today, the transition grant in Head Start's recent reauthorization calls for a continuation of the effort.

High/Scope

Under the leadership of David Weikart, the High/Scope Foundation has become a major source of applied educational research and practical work with teachers. Chief among their accomplishments are the Perry Preschool Project (described earlier) and a cognitively oriented approach to teaching and curriculum, using Piagetian theory.

The High/Scope curriculum stresses active learning through a variety of learning centers with plenty of materials and developmentally appropriate activities. Active problem solving is encouraged as children plan, with teacher's assistance, what they will do each day, carry out their plan, and review what they have done. Appropriately, this is known as the "plan–do–review" process. Teachers use small groups to encourage, question, support, and extend children's learning while emphasizing their communication skills.

There is a balance between child-initiated experiences and teacher-planned instructional activities. Teachers use observational techniques to focus on children and to understand children's play. Teachers are responsible for planning *key experiences* that reinforce and extend the learning activities the children select for themselves. These key experiences are eight concepts that form the basis of the Cognitively Oriented Curriculum, another term for the High/Scope approach, and include creative representation, language and literacy, initiative and social relations, movement, music, classification, seriation, number, space, and time (Hohmann & Weikart, 1995).

Children with special needs are integrated readily into High/Scope programs and with a curriculum developed especially for K–3 grades, High/Scope extends its active learning philosophy into the early elementary school years.

High/Scope's approach to children's learning is deeply rooted in Piagetian theory and supports Vygotsky's theory of social interaction and cognition: children learn when interacting with the people and materials in their environment. Core elements of the High/Scope philosophy are shared by the schools of Reggio Emilia. Both philosophies stress the importance of children's constructing their knowledge from activities that interest them; team teaching is an important concept, to allow the children access to adult support; and the process of planning, acting, recording, and reassessing is one that both approaches use to foster critical-thinking skills.

Bank Street Developmental-Interaction Approach

Bank Street was founded by Lucy Sprague Mitchell (see Chapter 1), and its roots reflect the thinking of Freud, Dewey, Erikson, Vygotsky, and Piaget, among others. There is a clear connection between education and psychology in its approach (Mitchell & David, 1992). Children are as seen as active learners who learn by interacting with and transforming the world about them. Play is seen as the primary vehicle for encouraging involvement between and among children, adults, and materials. The teacher's primary role is to observe and respond to activities initiated by the children. Classrooms are organized into specific areas, where children can work individually or in groups. Units and themes are used to focus the curriculum. There is a freedom of movement and choice and easy access to materials (Epstein, Schweinhart, & McAdoo, 1996).

A teacher's knowledge and understanding of child development principles is crucial to this approach. Educational goals are set in terms of developmental processes and include the development of competence, a sense of autonomy and individuality, social relatedness and connectedness, creativity, and an integration of different ways of experiencing the world.

Open Schools

Open education—sometimes called open schools or informal education—is a term used to describe child-centered learning environments often associated with the British infant schools (see discussion of this type of school in Chapter 1, as well as references to Summerhill and Waldorf). It is based on the belief that children learn and grow at different rates, that they are eager and curious about learning, and that they learn best when they are able to pursue their own interests. Open school philosophy uses play as the principal means for learning. Not only do children learn from each other as they play in a mixed-age group; they also grow through a rich and varied learning environment.

If this description sounds vaguely familiar, it should because it applies to many typical nursery schools and kindergartens. The philosophy has a familiar ring to it. Didn't John Dewey speak of self-initiated learning, social cooperation, active education, and respect for the individual? And before him, Comenius, Rousseau, Pestalozzi, and Froebel all promoted similar concepts. In some ways, open education is the Progressive Movement revisited.

The British infant school movement aided the revival of open education in the United States in the 1970s, and today many schools still pattern themselves after the British model. The open school has come to mean an approach, a philosophy, that is practiced in many types of early childhood settings—nursery schools, child care centers, and elementary schools.

The open school is not without criticism, much of which centers around the lack of formal instruction. The deemphasis of direct instruction of reading and writing is questioned. Supporters of open schools counter that the child-centered approach in fact leads to a high motivation to read and write.

Open education allows for a child to respond individually and personally to the experience. The freedom of choice, the development of problem-solving skills, and the respect for initiative are all based on the strong belief that allowing children this kind of involvement reflects back to them their worth and dignity. For that reason alone, open classrooms continue to exemplify the best in humanistic education (Elkind, 1993). See Chapter 11, "Open Education Revisited," for futher discussion."

The Schools of Reggio Emilia

Respect for children's investigative powers and for their ability to think, plan, criticize, collaborate, and learn from all they do is the hallmark of the Reggio

Emilia approach and is a good example of an open education approach to learning. This collection of schools in Italy, with separate programs for infants to 3-year-olds and 3- to 6-year-olds, has commanded worldwide attention for its philosophy and practices. "Nowhere else in the world," states Gardner (Edwards, Gandini, & Forman, 1993), "is there such a seamless and symbiotic relationship between a school's progressive philosophy and its practices."

Influenced by Dewey's progressive education movement, the philosophies and practices of Reggio Emilia owe a great deal as well to Piaget's constructivist theory, Vygotsky's belief in social discourse as a method of learning, and Gardner's own theory of multiple intelligences (see Chapters 1, 4, and 13). Therefore, children are actively engaged in long-term projects that they initiate, design, and carry out with the support of the teacher. Art is the primary medium for learning.

Some of the key components of the Reggio Emilia approach are: a materials-rich environment that is aesthetically appealing; a community-based attitude involving the entire city; a family support system; and a commitment to process. These elements are manifested in the program through astonishingly beautiful school settings, replete with the work of children and evidence of their projects elegantly displayed throughout; by support realized through a large portion of the city's budget; through small groups of children who stay together for a 3-year period with the same teacher; and through intentionally bringing the children's culture into school life.[1]

The teacher's role is unique: two coequal teachers work with a class of 25 children. There is no head teacher or director of the school. The teachers are supported by a *pedigogista*, a person trained in early childhood education, who meets with the teachers weekly. Also on the staff of every school is an *atelierista*, a person trained in the arts who teaches techniques and skills the children learn for their projects.

Process is highly respected as the way to plan and work together. Teachers and children, cocollaborators, listen to one another, and many points of view are encouraged. Debate and discussion are key elements in the process of deciding what project to do and how to go about it. The attitude that a child is a natural

OUR DIVERSE WORLD OUR DIVERSE WORLD OUR DIVERSE WORLD OUR DIVERSE WORLD OUR DIVERSE WORLD OUR DIVERSE WORLD OUR DIVERSE WORLD OUR DIVERSE WORLD

[1] For example, common household objects and displays of pasta, fruits, and vegetables representing locally produced foods are often arranged in the lunch area.

researcher as well as an able learner and communicator has molded the organization and structure of the schools. The schools of Reggio Emilia are worth knowing about just for the strong and powerful view they hold of the child and the concept of teacher and student learning from one another. There are a growing number of American models as well.

Montessori

In Chapter 1, the person who started this important movement, Maria Montessori, was discussed in relation to the history of early childhood education. What follows here is an explanation of the Montessori method as a program for young children.

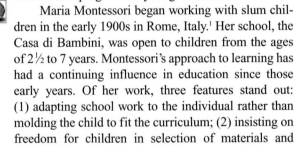

Maria Montessori began working with slum children in the early 1900s in Rome, Italy.[1] Her school, the Casa di Bambini, was open to children from the ages of 2½ to 7 years. Montessori's approach to learning has had a continuing influence in education since those early years. Of her work, three features stand out: (1) adapting school work to the individual rather than molding the child to fit the curriculum; (2) insisting on freedom for children in selection of materials and choice of activities; and (3) training of the senses and on practical life issues.

The Program

A common misunderstanding is that all schools with the Montessori name are the same; they are not. There are many variations and types of Montessori schools throughout the United States, reflecting an infinite variety of interpretations of the Montessori method. Within the Montessori movement itself, there are at least two factions claiming to be the voice of the true Montessori approach to education.

Although, the most common form of Montessori program is one in which 3- to 5-year-olds are grouped together, there are a growing number of schools for 6- to 9-year-olds and even 9- to 12-year-olds. New teacher education programs now prepare Montessori teachers to work with infants and toddlers as well as high schoolers.

The most striking feature of the Montessori classroom is its materials. Many are made of wood and designed to stress the philosophy of learning through the senses. Color, texture, and quality of craftsmanship of the materials appeal to the hand as well as the eye; they demand to be touched. "Smooth" and "oval" take on new meaning as a child runs a finger around Montessori-designed puzzle shapes.

Montessori materials have other unique characteristics besides their tactile appeal. They are self-correcting; that is, they fit together or work in only one way so that children will know immediately whether they are successful. The Montessori curriculum presents the materials in a sequence, from simplest to most difficult. Many of the learning tasks have a series of steps and must be learned in a prescribed order. Whether sponging a table clean or using the number rods, the child is taught the precise order in which to use the materials. Montessori developed curriculum materials and tasks that are related to real life. "Practical life" activities range from cleaning tasks (hands, tables) to clothing tasks (lacing, buttoning, or tying garment closures).

In a Montessori classroom, children work by themselves at their own pace. They are free to choose the materials with which they want to "work"—the word used to described their activity. Children must accomplish one task before starting another one, including the replacing of the materials on the shelf for someone else to use.

The prepared environment in a Montessori program has child-sized furniture and equipment—one of Froebel's ideas that Montessori used. Materials are set out on low shelves, in an orderly fashion, to encourage children's independent use. Only one set of any materials—their shape, form, and the way they are presented for children to use—are the vehicles for learning.

The teacher in the Montessori setting has a prescribed role, one of observing the children. Teachers become familiar with skills and developmental levels, then match the children to the appropriate material or task. There is little teacher intervention beyond giving clear directions for how to use the materials. Group instruction is not common; learning is an individual experience.

OUR DIVERSE WORLD OUR DIVERSE WORLD OUR DIVERSE WORLD OUR DIVERSE WORLD OUR DIVERSE WORLD OUR DIVERSE WORLD OUR DIVERSE WORLD OUR DIVERSE WORLD

[1] Montessori exemplified inclusivity. Her theories evolved from her work with children who were considered developmentally delayed and with children from the slums of Rome.

The Controversy

Some controversy surrounds the Montessori method, its schools, and its training. Four limitations of the Montessori philosophy most frequently cited are:

● *Lack of social interaction among children and between teachers and children.* Notably absent is dramatic play equipment that would foster peer interchange. This is the area in which there is the largest single disagreement between Montessori and traditional schools (Chattin-McNichols, 1992).

● *Lack of self-expression.* In some schools, children are still discouraged from exploring and experimenting with materials in their own way. Creative arts are not part of the pure Montessori method. No vehicle is provided for self-expression through fantasy, imagination, or creative play.

● *Lack of stimulation for language development.* Because children are encouraged to work alone and teachers interact with them in fairly structured ways, many opportunities for verbal exchange are lost. Again, creative arts and dramatic play provide options, if they are available.

● *Lack of gross-motor equipment or emphasis.* Only fine-motor skills are emphasized in most of the Montessori materials. Outdoor play is not an integrated part of the Montessori curriculum.

Research, although not extensive, does show that children from Montessori programs perform as well as children from other types of preschool programs in most areas, such as school readiness and intelligence (Chattin-McNichols, 1992). Continued research is needed to answer more fully the questions concerning the effect of a Montessori school experience.

Many changes have taken place in Montessori practices over the years, and today's best Montessori programs are those that are true to philosophical traditions of the Montessori method but constantly make small changes and adjustments. Many Montessori schools are adding curriculum areas of art, dramatic play, gross-motor development, and computers. There is also greater teacher flexibility to promote social interaction.

For years, Montessori has been separated from the mainstream of American education. Today that is changing, with over 100 public school districts offering Montessori programs in their elementary schools and with the increased interaction between Montessorians and other early childhood professionals.

Maria Montessori has found her way into nearly every early education program in existence today. Whether labeled so or not, much of the material and equipment as well as many of the teaching techniques in use today originated with this dynamic woman nearly 100 years ago.

She is firmly established in early childhood history of the past and of the future. The Montessori method should be weighed in light of contemporary knowledge and should be tailored to meet the needs of vigorous, eager, often needy children of the 21st century.

John Chattin-McNicols offers a current perspective in the following Focus Box.

EXTENDING THE AGE RANGE

Infant/Toddler Programs

There has been a dramatic rise in recent years in the demand for and availability of group care for infants and toddlers. The early 1970s produced a great deal of research concerning the infant/toddler, enhancing public awareness of the potential of children this age. Greater resources and information became available, creating an awareness of the implications for programs that focus specifically on the infant or toddler. Research by Brazelton, White, Honig, Caldwell, Lally, and others has informed us where and how and why we can offer enrichment and learning opportunities to the youngest of children. And we know that this can occur in group care settings under professional guidance.

The trend toward group care for infants and toddlers was affected by the rising number of women in the work force who combine child rearing and careers and by the increasing number of single-parent families in which the parent must work.

Gonzalez-Mena and Eyer (1993) define the infant/toddler age group: infancy is from babyhood until the child learns to walk. Then he or she is called a toddler until almost 3 years old.

Infant/toddler centers fall into several categories. They may be full-day centers or they may be part-time. They may be more educational, with parent involvement programs, than centers for group care. Most are a combination of physical care coupled with intellectual simulation and development.

Parent relationships are an important part of any program for young children, but especially so when babies and toddlers are involved. The general intention

Montessori in the United States, Then and Now

John Chattin-McNichols

Dr. Maria Montessori founded the first Montessori school *(Casa di Bambini)* in Rome, in 1907. Montessori was introduced in the United States by Jenny B. Merrill, Ph.D., in the *Kindergarten-Primary Magazine* (December 1909).

Poor or uncomprehending reception of Montessori's methods by the educational leadership, adaption of her methods in a variety of ways, a focus on academics by demanding middle-class parents, and a flood of "trainers" and authors eager to capitalize on Monstessori contributed to a rapid downfall of Montessori schools in the United States by 1925 or so. J. McVicker Hunt, in his introduction to *The Montessori Method*, claims that a *mismatch* existed between the educational and psychological leaders of the day and Montessori. In important areas such as the importance of school experience for 3- and 4-year-olds, the belief in fixed intelligence (nature rather than nurture), and the idea that all behavior had to be (externally) motivated by drives, Montessori was ahead of her time and so in complete opposition to the educational and psychological thought of the day. Montessori's ideas that children would be motivated by a desire for mastery, now recognized as "competency motivation," was seen as nonsense by early theorists. Hunt also claimed that the new role for the teacher that Montessori advocated and the greater freedom for children to choose their own activity threatened traditional ideas of teaching.

In the late 1950s and early 1960s, parents saw Montessori schools in Europe and ... set out to create their own. Teachers were hired from Holland, England, and Ireland, materials were brought in, and the second American Montessori movement began. A basic difference in perspective on Montessori between European experts and Americans was brought to a head in a controversy over control of Montessori teacher preparation programs. The American Montessori Society grew out of the conflict and has become the largest Montessori organization in the United States.

Today with a much wider range of children than ever before, the majority of Montessori schools are private preschools and child care centers, serving 3- to 6-year-old children. But many also serve elementary students, and a small (but growing) number of infants, toddlers, and middle-school students. Some 100 school districts nationwide have public Montessori programs today, primarily as magnet programs. The American Montessori Society has its own accreditation process for ensuring quality in its teacher education programs and the Teachers' Research Network, dedicated to fostering ongoing examination of Montessori practices. The word *Montessori*, however, remains in the public domain, so that Montessori in the name of a school or teacher education program does not guarantee any adherence to Montessori's original ideas.

Dr. John Chattin-McNichols of Seattle University is an internationally known Montessori educator and author.

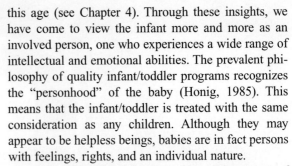

Figure 2.9 ● The need for quality child care has increased as thousands of mothers enter the work force.

of these centers is to provide care that is supplemental to family life and that supports the child's family structure. To do that, the caregiver at an infant/toddler center involves the parents in the everyday decisions about the care of their child, provides them with information about the child's day, and strengthens the child's sense of belonging to that particular family.[1]

Philosophy of Infant/Toddler Care

Research has enlarged our understanding of the growth process of babies. Piaget defined this time as the sensorimotor stage, and Erikson states that trust and autonomy are the critical lessons to be learned at this age (see Chapter 4). Through these insights, we have come to view the infant more and more as an involved person, one who experiences a wide range of intellectual and emotional abilities. The prevalent philosophy of quality infant/toddler programs recognizes the "personhood" of the baby (Honig, 1985). This means that the infant/toddler is treated with the same consideration as any children. Although they may appear to be helpless beings, babies are in fact persons with feelings, rights, and an individual nature.

This philosophy implies that taking care of infants or toddlers is not just a case of thrusting bottles in their mouths when they are hungry or putting them in a playpen to amuse themselves. The caregiver in a quality infant/toddler center understands that feeding, diapering, and playing are, in fact, the curriculum of this age group. Caregiving routines are at the heart of the infant/toddler program. The challenge for the caregiver is to find ways to use these daily routines to interact, develop trust and security, and provide educational opportunities. In many cases, the caregiver's (or educarer's) role extends to helping parents use these same common occurrences to promote the optimal development of their child.[2]

Magda Gerber has been a pioneer in infant care. She coined the term **educaring** to describe the relationship between an infant and an adult. Gerber's philosophy is based on a respect for babies and the use of responsive and reciprocal interactions in which baby and caregiver learn about each other. Communicating through caregiving routines (diapering, feeding) in one-to-one intense and focused interactions is a foundation of Gerber's approach to caring for infants and toddlers (Gerber, 1979). Observing, listening, and reading babies' cues are key elements in educaring.

Differences from Preschool

Infant and toddler education differs from preschool education in several important ways. These differences stem from the very nature of infants and toddlers and their needs. According to Cataldo (1983) infant and toddler education is "more intense . . . more

1 The early childhood educator should respond to the child and parent as individuals in a unique family context and foster healthy family relationships.

2 The caregiver must be culturally sensitive to the parent's background. There are many cultural differences about caring for infants, such as the amount of vocalizations, how and when babies are held, and sleep routines.

physical . . . more personal" than working with preschoolers. Infant/toddler education owes its overall philosophy to the traditional tenets of early childhood education; these basic principles are extended to meet the specific requirements of this more vulnerable age group.

In infant and toddler programs as compared with preschool programs, there is a need for:

● More one-to-one physical care

● Immediate response from adults

● More follow-up to experiences and activities

● Use of ordinary routines as learning opportunities

● Skills that go beyond teaching: mothering, being a playmate

● Intentional rather than discovery learning

● Keener attunement to interpreting need and distress signals in young children

Figure 2.10 ● Active involvement with people and objects help infants and toddlers develop feelings of self-identity, curiosity, and creativity.

The distinction between programs for infants and those for toddlers is also important to note. Just as a scaled-down version of preschool is not a toddler program, neither is a scaled-down version of a good day for toddlers an appropriate model for infants. The mobility of the toddler, for instance, requires different amounts of space and time in the schedule than are required for infants. Babies sleep more their first year of life; their rhythm of eating, sleeping, and playing must be met. Babies thrive when someone responds to their smiles and developing skills. Common routines such as diapering create the curriculum as caregivers talk with the babies about what they are doing and what is happening to them. Caregivers get babies to focus on themselves through gentle, extensively personal involvement. Good programs for babies recognize their capacities and the extent of their awareness of themselves and others in their environment.

Routines again become the focus of the toddler's day but in a somewhat different way. Mealtimes and toileting provide daily opportunities for toddlers to explore and to express their emerging sense of self. Handwashing—even eating—becomes a time to fill, to taste, to dump, to pick up. Again, the curriculum emerges from a developmental need toddlers have of "Me! Mine!" To foster that independence, that wanting to "do it myself," routines that allow for experimentation, mistakes, and messes make a good toddler curriculum.

Good programs for infants and toddlers, then, are distinctly arranged for them and are not simply modified versions of what works well in a program for 3-year-olds.

What Is Good Quality Infant/Toddler Care?

Infants and toddlers need attention to their physical and psychological needs; a relationship with someone they can trust; respect; a safe, healthy, and developmentally appropriate environment; chances to interact with other infants and toddlers; and freedom to explore using all their senses (Gonzales-Mena & Eyer, 1989).

The high level of dependency on adults, the rapid growth changes from birth to age 3, and the interrelationship among developmental areas (see Chapter 3) call for certain elements to ensure high-quality infant and toddler programs. Honig (1985) calling infant/toddler caregiving "the scarcest commodity in the world of child care," lists key elements for quality programs:

● The quality of the caregiver

● The stability of the staff

● The expensive staff-infant or staff-toddler ratio of at least 1 to 4

● The need for a rich language experience integrated into daily routines

● The need to build a prosocial curriculum that promotes children to care for and about one another

● The necessity for caregivers to devote individual attention for both learning and caregiving, balancing between the group and the individual child

● The need to support and renew staff so they in turn will be supportive to parents and serve as appropriate resources

● The need to promote a sense of choice and control to young children throughout the curriculum and routines of caregiving

● The critical need for ongoing training for caregivers

Issues. There are many important issues surrounding quality infant/toddler care. First, good care costs money. The factors that combine to make a quality program—low teacher-child ratio, small groups, individual attention—raise the costs to make infant/toddler care one of the most expensive child care programs. Second, critics of child care—any child care—raise even greater fears about the negative effects on family life and the harmful aspects of group care for the very young. Ignoring the statistics, they do not seem to realize that the question is hardly one of whether child care should exist. The need for child care for young children was well documented earlier in this chapter.

The most critical question is in regard to infant attachment. It is an accepted conclusion today that children who first enter child care situations at the age of 18 months to 2 years or older show no loss of attachment to their parents. Some studies (Belsky & Braungart, 1991) concerning children who are placed in child care outside the home before the age of 1, however, have raised questions about the higher level of insecurity attachment they show compared with infants who were raised at home. Berk (1994), who suggests that this small number of children is at risk for attachment insecurity because of poor-quality day care, calls for high-quality day care and parent education in infant emotional development.

The task for the early childhood professional seems clear. Learn what the issues are, defend policies that reflect high standards, and be prepared to further influence group care for infants and toddlers that is of the highest quality.

Kindergarten

Kindergarten programs are universally available throughout the United States and have a significant impact in early education. They are found in elementary public and private schools, churches, and as part of preschool child care centers. Forty years ago only 47% of 5-year-olds were enrolled in kindergarten (Spodek, 1986). Today that number has doubled (National Center for Education Statistics, 1998), which means that almost all children attend kindergarten before entering elementary school. All states now have publicly supported kindergarten, but attendance is mandatory in only 22 of them.

Length of Day

The length of kindergarten programs is a prime example of the diversity and division in this critical area of early childhood education. Children attend kindergarten programs that operate for:

● Half day, every day

● Full school day, every day

● Full school day, alternate days

● Half day, followed by child care/extended day program

● Full school day, followed by child care/extended day program

The debate in many school boards focuses on whether to offer a 5-day-a-week full-day kindergarten. Only a few states fund full-day programs. Too often the arguments regarding the costs of such programs overshadow a more basic question: What are the best and most appropriate kindergarten programs and curricula, regardless of the length of day? Areas that need to be considered in response to this question and the debate on length of day are:

1. *The purpose of the kindergarten program.* What are the goals, and how will kindergarten serve the whole of the child's development? How will the program foster the goals in appropriate programming and adapt to the needs of children? The purpose of a full day, every day does not have to mean more academics that will be measured by more testing. It can mean developing a curriculum that is

aimed at a wide range of developmental levels, yet that can be individualized, a curriculum that fits the growing and changing 5- to 6-year-old. The goal should begin with the child and build the program to fit the child's needs, skills, and developing abilities.

2. *The effects of a full day on children.* Many children have already been in a child care setting for up to 10 hours a day and have shown they thrive in programs that are suited to their ages, development styles, and needs. There is no question that most children can handle a full-day kindergarten program, providing it is adapted to their age, interests, and abilities.

3. *The needs and concerns of parents.* Some parents may want a full-day program because they work and need a safe and nurturing place for their children. Others who do not work outside the home may want to keep their children with them a while longer.[1] Parents clearly need to have a choice about the type of program that best suits their family.

4. *The effect on teachers.* If a full-day kindergarten means that a teacher's class is extended for a longer period of time, that provides an opportunity to improve the quality of the program by individualizing the curriculum and better serving the children and their families who are enrolled. Half-day kindergartens, however, are many times staffed by teachers who have two separate classes of 20 to 25 students, one in the morning and one in the afternoon. The negative effects on planning, continuity, parent relationships, and individualizing curriculum are obvious, not to mention teacher burnout.

5. *The concerns of the administration.* The cost effectiveness of extending a kindergarten program all day will undoubtedly require more staff, more supplies and equipment, and greater food service costs. The policymakers in any school setting must take these into account along with the other issues, but one would hope they would not be limited by them.

6. *The nature and quality of the extended-day program.* Often, in programs in which children are in half-day kindergarten, the quality of the extended-care part of their day is not equal to their school experience. In many extended-day programs, the staff is untrained, has a high turnover rate, and does not reflect the same program goals for the kindergartener.

7. *Research findings.* Gullo and Clements (1984) measured academic achievement and social behavior of children enrolled in half-day (every day) and full-day (alternate day) kindergartens and found no significant differences. Further research (Gullo, Bersani, Clements, & Bayless, 1986) suggests that 5-year-olds benefit socially, emotionally, and academically in full-day programs.

School Entry Age

Every state establishes an arbitrary date (e.g., September) by which children must be a certain age to enter kindergarten. In the United States, compulsory age for kindergarten ranges from 5 to 8. Lowering and raising the age for beginning school is debated periodically; currently, the trend is to move the date later into the year in the hopes of enrolling more "mature" kindergarteners. It has long been noted that the youngest children in kindergarten have more academic problems than do their peers, are more likely to be labeled slow learners, and are asked to repeat the year. The "birthdate effect," as it is sometimes called (Peck, McCaig, & Sapp, 1988), has led to a number of questionable practices regarding kindergarten entrance: parents hold children out for 1 year and enroll them when they are 6; teachers retain many children each year in kindergarten; and administrators have created an array of kindergarten-substitute programs called trendy names such as "developmental," "extra-year," or "transitional" kindergartens. By the time they finally reach kindergarten, children are now in class with late-4-year-olds, 5s, and 6s—a vast developmental span under one roof.

An "alarmingly" high rate of children failing kindergarten (Peck et al., 1988) has given rise to a number of these questionable solutions. Yet research shows that children who are held back a year may perform less well academically in the future and that

OUR DIVERSE WORLD OUR DIVERSE WORLD OUR DIVERSE WORLD OUR DIVERSE WORLD OUR DIVERSE WORLD OUR DIVERSE WORLD OUR DIVERSE WORLD OUR DIVERSE WORLD
[1] This may or may not be culturally related.

Figure 2.11 ● Kindergartners are able to enjoy close friendships.

kindergarteners who are retained show harmful effects on their social and emotional development as well as their self-esteem. Children from minority groups and from poor homes are more likely to be held back a year than others[1] (Meisels & Sternberg, 1989). Further, research shows that kindergarten retention does nothing to boost subsequent academic achievement, that there is social stigma for children who repeat a year, and that curricular expectations will be geared to the fastest learners (Shepard & Smith, 1988).

In studies of kindergarten alternatives, no differences in math or reading scores were found between third-graders who had attended a "developmental/ transitional" kindergarten and those who had been enrolled in a traditional kindergarten (Meisels &

Sternberg, 1989). The "holdout phenomenon" of giving the potential kindergartner an extra year does not seem to be justified in the long run considering that many of the child's needs will not be addressed and that, as older children in a kindergarten class, they may become bored and less motivated.

Curriculum: Developmental or Academic?

Critical issues such as school-entry age and length of school day are deeply related to kindergarten curriculum issues. At the present, kindergarten programs range from relatively traditional classes to highly structured, academically oriented classes. Over the last 20 years, the push to teach separate skills, such as

[1] Poverty puts children at a greater risk of falling behind in school than does living in a single-parent home or being born to teenage parents (Children's Defense Fund, 1998).

reading, writing, and math, has created more and more academically focused kindergartens where worksheets and teacher-directed lessons are the norm. This movement has caused deep concern in the early childhood field because most of these programs seem inconsistent with the developmental and learning styles of 5- and 6-year-olds and are viewed as preparation for advancement to first grade rather than as high-quality programs aimed at the development of the whole child.

It is clear that the "children's garden," as Froebel pictured this experience to be, has wandered far from its child development roots. Curricula in which play is not respected as a vehicle for learning, reading is taught as a separate skill, and attempts are made to accelerate children's learning are at odds with kindergarten history. Revisit Chapter 1 and read again about Froebel, Dewey, Piaget, Patty Smith Hill, Susan Blow, and other pioneers and their approach to learning. Educating the whole child is very much in evidence in their work, as is their basic connection to child development theory and research. Historically developed curricula, based on interaction and involvement of children in their own learning, with methods and materials to match the child's age level, are at the core of developmentally appropriate practice. The current system of frequently labeling children "immature," "slow," or "not ready" means that the program is not ready for the children; yet we know that young children are ready to learn and grow.[1] It is time to fix the program, not the children.

Differences in teacher training have led to some of the problems associated with kindergarten. Most kindergarten teachers are trained in education schools with methods more appropriate to elementary school teaching. They receive little or no training in early childhood philosophy or child development theory. Qualified teachers are the core of any educational reform, and kindergarten teachers must be educated and credentialed in early childhood education (Peck et al., 1989).

For further discussion on the negative effects of early academics, see Chapter 3 for developmental ranges and Word Pictures for appropriate expectations. In Chapter 10, the related questions of standardized testing and screening are discussed. In Chapters 11 and 15, related issues are explored.

Primary Grades

Early childhood is defined as children from birth through 8. Often overlooked as part of a comprehensive view of young children are grades one, two, and three, serving children who range from 6 to 8 years old. Primary grades, in both public and private schools, focus on the basic academic skills of reading, writing, math, science, social studies, art and drama, health and safety, and physical education. They are usually part of a larger school with grades up to six or eight.

"Years of Promise: A Comprehensive Learning Strategy for America's Children," a report from the Carnegie Corporation (1996), noted that by the fourth grade, most primary school students did not meet the basic achievement levels in reading and math. According to the report, the reasons that primary children nationwide achieve far below their potential is related to ineffective teaching strategies, poorly trained teachers, outmoded curricula, and inadequate home–school partnerships. Linking success in the primary years with good early childhood education and high-quality child care programs prior to kindergarten, the study suggests reforms that promote children's learning in families and communities, expansion of high-quality early learning opportunities, and the creation of a comprehensive, coordinated education system (Jacobson, 1996a).

As the NAEYC position statement on developmentally appropriate practice states, "too many schools . . . adopt instructional approaches that are incompatible with . . . how young children learn and develop . . . emphasizing rote learning of academic skills rather than active, experiential learning in a meaningful context," with the result that children "are not learning to apply those skills to problems . . . and they are not developing more complex thinking skills" (Bredekamp & Copple, 1997).

The importance of the primary years and their relationship to the preschool years bear further attention by educators and policymakers. Too often, pre-primary curricula and methodology are ignored by administrators when planning for grades one, two, and three. Bredekamp & Copple (1997) underscore the necessity to integrate teaching practices for children from birth through age 8:

 OUR DIVERSE WORLD OUR DIVERSE WORLD OUR DIVERSE WORLD OUR DIVERSE WORLD OUR DIVERSE WORLD OUR DIVERSE WORLD OUR DIVERSE WORLD OUR DIVERSE WORLD

[1] If programs are to be based on democratic and inclusive values, then perhaps school should be thought of as being ready for all children.

Along with the home, church, and community,[1] primary-grade schools and school-age care programs are among the key settings in which children's character is shaped. Therefore, the primary-grade years are an important time not only to support children's intellectual development but also to help them develop the ability to work collaboratively with peers; express tolerance, empathy, and caring for other people; function responsibly; and gain positive dispositions toward learning, such as curiosity, initiative, persistence, risk taking, and self-regulation.

Class Size

As part of his 1998 State of the Union address, President Clinton proposed a $12 billion initiative over a 7-year period to reduce class size in grades one to three to a nationwide average of 18 students in each class. The goals of this proposal are to provide the funds for additional teachers and teacher training and to ensure that every child receives personal attention and learns to read independently by the end of third grade. A U.S. Department of Education report, "Reducing Class Size: What Do We Know?" (1998), concluded that reducing class size to below 20 students leads to higher student achievement. Critics of the proposal cite the high cost of lowering student-teacher ratios and the objectivity of the research data. If the initiative were successful, class size would be more in keeping with NAEYC standards for staff-child ratios in primary programs. Optimal group size for first, second, and third grade classes are 15 to 18 children with one adult or 25 children with a second adult (Bredekamp & Copple, 1997).

Out-of-School–Time Care

Before-school and **after-school programs** are designed for children before they start or after they finish their regular academic day. This type of care is usually available for children from ages 6 to 16, with the vast majority (83%) in the kindergarten to third grade age group (Neugebauer, 1996). Over 2 million children attend programs in child care centers, public and private schools, churches and synagogues, family child care homes, community centers, and work sites. School-age care is the fastest growing segment of early education and care, particularly for middle-school-age children. Over two thirds of all school-age programs provide services both before and after school hours (Neugebauer, 1996).

Staff for after-school programs come from a variety of backgrounds, most of which include some experience with children, such as teachers, recreation specialists, or specialists within the arts. As with most child care programs, however, high turnover and low wages affect the quality of the service.

Two national organizations, the National School-Age Care Alliance and the School-Age Child Care Project (now called the National Institute on Out-Of-School Time) joined forces in 1996 to create an accreditation system for after-school care. Their goals are to set professional standards, accredit high-quality programs, and support program improvement. Categories assessed include human relationships, indoor environment, outdoor environment, activities, health, safety and nutrition, administration, and limiting group size to 30 students (Jacobson, 1996b).

There is a critical need for safe, recreational programs for **after-school care**. According to one source, nearly 5 million school-age children of employed mothers were "**self-care**" children, a term that replaces "**latchkey**" (Seligson, 1997).

What happens to these children after school? For the kindergartener, school may be over at noon. From 1:30 to 3:00 PM, first-, second-, and third-graders are released from their school day. Too often these children are sent home with a house key around their necks or in their pockets. They are instructed to look after themselves and possibly a younger sibling until the parent (or parents) comes home from work. These **self-care children**, as they are known, are a young and vulnerable population. Recent studies (Seligson, 1997) indicate that children unsupervised during out-of-school time are likely to engage in risky behaviors, receive poor grades, be truant, and abuse substances. Half the teachers questioned in a survey cited "children left on their own after school" as the primary cause of school failure. The value of good programs is also being recognized. Seligson (1997) cites a University of Wisconsin study that linked good after-school pro-

OUR DIVERSE WORLD OUR DIVERSE WORLD OUR DIVERSE WORLD OUR DIVERSE WORLD OUR DIVERSE WORLD OUR DIVERSE WORLD OUR DIVERSE WORLD OUR DIVERSE WORLD

1 This presents a broad, ecological view of the child's socialization in a family and community context.

grams with improved reading scores and self-esteem. Unfortunately, the United States Government Accounting Office (1997) estimates that in the year 2002, the current school-age care supply will meet as little as 25% of the demand in some urban areas.

The essentials of out-of-school care reflect the needs of the parents, teachers, and children involved. Flexible hours, reasonable tuition rates, and clear lines of communication are of primary importance to parents. To ensure continual care, scheduling must take into consideration the elementary school calendar. Holidays, conference times, and minimum-day schedules of schools must be considered. Opportunities to extend the after-school program can originate from the use of community resources such as library story hours, swimming facilities, and parks.

Out-of-school care is not intended to be an extension of a regular school day. Ideally, the program should supplement and support the regular school program. Many are called "enrichment programs" to distinguish them from the child's academic school day.

The teaching staff is usually different from the regular school faculty and should be specially trained in how to operate extended programs for young children. They must know how to create a homey, relaxed, and accepting atmosphere in an environment that supports large blocks of time for free play, where children can be self-directed and self-paced, where there are many opportunities for creative expression, where cooperation is emphasized and competition is limited, and where children may form small groups or find private spaces and places to play.

A national study of out-of-school programs compiled in 1991 offered the first nationwide picture of these programs: approximately 1.7 million children in kindergarten through eighth grade were enrolled in nearly 50,000 before- and/or after-school programs in the United States in 1991; 84% of those were licensed or regulated by a state agency; and the three most common program locations were child care centers (35%), public schools (28%), and religious institutions (14%). Less than 20% of the programs had access to necessary space, and 27% reported that they did not have access to a playground or a park on at least a weekly basis (U.S. Department of Education, 1993). The study concludes that training and retaining staff are critical issues if continuity and quality of program are to be maintained.

Programs for school-age children need their own permanent space to support the type of long-term

group projects that children of this age enjoy. Some programs may offer homework assistance, but care must be taken not to simply extend an already structured day with more restrictions.

Children need the safety, the creative opportunity, and the emotionally supportive relationships that out-of-school care can provide. These programs are natural extensions of responsible child care and are essential services to children and their families.

FEATURES OF EARLY CHILDHOOD

Many factors determine exactly what type of program will best serve young children. Some of these variables emerged through the descriptions of the many kinds of settings available for children today. Programs in early childhood are defined by

- Age of the children served
- Philosophy or theoretical approach taken
- Goals the program hopes to meet
- Purpose for which it was established
- Requirements of sponsoring agency
- Quality and training of teaching staff
- Shape, size, and location of physical environment
- Cultural, ethnic, economic, and social makeup of community
- Financial stability

Programs in early childhood settings are defined by these elements, and each factor has to be taken into consideration regarding its impact on the program. Any given program is a combination of these ingredients.

MIXED-AGE GROUPINGS

One factor that may cut across program considerations is that of placing children of several age levels, generally separated by a year, into the same classroom. In these classes, younger children learn from older children and older children learn by teaching younger children. This practice is often referred to as family, heterogeneous, vertical, or ungraded grouping (Katz, Evangelou, & Hartman, 1990) and, though not a new

Figure 2.12 ● After-school programs provide opportunities to make new friends and try new skills.

idea, is emerging as an area of considerable interest to early childhood educators.

Although reminiscent of the British infant schools' open classroom model, mixed-age groupings have been a practice in Montessori programs, in the schools of Reggio Emilia, and in one-room school-houses for many years. Advocates of mixed-age groups point to a number of developmental advantages when children interact with peers above and below their age level:

● The child's own developmental level and pace are accommodated, allowing children to advance as they are ready.

● Age and competition are deemphasized, as cooperative learning is enhanced.

● Caring and helping behaviors toward younger children and a sense of responsibility toward one another are fostered.

● Diverse learning styles and multiple intelligences are appreciated.

● A variety and number of different models for learning and for friendships are available.

● Children grow in independence in their work and in socialization.

The academic and social advantages of mixed-age grouping cannot occur without a variety of activities from which children may freely choose and the opportunity for small groups of children to work together. Teachers must be intentional about encouraging children to work with others who have skills and knowledge they do not yet possess. Other considerations are the optimal age range, the proportion of older to younger children, the amount of time spent in mixed-age groups, and the implementation of a project-oriented curriculum (Katz et al., 1990).

It is easy to see how mixed-age groupings reflect the principles of Dewey, Piaget, Gardner, and Vygotsky, whose "zone of proximal development" is made more available through the interactions of peers as well as adults. The practice of mixed-age grouping has much to commend it and must be seriously addressed as an issue in programs for young children.

Summary

Educational facilities for young children reach a broad population. They serve children from infancy through elementary-school age. An array of programs is available; each varies for philosophical reasons as well as because of the ages of children enrolled. Early childhood teachers have a wide range of programs from which to choose—as do parents.

The traditional nursery school and its sister programs of child care, laboratory schools, and parent cooperatives form the core of early childhood programs. Many different agencies and people sponsor early childhood programs, including employers, churches, universities, and hospitals. Some are located in family homes as a business. The intervention models of the 1960s and 1970s—Head Start and Follow-Through—are variations on the theme. They are specific attempts to provide early education and intervention to children caught in poverty's cycle. Other schools, such as Montessori or High/Scope, are based on clearly stated principles with outlined procedures for teachers and children.

Reflecting the needs of society, extended day programs have been created. Not only are children being cared for in group situations before and after school hours; they are also being placed in the group settings at an earlier age. Infant/toddler programs are common, and out-of-school care is a service that meets the demands for good, safe, and challenging programs for children who need care on either side of their school day.

As varied as they are, there is also a certain similarity among all programs for young children. Consideration must be given to a number of factors when reviewing the needs of young children and their families. Some of these elements are the ages of the children the program will serve, the qualifications and experience of the teaching staff, the funding base and financial support available, and the goals of the program to meet the needs of all children and their families. With so many choices, those who desire child care will find options that suit their specific needs.

Review Questions

1. What are the three most important factors that determine the quality of an early childhood program?

2. Match the type of program with the appropriate description:

Montessori	Key experiences
Infant/toddler	Staggered staff schedules
All-day child care	Comprehensive programs
Church-based	Teacher training
Head Start	In home
Employer-supported	Prepared environment
Proprietary	Benign landlord
High/Scope	For profit
Laboratory schools	Educaring
Family child care	Fringe benefit

3. Why are some early childhood programs called "intervention" schools?

4. Are there differences between preschool and kindergarten programs? Between infant and toddler programs? What are they? Should there be a difference? Why?

5. What are some of the features that affect all children's programs?

6. What has been the unique contribution of the Perry Preschool Project, and how do you see this affecting legislation, program development in early childhood, and the early childhood profession?

7. What is the controversy regarding for-profit care centers? Are you for or against the idea of child care centers making a profit? Why?

8. Describe the influence of Piaget, Gardner, and Vygotsky on three types of early childhood programs.

Learning Activities

1. Choose one program and describe how you would operate that type of class. Include the daily schedule, number and skill level of teachers, types of parent contacts, and the activities of children.

2. Visit a family child care home. Look at the home as if you were a prospective parent. What did you like most? Least? Is the home licensed? If so, for how many children? After talking with the family child care provider, what do you think are the disadvantages of this type of program? What do you think are possible solutions to these problems?

3. What role would children's social skills play in these settings?

Traditional nursery school

Montessori

Kindergarten

Infant/toddler

4. What are the licensing regulations for child care in your area? Describe the steps necessary in your town to open a nursery school, child care center, and a family child care home.

5. Which government agencies are involved in the licensing procedure?

6. Visit a Head Start program and a local kindergarten. Compare their programs in terms of appropriate or inappropriate curriculum. What are the major concerns of the teaching staff in each type of setting? What are the controversies about each of these programs in your community?

Bibliography

Accreditation Criteria and Procedures of the National Association for the Education of Young Children. (1998). Washington, DC: National Association for the Education of Young Children.

Baker, K. R. (1955) *The Nursery School.* Philadelphia, P.A.: W. B. Saunders.

Belsky, J., & Braungart, J. M. (1991). Are insecure-avoidant infants with extensive day-care experience less stressed by and more independent in the strange situation? *Child Development, 62,* 567–571.

Berk, L. E. (1994). *Infants and children.* Boston: Allyn & Bacon.

Berrueta-Clement, J. R., Schweinhart, L. J., Barnett, W. S., Epstein, A. S., & Weikart, D. P. (1984). *Changed lives: The effects of the Perry Preschool Program on youths through 19.* Ypsilanti, MI: High/Scope Press.

Bredekamp, S. (1997). Developmentally appropriate practice: The early childhood educator as decisionmaker. In S. Bredekamp & C. Copple (Eds.), *Developmentally appropriate practice in early childhood programs.* Washington, DC: National Association for the Education of Young Children.

Bredekamp, S., & Copple, C. (Eds.). (1997). *Developmentally appropriate practice in early childhood programs.* Washington DC: National Association for the Education of Young Children.

Bredekamp, S., & Glowacki, S. (1996). The first decade of NAEYC accreditation: Growth and impact on the field. In S. Bredkamp & B. A. Willer (Eds.), *NAEYC accreditation: A decade of learning and the years ahead.* Washington, DC: National Association for the Education of Young Children.

Brown, B. (1985, July). Head Start—How research changed public policy. *Young Children,* 9–13.

Carnegie Corporation. (1996). *Years of promise: A comprehensive learning strategy for America's children.* New York: Author.

Cataldo, C. Z. (1983). *Infant and toddler programs.* Reading, MA: Addison-Wesley.

Chattin-McNichols, J. (1992). *The Montessori controversy.* Albany, NY: Delmar.

Child Care Information Exchange. (1986, November), 7–8.

Children's Defense Fund. (1991). *The state of America's children, yearbook 1991.* Washington, DC: Author.

Children's Defense Fund. (1998). *The state of America's children, yearbook 1998.* Washington, DC: Author.

Cohen, D. L. (1993a, November 10). Stress Head Start quality, but spotlight 0–3, panel says. *Education Week,* p. 20.

Cohen, D. L. (1993b, April 21). Perry preschool graduates show dramatic new social gains at 27. *Education Week,* p. 1.

Cohen, D. L. (1994a, April 24). Head Start measure appears to be on Congressional fast track. *Education Week,* p. 14.

Cohen, D. L. (1994b, February 16). Bill to authorize Head Start is introduced. *Education Week,* p. 21.

Cost, Quality, and Child Outcomes Study Team (1995). *Cost, quality and child outcomes in child care centers.* Denver: Department of Economics, University of Colorado at Denver.

Creating a 21st century Head Start. Public Policy Report. (1994, March). *Young Children,* p. .

Edwards, C., Gandini, L., & Forman, G. (1993). *The hundred languages of children: The Reggio Emilia approach to early childhood education.* Norwood, NJ: Ablex.

Elkind, D. (1993). *Images of the young child.* Washington, DC: National Association for the Education of Young Children.

Epstein, A. S., Schweinhart, L. J., & McAdoo, L. (1996). *Models of early childhood education.* Ypsilanti, MI: High/Scope Press.

Galinsky, E., Howes, C., Kontos, S. & Shinn, M. (1994). *The study of children in family child care and relative care: Highlights of findings.* New York: Families and Work Institute.

Gerber, M. (1979). Respecting infants: The Loczy model of infant care. In E. Jones (Ed.), *Supporting the growth of infants, toddlers, and parents*. Pasadena, CA: Pacific Oaks.

Gonzalez-Mena, J., & Eyer, D. W. (1989, 1993). *Infants, toddlers, and caregivers*. Mountain View, CA: Mayfield Publishing.

Greenberg, P. (1990, September). Before the beginning: A participant's view. *Young Children*, pp. 41–52.

Gullo, D. F., & Clements, D. H. (1984). The effects of kindergarten schedule on achievement, classroom behavior, and attendance. *Journal of Educational Research*, 78, 51–56.

Gullo D. F., Bersani, C., Clements, D. H., & Bayless, K. M. (1986). A comparative study of all-day, alternate-day, and half-day kindergarten schedules: Effects on achievement and classroom social behaviors. *Journal of Research in Childhood Education*, 1, 87–94.

Head Start Program Performance Standards and Other Regulations. (1998). Head Start Bureau, Administration on Children, Youth and Families, Administration for Children and Families, United States Department of Health and Human Services. Washington, DC: U.S. Government Printing Office.

Hohmann, M., Weikart, D. P. (1995). *Educating young children: Active learning practices for preschool and child care programs*. Ypsilanti, MI: High/Scope Press.

Honig, A. S. (1985, November). High quality infant/toddler care: Issues and dilemmas. *Young Children*, pp. 40–46.

Hyun, E. (1998). *Making sense of developmentally and culturally appropriate practice (DCAP) in early childhood education*. New York: Peter Lang Publishing.

Jacobson, L. (1996a, September 18). Carnegie offers reform strategy for ages 3 to 10. *Education Week*, p. 1.

Jacobson, L. (1996b, October 23). Standards for after-school care piloted. *Education Week*, p. 1.

Katz, L. G., Evangelou, D., & Hartman, J. A. (1990). *The case for mixed-age groupings in early education*. Washington, DC: National Association for the Education of Young Children.

Lindner, E., Mattis, M. C., & Rogers, J. (1983). *When churches mind the children*. Ypsilanti, MI: High/Scope Press.

Meisels, S. J., & Sternberg, L. S. (1989, June). Quality sacrificed in proprietary child care. *Education Week*, p. 36.

National Association for the Education of Young Children Position Statement. (1997). Developmentally appropriate practice in early childhood programs serving children from birth through age 8. In S. Bredekamp & C. Copple (Eds.), *Developmentally appropriate practice in early childhood programs*. Washington, DC: National Association for the Education of Young Children.

National Association for the Education of Young Children. (1998, January). NAEYC position statement on licensing and public regulation of early childhood programs. *Young Children*, pp. 43–50.

National Association for the Education of Young Children. (1998). *Accreditation criteria and procedures of the National Academy of Early Childhood Programs*. Washington, DC: Author.

National Center for Education Statistics. (n.d.). *Digest of Education Statistics: 1998*. Washington, DC: U.S. Government Printing Office.

National Institute on Out-of-School Time. (1998). Wellesley MA: Center for Research on Women, Wellesley College.

Neugebauer, R. (1991, September/October). Churches that care: Status report #2 on church-housed child care. *Child Care Information Exchange*, pp. 41–45.

Neugebauer, R. (1995, May/June). Employer child care report: Drawing and consolidating. *Child Care Information Exchange*, pp. 67–76.

Neugebauer, R. (1996, July). Promising development and new directions in school-age care. *Child Care Information Exchange*, pp. 7–13.

Neugebauer, R. (1997, May/June). How's business? Status report #10 on for-profit child care. *Child Care Information Exchange*, pp. 65–69.

Neugebauer, R. (1998, January/February). Sesame Street meets Wall Street. Eleventh annual status report on for-profit child care. *Child Care Information Exchange*, pp. 12–16.

Peck, J. T., McCaig, G., & M. E. Sapp, (1988). *Kindergarten policies—What is best for children?* Washington, DC: National Association for the Education of Young Children.

Schnaiberg, L. (1996, June 12). Staying home from school. *Education Week*, pp. 24–33.

Schweinhart, L. J., & Weikart, D. P. (1993, November). Success by empowerment: The High/Scope Perrry Preschool Study through age 27. *Young Children*, pp. 54–58.

Seligson, M. (1997). School-age child care comes of age. *Child Care ActioNews*, 14(1).

Shepard, L. A., & Smith, M. L. (1988). Escalating kindergarten curriculum. Urbana, IL: ERIC Digest.

Snow, C. W., Teleki, J. K., & Reguero-de-Atiles, J. T. (1996, September). Child care center licensing standards in the United States: 1981 to 1995. *Young Children*, pp. 36–41.

Spodek, B. (Ed.). (1986). *Today's Kindergarten*. New York: Teacher's College Press.

Trawick-Smith, J., & Lambert, L. (1995, March). The unique challenges of the family child care provider: Implications for professional development. *Young Children*, pp. 25–32.

United States Bureau of the Census. (1996). *Who's minding our preschoolers*. Washington, DC: U.S. Government Printing Office.

United States Department of Education. (1990). *A profile of child care settings: Early education care in 1990*. Washington, DC: U.S. Government Printing Office.

United States Department of Education. (1993). *National study of before and after school programs*. Washington, DC: U.S. Government Printing Office.

United States Department of Education, National Center for Education Statistics. (1995). *National household education survey*. Washington, DC: U.S. Government Printing Office.

United States Department of Education. (1998). *Reducing class size: What do we know?* Washington, DC: U.S. Government Printing Office.

United States Department of Health and Human Services. (1998). *Project Head Start statistical fact sheet*. Washington, DC: U.S. Government Printing Office.

United States Government Accounting Office. (1997, May). GAO/HEHS-97-95. Washington, DC: U.S. Government Printing Office.

Viadero, D. (1997, March). Home-schooled pupils outscore counterparts. *Education Week*, p. 7.

Whitebrook, M., Howes, C., & Phillips, D. (1997). *National Child Care Staffing Study: Who cares? Child care teachers and the quality of care in America: Final report*. Washington, DC: Center for the Child Care Workforce.

Whitebrook, M., Phillips, D., & Howes, C. (1993). *The National Child Care Staffing Study revisited*. Oakland, CA: Child Care Employee Project.

SECTION *Two*

Who Is the Young Child?

Olivia N. Saracho

American schools have shown an increased percentage of linguistically and culturally diverse (LCD) children in the last several years. The linguistic differences integrate the explicit cultural differences in various ethnic groups that constitute our plural society. Each predominant ethnic group possesses its own heritage, pattern of traditions, values, and convictions about what is right and proper. Ethnic groups transmit their traditions from generation to generation as part of the informal family or peer group socialization process (Saracho & Spodek, 1995).

American schools presently serve these LCD children, who usually find unfamiliar the language patterns, social interactions, and manifestations of values and culture that are found in the schools (Saracho & Spodek, 1995). As American schools are challenged to educate all children, their educational goals have forced children to give up their cultural identity and ancestral language. LCD children learn their own family language and culture and are compelled to learn in the school a language and culture that are foreign to them. Many LCD children infer that they must reject their home language and culture and replace them with those of the school, which are patterns of behavior and language of the middle class, white, English-speaking society. These beliefs may cause LCD children to experience bewilderment, rejection, and a loss of ethnic identity (Saracho, 1986). Recurrently, these children become confused in school and are not able to gain a new acceptable identity.

Young children's socialization into the dominant society is a meaningful and appropriate goal of early childhood education. The family is an integral socializing agency in our society, although the school introduces LCD children to the predominant society outside the family and assists children to learn its social processes. For example, LCD children learn the individuals' roles, purposes, and interrelationships in our society that exist outside the home. They learn how to gain personal satisfaction in a manner that is regarded as correct and learn to behave toward others, including using proper language and behavioral patterns in getting along with others (Saracho & Spodek, 1983).

Although the education of LCD children has prospered, there is a need for substantive improvement. Researchers, educators, and child development specialists have increased their knowledge about the importance of family language and cultural values, especially how each culture has contributed to our American heritage. It is important that the unique language and culture of each cultural group be cherished and praised in the classroom. Teachers need to use the LCD children's language and cultural background as a foundation for learning. Children need to experience learning in more than one language and culture. They need to become flexible and proficient in the language and culture of both the home and the school. Such modifications can enrich the LCD children's life, and their socialization can welcome a new meaning in such a context.

Dr. Olivia Saracho is a Professor of Education at the Department of Curriculum and Instruction at the University of Maryland.

References

Saracho, O. N. (1986). Teaching second language literacy with computers. In D. Hainline (Ed.), *New developments in language CAI* (pp. 53–68). Beckenham, Kent, England: Croom Helm.

Saracho, O. N., & Spodek, B. (1983). The preparation of teachers for bilingual bicultural early childhood classes. In O. N. Saracho & B. Spodek (Eds.), *Understanding the multicultural experience in early childhood education* (pp. 125–146). Washington, DC: National Association for the Education of Young Children.

Saracho, O. N., & Spodek, B. (1995). The future challenge of linguistic and cultural diversity in the schools. In E. E. García, B. McLaughlin, B. Spodek, & O. N. Saracho, O. N. (Eds), *Yearbook of early childhood education: Meeting the challenge of cultural diversity in early childhood education* (vol. 6, pp. 170–173). New York: Teachers College Press.

Defining the Young Child

CHAPTER 3

Questions for Thought

What are some of the basic characteristics of each age?

How does the development of one area of growth affect other areas?

What are the implications for teaching children of varying levels of development?

What are some cautions to take when interpreting age-level characteristic charts? How are they useful?

Who is the whole child?

Who are children with special needs?

What are some of the common types of disabilities found in young children?

What is an inclusive classroom?

What issues are related to the inclusion of young children in early childhood classrooms?

Figure 3.1 ● Children: alike, yet different.

DEFINING THE CHILD

Children—who are they? When entering a classroom, teachers might find themselves asking questions about the youngsters they see:

● What do children say?

● What can children do?

● What do children think?

● How do children feel?

Glancing around the room brings an awareness of the group as a whole. Individuals blur among a number of children, all the same size and same age. At this point, they are hardly more than a list of names with ages attached. Quickly, however, a teacher becomes conscious of a single child here and there. In this assortment of small people, different sizes, shapes, languages, and colors emerge.[1]

Through the Teacher's Eyes

Physical Impressions

Teachers usually begin to define children by their physical characteristics. Initially, their differences are most obvious by the way they look.

Eric is a tall blond. He is much larger than his just-3 age would indicate. He has long slender fingers and arms to match. His movements are fluid; he lopes across the room toward the easel.

OUR DIVERSE WORLD OUR DIVERSE WORLD OUR DIVERSE WORLD OUR DIVERSE WORLD OUR DIVERSE WORLD OUR DIVERSE WORLD OUR DIVERSE WORLD OUR DIVERSE WORLD
[1] Quality early childhood programs can provide the opportunity to celebrate OUR DIVERSE WORLD!

Lamar's short stocky build and constant swagger lend the impression that he is a pretty tough character. His twinkling eyes and infectious smile offset that image.

Natalie at 4 is a study in perpetual motion. Green eyes flashing, arms and legs waving, she ignores the bulk of her diaper as she propels herself down the slide. There is little indication that the mild case of spina bifida she has inhibits her motor activities. It certainly hasn't affected her daring.

Nothing will heighten an awareness of the individuality of each child more than working in the classroom. Teachers quickly learn what makes each child special. By watching and observing children, teachers accumulate a great deal of detailed information. Adults learn what children really look like as children move their bodies, change expressions, and assume a posture. A teacher can sense whether Sonja is happy, hurt, or hurried by the way she moves and how she looks. Rodrigo's face mirrors his distress or his delight. The observant teacher learns to read children for evidence of their social, emotional, physical, and intellectual growth. Children quite naturally express these characteristics with their whole body; each child's response is unique.

Children's Behaviors

Children's behaviors are so individual; children show their own personal responses to life. They relate to people in ways that express their original nature. Dina has an ability to get her peers to wait on her; Sean trails the teachers for constant companionship. Their responses to the classroom environment are also singular. Ginny becomes overstimulated and loses control; Clark stands and watches over children for long periods of time before he joins in. Teachers become aware of individual differences in the skill level of children. They notice that of the five children at the art table, for instance, only one of them is holding scissors correctly and cutting paper.

How Children Are Alike

The similarities of the many children in a class are striking. Teachers can see the differences—wide differences—yet there are common characteristics within the age group itself. Six toddlers working on an art project exhibit six different personal styles, yet typically, they all become distracted and leave their projects half finished. Observation of children—how they look and how they act—helps the teacher see each child as an individual. When many children in a classroom are observed, behaviors common to that age become clear. There is enough standard behavior appropriate to certain age levels that allows for some generalizations about children's behavior.

Caldwell (1993) cites three universal characteristics that unite children of the world. Each child is like every other in that (1) they all have the same needs, the most important of which are food, shelter, and care; (2) they all go through the same developmental stages; and (3) they all have the same developmental goals, although the timing and the cultural influences will differ.

Descriptions of these common characteristics date back to a classic collection of research by Gesell and Ilg. See both Chapters 1 and 4 for related discussions. See Figures 3.5 through 3.12 for a series of "word pictures" depicting these age-level characteristics from infancy through age 8. In looking at individual children or a group, these descriptions are helpful in understanding the nature of the child and normal growth.

Why Children Differ

Watching and working with children exposes how very different each child is. What makes children differ so, especially when they have so many features in common? Megan gives the tire swing a big push. Ariel shrieks with delight, but Hans bursts into tears and screams to get off. What accounts for the wide range of behaviors evident when you observe any group of children?[1]

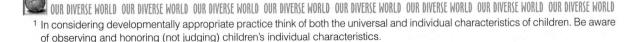

OUR DIVERSE WORLD OUR DIVERSE WORLD OUR DIVERSE WORLD OUR DIVERSE WORLD OUR DIVERSE WORLD OUR DIVERSE WORLD OUR DIVERSE WORLD OUR DIVERSE WORLD

1 In considering developmentally appropriate practice think of both the universal and individual characteristics of children. Be aware of observing and honoring (not judging) children's individual characteristics.

Genetic Makeup. This certainly accounts for some of the differences. Each child is a unique combination of genes that "contributes to the emergence and nature of every human trait from the color of the eyes . . . to the individual's ultimate intelligence and creativity" (Gardner, 1982). This also influences a child's hair color, height, body shape, and rate of growth (Bee, 1997).

Environment. The effects of the world on inherited genes also play a role. The number and kinds of experiences children have affect how they develop. The attitudes with which children are raised, their culture, their socioeconomic status, the kinds of caregiving they experience, and their community combine in countless ways to affect growth.[1] In Chapter 15, this subject is more thoroughly discussed as the "ecology of the family." Nutrition, safety, play space, adult relationships, neighborhood, and family stability affect individual development. Whether a child lives in the South Bronx or Beverly Hills, environmental factors interact with genes to create a single, individual person.

The small child who stands at the classroom door is the sum total of the physical, intellectual, social, and emotional factors of home and heredity. What nature provides, the world shapes and bends. Using intelligence as an example, Gardner (1993) states the interdependency of environment and genetics this way: "The limit of intelligence is fixed by genetics, but the actual intelligence achieved reflects the diverse environments."

There are four other factors concerning the developmental scheme of things that account for individual differences.

Children Grow and Develop at Different Rates. Each child has an inner mechanism for monitoring growth. It is a timetable that varies from child to child. It means that each child is ready to learn at a given time, which may or may not coincide with the rest of the group. This readiness factor must be respected.

Development Is Predictable and Follows a Sequence. Even as the rate varies, the sequence remains the same for all children, even those who are disabled (Chandler, 1994). Physical development tends to be from the head downward (notice how large a newborn baby's head is in relation to the rest of its body) and from the center outward (a young child gains control over arm movements before mastering finger control).

A review of maturational theory (Chapter 4) and physical growth and development (Chapter 12) might be helpful. Periods of rapid growth and activity are followed by periods of calmness and consolidation. Behavior swings at the half-year mark are common in many children. The pleasant, well-balanced 3-year-old may become shy and begin to stutter at 3½. The age at which this change occurs is not as important as the sequence in which it happens. The important thing to remember is that children will exhibit markedly different behaviors in one short year. Teachers prepare for these times and appreciate them as a normal course of events for the growing child.

Gender and Race Differences. Girls and boys differ in both the rate and the pattern of growth, especially in adolescence. African American and Asian American children seem to have a more rapid tempo of growth than do Euro-American children, and children who are raised at poverty level or below develop more slowly than others (Bee, 1997).[2]

Using the Word Pictures (pp. 96–103) and a frequent review of developmental theory help remind teachers and parents to take a long-range view regarding children's behavior. Chapters 4 and 7 will provide further insights.

Janice Hale's Focus Box offers timely suggestions on how teachers can be more effective in teaching African American children. Her ideas can be applied to other cultural groups as well.

Implications for Teaching

The differences in children's development must be accounted for when planning a program for a group. Teachers consider all these factors as they meet the needs of the individual child while addressing the concerns and interests of the total group.

OUR DIVERSE WORLD OUR DIVERSE WORLD OUR DIVERSE WORLD OUR DIVERSE WORLD OUR DIVERSE WORLD OUR DIVERSE WORLD OUR DIVERSE WORLD OUR DIVERSE WORLD

[1] This interaction also results in an ever-growing understanding of the world.

[2] See footnote 1 on page 88 and be reminded of the importance of noticing and knowing, but not judging, children's individual differences.

Culturally Appropriate Pedagogy and the African American Child

Janice E. Hale

Corporate marketing and advertising executives know that there is a distinctive African American culture. Madison Avenue has discovered a psychological truism: you can get your message across more effectively if you use a culturally salient vehicle.

McDonald's, for example, uses a rapping french fry, hip hop cheerleaders, and the McDonald's Breakfast Club, which markets to upscale African American professionals. A Kodak ad, showing an African American man holding an infant tenderly, depicts a warm relationship between an African American father and child. Advertisements that are directed to the African American community use music, dance, symbols, and images that tap into the African American culture.

Politicians who speak to African American congregations in an attempt to win votes utilize the rhetorical styles that African Americans resonate toward—call and response, rhythm, inflection, intonation. They touch bases with the images and symbolism of African American culture—for example, evoking the memory of Dr. Martin Luther King Jr.

Educators are the last ones to consider the idea that we can get our message across more effectively if we use a culturally salient vehicle. We know that the distinctive *preaching style* and message of the African American preacher incorporates distinctive features of African American culture.

Why, therefore, would it be a big leap to suggest that there could be a *teaching style* that would inspire, motivate, and capture the interest of African American children? Just as homiletics—the science of writing and preaching sermons—is taught from an African American perspective in seminaries, it is important to teach pedagogy in teacher training institutions from the perspective of African American culture.

Culturally appropriate pedagogy would expose African American children to Anglocentric and Afrocentric literature at each grade level. Exposure to Anglocentric literature would provide them with the vocabulary, history, and information about the cultural orientation of mainstream America. This exposure is essential for African American children to be able to negotiate the mainstream.

Exposure to Afrocentric literature would broaden their vocabulary, provide them with information about African American cultural values, enhance their selfesteem, and provide motivation and inspiration.

To educate African American children in a culturally appropriate manner, requires a kind of dual educational process. In this culturally appropriate pedagogy, there should be no difference in the academic standards that presently exist in mainstream settings. The difference lies in the *manner* in which those standards are met. There is also a need to infuse the content of public and private school curricula for all children in America with a multicultural focus.

Dr. Janice E. Hale is a professor of early childhood education at Wayne State University.

Figure 3.2 ● In our diverse world, teachers should be sensitive to the influence of sex, race, and individual patterns of development.

Program Planning. Teachers generally begin by planning individual and group activities according to the age level of the class they teach, knowing that certain behavior patterns exist. Planning begins around the known similarities, the developmental tasks and age-appropriate behavior common to that group of children, including planning for children with special needs.[1] Goals based on these general characteristics are set for the children. As the school year progresses, teachers observe individuals and the group and change the developmental goals as needed. Individual differences in children are incorporated into the planning; activities selected allow for a variety of responses from children at different stages of development. A pasting activity encourages creativity in the most adept 3-year-old and still allows the less-skilled 3-year-old to explore the feel of the paste on fingers and hands. The activity may need to be modified to make it more accessible or appropriate for children with special needs.[2] Programs are planned to meet the needs and challenges of the whole group.

Grouping of children by rigid age levels seems contrary to our understanding of individual rates of growth, readiness factors, and wide ranges of abilities. It is a convenient, though **arbitrary**, system of teaching children. The implication for teachers is clear: plan for the age level with the understanding and appreciation of the variations in development even within a 1-year span. Know the child; know what to expect and what development has occurred. Look at the stages of growth for the age level just below and just above the one in which you teach.

Teachers' Response. The key word for teachers is *acceptance*. Teachers must not only accept the differences in children; they must plan for them. In doing so, they show respect for the individuality of each child in the class. Accepting the way children reveal themselves fosters the uniqueness that makes each one a special person.

See Chapter 5 for specific suggestions on how teachers plan to accommodate the individuality of

 OUR DIVERSE WORLD OUR DIVERSE WORLD OUR DIVERSE WORLD OUR DIVERSE WORLD OUR DIVERSE WORLD OUR DIVERSE WORLD OUR DIVERSE WORLD OUR DIVERSE WORLD

[1] Planning for children with special needs always begins by looking at typical development.
[2] The learning environment can be arranged so that children of every skill level can work and play together.

children, particularly the sections Self-awareness; Attitudes and Biases; Ten Essentials to Successful Teaching; and A Student Teacher's Guidelines for Beginning. The curriculum chapters, 11 through 15, demonstrate other examples of planning for a wide range of skills. It might be useful, too, to read Chapter 9, particularly the self-help environment and the anti-bias curriculum.

Through Children's Eyes

Another way to define children is to look at them from their own point of view. What does it mean to look at the world through children's eyes? What is a child's perspective on the world?

Adults carry into the classroom a great many perceptions about children. Having the advantage of many more years of experience, they tend to forget how much they know! The child they see is sometimes blurred through a great many filters. These filters are attitudes, concepts, experiences, and prejudices.[1] What looks mundane to an adult, such as a trip on the subway, fills children with the joy and wonder of discovery.

To view a classroom through the eyes of a child, one must set aside the filtered lenses of the grown-up world. The young child in the classroom is of the here and now and likes what is familiar and known. The preschooler takes pleasure in common, everyday experiences, learns by doing, and uses all five senses. Children this age are interested in dabbling in a great many things, yet when given time and opportunity to explore something that catches their eye, they are capable of a great depth of learning, as the children of Reggio Emilia demonstrate. (See Chapters 1, 9, 11, and 13 for further examples.)

The teacher learns to look through children's eyes—what interests them, what they avoid, who their friends are, how they respond in a variety of situations, and how they learn. When Kitty must play it safe with a friend who is less timid than she or Jacques puts together facts in ways that make sense to him, the teacher recognizes these as expressions of individuality.

Adults find that by looking at the world through the eyes of a child, they gain a different and valuable perspective as teacher.

DEVELOPMENTAL RANGES

As children grow and change, they move through predictable stages of development. Each developmental phase has characteristic traits. In the following pages some of the classic normative data collected by Gesell are combined with theories of Piaget, Elkind, Erikson, and Vygotsky (see Chapter 4) to demonstrate what children have in common at various ages. Despite the wide range of individual differences at all ages, there are some characteristics children share that are worth keeping in mind. These common behaviors help teachers prescribe programs and plan activities and curricula. They lend perspective.

Most classes are labeled "the two's," "the three's," and so on. Schools enroll children according to a chronological order based on whether a birthday falls before or after an arbitrary deadline. Yet most child development texts no longer use the narrow 1-year age span when setting out behavior characteristics. Larger, more inclusive groupings of infant, toddler, preschooler, and so on are common. The reason is that children's growth patterns and individual differences can be so great that a narrow definition of behaviors would lead to inaccurate assessment of a child's development. For this reason, age-level charts can be misunderstood unless used with discretion.

The Value of Word Pictures for Teachers

In Behavior and Guidance

One consideration is what use teachers will make of the charts. It is important to know what range of behaviors occur and to be able to recognize them as normal patterns of growth, whether teaching children with special needs or children whose growth is typical.[2] This awareness helps to define and interpret the child's action in light of what is considered typical. Guidance and discipline are based on an awareness of the expected behaviors common to a given age range. Many so-called problem behaviors are normal behaviors of the age at which they occur: for example, the difficulty some toddlers and 2-year-olds have with sharing their toys. This does not imply a passive approach; teachers and parents do not ignore undesirable behav-

 OUR DIVERSE WORLD OUR DIVERSE WORLD OUR DIVERSE WORLD OUR DIVERSE WORLD OUR DIVERSE WORLD OUR DIVERSE WORLD OUR DIVERSE WORLD OUR DIVERSE WORLD OUR DIVERSE WORLD

1 Individual judgments may be based on these filters. Keep developing an awareness of yourself and your particular filters.

2 Children are more alike than they are different.

Figure 3.3 ⬤ Adults see children through many filters. What is it like to look through children's eyes?

ior because the child is "going through a stage." Instead adults seek to guide and direct children in ways that enhance their overall growth. Four-year-olds test limits and are resistant to controls. The wise teacher accepts the testing of power and individuality, yet still maintains necessary limits to behavior.

Word pictures of a child, taken from age-level charts, help teachers know what to expect and when to expect it. By using the charts as a reference, teachers lessen the risk of expecting too much or too little of children at any given age. If, for instance, 4-year-olds typically "tell tall tales," teachers' responses to their stories reflect an awareness of that tendency. The fun of making up a story and the use of imagination are acknowledged, but there is not a concern that the child is lying. Age-level characteristics give a frame of reference with which to handle daily situations and a basis for planning appropriate guidance measures.

In Curricula

The expression "hurried child," so aptly used by David Elkind (1989) in his book of the same name has come to mean a disregard for activities and curriculum geared to a child's appropriate developmental level. Instead, children are forced to sit and pay attention far longer than their bodies or minds can tolerate; attempts

are made to teach reading and writing before children are developmentally prepared; and curricula for fours, fives, and sixes include content best suited for later years. The following charts can be invaluable in helping early childhood professionals plan appropriate curricula and activities for young children. Word pictures can be used to tailor curriculum planning to an individual child or a particular class or group on the basis of known developmental standards. See also The Importance of Childhood in Chapter 15.

Guidelines

Use the charts with care. A profile of the whole child is helpful, but avoid the tendency to overclassify.[1] Look and listen to the children in the classroom to interpret theory. Balance your impressions with classroom experience of real children. Interpretation of the charts must not focus on what the child *cannot* do. Instead, use them to get a perspective on the wide range of developmental norms a child exhibits over several of the chronological age groupings. Always look at the word picture for the group just below and just above the age level of the children you are assessing. Those children will undoubtedly exhibit some of the developmental behaviors appropriate to all three groups you check.

[1] Culture notwithstanding, all children grow at their own rate.

There are several things to keep in mind for the age-level charts to be a valuable teaching tool. It is very important to realize that these norms of development refer to average or typical behavior. They cannot be applied to an individual child too literally. If you were to look at a class of 6-year-olds, for instance, you would find that probably half or the children would fit the majority of the description in the profile. Some of them would not yet have reached this level of development, and some would have already gone through this stage. Shawna might well fit the general description of the 6-year-old at a physical level. Her language and intellectual levels may be closer to a 7-year-old, while her social skills may be typical of many 4-year-olds. There may very well be characteristics that Shawna will *never* exhibit. It won't work to use the chart as a measuring stick, comparing one child with another, because children develop at their own rates and in their own ways.

Remember that children probably go through most of the stages described, and in the same sequence. But they will do so in ways that reflect their own rate of growth and their own background. Use these characteristics not to pit children against each other to see who is developing faster, but to compare the child with himself. Looking at Dwayne, it helps to know where he is in relation to most 2-year-olds, but more important, where he is now, 6 months from now, a year from now, and what he was like a year ago. A clear picture of his rate of growth emerges. See also Child Development and Cultural Diversity in Chapter 4.

The word picture on the infant to 1-year-old is deliberately vague on the ages when some developmental characteristics might appear. The rapid rate of growth combined with individual growth patterns make it difficult to predict with any surety when Garth will indeed sit up by himself unaided, but he is likely to accomplish that task within 1 or 2 months on either side of the average age cited.

Derman-Sparks and the ABC Task Force (1989) point out that children become aware of and form attitudes about racial and cultural differences at a very early age. Their experiences with their bodies, social environment, and cognitive developmental stage combine to help them form their own identity and attitudes. What they learn about themselves is reflected in their behavior and attitudes toward others. As they develop cognitively, children become aware of differences and similarities in people. Concurrently, they are developing feelings of trust, fear, joy, anger, and love. This interplay of developmental tasks can be influenced by societal stereotyping and bias, which can affect a child's self-concept and attitude toward others. These cultural milestones are included in the Word Pictures to indicate how, as children come to a sense of themselves as individuals, their attitudes and behaviors toward others can be influenced.[1]

Word Pictures

Five basic developmental areas are included in the Word Pictures:

● *Social-Emotional Development.* Includes a child's relationship with himself and others, self-concept, self-esteem, and the ability to express feelings.

● *Language Development.* Includes children's utterances, pronunciation, vocabulary, sentence length, and the ability to express ideas, needs, and feelings. It includes receptive language (do they understand what they hear?) and verbal levels (what do they say?)

● *Physical-Motor Development.* Includes gross motor, fine motor, and perceptual motor.

● *Intellectual Development.* This generally means the ability to perceive and think. Includes curiosity, memory, attention span, general knowledge, problem solving, analytical thinking, beginning reading, computing skills, and other cognitive processes.

● *Cultural Identity Development.* This suggests the interconnections between developmental stages and a growing awareness of one's own culture as well as attitudes toward others of differing cultures. Various cultural milestones appear in each age group which, when appropriately fostered, can increase a child's sensitivity to differences.[2]

The following Word Pictures are designed to help classroom teachers. Characteristics listed are:

● Behaviors most common to the age group

● Those that have implications for children in group settings

OUR DIVERSE WORLD OUR DIVERSE WORLD OUR DIVERSE WORLD OUR DIVERSE WORLD OUR DIVERSE WORLD OUR DIVERSE WORLD OUR DIVERSE WORLD OUR DIVERSE WORLD

[1] Racial, cultural, gender, and ability biases have a profound effect on children's developing sense of self and others.
[2] Very early in the course of normal development, children develop attitudes about differences in people.

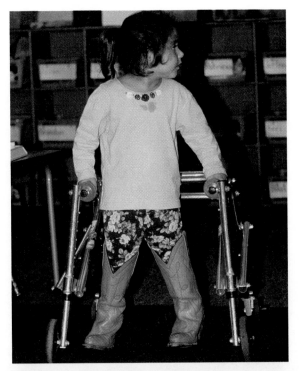

Figure 3.4 ● There is a wide range of individual differences in the way children grow and develop.

● Those that suggest guidance and disciplinary measures

● Those that have implications for planning a developmentally appropriate curriculum

● Those that are cultural milestones, which are highlighted to suggest the interaction of children's development and their awareness of attitudes toward race and culture[1]

In Chapter 4, students will come to appreciate the importance of research and significant theories from which these word pictures are drawn.

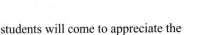 OUR DIVERSE WORLD OUR DIVERSE WORLD OUR DIVERSE WORLD OUR DIVERSE WORLD OUR DIVERSE WORLD OUR DIVERSE WORLD OUR DIVERSE WORLD OUR DIVERSE WORLD

[1] In order to build attitudes that go beyond mere tolerance, we must help children gain more accurate pictures of persons and cultures different from their own.

INFANT

SOCIAL-EMOTIONAL

0–1 month: cries to express emotions; bonding begins
4–10 weeks: social smiles
2 months: begins social games
3 months: distinguishes familiar faces
    turns head toward human voice
    smiles in response to a smile
    kicks, smiles, waves in response
    cries when left alone
    recognizes parent
4 months: genuine laugh
    smiles when spoken to
    loves attention
5 months to 1 year: stranger anxiety
6 months: distinguishes between voices
    smiles, babbles at strangers
    develops attachment
    begins to play imitation games
    plays peek-a-boo
    sensitive to parental moods
8 months: laughs out loud
9 months: screams to get own way

Play is activity only for present moment.
Fears unfamiliar: people, places, things.
Beginning sense of separate self.

LANGUAGE

0–1 month: turns head in response to voices
    cries to express needs
6–8 weeks: coos
Gestures to communicate:
 pushes objects away, squirms,
 reaches out to people, pouts,
 smacks lips, shrieks, points
2 months: voluntary vocal sounds
3 months: babbles
6–12 months: imitation sound games
Responds to variety of sounds
Makes vowel sounds
Acquires receptive language
Cries to communicate
12 months: first words

PHYSICAL-MOTOR

By 1 year: grows 10 to 12 inches, triples birth weight,
    lengthens by 40%, doubles brain size, grows full
    head of hair
Bounces in crib
Uses whole-body motions

Figure 3.5 ● By 8 months, the infant focuses eyes on small objects and reaches for them.

4 months: sees, grasps objects
5 months: examines fingers
    sits when propped
6 months: rolls over
    discovers feet
    teething begins
7 months: crawls
8 months: sits up unaided
    pulls to standing position
    pincer grasp established
9 months: creeps
10 months: feeds self with spoon
11 months: stands alone, cruises
12 months: first steps
Late infancy: can move hands in rotation to turn knobs
Newborn motor activity is mostly reflexes.

INTELLECTUAL-COGNITIVE

0–1 month: responds to mother's voice:
    senses function, especially pain, touch
10 weeks: memory is evident
4 months: smiles of recognition
7–10 months: solves simple problems (knocks over box
    to get toy)
8 months: begins to believe in permanence of objects;
    follows a simple instruction
8–12 months: intentionality in acts
11 months: begins trial-error experimentation
12 months: plays drop/retrieve games, pat-a-cake
Explores with hands and fingers
Smiles, vocalizes at image in mirror

Key characteristics of cultural awareness.

TODDLER

SOCIAL-EMOTIONAL

Almost totally egocentric
Likes to be noticed; loves an audience
Lacks inhibitions
Insists on own way, assertive
Likes doing things by self
Independent, has self-identity
Adapts easily
Plays by self in playpen
Refers to self by name
Laughs loudly at peek-at-boo
Cries when left alone
Curious
Relates to adults better than children
Active, eager
Talks mostly to self
Usually friendly
Strong sense of ownership
Mimics adult behavior
Experiences and shows shame

Figure 3.6 ● Toddlers enjoy pointing out objects in a book.

LANGUAGE

Some two-word phrases
Enjoys vocalizing to self
Babbles in own jargon
Uses "eh-eh" or "uh-uh" with gestures
Names closest relatives
Repeats adults' words
Points to communicate needs, wants
Shakes head "no" to respond
Responds to directions to fetch, point
Obeys verbal requests
Answers "What's that?"
Understands simple phrases
Uses 5 to 50 words

Loves to pull/push objects
Runs with stiff, flat gait
Uses whole-arm movements
Carry and dump becomes a favorite activity
Scribbles
Turns pages two or three at a time
Zips/unzips large zipper
Likes holding objects in both hands

INTELLECTUAL-COGNITIVE

Points to objects in a book
Matches similar objects
Fits round block in round hole
Loves opposites: up/down, yes/no
Imitates simple tasks
Interest shifts quickly
Short attention span
Follows one direction
Gives up easily, but easily engaged
Conclusions are important: close doors, shut books
Thinks with feet; action-oriented
Builds tower of three or four small blocks

PHYSICAL-MOTOR

Awkward coordination; chubby body
Tottering stance
Creeps when in a hurry
Walks with increasing confidence
Walks with feet wide apart, arms out, head forward
Finds it difficult to turn corners
Goes up and down stairs holding on
Backs into chair to sit down
Can squat for long periods of time
Motor-minded: constant motion

Key characteristics of cultural awareness.

TWO-YEAR-OLD

SOCIAL-EMOTIONAL

Self-centered
Unable to share, possessive
Clings to familiar; resistant to change
Ritualistic; insists on routines
Dependent
Likes one adult at a time
Quits readily; easily frustrated
Goes to extremes
Impulsive; shifts activities suddenly
Easily distracted
Pushes, shoves
Finicky, fussy eater, some food jags
Refers to self by given name
Treats people as inanimate objects
Dawdles; slow-geared
Plays parallel
Watches others
Likes people
Excited about own capabilities

LANGUAGE

Uses two- or three-word sentences
Telegraphic sentences: "Throw ball"
Has difficulty in pronunciation
"Me," "Mine" most prominent pronouns
Spontaneous language; rhythmic, repetitive
Constant talking; interested in sound
Sings phrases of song, not on pitch
Can't articulate feelings
Frustrated when not understood
May stutter
Asks "Whassat?" about pictures
Can match words with objects
Repeats words and phrases
Uses 50 to 300 words

PHYSICAL-MOTOR

Uses whole-body action
Pushes, pulls, pokes
Climbs into things
Leans forward while running
Climbs stairs one by one
Dependent on adults for dressing
Can help undress
Has reached one-half potential height
Bladder/bowel control begins
Feeds self
Thumb-forefinger opposition complete
Grasps cup with two hands

Awkward with small objects
Lugs, tumbles, topples; unsteady
Alternates hands; preference developing
Can rotate to fit objects
Expresses emotions bodily
Sensory-oriented
Cuts last teeth
Has difficulty relaxing

INTELLECTUAL-COGNITIVE

Recognizes, explores physical characteristics
Investigates with touch and taste
Intrigued by water, washing
Likes to fill and empty things
Has limited attention span
Lives in present
Understands familiar concepts
Can tell difference between black and white
Needs own name used
Likes simple make-believe
Does one thing at a time
Remembers orders of routines
Recalls where toys are left
Classifies people by gender
Names familiar objects in books

Figure 3.7 ● The 2-year-old watches others.

Key characteristics of cultural awareness.

THREE-YEAR-OLD

SOCIAL-EMOTIONAL

Highly imitative of adults
Wants to please adults; conforms
Responds to verbal suggestions
Easily prompted, redirected
Can be bargained with, reasoned with
Begins to share, take turns, wait
Avid "me-too"er
Exuberant, talkative, humorous
Has imaginary companions
Has nightmares, animal phobias
Plays consciously, cooperatively with others
Plays spontaneously in groups
Dramatizes play
Goes after desires; fights for them
Asserts independence often
Often stymied, frustrated, jealous
Sympathizes
Strong sex-role stereotypes

LANGUAGE

Talkative with or without a listener
Can listen to learn
Likes new words
Increases use of pronouns, prepositions
Uses "s" to indicate plural nouns
Uses "ed" to indicate past tense
Uses sentences of three or more words
Says "Is that all right?" a lot
Talks about nonpresent situations
Put words into action
Moves and talks at the same time
Substitutes letters in speech: "w" for "r"
Intrigued by whispering
Uses 300 to 1000 words

PHYSICAL-MOTOR

Well-balanced body lines
Walks erect; nimble on feet
Gallops in wide, high steps
Alternates feet in stair climbing
Suddenly starts, stops
Turns corners rapidly
Swings arms when walking
Jumps up and down with ease
Uses toilet alone
Loses baby fat
Achieves bladder control
Rides a tricycle
Puts on, takes off wraps with help

Figure 3.8 ● The 3-year-old is refining finger movement.

Unbuttons buttons
Has some finger control with small objects
Grasp with thumb and index finger
Holds cup in one hand
Pours easily from small pitcher
Washes hands unassisted
Can carry liquids
Has activity with drive and purpose
Can balance on one foot

INTELLECTUAL-COGNITIVE

Matches people according to physical characteristics
Estimates "how many"
Enjoys making simple choices
Alert, excited, curious
Asks "why?" constantly
Understands "It's time to . . ."
Understands "Let's pretend . . ."
Enjoys guessing games, riddles
Has lively imagination
Often overgeneralizes
Has short attention span
Carries out two to four directions in sequence
Often colors pages one color
Can't combine two activities
Names and matches simple colors
Has number concepts of one and two
Sees vague cause-and-effect relationships
Can recognize simple melodies
Distinguishes between night and day
Understands size and shape comparisons

Key characteristics of cultural awareness.

FOUR-YEAR-OLD

SOCIAL-EMOTIONAL

Mood changes rapidly
Tries out feelings of power
Dominates; is bossy, boastful, belligerent
Assertive, argumentative
Shows off; is cocky, noisy
Can fight own battles
Hits, grabs, insists on desires
Explosive, destructive
Easily overstimulated; excitable
Impatient in large groups
Cooperates in groups of two or three
Develops "special" friends but shifts loyalties often
In-group develops; excludes others
Resistant; tests limits
Exaggerates, tells tall tales
Alibis frequently
Teases, outwits; has terrific humor
May have scary dreams
Tattles frequently
Has food jags, food strikes

LANGUAGE

Has more words than knowledge
A great talker, questioner
Likes words, plays with them
Has high interest in poetry
Able to talk to solve conflicts
Responds to verbal directions
Enjoys taking turns to sing along
Interested in dramatizing songs, stories
Exaggerates, practices words
Uses voice control, pitch, rhythm
Asks "when?" "why?" "how?"
Joins sentences together
Loves being read to

PHYSICAL-MOTOR

Longer, leaner body build
Vigorous, dynamic, acrobatic
Active until exhausted
"Works": builds, drives, pilots
Can jump own height and land upright
Hops, skips
Throws large ball, kicks accurately
Hops and stands on one foot
Jumps over objects
Walks in a straight line
Races up and down stairs
Turns somersaults

Walks backward toe-heel
Accurate, rash body movements
Copies a cross, square
Can draw a stick figure
Holds paint brush in adult manner, pencil in fisted grasp
Can lace shoes
Dresses self except back buttons, ties
Has sureness and control in finger activities
Alternates feet going down stairs

INTELLECTUAL-COGNITIVE

Does some naming and representative art
Gives art products personal value
Can work for a goal
Questions constantly
Interested in how things work
Interested in life-death concepts
Has an extended attention span
Can do two things at once
Dramatic play is closer to reality
Judges which of two objects is larger
Has concept of three; can name more
Has accurate sense of time
Full of ideas
Begins to generalize; often faulty
Likes a variety of materials
Calls people names
Has dynamic intellectual drive
Has imaginary playmates
Recognizes several printed words

Figure 3.9 ● Having special friends is part of being age 4.

Key characteristics of cultural awareness.

FIVE-YEAR-OLD

SOCIAL-EMOTIONAL

Poised, self-confident, self-contained
Sensitive to ridicule
Has to be right; persistent
Has sense of self-identity
May get silly, high, wild
Enjoys pointless riddles, jokes
Enjoys group play, competitive games
Aware of rules, defines them for others
Chooses own friends; is sociable
Gets involved with group decisions
Insists on fair play
Likes adult companionship
Accepts, respects authority
Asks permission
Remains calm in emergencies

LANGUAGE

Uses big words and complete sentences
Can define some words
Spells out simple words
Takes turn in conversation
Has clear ideas and articulates them
Uses words to give, receive information
Insists "I already know that"
Asks questions to learn answers
Makes up songs
Enjoys dictating stories
Uses 1500 words
Tells a familiar story
Defines simple words
Answers telephone, takes a message
Thinks out loud

PHYSICAL-MOTOR

Completely coordinated
Has adultlike posture
Has tremendous physical drive
Likes to use fine-motor skills
Learns how to tie bow knot
Has accuracy, skill with simple tools
Draws a recognizable person

Dresses self completely
Cuts on a line with scissors
Begins to color within the lines
Catches ball from 3 feet away
Skips using alternate feet
Enjoys jumping, running, doing stunts
Rides a two-wheeler
Balances on a balance beam
Jumps rope
Runs lightly on toes
Likes to dance; is graceful, rhythmic
Sometimes roughhouses, fights

INTELLECTUAL-COGNITIVE

Curious about everything
Wants to know "how?" "why?"
Likes to display new knowledge, skills
Somewhat conscious of ignorance
Attention span increases noticeably
Knows tomorrow, yesterday
Can count 10 objects, rote counts to 20
Sorts objects by single characteristic
Knows name, address, town
Makes a plan, follows it, centers on task
Sorts objects by color, shape
Concepts of smallest, less than, one-half
May tell time accurately, on the hour
Knows what a calendar is used for

Figure 3.10 ● Five-year-olds are coordinated; they are graceful and rhythmic.

Key characteristics of cultural awareness.

SIX- AND SEVEN-YEAR-OLDS

SOCIAL-EMOTIONAL

Six-year-old
Likes to work, yet often does so in spurts
Does not show persistence
Tends to be a know-it-all
Free with opinions and advice
Brings home evidence of good schoolwork
Observes family rules
Gender-role stereotypes are rigid
Friends easily gained, easily lost
Tests and measures self against peers
Makes social connections through play
Friends are of same sex
Believes in rules except for self
Active, outgoing
Charming
Proud of accomplishments
Shows aggression through insults, name-calling

Seven-year-old
More serious
Sensitive to others' reactions
Eager for home responsibilities
Complaining, pensive, impatient
Shame is common emotion
Leaves rather than face criticism, ridicule, disapproval
Complains of unfair treatment, not being liked
Shows politeness and consideration for adults
Enjoys solitary activities
First peer pressure: needs to be "in"
Wants to be one of the gang
Relates physical competence to self-concept

LANGUAGE

Six- and seven-year-olds
Enjoy putting language skill to paper
Talk *with* adults rather than *to* them
Chatter incessantly
Dominate conversations
Speech irregularities still common
Learning to print/write
Acquisition of new words tapers off
Bilingual capacities nearly complete if English is second language
Ability to learn new language still present

PHYSICAL-MOTOR

Six- and seven-year-olds
Basic skills develop; need refinement

Like to test limits of own body
Value physical competence
Work at self-imposed tasks
Need daily legitimate channels for high energy
Learn to ride two-wheeler, skate, ski
Motor development is tool for socializing
Boisterous, enjoy stunts and roughhousing
Susceptible to fatigue
Visual acuity reaches normal
Hungry at short intervals, like sweets
Chew pencils, fingernails, hair

INTELLECTUAL-COGNITIVE

Six- and seven-year-olds
Work in spurts, not persistent
Letter and word reversal common
Learn to read, beginning math skills
Can consider others' point of view
Use logic, systematic thinking
Can plan ahead
Enjoy collecting: sorting, classifying
Can sequence events and retell stories
Concepts of winning and losing are difficult
Like games with simple rules
May cheat or change rules
Want "real" things: watches and cameras that work
Sift and sort information
Can conceptualize situations
Enjoy exploring culture of classmates

Figure 3.11 ● An important milestone, learning to read.

Key characteristics of cultural awareness.

EIGHT-YEAR-OLD

SOCIAL-EMOTIONAL

Outgoing, enthusiastic
Enormously curious about people and things
Socially expansive
Judgmental and critical of self and others
Ambivalent about growing up
Often hostile but attracted to opposite sex
Growing self-confidence
Learns about self through others: peers, parents
Aware of and sensitive to differences from other children
Begins to evaluate self and others through clothing,
    physical attraction, social status
Likes to meet new people, go new places
Emerging sensitivity to personality traits of others
Eager for peer approval and acceptance
Growing sense of moral responsibility
Joins clubs
Chooses same-sex playmates
Struggles with feelings of inferiority
Likes to work cooperatively
Responds to studies of other cultures
Growing interest in fairness and justice issues

LANGUAGE

Talks *with* adults
Attentive and responsive to adult communication
Teases members of opposite sex
Talks about "self"
Talkative, exaggerates
Likes to explain ideas
Imitates language of peers
Enjoys story telling and writing short stories

PHYSICAL-MOTOR

Beginning to engage in team sports
Often a growth spurt year
Speedy, works fast
Restless, energetic, needs physical release
Plays hard, exhausts self
Eye–hand coordination matures; learning cursive
    handwriting
Enjoys competitive sports
Hearty appetite, few food dislikes
Repeatedly practices new skills to perfect them

INTELLECTUAL-COGNITIVE

Criticizes abilities in all academic areas
Seeks new experiences
Likes to barter, bargain, trade

Enjoys creating collections of things
Interested in how children from other countries live
Thinks beyond the here-and-now boundaries of time and
    space
Enjoys role-playing character parts
Tests out parents to learn more about them
Needs direction, focus
Enjoys all types of humor
Full of ideas, plans
Gaining competence in basic skills
Concrete operations are solidifying
Industrious, but overestimates abilities
Interested in process as well as product of schoolwork
Growing interest in logic and the way things work
Takes responsibility seriously

Figure 3.12 ● Eight-year-olds prefer same-gender friendships

Key characteristics of cultural awareness.

THE WHOLE CHILD

The concept of "the whole child" is based on the accepted principle that all areas of human growth and development are interrelated. It is only for the purpose of studying one area or another in depth that such categories are created. The four developmental areas labeled in the preceding Word Pictures help focus on certain aspects of a child's normal development. In reality, all areas of growth are "intertwined and mutually supportive" (Allen & Marotz, 1994).

Each Child Is Unique

There are several reasons to consolidate the different developmental areas when looking at children. The first is the uniqueness of each child. Each one is a sum total of a multitude of parts and, as such, is different from anyone else. Individual natures and learning styles affect the way teachers will teach any two children of the same age in the same class.

Growth Is Interrelated

One area of development affects the other. A child with a hearing loss is likely to have language delay as well; thus, the physical development affects the language part of growth.[1] The child who has trouble making friends (social) is likely to exhibit his unhappiness (emotional) in the schoolyard (physical) and in the math period (intellectual). The interdependence of the areas of development have some positive aspects as well. The child who has a good breakfast and starts the school day with parent interest is ready to tackle new puzzles and new relationships. The kindergartener who masters using scissors is ready to try printing: the fine-motor skills enhance the cognitive task of learning the alphabet.

One way for new teachers to look at this concept of development is to plot the relationships visually. Think of each area of development as a circle. There are four of them: physical-motor, language, intellectual, and social-emotional. Try to connect them so that they intersect one another, as shown in Figure 3.13.

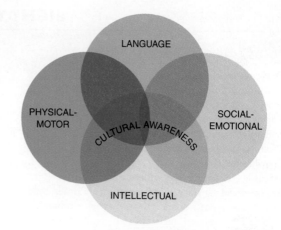

Figure 3.13 ● How areas of growth are interrelated: each area of growth is affected by and influences every other area of development.

Think how each area might affect or interact with the others. Can physical development affect how children feel about themselves? Of course; children who appreciate their body and its power feel confident in what they can do. How do intellectual skills interact with language development? When children have mastered their primary language, they can then clarify some of their thought processes. The emphasis on the circularity of the child's growth and development is a primary concept.

Normal physical development, for instance, depends on meeting not only the child's physical (adequate nutrition) needs but pyschological (nurturing caregivers/parents) and social (adequate play/exploration) needs as well. Social development is aided by the ability to communicate verbally; a well-developed attention span helps the child develop fine-motor skills; relating to others is more successful if intellectual problem-solving skills are already mature.

Three-year-olds frequently pose the question "Why?" as part of their intellectual curiosity. A teacher matches that understanding with the age-level characteristic of "listening to learn" and knows that the child understands some explanations. Thus, intellectual and language development areas influence one another.

OUR DIVERSE WORLD OUR DIVERSE WORLD OUR DIVERSE WORLD OUR DIVERSE WORLD OUR DIVERSE WORLD OUR DIVERSE WORLD OUR DIVERSE WORLD OUR DIVERSE WORLD

[1] Be aware of the full range of child development. Remember to keep working with the whole child, continuing to notice how children are similar *and* how each child is unique.

Two-year-old Gabe, who has difficulty relaxing, responds better at naptime if allowed to cling to a familiar object or toy. Motor and emotional growth interact with each other in this case.

Valuing Wholeness

The whole-child approach is seen from a medical point of view as well. **Holistic** medicine is basically an attempt to view health care from a "wellness" rather than an illness perspective. From this comes the idea of preventive medicine, which attempts to maintain the body in a healthy state, rather than wait for treatment until infection or disease has invaded.

This has a great deal to do with educating children. It is an attitude that begins with a belief in the "wellness" of children, their innate goodness and trustworthiness. A 2-year-old who says "No!" exhibits signs of wellness and is to be accepted as behaving normally. Young children wiggle and squirm during naptime. The deadly quiet of 25 kindergarteners in a room may indicate anxiety and concern rather than accomplishment. In other words, rather than viewing behavior as "wrong," it is important to notice and value whether what a child is doing is a sign of wellness.

The concept of the whole child strongly suggests the uniqueness of the person. Although they are often discussed separately, the areas of development (social-emotional, physical, language, cultural awareness, and intellectual) cannot be isolated from one another. They each make a valuable contribution to the total child.

CHILDREN WITH SPECIAL NEEDS

Approximately 15% to 20% of all children in the United States will exhibit some form of atypical development and need special services (Bee, 1997). These are children who did not develop according to normal standards. They exhibit a wide range of atypical disorders ranging from short-term behavior problems to long-term physical, mental, and emotional disabilities.[1]

Two types of children come under the category of children with special needs. Children who are disabled and children who are gifted extend the definition of "Who is the child?"[2] They are discussed separately in this section.

Children Who Are Disabled

More and more of the children in early childhood classrooms have a disabling condition. Five-year-old Pete, blind from birth, has been in nursery school for 3 years. Chrissy, a multihandicapped 4-year-old, has her daily program in a special school supplemented by attending the child care center three afternoons each week. Travis is a child with **Down syndrome**, and this is his first experience in a school not restricted to *atypical* children.

These child have some obvious characteristics that qualify them for special-needs status. Other children with less apparent **disabilities** also fall into this category. The term **special needs** includes a great many conditions that may or may not be noticeable.

Allen and Schwartz (1996) suggest three conditions under which a child is considered disabled. To be so designated, a child's normal growth and development is (1) delayed; (2) distorted, atypical, or abnormal; or (3) severely or negatively affected. This definition includes the physical, mental, emotional, and social areas of development.

A variety of disabilities may be encountered by teachers of young children:

- *Speech and language:* hearing impairment, stuttering, articulation problems, cleft palate, chronic voice disorders, learning disabilities

- *Physical-motor:* visual impairment, blindness, perceptual motor deficits, orthopedic disabilities such as cerebral palsy, spina bifida, loss of limbs, muscular dystrophy

- *Intellectual:* cognitive delays, brain injury, brain dysfunction, dyslexia, learning disabilities

OUR DIVERSE WORLD OUR DIVERSE WORLD OUR DIVERSE WORLD OUR DIVERSE WORLD OUR DIVERSE WORLD OUR DIVERSE WORLD OUR DIVERSE WORLD OUR DIVERSE WORLD

[1] More and more early care and education programs are reflecting diversity by creating groups of children exhibiting a wide range of developmental abilities.

[2] Our picture of what to consider while thinking about diversity continues to expand—race, gender, ethnicity, social class, physical and cognitive ability.

● *Social-emotional:* self-destructive behavior, severe withdrawal, dangerous aggression toward self and others, noncommunicativeness, moodiness, tantrums, attention-deficit hyperactivity disorder, severe anxiety, depression, phobias, psychosis, autism

● *Health impairments:* severe asthma, epilepsy, hemophilia, congenital heart defects, severe anemia, malnutrition, diabetes, tuberculosis, cystic fibrosis, Down syndrome, sickle cell anemia, Tay-Sachs disease, AIDS (Wolery & Wilbers, 1994)

● *Specific learning disabilities:* difficulties with language use and acquisition, spoken and written language affected, perceptual handicaps, brain injury, minimal brain dysfunction, dyslexia, developmental aphasia (Baron, 1995)

These disorders may range from mild to severe, and children will exhibit a wide variety of abilities and needs, even if they are diagnosed with the same condition. For further information concerning a specific one, the student will want to consult a special education textbook.

In the course of normal development, any one area of a child's growth is affected by the development of the whole child. This is true for children who are disabled also; the disability may have led to problems in other areas of growth. A child with a profound hearing loss is often delayed in speech production or language abilities and suffers social isolation due to the inability to hear and speak with peers. A child with a speech impairment or cleft palate may have the intellectual capacity to put simple puzzles together but may not yet have the language to engage verbally in songs and fingerplay.

Some disabilities are in and of themselves multihandicapping, affecting several growth areas. Typically, a child with Down syndrome may have congenital heart defects, intellectual impairments, eye abnormalities, or poor physical coordination. Children who have cerebral palsy, a central nervous system disorder, often have other disabling conditions such as intellectual delays, epilepsy, and hearing, visual, and speech problems (Kiernan et al., n.d.).

Learning Disabilities

Children with learning disabilities are found in almost every classroom; they have no discernable disability condition but nevertheless are having problems with one or more basic skills or learning.[1] These children may have, among other things, poor memory skills, difficulty in following directions, eye–hand coordination problems, and trouble discriminating between letters, numbers, and sounds. These keep them from storing, processing, and producing information (Kelly, 1988). Dyslexia, the most common specific learning disability, occurs when children have difficulty in learning to read. They may reverse letters (such as *d* and *b*) or words (such as *was* and *saw*), although many children do this who are not dyslexic. A child with a learning disability may have a strength in one area, such as math, and yet have a disability in another area, such as language. A learning disability does not mean that a child is intellectually impaired or delayed.

As we learned earlier in this chapter, growth is interrelated, and each area of growth is influenced by and influences other areas of growth. It will come as no surprise to discover that learning disorders are usually not a singular dysfunction. Children who exhibit problems with reading and writing will often have difficulties with spatial relationships and body coordination. Observations of these behaviors can give teachers some of the first warning signs of learning disorders.

There is continuing controversy on how to define and identify these children; a broad use of the term *learning disorder* is commonplace, sometimes to qualify for special education funding. Although some experts consider minimal brain damage to be the cause of learning disabilities, there is not consensus yet on why children have these problems.

According to Bee (1997), a child with a learning disorder develops normally in other respects and has no obvious brain damage, but the task of reading seems to highlight several areas of difficulty: problems of visual perception, inability to integrate visual and auditory information, impaired memory, problems with language, and difficulty distinguishing the separate sounds in words. This wide range of symptoms, the number of potential causes, and the varying degrees to

[1] Children with special needs cut across social, economic, and cultural lines.

which children exhibit the symptoms make learning disorders difficult to diagnose.

Attention-Deficit Disorder

Do you remember a classmate who could never sit still—one who was constantly on the move, talked excessively, and disrupted classroom activities? You may have also seen a preschool counterpart in the form of a child who couldn't finish a puzzle, take a nap, or wait for a turn. These children are typical of children with a condition known as attention-deficit hyperactivity disorder (ADHD), which affects up to 5% of children under 18 years of age (Wallis, 1994).

This disorder, previously called hyperactivity, was renamed by the American Psychiatric Association in 1987. When it exists without the hyperactive components it is called attention-deficit disorder, or ADD. ADHD is commonly thought to appear more often in boys; however, according to Hallowell and Ratty (1994), girls may go undiagnosed because they may not exhibit the hyperactive behavior.

As with learning disabilities, experts do not agree on the cause of this emotional disorder, but it does not appear to be caused by brain damage (Bee, 1997).

Children with ADHD are difficult to manage, both at home and in the classroom. They are prone to restlessness, anxiety, short attention spans, and impulsiveness. Hyperactive children have difficulty remaining seated, they are in constant motion, do not listen well, may talk excessively, are easily distracted, and have difficulty with social relationships. This constellation of behaviors may apply at some level to many children, but teachers must be cautious about labeling the normally active, somewhat disruptive child as hyperactive. The child with ADHD exhibits these behaviors in extreme, usually before age 7.

Medication with a drug, Ritalin, is a common treatment for children with ADHD, but because its effects are short term and its side effects can be serious, it is controversial as a remedy. Research does not support a popular theory that eliminating food additives, preservatives, and refined sugar from the child's diet will alter behavior significantly (Kelly, 1988). There is no easy solution for dealing with children who are hyperactive; further research into the cause of this disability and development of safe effective treatments are clearly called for.

Effective guidance strategies for children with ADHD include:

● Regular and consistent routines: "Remember, Sitara, we always wash hands before snacks."

● Consistent rules: "That's right, Ethan. Walk inside and run outside."

● Realistic expectations: "I know it is hard for you to wait a long time. Why don't you go over to the other cabinet and see if the pencils you want are in there?"

● Eye contact when giving directions and clear and simple explanations: 'Look at me, Toby, so I know that you are listening. Good. Now let's go over the assignment together."

● Allowing time for transition and giving a plan for the next step: "In 3 minutes it will be time to get ready to go home. When the other children begin to leave, I want you to get your coat and come back here to sit with us."

● Selecting jobs in which the children can be successful: "Connie, please pass the napkins out to this table today."

● Recognition of accomplishments: "Good work, Connie. You gave everyone a red napkin and then sat down with one for yourself."

Role of Parents and Teachers

Parents are usually the first to notice that their child is not developing according to the norms. They may ask the child's teacher to watch for signs of hearing impairments, lack of necessary motor skills, or language imperfections. Because early diagnosis and intervention are important, teachers should take these requests seriously and should begin to assess the child's overall skills.[1] With the parents, they can then plan appropriate follow-through. This may include a consultation with a physician for further developmental screening and testing. If both parents and teachers feel there is a potential problem, the task is to help identify it and secure the services needed.

OUR DIVERSE WORLD OUR DIVERSE WORLD OUR DIVERSE WORLD OUR DIVERSE WORLD OUR DIVERSE WORLD OUR DIVERSE WORLD OUR DIVERSE WORLD OUR DIVERSE WORLD

[1] Early childhood professionals need to be skilled at carefully observing and documenting the growth and development of individual children.

The teacher's role is to observe the child and provide current information, to support the parents through their concern, to find appropriate resources for them (such as social service agencies, public health offices, private and public schools), to assist with future placement for child care, and to be available for consultation with others who are working in the best interests of the child. The early childhood professional is not an expert in diagnosing learning disabilities but can be effective in helping parents secure proper referrals and treatment.

Public Recognition

Attention to the problems of people with disabilities in our society has reached national proportion only recently. Since the mid-1960s there has been significant public recognition of and the advent of public funding for the education programs for disabled persons. Prior to that, public—and private—attitudes seemed to be ones of shame and segregation. Past generations hid adults and children with disabilities in their homes or secluded them in institutions. Slowly, reform took place. Keeping special populations out of sight gave way to providing separate opportunities for them. Schools, classes, and recreational programs were started exclusively for people with special needs. Public consciousness is now sufficient to understand that not all people with special needs are necessarily mentally impaired. The current practice of integrating children with disabilities into ongoing programs in schools—the mainstream of American life—is not only more humane, but practical as well.[1]

Over the years a small number of schools had routinely accepted children with special needs. The idea gained national attention in 1972 when Head Start required that a minimum of 10% of its enrollment be reserved for children with disabilities. Head Start led the way toward large-scale inclusion. In 1975, Public Law 94-142, the Education for All Handicapped Children Act, was passed. This so-called Bill of Rights for the Handicapped guarantees free public education to disabled persons from 3 to 21 years of age. An individualized program for each person is mandatory, to be worked out in concert with the child's parents. Early childhood educators are fulfilling the requirements of that legislation. Public school systems faced with providing preschool programs for children with disabilities are turning to private preschools to fill the need when their own services are unavailable or inadequate.

The success of P.L. 94-142 means that thousands of children who are disabled who would have been denied any educational opportunities are now in school with their nondisabled peers.[2]

P.L. 99-457, the Education of the Handicapped Amendments Act of 1986, has had an even more profound impact for early childhood educators. Sections of this law provide funding for children who were not included in the previous law: infants, toddlers, and 3- to 5-year-olds. Before P.L. 99-457 was passed, only six states offered any services to infants with special needs at birth.

Since the initial law in 1975, parents of children with special needs have been part of the development of their child's Individualized Education Plan (IEP). This role has been strengthened recently to include a more family-centered approach. The family's strengths and needs are considered as specific services are arranged for the child, providing a more supportive atmosphere in which the child's unique needs will be met.

The preschool programs of P.L. 99-457 are essentially an extension of P.L. 94-142 services, which provide for the least restrictive environments for educating children with disabilities. The infant/toddler amendment is new, however. Another critical aspect of this law is that it allows for the inclusion of "developmentally delayed" youngsters and leaves local agencies the opportunity to include the "at-risk" child in that definition. The vague definitions give local agencies the opportunity to define disabling conditions in terms of local needs.

In 1990, Congress reauthorized P.L. 94-142 and renamed it the Individuals with Disabilities Education Act (IDEA) (P.L. 101-576). Two new categories, autism and traumatic brain injury, were included, and children from birth to age 5 years were now eligible to receive services.

OUR DIVERSE WORLD OUR DIVERSE WORLD OUR DIVERSE WORLD OUR DIVERSE WORLD OUR DIVERSE WORLD OUR DIVERSE WORLD OUR DIVERSE WORLD OUR DIVERSE WORLD OUR DIVERSE WORLD OUR DIVERSE WORLD

[1] See footnote 2 on page 60
[2] We need to remember that inclusion refers to abilities and gender as well as race and culture.

The importance of this legislation cannot be underestimated by those in and entering the field of early childhood. Clearly, the integration and transition of children with disabilities into early childhood programs require knowledgeable teachers. Early childhood educators would be wise to avail themselves of special education courses now to meet this challenge. Many states require such course work before certification; others will surely follow to fulfill these mandates.

Many programs may be affected by another piece of legislation, P.L. 101-336, the American with Disabilities Act (ADA), which was passed in 1990. This civil rights act makes it unlawful to discriminate against people with disabilities because of their disability and requires that people with disabilities have equal access to public and private services, as well as reasonable accommodations.[1] This law has had an impact on hiring practices in early childhood centers and family child care homes and may require adaptations to facilities and work environments to make them more accessible to individuals with disabilities. Although not specifically an education law, ADA is another step toward respecting the dignity and worth of all individuals.

Inclusion of Children with Special Needs

Allen and Schwartz (1996) differentiate between the terms **inclusion** and **mainstreaming**. In the past, children with special needs were integrated into classrooms only after they had met certain standards and expectations. Often they were assigned to separate special education classes. When ready, they were mainstreamed into classrooms with typically developing children. Inclusion means that a child with a disability is a full-time member of a regular classroom, a more natural environment, with children who do, as well as those who do not, have special needs.

More than a word definition is at stake, however. Allen and Schwartz (1996) go on to point out that inclusion is about belonging, having worth, and having choices. An inclusive classroom is about "accepting valuing human diversity and providing support so that

all children and families can participate in the program of their choice."

Placement in the classroom is not all there is to inclusion. Planning and care must be given to ensure that

● Teachers foster interactions between children who are disabled and children who are not disabled that promote healthy social relationships.

● Teachers recognize that every child with special needs has strength as well as deficits and build on those strengths.

● Teachers receive training and guidance in the critical task of working with children who have special needs and are *developmentally disabled* in their classes.

● Teachers work with parents to plan and implement the child's individualized program.

● Children with disabilities are actively involved and accepted in the total program.

● Children with special needs are helped to take advantage of, to the fullest extent of their capabilities, all the activities the school has to offer.

● Children's individual disabilities are addressed and considered in program planning and that procedures and curriculum are adapted to fit the children with special needs.

Inclusion is an important concept for all children. For the children without disabilities it is an opportunity to learn to accept differences in people.[2] In the early education center much of the curriculum is directed toward fostering the child's self-esteem and self-worth. Teaching is dedicated to helping youngsters see themselves and others as important and valuable. Inclusion presents an opportunity to extend that principle to the full range of human characteristics.

For the child with disabilities, the large numbers of typically developing children who serve as age-appropriate behavior models is important. Many children have not had an opportunity to hear the language of their normal peer group. They may not know how

 OUR DIVERSE WORLD OUR DIVERSE WORLD OUR DIVERSE WORLD OUR DIVERSE WORLD OUR DIVERSE WORLD OUR DIVERSE WORLD OUR DIVERSE WORLD OUR DIVERSE WORLD

[1] Each person's needs are assessed on an individual basis.

[2] One needs to see creating diverse learning situations as a benefit to everyone—everyone has something to learn. It is not a one-way street—those born with more abilities are not simply helping "others" (e.g., in an inclusive classroom of 3-year-olds, the "special needs child" having had numerous hospitalizations may easily separate from a parent, while the "typically developing" child may still be clinging to his mother's leg at the doorway and gain support from the "special needs child").

Figure 3.14 ● The inclusive classroom fosters children's interactions with one another.

to play with another child or how to communicate in socially acceptable ways. In the inclusive classroom, with sensitive and knowledgeable teachers, children with disabilities are helped to realize their potential as growing and learning children.

Teachers are a key factor in the successful integration of children with disabilities. Their attitude is critical; they must be committed to teaching all children, regardless of their intelligence or skill levels, with equal caring and concern.

Legislation makes strong demands on parents to be intimately involved with their child's program. Parent involvement greatly improves the child's chances for success (Allen & Marotz, 1994). Teachers and parents work together on a planned, consistent set of expectations. The child's confidence is reinforced at home and at school for the same achievements. Parents of children with disabilities find support from other parents since they share common child-rearing concerns.[1] Teachers learn a great deal about disabilities from the parents of the children who have special needs. This helps them become more effective teachers and aware of the special needs of the child.

Fortunately, the preschool teacher rarely needs to face the task of inclusiveness alone. Almost every early

childhood center has access to a team of professionals who can provide the child, the family, and the teaching staff with effective therapeutic activities. Their combined knowledge helps teachers understand the specific disability and plan an appropriate curriculum for each child. Together, teachers, clinicians, and parents work out a well-rounded program. This is called an **interdisciplinary approach** to teaching.

In 1993, NAEYC endorsed a Position on Inclusion, written by the Division of Early Childhood of the Council for Exceptional Children. This statement, which follows, offers guidelines for implementation.

(Reprinted with permission from NAEYC)
Position on Inclusion

Division for Early Childhood (DEC) of the Council for Exceptional Children

Adopted April 1993
(Endorsed by NAEYC November 1993)

Inclusion, as a value, supports the right of all children, regardless of their diverse abilities, to participate actively in natural settings within their communities. A natural setting is one in which

OUR DIVERSE WORLD OUR DIVERSE WORLD OUR DIVERSE WORLD OUR DIVERSE WORLD OUR DIVERSE WORLD OUR DIVERSE WORLD OUR DIVERSE WORLD OUR DIVERSE WORLD

[1] See footnote 2 on page 109.

the child would spend time had he or she not had a disability. Such settings include but are not limited to home and family, play groups, child care, nursery schools, Head Start programs, kindergartens, and neighborhood school classrooms.

DEC believes in and supports full and successful access to health, social service, education, and other supports and services for young children and their families that promote full participation in community life. DEC values the diversity of families and supports a family-guided process for determining services that are based on the needs and preferences of individual families and children.[1]

To implement inclusive practices, DEC supports (a) the continued development, evaluation, and dissemination of full inclusion supports, services, and systems **so that the options for inclusion are of high quality;** (b) the development of preservice and inservice training programs that prepare families, administrators, and service providers to develop and work within inclusive settings; (c) collaboration among all key stakeholders to implement flexible fiscal and administrative procedures in support of inclusion; (d) research that contributes to our knowledge of state-of-the-art services; and (e) the restructuring and unification of social, education, health, and intervention supports and services to make them more responsive to the needs of all children.

Children Who Are Gifted

The child who is gifted demonstrates an intellectual and creative potential superior to that of most children in the same age range and may exhibit an exceptional in-depth knowledge or skill of one or more specific areas (Bee, 1997; Lupkowski & Lupkowski,

1985). Traditionally, children have been identified as gifted if they score between 130 and 150 on standard IQ tests. Today, more and more programs for **gifted children** are open to those who exhibit exceptional talent in other than just intellectual superiority—children who are gifted in music, art, and physical skills. Today's definition must include children with disabilities as well because a child may be hearing-impaired and gifted or learning-disabled and gifted. Children who are gifted come from all social, economic, and cultural groups; however, there is increasing concern that children from low-income populations, children who are ethnically and culturally in the minority, children who have disabilities, and children who are bilingual are underrepresented in the gifted category.[2]

Early childhood teachers should be aware of some traits children who are gifted display so they can recognize potentially gifted children in their care.

In intellectual and academic areas, gifted children have long attention spans, learn rapidly, and have good memories and advanced vocabularies. They ask a lot of questions and are able to express their ideas easily. Independent and imaginative, gifted children may be bored by normal activities.

Socially, the gifted child is sought after by peers yet may be uneasy about relationships with other children. Planning and organizing skills are evident in their artwork and other creative endeavors. The gifted child is content to be alone, spending time in purposeful activity. Their use of humor is more advanced than children the same age; originality is typically characteristic of the gifted.

One of the most fascinating studies of gifted children—in fact, the study that is the cornerstone of the gifted child movement—is the Terman Study of the Gifted, which began at Stanford University in 1921. Lewis M. Terman, who developed the Stanford-Binet intelligence test, picked 1500 California public school children who had scores ranging between 135 and 200 on the test. This longitudinal study is now in its seventh decade; many of the participants are in their seventies and eighties. It is the longest psychological study ever conducted. This body of work has provided the most complete information to date on gifted children, span-

OUR DIVERSE WORLD OUR DIVERSE WORLD OUR DIVERSE WORLD OUR DIVERSE WORLD OUR DIVERSE WORLD OUR DIVERSE WORLD OUR DIVERSE WORLD OUR DIVERSE WORLD

[1] The child's family helps determine what program best suits the needs of their child, ensuring that their cultural beliefs will be noted.

[2] This information provides another opportunity to examine the impact of bias in thinking about children (i.e., do the existing instruments for identifying giftedness identify only particular strengths for a particular segment of the population?)

ning the grade school years through retirement. Its initial purpose was to dispel the perception, common at that time, that bright children grow into maladjusted and eccentric misfits.

Instead, the study found that the exceptionally bright child is, in later life, more successful, better educated, better satisfied, healthier, more socially adept and popular with peers, better adjusted, and a more productive member of society than the average American. It must be noted that the families from which these exceptional children came were middle class, advantaged, and with an enriched environment.

A study by the Sid W. Richardson Foundation highlights a common concern about gifted programs and the exclusion of children from backgrounds other than those cited in the Terman study. The Richardson study calls for opening programs for the gifted to a larger group of "able learners" (Olson, 1985), dropping labels such as "gifted" and "talented," promoting students on the basis of their mastering a subject or skill, and looking for eligible students among populations "excluded from opportunity by ethnic or economic circumstances" (Olson, 1985). Other reports similarly call for making nontraditional students a priority in programs for gifted children.

The current definition of "gifted" too often limits programs to those children who are intellectually exceptional. There is a call among other gifted-education experts to enlarge the definition to include, for example, children who are gifted in music, art, and physical skills as well as children who have handicaps, bringing to mind Gardner's multiple intelligences (Gardner, 1993). The eight different kinds of knowing that Gardner lists (see p. 447) foster a more open, inclusive approach to the definition of "gifted."

Gifted children, once identified, need to be challenged. In some cases the children may be advanced to an older group, moving on to kindergarten or first grade. A more common approach in early childhood has been in the area of curriculum enrichment. In this way the child remains with age-level peers to develop social skills. Some schools segregate gifted children by placing them in special classes exclusively for those identified as being gifted.

The Role of the Early Childhood Educator

Early childhood teachers are well prepared to work with children at their own pace—a key factor in teaching children who have disabilities and children who are gifted, and an underlying principle of early childhood education. The good early childhood teacher is familiar with and endorses an individualized approach to learning, emphasizes discovery learning through self-direction and independence, and accepts and appreciates the unique and individual differences in all children. These are qualities and beliefs that work well with all children, including any who have disabilities.

With Children Who Are Gifted

The teacher's role with the gifted preschool child is that of providing challenge and stimulation. Curriculum areas are developed in more complex ways. The gifted child is ready to learn in greater depth; the teachers provide added materials and activities that will help the children probe the extent of their interests. The nongifted children in the same classroom benefit from this enrichment; each responds according to his or her abilities. Teachers of children who have special gifts and talents can meet their unique needs in a regular school setting at the same time they provide a rich curriculum for the nongifted student.

Parents of the gifted child will need support and encouragement as well as guidance in dealing with their child's exceptionality. Together, teachers and parents can explore what will best suit each individual child so that this giftedness may be nurtured and challenged at home and at school.

With Children Who Have Special Needs

Integrating children with special needs into classroom settings can pose problems if teachers are not aware of how to deal with children who represent both ends of the broad spectrum of normal development. Individual attention is a necessity; so is a climate that supports self-help, interdependence, and responsibility. In kindergarten and early elementary grades, it is important to foster cooperative learning so that students of mixed abilities work together and each child finds an appropriate pace at which to work within the team. Successful inclusion requires more planning and preparation on the part of the teaching staff to see that the needs of all the children are being met. Teachers are called on to facilitate and support peer interaction between the children with special needs and those without disabilities on a more frequent and consistent basis.[1] The average early childhood teacher can learn from special education courses, from the parents of children with special needs, and from medical specialists how to adapt teaching strategies for an integrated program. Knowing how to work with the parents, especially in the area of communication, is a critical factor for teachers. It is also important to keep in mind that most early childhood professionals are not trained diagnosticians but can assist parents in identifying potential problems as they observe children in the classroom setting.

With Bias and Stereotypes

Vincent is a husky 5-year-old boy whose physical skills match those of his classmates. When he was born Vincent was diagnosed with spina bifida, a spinal cord injury, which left him with no bladder or bowel control. As a result, he wears diapers. Noah watched Vincent changing his diapers and later refused to let Vincent join him at the art table. Noah taunted: "I don't like him. He's a baby. He's not like us big guys. He wears diapers. He can't sit here. I'm not gonna play with no babies." Vincent looked both surprised and hurt (Gordon & Browne, 1996).

One of the greatest needs a child with disabilities has is to be accepted (Chandler, 1994). Rejection by their nondisabled peers may occur. Young children are known for their forthrightness in commenting on and asking questions about what confuses and frightens them. They may be anxious about what another child's disability means to them. Although this is a common reaction and age appropriate, we cannot allow an individual to be rejected on the basis of a disability. Derman-Sparks and colleagues' (1989) suggestions follow, along with examples of supportive and sensitive teacher interactions (Gordon & Browne, 1996).

● The rejection must be handled immediately, with support and assurance given to the child who was rejected that this type of behavior will not be permitted.

Example: The teacher put her arm around Vincent, and said, "Noah, what you said about Vincent is very hurtful. Tell me more about what you meant." Noah began to deny that he had said anything, then admitted that Vincent looked funny in diapers because he was so big. The teacher asked Vincent if he would like to tell Noah why he wore diapers. Vincent agreed and responded, "When I was born there was something wrong with my spine so I don't feel it when I have to go to the bathroom. I wear diapers so that I don't wet my pants." "Does it hurt"? asked Noah. "No way," answered Vincent. "I just have to remember to change so I don't get a rash." The teacher then said to Noah, "It's okay for you to ask questions about why Vincent wears diapers, but you can't tell him he can't sit at the table with you. In our class, everybody gets to play and work together."

● It is important to help children recognize how they are different and how they are alike.

Example: "Noah, both you and Vincent have to go to the bathroom during the day. Your body tells you when it is time to go and since Vincent's doesn't, he has to wear protection. You are both good at drawing dinosaurs, too."

● Children need to have their fears about disabilities taken seriously and to have adults understand their concerns.

Example: Noah was approached by the teacher in a way that allowed him to admit part of his concern. The teacher understood his unstated fear: "Noah, what happened to Vincent took place before he was born. It can't happen to you."

● Questions must be answered promptly, truthfully, and simply. Use the children's own natural curiosity and let the child with disabilities answer for himself whenever possible.

Example: Before leaving the art table, the teacher spoke to Noah, "Are there any more questions you have for Vincent?"

All children benefit when adults are willing to confront bias and deal with children's prejudice and misconceptions.[2] This example could have been about

[1] Strategies include assisting children in enjoying an activity together, providing social reinforcement, and teaching children how to play.

[2] Children need correct information, appropriate language, brief answers, and adults who are comfortable answering their questions and talking about their fears.

girls rejecting boys or one child being rejected because of skin color. When we provide opportunities for children to interact with people who look and act differently than they do, we actively foster acceptance and respect for the individual. See Derman-Sparks's Guest Editorial in Section V for further insights. More gender diversity issues are found in Chapter 15.

CULTURAL, RACIAL, AND ETHNIC CONSIDERATIONS

The answer to "Who is the young child?" takes on a powerful new meaning as the last decade of this century comes to a close. A multicultural explosion has swept across the nation, filling early childhood programs with children from many different cultural backgrounds. A dramatic shift in demographics is of importance to the early childhood professional if the needs of individual children are to be served. Some indicators of the population changes are:[1]

● Enrollment in public schools increased between 1985 and 1991 by just over 4%, yet the number of students with little or no English language skills increased 50% (Gray, 1993).

● Over 127 languages and dialects are spoken by students in the Washington, D.C., school system (Gray, 1993).

● One of six children in California public schools is born outside the United States, and one third of them speak a language other than English at home (Gray, 1993).

● By 2010, Hispanics, who can be of any race, will become the largest minority population (Gray, 1993).

For a teacher of young children, these statistics have some important implications. There will be more students in the classroom who are culturally and linguistically different. Unless teachers are informed and educated about these differences, they may misinterpret a child's abilities, learning, and needs. Too often, language barriers between a teacher and a child lead to the conclusion that the child is a slow learner or has a disability.

Working with parents will become more challenging to a teacher's ingenuity and communication skills. Many parents are unfamiliar with school culture in the United States and the expectations schools have about parent involvement and participation. Some parents are illiterate in their own language. An informed and supportive teacher can help parents help their children succeed under these circumstances. (See Chapter 8, Needs of Immigrant Parents).

A lack of understanding about the culture, history, beliefs, and values of the children is harmful to their self-concept (see Derman-Sparks et al., 1989, and other references in this book). Interracial marriages have increased in the United States 120% since 1980 (U.S. Bureau of the Census, 1995). The ranks of multiracial children are swelling. Francis Wardle, in his Focus Box on page 115, raises some of the critical issues inherent in working with young children who claim more than one or two ethnic backgrounds. He challenges the early childhood teacher to support interracial families in embracing their varied heritage and offers some ways to begin that process. When there are no assessment tools or instructional materials that are in the language of the children or depict their native heritage, they are placed at a distinct disadvantage. Minorities have argued for years that testing instruments that determine IQ and placement in special programs for children who are gifted or disabled are biased because they are not written in the predominant culture of the child being tested. As a result, minority children are underrepresented in programs for children who are gifted. Yet they are overrepresented in programs for children with disabilities, a fact that some relate to a lack of sensitivity to a child's cultural and linguistic heritage.

Cultural Sensitivity

Cultural and linguistic sensitivity means that each child's heritage is honored, that it is understood as unique from other cultures, and that it is respected. It means that teachers must become familiar with the cultural norms of the children in their classes and build bridges for children and their families into the more dominant culture.

OUR DIVERSE WORLD OUR DIVERSE WORLD OUR DIVERSE WORLD OUR DIVERSE WORLD OUR DIVERSE WORLD OUR DIVERSE WORLD OUR DIVERSE WORLD OUR DIVERSE WORLD OUR DIVERSE WORLD

[1] Early childhood educators need to move from an ethnocentric orientation (based on their own or the dominant culture experience) and move toward a more multicultural approach. Examination is needed of terms such as *minority* and *majority*.

Children of Mixed Heritage

Francis Wardle

Trell's first grade teacher asked him to research the life of one of his grandparents for a Black History Month project. Trell enthusiastically collected photographs, old letters, and newspaper clippings of his favorite grandfather. He asked his parents for anecdotal information; he also remembered his favorite times with his grandfather. He spent hours preparing.

Before the important day Trell went over the report with his teacher. He knew she would be as excited as he was about his grandfather, who had been a famous politician in his day. Much to Trell's disappointment, his teacher rejected the report. Trell, a biracial boy, had chosen to tell about his white/Carib grandfather. The teacher only wanted black people presented. Trell was devastated.

Anti-bias, multicultural education has found a permanent place in our early childhood programs. Psychologists have recognized that a crucial part of children's self-esteem is contingent on a positive view of their racial and ethnic heritage and that children with a high self-esteem do better in school. So programs now provide materials, books, dolls, activities, content, and discussion to help support the ethnic and racial identity of their children.

Multicultural approaches place children within five distinctive groups: African American, Hispanic, Native American, Asian American, and white. Programs then respond to children on the basis of the group they belong to. For children like Trell, whose parents represent more than one of these categories, this does not work. And teachers who work with the growing number of multiracial and multiethnic students find themselves without tools to support these children. Where do they fit in? How should teachers support and nurture their identities?

Children of mixed heritage—multiracial and multiethnic—have a racial and cultural heritage that includes both biological parents' complete backgrounds. Educators must carefully help these children develop a pride and positive self-esteem in their *total* multiracial heritage, culture, and identity.

There are no multiracial holidays, no heroes, no puzzles, no multiracial families, very few books, no posters, and no curriculum activities. Here are a few suggestions to help teachers begin to fill this void:

- Use interracial and interethnic families in your program to help with information, photographs, holidays, stories, histories, and curriculum resources.

- Create your own posters, materials, and books that show interracial families (including foster, adoptive, and blended families).

- Pressure companies that provide books and curriculum materials to include multiracial and multiethnic materials in their selections.

- Provide an immediate response to any language or behavior that in any way negates a multiethnic or multiracial child's identity, heritage, or pride. This includes comments that imply the child cannot embrace his full multiracial identity.

- Research multiracial and multiethnic heroes (e.g., composer Gottschalk, ornithologist Audubon) and present material to your class.

- Never celebrate an activity that requires a child to select only part of his heritage. If you celebrate cultural days, such as Cinco de Mayo and Martin Luther King Day, present them in a way all children can benefit. Make sure a multiracial child is comfortable identifying both with Cinco de Mayo *and* Martin Luther King Day, if the child has those combined heritages.

- Contact a local multiracial support group to get ideas, information, and advice.

- Do not teach about race, ethnicity, and culture in a way that excludes children and people. We should teach about culture and heritage as a way to give individuals strength, traditions, and values, not to group and exclude people.

Francis Wardle, Ph.D., is Executive Director of the Center for the Study of Biracial Children. He has written extensively on this topic, including, *Proposal: An Anti-Bias and Ecological Model for Multicultural Education*, an article that presents a multicultural model inclusive of children with multiracial and multiethnic heritages.

The following are examples of different cultural groups and some of the values and beliefs of their culture. These represent traditional influences along with adaptations to U.S. culture. These cultural factors should be addressed as teachers work with parents and children toward a partnership in education.[1]

A word of caution: like the Word Pictures, these characteristics are not to be taken stereotypically. They are meant as an introductory, general overview of a culture. Be careful not to overgeneralize about families from the following examples. There is a tendency to stereotype if we believe that *all* Asians, Hispanics, Native Americans, and African Americans are represented by such an overview. In fact, there are any number of different cultures represented by the broad categories listed here. Korean, Japanese, and Vietnamese are distinct cultures within the broad category of "Asian," just as Haitian and South African are unique cultures within the designation of "African American." The culturally sensitive teacher will get to know each of the families as a separate entity and become familiar with their individual expressions of culture and heritage.

Asian Americans

● Teachers are accorded great respect (Yee, 1988).

● Father is head of household, decisions should include him (Yee, 1988).

● The structure and use of first and last names among Asian subgroups vary (Morrow, 1989).

● Child represents the family's good name for the future; family may have difficulty accepting a child's disability and see it as a disgrace to the family name (Yee, 1988).

Hispanic Americans

● Children are highly valued (Valero-Figueira, 1988).

● Others accorded great respect are clergy, teachers, and community leaders (Valero-Figueira 1988).

● Children work best in cooperative situations (Beacher, Castillo, and Cruz, in Charlesworth, 1996).

● Sensitive to authority figures and their feelings about them (Beacher, Castillo, and Cruz, 1996).

Native Americans

● Family encourages independent decision-making by children.

● Being recognized as a part of peer group is more important for child than individual recognition.

● Extended family members, especially grandmothers, are involved with children and their education.

● Value cooperation and sharing.

● Respect the dignity of the individual.

● Wisdom of the elders is held in high esteem.

● Strong oral tradition, especially storytelling (Walker, 1988).

African Americans

● Parents are highly motivated for their children to achieve.

● Children have high degree of stimulation from the creative arts.

● Children tend to be active.

● Are expressive in music, dance, and drama.

● Raised with an emphasis on feelings and intense interpersonal relationships.

● Learn from people rather than objects (Hale, 1989).

European Americans

● Respect is earned in adult–child relationships; boys are allowed to be more open in disagreements with adults; disagreements are often passive and hidden.

● Children are encouraged to challenge adult opinions.

● Working independently is valued as is individual accomplishment; individual freedom is the most cherished value.

● In both academics and athletics, boys are encouraged to excel; physical appearance and friendliness are valued in girls.

OUR DIVERSE WORLD OUR DIVERSE WORLD OUR DIVERSE WORLD OUR DIVERSE WORLD OUR DIVERSE WORLD OUR DIVERSE WORLD OUR DIVERSE WORLD OUR DIVERSE WORLD OUR DIVERSE WORLD

[1] Examine your own culturally biased assumptions and note sources of conflict with your cultural influences.

● Logical, analytical thinking is encouraged in boys; girls are perceived as more subjective and intuitive.

● Children are encouraged to compete to get ahead.

● Civic mindedness and religious freedom are important cultural concepts (Della-Dora & Blanchard, 1979).

Each of these cultural factors has implications for teaching and forming relationships with people from varying backgrounds and cultures. The teacher of the future will be called on to integrate these insights into curriculum planning as well as home and school relationships. (See also "Attitudes and Biases" in Chapter 5).

Summary

The child in early childhood programs ranges from the dependent infant to the outgoing 8-year-old. In those few short years teachers witness tremendous physical, intellectual, social, and emotional gains.

The child learns to crawl, walk, run, climb, throw a ball, write with a pencil, use scissors, hold a spoon, and manipulate toys. Both large and small muscles are called into play throughout each stage of development.

Language development is equally impressive. The babbling infant becomes fluent, sometimes in more than one language. Intellectual gains coincide as children become able to express thoughts, solve problems, and exhibit growth in their reasoning powers.

Socially, the child learns to relate to family members, schoolmates, teachers, and other adults. Every range of human emotion is developed during these early years as children learn appropriate ways to express and release their feelings.

Teachers notice that children share many common characteristics at the same time they display wide individual differences. Profile charts—Word Pictures—describing normal development help teachers understand when a particular behavior is likely to occur. With advance notice, then, teachers can plan activities and curricula that appeal to children at every age level; disciplinary and guidance measures can match the child's specific level of development.

Yet it is obvious that growth and development do not proceed normally for all children. Two groups of children have special needs within the early childhood classroom. Children with disabilities who are mainstreamed require particular attention to their individual disabilities, and teachers need special skills to nurture children who are handicapped and nonhandicapped. Gifted children also require attention; their exceptional abilities must be challenged and stimulated within the regular early childhood program.

The changing demographics that bring more and more culturally and linguistically diverse children into early childhood settings require that teachers become familiar with the specific cultural norms represented in America today. This will call for new teaching strategies, culturally appropriate curriculum, and special efforts to work with parents from a multicultural perspective.

Review Questions

1. Match the word picture to the age group in which it belongs:

Observe family rules	toddlers
Plays peek-a-boo	fives
Has dynamic intellectual drive	sixes and sevens
Is intrigued by whispering	infants
Needs to be "in"	twos
"Mine" most prominent pronoun	fours
Backs into chair to sit down	sixes
May get silly, high, wild	threes
Can balance on one foot	threes
Letter, word reversal common	fours
Mood changes rapidly	sevens

2. Name one way children are alike and one way they differ from one another. Describe the curriculum planning implications for the teacher of these differing children.

3. One area of development affects another. List two ways that social or emotional problems can affect other areas of growth.

4. What are some of the reasons for using the concept of the whole child in early education?

5. What are some of the advantages of including children with special needs? What are some of the difficulties that must be overcome for successful integration of children with special needs?

6. Why is it important for teachers to know about attention-deficit hyperactivity disorder (ADHD)?

7. How important is it to know and understand the culture of children we teach?

8. How are inclusion and mainstreaming different?

Learning Activities

1. Select two children who are approximately the same age. Compare their physical and social development. How are they alike? How are they different? What do you think accounts for these differences?

2. Review the cultural factors noted for Asian American, Hispanic American, Native American, European American, and African American children. Suggest a teaching strategy that would be appropriate in response to each of the characteristics.

3. Look at the Word Picture for a 3-year-old. Compare it with a 3-year-old you know. What behavior do you observe in the real 3-year-old that falls within the range of the chart? What is different? Are there cultural differences?

4. Observe a class of children with special needs in an inclusive classroom. What would you do to foster interactions between the children who are disabled and the children who are not? What verbalizations are used about a child's handicapping condition, and do the nondisabled children seem to understand how their friends are similar to them as well as different? Do you think inclusion is a good idea? Why or why not?

5. Using the Word Pictures, how would you design an appropriate art activity for children who are 18 months old? What kind of playground experience would you provide for a 3-year-old? How would you schedule a day for a 6-year-old you were babysitting? Justify your answers by citing specific developmental references.

Bibliography

Allen, K. E., & Marotz, L. (1994). *Developmental profiles: Birth to eight.* Albany, NY: Delmar.

Allen, K. E., & Schwartz, I. (1996). *The exceptional child: Inclusion in early childhood education.* Albany, NY: Delmar.

Ames, L. B., & Ilg, F. L. (1983). *Your One-Year-Old.* New York: Dell.

Ames, L. B., & Ilg, F. L. (1976). *Your Two-Year-Old.* New York: Dell.

Ames, L. B., & Ilg, F. L. (1976). *Your Three-Year-Old.* New York: Dell.

Ames, L. B., & Ilg, F. L. (1976). *Your Four-Year-Old.* New York: Dell.

Ames, L. B., & Ilg, F. L. (1976). *Your Five-Year-Old.* New York: Dell.

Ames, L. B., & Ilg, F. L. (1976). *Your Six-Year-Old.* New York: Dell.

Bailey, D. B., Jr., & Wolery, M. (1992). *Teaching infants and preschoolers with disabilities.* New York: Merrill.

Baron, R. A. (1995). *Psychology.* Boston: Allyn & Bacon.

Bee, H. (1997). *The developing child.* Menlo Park, CA: Addison-Wesley.

Caldwell, B. M. (1993). One world of children. In A. Gordon & K. W. Browne *(Eds.), Beginnings and beyond: Foundations in early childhood education* (3rd ed.). Albany, NY: Delmar.

Chandler, P. A. (1994). *A place for me.* Washington, DC: National Association for the Education of Young Children.

Charlesworth, R. (1996). *Understanding child development.* Albany, NY: Delmar.

Della-Dora, D., & Blanchard, L. J. (Eds.) (1979). *Moving toward self-directed learning.* Alexandria, VA: Association for Supervision and Curriculum Development.

Derman-Sparks, L., & the ABC Task Force. (1989). *Anti-bias curriculum: Tools for empowering young children.* Washington, DC: National Association for the Education of Young Children.

Elkind, D. (1989). *The hurried child: Growing up too fast, too soon* (Rev. ed.). Reading, MA: Addison-Wesley.

Froschl, M., Colon, L., Rubin, E., & Sprung, B. (1984). *Including all of us: An early childhood curriculum about disability.* New York: Educational Equity Concepts.

Gardner, H. (1982). *Developmental psychology.* Boston: Little, Brown.

Gardner, H. (1993). *Frames of mind: The theory of multiple intelligences.* New York: Basic Books.

Gordon, A. M., & Browne, K. W. (1996). *Guiding young children in a diverse society.* Boston: Allyn & Bacon.

Gray, P. (1993, Fall). Teach your children well. *Time,* Special Issue, pp. 69–71.

Hale-Benson, J. (1986). *Black children: Their roots, culture and learning styles*. Baltimore: The Johns Hopkins University Press.

Hale, J. (1989, April 12). Designing instruction for black children. *Education Week*, p. 26.

Hallowell, E., & Ratty, J. (1994). *Driven to distraction*. New York: Pantheon Books.

Kelly, E. B. (1988, August). Learning disabilities: A new horizon of perception. *The World and I*, pp. 314–321, The Washington Times Corp.

Kiernan, S., et al. (n.d.). *Mainstreaming preschoolers: Children with orthopedic handicaps*. Washington, DC: U.S. Department of Health, Education, and Welfare.

Lupkowski, A., & Lupkowski, E. (1985, March/April). Meeting the needs of gifted preschoolers. *Children Today*, pp. 10–14.

Morrow, R. D. (1989). What's in a name: In particular, a Southeast Asian name? *Young Children*, pp. 20–23.

Olson, L. (1985, January 16). Programs for gifted students fragmented, inadequate, study says. *Education Week*, p. 5.

Ramirez, B. A. (1988, Summer). Culturally and linguistically diverse children. *Teaching Exceptional Children*, pp. 45–51.

Soto, L. D. (1991, January). Understanding bilingual/bicultural young children. *Young Children*, pp. 30–36.

U.S. Bureau of the Census. (1995, 1997).

Valero-Figueira, E. (1988, Summer). Hispanic children. In B. Ramirez, Culturally and linguistically diverse children. *Teaching Exceptional Children*, pp. 45–51.

Walker, J. L. (1988, Summer). Young American Indian children. In B. Ramirez, Culturally and linguistically diverse children. *Teaching Exceptional Children*, pp. 45–51.

Wallis, C. (1994, July 18). Life in overdrive. *Time*, pp. 43–50.

Wolery, M., & Wilbers, J. S. (Eds.). (1994). *Including children with special needs in early childhood programs*. Washington, DC: Research Monograph of the National Association for the Education of Young Children.

Wood, C. (1994). *Yardsticks*. Greenfield, MA: Northeast Foundation for Children.

Woolfolk, A. E. (1993). *Educational psychology*. Boston: Allyn & Bacon.

Yee, L. Y. (1988, Summer). Asian children. In B. Ramirez, Culturally and lingustically diverse children. *Teaching Exceptional Children*, pp. 45–51.

York, S. (1991). *Roots and wings: Affirming culture in early childhood programs*. St. Paul, MN: Redleaf Press.

Developmental and Learning Theories

CHAPTER 4

Questions for Thought

What are the basic questions of developmental and learning theories?

What is the role of culture in development and learning?

Who are the main speakers for each school of thought?

What are the psychosocial stages of early childhood?

What are the tenets of behaviorist theory?

How does a cognitive/constructivist theory explain children's thinking processes?

How does sociocultural theory affect early childhood practices?

What is the theory of multiple intelligences?

How can humanist theory apply to education?

How does maturation theory describe growth?

What research and other theoretical viewpoints are important for educators?

How can development and learning theories be applied to the classroom and work with young children?

INTRODUCTION

Why do we need to know anything about theory or research? Isn't direct experience with children enough to plan good programs? Certainly the practical aspects of teaching young children are important. However, "only through a genuine understanding of why a practice is conducted may an educator achieve meaningful and effective intervention" (Glascott, 1994). If the processes involved in development are not random, then we must try to know them. As complex as the system of children's growth, thinking, feeling, and behaving may be, we cannot consider ourselves responsible professionals until we understand the theory behind the practice.

Early childhood education draws from several fields of study. The connection with the field of psychology is particularly strong. Much of what we know about children today comes from child development and child psychology research. As educators, we apply those findings in the classroom. Our knowledge base comes directly from psychological studies.

● How do children develop?

● What do they learn, and in what order?

● What do people need to be ready to learn?

● What affects learning?

● Do all people develop in the same ways?

● What are the similarities and differences in growth and development?

To begin to answer these questions, we need some way to look for information and then choose and organize the facts so that we can understand what we see. In other words, we need a **theory.** Psychologists and educators have been doing just that for years, and in the 20th century a great deal has been discovered about these issues. Theories are especially useful in providing a broad and consistent view of the complexity of human development. They allow us to make educated guesses (called **hypotheses**) about children's behavior and development. Because these theories are based on experience, their validity can be checked by teachers as they observe children every day. Thus, the basic quest for sound theories about development and knowledge, for systematic statements about behavior and development, has given educators much to consider in bringing forth their own ideas about children.

A key question that is central to all developmental and learning theories is about the source of influence. Are the changes we see in children over time due to internal or external influences? Do children change because of innate, biologic, or genetic patterns built into the human being, or are they shaped by the environment and experiences (such as parents, materials, TV, school, and so on) of life? This argument is often referred to as the **nature/nurture controversy,** also known as the problem of heredity versus environment. As you will remember from Chapter 1, this issue has been discussed for centuries. On the "nature" side, Rousseau argued that the child is born with natural, or innate, goodness. John Locke, however, asserted that it was "nurture" that mattered. He contended that children entered the world with a **tabula rasa,** or clean slate, on which all experience and learning was then written. Today, most psychologists and educators agree that the patterns of development and learning are complex and not so simply explained. Modern theories are not set in such black-and-white terms but rather focus on variations that emphasize one or the other.

In previous generations, little scientific information was available by which parents (and teachers) could assess the validity of theories. Many beliefs were espoused by adults about children, such as "You'll spoil the baby if you respond to his demands too quickly," or "Children who suffer early neglect and deprivation will not realize their normal potential" (Segal, 1989). Such myths can be powerful, particularly as they are passed on to you by your family (and talk-show guests on TV). However, some adult ideas are rooted in myth rather than reality. Child development researchers and theorists have accumulated a rich store of knowledge, based on scientific evidence.

Initially, the study of child development was mostly confined to the study of trends and descriptions of age changes. As this century has progressed, the scope and definition of child development have changed radically. Developmental psychologists now study how psychological processes begin, change, and develop. Child development now focuses on language acquisition, various early effects on later intellectual development, and the process of attachment to others. Early childhood teachers should know how children develop and how they learn. Knowing how children develop is critical in making the daily decisions about curriculum, the classroom setting, and children. To be effective with children, teachers need a thoughtful philosophy and approach that is based on what we know about how children develop and what works to help them learn and understand. The teacher who is well versed in theory has invaluable tools to work with parents, advise the family of the range of typical behavior, and talk to parents about concerns that are beyond the norms. Therefore, it is important to have a background in both developmental psychology and learning theories.

No one set of principles encompasses all developmental and learning theories. We have chosen seven theories. Five of these are commonly accepted as major components of the child development field. A sixth comes from a medical model and outlines developmental norms of growth and behavior. A seventh does not always appear in child psychology texts but highlights some of the processes of working with children. The seven theories we will outline are commonly known as (1) psychodynamic theory, (2) behaviorist theory, (3) cognitive and constructive theory, (4) sociocultural theory, (5) multiple intelligences theory, (6) maturation theory, and (7) humanistic theory.

Because the field of child development is broad, encompassing a wide variety of opinion and fact, not all the experts agree, or even think alike. Indeed, there are differences among them about how children grow, think, and learn, and what motivates them. Each theory describes children and their processes in a different way. The teacher thus has a diversity of thought on which to establish a professional philosophy.

CHILD DEVELOPMENT AND CULTURAL DIVERSITY

Before learning about the individual theories, early childhood educators need a broad orientation to children. Development, as Rodd (1996) reminds us, can be fully understood only when it is "viewed in the larger cultural context. . . . [Indeed] while culture's important role in shaping child rearing and family interaction is well understood, its effect on education opportunities is not always recognized."

What this means is that we must know about children in their own setting, their own context, to understand them well enough to teach them. Every child lives "deeply rooted in a cultural milieu" (Hilliard & Vaughn-Scott, 1982), and the ecology of a child's life must be acknowledged and brought into our work. Think about these international examples of how cultural orientation might influence how you teach or these children might learn (Rodd, 1996):

The primary curricular emphasis in England is upon children's social development until age 3, after which academic competence is emphasized. Swedish educators focus on developmental issues, particularly socio-emotional development. . . . In Asian countries (where children's physical well-being and primary health care have improved to the point where they are no longer issues), the focus is upon academic achievement and excellence. While academic achievement is not stressed in the Czech Republic, young children are taught the value and importance of work and aesthetics, and they participate in cultural programs by the time they are 3.

Let us turn to the United States. An important issue for teachers is the fact that "large numbers of children are members of one cultural group while being taught or cared for by members of other cultural groups. Although this need not create problems, research shows that special problems can arise in many cross-cultural teaching settings" (Hilliard & Vaughn-Scott, 1982). In fact, Lightfoot (1978) has documented four problems that tend to develop:

1. There are problems when the *language* that is spoken by the child is not understood by caregivers from another culture.

2. There are problems when caregivers have low *expectations* for children based largely on the children's membership in a low-status cultural group, rather than on the actual abilities of the children.

3. There are problems when caregivers are unprepared to deal with children whose general *behavioral style* is different from that of the caregivers.

4. There are problems when standard *testing* and *assessment* techniques are applied to certain cultural groups with insufficient recognition of, or respect for, the cultural patterns of the group.

The range of existing differences makes more research—and also more teacher interest in individual family cultures—essential. Creating a culturally responsive education is the only way we can implement truly developmentally appropriate practices.

In many ways, each child is like every other. Certain universals hold for all children, and knowing them, teachers can apply child development and learning theories. Chapter 3 will help you identify these universals. While reading all these theories, try to look

Figure 4.1 ● All children are affected by the socializing experiences they have early in life.

beyond any one model, and "work to define a set of principles that are fundamental to good practice and that can be responsive to and can incorporate varied cultural patterns and values" (Rodd, 1996). This is especially important because there are limits to applying universals in these theories.

One limit is the fact that most early theories were based on observations of male or white subjects. We encourage you to read more recent studies of development that include other ethnic populations, such as Ramirez and Casteneda (1974) and Hale (1986) and the writings of Hilliard and Vaughn-Scott (1982), Gura (1994), and York (1991). Another limitation is that some differences among children exist as a result of cultural commonalities and each child's uniqueness. Caldwell (1983) outlines three areas so that teachers can make child development useful without over-generalizing:

First, all children have the same needs and rights, go through the same developmental stages, and have the same developmental goals. Cross-cultural research on Piagetian theory has demonstrated that the stages of development are invariant and hold true worldwide, although the ages vary between cultures and among individuals.

Second, children are like each other in some ways; for example, there are similarities within cultural groups. Certain cultural and social expectations will bring about commonalities in how soon youngsters use writing tools or in ways of self-expression. This means that, while all 2-year-olds are in the process of developing language, the actual rate of vocabulary increase will differ according to how important language expression is to the cultural and familial groups. What certain children have in common may be broad—from patterns of socializing to cognitive style—but is culture bound. Teachers without appropriate knowledge of their students' cultures run a risk of misapplying developmental theories and norms.

Third, each child is like no other in many respects. What is unique comes from genetic makeup, temperament, energy level, sensory sensitivity, interests, and motivation, to name several. Child development and learning theories have limits. They can foster a global outlook about children in general, but these theories must be viewed in light of both cultural diversity and a respect for individuality. With the theoretical underpinnings presented here, teachers have the tools with which to make their own way into the world of children and of early childhood education.

PSYCHODYNAMIC THEORY

Psychodynamic theory is about personality development and emotional problems. **Psychodynamic**, or psychoanalytic, **theories** look at development in terms of internal drives that are often **unconscious**, or hidden from our awareness. These motives are the underlying forces that influence human thinking and behavior and provide the foundation for universal stages of development. In psychoanalytic terms, children's behavior can be interpreted by knowing the various stages and tasks within those stages.

Sigmund Freud

Sigmund Freud began his career as a medical doctor and became interested in the irrational side of human behavior as he treated "hysterics." His technique, asking people to recline on a couch and talk about everything, was ridiculed by the medical establishment as the "talking cure." Then, as patients revealed their thoughts, fantasies, and problems, he began to see patterns. According to Freud, people possess three basic drives: the sexual drive, survival instincts, and a drive for destructiveness. Of the first, childhood sexuality, Freud outlined development in terms of psychosexual stages, each characterized by a particular part of the body. In each stage, the sensual satisfaction associated with each body part is linked to major challenges of that age. For instance, think about how some of the issues of toddlers, such as biting or thumbsucking, and the preschool concerns with "doctor play," masturbation, or gender identification in the dress-up corner might be seen in a psychosexual context. Each stage also has its own conflicts between child and parent, and how the child experiences those conflicts will determine basic personality and behavior patterns.

Freud first put forth this theory, and his ideas were expanded on by Anna Freud (his daughter), Carl

Stage	Age	Description/Major Area
Oral	Birth to 2	Mouth (sucking, biting) source of pleasure Eating and teething
Anal	2–3	Bowel movements source of pleasure Toilet learning
Phallic	3–6	Genitals source of pleasure Sex role identification and conscience development
Latency	6–12	Sexual forces dormant Energy put into schoolwork and sports
Genital	12–18	Genitals source of pleasure Stimulation and satisfaction from relationships

Figure 4.2 ● Freud's psychoanalytic theory of childhood sexuality. Freud's stage theory contends that each stage has its own area of pleasure and crisis between the child and parent or society.

Jung, Karen Horney, and others. Although Freud's interest was abnormal adult behavior and its causes, his conclusions have had a major effect on our conception of childhood and its place in the life span.

To Freud, the personality was the most important aspect of development, more central to human growth than language, perception, or cognition. Personality was defined by three structures. These are the *id*, which is the instinctive part that drives a person to seek satisfaction, the *ego*, the rational structure that forms a person's sense of self, and the *superego*, the moral side that informs the person of right and wrong. He thought that the personality developed in a fixed pattern of stages that emerged as the body matured naturally. But even though the sequence of the stages might be firm, how children were treated while going through those stages determined whether they developed healthy or abnormal personalities. In particular, the mother–child relationship was important in each stage. Thus, the interaction between the child's wishes and needs and how these were treated (by the mother or other adults) was a focal point for proper development.

All psychoanalytic explanations of human development emphasize the critical importance of relationships with people and the sequence, or stages, of personality development. The psychoanalyst Erik Erikson expanded and refined Freud's theory of development.

It is Erikson whose ideas have most affected early childhood education.

Erik Erikson

Erik Homberg Erikson is perhaps the most influential psychoanalyst alive today, certainly a key figure in the study of children and development. His interests in children and education has been a lifelong one, including a teaching background in progressive and Montessori schools in Europe. After clinical training in psychoanalysis, he remained interested in the connections between psychotherapy and education. Erikson became the first child analyst in the Boston area and worked for years in several universities in the United States.

Erikson's Theory of Human Development

Erikson's theory of human development, like those of Freud and Piaget, states that life is a series of stages through which each person passes, with each stage growing from the previous ones. He proposes eight stages of psychosocial development, each representing a critical period for the development of an important quality or virtue. Positive growth allows the individual to integrate his or her physical and biologic

Stage	Description	Challenge
Stage One	The newborn	Trust vs. Mistrust
Stage Two	Toddlers	Autonomy vs. Shame and doubt
Stage Three	Childhood	Initiative vs. Guilt
Stage Four	School	Competence (or industry) vs. Inferiority
Stage Five	Adolescence	Search for identity vs. Role confusion
Stage Six	Young adulthood	Intimacy (love and friendship) vs. Isolation (loneliness)
Stage Seven	Grown-ups	Generativity (caring for the next generation) vs. Stagnation
Stage Eight	Old age	Integrity vs. Despair

Figure 4.3 ● Erikson's theory of psychosocial development centers on basic crises that people face from birth to old age. This stage theory of development proposes that these conflicts are part of the life process and that successful handling of these issues can give a person the "ego strength" to face life positively. (Adapted from Hubley and Hubley, 1976.)

development with the challenges that the social institutions and culture present. Each stage is characterized by a pair of basic emotional stages. *Balance* is the key word in Erikson's framework: the forming of a balance between a child's wishes and the demands of the environment, of a mentally healthy dose of each emotion, is essential for personality strength.

In other words, every growing organism passes through certain developmental stages. A stage is a period during which certain changes occur. What one achieves in each stage is based on the developments of the previous stages, and each stage presents the child with certain kinds of problems to be solved. When children succeed, they go on to attack new problems and grow through solving them.

Everyone has certain biologic, social, and psychological needs that must be satisfied to grow in a healthy manner. Medicine has learned much about physical needs—diet, rest, exercise. Basic intellectual, social, and emotional needs also must be met for an organism to be healthy. Psychology, such as Eriksonian theory, can speak to these needs. Whether these needs are met or unfulfilled will affect development.

Erikson's stage theory is expanded here because of its importance to the field of early childhood education.

Stage 1: Trust vs. Mistrust (Birth to 1 Year)

Erikson's first stage is roughly the first year of life and parallels Freud's oral–sensory stage. Attitudes important to development are the capacity to trust—or mistrust—inner and outer experiences. By providing consistent care, parents help an infant develop a basic sense of trust in self and an ability to trust other people. They give affection and emotional security as well as provide for physical needs. Inconsistent or inadequate care prevents the infant from trusting the world. In extreme cases, as shown by Spitz's classic studies on infant deprivation (Spitz & Wolf, 1946), lack of care can actually lead to infant death. A less extreme case might form isolation or distrust of others. Recent studies suggest a strong hereditary element in this disorder rather than environmental (Myers et al., 1984). Given a solid base in early trust, though, the typical infant develops the virtue, or strength, of hope.

When working with infants and toddlers, teachers must take special care to provide a predictable environment and consistent caregiving. Babies are totally dependent on adults to meet their needs; they are particularly vulnerable to difficulties because they have few skills for coping with discomfort and stress. It is critical, therefore, that they be cared for by warm, positive adults who are sensitive and respond affectionately to an infant's needs as soon as they arise. In this way, the very young develop the trust in the world that will support their growth into the next stage.

Stage 2: Autonomy vs. Doubt (2–3 Years)

The second stage, corresponding to the second and third years of life, parallels the muscular-anal period in Freudian theory. The child learns to manage and control impulses and to use both motor and mental skills. To help a child develop a healthy balance between autonomy and shame, parents should consider how to handle their toddlers' toilet training and growing curiosity to explore. Restrictive or compulsive parents may give the child a feeling of shame and doubt, causing a sense of insecurity. Successful growth in this stage gives a child strength of will. "This stage, therefore, becomes decisive for the ratio of love and hate, cooperation and willfulness, freedom of self-expression and its suppression. From a sense of self-control without loss of self-esteem comes a lasting sense of good will and pride; from a sense of loss of self-control and of foreign overcontrol comes a lasting propensity for doubt and shame" (Erikson, 1963).

When teaching children of this age, adults help children feel ready to explore their world through a full range of activities that use their senses. Play is encouraged, with plenty of "yes" in the environment. Budding curiosity means high energy, so the daily schedule should include plenty of time for active movement and flexibility to deal with fluctuating energy and mood. Toileting is a learned behavior just as eating, dressing, painting, and singing are; a relaxed attitude about this area helps the child gain mastery without shame. Allowing for plenty of "two steps forward, one back" acknowledges the child's natural doubts and the balancing that happens in this stage.

Stage 3: Initiative vs. Guilt (3–5 or 6 Years)

The third stage of Eriksonian theory corresponds to the preschool and kindergarten years and parallels

Figure 4.4 ● An Eriksonian crisis in a young child's life. The child who has successfully mastered the first of Erikson's psychosocial conflicts will then be able to cope with future challenges. In this instance, the child who takes initiative (grabbing a toy) also can feel guilt (returning it).

Freud's phallic stage of development. Out of a sense of autonomy grows a sense of initiative. The child is ready to plan and carry out thoughts and ideas. The parent can encourage the child's natural curiosity to plan and execute activities that are constructive and cooperative. An overly restrictive parent may raise a child with an excessive sense of guilt and inhibition. On the other hand, parents or teachers giving no restraints signal to the child no clear idea of what is socially acceptable and what is not. The key strength that grows out of this stage is purpose.

Teaching children of this age is both exhilarating and exasperating. The child who takes initiative is ready to meet the world head-on and wants to do it "all by myself," which may include both putting on a jacket and hitting someone who has said something unkind. The environment that can respond to a child's interests, both in theme and at the moment, will be interesting and successful. At the same time, teachers must be prepared with a small set of logical limits (or "rules") and the means to follow through kindly and firmly when those limits are tested. Socializing at this age is the very point of the emotional states of initiative and guilt; children must have enough freedom to develop their own ways to deal with one another and still develop a sense of fairness and conscience.

Stage 4: Industry vs. Inferiority (6–12 years)

Erikson's fourth stage, beginning with the primary school years and ending with puberty, parallels Freud's latency period. The major theme in this stage is mastery of life, primarily by adapting to laws of society (people, laws and rules, relationships) and objects (tools, machines, the physical world). The child, according to Erikson, "begins to envisage goals for which his locomotion and cognition have prepared him. The child also begins to think of being big and to identify with people whose work or whose personality he can understand and appreciate" (Evans, 1967). For most children, this means finding a place in one's own school, be it in a classroom, on a soccer field, or at a club meeting. Children are ready to apply themselves to skills and tasks and to receive systematic instruction in the culture. They also need to handle the "tools of the tribe" (Erikson, 1963) and to experience both achievement and disappointment. In the United States, these tools include pencils, reading and arithmetic books, and computers, as well as balls and bats. The danger for the child lies in feeling inadequate and inferior to such tasks. A parent or teacher who over-emphasizes children's mistakes could make them despair of ever learning, for instance, the multiplication tables or cursive handwriting. At the same time, adults must encourage children to work toward mastery. Parents must not let their children restrict their own horizons by doing only what they already know. Particularly in social situations, it is essential for children to learn to do things *with* others, as difficult and unfair as this may sometimes be.

Applying Erikson's Theory to Work with Children

How can teachers apply Erikson's theory of psychosocial development to young children? First, Erikson has a clear message about the importance of play. Second, the theory helps shape guidelines for the role of adults in children's life.

Early childhood teachers have long held that play is a critical part of children's total development. Most schools for children under age 6 have periods of time allotted for play called "choice time" or "free play." Erikson supports these ideas explicitly by stating that the sense of autonomy and of initiative are developed mainly through social and fantasy play. He suggests that child's play is "the infantile form of the human ability to deal with experiences by creating model situations and to master reality by experiment and planning. . . . To 'play it out' in play is the most natural self-healing measure childhood affords" (Erikson, 1964).

The adult, from a psychoanalytic point of view, is primarily an emotional base and a social mediator for the child. That is, the adult is the interpreter of feelings, actions, reasons, and solutions. The adult helps children understand situations and motives so that they can solve their own problems. The adult looks at each child's emotional makeup and monitors the progress through developmental crises. Because the infant must learn to trust the world, the parent needs to be responsive and satisfy the basic needs of food, warmth, and love. In a toddler's world, the teacher and parent must allow the child, in Erikson's words:

> . . . to experience over and over again that he is a person who is permitted to make choices. He has to have the right to choose, for example, whether to sit or whether to stand, whether to approach a visitor or to lean against his mother's knee . . . whether to use the toilet or to wet his pants. At the same time he must learn some of the

Figure 4.5 ● In Erikson's theory the adult serves as a social mediator for the child.

boundaries of self-determination. He inevitably finds that there are some walls he cannot climb, that there are objects out of reach, that, above all, there are innumerable commands enforced by powerful adults (Erikson, 1969).

In preschool and kindergarten, a teacher allows children to take initiative and does not interfere with the results of those actions. At the same time, teachers and parents provide clear limits so that the children can learn what behaviors are unacceptable to society.

The issues of early childhood, from Eriskson's theory, are really our own issues. Because the remnants of these crises stay with us all our lives, teachers must be aware of their own processes to fully appreciate the struggles of children.

BEHAVIORIST THEORY

Behaviorism is the most pragmatic and functional of the modern psychological ideologies. **Behaviorist theories** describe both development and learning. Developed during the 1920s and continually modified today, behaviorism is "the most distinctively American contribution to psychology" (Suransky, 1982). Countless developmental psychologists and researchers have defined and expanded on this idea, several of whom are mentioned later in this chapter. To summarize the behaviorist theory, we have chosen five theorists: John Watson, Edward Thorndike, Benjamin Bloom, B. F. Skinner, and Albert Bandura.

The Behaviorists

What is known today as "behaviorism" begins with the notion that a child is born with a "clean slate," a *tabula rasa* in John Locke's words, on which events are written throughout life. The condition of those events cause all important human behavior.

John B. Watson was an American theorist who studied the animal experiments of Russian scientist Ivan Pavlov. He then translated those ideas of conditioning into human terms. In the first quarter of this century, Watson made sweeping claims about the powers of this classical conditioning. He declared that he could shape a person's entire life by controlling exactly the events of an infant's first year. One of his ideas was to discourage emotional ties between parents and children because they interfered with the child's direct learning from the environment (though he later modified this). Nonetheless, he gave scientific validity to the idea that teachers should set conditions for learning and reward proper responses.

Edward L. Thorndike also studied the conditions of learning. Known as the "godfather of standardized testing," Thorndike helped develop scales to measure student achievement and usher in the era of standardized educational testing (see Chapter 10). After working with animals and their problem-solving abilities, he decided that people took an active part in their learning. He set forth the famous "stimulus–response" technique. A stimulus will recall a response in a person; this forms learned habits. Therefore, it is wise to pay close attention to the consequences of behavior and to the various kinds of reinforcement.

Benjamin Bloom was a pioneer in the development of categorizing educational objectives. His purpose was to build a classification scheme to describe teacher behavior, instructional methods, and intended "pupil behaviors." His work on "mastery learning" and his classification of educational outcomes became the basis of behavioral objectives in American curriculum and instruction in the 1970s and 1980s. His work is still used in describing the cognitive domains of learning, such as knowledge comprehension, analysis, and evaluation.

B. F. Skinner took the idea of "tabula rasa" one step further. He created the doctrine of the "empty organism." That is, a person is like a vessel to be filled by carefully designed experiences. All behavior is under the control of one or more aspects of the environment. Furthermore, Skinner maintained that there is no behavior that cannot be modified.

Behaviorists often insist that only what can actually be observed will be accepted as fact. Only behavior can be treated, they say, not feelings or internal states. This contrasts to the psychodynamic approach, which insists that behavior is just an indirect clue to the "real" self, that of inner feelings and thoughts.

Skinner's ideas probably stirred up more controversy, and caused more emotional responses, than those of any other psychologist of our time. Some people might argue that Skinnerian concepts tend to depersonalize the learning process and treat people as puppets. Others say that behaviorist psychology has made us develop new ways to help people learn and cope effectively with the world.

Albert Bandura has developed another type of learning theory, called social learning. As behaviorists began to accept that what people said about their feelings and internal state was valid, they looked at how children became socialized. Socialization is the process of learning to conform to social rules. Social-learning theorists watch how children learn these rules and use them in groups. They study the patterns of reinforcement and reward in socially appropriate and unacceptable behavior.

According to Bandura:

Children acquire most of their social concepts—the rules by which they live—from models whom they observe in the course of daily life, particularly parents, caregivers, teachers, and peers. Social learning theory [suggests] the models most likely to be imitated are individuals who are nurturant—warm, rewarding, and affectionate. Attachment also affects the process: the most significant or influential models are people to whom the child is emotionally tied (Fong & Resnick, 1986).

From this arose a new concept known as modeling. This is what used to be known as learning and teaching by example. For instance, children who see their parents smoking will likely smoke themselves. In fact, Bandura's studies provided "strong evidence that exposure to filmed aggression heightens aggressive reactions in children. Subjects who viewed the aggressive human and cartoon models on film exhibited nearly twice as much aggression than did subjects in the control group who were not exposed to the aggressive film content" (Bandura, 1963). This work suggests that pictorial mass media—television, video games, and computer activities—serve as important sources of social behavior. Any behavior can be learned by watching it, from language (listening to others talk) to fighting (watching violence on television).

Theory of Behaviorism and Learning

What is behavior, or learning, theory all about? Many texts have been written on this set of principles; every child development text of the day cites behavior and social-learning concepts. Most early education texts will make mention of the system of positive reinforcement: that is, how to praise children so that they are likely to repeat the desired behavior.

Learning occurs when an organism interacts with the environment. Through experience, behavior is modified or changed. In the behaviorist's eyes, three types of learning occur: (1) classical conditioning; (2) operant conditioning; and (3) observational learning or modeling. The first two are based on the idea that learning is mostly the development of habit. What people learn is a series of associations, forming a connection between a stimulus and response that did not exist before. The third is based on a social approach. Figure 4.6 summarizes these three types of behaviorist learning processes.

Classical Conditioning

Classical conditioning can be explained by reviewing Pavlov's original experiments. A dog normally salivates at the sight of food but not when he hears a bell. When the sound of a bell is paired with the sight of food, the dog "learns" to salivate when he hears the bell, whether or not food is nearby. Thus, the dog has been conditioned to salivate (give the response) for both the food (unconditioned stimulus) and the bell (conditioned stimulus).

Operant Conditioning

Operant conditioning is slightly different from classical conditioning in that it focuses on the response rather than the stimulus. In operant conditioning, the process that makes it more likely that a behavior will recur is called **reinforcement**. A stimulus that increases the likelihood of repeated behavior is called a **reinforcer**. Most people are likely to increase what gives them pleasure (be it food or attention) and decrease what gives them displeasure (such as punishment, pain, or the withdrawal of food or attention). The behaviorist tries to influence the organism by controlling these kinds of reinforcement.

A **positive reinforcer** is something that the learner views as desirable. These can be "social reinforcers," such as attention, praise, smiles or hugs, or "nonsocial reinforcers," including tokens, toys, food, stickers, and the like. For example, you would like Claire to begin to use a spoon instead of her hands to eat. Before

	Classical Conditioning	Operant Conditioning	Social Learning
Kind of behavior	Reflexive	Voluntary	Voluntary
Type of learning	Learning through association	Learning through reinforcement	Learning through observation and imitation
Role of learner	Passive	Active or passive	Active

Figure 4.6 ● Behaviorist learning processes. Classical conditioning, operant conditioning, and social learning are three ways to develop learned behavior. Each describes how certain kinds of behavior will be learned and what role the learner will take in the process.

conditioning, you talk to her whenever she eats. During the conditioning period, you can give attention (a *positive reinforcer*) each time she picks up a spoon during feeding times and ignore her when she uses her hands. Afterward, she is more likely to use a spoon, and less often her hands. This is an example of a positive reinforcer, something that increases the likelihood of the desired response.

The reinforcers can be either positive or negative. A **negative reinforcer** is removal of an unpleasant stimulus as a result of some particular behavior. Circle time is Jimmy's favorite activity at school. Yet he has difficulty controlling his behavior and consistently disrupts the group. Before conditioning, he is told that if he talks to his neighbors and shouts responses at the teacher, he will be asked to leave the circle. During the conditioning period, Jimmy is praised whenever he pays attention, sings songs, and does not bother those around him (positive reinforcement). When he begins to shout, he is told to leave and return when he can sing without shouting (negative reinforcement). A negative reinforcer is used to stop children from behaving in a particular way by arranging for them to end a mildly adversive situation immediately (in this case, the boy has to leave the group) by improving their behavior. Jimmy, by controlling his own behavior, could end his isolation from the group.

A negative reinforcer is different from punishment. **Punishment** is an unpleasant event that makes the behavior *less* likely to be repeated; that is, if Jimmy were spanked every time he shouted, then his shouting would be the punished behavior and it is likely he would begin to shout less. However, when leaving the group is the reinforcer for shouting, he tries to stop shouting to increase the likelihood of being able to stay, and not being taken away from the group. *Negative reinforcement* thus increases the likelihood that the desired behavior will be repeated (staying in the group) and removes attention from the less desirable behavior (the shouting). The "time out" chair, for instance, could be viewed as either a punishment or a negative reinforcer. If used as exclusion from the group or a withdrawal of playing privileges, a child would find the time-out as a punishment. If, on the other hand, a child could leave the time-out more quickly if she exhibited certain behaviors (instead of the "bad" behavior), it might be seen as a negative reinforcer.

Reinforcement, both positive and negative, is a powerful tool. It is important for adults to realize that it can be misused. It is wise to be careful, particularly in the case of negative reinforcement. An adult may not

Figure 4.7 ● A shared smile is a simple and powerful reinforcer.

be gentle with a negative reinforcer when angry with a child's inappropriate behavior. Educators and parents should be aware of the possibilities and check their own responses.

Modeling

The third kind of conditioning is called *observational learning* or *modeling*. Social behavior is particularly noteworthy to early childhood professionals, as most work with children in groups and thus witness social behavior constantly. Any behavior that involves more than one person can be considered social. One of the most negative social behaviors is aggression. It is this type that Albert Bandura researched, finding that much of it is learned by watching others.

Aggression is a complex issue, involving various definitions and behaviors. To illustrate social learning theory, Bandura and others interpret aggression to mean behavior intended to inflict harm or discomfort to another person or object. Bandura showed a short film of aggressive behavior to young children. The original mid-1960s studies are summarized below:

Each child in Bandura's experiment viewed one of three films. In all three films, a man hit, kicked, and verbally abused an inflated Bobo doll in ways that young children are unlikely to do spontaneously. The films differed in what happened to the model after the aggressive sequence. In one film the model was lavishly rewarded with praise and foods that appealed to preschoolers, such as candy and caramel popcorn. In another film the model was punished in a dramatic way, including severe scolding and a spanking. The third film simply ended after the model's aggressive behavior, with no consequences following the aggression. After viewing one film, each child in the experiment was allowed to play in a room with a Bobo doll, all the toys used in the aggression film, and a variety of other toys (McClinton & Meier, 1978).

The results are most impressive, especially to those working with young children. The level of aggression expressed by each child was directly related to what the children saw as the consequences in the film. When offered prizes, they imitated almost exactly what their model had done. Also, children appeared more likely to attack one another child after viewing the attacks on the Bobo doll in film. Further studies have shown that children's level of aggression is higher right after viewing the film, but less so when shown it again 6 months later (McClinton & Meier, 1978). Regardless of the controversy that may surround any study of children's aggression, or the effects of watching filmed violence on youngsters, the social-learning theory deserves serious consideration. The effect of television watching on children is extremely important and will be discussed in Chapter 15.

Applying Behaviorist Theory to Work with Children

Behaviorist theories make a strong case for how the environment influences our behavior. A teacher, a parent, any adult who works closely with children, can use this knowledge to arrange the environment in such a way that positive learning is enhanced. Thus, early childhood educators pay close attention to how to arrange furniture, materials, and the daily schedule. The way teachers interact with children is critical to changing their behavior.

Adults are powerful reinforcers and models for children. A learning situation comprises many cues; it is up to adults to know what those cues are and how to control them. Teachers who use behavior modification techniques know both what children are to do and how they will be reinforced for their behavior. The issues of

using this kind of control, and the ethics involved, are of deep concern to everyone. The extremes of behaviorist theory suggest programmed instruction and interaction that many early educators reject. Each teacher and program must consider the impact of this theory and how to apply it to classroom and client. Chapter 7, which deals with behavior management and discipline issues, has examples of this theory as it applies to behavior modification techniques.

The implications of behaviorist theory for teachers are far-reaching. What children learn is shaped by the circumstances surrounding the learning. Experiences that are enjoyable are reinforcing. From the peek-a-boo game with an infant to a 7-year-old's first ride on a skateboard, an experience is more likely to be repeated and learned if it is pleasant. Social learning is particularly powerful in the lives of young children. Adults must be mindful of their own behavior, and that it is a source of learning. Watching children as young as 2 years old play "family" or "school" will convince the most skeptical critic that any behavior is learnable and can become part of children's behavioral repertoire.

COGNITIVE THEORY

Adult: What does it mean to be alive?
Child: It means you can move about, play—that you can do all kinds of things.
Adult: Is a mountain alive?
Child: Yes, because it has grown by itself.
Adult: Is a cloud alive?
Child: Yes, because it sends water.
Adult: Is wind alive?
Child: Yes, because it pushes things.

How can we tell what children are thinking? How do children learn to think, and what do they think about? Once we begin to ask these questions, we enter the realm of knowledge about how people "know" and "think," and how they learn to do it. The focus of cognitive theory is the structure and development of human thought processes and how those processes affect the way a person understands and perceives the world. Piaget's theory of cognition forms a cornerstone of early childhood educational concepts about children; the works of Howard Gardner (see Chapter 13) in intelligence enrich our knowledge of intellectual development and how to translate theory into educational practice.

Jean Piaget

Jean Jacques Piaget (1896–1980) was one of the most exciting research theorists in child development. A major force in child psychology, he studied both thought processes and how they change with age. Piaget's ideas serve as our guide to the cognitive theory because of the thoroughness of his work. He had great influence on child psychology, theories of learning, intellectual development, and even philosophy. He became the foremost expert on the development of knowledge from birth to adulthood.

How did Piaget find out about such matters? A short review of his life and ideas reveals a staggering volume of work and a wide scope of interests. Born at the turn of the century, Piaget built on his childhood curiosity in science and philosophy by working with Dr. Simon at the Binet Laboratory (Simon and Binet devised the first intelligence test). While recording children's abilities to answer questions correctly, he became fascinated with children's incorrect responses. He noticed that children tended to give similar kinds of wrong answers and that they made different kinds of mistakes at different ages.

Thus, Piaget launched into a lifelong study of intelligence. He believed that children think in fundamentally different ways from adults. He also developed a new method for studying thought processes. Rather than using a standardized test, he adapted the psychiatric method of question and response. Called the methode clinique, it lets people's answers guide the questions. Therefore, it focuses on the child's own natural ways of thinking. This method is discussed in detail in Chapter 6.

Piaget then began studying children's thought processes. With his wife, one of his former students, he observed his children. He also began to look closely at how actively children engage in their own development. He studied the development of logic and looked at children's understanding of scientific and mathematical principles. In his final works, he returned to his original interest, that of the study of knowledge itself. Prolific his entire life, Piaget gave us a complex theory of intelligence and child development that will influence us for some time. He recorded, in a systematic way, how children learn, when they learn, and what they learn.

Piaget's Theory of Cognitive Development

What are the concepts of cognitive theory? Detailing all Piaget's ideas is impossible. What follows are several tenets that explain the nature of intelligence and its functions.

Piaget's theory relies on both maturational and environmental factors. It is called maturational because it sets out a sequence of cognitive (thinking) stages that is governed by heredity. For example, heredity affects our learning by (1) how the body is structured biologically and (2) automatic, or instinctive, behavior, such as an infant's sucking at birth. It is an environmental theory because the experiences children have will directly influence how they develop.

Thinking and learning is a process of interaction between a person and the environment. Piaget also sets out that all species inherit a basic tendency to organize their lives and adapt to the world around them. This is known as a constructivist theory; that is, children actively construct knowledge on an ongoing basis. On the basis of both innate cognitive structures and experience, they are developing—and constantly revising—their own knowledge. In doing so, an organism "figures out" what the world is all about and then works toward surviving in that world. Regardless of their age, all people develop schemas, or mental concepts, as a general way of thinking about, or interacting with, ideas and objects in the environment. For instance, the infant learns about the world first through sensorimotor schemas such as sucking and grasping. Young children learn perceptual schemas and then more abstract ones such as morality schemas that help determine how to act in different situations. Throughout, we use three basic processes to think: these are known as the adaptive processes of assimilation and accommodation and the balancing process of equilibration. Figure 4.8 demonstrates how these work.

Piaget theorized that thinking develops in a certain general pattern in all human beings. People tend to organize themselves and their thinking to make sense of their world. These stages of thinking are the psychological structures that go along with trying to adapt to the environment. Such a series of stages goes beyond individual differences in thinking styles. It focuses on internal structures rather than on external conditions as behavioral theory does. Piaget identified four major stages of cognitive development:

Assimilation: Taking new information and organizing it in such a way that it fits with what the person already knows.

Example: Juanita sees an airplane while walking outdoors with her father. She knows that birds fly. So, never having seen this flying thing before, she calls it a "bird (pájaro)." This is what we call *assimilation.* She is taking in this new information and making it fit into what she already knows. Children assimilate what they are taught into their own worlds when they play. This happens when children play "taking turns" or "school" and "house" with their dolls and toy figures. Another way to see assimilation at work is during carpentry, as children hammer and nail triangles and squares after being shown shape books and puzzles by their teacher.

Accommodation: Taking new information and changing what is already thought to fit the new information.

Example: Aaron is at the grocery store with his mother and newborn baby. He calls the woman in the line ahead of them "pregnant" although she is simply overweight. After being corrected, he asks the next person he sees, "Are you pregnant or just fat?" This is what we call *accommodation.* Having learned that not all people with large bellies are pregnant, he changes his knowledge base to include this new information. Children accommodate to the world as they are taught to use a spoon, the toilet, a computer.

Equilibration: A mental process to achieve a mental balance, whereby a person takes new information and continually attempts to make sense of the experiences and perceptions.

Example: Colby, age 7, gets two glasses from the cupboard for his friend Ajit and himself. After putting apple juice into his short, wide glass he decides he'd rather have milk, so he pours it into Ajit's tall, thin glass. "Look, now I have more than you!" says his friend. This puzzles Colby, who is distressed (in "disequilibrium"): how could it be more when he just poured it out of his glass? He thinks about the inconsistency (and pours the juice several times back and forth) and begins to get the notion that pouring liquid into different containers does not change its amount (the conservation of liquids). "No, it isn't," he says, "it's just a different shape!" Thus, Colby learns to make sense of it in a new way and achieve equilibrium in his thinking. Children do this whenever they get new information that asks them to change the actual schemas, making new ones to fit new experiences.

Sensorimotor stage	zero to 2 years
Preoperational stage	2–6 or 7 years
Concrete operational stage	6–12 years
Formal operational stage	12 years to adulthood

Each person of normal intelligence will go through these stages in this order, although the rate will change depending on the individual and his or her experiences. Figure 4.9 details the stages of early childhood, and Figure 4.10 illustrates some research that has validated Piaget's theory.[1]

Piaget's theories revolutionized our thinking about children's thinking and challenged psychologists and educators to focus less on *what* children know than *the ways they come to know*. But was Piaget right? Researchers have been exploring and debating the ideas of cognitive theory for many years, often engaging in what Piaget himself called "the American question"; can you speed up the rate in which children pass through these intellectual stages of development? Certainly there are problems with the theory, as articulated in Helen Bee's Focus Box.

Now, developmental psychologists believe that Piaget's theory of distinct stages is not correct, but the idea of a sequence in thinking is. Furthermore, current research on the brain supports Piagetian theory; brain maturation, as reflected in the development of neurons, called **myelination**, seems to follow a sequence that parallels the various thinking stages of development. Figure 4.10 illustrates some of the research results from one of America's outstanding cognitive psychologists, Dr. John Flavell. Brain-based research and its implications for early childhood teachers is discussed at the end of this chapter.

What we do know is that children progress from one stage to the next, changing their thinking depending on their level of maturation and experience with the environment. Certain physical skills, such as fine-motor coordination, determine how much a child is capable of doing. Certain environmental factors, such as the kinds of experiences the world and adults

Figure 4.8 ● In Piagetian theory, the processes of assimilation, accommodation, and equilibration are basic to how all people organize their thoughts and, therefore, to all cognitive development.

OUR DIVERSE WORLD OUR DIVERSE WORLD OUR DIVERSE WORLD OUR DIVERSE WORLD OUR DIVERSE WORLD OUR DIVERSE WORLD OUR DIVERSE WORLD OUR DIVERSE WORLD

[1] Piaget's stages have been validated in cross-cultural studies (Dasen, 1977; Mali & Howe, 1980; Voyat, 1983).

Criticisms of Piaget's Theory

Helen Bee

The most obvious criticism of Jean Piaget's cognitive-developmental theory is that he seems to have been wrong about just how *early* many cognitive skills develop. For example, virtually all the achievements of the concrete operational period are present in at least rudimentary or fragmentary form in the preschool years. This might simply mean that Piaget just had the ages wrong—that the concrete operations stage really begins at age 3 or 4. But I think by now there is agreement even among modern Piaget enthusiasts that the problem goes far deeper than that. The fact that younger children demonstrate some types of apparently complex logic if the problems are made simple calls this whole assumption into serious doubt.

A second blow to the notion of completely separated stages comes from research on *expertise*. If children are applying the same broad forms of logic to all their experiences, then the amount of specific experience a child has had with some set of material should not make a lot of difference. A great deal of research now shows that specific knowledge makes a huge difference. Children and adults who know a lot about some subject or some set of materials (dinosaurs, baseball cards, mathematics, or whatever) not only categorize information in that topic area in more complex and hierarchical ways; they are also better at remembering new information on that topic and better at applying more advanced forms of logic to material in that area.

In the most famous study to demonstrate this effect, Micheline Chi (1978) showed that expert chess players can remember the placement of chess pieces on a board much more quickly and accurately than can novice chess players, *even when the expert chess players are children and the novices are adults.* Experts thus look very "cognitively mature," very smart, and novices operate in ways that we used to think of as cognitively "immature." And the same individual can be an expert on one task and a novice on another. Because young children are novices at almost everything, perhaps the difference in apparent thinking strategies or functioning between younger and older children is just the effect of accumulating expertise, rather than stagelike changes in fundamental cognitive structures.

Arguments like these have persuaded virtually all developmental psychologists that Piaget's version of structurally distinct stages of cognitive development is incorrect. Instead, it looks as if cognitive development is made up of a large number of apparently universal *vertical sequences.* That is, in any given concept area, such as number concepts, or concepts of gender, or ideas about appearance and reality, or in hundreds of other areas, children seem to learn the basic rules or strategies in the same order.

Thus, though Piaget appears to have been off-target in talking about stages, he was very much on-target in talking about *sequences.* Further, I am convinced that Piaget was right in arguing that the changes in cognitive skill are more than merely quantitative increases in specific task knowledge and experience. There seem to be real differences in the way 2-year-olds and 10-year-olds approach problems that are not merely differences in experience.

Adapted from The Developing Child, *6th ed. by Dr. Helen Bee (HarperCollins, 1997)*

Stage	Age	What Happens
Sensorimotor	Birth to 1½–2	Initial use of inherent reflexes (sucking, crying)—at birth.
		Out of sight, out of mind, at the beginning; object permanence is learned by experience by around 1 year.
		Movements from accidental and random to more deliberate and intentional—throughout stage.
		Learns to coordinate perceptual and motor functions (such as seeing object and then grabbing it).
		Learns relationship between means and ends (pushes aside barrier to get a toy).
		Beginning forms of symbolic behavior (opens and closes mouth when doing same to a jar).
Preoperational	2–6 or 7	Gradual acquisition of language (new words, such as "yummed it up," or "my ponytail was keeping me in bothers").
		Symbolic (play doll as baby, stick as sword).
		Egocentric (not aware of another point of view, only one's own).
		Physical characteristics, such as size, judged by appearance only (a ball of playdough *looks* bigger when made into a long roll, so therefore it *is* bigger).
		"Conservation" develops slowly; ability to reverse operations is not understood (the milk cannot be visualized as being poured back into the first glass).
		Inability to think of the whole and its parts at the same time (given a set of blue and red wooden beads, the child will say that the blue beads will make a longer necklace than the wooden beads).
Concrete operational	6–12	Begins to "conserve" (can see that quantity, size, length, and volume remain the same no matter how they are arranged).
		Can handle several ideas at the same time (given an array of objects of various colors and shapes, can find all the "red, square, small ones").
		Starts to remove contradictions (can understand and follow rules, and make up own).
		Can understand other points of view, although needs to be in real situations, rather than abstract ones.

Figure 4.9 ● In their early childhood, children will pass through the sensorimotor and preoperational stages and enter the stage of concrete operations.

provide, influence the rate of growth. Yet throughout the process, children take in new knowledge and decide how it fits with what they already know. As new information comes in, the child learns and grows.

Special Topic: Constructivist Theory

For the better part of this century, there has been regular debate about how children learn and concerning the best methods of teaching. Traditional methods of teaching, particularly for school-age children, are based on behaviorist views of learning. Articulated by Thorndike and Skinner (see the behaviorist section in this chapter), these methods emphasize learning by association and in a stimulus–response manner. With this **transmission model** of teaching, the teacher possesses the knowledge and transmits it directly to the children.

In contrast, a method called **constructivism** is emerging. Based on ideas from Dewey and Piaget and supported by sociocultural theory, this **transactional model** of teaching actively engages a child in tasks

Figure 4.10 ● Children have different ways in which they mentally represent the same things. The older child recognizes that, although the contents of the box are only one thing out in the world, they can be represented in people's heads in more than one way—a possibility that escapes the younger child. (Special thanks to John Flavell for the example and the research.)

designed to create personal meaning. Learning is an active process, based on the belief that knowledge is constructed by the learner rather than transferred from the teacher to the child.

"Constructivism is a theory of learning which states that individuals learn through adaptation. What they learn or adapt to is directly influenced by the people, materials and situations with which they come into contact" (Meade-Roberts & Spitz, 1998). People build on preexisting knowledge, be it intellectual, social, or moral. One of its basic tenets is that "knowledge is subjective; that is, everyone creates his own meaning of any particular experience, including what he hears or reads (Heuwinkel, 1996). Another basic idea is that children learn by taking new ideas and integrating them into their existing knowledge base. This is exactly in line with Piaget's processes of assimilation and accommodation.

The teacher's role is to build an environment that is stimulating and conducive to the process of constructing meaning and knowledge. The preprimary schools of Reggio Emilia (see Chapters 2, 9, 11, 14)

encourage children to create their own material representations of their understanding by using many types of media (drawing, sculpture, stories, puppets, paper). At kindergarten and school-age levels, learning literacy and mathematics is considered a developmental process that the teacher "facilitates by providing modeling, authentic experiences, mini-lessons on specific topics and frequent opportunities for students to consult with and learn from each other" (Heuwinkel, 1996). Many constructivist classrooms work on creating community through rule-creating; in fact, those teachers would tell us that "the only way to help students become ethical people, as opposed to people who merely do what they are told, is to have them construct moral meaning" (Kohn, 1993).

Every classroom will look different because the style and cultures of the teacher and children will prevail. Furthermore, a constructivist class will sound different. Children will have choices and make decisions on significant parts of their learning, as they are to be actively engaged mentally and physically. There may be more "arguments," about how children are to play, to build, with children leading discussions and many participating in solutions. The teacher becomes a facilitator and must continually ask genuine questions that will challenge learners to think. A teacher may do less talking, while the learners do more, and provide guidance and written observations rather than rules and standardized tests.

Although there may still be direct instruction and demonstrations as in classes based on behaviorist views, a constructivist theory has fundamental differences about teaching and learning, about how children learn best, who and how they should be taught, and who has the answers. Constructivist classrooms may do a better job promoting children's social, cognitive, and moral development than do more teacher-centered programs (DeVries & Kohlberg, 1990). It is a theory worthy of a closer look.

Applying Cognitive Theory to Work with Children

What can teachers learn from the complicated cognitive theory? Piaget's writings do not apply directly to classroom methods or subject matter per se, and therefore careful interpretation is required. In fact, he never claimed to be an educator. However, Piaget's theories provide a framework, or philosophy, about children's thinking. Piagetian theory has some implications for both environment and interactions.

Materials

Children need many objects to explore, so that they can later incorporate these into their symbolic thinking. Such materials need to be balanced among open-ended ones (such as sand and water activities, basic art and construction materials), guided ones (cooking with recipes, conducting experiments, classification and seriated materials), and self-correcting ones (puzzles, matching games, such as some of the Montessori materials). It is important to remember that young children need to be involved with concrete objects and to explore and use them in their own ways, which include both sensorimotor and beginning symbolic play.

Scheduling

Children need lots of time to explore their own reality, especially through the use of play. A Piagetian classroom would have large periods of time for children to "act out" their own ideas. Also, time should be scheduled for imitation of adult-given ideas (songs, fingerplays, and stories).

Teachers

Children need teachers who understand and agree with a developmental point of view. The teacher who knows the stages and levels of thinking of the children will be one who can guide that class into new and challenging opportunities to learn and grow.

What are the implications for early childhood teachers and parents? In working with children under age 5, we must remember that, because they do not understand mental representations very well, they will have trouble recognizing that another person may view or interpret things differently than they do. This egocentric viewpoint is both natural and normal but must be factored into teachers' thoughts as they work with children. For instance, you may be able to ask a 6- or 7-year-old "How would you feel if you were in that situation?" For a younger child the question is incomprehensible. For the same reason, the younger child may have trouble distinguishing how things seem or appear from how they really are. As Flavell puts it,

> For them, if something *seems* dangerous (the menacing-looking shadow in their unlit bedroom), it *is* dangerous, and if it *seems* nondangerous (the friendly acting stranger) it *is* nondangerous. We often think of young children as naive, credulous, gullible, trusting, and the like. Their inadequate understanding that things may not be as they appear might be partly responsible for this impression (Flavell, Green, & Flavell, 1989).

To encourage thinking and learning, teachers should refrain from telling children exactly how to solve a problem. Rather, the teacher should ask questions that encourage children to observe and pay attention to their own ideas. Teachers:

- Use or create situations that are personally meaningful to children.

- Provide opportunities for them to make decisions.

- Provide opportunities for them to exchange viewpoints with their peers.

Awareness

Perhaps more important is the awareness on the part of all adults that all children have the capability to reason and be thinkers if they are given appropriate materials for their stage of development. Teachers must remember that young children:

1. Think differently from adults.

2. Need many materials to explore and describe.

3. Think in a concrete manner and often cannot think out things in their heads.

4. Come to conclusions and decisions based on what they see, rather than on what is sensible and logical.

5. Need challenging questions and the time to make their own decisions and find their own answers.

The thoughts and ideas of Jean Piaget are impressive, both in quantity and quality. The collective works of this man are extremely complex, often difficult to understand. Yet they have given us a valuable blueprint. Clearly, Jean Piaget has provided unique and important insights into the development of intelligence and children.

It is Piaget's genius for empathy with children, together with true intellectual genius, that has made him the outstanding child psychologist in the world today and one destined to stand beside Freud with respect to his contributions to psychology, education, and related disciplines. Just as Freud's discoveries of unconscious motivation, infantile sexuality, and the stages of psychosexual growth changed our ways of thinking about human personality, so Piaget's discoveries of children's implicit philosophies, the construction of reality by the infant, and the stages of mental development have altered our ways of thinking about human intelligence (Elkind, 1977).

SOCIOCULTURAL THEORY

In the last decade, one theory (and theorist) has received renewed attention. The sociocultural theory of development of Lev Vygotsky focuses on the child as a whole and incorporates ideas of culture and values into child development, particularly the ideas of the development of language and self-identity. Although his theory was developed in the 1920s, it did not receive attention in the United States until his seminal work, *The Mind in Society*, was translated into English in 1978. Since that time, many developmental psychologists, sociologists, and educators have noticed the implications it has for our thinking about children and culture. For instance, work by Janice Hale (see Chapter 3) has identified and applied sociocultural theory to the development of the African American child. Ramirez and Castaneda (1974) have identified particular cognitive and language patterns among young children in selected Hispanic populations. In both cases, these patterns are linked to family and cultural styles of relating and problem-solving.

Lev Vygotsky

Born in 1896 in Byelorussia, Lev Vygotsky graduated from Moscow University with a degree in literature in 1917. For the next 6 years he taught literature and psychology and directed adult theater as well as founding a literary journal. In 1924 he began work at the Institute of Psychology in Moscow, where he focused on the problems of educational practice, particularly those of handicapped children. Toward that end, he gathered a group of young scientists during the late 1920s and early 1930s to look more closely at psychology and mental abnormality, including medical connections. His roots lie with experimental psychology, American philosopher William James, and contemporaries Pavlov and Watson (see the behaviorist theory section of this chapter). A scholar with interests in art and creativity as well as philosophy, psychology, and politics, Vygotsky died in 1934 of tuberculosis.

Vygotsky's Sociocultural Theory

Vygotsky's work is considered as **sociocultural** theory because it focuses on how values, beliefs, skills and traditions are transmitted to the next generation. Like Erikson, Vygotsky believed in the connection between culture and development, particularly the interpersonal connection between the child and other important people. Like the humanists (see later in this chapter), he considered the child as a whole, taking a humanistic, more qualitative approach to studying children. And though he understood the primary behaviorists of his day, he differed from them in that he emphasized family, social interaction, and play as primary influences in children's lives, rather than the

Vygotsky's Sociocultural Theory

Laura E. Berk

The ideas of the Soviet developmental psychologist Lev Vygotsky, who early in this century forged an innovative theory granting great importance to social and cultural experience in children's development, have gained increasing visibility over the past decade. In Vygotsky's *sociocultural theory*, cooperative dialogues with more knowledgeable members of society are necessary for children to acquire the ways of thinking that make up a community's culture. Also, language plays a crucial role in the formation of the child's mind because it is our primary way of communicating, serves as the major means by which social experience is mentally represented, and is an indispensable tool for thought.

According to Vygotsky, the aspects of reality a child is ready to master lie within the *zone of proximal (or potential) development*—a range of tasks that the child cannot yet do alone but can accomplish with help from others. When a child discusses a challenging task with a mentor, that person offers spoken directions and strategies. Then children incorporate the language of those dialogues into their self-directed speech and use it to guide independent efforts. Listen closely to young children and you will hear them talk aloud to themselves as they play, explore, and solve problems. Recent research shows that this *private speech* is a vital bridge between social experience and inner thought and helps children learn.

Vygotsky's ideas are stimulating new ways to educate children that emphasize discussion and joint problem-solving. Adult guidance that creates a *scaffold* for children by sensitively adjusting to their momentary progress is essential for cognitive development. Cooperative learning, in which small groups of peers at varying levels of competence work toward a common goal, also fosters more advanced thinking. In a Vygotskian classroom, learning is highly interactive and simultaneously considers where children are and what they are capable of becoming.

From Berk, L.E. (1996). Infants, children and adolescents (2nd ed.). Boston: Allyn & Bacon, and Berk, L.E. (1994, November). Why children talk to themselves. Scientific American, 271(5), pp. 78–83. Dr. Berk is Professor of Psychology at Illinois State University, consulting editor for Young Children, *and author of child development texts.*

142

stimulus–response and schedules of reinforcement that were becoming so popular in his day.

Vygotsky believed that the child was embedded in the family and culture of his community and that much of a child's development was culturally specific. Rather than moving through certain stages or sequences (as Piaget proposed), children's mastery and interaction differ from culture to culture.[1] Adults, Vygotsky noted, teach socially valued skills at a very early age; children's learning is, therefore, quite influenced by what their social world values. One way he explained this was by this theory of the zone of proximal development. If meaningful learning happens in a social context, the learning is interpersonal and dynamic and depends on who and how much a child's experiences interact with others. This zone has an upper and lower limit. Tasks in the zone are too difficult for a child to learn alone, so he needs the assistance of another who has mastered the task. The lower limit of the zone is where the child has reached working and problem-solving independently. The upper limit is the level of mastery the child can reach with assistance from a skilled person.

Who can be part of a child's zone of proximal development, sharing experiences and developing a cooperative dialogue with the child? Initially, of course, it is the family. For instance, a young girl is carried even as a toddler to the open market with her mother. There she watches and is guided toward learning how to touch cloth, smell herbs, taste food, and weigh and compare amounts. Is it any wonder she learns advanced math skills and the language of bargaining early on?

The reciprocal relationships in the child's zone of proximal development can also include the teacher. Think about your role, for example, in helping a child in your program learn problem-solving skills in completing a puzzle, putting on mittens, or resolving a conflict. Finally, other children—older ones who have more expertise or peers who may have superior skills or simply offer help—can be part of a child's learning in this sociocultural theory. Vygotsky's theory dictates that learning is active and constructed, as did Piaget's. He differs from Piaget, however, in the nature and importance of interaction. Piaget insisted that the child needed to interact with people and objects to learn but that the stages of thinking were still bound by maturation. Vygotsky's claim was that interaction and direct teaching are critical aspects of a child's cognitive development and that a child's level of thinking could be advanced by such interaction.

Further, sociocultural theory challenges Piagetian ideas of language and thought. Vygotsky believed that language, even in its earliest forms, was socially based. Rather than egocentric or immature, children's speech and language development during the years of 3 to 7 is merged and tied to what children are thinking. During these transitions years, the child talks aloud to herself; after a while, this "self-talk" becomes internalized so that the child can act without talking aloud. Vygotsky contended that children speak to themselves for self-guidance and self-direction and that this private speech helps children think about their behavior and plan for action. With age, private (inner) speech (once called "egocentric speech"), which goes from out loud to whispers to lip movement, is critical to a child's self-regulation.

Applying Sociocultural Theory to Work with Children

Sociocultural theory has several implications for the classroom teacher. First, teachers work to understand and incorporate a *child's family and culture* into their teaching.[2] This lends credence to the notion of multicultural education, as noted throughout this text in the "Our Diverse World" ideas. This is also a growing specialty in psychology, with several minority scholars at the forefront. Many teachers and researchers have observed that children of color in this society are socialized to operate in "two worlds," and thus must achieve a kind of "bicognitive development," along with bicultural and bilingual skills. Such work led the way for the popular "learning styles" movement of the 1970s and 1980s. Research done with different cultural groups has reinforced the importance of looking at culture as part of the context in which the child lives and learns.

---

[1] Vygotsky understood the importance of diversity nearly 75 years ago.

[2] The whole area of racial/ethnic identity development is a growing field; works by B. D. Tatum (1995) and Stacey York (1991) are of interest here.

Second, because learning is considered essentially an interpersonal and dynamic process, teachers must develop comfortable and cooperative *relationships* with their children. The teacher and learner adjust to one another; teachers use what they know about children to guide their teaching and plan their curriculum. Sociocultural theory supports both the "emergent curriculum" (see Chapter 11) and the i dea of spontaneous, teachable moments such as are advocated by proponents of an anti-bias curriculum (see Chapters 9, 12, 13, and 14). Further, Vygotsky's theory supports the power of the individual teacher–child relationship, a cornerstone of this text (see Chapter 5) and of developmentally appropriate practices (see Chapters 1, 2, and 11). Not all learning is spontaneous, nor is it enough to simply provide interesting objects and expect children to learn all there is to know. Children need adults to mediate, not only to ask questions but also to analyze where the child is with the questions that are asked. In this way, adults help children learn; when a task is mastered so that the child can do it independently, the adults see the shift from the upper to the lower limit of the zone and can offer a new challenge to enter.

 Third, teachers pay close attention to the *psychological "tools"* used to learn.[1] These include those of the culture, such as how in the United States children are taught to tie a string around their fingers as a memory device whereas in Russia they tie a knot in their handkerchief. They also include the universal tools of drawing, of language, and of mathematics. Lower mental functions such as using the senses take little effort to do, but the higher mental functions need the help of a person who knows the tools of the society to learn.

Teachers realize that there is much value in *play.* It is in play that the child can practice operating the symbols and tools of the culture. Vygotsky (1978) puts it this way:

> Action in the imaginative sphere, in an imaginary situation, the creation of voluntary intentions, the formation of real-life plans and volitional motives—all appear in play and make it the highest level of preschool development. The child moves forward essentially through play activity. Only in this sense can play be considered a leading activity that determines the child's development.

For instance, children might build a structure with blocks; the teacher encourages them to draw the building and then map the entire block corner as a village or neighborhood. The adult serves an important role as an intellectual mediator, continually shifting to another set of symbols to give children a different way of looking at the same thing.

In a Vygotskian classroom there will be activity and an awareness of individual differences. A teacher with this perspective will likely have planned activities that encourage assisted and cooperative learning. Moreover, these classrooms will work best with multi-aged grouping, or at least with plenty of opportunity for older "buddies" or siblings younger and older to be present. Laura E. Berk's Focus Box offers more insight into Vygotsky's theory.

MULTIPLE INTELLIGENCES THEORY

Howard Gardner

Howard Gardner, a professor of human development at the Harvard Graduate School of Education, has been very influential in the ongoing debate about the nature of intelligence. Born in Pennsylvania, he earned both bachelor's and doctorate degrees at Harvard University. Influenced by the works of Piaget and Bruner, Gardner's ideas are best read in his books *Frames of Mind: The Theory of Multiple Intelligences* (1983), *The Unschooled Mind* (1991), and *Multiple Intelligences: The Theory in Practice* (1993).

Gardner's Theory of Multiple Intelligences

The century-old argument that Gardner presents is whether intelligence is a single, broad ability (as measured by an IQ test) or is a set of specific abilities (more than one intelligence). His theory of multiple intelligences asserts that there is strong evidence, both from the brain-based research (see discussion in this chapter) and from the study of genius, that there are at least seven (now eight) basic different intelligences.

Gardner's new view of the mind (1993) claims that:

> human cognitive competence is better described in terms of sets of abilities, talents, or mental

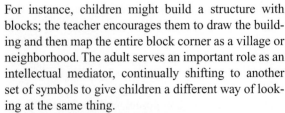

[1] Sociocultural theory recommends that teachers learn the culture of the children they teach.

skills, which we call 'intelligences.' All normal individuals possess each of these skills to some extent; individuals differ in the degree of skill and the nature of their combination. . . . Multiple intelligences theory pluralizes the traditional concept.

Intelligence becomes the ability to solve a problem or to create a product that is in a culture. This is a key point that needs an explanation.

Solving a problem includes the ability to do so in a particular cultural setting or community. Thus, the skill needed and developed depends very much on the context in which the child lives. For example, we all know now that certain parts of the brain are designated for perception, bodily movement, language, or spatial processing. Everyone who has a functional brain will be able to demonstrate some skill in these areas. But the child who has special "musical intelligence," for instance, will hear a concert and insist on a violin (as did Yehudi Menuhin). Or the child whose culture depends on running for its daily living (as do some people of Kenya) is more likely to have children well developed in that area of intelligence. Gardner writes of Anne Sullivan, teacher of blind and deaf Helen Keller, as an example of interpersonal intelligence, for she could understand what Helen needed in a way no one else could.

Gardner's descriptions of the various intelligences are described in Figure 4.11.

Applying Multiple Intelligences Theory to Work with Children

Gardner's theory of multiple intelligences has had a big impact on schools, transforming curricula and teaching methods from preschool to high school. Even Sesame Street has taken to applying the theory to developing its programs (Blumenthal, 1995). Teachers in early childhood use the theory daily as they individualize their environments, curricula, and approaches. The child whose facility with puzzles excels that of his classmates is given a chance to try more complex ones. The children who thrive in dramatic play are offered a time to put on a puppet show for the class. The child whose mind works especially musically, or logically, or interpersonally is encouraged to develop those special gifts.

At the same time, there is no one right way to implement multiple intelligences. The theory is both culture and context specific, so that, in a similar way

to a constructivist classroom, "multiple intelligence classes" would have teachers developing their own strategies, developing curricula and assessment methods based on both their own and their children's culture and priorities and on the individual children's intelligences. Chapter 13 will give examples of the multiple intelligences curriculum.

MATURATION THEORY

Arnold Gesell

As noted in Chapter 1, Arnold Gesell was a physician intrigued with the notion that children's internal clock seemed to govern their growth and behavior. In the 1940s and 1950s, Gesell established norms for several areas of growth and the behaviors that accompany such development:

Our first task will be to characterize ascending levels of maturity in terms of typical behavior patterns. Such characterizations will provide a series of normative portraits outlining the directions and trends of psychological growth. In order that the lines of growth may be more apparent, each portrait will consider in turn four major fields of behavior, namely (1) Motor Characteristics, (2) Adaptive Behavior, (3) Language Behavior, (4) Personal-Social Behavior (Gesell, 1940).

The Gesell Institute, which fosters the work of Dr. Louise Bates Ames and others, continues to provide guidelines for how children mature from birth to puberty. The Word Pictures in Chapter 3 are an excellent example of the information maturational theory and research have provided.

Theory of Maturation

Maturation, by definition, is the process of physical and mental growth that is determined by heredity. The maturation sequence occurs in relatively stable and orderly ways. Maturation theory holds that much growth is genetically determined from conception. This theory differs from behaviorism, which asserts that growth is determined by environmental conditions and experiences, and cognitive theory, which states that growth and behavior are a reflection of both maturation and learning.

Musical Intelligence	is the capacity to think in music, to be able to hear patterns, recognize, and then remember them. Certain parts of the brain help in the perception and production of music. Gardner cites as evidence of this as an intelligence the importance of music in cultures worldwide, as well as its role in Stone Age societies.
Bodily-Kinesthetic Intelligence	is the capacity to use parts or all of your body to solve a problem or make something. As bodily movements became specialized over time, it was an obvious advantage to the species. We can see this in a person's ability in sport (to play a game), in dance (to express a feeling, music or rhythm), in acting, or in making a product.
Logical-Mathematical Intelligence	is the capacity to think in a logical, often linear, pattern and to understand principles of a system. Scientists and mathematicians often think this way. Gardner asserts that there are two essential facts of the logical-mathematical intelligence. First, in the gifted individual, the process of problem-solving is often remarkably rapid, and the second is the often *nonverbal* nature of the intelligence (the familiar "Aha!" phenomenon).
Linguistic Intelligence	is the capacity to use language to express your thoughts, ideas, feelings, and the ability to understand other people and their words. The gift of language is universal, as evidenced by poets and writers as well as speakers and lawyers. The spoken language constant across cultures, and the development of graphic language, is one of the hallmarks of human activity.
Spatial Intelligence	is the capacity to represent the world internally in spatial terms. Spatial problem-solving is required for navigation, in the use of maps, and relying on drawings to build something. Playing games such as chess and all the visual arts—painting, sculpting, drawing—use spatial intelligence, and sciences such as anatomy, architecture, and engineering emphasize this intelligence.
Interpersonal Intelligence	is the capacity to understand other people. Master players in a nursery school notice how others are playing before entering; some children seem to be born leaders; teachers, therapists, religious or political leaders, and many parents seem to have the capacity to notice distinctions among others. This intelligence can focus on contrasts in moods, temperaments, motivations, and intentions.
Intrapersonal Intelligence	is the capacity to understand yourself, knowing who you are, how you react. Intrapersonal intelligence is a knowledge of the internal aspects of one's self. These people have access to their own feeling life, a range of emotions they can draw on as a means of understanding and guiding their own behavior. Children who seem to have an innate sense of what they can and cannot do often know when they need help.
Naturalist Intelligence	is the capacity to discriminate among living things (plants, animals) as well as a sensitivity to other features of the natural world (clouds, rock configurations). This intelligence is clearly of value in our roles as hunters, gatherers, and farmers and is important to those who are botanists or chefs.

Figure 4.11 ● In his book *Multiple Intelligences* (1993) and subsequent work, Howard Gardner describes a new way of looking at intelligence that has serious implications for teaching.

Maturation and growth are interrelated and occur together. Maturation describes the *quality* of growth; that is, while a child grows in inches and pounds, the nature (or quality) of that growth changes. Maturation is qualitative, describing the way a baby moves into walking, rather than simply the age at which the baby took the first step. Growth is *what* happens; maturation is *how* it happens.

Studies have established that the maturation sequence is the same for all children, regardless of culture, country of origin, or learning environment. But there are two vital points to remember:

● Although maturation determines the sequence of development, the precise age is *approximate*.[1] The sequence of developmental stages may be universal, but the rate at which a child moves through the stages varies tremendously.

● Growth is *uneven*. Children grow in spurts. Motor development may be slow in some stages, fast in others. For instance, a baby may gain an ounce a day for 2 months, then only half a pound in an entire month. Usually there is a growth spurt at puberty, with some children at 13 nearly their adult height, others not yet 5 feet tall. This unpredictability brings, again, much individual variation.

Applying Maturation Theory to Work with Children

Maturation theory is most useful in describing children's growth and typical behavior. In Chapter 3, these normative data are used to develop Word Pictures that describe common characteristics of children at different ages. Such charts will help adults understand behavior better and will keep them from expecting too much or too little. Teachers can use developmental norms to understand typical growth by remembering that there is great individual variation and uneven growth. However, both teachers and parents must be cautious in overgeneralizing from these normative charts. Also, Gesell's initial data were focused on a narrow portion of the population and were derived from American children only. Further work in the last two decades has adjusted the ranges with succeeding generations of children and an ever-larger and more

Figure 4.12 ● Young children need materials and time to explore the world on their own. (Courtesy of American Montessori Society.)

diverse population. Further, maturation theory has inspired excellent developmental norms that help parents, teachers, and physicians alike determine whether a child's growth is within the normal range.

HUMANISTIC THEORY

The Humanists

As the field of psychology began to develop, various schools of thought arose. By the middle of this century, two "camps" dominated the American psychological circles. The first, known as psychodynamic, included the Freudians and is best known to us through the works of Erik Erikson. The second, called behaviorism, began with Watson and Thorndike and was later expanded by Skinner and Bandura.

In 1954, Abraham Maslow published a book that articulated another set of ideas. He called it the Third Force (or Humanistic Psychology), which focused on what motivated people to be well, successful, and mentally healthy.

OUR DIVERSE WORLD OUR DIVERSE WORLD OUR DIVERSE WORLD OUR DIVERSE WORLD OUR DIVERSE WORLD OUR DIVERSE WORLD OUR DIVERSE WORLD OUR DIVERSE WORLD

[1] There are so many ways in which children differ; their maturation is one aspect of their development that is universal.

This **humanist theory** has a place in early childhood education because it attempts to explain how people are motivated. Specifically, humanistic theory is centered on people's needs, goals, and successes. This was a change from the study of mental illness, as in psychotherapy, or the study of animal behavior, in the case of much behaviorist research. Instead, Dr. Maslow studied exceptionally mature and successful people. Others, such as Carl Rogers, Fritz Perls, Alan Watts, and Erich Fromm added to what was known about healthy personalities. The humanists developed a comprehensive theory of human behavior based on mental health. It must be noted, however, that many of the humanist theories, and in particular Maslow's theory of human needs, is clearly a "Western" philosophy, although it is often presented as a universal set of ideas. In fact, other cultures would see life differently. An African world view might see the good of the community as the essential goal of being fully human. Cultures with more of a "collective" orientation, rather than an emphasis on the individual or self, would see serving the family or group as the ultimate goal of humanity. Humanistic psychology can also be seen as being at odds with more orthodox religions that seek ultimate reliance on a supreme deity, putting "God" rather than "self" at the top of the hierarchy.

Maslow's Theory of Human Needs

Maslow's theory of **self-actualization** is a set of ideas about what people need to become and stay healthy. He asserts that every human being is motivated by a number of basic needs, regardless of age, sex, race, culture, or geographic location. According to Maslow (1954), a basic need is something:

● Whose absence breeds illness

● Whose presence prevents illness

● Whose restoration cures illness

● Preferred by the deprived person over other satisfactions, under certain conditions (such as very complex, free-choice instances)

● Found to be inactive, at a low ebb, or functionally absent in the healthy person

These needs, not to be denied, form a theory of human motivation. It is a hierarchy, or pyramid,

because there is a certain way these needs are interrelated, and because the most critical needs form the foundation from which the other needs can be met.

Applying Humanistic Theory to Work with Children

The basic needs are sometimes called **deficiency needs** because they are critical for a person's survival, and a deficiency can cause a person to die. Until those are met, no other significant growth can take place. How well a teacher knows that a hungry child will ignore a lesson, or simply be unable to concentrate. A tired child often pushes aside learning materials and experiences until rested. The child who is deprived of basic physiologic needs may be able to think of those needs only; in fact, "such a man can fairly be said to live by bread alone" (Maslow, 1954). The humanists would strongly advocate a school breakfast or lunch program and would support regular rest and naptimes in programs with long hours.

Once the physiologic needs are satisfied, the need for safety and security will emerge. Maslow points at insecure and neurotic people as examples of what happens when these needs are left unfulfilled. These people act as if a disaster is about to occur, as if a spanking is on the way. Given an unpredictable home or school, a child cannot find any sense of consistency, and so is preoccupied with worrying and anxiety. Maslow would advise teachers to give freedom within limits, rather than either total neglect or permissiveness.

The growth needs begin to emerge when the basic needs have been met. Higher needs are dependent on those primary ones. They are what we strive for to become more satisfied and healthy people.

The need for *love and belonging* is often expressed directly and clearly by the young children in our care. A lack of love and sense of belonging stifles growth. To learn to give love later in life, one has to learn about love by receiving it as a child. This means learning early about the responsibilities of giving as well as receiving love.

The *need for esteem* can be divided into two categories: self-respect and esteem from others. "Self-esteem includes such needs as a desire for confidence, competence, mastery, adequacy, achievement, independence, and freedom. Respect from others includes

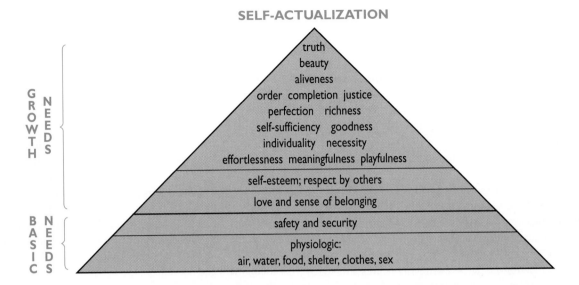

Figure 4.13 ● Abraham Maslow studied healthy personalities and theorized that what people need for growth is a hierarchy of basic and growth needs. (Adapted from Abraham Maslow, 1954.)

such concepts as prestige, recognition, acceptance, attention, status, reputation, and appreciation" (Goble, 1970).

Self-actualization is what gives a person satisfaction in life. From the desire to know and understand the world and people around us comes a renewal of self-knowledge. For the early childhood educator, these needs are expressed in the enthusiasm, curiosity, and natural "drive" to learn and try. In meeting these needs, a person finds meaning for life, an eagerness to live, and a willingness to do so. Figure 4.13 describes both basic and growth needs in detail.

Children must have their physical and basic emotional needs met before these requirements of higher cognitive learning can be fulfilled. Moreover, the child who seems stuck in a particular "needs area" will likely stay there until that basic need is satisfied. A hungry, insecure, or hurt child is a poor learner. Teachers must continually advocate better physical and social conditions for all children.

Maslow's theory has important implications for child care. Children's basic needs are teachers' first concern: Teachers must ensure that children are properly clothed, fed, and rested as well as safe and secure. Only then are they ready to address curriculum and skill development.

RESEARCH AND OTHER THEORETICAL VIEWPOINTS FOR EDUCATORS

To complete our discussion of psychology and early education, the contributions of several other aspects are noteworthy. All have added to our knowledge about how people think and learn, how personality and social attitudes develop, and how early attachment and learning affect the developing child. The number of excellent researchers who have contributed to the knowledge of early childhood development far exceeds the space we have here. We include these viewpoints to emphasize the vital links between psychology, developmental research, and education.

Attachment

A key concept in the development of the self and the study of social relationships is that of **attachment**, a term used particularly in the works of John Bowlby and Mary Ainsworth, and a concept used in Burton White's descriptive work and Magda Gerber's Resources for Infant Educarers (RIE) programs for infants and toddlers. Attachment is the emotional connection, an "affectional bond" in Bowlby's terms, between two people. The child or adult who is attached to another uses that person as a "safe base" from which to venture out into the world, a source of comfort when distressed or stressed, and a support for encouragement. **Attachment behaviors**, therefore, are anything that allows a person to get and stay attached. These include smiling, eye contact, talking, touching, even clinging and crying.

Bowlby's theory includes the idea that infants are preprogrammed to form attachments to adults, thus ensuring their survival. "It is an essential part of the ground plan of the human species—as well as that of many other species—for an infant to become attached to a mother figure. This figure need not be the natural mother but can be anyone who plays the role of the principal caregiver" (Ainsworth, 1979). Research does show that human and animal babies do indeed send signals to their mothers very early on. In fact, the human infant's early signals include crying and gazing, both of which are powerful to adults, and a kind of rhythmic sucking that appears to keep the mother engaged. Soon after appears the social smile, which is a thrill for parents and a boost in communication skills for the baby.

The nature of children's attachment has been researched extensively by Mary Ainsworth and colleagues. Developmentally, children develop an initial bond, then proceed to develop real mutuality—that is, to learn and practice almost a "dance" between themselves and their favored loved one. She found that, although virtually all infants develop attachments, including to multiple caregivers, they differ in how secure they are in those attachments. Furthermore, attachment can be measured in the infant and toddler, as seen in children's response to a stranger both in and out of the parent's presence. Figure 4.14 illustrates these patterns of attachment. This research was important to early educators. As Ainsworth (1979) reports,

It is clear that the nature of an infant's attachment to his or her mother as a 1-year-old is related both to earlier interaction with the mother and to various aspects of later development. The implication is that the way in which the infant organizes his or her behavior towards the mother affects the way in which he or she organizes behavior towards other aspects of the environment, both animate and inanimate. This organization provides a core of continuity in development despite changes that come with developmental acquisitions, both cognitive and socioemotional.

Researchers have found that a majority of American infants tested in the stranger situation demonstrated secure attachment. Still, when attachment fails, children are placed at tremendous risk.

For instance, this two-part dance requires both infant and parent (or caregiver) to have the skill to connect. Premature infants often lack these skills at first, as their systems are underdeveloped and they often are separated in the first weeks or months, causing parents to report them as quite unresponsive. Some parents of blind infants, who cannot engage in gazing, may wonder if they are being rejected by their babies. Failure of attachment can come from the parent, too. Parents who themselves did not have secure attachments as children may not know the needed behaviors. Abusing parents are not doing their part to encourage bonding. Other neglectful conditions, such as depression, abject poverty, and other stresses, increase the likelihood that there will be a failure of attachment. Intervention can help unattached persons, teaching specific interactive techniques with ongoing supports such as crisis hotlines and personal counseling.

Also, parents and researchers have asked careful questions about full-day child care, particularly for infants, wondering if such care undermines children's attachment to their parents. The debate, reaching its height in the latter half of the 1980s, has spurred research into both parent–child attachment and child care programs. Whether concerns about infant child care prove valid or not, as of this date we can conclude that children are not at any higher risk in high-quality child care. This highlights the need for such programs, as will be addressed further in Chapters 9, 10, and 15.

Sex Differences

Are girls and boys different in terms of development and learning? What are these differences, and how do they occur? More important, what differences are caused by "nature" and which ones by "nurture"? Should we treat our girls and boys the same or differently? The realities and the myths surrounding sex differences and their effect on behavior from infancy to adulthood is the subject of interest, controversy, and research. The work of Eleanor Maccoby and others have provided both hard data and an open forum for

	Exploratory Behavior before Separation	Behavior during Separation	Reunion Behavior	Behavior with Stranger
Secure	Separates to explore toys; shares play with mother; friendly toward stranger when mother is present, touches "home base" periodically.	May cry; play is subdued for a while; usually recovers and is able to play.	If distressed during separation, contact ends distress; if not distressed, greets mother warmly; initiates interaction.	Somewhat friendly; may play with stranger after initial distress reaction.
Anxious/ambivalent (resistant)	Has difficulty separating to explore toys even when mother is present; wary of novel situations and people; stays close to mother and away from stranger.	Very distressed; hysterical crying does not quickly diminish.	Seeks comfort and rejects it; continues to cry or fuss; may be passive—no greeting made.	Wary of stranger; rejects stranger's offers to play.
Anxious/avoidant	Readily separates to explore toys; does not share play with parent; shows little preference for parent versus stranger.	Does not show distress; continues to play; interacts with the stranger.	Ignores mother— turns or moves away; avoidance is more extreme at the second reunion.	No avoidance of stranger.

SOURCE: Compiled from Ainsworth, M.D.S., & Wittig, B.A. (1969). Attachment and exploratory behavior of one-year-olds in a strange situation. In B.M. Foss (Ed.), Determinants of infant behavior (Vol. 4). London: Methuen.

Figure 4.14 ● Patterns of attachment in 12- to 18-month-olds in Ainsworth's "Strange Situation" show how critical the interpersonal environment is for young children. (From *Understanding Children* by Judith Schickendanz by permission of Mayfield Publishing Company. Copyright © 1993 by Mayfield Publishing Company.)

discussions about how people grow and the complex interaction between heredity and environment that makes child development so fascinating.

The child's emerging sense of self has several elements, including an awareness of a separate self and in comparison to others (as discussed in Chapter 14). One aspect of self is gender identity. Children generally acquire the ability to label themselves and others correctly by age 2 or 3; they develop gender stability (the understanding of staying the same sex throughout life) by age 4 and gender constancy (a person keeps the same gender regardless of appearance) by about 5 or 6.

As they grow, children begin to develop ideas about gender roles, what girls/women and boys/men do. Sex-typed behavior begins to appear at 2 or 3, when children tend to choose same-sex playmates and sex-typed toy preferences. Research indicates that there are

no significant differences between girls and boys in intelligence or reasoning behavior. Some cognitive functioning and personality differences do exist, but overall the differences are small and there is no overall pattern.

So, why are there these sex differences in behavior? Theorists of several different schools of thought have tried to explain the patterns. Freud's explanation is based on the concept of identification, whereby the child learns to imitate the same-sex parent and acquires the appropriate role. Behaviorists emphasize the role of reinforcement and modeling, and parents do appear to treat boys and girls in systematically different ways. A cognitive-developmental model, by Kohlberg, theorizes that children imitate same-sex models after they develop gender constancy. Current theorists now propose a "schema" model (see the discussion of cognitive theory); that is, children develop theories about the world from an early age, especially in the preoperational stage, and therefore develop general rules about what girls and boys do as soon as they figure out that there is a difference. The application of such rules would be particularly strong in the preschool and early elementary years, until a child develops an ability to see beyond appearance and can think in more abstract ways to deeper characteristics and broader categories.

Researchers have found two characteristics of boys—better spatial ability and greater aggressiveness—but have been unable to demonstrate a clear biologic connection. Because girls and boys are treated differently by parents and teachers, and are presented with sex stereotypes in the mass media and children's books, they clearly receive different messages. Adults who work with children are thus well-advised to pay careful attention to the messages they give children.[1]

In the environments we prepare for them, the materials they use, and the examples we model, children create their own ideas and learn behavior that works for them in the world. Socialization, then, probably accounts for most of the sex-typed behavior we see in children.

Moral Development

People used to assume that young children needed to be taught exactly what was "right" and "wrong" and that was enough. In the last 20 years, research has shown that moral development is a more complex process with both a cognitive and an emotional side to it. Several theorists and researchers have proposed how to think about children's moral development. Jean Piaget, Lawrence Kohlberg, Nancy Eisenberg, and Carol Gilligan are discussed here.

Piaget investigated children's moral reasoning by presenting children with pairs of stories and asking them which child was "naughtier." From this, he discovered that children under age 6 base their judgment on the amount of damage done, not the child's intentions. By middle childhood, children are beginning to take intent into account, so that one can begin to see a

shift in moral reasoning toward the end of the early childhood period from objective judgments, based on physical results and concrete amounts, to more subjective considerations (such as the purpose of the perpetrator or psychological factors). The connections to children's cognitive stage of development is interesting, and adults might consider that a child's protests over wrongdoing ("I didn't mean to do it!") may very well signal a new level of reasoning, with the realization that one's intentions *do* matter.

Lawrence Kohlberg is best known as a theorist in social development, addressing educational practice and gender constancy as well. Building on Piagetian dimensions, Kohlberg's theory of moral development involves both social growth and intellectual reasoning. People move from stage to stage as a result of their own reasoning power and they see for themselves the contradictions in their own beliefs. As with Erikson and Piaget, Kohlberg's stages are hierarchical—a person moves forward one by one, and no stage can be skipped. On the basis of children's responses to moral dilemmas similar to those of Piaget, Kohlberg identified three levels of moral development, as illustrated in Figure 4.15. For early childhood educators, research shows that preconventional reasoning (stages 1 and 2) is dominant into elementary school.

Most of the stories, or dilemmas, that Piaget and Kohlberg used were about stealing, lying, disobeying rules, and the like. More recently, researcher and theorist Nancy Eisenberg has explored the kinds of reasoning children use to justify good (**prosocial**) behavior. She asks children what they would do in situations with a moral dilemma. One of her stories involves a child on the way to a friend's birthday party. The child encounters someone who has fallen and is hurt. What should the child do, help the hurt child and miss cake and ice cream, or leave the child and go on to the party?

Such questions brought to light several levels of prosocial reasoning. In the early childhood years, children seem to be engaged in level 1 (*hedonistic reasoning*) in which the individual's own needs are put first. In the case mentioned above, the child would leave the hurt person and go to the party ("I won't help because I have to go to the party.") As children move through

OUR DIVERSE WORLD OUR DIVERSE WORLD OUR DIVERSE WORLD OUR DIVERSE WORLD OUR DIVERSE WORLD OUR DIVERSE WORLD OUR DIVERSE WORLD OUR DIVERSE WORLD

[1] Working with young children and their families invites early childhood educators to carefully examine their own upbringing, values, beliefs, and biases, especially about gender roles.

I. **Preconventional morality**

Stage 1: Punishment and obedience orientation
Might makes right; obey authority to avoid punishment

Stage 2: Individualism and relativist orientation
Look out for number one; be nice to others so they will be nice to you

II. **Conventional morality**

Stage 3: Mutual interpersonal expectations
"Good girl, nice boy"; approval more important than any reward

Stage 4: Social system and conscience
"Law and order"; contributing to society's good is important

III. **Postconventional morality**

Stage 5: Social contract
Rules are to benefit all, by mutual agreement; may be changed same way; the greatest good for the greatest number

Stage 6: Universal ethical principles
Values established by individual reflection, may contradict other laws

Figure 4.15 ● Kohlberg's Stages of Moral Development. Fairly broad cross-cultural data and extensive American research indicate a persuasive universality and a strong sequence of stage development in children's moral development.

middle childhood, they tend to move to level 2, in which the needs of another begin to be considered and increase in importance. Answers to the story would begin to shift toward including others ("I'd help because they'd help me next time."). Eisenberg's stages roughly parallel Kohlberg's and help broaden these concepts without contradicting the fundamental arguments.

 Carol Gilligan, however, challenges Kohlberg's strong emphasis on justice and fairness and his omission of caring for others. In her book *In a Different Voice* (1982), Gilligan points out that mostly males were studied for such work, and that, because girls and boys are socialized differently, their moral judgments will be quite different. For instance, boys may be raised with the idea that justice and fairness are the key moral basis, whereas girls may be taught that caring and responsibility to others are central.[1] Buzzelli (1992)

has also worked extensively on young children's moral understanding and has applied recent research to children's development of peer relationships. Although this claim of different moral ideas based on gender differences has yet to be fully researched, it is an important thought to keep in mind, particularly when teaching and raising young children.

Brain-Based Research

Some of the most exciting research discoveries in the last part of this decade have been in the area of brain-based research. The development of new research tools has coupled with a growing concern about children in America. Over the last three decades, early intervention programs and their advocates have been pressing for a deeper, broader knowledge base about child development, adult–child relationships,

OUR DIVERSE WORLD OUR DIVERSE WORLD OUR DIVERSE WORLD OUR DIVERSE WORLD OUR DIVERSE WORLD OUR DIVERSE WORLD OUR DIVERSE WORLD OUR DIVERSE WORLD

[1] These characteristics may not be *gender specific* (i.e., "only girls do this and only boys do that"), but be *gender related* (i.e., "many girls often . . . and some boys may do the same"). What is important to remember in our diverse world is that one way is *not necessarily better* than another way, just *different*.

and educational programs. Political pressure has mounted both from an educational front (such as Children's Defense Fund, NAEYC, Head Start, the Carnegie Foundation) and a politicomoral one (such as the abortion debate, women's rights, state versus federal funding, etc.). In academic circles, neuroscience research has developed sophisticated technologies, such as ultrasound, magnetic resonance imaging (MRI), position emission tomography (PET), and effective, noninvasive ways to study brain chemistry (such as the steroid hormone cortisol). In short, brain scans and other technologies that have made it possible to investigate the intricate circuitry of the brain and a favorable social and political climate have made such research compelling and supported.

What have we learned? The brain seems to operate on a "use it or lose it" principle. At birth, one has about 100 billion brain cells and 50 trillion connections among them. With use, these cells grow branches, called dendrites, that reach out to make connections with other cells. With impoverishments, you lose the dendrites. Over the first decade of life, the number of connections begins to decline, and by the teenage years about half have been discarded (this number will remain relatively stable throughout life). As Galinsky (1997) tells us, "the connections that have been reinforced by repeated experience tend to remain while those that are not are discarded. Thus, a child's early experiences—both positive and negative—help shape the brain, affecting to some degree how he thinks, feels and relates to others throughout his life." Figure 4.16 summarizes these research findings.

Every environment has opportunities for interaction with a variety of objects, people, and circumstances that can stimulate brain growth. Conversely, any environment can be impoverished. This is less about toys than it is about interactions and the atmosphere. When the brain perceives a threat or stress, the body reacts, and a kind of **downshifting** (Caine & Caine, 1994) occurs that can compromise the brain's capabilities. A chronic threat of emotional embarrassment, social disrespect, or simply hurried, restrictive time settings can all trigger this downshifting.

Applying brain research to the early childhood classroom is important and will be a challenge. A framework for action was proposed at the recent conference with three key principles.

First, do no harm. Let us do everything to help parents and caregivers form strong, secure attachments. At the same time, we need to provide parent education and information about what does help their children's brain and well-being to grow. Finally, we must educate ourselves so the quality of child care and early education is ensured.

Second, prevention is best, but when a child needs help, intervene quickly and intensively. The brain is a work in progress, and children can recover from serious stress. But the list of preventable conditions is clear, and it is everyone's job to work toward eliminating the unnecessary traumas.

Third, promote the healthy development and learning of every child. "Risk is not destiny," reminds Shore (1997), "The medical, psychological, and educational literatures contain a sufficient number of examples of people who develop or recover significant capacities after critical periods have passed to sustain hope for every individual." Figure 4.17 gives 12 suggestions for teachers in early childhood classrooms.

USING DEVELOPMENTAL AND LEARNING THEORIES

As a teacher, you must think about what you believe about children, development, and learning. This chapter gives much food for thought in this regard, and students are often overwhelmed. Two critical questions arise: (1) Why do contradictions exist among the theories, and (2) How can I decide which is the "right" one? To answer the first question, remember that each theory addresses a particular aspect of development. For instance, psychodynamic theory focuses on the development of personality, behaviorist on the conditions of learning, cognitive on how children think and learn, maturation on how development progresses, and humanist on the conditions for overall health. Each has its avid proponents with a body of research that supports it. Because every theory has its own focus and advocates, each viewpoint is rather subjective and somewhat narrow. In other words, no one theory tells us everything . . . and that is the answer to the second question. Thoughtful teachers develop their own viewpoints. Begin to decide what you believe about children, learning, and education. Try to avoid the pitfall of taking sides. Instead, integrate theory into your teaching practices by comparing the major developmental and learning theories with your own daily experiences with young children.

Key Finding	Implications for Educators
"1. Human development hinges on the interplay between nature and nurture."	Remember the nature/nurture controversy described in Chapter 1 and this chapter? Think, too, about the contributions of Piaget, the constructivists, and sociocultural theorists in regard to the dynamic interplay between the environment and learning. We now know that the brain is affected by all kinds of environmental and interactive conditions. The impact is both specific and dramatic, influencing both the general direction and the actual circuitry of the brain.
"2. Early care has a decisive and long-lasting impact on how people develop, their ability to learn, and their capacity to regulate their own emotions."	This finding confirms the work on attachment (see this chapter) and underscores the importance of warm and responsive care. It is in the daily interaction with nurturing adults that children develop the network of brain cells that help them learn to regulate and calm themselves, which actually helps the brain turn off a stress-sensitive response quickly and efficiently.
"3. The human brain has a remarkable capacity to change, but timing is crucial."	Sound familiar? Montessori's *critical periods* and Steiner's belief in a 7-year cycle of growth (see Chapter 1) both stress the notion of timing. Brain research is helping us pinpoint those periods. Experiments have proven that there are certain "windows of opportunity" for the proper development of vision and language, and studies show certain effective times in the learning of music. There are limits to the brain's ability to create itself, and researchers have found that these limitations have some time periods to them that we ought not to ignore.
"4. There are times when negative experiences or the absence of appropriate stimulation are more likely to have serious and sustained effects."	Consider the impact of trauma and neglect, of maternal depression, of substance abuse, and of poverty. The parts of the brain associated with expression and regulation of emotions seem to show the most effect. Brain activity and children's behavior can improve when some of these problems, such as maternal depression, are treated. However, many of the risk factors occur together.
"5. Evidence amassed over the last decade points to the wisdom and efficacy of prevention and early intervention."	We know this in our hearts and we know this from the research on Head Start (see Chapters 1 and 2). Now the studies of brain research point to the value of timely, well-designed and intensive intervention.

Figure 4.16 ● Decades of brain-based research is summarized here from the 1996 Conference on Brain Development in Young Children, sponsored by the Families and Work Institute (Shore, 1997).

Key Principles of Brain-Based Learning

1. Each brain is unique. It develops on different timetables; normal brains can be as much as 3 years apart in developmental stages. We should not hold each age or grade level learner to the same standards.

2. Stress and threat impact the brain in many ways: They reduce capacity for understanding, meaning, and memory. They reduce higher order thinking skills. Learners are threatened by loss of approval, helplessness, lack of resources, and unmeetable deadlines.

3. Emotions run the brain. Bad ones flavor all attempts at learning. Good ones create an excitement and love of learning. More importantly, we only believe something and give it meaning when we feel strongly about it.

4. The neocortex is strongly run by patterns, not facts. We learn best with themes, patterns, and whole experiences. The patterns of information provide the understanding learners seek.

5. We learn in a multipath, simultaneous style. It's visual, auditory, kinesthetic, conscious, and nonconscious. We do most poorly when we "piecemeal" learning into linear, sequential math facts and other out of context information lists.

6. Our memory is very poor in rote, semantic situations. It is best in contextual, episodic event-oriented situations.

7. All learning is mind–body. Physiology states, posture, and breathing affect learning. Teachers should learn how to better manage students' states as well as teach students how to manage their own states.

8. Feed the brain. Our brains are stimulated by challenge, novelty, and feedback in our learning environments. Creating more of these conditions is critical to brain growth.

9. Ritual is a way for the reptilian brain to have a productive expression. More positive and productive rituals can lower the perceived stress and threat.

10. The brain is poorly designed for formal instruction. It is designed to learn what it needs to learn, to survive. It can usually learn what it wants to learn. By focusing on learning, not instruction or teaching, we can allow the brain to learn more.

11. Cycles and rhythms. Our brain is designed for ups and downs, not constant attention. The terms "on" or "off task" are irrelevant to the brain.

12. Assessment. Most of what is critical to the brain and learning cannot be assessed. The best learning is often the creation of biases, themes, models, and patterns of deep understanding.

Figure 4.17 ● All early childhood teachers can benefit from the knowledge of the brain and how it works (Jensen, 1995).

Similarities among the Theories

All seven theories we have discussed attempt to explain how children grow, more in the socioemotional and cognitive areas than in the pysical and motor areas. Maturation theory is the only one of the five that includes physical growth and motor development. In other words, these theories do not try to explain the workings of the body as much as the mind and heart.

In general, the theories do not dictate the curriculum for the classroom, though behaviorism does recommend teaching/learning techniques. Piagetian, multiple intelligences, and Vygotsky's theories support important programmatic elements of good early childhood education, such as the creative collaboration of Reggio Emilia (see Chapters 1, 9, and 14) and Gardner's recommendations for intellectual development in the schools (see Chapter 13). Each theory posits that learn-

Theory	Major Theorists	Important Facts
Psychosocial	Erik Erikson	Maturational emphasis Stage theory of social and emotional development Crises at each level Teacher: Emotional base, social mediator
Behaviorist	John Watson Edward Thorndike B. F. Skinner Albert Bandura	Environmental emphasis Stimulus–response Conditioning (classical and operant) Reinforcement (positive and negative) Modeling Teacher: Arranger of environment and reinforcer of behavior
Cognitive	Jean Piaget	Maturational and environmental emphasis Assimilation and accommodation Stage theory of cognitive development Teacher: Provider of materials and time and supporter of children's unique ways of thinking
Sociocultural	Lev Vygotsky	Zone of proximal development Private speech Collaborative/assisted learning
Multiple intelligences	Howard Gardner	Many kinds of intelligence Problem-solving and product-creating
Maturation	Arnold Gesell	Emphasis on heredity Normative data Teacher: Guider of behavior based on what is typical and normal
Humanist	Abraham Maslow	Environmental emphasis Mental health model Hierarchy of human needs Teacher: Provider of basic and growth needs
Others	Mary Ainsworth John Bowlby Nancy Eisenberg Carol Gilligan Lawrence Kohlberg Eleanor Maccoby	Attachment and categories research Attachment theory Expands moral development to prosocial Questions categories of moral development Moral, cognitive, and sex-role development Sex differences research
Brain-based research	Neuroscientists	New insights into early development "Use it or lose it" principle Warm and responsive care matters

Figure 4.18 ● The major theories of and research on development and learning describe children and their growth in different ways.

ing follows an orderly, if not always smooth, path from birth to adulthood. They all see later learning as growing from previous experiences. They all agree that learning must be real, rewarding, and, except in extreme cases, connected to an important person or people in early life. Figure 4.18 summarizes the seven major theories and principal theorists.

Differences among the Theories

More obvious are the differences among the various theories. All seven have a particular focus, but not the same one. In development terms, Erikson covers the psychosocial area. The behaviorists and Piagetians tend to concentrate on cognitive growth. The constructivists, Gardner, and sociocultural theories all emphasize the importance of culture in development and learning. Maturational theory rests on physical-motor development, although theorists have derived behavior in other areas as well. Gesell's maturation theory concentrates on the larger behaviors that heredity dictates. Maslow builds a framework including physiologic, affective, and intellectual needs. Three of the seven are developmental theories; that is, they describe changes in children as a result of a combination of growth (controlled mostly by maturation and heredity) and interaction with the environment. The new brain-based research shows the importance of a child's relationships and interactions, as do the psychodynamic, sociocultural, and humanist theories. Maslow's theory of self-actualization is less developmental than descriptive of overall human needs, though it is clear that in early childhood the basic needs predominate over higher ones that occur later in life.

Behaviorist theory emphasizes changes that occur in the environment. Cognitive and psychosocial ideas are stage theories, explaining growth as a series of steps through which all children pass, regardless of environment. Behaviorists spell out how the children learn no matter what age or stage they may have achieved, while the two stage theorists claim that what and how a child learns are tied to a stage of development. Humanists tend to look at learning as paralleling the child's internal affective stage, rather than a stage of growth or external environmental conditions.

Most early childhood educators are eclectic in their theoretical biases. That is, they have developed their own philosophies of education based on a little of each theory. Each teacher has an obligation to develop a clear set of ideas of how children grow and learn. We are fortunate to have choices. Most educators agree on some basic tenets based, in part, on theories of development and learning.

1. Children's basic physiologic needs and their needs for physical and psychological safety must be met satisfactorily before they can experience and respond to "growth motives." [Maslow and brain-based research]

2. Children develop unevenly and not in a linear fashion as they grow toward psychosocial maturity and psychological well-being. A wide variety of factors in children's lives, as well as the manner in which they interpret their own experiences, will have a bearing on the pattern and rate of progress toward greater social and emotional maturity. [Erikson, Vygotsky, the behaviorists, maturationists]

3. Developmental crises that occur in the normal process of growing up may offer maximum opportunities for psychological growth, but these crises are also full of possibilities for regression or even negative adaptation. [Erikson]

4. Children strive for mastery over their own private inner worlds as well as for mastery of the world outside of them. [Erikson, Piaget]

5. The child's interactions with significant persons in his life play a major part in his development. [Erikson, the behaviorists, Vygotsky, and Maslow]

Developmental Research Conclusions

Results

Research, and the information it yields, must serve the needs of the practitioner to be useful. Teachers can combine researchers' systematic data with personal observations and experiences, including the significance of relationships, language and thinking, biologic factors, and special needs (see also Chapters 6, 10, and 12–14). To keep in mind the real child underneath all these theories, teachers apply developmental research to their own classroom settings. Figure 4.19 consolidates what developmental research has found and how it can be put into practical use with young children.

Moreover, it is important for both teachers and parents to know something about the latest research to

Developmental Research Tells Us:	Teachers Can:
1. Growth occurs in a sequence.	Think about the steps children will take when planning projects. Know the sequence of growth in their children's age group.
2. Children in any age group will behave similarly in certain ways.	Plan for activities in relation to age range of children. Know the characteristics of their children's age group.
3. Children grow through certain stages.	Know the stages of growth in their class. Identify to family any behavior inconsistent with general stages of development.
4. Growth occurs in four interrelated areas.	Understand that a person's work in one area can help in another. Plan for language growth, while children use their bodies.
5. Intellectual growth: Children learn through their senses. Children learn by doing; adults learn in abstract ways, while children need concrete learning. Cognitive growth occurs in four areas: perception (visual, auditory, etc.)	Have activities in looking, smelling, tasting, hearing, and touching. Realize that talking is abstract; have children touch, Provide materials and activities in matching, finding same/different, putting a picture with a sound, taste, or with a symbol.
language	Provide opportunities to find and label things, talk with grown-ups, friends, tell what it "looks like," "smells like," etc.
memory	Know that by age 3, a child can often remember 2–3 directions. Know that memory is helped by seeing, holding objects and people.
reasoning	Recognize that it is just beginning, so children judge on what they see, rather than what they reason they should see. Be sure adult explanations aid in understanding reasons. Practice finding "answers" to open-ended questions such as 'How can you tell when you are tired?"
6. Social growth: The world *is* only from the child's viewpoint. Seeing is believing.	Expect that children will know their ideas only. Be aware that the rights of others are minimal to them. Remember that if they cannot set the situation, they may not be able to talk about it.
Group play is developing.	Provide free-play sessions, with places to play socially. Understand that group play in structured situations is hard, because of "self" orientation.

Figure 4.19 ● Developmental research tests theories of growth and learning to find out about children and childhood.

Developmental Research Tells Us:

Independence increases as competence grows.

People are born not knowing when it is safe to go on.
Adult attention is very important.

Young children are not born with an internal mechanism that says "slow down."

7. Emotional growth:
Self-image is developing.

8. Physical growth:
Muscle development is not complete.
Muscles cannot stay still for long.
Large muscles are better developed than small ones.
Hand preference is being established.

A skill must be done several times before it is internalized.
Bowel and bladder control is not completely internalized.

Teachers Can:

Know that children test to see how far they can go.
Realize that children will vary from independent to dependent (both among the group, and within one child).
Understand that children will need to learn by trial and error.
Know the children individually.
Be with the child, not just with the group.
Move into a situation before children lose control.

Watch for what each person's self-image is becoming.
Give praise to enhance good feelings about oneself.
Know that giving children responsibilities helps self-image.
Talk to children at eye level. Children learn by example.
Model appropriate behavior by doing yourself what you want the children to do.

Not expect perfection, in either small- or large-muscle activity
Plan short times for children to sit.
Give lots of chances to move about, be gentle with expectations for hand work.
Watch to see how children decide their handedness.
Let children trade hands in their play.
Have available materials to be used often.
Plan projects to use the same skill over and over.
Be understanding of "accidents."
If possible, have toilet facilities available always, and keep them attractive.

Figure 4.19 ● *Continued.*

be current about issues critical to children's development. For instance, are there critical periods in child growth? Is there a special time for the development of attachment, or of certain intellectual skills, or other matters? Research has revealed that animals such as ducks will become attached to any quacking or moving object approximately 15 hours after hatching. Therefore, that time is a critical period for ducks to develop "following" behavior.

Are there parallels in child development? Clearly, the brain-based research presented here has many possibilities. It is harder to find such precise periods in human development, but many psychologists hold that looser, broader sensitive periods may exist. The period from 6 to 12 months may be a sensitive period

for the formation of attachment to parents, and the period from 18 to 60 months may be one for motor skills.

Bloom (1971) asserts that 50% of a child's intellectual capacity is attained by age 5; multiple intelligences theory might take issue with that statement.

However, other psychologists argue that children are more resilient and flexible than that, and such periods are not all that crucial. Jerome Kagan and many psychotherapists, for instance, assert that there is a potential for *plasticity* (change or growth) throughout the life span. Abused children, for instance, can recover if their environment is improved and if they have the support (therapy, remedial education, and so on) to make those changes.

We suggest that there are good reasons and research to support both positions. The entire period of early childhood is considered a kind of sensitive or critical one by many in this field. At the same time, programs such as Head Start believe in the worthiness of enrichment and intervention. Teachers use research and theory to help them make appropriate decisions in their teaching.

Decision-Making in Teaching

Knowledge of child development can help teachers in the many decisions they must make daily concerning their classrooms, the curriculum, and, most important, the children. Consistent and effective teachers have a solid foundation in learning and developmental theory. Instead of basing a decision on whim or the heat of the moment, the thoughtful teacher can use theory along with sharp observation skills to set realistic goals for each child.

Consider, for instance, how useful child development information is in the following circumstances:

15-month-old Kenya and Peter are crying and fussy this morning. The teacher pauses, then realizes that neither has been outdoors yet or eaten a snack. Scheduling regular times for active movement keeps children comfortable; knowing children's physical developmental needs (maturation theory) will help these children.

Mario and Therese, both in wheelchairs, joined the first grade class last month, but their parents report that neither wants to come to school. The teacher, recognizing their need to feel part of the class and their classmates' need to get acquainted with newcomers (sociocultural theory), pairs children in a project to design and build wheel toys for pets. By knowing the children's need for competence (Erikson) and level of cognitive thinking (Piaget), she encourages these 6-year-olds toward greater mutual understanding and social skills.

Preschoolers Jared and Panya have been arguing about who has brought the "best" toy to child care. Knowing of their egocentrism (Piaget), the teacher realizes that both are right, but that they may be unable to see this themselves. By praising each child's toy in their presence, the teacher

uses herself as a model (behavioral social learning theory) and as an example of how to behave appropriately (sociocultural theory), as she demonstrates how the two children—and their toys—can play together.

Finally, the teacher well versed in child development theory can offer this information to parents. Parents can share the intimate, in-depth view of their children while teachers offer their perspective regarding learning and growth. Together, parents and teachers can make decisions about the child on the basis of concrete, accurate information.

Conditions for Learning

Teachers also look for the best conditions for learning. Caring for children means providing for total growth, in the best possible environment. Developmental theory helps define conditions that enhance learning and from which positive learning environments are created. Research on all theories extends the knowledge of children and learning.

Coupled with practical application, both theory and research have helped all to recognize that:

1. *Learning must be real.* We teach about the children's bodies, their families, their neigborhoods, and their school. We start with who children are and expand this to include the world, in their terms. We give them the words, the ideas, the ways to question and figure things out for themselves.

2. *Learning must be rewarding.* Practice makes better, but only if it is all right to practice, to stumble and try again. We include the time to do all this, by providing an atmosphere of acceptance and of immediate feedback as to what was accomplished (even what boundary was just overstepped). Also, practice can make a good experience even better, as it reminds children in their terms of what they can do.

3. *Learning must build on children's lives.* We help connect the family to the child and the teacher. We realize that children learn about culture from family and knowledgeable members of the community, such as teachers, librarians, grocers, and the like. We know important family events and help the family support happenings at school. For children, learning goes on wherever they may be, awake and asleep. Parents can learn to value learning and help it happen for their child.

4. *Learning needs a good stage.* Healthy bodies make for alert minds, so good education means caring for children's health. This includes physical health, and emotional and mental health, too. Psychological safety and well-being are theoretical terms for the insight, availability, and awareness teachers bring to their classrooms. On the lookout for each child's successes, we prevent distractions in the way furniture is arranged, how noisy it is, how many strangers are around. Mental health is both emotional and intellectual. We try to have a variety of materials and experiences, and a flexible schedule, when someone is pursuing an idea, building a project, finishing a disagreement. As long as we care for children, we will have our hands full. With the theoretical underpinnings presented here, we have the tools with which to make our own way into the world of children and of early childhood education.

Summary

The 20th century has been called "the century of the child." Developmental and learning theories of this century form the cornerstone of our knowledge about children. What we know about how children grow, learn, and adapt to the world around them is critical in our quest for greater understanding of the people we serve. Our field is greater for the contributions of several schools of study. Erikson's theory of psychosocial development gives us insight into children's feelings and how their emotional and social lives affect their learning. The behaviorists, a distinctively American group of psychologists, demonstrate how much we can learn of human affairs by applying the methods of science. Piaget, a "giant in the nursery school" (Elkind, 1977), opens our eyes to a stage theory of growth and shows us how active children are in their own learning. Vygotsky reminds us of how values, beliefs, skills, and traditions are transmitted to the next generation within a "zone of proximal development" based on relationships with other people. Gardner suggests multiple kinds of intelligence, rather than seeing the mind as a static "black box" or empty vessel. Gesell offers us developmental norms. Maslow, a humanistic psychologist, establishes a hierarchy of needs, reminding us that the basic physical and psychological needs must be met before higher learning can take place. The brain-based research opens doors to new vistas of possibility and better teaching and learning.

In learning about these theories, we are more able to formulate our own philosophy of education. By consistently applying the insights from research and theory, we show our willingness to make a commitment to children. What we know about growth and development helps us fight for our most important resource—our children.

Review Questions

1. Match the theorist with the appropriate description:

B. F. Skinner	Multiple intelligences
Abraham Maslow	Sex differences
Jean Piaget	Attachment
Albert Bandura	Social learning
Mary Ainsworth	Zone of proximal development
Eleanor Maccoby	Psychosocial development
Erik Erikson	Behaviorism
Arnold Gesell	Developmental norms
Lev Vygotsky	Cognitive theory
Howard Gardner	Self-actualization

2. Describe Piaget's four stages of cognitive development and their implications for each childhood education.

3. Name at least three psychologists who have contributed to the knowledge of development. Describe your reaction to each.

4. Given five theories of learning and development, which one would most likely advocate large blocks of free play? An early academic program? Open-ended questioning by teachers? Regular early mealtime?

5. Who said it? Match the theorist to the relevant quotation.

Lev Vygotsky	"The first organ to make its appearance as an erotogenic zone and to make libidinal demands upon the mind is, from the time of birth onwards, the mouth."
Erik Erikson	"There are problems when caregivers have low *expectations* for children based largely upon the children's membership in a low-status cultural group, rather than on the actual abilities of the children."
Jean Piaget	"From a sense of self-control without loss of self-esteem comes a lasting sense of good will and pride; from a sense of loss of self-control and of foreign overcontrol comes a lasting propensity for doubt and shame."
Sigmund Freud	"Children acquire most of their concepts—the rules by which they live—from models who they observe in the course of daily life."
Sara Lawrence Lightfoot	"The young child's thinking manifests considerable activity that is frequently original and unpredictable. It is remarkable not only by virtue of the way it differs from adult thinking but also by virtue of what it teaches us."
Albert Bandura	"No matter how we approach the controversial problem of the relationship between thought and speech, we shall have to deal extensively with *inner speech*."

Learning Activities

1. You are a teacher in a large urban child care center. Your children arrive by 7:00, and usually stay until after 5:00 each day. What would you do first thing in the morning? Use Maslow's hierarchy of needs to justify your answer.

2. What do you think of the influence of television on children's behavior? Consider the typical cartoons that the children you know are watching. From a social learning perspective, what are they learning? What else would you have them watch?

3. You are a teacher in a middle-class suburban preschool. What do you know about your group's needs and developmental stage? What assumptions, if any, can you make about development and social class? What does their cultural background tell you about what to teach? How will you find out about what each child is ready to learn?

4. Observe children in a child care center as they say goodbye to their parents. What can your observations tell you about their attachment levels? What can teachers do to support attachment and also help children separate?

Bibliography

General Texts

Bee, H. (1997). *The developing child.* Menlo Park, CA: Addison-Wesley.

Berger, K. S. (1995). *The developing person* (4th ed.). New York: Worth.

Berk, L. (1996). *Infants, children, and adolescents.* Boston, Allyn & Bacon.

Cole, M., & Cole, S. (1993). *The development of children.* New York: Scientific American Books.

Diessner, R., Paciorek, K. M., Munro, J. H., & Schultz, F. (1995–1997). *Sources: Notable selections in human development.* Guildford, CT: Dushkin/McGraw-Hill.

Fong, B., & Resnick, M. (1986). *The child: Development through adolescence.* Palo Alto, CA: Mayfield.

Gardner, H. (1982). *Developmental psychology.* Boston: Little, Brown.

Glascott, K. (1994, Spring). A problem of theory for early childhood professionals. *Childhood Education,* pp. 190–192.

McClinton, B. S., & Meier, B. G. (1978). *Beginnings: Psychology of early childhood.* St. Louis: Mosby.

Schickendanz, J., Hansen, K., & Forsyth, P. (1993). *Understanding children.* Mountain View, CA: Mayfield.

Segal, J. (1989, July). Ten myths about child development. *Parents,* pp. 96.

Child Development and Cultural Diveristy

Caldwell, B. (1983). *Child development and cultural diversity.* Geneva, Switzerland: OMEP World Assembly.

Gura, P. (1994). Childhood: A multiple reality. *Early Childhood Development and Care, 98.*

Hilliard, A., & Vaughn-Scott, M. (1982). The quest for the 'minority' child. In S. Moore & C. Cooper (Eds.), *The young child: Review of research* (Vol. 3). Washington, DC: National Association for Education of Young Children.

Lightfoot, S. L. (1978). *Worlds apart*. New York: Basic Books.

Rodd, J. (1996). Children, culture and education. *Childhood Education*, Intenational Focus Issue.

Tatum, B. D. (1995, February). *Stages of racial/ethnic identity development in the United States*. Paper presented at the National Association for Multicultural Education, Washington, DC.

York, S. (1991). *Roots and wings: Affirming culture in early childhood programs*. St. Paul, MN: Redleaf Press.

Psychodynamic Theory

Erikson, E. H. (1963). *Childhood and society* (2nd ed.). New York: Norton.

Erikson, E. H. (1964). Toys and reasons. In M. R. Haworth (Ed.), *Child psychotherapy: Practice and theory*. New York: Basic Books.

Erikson, E. H. (1969). A healthy personality for every child. In P. H. Mussen, J. J. Conger, & J. Kagan (Eds.), *Child development and personality* (3rd ed.). New York: Harper & Row.

Evans, R. I. (1967). *Dialogue with Erik Erikson*. New York: Harper & Row.

Freud, S. (1968). *A general introduction to psychoanalysis*. New York: Washington Square Press.

Hubley, J. & Hubley, F. (1976). *Everyone rides the carousel*. Santa Monica, CA: Pyramid Films.

Myers, J. K., et al. (1984). *Archives of General Psychiatry, 41*, 259–267.

Spitz, R. A., & Wolf, K. M. (1946). Analytic depression: An inquiry into the genesis of psychiatric conditions in early childhood, II. In A. Freud, et al. (Eds.), *The psychoanalytic study of the child* (Vol. II). New York: International Universities Press.

Behaviorist Theory

Bandura, A. (1963). Imitation of film-mediated aggressive models. *Journal of Abnormal and Social Psychology*.

Bandura, A. (1986). *Social foundations of thought and action: A social cognitive theory*. New York: Prentice Hall.

Bloom, B. (Ed.). (1971). *Handbook of formative and summative evaluation of student learning*. New York: McGraw-Hill.

Bloom, B. (1973). Every kid can: *Learning for mastery*. College/University Press.

Carpenter, F. (1974). *The Skinner primer*. New York: The Free Press.

Fong, B., & Resnick, M. (1986). *The child: Development through adolescence*. Palo Alto, CA: Mayfield.

Levin, R. A. (1991, Winter). The debate over schooling: Influences of Dewey and Thorndike. *Childhood Education*.

Skinner, B. F. (1953) *Science and human behavior*. New York, NY: MacMillan Co.

Suransky, V. P. (1982, Autumn). A tyranny of experts. *Wilson Quarterly*.

Cognitive/Constructivist Theories

Castle, K., & Rogers, K. (1993/94, Winter). Rule creating in a constructivist classroom community. *Childhood Edcuation*.

Chi, M. T. (1978). Knowledge structure and memory development. In I. M. Siegler (Ed.), *Children's thinking: What develops?* Hillscale, NJ: Erlbaum.

Dasen, P. R. (Ed.). (1977). *Piagetian psychology: Cross-cultural contributions*. New York: Gardner Press (division of John Wiley).

DeVries, R., & Kohlberg, L. (1990). *Constructivist early education: An overview and comparison with other programs*. Washington, DC: National Association for Education of Young Children.

DeVries, R., & Zan, B. (1994). *Moral classrooms, moral children: Creating a constructivist atmosphere in early education*. New York: Teachers College Press.

Elkind, D. (1977). Giant in the nursery school—Jean Piaget. In E. M. Hetherington & R. D. Parke (Eds.), *Contemporary readings in psychology*. New York: McGraw-Hill.

Elkind, D., & Flavell, J. (Eds.). 1996. *Essays in honor of Jean Piaget*. New York: Oxford University Press.

Flavell, J. H., Green, F. L., and Flavell E. R. (1989). Young children's ability to differentiate appearance-reality. *Child Development, 60,* 201–213.

Forman, G. (1996). A child constructs an understanding of a water wheel in five media. *Childhood Education,* Annual Theme.

Heuwinkel, M. K. (1996, Fall). New ways of learning = new ways of teaching. *Childhood Education,* pp. 313–342.

Kohn, A. (1993). *Punished by rewards.* New York: Houghton Mifflin.

Labinowicz, E. (1980). *The Piaget primer: Thinking, learning, teaching* (pp. 41–46). Menlo Park, CA: Addison-Wesley.

Mali, G., & Howe, A. C. (1980, April). Cognitive development of Nepalese children. *Science Education, 64*(2),

Meade-Roberts, J., & Spitz, G. (1998). Under construction. Unpublished documents.

Voyat, G. (1983). *Cognitive development among the Sioux children.* New York: Plenum Press.

Sociocultural Theory

Badrava, E. (1992, November). *Vygotsky's theory.* Paper presented at seminar, National Association for the Education of Young Children, New Orleans, LA.

Hale, J. (1986). *Black children: Their roots, culture and learning styles.* Baltimore, MD: The Johns Hopkins University Press.

Ramirez, M., & Casteneda, A. (1974). *Cultural democracy, biocognitive development and education.* New York: Academic Press.

Rogoff, B. (1990). *Appreciation in thinking: Cognitive development in a social context.* New York: Oxford University Press.

Vygotsky, L. S. (1978). *Mind in society: The development of higher psychological processes.* Cambridge, MA: Harvard University Press.

Vygotsky, L. S. (1987). *Thinking and speech.* (N. Minick, Trans.). New York: Plenum Press.

Multiple Intelligences Theory

Blumenthal, R. (1995, November 19). Curriculum update for Sesame Street. *New York Times,* pp. 43–44.

Gardner, H. (1983). *Frames of mind.* New York: Basic Books.

Gardner, H. (1991). *The unschooled mind.* New York: Basic Books.

Gardner, H. (1993). *Multiple intelligences.* New York: Basic Books.

Maturation Theory

Ames, L. B., and Ilg, F. (1979). *The Gesell Institute's child from one to six. The Gesell Institute's child from five to ten,* and *The infant in today's culture.* New York: Harper & Row.

Gesell, A. (1940). *The first five years of life.* New York: Harper & Row.

Humanist Theory

Goble, F. G. (1970). *The third force: The psychology of Abraham Maslow.* New York: Grossman Publishers.

Maslow, A. H. (1954). *Motivation and personality.* New York: Harber & Row.

Maslow, A. H. (1962). *Towards a psychology of being.* New York: Van Nostrand.

Other Education Theories

Attachment

Ainsworth, M. (1979, October). Infant-mother attachment. *American Psychologist,* pp. 131–142.

Bowlby, J. (1969, 1973). *Attachment and loss* (Vols. I & II). New York: Basic Books.

Brain-Based Research

Armstrong, T. (1987). *In their own way*. Los Angeles: Jeremy Tarcher.

Caine, G., & Caine, R. (1994). *Making connections: Teaching and the human brain*. New York: Addison-Wesley.

Caine, G., & Caine, R. (1997). *Education on the edge of possibility*. Alexandria, VA: Association for Supervision and Curriculum Development.

Diamond, M., & Hopson, J. (1998). *Magic trees of the mind*. New York: Dutton.

Galinsky, E. (1997, Winter). New research on the brain development of young children. *CAEYC Connections*.

Jensen, E. (1995). *Brain-based learning and teaching*. New York, NY. Bain Store, Inc.

Neuberger, J. J. (1997, May). New brain development research—A wonderful window of opportunity to build public support for early childhood education? *Young Children, 52*, 4.

Phipps, P. A. (1998). *Applying brain research to the early childhood classroom*. New York: McGraw-Hill.

Shore, R. (1997). *Rethinking the brain: New insights into early development*. New York: Families and Work Institute.

Sex Differences

Bee, H. (Ed.). (1978). *Social issues in development psychology*. New York: Harper & Row.

Maccoby, E. (1980). *Social development*. New York: Harcourt Brace Jovanovich.

Maccoby, E. E., & Jacklin, C. N. (1974). *The development of sex differences*. Stanford, CA: Stanford University Press.

Matthews, W. S. (1979). *He and she: How children develop their sex role identity*. Englewood Cliffs, NJ: Prentice-Hall.

Tavris, C., & Offir, C. (1977). *The longest war:* Sex differences in perspective. New York: Harcourt Brace Jovanovich.

Moral Development

Buzzelli, C. A. (1992, September). Young children's moral understanding: Learning about right and wrong. *Young Children*, pp. 47–53.

Eisenberg, N., Lenon, R., and Roth, K. (1983). Prosocial development in middle childhood: A longitudinal study. *Developmental Psychology, 23*, 712–718.

Gilligan, C. (1982). *In a different voice*. Cambridge, MA: Harvard University Press.

Kohlberg, L. (1981). *The philosophy of moral development*. New York: Harper & Row.

Who Are the Teachers?

Guest Editorial WHO ARE THE TEACHERS OF THE YOUNG CHILD?

Elizabeth Jones

Teachers of 3-, 4-, and 5-year-olds are people who help children become *master players*. When children are under age 3, they are engaged primarily in sensory-motor *exploration* of the world, of things and people including themselves, and what can be done with them. When children are over 5, they are undertaking more systematic *investigation* of the rules that govern the natural and social worlds and the symbol systems human beings use to represent and communicate them. In preschool and kindergarten, children's task is the mastery of *play*. In play they are representing, through spontaneous dramatization, language, and construction, the "scripts" of their real and fantasy worlds. They are recreating the world in order to understand it for themselves.

Marina, Ruben, and Daniel are 3 years old, and they go to child care every day. They all like blocks, and so does their teacher. In her role of *stage manager,* she carefully organizes the blocks, and the cars and animal and people figures that enrich block play, just as she does all the materials in the environment, both indoors and outdoors. Observing children as they play, she continues to order and enrich the props that focus the action taking place on the children's stage.

Marina is carefully building a platform of blocks for her cars, with a ramp leading off the platform. Ruben's fast car crashes into the ramp. Marina hits Ruben. "No, no, no!" she yells. Ruben runs to the aide: "Marina hit me!"

"Marina, come over here," calls the aide. "You can't play if you can't share. Use your words. Don't just say no, no, no."

Marina tries to twist away. The aide restrains her: "When I call you, I expect an answer."

Marina frees herself and runs back to the blocks, where she continues to build.

Ruben starts to run his car down the ramp. Marina pushes the car away, and the ramp falls down. "Marina, remember what we talked about," warns the aide.

Marina runs to the teacher, who comes to see what's going on. "Marina, what do you want to tell Ruben?" she asks, with an arm around each child. "I don't like him. He's a dumb-dumb," says Marina.

"You're mad at Ruben. Can you tell him what he did to make you mad?"

"My road!" wails Marina. "He keeps messin' my road!" She tries to hit Ruben again. The teacher keeps both children safe while asking, "Ruben, what you want to do?"

"Run my car there," Ruben explains. "I gotta fast car. That's a fast hill." He smiles winningly at Marina.

"Be careful, then," Marina says sternly. He is, and soon they are building together.

In her role of *mediator*, the teacher has shown respect for both children's intent. She has asked questions to help them solve their very real problem and continue the play. The play is the important thing that's happening; problem-solving strategies need to support, not interrupt it. In contrast, reiteration of adult rules—"You can't play if you can't share"—risks destroying the play and fails to give young children useful strategies for solving either this problem or the next one that comes along.

No one is playing in the blocks. Daniel, who has been home sick for several days, tentatively approaches and takes a bus off the shelves. He doesn't seem to know what to do next. The teacher, alert to children's needs, brings over a container of tiny teddy bears as possible bus passengers. "Can I ride in your bus?" she asks in a squeaky voice, animating a red teddy bear. Daniel smiles wanly but doesn't respond.

The teacher decides to offer more ideas. She sits on the floor and quietly starts building a road of blocks. Daniel watches. When the teacher asks softly, "Toot toot, would you like to go on my road?" Daniel decides it's a good road for a bus. He drives slowly along it.

The teacher may move into the role of *player* to help get play under way or to enrich it when that seems like a good idea. She makes such decisions while observing to see what's going on. Her goal is to support the development of high-quality play—increasingly complex representation by children of their understandings of the world.

With children who have mastered play, the teacher is free to move into the role of *scribe*— someone who records information about play for her own uses as *assessor* of children's growth, *planner* of program for children, and *communicator* both to children themselves and to other adults, including parents.

Now that Marina and Ruben are building together, the teacher is free to observe them. They are building a tower. She decides to draw a picture of it; it's a fine tall tower.

Dr. Elizabeth Jones is on the faculty of Pacific Oaks College, a frequent contributor to NAEYC, and the author of The Play's the Thing *and* Teaching Adults Emergent Curriculum *among many other works.*

The Teacher's Role

CHAPTER 5

Questions for Thought

What makes the teacher's role complex?

What qualifications does a good teacher possess?

What is team teaching in early childhood?

What are the essentials for successful teaching?

How is my own personal development related to my growth as a teacher?

What is a professional code of ethics, and why should we have one?

What are some of the common problems associated with beginning teaching, and how can I avoid them?

What does it mean to be a member of the teaching profession?

How can teachers be culturally competent?

WHO ARE THE TEACHERS OF THE YOUNG CHILD?

Margarita had always wanted to be an early childhood teacher. Right after high school she went to a community college and earned her AA degree. Shortly after her first child was born, she became a licensed family child care provider and cares for infants and toddlers in her own home. It is important to Margarita that she feels she is making a contribution to the family's well-being as well as enjoying a satisfying career. She plans to pursue her BA degree in the evenings when her children are older.

Paul recently spent several years teaching in a school for emotionally disturbed children. He has been a lead teacher for 4-year-olds at the child care center for 2 years, gaining experience with children whose developmental patterns are typical. Paul wants to remain a teacher but is concerned about the salary levels. He has given himself one more year before he will make a decision.

Kendra's four children were in parent cooperative nursery schools, where she enjoyed the companionship of so many other parents of young children. After a few years of teaching elementary school, she is now director of a parent co-op and teaches children from ages 2 to 5. She particularly enjoys leading weekly parent discussion groups.

Elva was the most sought after parent-aide in the school after she began helping out when her two boys were ages 4 and 5. This success stimulated her to get an AA degree in early childhood education, then a Bachelor's degree in child development. She is now a kindergarten teacher in a bilingual program.

Although, all of these people had different motivations, they all were drawn to the early childhood classroom. They may teach in different settings, have different educational backgrounds and skills, yet they do share common everyday experiences of the teacher of young children. They plan, observe, listen, help, learn, play, console, discipline, confer, comfort, and teach the children and adults who make up their particular world of early childhood.

Teacher Diversity

The National Child Care Staffing Study (Whitebook, Howes, & Phillips, 1990) gives a glimpse of the diversity among teachers and caregivers in early childhood settings. A survey of nearly 230 child care centers in five different cities compared demographics with a study made 10 years previously in which few changes were noted. In 1988, the following picture emerged:

● 97% of the teachers were women

● 81% were over 40 years of age

● 50% were single

● 33% were members of minority groups

The percentage of minority teachers was usually higher than the percentage of minorities in the community at large. Ethnicity also played a role in the level of education and the staff position. White and African American teachers and caregivers were more likely to hold teacher or teacher/director positions compared with other minorities. African American teachers more than likely received their early childhood training in vocational schools rather than in college; other minorities tended to receive their training at the college level. The study also noted that many child care teachers, particularly lower paid assistant teachers and aides were members of minorities (Whitebook, Howes, & Phillips, 1990).[1]

Comparison with Teaching in Other Educational Settings

The nature of teaching in the early years is unlike that of other age groups. At first glance, the differences in teaching preschool and older children may outweigh any similarities. There are some common elements, however, that link the two. Early childhood teachers teach what other teachers teach. The curriculum in the early years is rich in math, science, social studies,

OUR DIVERSE WORLD OUR DIVERSE WORLD OUR DIVERSE WORLD OUR DIVERSE WORLD OUR DIVERSE WORLD OUR DIVERSE WORLD OUR DIVERSE WORLD OUR DIVERSE WORLD

[1] We must continue to collect and use ethnic data on children and teachers in early childhood programs to ensure that we continually address equity and justice issues in the early childhood field.

history, language, art, and geography, as it is in any other grade. Early childhood teachers and their elementary and high school counterparts share many of the frustrations of the teaching profession—long hours, low pay, and a people-intensive workplace. They also share the joy of teaching—the opportunity to influence children's lives and the satisfaction of meeting the daily challenges that teaching children provides. Figure 5.1 highlights the similarities and differences between early childhood teachers and others.

THE TEACHER'S ROLE

Definitions

Over the years the teacher's role in the early childhood classroom has been defined in many ways. Two 30-year-old descriptions are still valid today when defining the innumerable variety of tasks teachers perform. Spodek (1972) noted that the teacher is part lecturer, storyteller, traffic director, conflict mediator, psychological diagnostician, custodian, and file clerk. Stanton (Beyer, 1968), a pioneer early childhood teacher, added plumber, carpenter, poet, and musician to the list, as well as degrees and training in psychology, medicine, and sociology. "Now, at 83, she's ready!" said Stanton.

This diversity is exactly what makes teaching in the early years so appealing. The multiple roles a teacher plays add challenge to the job. Nor are these descriptions exhaustive; the list could include adult educator, parent resource, faculty member, chief purchasing agent, nurse, program planner, staff supervisor, business manager, treasurer, personnel director, employee, and employer. (The role of the teacher in relationship to parents and programs as a whole will be further discussed in Chapters 8 and 10, respectively.)

Two prominent early childhood teacher educators reinforce the value of having teachers who have a theoretical and historical grounding. Jones (1994) tells us that teachers, like young children, are constructivists. The complexity and unpredictability of teaching, she says, call for on-the-spot decisions, and those decisions are based on developmental and learning theory and constructed from the teacher's own experience and practice. Spodek (1994) calls for teachers to know the

history and traditions of the field along with theory but also stresses the need to know "the cultural, social and political contexts in which early childhood education functions."

Teaching is defined as those daily "acts of creation" (Phillips, 1994) that are constructed from the teacher's own repertoire of skills, knowledge, and training, added to what he or she observes about children and his or her interactions with their families. The teacher as a collaborator is a significant part of the teacher's role definition in the schools of Reggio Emilia, Italy (see Chapter 11). Collaboration reinforces the notion underlying many definitions that teachers are, first and foremost, lifelong teachers.

Perhaps the job would seem more manageable and less overwhelming to the new teacher if some of the responsibilities were categorized. What teachers do with children is not all there is to teaching. Much of the work occurs outside the classroom. It is helpful to look at the teacher's role in another way. What are the things a teacher does with children? What are the things a teacher does after the children go home? How does the teacher interact with other adults in the early childhood setting?

In the Classroom

Interacting with Children

It is no secret that most teachers find their greatest satisfaction and challenges in the first role—who and what they are with children. The teacher–child interactions, the spur-of-the-moment crises, the intense activity, the on-the-spot decisions, the loving and nurturing, go far in making one "feel" like a real teacher. Helping Rhonda get a good grip on the hammer, soothing Josh and Benno after they bump heads, and talking with Alexa about her drawing are at the heart of teaching young children. These encounters are enjoyable and provide moments for interactive teaching opportunities.[1] These times help establish good relationships with the children. It is during these spontaneous, anything-can-happen-and-probably-will times that teachers display their craftsmanship. The real art of teaching comes on the floor of the classroom. All teaching skills are called on. Responses are automatic and sometimes unplanned. Teachers intu-

[1] Teaching about the rich diversity that makes up our world can be an integral and spontaneous response when interacting with children.

Elements of Teaching and Learning	Early Childhood Settings	Elementary and High School Settings
How teaching and learning occur	Through teacher–child interactions and concrete use of materials	Through lectures and demonstrations that are teacher dominated
	Guides children toward discovery	Teaches subject matter
Play opportunities	Primary learning medium is play	Usually just at recess
Opportunity for child to make choices	Many choices throughout the day both inside and out	Few options—students do same activity most of the day
Classroom environment	Abundant floor space, many activity centers, variety of materials	Rows of desks and tables
Daily schedule	Large blocks of time for unlimited exploration of materials and for play	45-minute to 1-hour periods on subject matter
Small group interactions	Majority of teaching	Much less frequent
Outdoor activity	Teachers involved as intensively as they are in the classroom	Others usually supervise play yard—little direct teacher interaction
Parents relationships	Frequent, if not daily, contact	May see them once a year
Working with other adults	Often works with aide, assistant teachers, and parents	Usually teaches alone
Educational materials	Toys, games, natural materials, blocks	Textbooks and worksheets
Evaluating students	Observational and anecdotal assessments	Grades, tests, and report cards
	Emphasis on growth of whole child	Standardized academic assessment
Age range of students	May have 2–2½ year age span or greater	Usually same age
Art, music, and physical education	Available throughout the day as an ongoing part of curriculum	Restricted to a special class, time, or teacher
Teacher training	Strong child development foundation	Emphasis on subject matter

Figure 5.1 ● The nature of teaching in the early years is unlike that of other age groups.

itively use their knowledge base, their experience, and their proven techniques. Almost unconsciously, they reach back in their minds for all those things they know about children. Throughout the school day they apply that combination of knowledge and know-how.

The creative genius of a teacher is in the ability to find ways to interact with each child according to that child's needs, to stretch an attention span, motivate a child to persist at a task, or provide opportunity to experiment with materials, actively and autonomously (Honig, 1979).

Managing the Classroom

A teacher spends a lot of time being a classroom manager. Being a successful manager is a little like being a successful juggler. Both require the ability to think about and react to more than three things at once. With a simple gesture, a significant look, or merely moving nearby, the teacher maintains the ongoing activity.

Anticipating a clash between Nathan and Julie, the teacher Miriam intervenes, redirects them, and

Figure 5.2 ● Teachers model learning, listening, and loving.

moves away. At the same time she has kept a watchful eye on Bobby at the bathroom sink. Passing close to Francie, she touches the child's shoulder in brief acknowledgment, smiling down as Francie struggles with the doll's dress. Miguel and Lea run up to her, grab her by the skirt and hand, and pull her toward the science display. They need to ask her something about the snake. . . . NOW! Jake, the handyman, has come into the classroom wanting to know exactly which of the climbers needs repair. Sarah, the parent volunteer, waves to her; it's time to check on the corn bread baking in the kitchen. Quickly, the teacher files a mental note of the names of the children who accompany Sarah to the kitchen. As she reaches for a copy of *Ranger Rick* (the one with the great snake pictures in it), she observes Angie and her father entering the room. They both look upset. Telling Miguel and Lea she will return, the teacher walks over to greet the latecomers. As she moves past Doug, the student teacher, she comments on how well his language game is going and suggests he continue for another five minutes. Glancing at the clock, she

realizes it is almost cleanup time. Her assistant, Chuck, watches her. She looks his way, and a non-verbal signal passes between them. Without a word, they both understand that snacks will be a little late today. Angie's father begins to explain their delay as the teacher bends down to invite the child to come and look at the new snake cage with her.

In this setting, the teacher has a major role in supervising a number of people. Aides and volunteers, student teachers, and visitors add to the richness of a program. But it is the teacher who coordinates and supervises their various functions. From the description, it is clear that the teacher's role as a supervisor and manager includes being:

● Caretaker for a safe environment

● Observer of and listener to children

● On-the-spot teacher trainer for students, aides, and volunteers

● On-site supervisor for student teachers

● A liaison and communicator with parents

Setting the Tone

Teachers, obviously, are at the center of activity. Directly or indirectly they control much of the action. Because teachers are responsible for what occurs in the classroom, they must have a finger on its pulse at all times. As part of the juggling act, the teacher takes the pulse while moving around the class or yard. But something else happens. Throughout the day, from the moment of arrival, the teacher puts into effect another vital element. The teacher sets the tone, creating an atmosphere in which teachers and children will work and play. The skill with which it is done can make the critical difference between a classroom that is alive and supportive and one that is chaotic or apathetic. Because personality has such impact in the early childhood setting, the teacher creates more than an environmental mood, does more than provide the setting and the learning activities.

The teacher establishes what will be the **emotional framework**. This is done with body movements, by the tone of voice, facial expressions or lack of them, and nonverbal as well as verbal gestures. The way the children respond reflects this tone.

This interaction between the atmosphere the teacher creates and the child's behavior sets the tone. Young children are very sensitive to adult moods and attitudes. The teacher who is upset or angry invites the children to react with their own tense brand of activity. A teacher who exudes calm and confidence, strength and support, will inspire a more relaxed, comfortable atmosphere in which children can learn and grow. If the teacher is punitive and harsh, the tone of the classroom will reflect that. On the other hand, if teachers act on their beliefs that children deserve respect and are intelligent, capable human beings, they will create an entirely different climate. And the children will respond in kind.

Normal behavior for the young child includes tantrums, crying, resistance, curiosity, impatience, emotional swings, noise, and self-centeredness. This is the time to achieve a sense of their own separate self. They need a place to work through the developmental stages that their needs and nature indicate. The atmosphere that a teacher creates is a key element in that process.

The way teachers handle fights, react to tears, the words they use, and the voices raised communicate a direct message to the child. The understanding, the soothing, the warmth, the acceptance, create a climate where children feel safe, secure, and guided. This requires teachers who respect childhood, the individuality of children, their growing patterns, their emerging feelings, and their special capacity to learn. Today we would also stress the need for teachers to become culturally competent: to accept and understand cultural differences, having a working knowledge of the cultural backgrounds of the children in the class, and appreciate that this may be the children's first experience outside their own culture.[1] The end result is that preschoolers will thrive in an atmosphere influenced by teachers who understand this time of tension and growth in their lives.

It is never too early to help children understand the rich diversity that makes up our world. Stacey York's Focus Box discusses strategies for setting the right tone for multiculturalism in early childhood settings.

Planning and Evaluating the Curriculum

As teachers move through the school day interacting with children, managing the classroom, sensing the tone, they consciously or unconsciously evaluate what is happening:

- The relay race outdoors produced more tears than cheers; most of the children were interested in participating when the game started but drifted away. Why?

- The Cuisenaire rods were never touched today. How can we make this a more inviting activity?

- The toddlers are beginning to participate fully in the "Eensy Weensy Spider" fingerplay. What might they like to learn next?

- Several children have asked why Miguel "talks funny." When would be a good time to talk about his language and teach the class a few words in Spanish?"[2]

The teacher notes where and how children played, the quality of their interactions, and possible "next steps" in curriculum. These notes are then discussed with other staff members at the end of the day or in weekly planning sessions.

Effective ways to develop curriculum planning are discussed in Chapter 11. It is important to note here, in discussing the role of the teacher, that the process has its roots in what the teacher sees happening in the classroom as children play and learn. It is constructivist theory in action: teachers watching and observing children to give meaning and support to their learning. Early childhood teachers use their observation skills, collect data as they work with children, and build curriculum around their knowledge of actual classroom practice and behavior.

Outside the Classroom

Certain after-hours tasks are a part of any total teaching effort. This part of the job may not be as gratifying as working directly with children, yet teachers must understand why it is important.

 OUR DIVERSE WORLD OUR DIVERSE WORLD OUR DIVERSE WORLD OUR DIVERSE WORLD OUR DIVERSE WORLD OUR DIVERSE WORLD OUR DIVERSE WORLD OUR DIVERSE WORLD OUR DIVERSE WORLD

[1] Emotional support is evident when children see that their family culture is valued.
[2] A goal of every early childhood program should be to foster positive attitudes and awareness of cultural differences.

Loving Children Isn't Enough: Putting Culture at the Core

Stacey York

Each fall, I ask our new students why they want to teach young children. The most common response is, "I love children." Ask a teacher why he or she stays in the field, despite the mediocre wages and poor working conditions, and we are likely to get the answer, "Because I love children."

A few years ago, I was discussing the teacher's role in culturally relevant education with a colleague. She caught me off guard when she said, "You know, loving children isn't enough." I've often thought about that statement and I've come to agree. Loving children isn't enough in a culturally diverse classroom.

Why not, you ask? Let me share a gardening analogy. A lot of people love flowers. Each spring, many of us make enthusiastic, yet ignorant, purchases of bedding plants and shrubs. We take our selections home and plop them into the ground. We hope the plants will like it in our yards. Too often they struggle, limp along, and some die. We shrug our shoulders and walk away, only to try the same thing again next year. A more responsible approach would recognize that every yard provides a certain type of growing environment and plants have different cultural requirements.

There are many things to consider regarding plant culture. There are different types of plants such as annuals, perennials, herbs, vines, shrubs, conifers, deciduous trees, bulbs, and ground covers. Plants have two names: a common and a botanical name. Plants have specific growing requirements that include the soil pH level, among of light, preferred soil type,

amount of water, feeding, and pruning requirements. Loving plants isn't enough. A successful gardener considers both the yard's culture and the plant's culture and either chooses to grow those plants that are consistent with what our yard offers or changes the conditions in the yard to provide a more hospitable environment for a variety of plants.

In a similar fashion, children have a home culture. Each one is growing up with a specific set of culturally specific values, beliefs, and traditions supported by their families and cultural communities. As teachers, we must recognize culture because it affects the parent–teacher relationship, teacher–child relationship, child–child relationship, children's learning style, children's communication style, children's expectations of adults, children's diet and mealtime behavior, children's sleep routines, and children's toileting habits.

Children's home culture may be very similar to or different from the culture of the early childhood classroom. Typically, classrooms project European American values, beliefs, and behaviors. For instance, individualism is promoted through separate cubbies and show and tell. Teaching self-help skills encourages independence and self-responsibility. Teachers want children to feed themselves, toilet themselves, separate from parents, and refrain from clinging or whining behavior. Children learn productivity and a strong work ethic through involvement in activities and staying on task. Wandering and onlooking are discouraged. Inviting children to choose their own activities and arranging the classroom so that children can help themselves encourages initiative and self-sufficiency. Messy play, messy art, and minimal use of adult demonstration foster ingenuity. Equality is fostered through practices that encourage boys and girls to play in all areas and to clean up in equal measure. Informal communication is practiced by encouraging children to call teachers by their first name. Direct and assertive communication is taught through common phrases like, "Use your words," "Tell him you don't like it when he hits you," and "Look at me when I talk to you." Freedom is celebrated by having children choose from a variety of activity options.

What happens to the child in our classroom whose family and home culture value interdependence? Collective responsibility? Interpersonal relations? Group rather than individual identity? Formal communication? Specific gender roles? How do we reach children from cultures other than our own, so that, like the gardener, we provide an environment that fosters the growth, development, and full potential of all the children in our classrooms?

Begin by developing dispositions and skills of a culturally competent teacher. Become aware of yourself as a cultural being, and learn about the historical social/political experience of diverse cultures in American history. Be flexible and open to change and new ideas. Decenter and take another perspective. Develop cross-cultural communication skills and a wide variety of teaching methods. Finally, be willing to learn about and from others.

An early childhood teacher who taught in a culturally diverse program avoided workshops on culturally relevant education. She had heard it all before and didn't feel the need for training in cultural diversity. After all, children are all the same and she loved children. At the same time, this teacher was preparing to purchase a new puppy. She went to the library and read all sorts of books about dogs. During her lunch break, she'd sit in the staff lounge reading about all the different breeds, trying to figure out which one's personality, size, activity level best matched her personality and lifestyle. She was willing to read and learn about dogs but she was not willing to learn about the home culture of the children in her classroom. She valued dogs more than her community's children. Loving children is not enough when culture is at the core.

Stacey York is an instructor of early childhood education at Minneapolis Community and Technical College and the author of Roots and Wings: Affirming Culture in Early Childhood Programs *(St. Paul, MN: Redleaf Press, 1991).*

Figure 5.3 ● The teacher determines the quality of the child's school experience by providing a supportive atmosphere in which children can learn.

A good classroom is often dependent on how teachers spend their time away from the children. Many of the tasks that give added strength and depth to a teacher's curriculum are those that, out of necessity, must be accomplished after hours. The two most obvious jobs that fall into this category are record keeping and meetings.

Record Keeping

Preschool teachers keep records on a variety of subjects; the type and kind will vary from school to school. The philosophy of the school, the number of children, the background of the teaching staff, and the purpose for the records will determine the amount the teachers will write. In schools that rely on government funding, record keeping is not optional. The children's progress, the teacher's performance, the program itself, must be evaluated on a regular basis. The data collected will be used to justify the continuation of the program; thus, the paperwork becomes critical to survival. Documentation is critical for

accreditation of early childhood programs. For years, CDA (Child Development Associates) candidates submitted a written portfolio of their experiences in the classroom as supportive evidence of their competency as teachers of young children. Laboratory schools, teacher training centers, and other programs consider periodic developmental reports on the children as a natural part of teaching; they guide the teacher in more objective ways than casual observations.

Although report writing and record keeping may be considered time-consuming, they are essential to any good early childhood program. The ultimate reason for collecting data is to give a more complete and up-to-date picture of each child. Recorded observations, notes, and similar data collected over a 6-month period, for instance, may show that Abraham is not participating in any strenuous physical activity and studiously avoids activities that involve balancing and climbing. This information could lead to a medical evaluation and diagnosis of possible perceptual motor problems.[1] Once teachers understand the importance

OUR DIVERSE WORLD OUR DIVERSE WORLD OUR DIVERSE WORLD OUR DIVERSE WORLD OUR DIVERSE WORLD OUR DIVERSE WORLD OUR DIVERSE WORLD OUR DIVERSE WORLD

[1] Early childhood teachers are in a unique position to support early identification, prevention, and treatment of developmental problems.

and value of ongoing records, they set about the task readily.

Children's progress reports demonstrate a school's commitment to good child development practices. Teachers see them as a means for parent education and information. Curriculum plans and learning activities sprout from such reports and records. It wasn't until such data were collected for entry into first grade that the kindergarten teachers realized most of the children were not sufficiently skilled with the scissors. They were able to plan curriculum experiences around this need and provide an opportunity for the classes to learn a necessary task.

Teachers also find that the social-emotional growth recorded periodically provides information from which insight and interpretation can develop. It may be just a brief note taken on the run, a thoughtful anecdote written at length after class, or a checklist of the child's favorite activities. All of these serve to give teachers a greater understanding of the role they play. If maintaining reports after school hours support that role, they accept the job willingly.

Meetings

Meetings are probably the most time-consuming of all out-of-class jobs. The teacher may need to communicate with the other people who are involved in the lives of the children, directly or indirectly. Parents, other teachers, baby-sitters, doctors, and social workers are some of the people with whom a teacher may want to confer. Teachers attend many different kinds of meetings. Figure 5.5 lists the most common.

Other Responsibilities

Some of a teacher's after-hours activities are intended to fortify and vitalize the classroom. Therefore, teachers:

● *Organize and collect materials* for use in class. They might collect space shuttle books from the library, find out if the bagel factory will allow field trips, or cut 18 pumpkin shapes while watching television. Teachers are also responsible for maintaining an

Figure 5.4 ● In addition to working with children, teachers support parents when they keep in touch. A brief, friendly phone call can make a family feel included in their child's education process.

Staff Meetings

Held usually once a week for individual teaching teams. Purpose is to plan curriculum, set goals, and discuss children's progress. Faculty meetings for all school personnel may be held less frequently.

Parent–Teacher Conferences

May be offered on a scheduled basis or they may be called by either parents or teachers as needed. Each school defines its own policy as to the number and frequency of parent contacts.

Parent Education Meetings

Many schools offer evening programs for parents. Teacher attendance may or may not be required.

Professional Meetings

Attendance at workshops, seminars, in-service training. Local, state, and national conferences are sponsored by the National Association for the Education of Young Children, Association for Childhood Education International, and Child Care Coordinating Council.

Student–Teacher Conferences

In schools used as training sites, teachers arrange time with individual students assigned to their classes.

Home Visits[1]

May or may not be optional. Some schools schedule them before opening day. Otherwise teachers must arrange them on their own time.

Figure 5.5 ● Teachers attend many different types of meetings, which help them create better programs, learn more about children, and learn how to become better teachers.

orderly classroom. They might add pictures to the bulletin board, obtain new books and records, or replenish curriculum materials.

● *Purchase materials and equipment* that cannot be ordered. They know that the kitchen needs new mixing bowls, the supply room is low on red construction paper, and someone has to pick up fabric for pillow covers.

● *Make phone calls.* This is a quick and efficient way of keeping in touch. Teachers may call parents to check on children who are sick or absent. For children with special needs, teachers may need to contact doctors, therapists, and other specialists.

● *Work with parents* on multicultural issues, organizing class fairs or school fund-raising events, or hold quick telephone conferences to update parents about a child's progress.[2] Further examples can be found in Chapter 8.

● *Attend professional conferences and workshops* and visit and observe other school settings. This type of ongoing professional education helps teachers keep abreast of the field.

● *Attend in-service training events* or study for an advanced degree in an area related to early childhood education.

These duties are a part of the job of teaching young children but many will be shared with other teachers on the team or at the school. Though time-consuming, these responsibilities add to the creativity and care that teachers express for their classes.

OUR DIVERSE WORLD OUR DIVERSE WORLD OUR DIVERSE WORLD OUR DIVERSE WORLD OUR DIVERSE WORLD OUR DIVERSE WORLD OUR DIVERSE WORLD OUR DIVERSE WORLD

1 Many parents welcome a teacher's visit. Others may fear criticism or judgment about their home environment or family practices.
2 Teachers are in a unique position to strengthen the bond between a child's school experience and family culture.

THE TEACHER AS A PERSON

Personal Qualities

A teacher's personality has influence and impact. When a teacher exhibits a sense of trust, security, and support, the children echo those feelings and behaviors. Children learn to trust by being trusted; they learn respect by being respected. Children learn to understand others by being understood themselves. They learn responsibility by being treated as responsible human beings. The personal qualities of their teachers should include traits that foster those learnings.

Good teachers should have dedication, compassion, insight, flexibility, patience, energy, and self-confidence. Teachers should also be happy people who can laugh and use their sense of humor wisely. Liking children is part of wanting to work with them; teachers then feel that the job they are doing is important. Teachers need to be fair-minded, showing concern for all, regardless of color or creed. Physical and mental well-being are important, as is a demonstrated sense of responsibility and reliability. Teachers who can be both warm and loving, yet firm when expressing disapproval, have good teaching qualities.

Today, the well-rounded teacher, while maintaining a professional commitment, has other interests as well. Good teachers have an involvement with the world outside the walls of the child care center. They want to help children understand some of the real-life issues and concerns. They know that their interest in the world at large transmits itself to children.

Quality teachers personalize teaching, integrating their individuality into their work in appropriate ways. By exposing the human qualities they possess, teachers strength the bond between themselves and the children.

This basic description is a framework, a checklist of personal attributes, a place to begin to look at the human side of teaching. Men and women who are able to nurture and comfort children treat them as real persons and value them as children. Expressing this takes practice so that teachers do not intrude on children's well-being. Teachers do not have to sentimentalize childhood or tolerate misbehavior because it is "cute." Children deserve teachers who understand their nature and respect the limits of behavior.

The best teachers are the ones who are struggling to become more than they are, on any given day, and who demonstrate to their students that this quest to learn and to grow, to accept failure and go on to new challenges, is what life is all about (LeShan, 1992).

Self-Awareness

To be the best teacher possible, understanding and accepting oneself is vital. **Self-awareness** will make a difference in the way teachers relate to children. Each teacher must ask, "Who and what and why am I? And how does knowing this bring some meaning into my life? How does it affect my life as a teacher?"

Teachers may also begin to realize something about themselves. They know how and why children learn as they do, but they may not know about themselves as learners. Teachers communicate an authentic appreciation of learning when they have a sense of it in their own lives. Teachers might well ask themselves: "Do I see myself as a learner? Where does my learning take place? How? What happens to me when something is hard or when I make a mistake? Do I learn from other teachers? Do I learn from children?" Teachers' recognition of themselves as learning, growing persons gives an added degree of sincerity to teaching.

Asking—and then answering—these questions helps teachers gain insights into their own behavior as adults and as professionals who work with children. In perceiving themselves as learners, for instance, they might see a similarity between their own learning style and that of some of the children in the class. Pausing to look at their own behavior when faced with a difficult task or in handling a mistake helps teachers remember what children experience each day. Opening themselves up to the possibility of learning from students stretches teachers' capacity to grow into relationships with children based on mutual respect and trust. This is especially important when teachers do not share the same cultural background or have no experience with a particular disability.[1] Opening themselves to learning from other teachers creates a foundation for mutual support, collegiality, professional mind-stretching, and

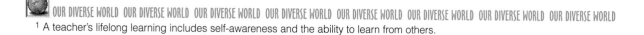
[1] A teacher's lifelong learning includes self-awareness and the ability to learn from others.

deepening of friendships. The first step is self-aware-ness; the second step is self-acceptance. Adults who work with young children weave these insights into what they are learning about children. They also adopt these insights into their relationships with parents and other staff members. When teachers take the time to look at their own style of behavior and how it affects others, they place themselves on a par with children as learning, growing people.

Self-knowledge—examining values and personal qualities—takes courage and a willingness to risk one-self. Children, other teachers, and parents will respond. Accepting oneself is where to begin in accepting children.

Attitudes and Biases

Knowingly as well as unintentionally, a teacher's values and attitudes weave their way into relationships with children, parents, and other staff members. This can be both positive and negative. One way it can be harmful is in the area of **prejudice**. Personal beliefs concerning race, culture, gender, handicaps, and eco-nomic status may negatively affect our teaching in ways of which we are not aware.[1] Facing prejudices about children and parents based on long-held beliefs may be one of the most difficult things for a teacher to do. Personal histories are filled with biases. Most teachers will not have lived through the significant and powerful experience of adapting to a new culture, or learning a new language, or surviving on food stamps and aid to dependent children, or living in a wheelchair; therefore, they may be uncomfortable with people who are labeled "different" because they have faced these issues.

Teachers have opinions, born of their own experi-ences, of what is "good" or "naughty" behavior (at least what their family thinks of as such). They also feel strongly about how parents should treat their children. Children who are messy, who have odors, whose clothes are too big or too small, who eat strange food, who don't do what girls or boys are supposed to do, bother some teachers. Some of these biases can be

Figure 5.6 ● A positive self-concept and a willingness to be open to new experiences are hallmarks of a good teacher of young children.

resolved, but only if a teacher takes the time to exam-ine personal beliefs and biases.

Anti-Bias Movement

There is a great deal of emphasis today on what is termed the "**anti-bias** approach"[2] to teaching young children. (See sections in Chapter 9, Chapter 11, and Chapter 15 for further discussion as well as Louise Derman-Sparks's Guest Editorial). This concerns stems from several issues: (1) significant changes in the ethnic makeup in the United States, especially in the last decade; (2) widespread racial and ethnic preju-dice still prevalent in this country (Armstrong, 1991); and (3) concern on the part of early childhood educa-tors of the harm being done to children's self-identity and self-esteem. This important movement promotes the concept that all children are born equal and are

OUR DIVERSE WORLD OUR DIVERSE WORLD OUR DIVERSE WORLD OUR DIVERSE WORLD OUR DIVERSE WORLD OUR DIVERSE WORLD OUR DIVERSE WORLD OUR DIVERSE WORLD

[1] Patricia Ramsey in her book *Teaching and Learning in a Diverse World* (1987) provides a format for the start of a thorough self-investigation of individual attitudes and biases.

[2] All early childhood programs should be examined for discrimination, bias, and ethnocentrism so that children can develop a positive self-identity.

Figure 5.7 ● Teachers' values and attitudes are reflected in the way they work with children.

worthy of our respect; it challenges teachers to examine beliefs, attitudes, and actions that might deny any child that unconditional respect. Some teachers may be forced into further soul searching and reflection before they can untangle their anxiety and attitudes about their prejudices. Our feelings show in our contacts with children, and we do not want those feelings to damage their self-acceptance and self-appreciation or to pass on biases to other children. The question is not one of liking or disliking any child, it is one of teacher understanding and acceptance. By achieving that level of acceptance, teachers are better able to accept all the children with whom they work, regardless of their "likeability."

The anti-bias approach affords teachers a tremendous opportunity to: confront their own anxieties and biases; work with parents of various religious and ethnic minority groups and learn some of their cultural norms and practices; work with parents of children with disabilities and learn more about how to improve each child's school experience; enrich the curriculum; represent accurately the broad ethnic makeup of this nation; influence the development of attitudes and values of young children toward the reality of the human condition; prevent irreparable harm to children's concept of themselves; and promote greater global understanding.

As a way to begin, teachers might ask themselves a few questions:

● Am I aware of my own identity and its influences on my beliefs and behaviors?

● Do I truly foster a respect for the value of those who are somehow different from me? How?

● Do I examine my biases and look at ways I can change my own attitudes? When? How?

● Do I show a preference for children who most closely fit my own ethnic, cultural, and religious background? When? How?

● Do I somehow pass along my biases to the children I teach? When? How? With whom?

● Do I truly enjoy differences in human beings? When? With whom?

Kuster (1994) suggests five critical issues for teachers who work with children and families who speak languages other than English. First and foremost, fluency in the child's language is critical to effective communication and to maximizing the child's learning experiences. A second concern is to focus on the family's competency and learn to value the family's child-rearing practices. A third point stresses a teacher's ability to preserve and enhance families' culture by learning and valuing their own first. Using the Latino culture's strong sense of family bonds,[1] Kuster's fourth point promotes the use of multiage grouping of children to foster social responsibility. The last is to confront one's own personal attitudes and biases.[2]

Teacher Burnout

Teacher burnout is an occupational hazard of substantial proportion and often results when a teacher is faced with a demanding workload, uncertain or inadequate rewards, and other pressures that damage work effectiveness. At its most extreme, teacher burnout can drive a good professional out of the field altogether, a common situation in early childhood settings and one that creates *one of the highest occupational turnover rates in the nation.*

 OUR DIVERSE WORLD OUR DIVERSE WORLD OUR DIVERSE WORLD OUR DIVERSE WORLD OUR DIVERSE WORLD OUR DIVERSE WORLD OUR DIVERSE WORLD OUR DIVERSE WORLD

[1] This may be a developmentally appropriate practice that complements many diverse cultural traditions.
[2] Teachers may need to learn new skills to effectively enhance a child's sense of self.

Burnout, according to Dresden and Myers (1989), "does not result from what we do or when we do it so much as it comes from a *sense of not being able to make a visible impact* . . . on children, . . . parents, . . . (other) teachers . . . in the working setting . . . or in society." This results in low morale, stress, and disillusionment in a profession where staff quality is the most important single factor in program quality. A school climate where open communication, trust, satisfying interpersonal relations, and clarity of roles and responsibilities exist helps create a positive atmosphere where burnout is less likely to occur (Jorde-Bloom, 1988a). In such a climate, where teachers can meet children's needs and program goals can be more effectively addressed, feelings of job satisfaction and productivity will prevail.

Recent search suggests a number of characteristics that produce healthy, happy, and positive school climates:

● Friendly, supportive, and trusting staff relationships

● Emphasis on personal and professional growth

● Leadership with clear expectations that encourages and supports staff

● Clearly defined roles and policies

● Fairness and equity regarding promotions, raises, and other rewards

● Staff involved in decision-making

● Agreement among staff on goals and objectives

● Emphasis on efficiency and good planning

● An equipped and cared-for physical environment to work in

● The ability to adapt to change (Jorde-Bloom, 1988b)

It is the responsibility of all the teachers on the staff to work together to create the kind of climate that enhances success and satisfaction in the workplace. Elsewhere in this text (Chapters 10 and 15) are related discussions.

BECOMING A TEACHER

A Collaborative Effort

The heart of teaching is, of course, what happens when you begin to work in a classroom every day. The teaching role is not restricted to working with children, though. Numerous adults must be met, tolerated, worked with, and included in the total teaching picture. Some of these people may be:

● Other professional teachers, aides, and student teachers

● Volunteers

● Program directors and administrators

● School support personnel; clerical and janitorial staffs, food service workers, bus drivers

● Parents

● Consultants and specialists

The majority of these interactions will be with other teachers, and these relationships are among the most important a teacher can have.

The beginning teacher may join a team of teachers or may teach in a small class alone. This will depend on many factors, including the age level of the children, licensing or accrediting requirements, the size of the classroom, and the school's philosophy and practices. In infant programs, for instance, there is a higher ratio of adults per child (NAEYC suggests as optimal a ratio of 1:4), so it is more likely there will be several teachers in one classroom. Together they will shape, direct, and participate in that program as a team of teachers. The team approach is common in many nursery schools and child care centers where larger groups of children attend. Kindergarten, first, and second grade teachers generally teach alone in self-contained classrooms, sometimes with an aide. In extended-day, after-school programs, high school and college students may make up the rest of the team.

Most teams of teachers are composed of people with varying skills, experience, and training. A typical group will have a lead or head teacher—someone who is trained in child development or early childhood education. Assistants with less experience and training add support. Student teachers, interns, and volunteers may round out the group. A resource teacher—someone who specializes in art, music, or physical development, for instance—may also be available on a part-time basis.

Many stage regulations mandate a minimum number of adults in the early childhood setting, and this minimum varies with the ages of the children. The prescribed ratio of adult to children changes as the children mature and become able to function in more independent ways.

There are many reasons why teaching in teams is such an integral part of so many early childhood programs. The advantages are numerous:

● *Variety of adult role models.* Teachers who are male, female, disabled, young, middle-aged, older, varying in ethnic backgrounds bring equally diverse attitudes, approaches to children, interests, skills, and knowledge to share, teaching children to accept differences in people as they watch adults interact with others on the teaching team.[1]

● *Support for children.* The absence of one teacher is not as disruptive when the children can count on other familiar faces. This enables children to learn to trust the teaching environment because someone they know is always there.

● *Collegiality.* Teachers can find friendship and support from one another as they share planning, problems, and achievements and grow in admiration and respect for one another.

● *Lightened workload.* There is a sharing of all the teaching tasks, from curriculum planning and clean-up to parent conferencing and record keeping.

● *Enriched program.* Talents and resources of the team are used to best advantage so that team members will teach to their strengths, adding richness to the program.

Most of the disadvantages of team teaching stem from communication problems among team members. The following 10 guidelines to successful teaching are particularly useful for team situations. Teachers new to the team teaching process will want to discuss them with other team members.

Good teachers are "complicated human beings with strengths and weaknesses, talents and limitations, good days and bad days" (LeShan, 1992). They work at becoming good teachers by developing skills in interpersonal relationships with other adults, just as they promote good social relationships between the young children they teach.

Communication problems and conflicts arise in every teaching situation. The following guidelines will help teachers promote good working relationships.

These guidelines focus on working with others in the school setting; parent–teacher relationships are discussed in Chapter 8.

Ten Essentials of Successful Teaching

Ten essential attributes of successful teaching are:

1. Professionalism
2. A satisfying role
3. Flexibility
4. Open and frequent communication
5. Self-awareness
6. Mutual respect and acceptance
7. Team spirit and empathy
8. A willingness to share the spotlight
9. Clearly defined roles
10. Evaluation

Each of these attributes is discussed in the following paragraphs.

Professionalism

Professional attitudes and behavior contribute to successful teaching. Teachers should relate to one another as peers, colleagues, and professionals, and keep personal grievances out of the classroom. There is no place in the early childhood setting for petty gossip, ill will, or exclusive cliques.[2] Through written personnel policies, most schools have established appropriate procedures through which teachers may address certain issues. The professional approach, however, is to first attempt to work out personal differences with the other person on a one-to-one basis.

Teachers should ask themselves: Do I behave in a professional manner? Can I keep confidences without being told to do so? Do I try to meet with those with whom I have differences in an attempt to work them out? Do I complain publicly about another member of the staff?

 OUR DIVERSE WORLD OUR DIVERSE WORLD OUR DIVERSE WORLD OUR DIVERSE WORLD OUR DIVERSE WORLD OUR DIVERSE WORLD OUR DIVERSE WORLD OUR DIVERSE WORLD

[1] The early childhood educator needs to remember to appreciate a DIVERSE WORLD in the professional community as well as in the community of children and their families.

[2] The teacher has an important role as a behavior model with other teachers as well as with children.

Figure 5.8 ● Members of a teaching team need frequent communication with one another.

A Satisfying Role

To teach successfully, each person must have a satisfying role to play. That means each person must be appreciated for the special something he or she brings to the classroom and the school. Beginning teachers might want to ask themselves: Is there a place in my school (or on my team) that is uniquely mine? How do my special talents and experiences contribute to the success of this program? These questions would make for a good staff meeting discussion so that all teachers could reflect on their special capabilities and share them with one another.

Flexibility

Just as it is important to change with and adapt to the varying needs of children, so is it crucial to respond to the needs of other staff members with a give-and-take approach. Flexibility involves a willingness to offer and accept negotiation and compromise to preserve the effectiveness of the whole staff's effort. Teachers should ask themselves: Do I demonstrate a willingness to change with the changing needs of my coworkers, or do I adhere rigidly to preset plans or attitudes? Am I open to new ideas proposed by others? Do I help children become comfortable with flexibility and change?

Open and Frequent Communication

The ability and opportunity to communicate honestly and openly thoughts, concerns, and feelings to others are perhaps the most important factors in promoting good interpersonal relationships. Communication takes many forms: verbal and nonverbal, written and spoken, even body language.

Teachers must seek out opportunities for formal and informal communication with others on the staff. This may mean taking advantage of the faculty lounge during lunch hour or arriving 5 minutes early to catch someone before children arrive. For those who work on teaching teams, set-up and cleanup times can be used to discuss issues, modify strategies, and resolve misunderstandings.

The three basic reasons for developing successful communication links with others on the teaching staff are:

1. *To share information*—about children and their families ("Sheila's grandmother died yesterday"), about changes in the schedule ("The dentist is unable to visit today; who wants to conduct group time?"), and about child development strategies ("Remember, we are all going to observe Leah's gross motor skills this week").

2. *To contribute new ideas*—teachers encourage one another to keep teaching fresh and alive when they share a recent article of interest, reports from a conference they attended, or a successful art activity.

3. *To solve problems*—accepting differences in opinions, approaches, personality, and style among people is part of the challenge of working closely with others. Open communication is an ongoing process in which people have honest and frequent discussion of their differences, respecting each other's

feelings and integrity and working together for mutually agreeable solutions.

Self-Awareness

Previously in this chapter, self-awareness as a qualification for a good early childhood teacher was discussed. The focus was primarily on the teacher's self-awareness in relationships with children. In this discussion, the focus is on the teacher's adult relationships. Beginning teachers may feel uncomfortable or inadequate in their relationships with others on the staff; once they know more about themselves and accept who they are, teachers can apply this self-awareness to their relationships with fellow workers.

To promote self-knowledge that contributes to success as a member of a faculty or teaching team, teachers might ask themselves: What are my strengths and weaknesses as a teacher, and how do they complement or conflict with others in this school? Do I prefer to follow or lead, to plan programs or carry out

Figure 5.9 ● Sharing insights with colleagues helps the early childhood professional become more self-aware.

the plans developed by others? In what teaching situations do I feel uncomfortable, and why? What have I done lately that caused me to learn more about myself?

Mutual Respect and Acceptance

Appreciating and accepting the individuality of other team members are as important to the success of the program as are appreciating and accepting the individuality of each child. The climate of trust and the nonthreatening atmosphere gained through mutual respect allow each staff member to contribute openly and innovatively to the program. To develop that appreciation for one another, teachers should ask themselves: What do I have in common with my coworkers? Are their teaching philosophies different from mine and, if so, in what way? What are their social and cultural values?[1] What are their previous experiences with young children? What do I want them to respect and accept about me?

Team Spirit and Empathy

A sense of being a team does not happen by accident, but by conscious effort. Every member of the staff must be committed to working together on a daily basis as well as to the long-term goals of the specific program and to being empathic to the feelings and needs of coworkers.

To develop staff relationships that enhance a team spirit, teachers should ask themselves: How can I show support to my coworkers? What can I do to promote and sustain high morale among my fellow teachers? Where and how can I offer help to another staff member?

A Willingness to Share the Spotlight

Tension among staff members can arise from a sense of competition. Teachers must be willing to admit that others are just as dedicated to children and deserving of their affections as they are. There must be a feeling of shared success when things work well, as there is a shared responsibility when problems arise. Teachers should ask themselves: How do I feel when another teacher is praised by a parent in front of me? How do I feel when a child prefers another teacher

Figure 5.10 ● Professional attitudes and behavior are crucial. Teachers and administrators work together in solving problems as colleagues and coworkers.

to me? Am I able to acknowledge my coworkers' achievements?

Clearly Defined Roles

A clear understanding of the roles and responsibilities a teacher has is essential for the teacher's own sense of well-being and for the smooth functioning of the program. A written job description helps teachers understand the scope of their own position as well as those of staff members. Clearly defined teacher roles also serve as a guard against legal and ethical problems, especially if children are injured at school. Teachers should ask themselves: Is my job description clearly written so I know the extent of my responsibilities? Do I fulfill my obligations, or are there areas where I am lax that might prove harmful to a child?

Evaluation

Evaluations are part of the privilege of claiming membership in the teaching profession. No teacher can become truly successful unless provisions are made for ongoing evaluations that provide a clear picture that confirms strengths and pinpoints areas for growth. (Evaluations are more thoroughly discussed in Chapter 10.) Teachers should ask themselves: Do I accept

OUR DIVERSE WORLD OUR DIVERSE WORLD OUR DIVERSE WORLD OUR DIVERSE WORLD OUR DIVERSE WORLD OUR DIVERSE WORLD OUR DIVERSE WORLD OUR DIVERSE WORLD

[1] When we learn something of the cultural norms and habits of our colleagues, we model a respect and concern for all.

evaluations as an essential part of teaching? Am I responsive to the suggestions made in my evaluations? When I evaluate others, am I fair and do I share my observations in a supportive way?

THE TEACHER AS A PROFESSIONAL

Attitudes and Background

There is a body of knowledge, an educational foundation, that is assumed of anyone entering the early childhood profession. Some basic teaching skills also are necessary. These include methods and techniques appropriate for teaching the very young child. Yet there is more if one is to be called a true *professional*.

Being a member of the teaching profession goes beyond an accumulation of methods, coursework, and teaching experiences. Being a professional teacher suggests an attitude about teaching. It is not simply an 8-hour-a-day job, or an occupation chosen lightly. Teachers are called to the profession when they believe they can indeed make a difference in the lives of the children. Although that may at first sound *altruistic*, it reflects a dedication to teaching that exceeds the desire for a job or a steady paycheck.

There are professional expectations, starting with having a common background with others in the field. This includes studying child development and human behavior, family relations, parent education and development, and curriculum planning. Some practical teaching experience under the guidance of a master teacher is assumed, as is a familiarity with observation and recording techniques. This foundation of knowledge and experience provides the framework for professional development. Teachers gradually acquire further skills on the job. They learn to juggle three or four interactions with children at once and develop the skill of stopping an argument by a mere look or a quick gesture. Thus, the process of becoming a professional teacher is an orderly progression along a continuum of development. Your state may have regulations or none at all; only half the states offer a specialized certification for early childhood professionals (Bredekamp, 1992). Professional expectations mandated by the states provide some degree of professionalization of early childhood teachers.

This progression of teaching skills has been described by Lilian Katz (1977) as consisting of four distinct stages of teacher development, ranging from Survival to Maturity. The beginning teacher often feels inadequate and ill-prepared during the first year of teaching (Survival) but soon begins to focus on individual children and specific behavior problems (Consolidation). By the third or fourth year (Renewal) the teacher is ready to explore new ideas and resources and, within another year or two, has come to terms with teaching and searches for insights and perspectives (Maturity). At each stage, teachers need differing degrees of on-site support (mentoring), with increased exposure to professional conferences and organizations.

Professional Development

Developing a Professional Code of Ethics

As teachers mature, they turn their attention to issues and concerns outside themselves. Many of these issues, whether they are called so or not, are related to ethical conflicts and moral principles. Teachers are, after all, human beings, and that entails genuine conflict about behavior. Doing what is right becomes difficult at times; knowing what is right may be elusive. Even identifying what is right—an ethical conflict—may not be obvious.

Every day, situations arise with parents, other teachers, and administrators that require teachers to make some hard choices. Some cases are clearly ethical dilemmas: suspected child abuse by a parent or teacher, talking about children and their families outside of school, or the firing of a staff member without due cause. Others, some of which are common occurrences, may not seem as obvious. Some everyday examples are:

When Parents:

● Ask you to advance their child into the next class against your advice

● Want you to use discipline practices common to their family and culture but at odds with your own sense of what children need[1]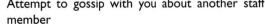

● Attempt to gossip with you about another staff member

[1] Teachers will need to become aware of child-rearing practices from many cultures.

When Another Teacher:

● Suggests a private staff meeting outside of school with a select group of teachers

● Refuses to take a turn cleaning out the animal cages

● Regularly is absent from staff meetings

● Disagrees with the school's educational philosophy and continues to teach in ways that differ from the approved methods in that setting

● Goes to the school administrator with an inappropriate complaint about a staff team member

When the Administrator:

● Insists on adding one more child to an already overenrolled class

● Makes personnel decisions based on friendship, not performance

● Backs a parent who complains about a teacher without hearing the teacher's side of the story

Surveys in the journal *Young Children* have identified some of the ethical issues of most concern to early childhood educators: (1) discussing a child or family outside of school; (2) implementing policies that are not good for children; (3) letting children do an activity that may not be worthwhile or appropriate; (4) knowing that a program is in violation of state regulations; and (5) dealing with conflicting requests from divorced or separated parents (Feeney & Sisko, 1986).

Teachers may find it helpful to discuss their ethical concerns with colleagues. Some staffs provide inservice programs for the staff where these issues are raised. Other schools have a code of ethics for their employees to follow.

Ethical problems occur daily in any teacher's life. They are not problems of an abstract or impersonal nature. Just what are ethics? Essentially, they are the moral guidelines by which we govern our own behavior and that of society. "Ethics is nothing more than

systematic critical reflection about our obligations," says philosopher Kenneth Kipnis (1987).

We can strictly define **ethics** as "the system or code of morals of a particular philosopher, religion, group, or profession." This definition suggests that a personal code of ethics can be supported by a professional code of ethics. A *code of ethics* is a set of statements that helps us deal with the temptations inherent in our occupations. It helps us act in terms of what is right rather than what is expedient (Katz & Ward, 1978).

Why might the early childhood profession need such a code? A primary reason is that the choices teachers make should be based not simply on personal values and preferences but "on values, judgments, and ethical commitments shared by the professional society or association of which they are a member" (Katz & Ward, 1978).[1]

A code of ethics provides collective wisdom and advice from a broad base in the profession. It states the principles by which each individual can measure and govern professional behavior. It says that a group or association has recognized the moral dimensions of its work. It provides teachers with a known, defined core of professional values—those basic commitments that any early childhood educator should consider inviolate. This protects teachers and administrators from having to make hard ethical decisions on the spur of the moment, possibly on the basis of personal bias. An established professional code supports the teacher's choice by saying, "It isn't that *I* won't act this way: *No early childhood educator* should act this way" (Kipnis, 1987).

The NAEYC has adopted a Code of Ethical Conduct that "offers guidelines for responsible behavior and sets forth a common basis for resolving the principal ethical dilemmas encountered in early childhood education" (Freeney & Kipnis, NAEYC, 1990). Four sections of the Code outline the major areas of the professional relationship: (1) working with children, (2) working with families, (3) relationships with colleagues, and (4) responsibilities to the community and society. The Statement of Commitment, an excerpt from the code, may be found in Appendix B at the back of this text.

OUR DIVERSE WORLD OUR DIVERSE WORLD OUR DIVERSE WORLD OUR DIVERSE WORLD OUR DIVERSE WORLD OUR DIVERSE WORLD OUR DIVERSE WORLD OUR DIVERSE WORLD

[1] One of the values in NAEYC's Code of Ethical Conduct is the recognition that children are best understood in the context of family, culture, and society.

Figure 5.11 ● Ethical questions arise daily. This child has been taught to hit back if anyone hits him. What does the teacher say to him? How should this situation be handled?

A basic list of core values has emerged from this work, values "that are deeply rooted in the history of our field" (Feeney & Kipnis, 1990). Core values form the basis of agreement in the profession about standards of ethical behavior. They are:

● Appreciating childhood as a unique and valuable stage of the human life cycle

● Basing our work with children on knowledge of child development

● Appreciating and supporting the close ties between the child and family

● Recognizing that children are best understood in the context of family, culture, and society

● Respecting the dignity, worth, and uniqueness of each individual (child, family member, and colleague)

● Helping children and adults achieve their full potential in the context of relationships that are based on trust, respect, and positive regard (Feeney & Kipnis, 1990)

Continuing Education

Creative and stimulating classes are the product of teachers who continue to learn more about how to teach. After the initial stage of teaching, many teachers begin to seek new challenges and new ways to improve the quality of their teaching. Usually, this search leads to some form of continuing education, such as participation in workshops, courses, or seminars. If time to pursue continuing education is not built into a teacher's schedule, there may be other options:

● In-service training programs may be brought into the school setting. Resource people can be invited to lead the staff in discussions about children's behavior, parent relationships, assessment charts, science curricula, creating multicultural classrooms.

● Various members of the teaching staff can develop a program of their own, offering their expertise to fellow faculty at an in-service meeting.

● A computer specialist, art resource teacher, or multicultural expert can be invited to visit the classrooms, instructing children and providing staff with some useful ideas and plans.

Figure 5.12 ● Through frequent contacts with teachers and administrators, parents can become aware of the importance of professional training and development for early childhood educators.

● A family therapist can be invited to speak at a staff meeting about strategies for supporting families in crisis.

● A library for teachers, stocked with professional books, journals (such as *Young Children*), and newspapers (such as *Education Week*) can provide a teacher with the means to keep up with current trends and practices and to improve teaching skills in the classroom.

● Parents who are professionals in a variety of fields can be utilized whenever possible to enrich the knowledge and skills of the staff.

Setting Professional Goals

As teachers raise their sights beyond "How will I survive?" to "Where am I going?", they begin to set goals for themselves and their teaching career. They develop both long- and short-term objectives for themselves, establishing a framework for professional growth.

The goals that are set will vary with individual teachers. For Jim, this could mean developing a brand new curriculum for his class of 2-year-olds. Susan might choose to work toward having greater parent support in her classroom. Yuriko and Frank might decide to develop a workshop on cultural sensitivity.[1] Stephanie wonders about using her skills with children and computers to go into business for herself. Cassie would like to create a calendar of parent meetings and events for the school year. Whether in the area of children's programs, administration, staff relationships, or their own professional development, teachers can learn, grow, and change. (See Chapter 10 for evaluation and goal-setting techniques.)

OUR DIVERSE WORLD OUR DIVERSE WORLD OUR DIVERSE WORLD OUR DIVERSE WORLD OUR DIVERSE WORLD OUR DIVERSE WORLD OUR DIVERSE WORLD OUR DIVERSE WORLD
[1] Peer-developed workshops are a good way to create an open climate for discussing diversity issues.

Professional Affiliations

Teachers who are beginning to perceive themselves as professionals may chose to join one of the professional organizations related to the early childhood field. One of the largest, the National Association for the Education of Young Children (NAEYC), has local and state affiliate groups through which one can become a member. NAEYC offers a range of services to its members, including conferences and publications such as the journal *Young Children*. The Association for Childhood Education International (ACEI) has a similar function, whereas the Society for Research in Child Development (SRCD) focuses on child psychology, research, and development.

There are a number of organizations concerned with young children, teachers, and issues related to the early childhood profession. Abundant resources are available from these groups, which are listed in Appendix D.

Career Options

The need for quality programs for young children has never been greater and the demand for early childhood specialists will continue, fostered by national attention to the issues of children and families. If you are considering a career in early childhood, the options are many and varied. Figure 5.13 lists some of the possibilities that exist in this profession.

Direct Services to Children and Families

Teacher in early childhood program
Director of child care facility, nursery school,
 Montessori program
Family day care provider
Nanny or au pair
Foster parent
Social worker/adoption agent
Pediatric nurse/school nurse
Family therapist/parent educator
Pediatrician
Parent educator
Early intervention specialist
Recreation leader
Play group leader
Home visitor

Indirect Services to Children and Families

Curriculum specialist
Instructional specialist—computers
Child development researcher
Early childhood education specialist
Program consultant
Consumer advocate
Teacher trainer—2- and 4-year colleges
Consultant

Community Involvement

State/local licensing worker
Legislative advocate
Child care law specialist
ECE environmental consultant
Interior designer for children's spaces
Government planning agent on children's issues
Consultant in bilingual education, multiculturalism
Nutrition specialist for children
Child care referral counselor

Other Options

Communications consultant
Script writer/editor
Freelance writer
Children's book author
Children's photographer
Microcomputer specialist/program consultant

Figure 5.13 ● There are many challenges in a variety of careers awaiting the early childhood professional. (Adapted from "Career Options in Early Childhood Education" by Dianne Widmeyer Eyer. In *Beginnings & Beyond: Foundations in Early Childhood Education*, Delmar, 1993. Third edition, p. 170.)

THE BEGINNING TEACHER

Beginning teachers of young children cannot expect to successfully blend all of the many facets of a teacher—personal, team, and professional identity—at once. Certainly, teaching young children carries with it the obligation to understand and accept the many roles and responsibilities associated with the title of "teacher." However, beginning teachers must also be committed to the time and energy need to *become* that total teacher.

Beginning teaching can be a great deal of fun as well as a unique learning experience. Textbook theories come alive as children naturally demonstrate child development concepts. New teachers expect to learn about individual child growth and development; many are surprised to discover that they also learn how children function in groups and with adults.

Planning and executing activities that fit the needs and abilities of the child are another part of the beginning teacher's role. They provide an opportunity to test curriculum ideas, to see what happens when child meets materials. Working with an experienced teacher who models highly polished skills is an important part of the new teacher's experience. Identification with a number of professionals can help the beginning find a teaching identity, and a team teaching situation can be especially supportive.

Yet we know that first-time teaching is not always fun. It is a time for intensive self-searching and self-revelations.[1] Many teachers' own school experiences loom before them and undermine their confidence. Planning lessons takes long hours. There may still be doubts about being a teacher at all. It is uncomfortable to feel judged and criticized by others. This is a time of anxiety for most beginning teachers. But remember, even the poised, confident, and always-does-the-right-thing master teacher was once a beginner.

The Student Teacher

Many teacher training programs require a formal period of supervised work with young children either in the college's child development center or in early childhood programs throughout the community. For

Figure 5.14 ● The beginning teacher invests herself emotionally as well as physically.

students in such a program, practice teaching may be the first hands-on opportunity to work with children.

Beginnings for student teachers are just as important as they are for young children. A child's first days of school are planned very carefully; likewise, there are some strategies for easing the transition from student to student teacher. The following guidelines will help to make the first days of student teaching a satisfying and positive experience.

Before School Starts

● Contact the teacher and meet before school begins. Find out what time school begins, where the classroom is located, what the age group is, the size and makeup of the class, the daily schedule and what hours you are expected to be on site. Ask if there are children with special needs and if there are cultural considerations of which you should be aware.[1] Find out what is expected of you the first few days. Be sure to meet the other administrative staff of the school.

OUR DIVERSE WORLD OUR DIVERSE WORLD OUR DIVERSE WORLD OUR DIVERSE WORLD OUR DIVERSE WORLD OUR DIVERSE WORLD OUR DIVERSE WORLD OUR DIVERSE WORLD

[1] This may be the first time some students confront their attitudes toward classroom diversity and inclusion.
[2] This may mark the beginning of a new teacher's pluralistic mindset.

● Visit the classroom to which you are assigned to become acquainted with its layout. Tour the yard as well. Find out where the janitor's room, kitchen, nurse's office, and storeroom are located.

● Share with the master teacher any special skills or talents you may have; let the teacher help you use these skills in new ways with young children. Let the teacher know about any other experiences with children: baby-sitting or camp counseling. Be sure to let the teacher know of any course requirements you must meet by this experience.

● Together, you, the master teacher, and your college instructor in student teaching will set goals and expectations for your student teaching experience. This will define more concretely what you would like to get out of the time you spend in the classroom, whether it is gaining experience with a group of children or learning to lead a group time by the end of the semester. By establishing common goals, the master teacher will be able to help guide a course so that these goals will be realized. An evaluation process related to those goals should be agreed on so that you will learn whether you have met the expectations of the teacher, the school, and the program.

Getting Started

After the first few days of teaching, routines will become familiar, you will know most of the children's names, and your presence in the classroom will have become standard procedure. Once a level of comfort is reached, some of the more challenging aspects of working with young children can be addressed. The following guidelines will help ease the first week's anxieties.

Student Behavior

Dress Appropriatly. Wear clothing that is comfortable, appropriate to the season, and easily covered by a smock or apron. Sturdy, waterproof shoes are good for outdoor activities.

Be Prompt. Arrive on schedule, and always inform the master teacher if you will be late or absent.

Know Where Things Are. Find out where important equipment and materials are stored.

Figure 5.15 ● Good teachers know when to help children learn new skills.

Use Professional Ethics. Avoid discussing children and families by name outside the school setting.

Interacting with Children

Move in Slowly. Sit back and watch to see what children are doing and if you are needed before getting involved.

Maintain Your Role As Teacher. Avoid playing adult-centered games with children or entertaining them so that you become the focus of their play. Keep their attention focused on each other or the activities.

Give Children Time. Allow plenty of time for children to do as much as they can possibly do without help.

Help Children Wait. Be alert to times when children may have to wait until the next activity or to move to another room. Have songs and fingerplays memorized or a short book ready to read.

Be Alert to the Whole Group. Know where the children and other teachers are and what they are doing even when they are not in the immediate area.

Never Leave Children Unsupervised. Notify the teacher in charge if you must leave the area, and work out arrangements that will provide full coverage of all the activities.

Figure 5.16 ● Through experience, teachers learn how to handle large groups of children. Learning to develop story time and reading skills is an ongoing process.

Maintain the Environment. Keep the room and yard in order as the day moves along, involving children in the cleanup process.

Use Your Voice and Tone Effectively. Go over to a child, bend down, and speak quietly, but distinctly, rather than shout from across the room or yard.

Never Shove or Use Force. Avoid picking up children to get them where they are supposed to go. Learn to use verbalizations, not force or threats of force, to get children to cooperate.

Relating to Other Adults

Never Interfere When Another Teacher Is Solving a Problem. Unless specifically invited to join in, allow other teachers the courtesy of dealing with the situation alone.

Ask Questions. Be sure to ask for help when needed. You are here to learn, so you may feel free to question teachers as to why and how they handle various situations.

Maintain Communication. Keep other staff members informed of significant events and problems that occur. Parents' questions and concerns should be redirected to the teacher staff.

Consult Your Master Teacher. Work together on selecting and evaluating age-appropriate activities that will fit in with the established curriculum goals.

Keep these guidelines in mind to avoid some of the common pitfalls of the beginning teacher, but remember they are only guidelines. Students must add their own experiences, insights, and interpretations. With the support of the teaching staff, confidence will grow, together with an understanding of what it means to be a total teacher. Further discussion related to guidance and discipline will be found in Chapter 7.

THE WHOLE TEACHER

At some point teachers emerge with their own point of view about teaching, based on self-knowledge of what calls them to teaching, why they teach the way they do, and what they know of the children they teach. This integration of knowledge and training, experience and life, is referred to by several names. Some say "real" teachers. Others refer to the "total" teacher. A common phrase is the "whole" teacher. Any one of these terms is an apt reflection of the relationship between how teachers view children and how they see themselves. There is a meshing of the emotional, physical, intellectual, and social aspects of each human being, adult or child.

Something happens when this blending occurs. During the first few years in the classroom, teachers consolidate their various official functions—merging their teacher training and experience with their personal style and nature. To discover and define the role of a teacher means to develop a personal teaching style. This is the sum of one's response to teaching, and it is unique to each teacher. When it happens, a beginning teacher becomes aware of "feeling" like a teacher. The strengths and convictions one has as a person blend with those one has as a teacher; they become inseparable. What teachers do and what teachers are become woven together. And in adding the personal teacher to the professional teacher, the sum becomes greater than two, allowing the whole teacher the freedom to grow in insight and understanding.

Summary

Teachers of young children share with other teachers a variety of subject matter. The curriculum in the early childhood school is rich in math, science, language, social studies, geography, and the like. The format for these learning experiences is a "hands-on" approach. Teachers set out materials, equipment, and activities that invite children's interest and interaction.

In some area the early childhood teacher differs from others in the field of education. Team teaching, teacher–child interactions, small-group emphasis, and adult relationships are more common in the early years than in other types of schools.

The teaching role is not restricted to working just with children. Teachers must learn to interact with numerous adults—primarily parents, other teachers, and administrators. Teaching roles will vary, depending on whether you teach alone or on a team. Team teaching is common in many early childhood programs and has many advantages. By keeping in mind 10 essentials for successful teaching, all early childhood teachers can ensure themselves of optimal working conditions in their setting.

Early childhood teachers have multiple roles. They supervise and manage the classroom, interact with children and a number of adults, and set the emotional tone. Much of what they do occurs away from children. There are meetings to attend, reports to write, parent conferences to hold, and materials to purchase. These after-hours duties add to the depth of classroom experiences the teacher provides for the children.

Ethical situations arise frequently, calling on the teacher or administrator to make difficult choices about children and their lives. A professional code of ethics sets out standards of behavior based on core values and commitments all early childhood professionals share. It can support decisions individuals have to make in the best interests of children.

The student teacher gains valuable experience working directly with children under the supervision of a mature teacher. Some of the initial anxieties are overcome by following general guidelines for student teaching. Further help comes from looking at some common problems and ways to avoid them.

As they grow and gain confidence, teachers pass through several stages of professional development and search for ways to be more effectively challenged. As they integrate teaching style and personality, they become whole teachers.

Review Questions

1. What do you think are the five most important qualifications a teacher of young children should have? Why? Which do you possess? Which are most difficult for you?

2. How does a teacher "set the tone" for a classroom? How does being culturally competent fit in?

3. Give several reasons why team teaching is important in the early years.

4. List some of the common problems associated with student teaching. How can you avoid them?

5. Why is self-awareness important?

6. What does having a code of ethics mean to a teacher?

7. You will note many similarities if you review the Ten Essentials of Successful Teaching and the characteristics of a good school climate found in the teacher burnout section. Why do you think these are interrelated?

Learning Activities

1. Draw a picture of the first classroom you remember. Place furniture in it and note where your friends sat, where you sat, where the teacher sat. Down one side of the paper write one-word descriptions of what you felt when you were in that classroom.

2. Survey a classroom where you teach or observe. How many different cultures are represented? How does the teacher respond to the cultural diversity?

3. Have you ever had a teacher who was "different"? Describe the person. What did you like most about that teacher? What did you like least? Would you hire that teacher? Why?

4. Write your own code of ethics.

5. Read the ethical situations posed in the section on professional development. Think about how you would solve them. Discuss your answers with a member of your class, a teacher, and a parent.

6. Observe a teacher working in a team situation and one who works alone in a classroom. What seem to be the advantages of each? Disadvantages? Which would you prefer for your first year of teaching? Why? Your third year? Your seventh year?

7. Do you disagree with any core values listed in the section Ten Essentials of Successful Teaching? What are they? How would you change them? Discuss your response with another teacher, another student, your class instructor.

8. In small groups, discuss the popular images of teachers as reflected in current movies and literature. Is there consensus of the portrait of teachers today? Where do early childhood professionals fit into the picture? Are issues raised about teachers being addressed anywhere? Where? How? By whom? What would you conclude about your role as a member of the teaching profession?

9. What elements would you add to Figure 5.1 on the basis of your observation of early childhood programs and teachers?

Bibliography

Armstrong, L. S. (1991, March 20). Census confirms remarkable shifts in ethnic makeup. *Education Week.*

Berk, L. E. (1994). *Infants and children.* Boston: Allyn & Bacon.

Beyer, E. (1968). *Teaching young children.* New York: Western Publishing.

Bredekamp, S. (1992, January). Composing a profession. *Young Children,* pp. 52–54.

Derman-Sparks, L. (1989). *Anti-bias curriculum: Tools for empowering young children.* Washington, DC: National Association for Education of Young Children.

Dresden, J., & Myers, B. K. (1989, January). Early childhood professionals: Toward self-definition. *Young Children.*

Eyer, D. (1989). Career options in early childhood education. In A. M. Gordeon & K. W. Browne (Eds.), *Beginnings and beyond: Foundations in early childhood education.* Albany, NY: Delmar.

Feeney, S., & Kipnis, K. (1985, March). Professional ethics in early childhood education. *Young Children,* pp. 54–58.

Feeney, S., & Kipnis, K. (1990). *Code of ethical conduct and statement of commitment.* Washington, DC: National Association for Education of Young Children.

Feeney, S., & Sisko, L. (1986, November). Professional ethics in early childhood education: Survey results. *Young Children*, pp. 15–20.

Gonzales-Mena, J. (1993). *Multicultural issues in child care.* Mountain View, CA: Mayfield.

Honig, A. (1979). *Parent involvement in early childhood education.* Washington, DC: National Association for the Education of Young Children.

Jones, E. (1994). Breaking the ice: Confronting status differences among professions. In J. Johnson & J. B. McCracken (Eds.), *The early childhood career lattice: Perspectives on professional development.* Washington, DC: National Association for the Education of Young Children.

Jorde-Bloom, P. (1998a). *A great place to work.* Washington, DC: National Association for Education of Young Children.

Jorde-Bloom, P. (1988b, September). Teachers need TLC too. *Young Children.*

Katz, L. G. (1977). *Talks with teachers.* Washington, DC: National Association for the Education of Young Children.

Katz, L. G., & Ward, E. H. (1978). *Ethical behavior in early childhood education.* Washington, DC: National Association for Education of Young Children.

Kipnis, K. (1987, May). How to discuss professional ethics. *Young Children*, pp. 26–30.

Kuster, C. A. (1994). Language and cultural competence. In J. Johnson & J. B. McCracken (Eds.), *The early childhood career lattice: Perspectives on professional development.* Washington, DC: National Association for the Education of Young Children.

LeShan, E. (1992). *When your child drives you crazy.* New York: St. Martin's Press.

Phillips, C. B. (1994). What every early childhood professional should know. In J. Johnson & J. B. McCracken (Eds.). *The early childhood career lattice: Perspectives on professional development.* Washington, DC: National Association for the Education of Young Children.

Ramsey, P. (1987). *Teaching and learning in a diverse world: Multicultural education for young children (early childhood education series).* New York: Teachers College Press.

Spodek, B. (1972). *Teaching in the early years.* Englewood Cliffs, NJ: Prentice-Hall.

Spodek, B. (1994). The knowledge base for baccalaureate early childhood teacher education programs. In J. Johnson & J. B. McCracken (Eds.), *The early childhood career lattice: Perspectives on professional development.* Washington, DC: National Association for the Education of Young Children.

Whitebook, M., Howes, C., & Phillips, D. (1990). *Who cares? Child care teachers and the quality of care in America. Final report: National Child Care Staffing Study.* Washington, DC: Center for the Child Care Workforce.

York, S. (1991). *Roots and wings: Affirming culture in early childhood programs.* St. Paul, MN: Redleaf Press.

Observation: Learning to Read the Child

CHAPTER 6

Questions for Thought

Why is observing children an important teaching tool?

How do observations help us understand people and their behavior?

What is the difference between fact and inference?

How can observations be used to compare individual behavior and general developmental growth?

How do we observe and record effectively?

What are useful recording techniques?

What are the guidelines to follow when observing and recording behavior?

Figure 6.1 ● These two children are seen playing together for the first time. What can teachers learn by observing them about their use of materials? The way they make friends? How they solve problems?

INTRODUCTION

Children are fascinating. They are charming, needful, busy, creative, unpredictable, and emotional. At school, at home, in the grocery store, and in the park, children demonstrate a variety of behaviors. There is the happy child pumping hard on the swing. The angry, defiant child grabs a book or toy and runs away. The studious child works seriously on a puzzle.

 These pictures of children flash through the mind, caught for an instant as if by a camera. These minipictures of children working, playing, and living together can be very useful to teachers.[1] Good observational skills can help teachers capture those moments in a child's life. Memory leaves just the impression. The written word is an opportunity to check impressions and opinions against the facts.

What Is Observation?

Teachers learn to make mental notes of the important details in each interaction:

That's the first time I've seen Karen playing with Bryce. They are laughing together as they build with blocks.

For 5 minutes now, Teddy has been standing on the fringes of the sand area where the toddler group is playing. He has ignored the children's smiles and refused the teacher's invitation to join in the play.

Antonio stops climbing each time he reaches the top of the climbing frame. He looks quickly around and if he catches a teacher's eye, he scrambles down and runs away.

OUR DIVERSE WORLD OUR DIVERSE WORLD OUR DIVERSE WORLD OUR DIVERSE WORLD OUR DIVERSE WORLD OUR DIVERSE WORLD OUR DIVERSE WORLD OUR DIVERSE WORLD

[1] A skilled observer, with an awareness of our diverse world, is reminded of the ways in which all children are the same, as well as the characteristics that make each child unique.

Figure 6.2 ● Observing children closely reveals their feelings and needs.

Through their behavior, these three children reveal much about their personalities. The teacher's responsibility is to notice all the clues and put them together in meaningful ways. The teacher sees the obvious clues as well as the more subtle ones. The way observations are put together with other pertinent information becomes critical. The first child, Karen, has been looking for a special friend. Now that she has learned some ways to approach other children that don't frighten and overwhelm them, children want to play with her. Teddy's parents divorced 2 weeks ago. It appears he is just beginning to feel some of that pain and has become withdrawn at school. At home, Antonio is expected to do things right the first time. Because climbing over the top of the frame might be tricky, he does not attempt it at all. At school, he generally attempts only what he knows he can do without making a mistake.

These simple observations, made in the midst of a busy morning at school, give vital information about each child's abilities, needs, and concerns. It is a more developed picture. Children are complex human beings who respond in many ways. Teachers can observe these responses and use their skills to help each child grow and learn.

The ability to observe—to "read" the child, understand a group, "see" a situation—is one of the most important and satisfying skills a teacher can have. As Cartwright (1994) tells us:

Really seeing means sensitive observation, keen listening, and simultaneous note-taking. It's not easy to master and it takes much practice, but the results are remarkable. The very process of learning skilled observation keeps teacher concern primarily with the children (where it should be!).

A consistent practice of observation will help teachers develop what Feeney, Christensen, and Moravicik (1996) describe as *"child-sense*—a feeling for how individual children and groups of children are feeling and functioning."

Observation is the basis of so much of a teacher's work. It influences how a teacher sets up the environment and how and when it will be changed. It helps a teacher create the daily schedule, planning appropriate time periods for various activities. It allows the teacher to make sense of and respond well to the many interpersonal exchanges that mean so much to parents and caregivers alike. Assessing children (see Chapter 10) can be done only on the basis of good observations. In more reflective and less structured ways, teachers will observe how they react and feel, observing themselves and their own values. Observations are used in nearly every chapter of this book.

Observation is more than ordinary looking. It takes energy and concentration to become an accurate observer. Teachers must train themselves to record what they see on a regular basis.[1] They need to discipline themselves to distinguish between detail and trivia as well as learn to spot biases that might invalidate observation (see Figure 6.3). Once acquired, objective observation techniques help give a scientific and professional character to the role of early childhood education.

Seeing Children through Observation

Play is the work of childhood. It is the way children express themselves and how they show what they are really like. By observing play, teachers can see children as they are and as they see themselves. Much of what children do gives clues to their inner beings.

The stage is set; the action begins as soon as the first child enters the room. Here, teachers can see children in action and watch for important behavior. All that is needed is to be alert to the clues and make note of them:

> Sierra, a toddler, walks up to Brooke. Sierra grabs Brooke's toy, a shape sorter, away from her. Then she begins to place shapes into the sorter. She has difficulty placing the shapes into the container. Sierra then throws the shapes, her face turns red, and she kicks the container away from her.

> Nico kneels on the chair placed at the puzzle table, selecting a 10-piece puzzle. He turns the puzzle upside down, allowing the pieces to fall on the table. He selects one piece at a time with his left hand and successfully puts every piece in the frame the first time. He raises both hands in the air and yells, "I did it!"

Developing sound observational skills enables teachers to better meet the social, emotional, and intellectual needs of each child.

What are children telling us about themselves? Which actions are most important to note? Understanding children is difficult because so many factors influence their behavior. A child's stage of development, culture, health, fatigue, and hunger can all make a difference in how a child behaves. Additionally, environmental factors such as the noise level, congestion, or time of day can add to the complex character of children's actions. Therefore, the teacher must make it a point to observe children at critical moments. For instance, an alert teacher will notice the way a child enters school each morning. Tina always clings to her blanket after her Dad leaves her at school. Lasauna bounces in each day ready to play the moment she walks in the door. David says good-bye to his grandmother, then circles the room, hugging each adult before settling into an activity. These children show the observant teacher something about their needs. A good observer will continue to watch, taking note of these early morning scenes. One can interpret these behaviors later, seeing how they apply to each child and how behavior changes over time.

Another important behavior to watch is how children use their bodies. The basic routines of eating, napping, toileting, and dressing show how they take care of themselves. Whether Chris knows how to put his jacket on by himself may indicate his skills in other areas that require initiative and self-sufficiency. It may also indicate how he is developing an awareness of himself as a separate, independent being.

Seeing children in relation to other people is a third area to notice. Teachers see whom children choose as playmates and whom they avoid. They can tell what children will look for in friends. The observant teacher will also make note of the adults in each child's life. Who does the child seek for comfort? For answering questions? Who takes care of the child outside of school? Who picks the child up from school each day?

Finally, in selecting play materials and equipment, children show what they like to do, how well they use the environment, and what they avoid. Specific observations about the various areas of skill development—physical-motor, intellectual, affective—can be mirrors of growth. Teachers observe whether a child picks materials that are challenging and the tendency toward the novel or the familiar. Bethany starts each morning

1 Early childhood educators are invited to study and learn about themselves as they learn about children.

Poor Observation

A. Julio walked over to the coat rack and dropped his sweater on the floor. He is <u>shy</u> (1) of teachers, so he didn't ask anyone to help him pick it up. He walked over to Cynthia <u>because she's his best friend</u> (2). <u>He wasn't nice</u> (3) to the other children when he started being <u>pushy and bossy</u> (4). He <u>wanted their attention</u> (5), so he <u>nagged</u> (6) them into leaving the table and going to the blocks <u>like 4-year-old boys do</u> (7).

Analysis and Comments

(1) Inference of a general characteristic.
(2) Inference of child's emotion.
(3) Observer's opinion.
(4) Inference with no physical evidence stated.
(5) Opinion of child's motivation.
(6) Observer's inference.
(7) Overgeneralization; stereotyping.

Good Observation

B. Emilio pulled out a puzzle from the rack with his right hand, then carried it with both hands to the table nearby. Using both hands, he methodically took each piece out of the frame and set it to his left. Sara, who had been seated across from Emilio with some table toys in front of her, reached out and pushed all the puzzle pieces onto the floor. Emilio's face reddened as he stared directly at Sara with his mouth in a taut line. His hands turned to fists, his brown furrowed, and he yelled at Sara in a forced tone, "Stop it! I hate you!"

Analysis and Comments

Emilio was clearly *angry* as demonstrated in his facial expressions, hand gestures, and body movements. What is more, the way a child speaks is as revealing as what a child says when one wants to determine what a child is feeling. Muscular tension is another clue to the child's emotions. But the physical attitude of the child is not enough; one must also consider the context. Just seeing a child sitting in a chair with a red face, one doesn't know if he is embarrassed, angry, feverish, or overstimulated. We need to know the events that led to this appearance. Then we can correctly assess the entire situation. By being open to what is happening without judging it first, we begin to see children more clearly.

Figure 6.3 ● Two observations. Example A contains numerous biases, which are underlined in the left column and explained in the right column. Example B has clear descriptions and is relatively free of biases.

in the art area, then plays with puzzles before taking care of the animals. Conor prefers the blocks and dramatic play areas and lately has been spending more time in the cooking corner. Observing children at play and at work can tell us how they learn and what methods they use to gain information.

Why Observe?

To Improve Your Teaching

Classrooms are busy places, especially for teachers, who plan many activities and share in hundreds of interactions every day. It is difficult to monitor our behavior while we are in the midst of working with children and time-consuming to reflect on that behavior afterward. Yet we know that teachers who are most effective are those who are thorough in their preparation and systematic in evaluating their own work. It takes a certain level of awareness—of self, of the children, and of the environment—to monitor our own progress. This includes carefully checking what is happening, looking for feedback, and then acting on it. Teachers can do this by asking others to observe them through videotaping, by observing each other at work with the children, and by self-observation.

Bias and Objectivity. Observing children helps teachers become *more objective* about the children in their care. When making observational notes, teachers look first at what the child is doing. This is different from looking at how a child ought to be doing something. The teacher becomes like a camera, recording what is seen without immediately judging it. This objectivity can balance the intense, personal side of teaching.

Bias is inherent in all our perceptions. We must acknowledge this truth without falling prey to the notion that because our efforts will be flawed, they are worthless. Observing is not a precise or wholly objective act. No two people will see something in identical ways. For instance, re-read the segments about Sierra and Nico. One teacher sees in Sierra a child demonstrating an age-appropriate response to frustration; another sees someone who is too aggressive; a third focuses on Brooke as a victim, rushing to comfort her and ignores Sierra altogether. And Nico? One teacher sees a 5-year-old boy who is flaunting his "power" over everyone at the table, and another notices a child swept up in the pride of accomplishment. As Seefeldt and Barbour (1994) put it

> It is a fact. Observing can never be totally objective or independent of the observer. Whatever is observed passes through the filter of the observer's beliefs, biases, assumptions, history, understanding, and knowledge. The individual observer's biases, beliefs, and ideas dictate what is observed, how, where, and when. The individual always brings his or her perception and interpretation to the observation.

 Teachers are influenced in their work by their own early childhood experiences.[1] They have notions about how children learn, play, grow, or behave because of the way they were raised and trained. For example, the same behaviors might be labeled "assertive and independent" by one teacher and "bossy and uncooperative" by another. The same applies to parents. "My husband and I just completed behavior rating scales for one of our children," a colleague writes. "Imagine my surprise at the disparity between our ratings on several characteristics. We live with the same child *daily*! How could we have made such different observations or inferences about the same child?" (Saxton, 1998).

Moreover, when teachers are in the thick of activity, they see only a narrow picture. To pull back, take some notes, and make an observation gives the teacher a chance to see the larger scene.

Teams of teachers help each other gain perspective on the class, an individual, a time of the day. Observations can be a means of validating one teacher's point of view. By checking out an opinion or idea through systematic observation, teachers get a sense of direction in their planning.

Additionally, all teachers develop ideas and impressions about children when they spend time with them. Some children seem shy, some helpful, some affectionate, aggressive, cooperative, stubborn, and so on. These opinions influence the way teachers behave and interact with children. The child thought to be aggressive, for instance, is more likely to be blamed for starting the quarrel when one occurs nearby. It is no accident that the children teachers consider more polite are the ones who are often given special considerations. The problem stems from teacher biases, and these can be misleading. Assumptions made about a child often stereotype rather than illuminate the child (or the group). This gives both teachers and children a narrow view of themselves and others.[2] In the Focus Box in this chapter Janet Gonzalez-Mena offers a multicultural perspective of observation of children.

Two guidelines come to mind as one begins to observe. The first is to practice "intensive waiting" (Nyberg, 1971): that is, to cultivate an ability to wait and see what is really happening instead of rushing to conclusions about what it means, where such behavior comes from, or what should be done. These hurried impressions hinder a teacher's work toward understanding. Try to suspend expectations and be open to what is really happening, whether this be about behavior, feelings, or patterns.

Second, Cohen and Stern (1978) suggest that to become a careful observer is to become in part a scientist. A good observer makes a clear distinction between fact and inference, between real behavior and an impression or conclusion drawn from it. Being aware of the difference between what actually happens and one's opinion and conclusions about those events is critical to good teaching. Refer to Figure 6.3 for an illustration of these differences. By separating what

OUR DIVERSE WORLD OUR DIVERSE WORLD OUR DIVERSE WORLD OUR DIVERSE WORLD OUR DIVERSE WORLD OUR DIVERSE WORLD OUR DIVERSE WORLD OUR DIVERSE WORLD

1,2 See footnote 1 on page 182.

happens from what you *think* about it or how you *feel* about it, you are able to distinguish between fact and inference. That does not mean teachers have to become aloof; their eyes can reflect both warmth and a measure of objectivity at the same time. The perception of a child from a teacher's view may be based on one or two events, not necessarily repeated or typical of the child. Thus, it is not a true picture of the child at all.

No one can be free from bias, nor is that the point. The impressions and influences made can provide valuable insights into children. The important first step in observation, though, is to separate what children *do* from what teachers think or feel about it. This can be done only with an awareness of one's own biases. Knowing personal influences and prejudices, coupled with observation and recording skills, prepares teachers to focus on actual behaviors.

To Construct Theory

Observations are a link between theory and practice. All teachers gain from making this connection. New teachers can see the pages of a textbook come alive as they watch a group of children. They can match what they see with what they read. By putting together psychology and medical research with in-class experiences, teachers gain a deeper understanding of the nature of children.

Early childhood education is the one level of teaching that systematically bases its teaching on child development. If we are to develop programs that work for young children—what they can do, how they think and communicate, and what they feel—we need to be able to apply sound child development knowledge to the classroom. Further, we can use what researchers have learned to understand the individual children in our care.

To Help Parents

Parents benefit from observations. A collection of notes about an individual child can be used in parent conferences. The teacher shares fresh, meaningful examples that demonstrate the child's growth and abilities. The child's teachers also gain a perspective when the notes are accumulated and discussed with parents. Problems become more clear, and plans can be made to work together. Results can be further tested through continuing observation.

Figure 6.4 ● Observations bring theory to life. What can this baby do with objects? Is the environment safe? Challenging? How does observing answer these questions?

To Use As an Assessment Tool

Notes, time samplings, and running records serve as an informal way to assess children's skills and capabilities. These methods are described later in this chapter, and a discussion of child assessment is detailed in Chapter 10. Observation can be used as a tool for teachers to check the accuracy of their own impressions. Comparing notes with other teachers, with parents, or with anyone familiar with the classroom or the child in question refines a teacher's own objective observation skills. The results lead directly into curriculum planning for the class. Teachers observe the room arrangement and use of space. Does the traffic flow easily, or are children stuck in play areas and unable to get out? Many classroom problems can be solved if teachers will take time to make observations. They can observe what happens in the block corner at cleanup time. Who always cleans up? Who avoids it? Or they look at play patterns and find out who children play with or who plays alone. Observations can clarify which children are having problems and give teachers a sense of when and where the trouble starts.

More frequently teachers are called on to set specific goals for the children in their classes and for the overall class performance. They justify what they do and why and document children's progress. In this way teachers are accountable to their clients: the children, the parents, and the public. Learning to assess children's skills and behavior and to document it is becoming increasingly important to the early childhood educator. Assessment techniques such as portfolios and screening are described in Chapter 10.

To Wonder Why and Solve a Problem

In the spirit of being a kind of scientist, teachers can become researchers in their own classrooms. A scientist, like a child, sees something and wonders why. This curiosity leads to thinking about the various components of a problem and looking at the parts as well as the whole. Next comes the "head-scratching" part— a time of reflection, developing hunches or intuitions about the problem, and generating alternatives. The teacher is then ready to try out an alternative, known in scientific terms as testing the hypothesis. Finally, the teacher gets results, which feeds back into rethinking the problem or celebrating the solution.

There are many ways the teacher can become a researcher. Certainly, systematic observation of children is one way to look at problems and situations. Without extensive training, teachers can engage in this kind of scientific thinking in their daily work. This kind of "action research" is easily adaptable to teaching.

To Communicate with Children

Observation of children's play is a way to encourage teachers to become interested observers-researchers. When teachers get more focused and interested in children's play, they improve their teaching with a heightened awareness of their own work and of the intricacies of children. At the same time, teachers can model the importance of writing. Furthermore, teachers support children in this process by *noticing* them.

See what happens when a teacher begins to write while children are playing:

Some of the children pay immediate attention. "What are you writing about?" asks four-year-old Nina as I sit down at the edge of the block area. "I'm writing about children playing," I explain. "You're writing about what I'm doing?" Nina asks. "Yes, I am." She's pleased. She goes back to building a careful enclosure with the long blocks (Jones & Carter, 1991).

In classrooms, the teacher can be the scribe, a kind of "literate helper" (Jones & Carter, 1991) who helps children become aware of the power of language, the written word, and their own importance. Observation helps keep most of the attention child-centered rather than teacher-directed and increases children's and adults' communication.

UNDERSTANDING WHAT WE OBSERVE

The goal of observing children is to understand them better. Teachers, students, and parents collect a great deal of information by watching children. Observational data help adults know children in several significant ways.

Children As Individuals

How do children spend their time at school? What activities are difficult? Who is the child's best friend? By watching individual children, teachers help them learn at their own pace, at their own rate of development, in their own time. By watching carefully, they find out each child's learning style. When teachers know how each child functions, they can choose activities and materials to match interests and skills. This is called **individualized curriculum**: tailoring what is taught to what a child is ready and willing to learn.

This kind of curriculum gives children educational experiences that offer **connected knowledge**: that is, a curriculum that is real and relevant to the individual child and is part of **developmentally appropriate practices** (see Chapters 1, 2, 9, and 11). It is also part of a program for children with special needs; in these cases an **individualized education plan (IEP)** is developed jointly by teachers, education specialists, and parents to better serve the child.

Observing helps a teacher spot a child's strengths and areas of difficulty. Once these are known, teachers plan intervention measures, helping to make the school experience successful for the child. The following example shows how individualizing the curriculum can bring about changes in behavior that help children succeed.

> The teachers were concerned about Jody, age 4½, who had minimal fine-motor skills. She used scissors in a "hedge-clippers" fashion and had an awkward grip when using a pencil. Jody also found it difficult to fit puzzle pieces together. She avoided all areas that required the use of those skills: art, table toys, woodworking, and cooking. A check with her parents revealed two important facts: Jody had trouble handling table utensils and couldn't button her sweater. They said there was no provision at home for her to pursue any fine-motor activities. Knowing of Jody's interest in airplanes, the teachers used that to draw Jody into areas of the curriculum she didn't ordinarily pursue. Small airplanes were added to the block corner, and airplane stencils were placed near the art table. A large mural of an airport was hung on the fence, and children were invited to paint on it. One day children cut airplane pictures out of magazines and used them on a collage. Simple airplane puzzles were placed on the puzzle table. Felt shapes and small plastic airplanes in the water table helped draw Jody toward activities requiring fine-motor skills. Jody's parents supplied her with a special art box at home, full of crayons, scissors, pens, water colors, and stencils. As her fine-motor skills increased and refined, Jody became a more confident and happier child. By the end of 3 months she was a regular participant in all areas of the school and seemed to be enjoying her newfound interest in art materials.

Dowley (n.d.) suggests that an observation of a child can be made on three levels. First, a teacher tries to report exactly what the child *does*: note exactly what actions the child takes. Second, express how the child seems to *feel* about what happened: note facial expressions, body language, the quality of the behavior. Third, include your own *interpretations*: add as a last and separate step some of your own personal responses and impressions.

Children in General

When recording behavior, teachers see growth patterns emerge. These trends reflect the nature of human development. Both Piaget and Erikson used this technique to learn how children think and develop socially and emotionally. Gesell studied large numbers of children to get developmental **norms** of physical growth. Parten (1932) and Dawes (1934) watched hundreds of preschoolers and arrived at the definitive description of children's play patterns and quarreling behavior. For today's early childhood educator, observing children can provide the answer to these questions:

● What might you expect when a 2-year-old pours juice?

● How will the second grade class respond to a field trip?

● What will children do when their parents leave them at school the first day?

● What is the difference between the attention span at storytime of a 2-year-old and a 5-year-old?

● What kind of social play is typical for the 4-year-old?

● How does an infant move from crawling to walking upright?

Observation gives a feeling for group behavior as well as a developmental yardstick to compare individuals within the group. Teachers determine age-appropriate expectations from this. It is important, for example, to know that most children cannot tie their own shoes at age 4 but can be expected to pull them on by themselves. A general understanding aids in planning a thoughtful and challenging curriculum. Teachers in a class of 3-year-olds, for instance, know that many children are ready for 8- to 10-piece puzzles but that the 20-piece jigsaw will most likely be dumped on the table and quickly abandoned.

Finally, knowledge of children in general gives teachers a solid foundation on which to base decisions about individuals. From observing many children comes an awareness of each child's progression along the developmental scale. Experienced teachers of toddlers will not put out watercolor sets, while the second-grade teacher will do so routinely. Teachers learn that it is typical of 4- and 5-year-olds to exclude others from their play because they will have seen it

Description	Interpretation/Inference
Jenny comes through the gate. She clutches her mother's hand. On the wall is a collection of road-building equipment; Jenny glances but does not stop or touch them. She is standing beside her mother and sucking her thumb.	Jenny is afraid of school. It's hard to let go of mom. She isn't interested because she is a girl. She doesn't like outdoor play.
Three children sitting at table doing art project. S and C sitting on one side, D on the other. D asks S if she can have the red paint; S doesn't respond. D asks again; again, no reply. D then yells, "Did you not hear me?!" and frowns. S looks startled, then pushes paint to D. C says, "Doncha know? She got an ear 'fection. You gonna break her heart." D clutches his chest—"No you breaking my heart." Everyone laughs as they all clutch chest and fall out of chairs.	Will D feel left out? D takes criticism well!
(Teacher asks: "How would you describe yourself?") I'm tall. My hair is very puffy. My two front teeth are very big. I have big feet. I have big muscles. I have a button nose. I have big black eyes. I like my very big cheeks.	Positive self-image
(Teacher asks: "What do you like about yourself?") I like that I'm good at karate. I like that I'm a nice girl. I'm good at school. I don't call people names. I like the way I approach people—I ask them how they're doing and their name. Hey, can you put this in? I like rice and lumpia.	Social success is important. Well-developed interpersonal awareness

Figure 6.5 ● Interpretation has its place in observation, but only after the behavior and description have been documented.

happen countless times. The 3½-year-old who is sure she is "too little" to use the toilet won't concern the knowledgeable teacher, who knows that this is developmentally appropriate behavior! Decisions about single children come from watching and knowing many children. This understanding is a valuable asset when talking to parents.[1]

Developmental Relationships

Observing brings about an understanding of the various developmental areas and how they are related. Development is at once **specific** and **integrated**. Children's behavior is a mix of several distinct developmental areas and, at the same time, an integrated

[1] Keen observers of young children come to realize that there is a wide spectrum of ways in which children develop with numerous ways in which parents support this growth—not good ways and bad ways, but many different ways.

whole whose parts influence each other. Reference to the *whole child* implies a consideration of how development works in unison.

When observing children, one must focus on these different developmental areas. What are the language abilities of 3-year-olds? What social skills do preschool children acquire? Which self-help skills can children learn before age 6? How does fine-motor development interact with intellectual growth? Does gross-motor skill effect successful cognitive learning? How does self-concept relate to all of the other areas?

Observing these separately brings a specific definition to the term "growth." Teachers see how the pieces fit together. When teachers have an understanding of children's thought processes, they can see why children have difficulty with the concept of dual-identity, for instance. When given a set of blocks in various sizes, colors, and shapes, a 4-year-old will have no difficulty finding the red ones or square ones, but may be puzzled when asked to find those that are both red and square. No wonder that same child has difficulty understanding that someone can be their best friend and like someone else at the same time.

Practiced observation will show that a child's skills are multiple and varied and have only limited connection to age. Derek has the physical coordination of a 4½-year-old, language skills of a 6-year-old, and the social skills of a 2-year-old—all bound up in a body that just turned 3. A brief picture such as this "whole child" can be helpful to both parents and teachers.

Influences on Behavior

Careful observation in the classroom and on the playground benefits an understanding of child growth and behavior. This includes an understanding of the influences and dynamics of that behavior.

Boaz has a hard time when he enters his child care each morning, yet he is competent and says he likes school. Close observation reveals that his favorite areas are climbing outdoor games and the sandbox. Boaz feels least successful in the construction and creative arts areas, the primary choices indoors, where his school day begins.

Mari, on the other hand, starts the day happily but cries frequently throughout the day. Is there a pattern to her outbursts? Watch what happens to Mari when free play is over and group time begins. She falls apart readily when it is time to move outdoors to play, time to have snacks, time to nap, and so on.

Environmental influences have an impact on both these children. The classroom arrangement and daily schedule influence children's behavior, because children are directly affected by the restraints imposed by their activities and their time. Boaz feels unsure of himself in those activities that are offered as he starts his day. Seeing only these choices as he enters the room causes him discomfort, which he shows by crying and clinging to his dad. By adding something he enjoys, such as a sand table indoors, the teacher changes the physical environment to be more appealing and positive. Boaz's difficulties in saying goodbye disappear as he finds he can be successful and comfortable at the beginning of his day.

The cause of Mari's problem is more difficult to detect. The physical environment seems to interest and appeal to her. On closer observation, her crying and disruptive behavior appear to happen just at the point of change, regardless of the activities before or afterward. It is the *time* aspect of the environment that causes difficulty for her. The teacher makes a special effort to signal upcoming transitions and to involve her in bringing them about. Telling Mari "Five more minutes until naptime" or "After you wash your hands, go to the snack table" gives her the clues she needs to anticipate the process of change. Asking her to announce cleanup time to the class lets her be in control of that transition.

Adult behavior affects and influences children. Annika has days of intense activity and involvement with materials; on other days she appears sluggish and uninterested. After a week of observation, teachers find a direct correlation with the presence of a student teacher. On the days the student is in the classroom, Annika calls out to him to see her artwork and watch her various accomplishments. It is on the days that the student is absent that Annika's activity level falls. Once a pattern is noticed, the teacher acts on these observations. In this case, the teacher and the student teacher work together to encourage Annika's daily involvement in school. The student teacher offers Annika ideas for activities she could demonstrate to him the following day. When he is absent, the teacher tries some of his activities that Annika especially enjoys.

Children also influence one another in powerful ways. Anyone who has worked with toddlers knows how attractive a toy becomes to a child once another has it. The 6-year-old who suddenly dislikes school may be feeling left out of a friendship group. Teachers need to carefully observe the social dynamics of the class as they seek to understand individual children.

Understanding of Self

 Observing children can be a key to understanding ourselves. People who develop observational skills notice human behavior more accurately. They become skilled at seeing small but important facets of human personality. They learn to differentiate between what is fact and what is inference. This increases an awareness of self as teacher and how one's biases affect perceptions about children.[1] Teachers who become keen observers of children learn to apply these skills to themselves. As Feeney and colleagues (1996) note:

In a less structured but no less important way, you also observe yourself, your values, your relationships, and your own feelings and reactions. When you apply what you know about observation to yourself, you gain greater self-awareness. It is difficult to be objective about yourself, but as you watch your own behavior and interactions you can learn more about how you feel and respond in various situations and realize the impact of your behavior on others.

 The values and benefits of observation are long-lasting. Only by practicing observations—what it takes to look, to see, to become more sensitive—will teachers be able to record children's behavior fully and vividly, capturing the unique qualities, culture and personality of each child.[2] The challenge of observation is high, but the benefits are well worth the effort.

Figure 6.6 ● Understanding the child is the goal of observation. Noticing how children interact with each other and the materials enriches the teacher's own knowledge of growth and behavior.

RECORDING OBSERVATIONS

Once teachers and students understand why observing is important, they must then learn how to record what they see. Although children are constantly under the teacher's eyes, so much happens so fast that critical events are lost in the daily routine of classrooms. Systematic observations aid in recording events and help teachers make sense of them.

In recording what you observe, you need to learn how to look and to learn the language of recording. The previous section helps by pointing out what to look for, and the concluding section of this chapter will give you some of the "nuts and bolts" of observing. *Learning to look,* however, requires a certain willingness to become aware and to do more than simply watch. Although it is

---

OUR DIVERSE WORLD OUR DIVERSE WORLD OUR DIVERSE WORLD OUR DIVERSE WORLD OUR DIVERSE WORLD OUR DIVERSE WORLD OUR DIVERSE WORLD OUR DIVERSE WORLD

[1] In the field of early childhood education, one is reminded repeatedly of the image of learning as a two-way, not a one-way, street. One teaches children *and* learns from children and families.

[2] The Focus Box by Janet Gonzalez-Mena gives a multicultural perspective to both observing children and understanding ourselves.

Understanding What We Observe: A Multicultural Perspective

Janet Gonzalez-Mena

When we observe young children, what we see is influenced by our culture. Even though we are objective, culture colors our description.

For example, I watch a 2-year-old scream "mine" and fend off a boy trying to grab the blanket she's holding. She is obviously protecting "her security blanket." What I see reveals my culture, because the "her" implies ownership and "security blanket" gives special meaning to the piece of cloth. My choice of words is related to my cultural perspective on property rights as I watch a girl "stand up for herself."

Through a different pair of cultural eyes, this scene might not make the same kind of sense. Suppose I didn't believe in private property or have the concept that an object could provide security. I might focus on the "selfishness" of this child. The way I understand the situation can affect the words I choose to describe it.

When I see a child shouting at another child in anger, I know he is just "expressing his feelings." I come from a culture in which individuality and self-expression are important. Someone from a culture that puts little focus on the individual may see self-expression in a different light. That person might describe the scene from the view of what the boy is doing to the harmony of the group.

If I observe children fingering rice at a "sensory table," I see their behavior differently from the person who thinks they are playing with food, especially if that person regards rice as sacred.

Mirrors in classrooms may also be regarded in a different light by two observers. One thinks that children are gaining a sense of self by looking at their reflections. Another may worry that they are becoming conceited.

Three observers looking at an infant asleep on his tummy in a crib may react very differently to what appears to be just a quiet scene. One sees a baby sleeping peacefully. The second may feel sorry for the baby because he is alone in a crib. In some cultures babies never sleep by themselves but are always with someone—asleep or awake. The third observer may see a baby at risk for crib death (sudden infant death syndrome, or SIDS). Although in her culture babies have traditionally slept on their stomachs, she now knows about the studies that correlate increased risk with sleeping position. She wants to turn the baby over!

Observers watching the same scene, seeing the same behavior, think of it in very different terms, thus affecting their reactions and descriptions.

Janet Gonzalez-Mena, of Napa Valley College, is co-author of Infants, Toddlers, and Caregivers *(Mountain View, CA: Mayfield, 1997) and author of* Multicultural Issues in Child Care *(Mountain View, CA: Mayfield, 1997),* The Child in the Family and the Community *(New York: Merrill, 1997), and* Dragon Mom: Confessions of a Child Development Expert *(Buffalo, NY: Exchange Press, 1995).*

Figure 6.7 ● Teachers balance observing with interacting. When a child asks a question, the teacher is available but not intrusive so that the child's play is uninterrupted and the teacher can resume observation.

true that teachers rarely have the luxury of observing uninterrupted for long periods of time, they can often plan shorter segments. Practice by paying attention to the content of children's play during free periods—theirs and yours.

Next, try your hand at jotting some notes about that play. It is easy to get discouraged, especially if you are unaccustomed to writing. The *language of recording* gets easier as you practice finding synonyms for common words. For instance, children are active creatures—how many ways do they run? They may gallop, dart, whirl, saunter, skip, hop. Or think of the various ways children talk to you: they shriek, whisper, whine, shout, demand, whimper, lisp, roar. Once you have a certain mastery of the language (and be sure to record what you see in the language that comes easiest to you), describing the important nuances of children's behavior will become easier. For an example of such descriptions, see Chapter 14 about children's feelings.

Common Elements of Observations

The key ingredients in all types of observations used in recording children's behavior are (1) defining and describing the behaviors and (2) repeating the observation in terms of several factors such as time, number of children, or activities. All observational systems have certain elements in common:

Focus

● What do you want to know?

● Whom/what do you want to observe? Child? Teacher? Environment? Group?

● What aspects of behavior do you want to know about? Motor skills? Social development? Problem-solving?

● What is your purpose?
Study the environment?
Observe the daily schedule?
Evaluate a child's skills?
Deal with negative behavior?
Analyze transitions?
Do research?
Confer with parents?
Train teachers?

System

● What will you do?

● How will you define the terms?

● How will you record the information you need?

● How detailed will your record be?

● Will you need units of measure? What kind?

● For how long will you record?

Tools

● What will you need for your observations?

● How will you record what you want to know?
Video or tape recorder? Camera? Pencil? Chart?

Environment

● Where will you watch?
Classroom? Yard? Home?

● What restraints are inherent in the setting?

Using these building blocks of observational systems, teachers seek a method that yields a collection of observable data that helps them focus more clearly on a child or situation. Four major methods of observing and two additional information-gathering techniques will be discussed. They are:

1. Narratives (diary descriptions, running records, specimen descriptions, anecdotal notes)

2. Time sampling

3. Event sampling

4. Modified child study techniques (checklists, rating scales, shadow study)

5. Experimental procedures

6. The clinical method

Types of Observations

Narratives

At once the most valuable and most difficult of records, **narratives** are attempts to record nearly everything that happens. In the case of a young child, this means all that the child does, says, gestures, seems to feel, and appears to think about. Narratives maintain a running record of the excitement and tension of the interaction while remaining an accurate, objective account of the events and behavior. Narratives are an attempt to actually recreate the scene by recording it in thorough and vivid language. Observers put into words what they see, hear, and know about an event or a person. The result is a full and dynamic report.

Narratives are the oldest and often most informative kind of report. Historically, as Arnold Gesell reported, they were used to set basic developmental norms. They are a standard technique in anthropology and the biologic sciences. Irwin and Bushnell (1980) provide a detailed historical background that traces the narrative back to Pestalozzi (1700s) and Darwin (1800s). Jean Piaget watched and recorded in minute detail his own children's growth. His observations resulted in a full report on children's thought processes and development of intelligence. **Baby biographies**, narratives written by parents, were some of the first methods used in child study and reached their peak of popularity in the early 1900s.

Diary descriptions are one form of narrative. Just as the term implies, they are, in diary form, consecutive records of everything children do and say and how they do it. The process is a natural one. In the classroom this means describing every action observed within a given time period. It might be a 5-minute period during free play to watch and record what one child does. The child who is a loner, the child who wanders, and the child who is aggressive are prime candidates for a diary description. Another way to use this type of **running record** is to watch an area of the yard or room, then record who is there and how they are using the materials.

A more common form of the narrative is a modified version of a running record, or a **specimen description** as it is often called in research terms. The procedure is to take on-the-spot notes of a specific child each day. This task lends itself easily to most early childhood settings. The teachers carry with them a small notebook and pencil, tucked in a pocket. They jot down whatever seems important or noteworthy during the day. They may focus on one specimen at a time:

● A part of the environment—how is the science area being used?

● A particular time of day—what happens right after naps?

● A specific child—how often is Lucy hitting out at other children?

This system may be even less structured, with all the teachers taking "on-the-hoof" notes as daily incidents occur. These notes then become a rich source of information for report writing and parent conferences.

Another form of narrative is a log or journal. A page is set aside for each child in the class. At some point, teachers write in details about each child. Because this is time-consuming and needs to be done without interruption, it helps to write immediately after school is over. Sometimes teaching teams organize themselves to enable one member of the staff to observe and record in the journal during class time. The important point is that each child's general behavior is recorded either while it is happening or soon afterward.

The challenging part of this recording technique, the narrative, is to have enough detail so the reader will be able to picture whole situations later. Using language as a descriptive tool requires a large vocabulary and skillful recorder. Whatever notes the teachers use, however brief, need to be both clear and accurate.

At the same time teachers are recording in a graphic way, they need to be aware of the personal biases that can influence observations. When we look at children, what we see is in part a result of our personal experiences, the theories we hold, and the assumptions we make.[1] Teaching is an intensely personal activity, and what the children look like, do, and say may arouse strong feelings and reactions. Figure 6.3 compares two observations to illustrate this point. By becoming aware of our biases and assumptions, we can become more accurate and objective in our work as teachers. Figure 6.9 is an example of the narrative type of observation.

Narratives are an observational technique with roots in psychology, anthropology, and biology. They can follow several formats and are an attempt to record all that happens as it happens. There are many advantages to this type of observation. Narratives are rich in information, provide detailed behavioral accounts, and are relatively easy to record. With a minimum of equipment and training, teachers can learn to take notes on what children do and say. To write down everything is impossible, so some selection is necessary. These judgment calls can warp the narrative. Also, observations of this kind require large amounts of time—just what teachers who are involved with a group of children lack. The main disadvantages of narratives, then, are the time they can take, the language and the vocabulary that must be used, and the biases the recorder may have. Even though the narrative remains one of the most widely used and effective methods of observing young children today, many teachers prefer more structured procedures because of these problems. These more definite, more precise techniques still involve some personal interpretation, but the area of individual judgment is diminished. The observational techniques discussed in the following sections also tend to be less time-consuming than the narrative.

Time Sampling

The time sampling method collects information other than that which a narrative provides. It is less descriptive, more specific, and requires different observational skills. A time sample is an observation of what happens within a given period of time. Developed as an observational strategy in laboratory schools in the 1920s, time sampling was used to collect data on large numbers of children and to get a sense of normative behaviors for particular age groups or sexes.

Time sampling appears to have originated with research in child development. It has been used to record autonomy, dependency, task persistence, aggression, and social involvement. Time sampling has also been used to study dependent, independent, and solitary play patterns and to record nervous habits of schoolchildren, such as nail biting and hair twisting (Prescott, 1973; Irwin & Bushnell, 1980). The defini-

OUR DIVERSE WORLD OUR DIVERSE WORLD OUR DIVERSE WORLD OUR DIVERSE WORLD OUR DIVERSE WORLD OUR DIVERSE WORLD OUR DIVERSE WORLD OUR DIVERSE WORLD

[1] It is a given we all have biases. It is not realistic to think one can be bias-free. The goal is to be conscious of the bias we bring to our work and be open to multiple interpretations of observed behavior. In this way we do not let our individual bias dictate our observations and interactions with children from diverse backgrounds.

Figure 6.8 ● A child plays alone.

tive study using time sampling is Mildred Parten's observation in the 1930s of children's play. The codes developed in this study have become classic play patterns: parallel, associative, and cooperative play. These codes are used throughout this text (see Chapters 3, 11, and 14), as well as in the professional field to describe the interactions of children.

In a time sample, behavior is recorded at regular time intervals. To use this method, one needs to sample what occurs fairly frequently. It makes sense to choose those behaviors that might occur, say, at least once every 10 minutes. Figure 6.10 demonstrates a time-sampling procedure.

Time sampling has its own advantages and disadvantages. The process itself helps teachers define exactly what it is they want to observe. Certainly it helps focus on specific behaviors and how often they occur. Time sampling is ideal for collecting information about the group as a whole. Finally, defining behaviors clearly and developing a category and coding system, reduce the problem of observer bias.

The Child Alone

Unoccupied Behavior. SH slowly walks from the classroom to the outside play area, looking up each time one of the children swishes by. SH stops when reaching the table and benches and begins pulling the string on the sweatshirt. Still standing, SH looks around the yard for a minute, then wanders slowly over to the seesaw. Leaning against it, SH touches the seesaw gingerly, then trails both hands over it while looking out into the yard. (*Interpretive comments:* This unoccupied behavior is probably due to two reasons: SH is overweight and has limited language skills compared with the other children. Pulling at the sweatshirt string is something to do to pass the time, since the overweight body is awkward and not especially skillful.)

Onlooker Behavior. J is standing next to the slide watching her classmates using this piece of equipment. She looks up and says, "Hi." Her eyes open wider as she watches the children go down the slide. P calls to J to join them but J shakes her head "no." (*Interpretive comments:* J is interested in the slide but is reluctant to use it. She has a concerned look on her face when the others slide down; it seems too much of a challenge for J.)

Solitary Play. L comes running onto the yard holding two paintbrushes and a bucket filled with water. He stops about 3 feet away from a group of children playing with cars, trucks, and buses in the sandbox and sits down. He drops the brushes into the bucket and laughs when the water splashes his face. He begins swishing the water around with the brushes and then starts wiggling his fingers in it. (*Interpretive comments:* L is very energetic and seems to thoroughly enjoy his outside playtime with water. He adds creative touches to this pleasurable experience.)

Figure 6.9 ● The narrative form of observation gives a rich sample of children's behavior; even though it risks teacher bias, it still records valuable information.

Child	9:00			9:05			9:10			9:20			9:25			9:30			Total
	P	A	C	P	A	C	P	A	C	P	A	C	P	A	C	P	A	C	
Jamal																			
Marty																			
Dahlia																			
Keith																			
Rosa																			
Cameron																			
Hannah																			

PLAY WITH OTHERS
P = Parallel
A = Associative
C = Cooperative
Time Unit

Figure 6.10 ● Time sampling of play with others involves defining the behavior and making a coding sheet to tally observations.

Yet, by diminishing this bias one also eliminates some of the richness and quality of information. It is difficult to get the whole picture when one divides it into artificial time units and with only a few categories. The key is to decide what it is teachers want to know, then choose the observational method that best suits those needs. When narratives or time samplings won't suffice, perhaps an event sampling will.

Event Sampling

Event sampling is one of the more intriguing techniques. With this method, the observer defines an event, devises a system for describing and coding it, then waits for it to happen. As soon as it does, the recorder moves into action. Thus, the behavior is recorded as it occurs naturally.

The events that are chosen can be quite interesting and diverse. Consider Helen C. Dawes's classic analysis of preschool children's quarrels. Whenever a quarrel began, the observer recorded it. She recorded how long the quarrel lasted, what was happening when it started, what behaviors happened during the quarrel (including what was done and said), what the outcome was, and what happened afterward. Her format for recording included duration (X number of seconds), a narrative for the situation, verbal or motor activity, and checklists for the quarrel behavior, outcome, and after-effects (Irwin & Bushnell, 1980).

Other researchers have studied dominance and emotions. Teachers can use event sampling to look at these and other behaviors such as bossiness, avoidance of teacher requests, or withdrawal.

Like time sampling, event sampling looks at a particular behavior or occurrence (Figure 6.11). But the unit is the event rather than a prescribed time interval. Here again the behavior must be clearly defined and the recording sheet easy to use. Unlike with time sampling, the event to be recorded may occur a number of times during the observation.

For these reasons, event sampling is a favorite of classroom teachers. They can go about the business of teaching children until the event occurs. Then they can record the event quickly and efficiently. Prescribing the context within which the event occurs restores some of the quality often lost in time sampling. The only disadvantage is that the richness of detail of the narrative description is missing.

Event Sampling Guidelines

1. Define the behavior to be observed.
2. Decide what information you want to know.
3. Make a simple recording sheet.

Children's accidents: spills,
knock-overs, falls.
Child(ren) involved, time,
place, cause, results.
To watch in early morning:

Time	Children	Place	Cause	Outcome
8:50	Shelley, Mike	playdough	M steps on S toes	S cries, runs to Tchr
9:33	Tasauna, Yuki	blocks	T runs through, knocks over Y's tower	Y hits T, both cry
9:56	Spencer	yard	S turns trike too sharply, falls off	S cries, wants mom
10:28	Lorena, Shelley	doll corner	L bumps table, spills pitcher S has just set there	S cries, runs to Tchr

Total 8:45–10:30 AM = 4

Figure 6.11 ● Event sampling can be helpful in determining how frequently a specific event takes place. For instance, sampling the number and types of accidents for a given child or time frame helps teachers see what is happening in class.

Modified Child Study Techniques

Because observation is the key method of studying young children in their natural settings, it makes good sense to develop many kinds of observational skills. Each can be tailored to fit the individual child, the particular group, the kind of staff, and the specific problem. Teachers who live in complex, creative classrooms have questions arise that need fast answers. Modified child study techniques can define the scope of the problem fairly quickly. Some of the techniques are: checklist systems, rating scales, shadow studies, and modified processes that reach both the group and the individuals in it.

Checklists contain a great deal of information that can be recorded rapidly. A carefully planned checklist can tell a lot about one child or the entire class. The data are collected in a short period of time, usually about a week. Figure 6.12 is an example of an activity checklist. With data collected for a week, teachers have a broad picture of how these children spend their time and what activities interest them.

Learning Center	Anna	Charlie	Leticia	Hiroko	Matt	Josie	Totals
Indoors							
Science Area					1		1
Dramatic Play	1	1	1			1	4
Art	1		1	1			3
Blocks		1					1
Manipulatives			1	1	1		3
Easels				1			1
Music			1		1		2
Outdoors							
Water/Sand/Mud		1	1			1	3
Blocks				1	1		2
Wheel Toys		1			1		2
Climbers	1		1			1	3
Woodworking				1			1
Ball Games	1						1
Animal Care	1	1				1	3
Totals	5	5	6	5	5	4	

Figure 6.12 ● An activity checklist. With data collected for a week, teachers have a broad picture of how children spend their time at school and what activities interest them.

If, however, teachers want to assess children's motor skills, a yes/no list is preferable. Figure 6.13 illustrates the use of such a chart.

Checklists can vary in length and complexity depending on their functions. To develop one, teachers first determine the purpose of the observation. Next they define what the children will do to demonstrate the behavior being observed. Finally comes designing the actual checklist, one that is easy to use and simple to set aside when other duties must take precedence.

Although they are easy to record, checklists lack the richness of the more descriptive narrative. For instance, by looking at the checklist in Figure 6.12, teachers will know which activities children have chosen, but they will not gain a sense of how they played in each area, the time spent there, or whether and with whom they interacted. The advantages of checklists are that they can tally broad areas of information and teachers can create one with relative ease. Checklists are often used in evaluation. Chapter 10 contains several examples.

Rating scales are like checklists, planned in advance to record something specific. They extend checklists by adding some quality to what is observed. The advantage is that more information is gathered. A potential problem is added because the observers' opinions are now required and could hamper objectivity.

Rating scales differ from checklists in several ways. Instead of simply recording where children are playing, the rating scales require the teacher to decide how they are playing. What is the extent of their

Motor Skills Observation (ages 2–4) Child _____ Date _____ Observer _____ Age _____	Yes	No
Eating:		
1. Holds glass with one hand		
2. Pours from pitcher		
3. Spills little from spoon		
4. Selects food with pincer grasp		
Dressing:		
1. Unbuttons		
2. Puts shoes on		
3. Uses both hands together (such as holding jacket with one hand while zipping with the other)		
Fine Motor:		
1. Uses pincer grasp with pencil, brushes		
2. Draws straight line		
3. Copies circles		
4. Cuts at least 2" in line		
5. Makes designs and crude letters		
6. Builds tower of 6-9 blocks		
7. Turns pages singly		
Gross Motor:		
1. Descends/ascends steps with alternate feet		
2. Stands on one foot, unsupported		
3. Hops on two feet		
4. Catches ball, arms straight, elbows in front of body		
5. Operates tricycle		

Figure 6.13 ● A yes/no checklist gives specific information about an individual child's skills.

involvement and the frequency or degree of their play? A rating scale may use word phrases ("always," "sometimes," "never") or a numerical key (1 through 5).

Developing a rating scale is simple, though a good scale can be difficult to make. The full range of behavior teachers will observe cannot always be easily reduced to discrete measurements. However, after deciding what to observe, teachers then determine what the children will do to demonstrate the action. A scale to measure attention at group times might include the categories in Figure 6.14. Each teacher's rating scale could include a series of checkmarks that record each group time for a period of 2 weeks. The staff pools information by comparing notes. The result is a detailed description of (1) each child's behavior as each teacher sees it; (2) the group's overall attention level; and (3) an interesting cross-teacher comparison.

The **shadow study** is a third type of modified technique. It is similar to the diary description and focuses on one child at a time. An in-depth approach, the shadow study gives a detailed picture.

Each teacher attempts to observe and record regularly the behavior of one particular child. Then after a week or so the notes are compared. Although the notes may be random, it is preferable to give some form and organization. Divide a sheet of paper in half lengthwise, with one column for the environment and the other column for details about the child's behavior or response. This will make it easy to glance at 15-minute intervals to collect the data. Figure 6.15 illustrates this process.

The data in a shadow study are descriptive. In this, it shares the advantages of narratives. One of its disadvantages is that teachers may let other matters go while focusing on one child. Also, the shadow study can be quite time-consuming. Still, one interesting side effect often noted is how the behavior of the child being studied improves while the child is being

NEVER ATTENDS (wiggles, distracts others, wanders away)

SELDOM ATTENDS (eyes wander, never follows fingerplays or songs, occasionally watches leader)

SOMETIMES ATTENDS (can be seen imitating hand gestures, appears to be watching leader about half the time, watches others imitating leader)

USUALLY ATTENDS (often follows leader, rarely leaves group, rarely needs redirection, occasionally volunteers, usually follows leader's gestures and imitations)

ALWAYS ATTENDS (regularly volunteers, enthusiastically enters into each activity, eagerly imitates leader, almost always tries new songs)

Figure 6.14 ● A rating scale measuring attention at group times requires data in terms of frequency, adding depth to the observation.

observed. Disruptive behavior seems to diminish or appear less intense. It would appear that in the act of focusing on the child, teacher attention has somehow helped to alter the behavior. Somehow the child feels the impact of all this positive, caring attention and responds to it.

Modified child study techniques are particularly useful because they are tailored to fit the specific needs and interests of the teachers. Teachers know what it is they want to observe and can develop a method of recording that matches their needs and the time available during school. Devising a new technique is neither easy nor quick. It takes hard work and dedicated teachers committed to improving their observational skills to record accurately what they see.

Additional Information-Gathering Techniques

Two additional strategies are used to obtain information about a child. Because they involve some adult intervention, they do not consist strictly of observing and recording naturally occurring behavior. Still, they are very helpful techniques for teachers to understand and use.

Experimental Procedures

Experimental procedures are those in which adult researchers closely control a situation and its variables. Researchers create a situation in which they can (1) observe a particular behavior, (2) make a hypothesis, or guess, about that behavior, and (3) test the hypothesis by conducting the experiment.

For instance, an experimenter might wish to observe fine-motor behavior in 7-year-olds to test the hypothesis that these children can significantly improve their fine-motor skills in sewing if given specific instructions. Two groups of children are tested. One group is given an embroidery hoop, thread, and needle and asked to make 10 stitches. The other receives a demonstration of how to stitch and is then given the identical task. The embroidery hoops created by both groups are then compared. Some previously agreed-on criteria are used to quantify the fine-motor skill demonstrated by the two groups' work. The major criteria for a scientific experiment may be applied to this procedure as follows:

1. The experimenters can control all relevant aspects of the behavior. (In this case, the materials can be controlled, although previous experience with embroidering cannot.)

2. Usually, only one variable at a time should be measured. (Only fine-motor skill as it relates to embroidery is observed, not other skills such as language or information processing, or even fine-motor proficiency in printing or drawing.)

3. Children are assigned to the two groups in a random manner. (In other words, the groups are not divided by sex, age, or any other predetermined characteristics.)

Few teachers working directly with children will use the stringent criteria needed to undertake a true scientific experiment. However, it is useful to understand this process because much basic research conducted to investigate how children think, perceive, and behave utilizes these techniques.

Clinical Method

The **clinical method** is another information-gathering technique that involves the adult directly with the child. This method is used in psychotherapy and in counseling settings, as the therapist asks prob-

Child's Name *Jeff*		

Time	Setting (where)	Behavior/Response (what and how)
9:00	Arrives—cubby, removes wraps, etc.	"I can put on my own nametag" (enthusiastically). Uses thumb to push sharp end of pin; grins widely. Goes to teacher, "Did you see what I did?"
9:15	Blocks	Precise, elaborate work with small cubes on top of block structure, which he built with James. "Those are the dead ones," pointing to the purple cubes outside the structure. Cries and hits Kate when her elbow accidentally knocks tower off.
9:30	Wandering around room	Semidistant, slow pace. Stops at table where children are preparing snack. Does not make eye contact with teacher when invited to sit; Ali grabs J's shirt and tugs at it. "The teacher is talking to you!" J blinks, then sits and asks to help make snack. Stays 10 minutes.

Figure 6.15 ● A shadow study will profile an individual child in the class. This method is especially useful for children who seem to be having trouble in school.

ing questions. The master of the **methode clinique** with children was Piaget, who would observe and question a child about a situation as described in Chapter 4. Two examples of this method are:

> Three-month-old Jenna is lying in a crib looking at a mobile. Her hands are waving in the air. The adult wonders whether Jenna will reach out and grasp the mobile if it is moved close to her hands. Or will she bat at the toy? Move her hands away? The adult then tries it to see what will happen.

> A group of preschoolers are gathered around a water table. The teacher notices two cups, one deep and narrow, the other broad and shallow, and asks, "I wonder which one holds more, or if they are the same?" The children say what they think and why. Then, one of the children takes the two cups and pours the liquid from one into the other.

In both examples, the adult does more than simply observe and record what happens. With the infant, the adult questions what Jenna's responses might be and then watches for the answer. The preschool teacher intervenes in the children's natural play to explore a question systematically with them, then listens for and observes the answers. The clinical method is not strictly an observational method, but it is an informative technique that, when used carefully, can reveal much about children's abilities and knowledge.

All these observation techniques help adults watch closely to see what is going on. Observation is used extensively in early childhood programs (and, increasingly, in elementary education) to assess children; Chapter 10 discusses assessment. Figure 6.16 summarizes these systems. It is safe to say that whenever a teacher encounters a problem—be it a child's behavior, a period of the day, a set of materials, or a puzzling series of events—the first step toward a solution is systematic observation.

Method	Observational Interval	Recording Techniques	Advantages	Disadvantages
1. Narratives				
Diary description	Day to day	Using notebook and pencil; can itemize activity or other ongoing behavior; can see growth patterns	Rich in detail; maintains sequence of events; describes behavior as it occurs	Open to observer bias; time-consuming
Specimen descriptions/running record	Continuous sequences	Same	Less structured	Sometimes need follow-up
Journal	Regular, preferred daily/weekly	Log, usually with space for each child; often a summary of child's behavior	Same as narratives	Difficult to find time to do
"On-the-hoof" anecdotes	Sporadic	Ongoing during class time; using notepad and paper in hand	Quick and easy to take; short-capture pertinent events/details	Lack detail; need to be filled in at later time; can detract from teaching responsibilities
2. Time sampling	Short and uniform time intervals	On-the-spot as time passes; prearranged recording sheets	Easy to record; easy to analyze; relatively bias free	Limited behaviors; loss of detail; loss of sequence and ecology of event
3. Event sampling	For the duration of the event	Same as for time sampling	Easy to record; easy to analyze; can maintain natural flow of class activity easily	Limited behaviors; loss of detail; must wait for behavior to occur
4. Modifications				
Checklists	Regular or intermittent	Using prepared recording sheets; can be during or after class	Easy to develop and use	Lack of detail; tell little of the cause of behaviors
Rating scales	Continuous behavior	Same as for checklists	Easy to develop and use; can use for wide range of behaviors	Ambiguity of terms; high observer bias
Shadow study	Continuous behavior	Narrative-type recording; uses prepared recording sheets	Rich in detail; focuses in depth on individual	Bias problem; can take away too much of a teacher's time and attention
5. Experimental procedures	Short and uniform	May be checklists, prearranged recording sheets, audio or video tape	Simple, clear, pure study, relatively bias free	Difficult, hard to isolate in the classroom
6. Clinical method	Any time	Usually notebook or tape recorder	Relevant data; can be spontaneous, easy to use	Adult has changed naturally occurring behavior

Figure 6.16 ● A summary chart of the major observational techniques that the early childhood professional can use to record children's behavior. (Adapted from Irwin, D.M., and Bushnell, M.M., *Observational Strategies for Child Study*. New York: Holt, Rinehart and Winston, 1980.)

HOW TO OBSERVE AND RECORD

Learning how to observe is a serious activity and requires a great deal of concentration. Some preparations can be made beforehand so that full attention is focused on the observation. Thinking through some of the possible problems helps the teacher get the most out of the experience.

Observing While Teaching

To make observing workable at school, the teacher must keep in mind that there is no one right way to observe and record. Some teachers find certain times of the day easier than others. Many prefer to watch during free play, whereas others find it easier to watch individual children during directed teaching times. Although some teachers keep a pencil and paper handy to write their observations throughout the day, others choose to record what they see after school is over for the day. The professional team that is committed to observation will find ways to support its implementation.

Finding an opportunity for regular observations is difficult. Centers are rarely staffed so well that one teacher can be free from classroom responsibilities for long periods of time. Some schools asks for parent volunteers to take over an activity while a teacher observes. In one center the snack was set up ahead of time to free up one teacher to observe during group time. The environment can be arranged with activities that require little supervision when a teacher is interested in making some observations.

Some question the reliability of the data collected when children know they are being observed. Initially, children may feel self-conscious, asking pointed questions of the observer and changing their behavior as if they were on stage. However, when effective observation strategies are used (see the section in this chapter entitled How to Observe Effectively) and regular observations are done by familiar adults, children will soon ignore the observer and resume normal activity.

Teachers can improve their observation and recording skills outside the classroom as well. Taking an "Observation of Children" class is helpful; so is visiting other classes in pairs and comparing notes afterward. Staff meetings take on added dimension when teachers role play what they think they've seen and others ask for details.

The teacher who makes notes during class time has other considerations. The need to be inconspicuous while note taking is important when trying to teach and record simultaneously. Wear clothing with at least one good pocket. This ensures the paper and pencil are available when needed and the children's privacy is protected. Take care not to leave notes out on tables, shelves, or in cupboards for others to see. They should be kept confidential until added to the children's records.

There is disagreement among professionals about the relative usefulness of the various kinds of record-keeping equipment. Some teachers find the "low-tech" materials of pen and notebook or 3×5 cards easiest to find, carry, use, and set aside. Others find a camera, tape recorder, and even a video camcorder helpful, although the expense, storage, and distracting nature of such equipment need to be considered. Regardless of what teachers use, they must organize themselves for success:

● Gather and prepare the materials ahead of time: This may mean getting everyone aprons with large pockets or a set of cards or labeled spiral notebook.

● Consider where you will observe: Set up observation places (chairs, stations); in a well-equipped yard and room, you can plan strategically.

● Plan when you will observe: In a well-planned day, teachers can have the freedom to practice observing regularly during play time.

● Prepare every adult to be an observer: Give every teacher some regular opportunities to observe and reflect on children's play.

Respect the privacy of the children and their families at all times. Any information gathered as part of an observation is treated with strict confidentiality. Teachers and students are careful not to use children's names in casual conversation. They do not talk about children in front of other children or among themselves. It is the role of the adults to see that children's privacy is maintained. Carrying tales out of school is tempting, but unprofessional.

Beginning to Observe

In some schools, observers are a normal part of the school routine. In colleges where there are laboratory facilities on campus, visitors and student

Figure 6.17 ● Observation skills are honed when teachers have opportunities to work with a few children at a time.

observers are familiar figures. They have only to follow established guidelines for making an observation.

Many times students are responsible for finding their own places to observe children. If so, the student calls ahead and schedules a time to observe that is convenient. Be specific about observation needs, the assignment, the ages of children desired, the amount of time needed, and the purpose of the observation.

If you are planning to observe in your own class, several steps are necessary for a professional observation and a believable recording. First, plan the observation. Have a specific *goal* in mind, and even put that at the top of your recording sheet. Goals can be general ("Let's see what activities Ajit chooses today.") or specific ("Watch for instances of quarreling in the sand area."). Second, *observe and record*. To be objective, be as specific and detailed as possible. Write only the behavior—the "raw data"—and save the analysis and your interpretation for later. After class, re-read your notes (transcribing them into something legible if anyone else might need to read them) and make some conclusions. Your observation was *what* happened; the

intepretation is the place for your opinions and ideas of *why* it happened. For instance, you may have found that three of the four quarrels were over holding the hose; this gives you a clear reason for the quarrels. The final step is implementing your solutions; plan what you will do next, and then *follow through* with your ideas. In our example, a five-pronged hose outlet could be purchased, a waiting list could be started for the "hose-holder job," or the teacher could be in charge of the hose.

Wherever an observation is planned, it is critical to maintain **professional confidentiality**. If observing at another site, call ahead for an appointment. Talk about the purpose and format of your observation with both director and teacher. Finally, in *any* discussion of the observation, change the names of the children and school to protect those involved.

How to Observe Effectively

The success of the observation depends on how inconspicuous the observer can be. Children are more

Figure 6.18 ● Learning to observe and record effectively takes time and practice. Remaining unobtrusive and recording quietly allow children to continue their natural behavior without distraction.

natural if the observer blends into the scenery. By sitting back, one can observe the whole scene and record what is seen and heard, undisturbed and uninfluenced. This distancing sets up a climate for recording that aids the observer in concentrating on the children.

There are two main reasons for an observer to be **unobtrusive**. First, it allows for a more accurate recording of the children's activities. Second, it does not interfere with the smooth functioning of the classroom, the children, or the teachers. In the case of teachers observing their own programs, you must plan ahead with coteachers and have materials at hand that can be set aside quickly if necessary. The following suggestions help effective observing:

● Enter and leave the area quietly. Ask the teacher where to sit. Keep in the background as much as possible. The good observer is so skilled at this that both children and teachers forget the presence of a stranger.

● Sit down in a low chair in an out-of-the-way place. Sit where the activity of the children is unobstructed. By keeping low, observers call less attention to themselves. Take care to sit outside traffic patterns so children will be able to carry on with play without interference or interruption.

● Sit at the edge of an activity rather than right in the middle of it. Against a wall or around the perimeter of the room are good vantage points for sitting. Outside, if no chair is available, blend against a wall, a fence, or a tree.

● Sometimes it may be necessary to follow children as they move from place to place. When that happens, be as inconspicuous as possible and be prepared for times when, for good reasons, the teacher might object.

● Children may occasionally ask, "What is your name? What are you doing? Why did you come here?" If asked a direct question, answer in a truthful, friendly manner, but be as brief as possible. A good response is, "I'm working." Avoid initiating conversations with children. Be as natural as possible if a child talks to you, but appear to be busy writing and observing.

● It is difficult to be in a busy classroom with children without being amused by them. Avoid a degree of response that will attract the children's attention. Laughing at them, smiling, talking, meeting their eyes—all distract them from play. They also make the observer, rather than the children's work or playmates, the center of attention.

● Avoid talking to other adults while observing. Sitting apart from others draws less attention to the tasks and lessens the temptation to chat. Request a brief conference before leaving to check accuracy.

● There is one time when it might be necessary to get involved with the children. If a child is in obvious danger and no one else is around, the observer should step in. Call for a teacher only if there is time. A child running out the gate toward the street or in the way of a swing needs immediate help. Two children fighting over a truck might need a teacher but are not in immediate danger.

Summary

Systematic observation and recording of children's behavior are fundamental tools in understanding children. What children do and say and how they think and feel are revealed as they play and work. By learning to observe children's behavior, teachers become more aware of the children's skills, needs, and concerns.

The ability to observe is a skill in itself; teachers examine their own beliefs, influences and attitudes to achieve a measure of objectivity. Recording the observations is another skill, one that requires facility with the written word and an understanding of the purpose for observing. To make a successful observation, teachers first decide what it is they want to find out about the child.

Key ingredients to successful observations include clear definitions of the behaviors to be observed and techniques for observing and recording them. These provide the tools for gaining a deeper understanding of individual children and the group. They also enhance knowledge about the interrelationships of developmental areas. Too, one gains insight into the dynamics of child behavior and what influences are brought to bear on it. Finally, observing children can give insight and greater understanding of self.

The general types of observational techniques explored in this chapter include narratives, time sampling, event sampling, and modified child study techniques, such as checklists, rating scales, and shadow studies. Additional information-gathering techniques include experimental procedures and the clinical method.

As teachers observe and record the behavior of young children, they are aware of professional guidelines that protect children. The guidelines help ensure accurate observation and help the observer respect the privacy of the individual or group.

Review Questions

1. List four observational methods. Describe the advantages and disadvantages of each. Which would you prefer? Why? Which one(s) might best suit a beginning teacher? A parent? An experienced teacher? The director of the school?

2. Poor observations usually contain inferences, overgeneralizations, and/or opinions that cloud a complete, objective sampling of a child's behavior. Read the segment below and underline the language segments that contain such passages.

> C is sitting on the rug with four friends and he is playing with cars and he starts whining about his car. He is just having a bad attitude about its not moving correctly. C is crying because he just got hit with the car. Let me tell you something about him. He is a big whiner about anything and he always wants it his way. Then he goes over to the book corner and is very quietly reading a book and he is happy by himself.

3. Put this chapter to the test! Match the behavior with the category it describes:

Category	Behavior
Children in general	Matthew cries when his grandma says goodbye.
Influences on behavior	Most 4-year-olds can pull up their pants on their own.
Understanding of self	To really know Celia, I'll have to observe her with scissors, at the climber, figuring out a problem, with her friends, in our small group time, when her mom leaves, and doing a painting.
Developmental relationships	I wonder why Mondays are so hard on Serena? Which weekends does she stay with her Dad?
Children as individuals	You know, I just overreact when I see children playing with their food.

4. Teachers have noticed that several children consistently interrupt at storytime with seemingly irrelevant questions and constantly grab onto children seated nearby. What's happening—and why? What observational tools would you use to find out? What clues from individual behavior would you look for? How would you look at the group as a whole? What other information would you need?

5. What do you consider to be the three most important guidelines to follow when observing young children? Why?

Learning Activities

1. Observe a children's quarrel. How did you feel when you watched? What does this tell you about your own influences in childhood? How did the teaching staff intervene? How would you? Why?

2. Try a time sample of children's play in your classroom. Observe 10 children for 1 minute each during free-play times, and record the type(s) of social behavior they show. Using Parten's categories, your chart would look like this one. Compare your results with the impressions of the other teachers with whom you work. Did you come to any conclusions on how children develop socially?

Child/Age	Unoccupied	Solitary	Onlooker	Parallel	Associative	Cooperative
1.						
2.						
3.						
4.						
5.						
6.						
7.						
8.						
9.						
10.						

Totals

3. Observe one child in your class and jot down a brief description of her language skills. Are they typical of her age level? How could you tell? Compare your notes with the perceptions of your supervising teacher.

4. Choose two children, one you think is doing well and one who is having trouble. Observe the adult–child interactions of each. What are the differences from the *children's* point of view in the quantity and quality of those relationships? What generalizations about the importance of such relationships in the early years can you make?

5. If you can, try a shadow study on a child in your class. Choose a child you don't know much about, you have trouble working with, or who is exhibiting inappropriate behaviors. How did this study help you to see the class and school from that child's point of view?

6. Observe a group of children for 10 minutes engaged in block play. Record your observations in running record form. Now, go back over that running record and make a list of things you want to know about the children's thinking and behavior. How could you construct this list, using the clinical method, to obtain the information you need? Would you intervene nonverbally? What questions could you ask the children directly?

7. Observe a child for 10 minutes. Using language as your paintbrush, make a written picture of that child's physical appearance and movements. Compare the child's size, body build, facial features, and energy level with those of other children in the class. Record as many of the body movements as you can, noting seemingly useless movements, failures, partial successes, as well as final achievements.

8. Perceptions of a person's character are in the eyes of the beholder. These perceptions affect how teachers behave with children. What color are your glasses tinted? Divide a piece of paper in half, lengthwise. On one side, list some words to describe your feelings about childhood, school, teachers, children, authority, making friends losing friends, hitting, playing. One the other side, describe how these feelings may have influenced your teaching and helped create your own biases.

Bibliography

Benjamin, A. C. (1994, September). Observations in early childhood classrooms. *Young Children, 46*(6), pp. 14–20.

Bentzen, M. (1995). *Seeing young children* (3rd ed.). Albany, NY: Delmar.

Brophy, J. E. (1979, May/June). Using observation to improve your teaching. *Young Children.*

Cartwright, S. (1994, September). When we really see the child. *Exchange,* pp. 5–9.

Cartwright, C. A., & Cartwright, G. P. (1984). *Developing observation skills* (2nd ed.). New York: McGraw-Hill.

Cohen, D. H., & Stern, V. (1978). *Observing and recording the behavior of young children.* New York: Teachers College Press.

Dawes, H. C. (1934). An analysis of two hundred quarrels of preschool children. *Child Development, 5,* pp. 139–57.

Dowley, E. M. (n.d.). *Cues for observing children's behavior.* Unpublished paper.

Feeney, S., Christensen, D., & Moravicik, E. (1996). *Who am I in the lives of children?* (2nd ed.). Englewood Cliffs, NJ: Prentice-Hall.

Irwin, D. M., & Bushnell, M. M. (1980). *Observational strategies for child study.* New York: Holt, Rinehart & Winston.

Jones, E. J., & Carter, M. (1991, January/February). The teacher as observer—Part 1, and Teacher as scribe and broadcaster: Using observation to communicate—Part 2. *Child Care Information Exchange,* pp. 35–38.

Nyberg, D. (1971). *Tough and tender learning.* Palo Alto, CA: National Press Books.

Parten, M. B. (1932). Social participation among preschool children. *Journal of Abnormal and Social Psychology, 27,* pp. 243–69.

Prescott, E. (1973). Who thrives in group day care? *Assessment of child-rearing environments: An ecological approach.* Pasadena, CA: Pacific Qaks College, ERIC 076 1229.

Rencken, K. S., Cartwright, S., Balaban, N., & Reynolds, G. (1996, November). Beginnings workshop: Observing children. Redmond, WA: *Child Care Information Exchange,* pp. 49–64.

Saxton, R. R. (1998, April). Personal communication.

Seefeldt, C., & Barbour, N. (1994). *Early childhood education: An introduction* (3rd ed.). New York: MacMillan College Publishing.

Special thanks to the following Early Childhood Education students for their observation samples: J. Gallero, C. Grupe, L. Hutton, C. Liner, C. Robinson, M. Saldivar.

Understanding and Guiding Behavior

Questions for Thought

Why do children behave the way they do?

What are some ways in which the classroom environment affects children's behavior?

What do teachers need to know about themselves so they can guide children with control and concern?

What is the difference between discipline and punishment?

Are behavior goals the same for all children? Why?

What are some common problem behaviors found in young children?

What are some effective ways to deal with behavior problems?

Why do some experts say spanking is harmful to children?

What should the teacher do if school and home guidance techniques differ?

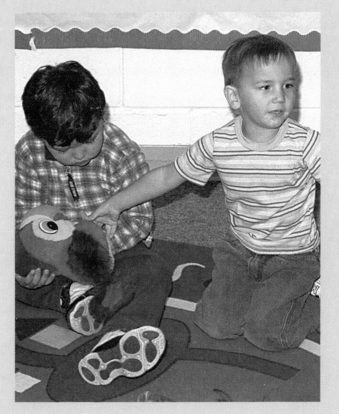

UNDERSTANDING BEHAVIOR

In the toddler class, 2-year-olds Shawnsey and Kim are playing in the dress-up area. Kim grabs at one of the many necklaces Shawnsey has draped around her neck. Startled, Shawnsey lets out a cry, grabs Kim's arm, and bites her.

Malcolm, a 5-year-old, rushes through the room, heading for the block area. For just a moment, he stands and watches Lorraine balancing blocks on top of one another in a tall column. With a swift wave of his arm, Malcolm topples the structure.

Mac, a 3½-year-old, is busy with a puzzle. When a teacher stops at the table to tell the children it is nearly time to clean up for snacks, Mac replies, "My daddy says that cleaning up is a girl's job and I don't have to do it." He throws the puzzle on the floor and dashes away from the teacher.

(*See Figures 7.13 and 7.17 for discussing solutions to these types of situations.*)

These are typical scenes in any early childhood center. No matter how plentiful the materials, how many or well-trained the adults, or how preplanned the program, conflicts are sure to occur. In this chapter, students will look at ways to recognize and handle such situations: how to understand and guide children's behavior in ways that will help them deal more effectively with their feelings. Helping children learn how to cope with their anger, their fears, their frustrations, and their desires is one of the most challenging jobs for a teacher.[1]

To teach children to respect themselves and each other is a complex and difficult task. It takes experience, skill, and love and is a critical part of caring for children. Look at the examples again. What do they say about children in general? What do they say about Shawnsey, Malcolm, and Mac? How should teachers respond to these children, and how does that response influence future behavior?

Figure 7.1 ● For guidance to be successful, a teacher must first understand children's behavior.

Theories

To guide children's behavior, a teacher must first understand it. This requires a solid background in child development, skills in observing, and understanding about *why* children behave and misbehave.

There are several ways of explaining what people do and why. One idea is that people's behavior is mainly a result of heredity (nature). Another is that experience and environment shape behavior (nurture). A third theory suggests that children go through "stages" at certain times of their lives regardless of their genes or home background.

Both sides have valid arguments in the nature/nurture debate. It is useful to remember that both heredity and experience affect behavior. Age and stage theory is also familiar. People speak of the "terrible two's" or say that all 4-year-old girls are silly. There may be some truth to those generalities, but that does not excuse the inappropriate behavior of the various developmental stages. Teachers and parents cannot ignore misbehavior (unless it is a specific guidance

[1] Different cultures have different ways of dealing with emotions. The educator needs an awareness of how he or she deals with particular emotions, as well as how the child's particular family culture deals with emotions.

strategy) just because children are the "right" age or because of their home situations. That attitude implies adults are powerless to help children form new behavior patterns. Not true!

Adults can do something about children's behavior if they understand what is happening to the child. Where does appropriate behavior come from? Why do children misbehave?

Factors That Affect Behavior

Knowing what affects children's behavior and feelings helps adults understand and manage the misbehaving child. Teachers can anticipate problems instead of waiting for them to occur; preventive guidance measures are part of guiding children's behavior.

At least five factors affect behavior: developmental factors, environmental factors, individual or personal styles, social and emotional needs, and cultural influences. These factors combine aspects of both nature and nurture theories, as well as the theories of ages and stages of development. The three vignettes at the beginning of the chapter provide examples of all five factors.

Developmental Factors

Children's growth is constant if not always smooth. Adults who work with children should be aware of developmental theory to know what type of behavior to expect of children at various ages.

The facts are that Shawnsey, Kim, Malcolm and Mac have been in a group setting for more than 3 hours and it is nearly snack time. Teachers know that preschoolers cannot be expected to be in control of themselves over extended periods of time. Conflicts and disagreements happen in any group of children. Hungry children are often ineffective problem solvers; Mac might not be as volatile after snack. It is also clear to the teacher that the toddlers do not have the language or social development skills to talk problems out with other children as does Malcolm, a 5-year-old.

Developmental theory helps teachers anticipate what children will do and how they might behave. To see behavior as predictable and developmentally appropriate is to understand it more completely. This understanding guides teachers in solving behavioral problems.

ON SPANKING

...Physical punishment such as hitting or spanking will mean two things: one, that you are bigger than she and you can get away with it, and two, that you believe in aggression.... Spanking is no good.... It says that you believe in settling things by force—and I don't believe in that (Brazelton, 1992).

...I think that the uneasiness after spanking a child is most telling.... subconsciously, we know that it is wrong, that it is not effective. Spanking does not accomplish the purpose for which it is intended. It teaches children to operate from fear rather than reason, and it breeds anger. The research evidence is also clear that physical force creates more resistance and much less cooperation (Galinksy & David, 1991).

Spanking may allow a parent to let off steam, but it doesn't teach a child the right way to behave. What's more, it is humiliating and emotionally harmful, and it can lead to physical injury. Worst of all, spanking teaches youngsters that violence is an acceptable way to communicate. The American Academy of Pediatrics strongly opposes hitting children (American Academy of Pediatrics, 1997).

Figure 7.2 ● Spanking children is a controversial issue. Do you agree or disagree with these authorities? Why?

Developmental guidelines also help teachers maintain reasonable expectations. When adults are aware of which behaviors are simply beyond the capabilities of children, they can help avert situations that will lead to conflicts. Asking a group of toddlers, for example, to sit quietly together for a 20-minute story is to invite misbehavior—wriggling, talking aloud, pushing, interrupting, walking away. Yet all of these are completely normal behaviors for a 2-year-old in that situation. The adult's insistence on a prolonged story time is asking these children to perform beyond their current physical, social, and cognitive abilities.

Environmental Factors

Environment for the young child is primarily home, school, or child care settings.[1] The term *environment* has three distinct parts: the physical, the **temporal** (timing and scheduling), and the interpersonal. Each has an impact on children's behavior.

The physical environment is a powerful tool in controlling children's behavior. Teachers can achieve a number of behavior goals through the physical facilities of the early childhood program. Child-size furniture that fits the preschool body encourages sitting and working behavior. Room arrangements that have no long, open spaces children could use as runways encourage children to walk from place to place. Low, open shelves create an expectation that children to help themselves in taking out and putting away the materials and equipment.

Chapter 9 contains a detailed discussion of many factors that should be considered when designing spaces for young children. Many of these environmental considerations directly influence children's behavior. See also the Classroom Checklist, Figure 7.9.

Materials. In addition to arrangement of room or yard, materials affect how children behave, whether in a family day care home or an after-school sports program. The materials provided can challenge children, overwhelm them, or bore them. If materials and equipment are suitable, children will feel more at ease with themselves and be more willing to accept adults' limits and controls.[2] The materials and equipment allow appropriate outlets for children's natural tendencies; they capture interest and attention, and this helps prevent many opportunities for misbehavior. When children are occupied with stimulating, age-appropriate materials, the amount of conflict and disruption lessens. Adding materials and equipment can help prevent fights over a favorite toy, create new interests and challenges in alternative activities, and extend children's play ideas and themes. Shawnsey and Kim's teacher will want to add more necklaces to the dress-up area if there aren't enough to outfit several children. Changing the environment when needed can help avert behavior problems. Removing attractive but

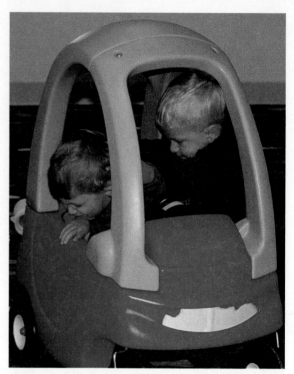

Figure 7.3 ● "I'm the boss here!"

breakable items reduces tears and conflicts. Some materials may prove to be too stimulating and may need to be removed for a while. Some activities may need to be limited to specific locations to control the level of activity and behavior.

Time. The temporal structure, that is, the timing and scheduling of daily events, describes the sequence of a program. When there are blocks of time to choose activities, children can proceed at their own pace without feeling pushed or hurried. They feel free to work, move, and play and are able to accept the teacher's control when it is necessary. Mac, for instance, had just settled in at the puzzle table when the teacher told him that it was time to clean up. The physical needs of eating, sleeping, and toileting are met by careful scheduling so that children are able to play without concern for the necessities of life. Schedules that do not allow enough time for cleanup,

 OUR DIVERSE WORLD OUR DIVERSE WORLD OUR DIVERSE WORLD OUR DIVERSE WORLD OUR DIVERSE WORLD OUR DIVERSE WORLD OUR DIVERSE WORLD OUR DIVERSE WORLD OUR DIVERSE WORLD

[1] One notable exception is the Israeli Kibbutz.

[2] Materials in the classroom reflect the attitudes of the teachers who select them. Those committed to multiculturalism will choose materials and equipment that reflect the diverse world in which we live.

Figure 7.4 ● Teachers are called upon to deal with a variety of emotional needs.

for instance, produce a frantic climate. It is when children are rushed and hurried by adults that arguments, accidents, and tears ensue. Uncooperative behavior is sometimes related to time pressures.

A consistent daily plan helps promote a feeling that the world is predictable and understandable. Children need time to work out their own problems. Hurrying and wondering what happens next create tension that results in behavior problems.

Relationships. These need special consideration because they determine how learning occurs. The interpersonal environment refers to all the "people" factors. An atmosphere of trust and support helps to create a sound learning environment. In early childhood centers the significant relationships are those between teacher and child, children and other children, teacher and parents, and teacher and other staff members and administrators. Each type of relationship affects and influences children's behavior.[1] When children sense a feeling of mutual support and accep-

tance, their play reflects that tone. Tension among adults is quickly transmitted to children, and their behavior patterns adjust to the negative influence. The teacher will want to support and comfort Kim at the same time she lets Shawnsey know that biting will not be tolerated. It is important to maintain a level of trust with Shawnsey so that she can help learn better ways to communicate her needs.

Other influences affect behavior. Weather seems to affect children. Wild, windy, gray, rainy days seem to stimulate children into high and excitable behavior. Bright, sunny days also seem to influence a child's mood and temperament. Problems that upset adults can make an impression on a child. A family crisis, a new baby, or a recent divorce have impact. Sharing a room, visits from relatives, illness, television and movie shows, brothers and sisters, nutrition and health cause children to behave in many different ways. The longer teachers work with children, the more adept they become at seeing how these various factors shape the behavior of the individual children in their class.

Individual Styles

People seem to come equipped with a style all their own. Pregnant women can describe a child's personality while the baby is still in the womb. Mothers know of the special way infants behave that sets them apart. Parents often comment on the differences among their own children. Raised by the same parents in the same house and neighborhood, each child is a singular and original being.

Each child in a classroom is also unique, an individual like no other. All have a personal style that needs to be acknowledged and valued.[2] Children who are not accepted for themselves may learn to hate themselves or not to trust their own instincts. A broken or timid spirit creates a timid or rebellious person.

Teachers of young children soon learn the temperamental characteristics of each child in the class.[3] Hondi works and plays with great intensity; Norman is easily distracted. Tawana fears any change, whereas Enrique thrives on challenges. The consistent patterns

OUR DIVERSE WORLD OUR DIVERSE WORLD OUR DIVERSE WORLD OUR DIVERSE WORLD OUR DIVERSE WORLD OUR DIVERSE WORLD OUR DIVERSE WORLD OUR DIVERSE WORLD

[1] Ask yourself: Do my classroom and teaching style reflect the patterns and relationships of one particular culture or many different cultures?

[2,3] Children's individual temperaments are an important consideration in developing an understanding of OUR DIVERSE WORLD. Differences in temperament may be less immediately obvious than differences in gender or race, but no less significant.

of temperament that emerge help define each child's individual style.

Research by Thomas and Chess (1977) has identified three types of temperament in babies: the easy child, the difficult child, and the slow-to-warm-up child. The traits used to classify these children were:

- The child's activity level—the amount of movement or inactivity

- The regularity and rhythm of bodily routines such as sleep, digestion, and elimination

- The ability to adapt to change

- Initial reaction to something new

- Physical sensitivity to the total environment—light, heat, noise

- Intensity of reaction and strength of response

- Ease of distraction

- Overall negative or positive mood

- Persistence and length of attention span

These differences were observed in very young infants and seem to remain consistent as the child grows.

The implications for teachers in these findings are several. First and foremost, the research supports the concept of individual differences that are present from birth and the importance of acknowledging those differences. If parents and teachers come to know the nature of a child's temperament, they can accept that as part of the wholeness of that particular child. Discipline and guidance measures can be tailored to meet the unique needs of a slow-to-warm-up child, for instance, or a difficult child. Those strategies will need to be different from techniques used to discipline the easy child. Recognition of traits enables teachers and parents to deal with quirks of personality. It is also useful to compare your own temperament with that of the children you teach.

Children's temperament also affects the way people deal with them. An easy child is easy to respond to; a slow-to-warm-up child may be harder to reach. Difficult children may tend to be blamed for things they did not do. Identifying traits can be useful so long as adults are careful not to label children unfairly or prematurely.

Malcolm is enthusiastic and plunges into activities spontaneously, sometimes without looking ahead or surveying the wreckage he leaves behind. His teacher is aware that he can be personable and cooperative if he is given options and a chance to make decisions. As they talk together about Lorraine's blocks, the teacher offers Malcolm a choice: to talk with Lorraine to see if she would like to have him help rebuild the same structure or start a new one. Both Malcolm and the teacher find satisfaction in working together in ways that acknowledge and respect Malcolm's personal style.

Emotional and Social Needs

Some behavior problems stem from the child's attempt to express social and emotional needs. These include the need to feel loved and cared for, the need to be included, the desire to be considered important and valued, the desire to have friends, and the need to feel safe from harm. Young children are still working out ways to express these needs and feelings. Typically, because they are only just learning language and communication skills, it is often through nonverbal or indirect actions that children let us know what is bothering them. Therefore, it is also important to provide children with models of language for resolving these conflicts. It is important to let children know that we recognize they can be angry, jealous, or hurt. The supportive adult will help children find satisfying ways to cope with their social and emotional feelings.

Figure 7.5 describes four categories of misbehavior that seem to stem from the child's social or emotional needs. Because children have something to gain from each type of misbehavior, Dreikurs labels the behaviors goals. These goals can apply to the child's interactions with adults or with other children. More than one goal may be involved, and the particular reason for misbehavior may not be obvious. Read again the three behavior situations described at the opening of the chapter. What do you think were the goals of Shawnsey, Malcolm, and Mac, and what role do their social and emotional histories play in their behavior?

The facts are that Shawnsey is an only child of older parents and has little opportunity outside of school to interact with others her age. Malcolm comes from a big, boisterous family where taking care of one's own desires and needs is instilled early on. Mac's parents are divorced and he is now living with his grandmother while his mother looks for work in another town. Their teachers understand their bids for

Dreikurs's Four Goals of Misbehavior

Attention	Children seek attention, believing they are worthwhile only when someone notices them. Their need causes them to gain attention in either positive or negative ways.
Power	Children who believe they are important only when they are "the boss" seek power and control over others.
Revenge	Children who believe they are unlovable and unimportant are hurt and try to hurt back. They seek revenge by hurting others so they may feel important.
Inadequacy	Children who feel they cannot succeed will rarely try anything new or persist in an activity when frustrated. They do not want others to expect anything from them for fear of failing.

Figure 7.5 ● Because children seem to gain something from each type of behavior, psychiatrist Rudolph Dreikurs calls the behaviors goals. Each goal fulfills a particular social or emotional need for the child. (From Dreikurs, R., & Stolz, V. [1964]. *Children: The challenge.* New York: Hawthorne Books.)

attention and weigh each child's social and emotional history as they guide them toward positive behavior.

In Chapter 14, the young child's social and emotional growth is further explored.

Cultural Influences

As we begin the 21st century, classrooms are filled with children who are growing up in a country of unparalleled diversity.[1] Many different cultures are converging and creating "a great national pool" of peoples, cultures, languages, and attitudes (America's Immigrant Challenge, 1993). Children and their teachers are living in a world of continual cross-cultural interactions. The ability to communicate across cultures is a critical skill to have when guiding children's behavior. (See also discussions in Chapters 2, 5, 8, and 15.) A review of Erikson's and Vygotsky's theories in Chapter 4 and Bronfenbrenner's in Chapter 15 underscores the connection between culture and behavior.

Discipline and guidance are deeply embedded within the values and beliefs of the family. The family's culture shapes how they raise their children, and each family is unique in the way it interprets its cultural values. Child-rearing practices ranging from the timing of toilet training to physical punishment are culturally influenced. The messages children receive about their behavior should be consistent between school and home. Yet conflict may be inevitable because the culturally influenced child-rearing practices of the family may be at odds with a teacher's ideas and expectations[2] (Gordon & Browne, 1996). In some cultures, for instance, children are encouraged to challenge adult opinions, where this would be considered disrespectful in other cultures. Kim (who was playing with Shawnsey) has a family culture that views the teacher as a respected authority figure and one who must be obeyed. This places Kim in an uncomfortable position if her teacher does not understand why Kim does not make activity choices easily and prefers to have the teacher tell her where to play and work each

 OUR DIVERSE WORLD OUR DIVERSE WORLD OUR DIVERSE WORLD OUR DIVERSE WORLD OUR DIVERSE WORLD OUR DIVERSE WORLD OUR DIVERSE WORLD OUR DIVERSE WORLD

[1] The ability to adapt to the needs of a diversified group of students will be the challenge for teachers of the 21st century.
[2] Culturally sensitive teaching strategies will recognize the parent's perspective and the child's family experiences.

Figure 7.6 ● Children are often able to work out their own solutions to conflict.

day. As teachers become familiar with the customs and beliefs of the families in the program, they will gain insights into children's behavior and understand the reasons for the way a child responds. Each child must be valued as part of a family system, no matter the origin of structure, and the teacher's role is to support the child's sense of security and identity within the family. Unconditional respect creates a climate in which positive behavior can thrive (Gordon & Browne, 1996).

As noted, children bring their unique individuality to the classroom. They are also bearers of the context in which they are being raised: their family, culture, ethnicity, religion, socioeconomic status, neighborhood, and so on. When we are aware of these influences we are better able to match who the child is with the most effective guidance approach (Gordon & Browne, 1996).

In some families, a sense of community is valued over individualism, a concept that can create difficulty in the early childhood classroom unless it is understood and appreciated. Early childhood educators, for the most part, do not force children to share personal possessions before they seem ready to, and they encourage children to become autonomous at an early age. This is at odds with families in which cooperation and sharing are valued concepts, as is dependency on other family members. Teachers of children of the 21st century will need to become culturally sensitive to some of the long-held assumptions of teaching young children.

Schools must be inviting and safe places in which families from all cultures can express their percep-

tions, concerns, and expectations about their children. Teachers will need to be flexible and nonjudgmental as they work with the cultural implications of children's behavior. Parents are the teacher's obvious resource and partner: they can say what is respectful and appropriate for their particular culture and work with the teacher for the most compatible resolution to any differences.

The sections on "Self-Awareness" and "Attitudes and Biases" in Chapter 5 suggest ways in which teachers can address stereotypes and prejudices that may interfere with their effectiveness in guiding children's behavior.

GUIDING BEHAVIOR

A Guidance Approach

The behavior of Shawnsey, Malcolm, and Mac is typical of children their age. The children we meet in early childhood programs are just learning how strong their emotions can be and what impact they have on their own behavior and on others. Behavior is the unspoken language through which children act out feelings and thoughts. Until they learn to express themselves vocally, they use a variety of behaviors to communicate such feelings as distress, anger, anxiety, fear, hurt, and jealousy. They don't yet know what kinds of behaviors are and are not acceptable and what adults expect of them. Using words (for instance, a resounding "No!" when someone takes a toy away) is slowly replacing biting, hitting, crying, and tantrums as a way to respond to frustration. Caring adults can help young children learn to behave responsibly and be respectful of others as they explore alternative behaviors, develop social skills, and learn to solve problems.

Because it is daily experiences that children use to construct their moral and social world, adults must look carefully at the guidance approach they take. The concept of guide is an important one (Gordon & Browne, 1996). A guide is one who leads, explains, and supports. A guide points out directions, answers questions, and helps you get where you want to go. This is what teachers do as they guide children. Implicit, too, is a sense of joint commitment of teaching and learning together. Relying on punishment as a guidance tool excludes the opportunity for teaching and learning to take place. A guidance approach to

Discipline	Punishment
Emphasizes what the child should *do*	Emphasizes what the child should *not* do
Is an ongoing process	Is a one-time occurrence
Sets an example to follow	Insists on obedience
Leads to self-control	Undermines independence
Helps children change	Is an adult release
Is positive	Is negative
Accepts child's need to assert self	*Makes* children behave
Fosters child's ability to think	Thinks *for* the child
Bolsters self-esteem	Defeats self-esteem
Shapes behavior	Condemns misbehavior

Figure 7.7 ● A guidance approach to discipline encourages children's interaction and involvement; punishment is usually something that is done to a child.

discipline requires the active participation of both child and adult in order to be successful.

A large part of an early childhood educator's role is to guide and direct children in learning the inner controls necessary for them to build positive relationships with others. Guidance and discipline are common concerns of parents and teachers and can be the basis for a strong partnership as they learn together why Dominick whines or Carrie dawdles or Cleo disrupts group time. Yet there is often confusion and uncertainty about guidance and discipline and what it really means.

What Are Guidance and Discipline?

Many people associate discipline with the word punishment. Discipline is generally thought of in negative terms, and to some, the words *discipline* and *punishment* are synonymous.

Figure 7.7 shows how these terms mean very different things. Discuss these differences in class, and plan intervention strategies for teachers to use with Shawnsey, Malcolm, and Mac in the situations described in the opening of this chapter. Match the

proposed solutions with the developmentally appropriate expectations found in the Word Pictures in Chapter 3.

The word *discipline* stems from disciple: a pupil, a follower, a learner. This suggests an important concept, that of following an example versus following rules. Children try to be like the adults they see; adults serve as models for children. How children see adults behave tends to become part of their own behavior. Adults help children learn appropriate behavior by setting good examples.[1]

Guiding and directing children toward acceptable behavior include everything parents and teachers do, everything they say, in an attempt to influence the child. The guidance process is something you do with children; it is an interaction, not something adults do *to* children. In caring and understanding ways, the effective teacher helps children gain control over their own behavior. To accomplish this, teachers maintain that delicate balance between children's attempts to be independent and their need for outer controls.

It is not so much the word *discipline* that is significant as it is the form it takes. Children are robbed of their self-respect when they are treated

OUR DIVERSE WORLD OUR DIVERSE WORLD OUR DIVERSE WORLD OUR DIVERSE WORLD OUR DIVERSE WORLD OUR DIVERSE WORLD OUR DIVERSE WORLD OUR DIVERSE WORLD

[1] Good role models deliberately vary their teaching styles and strategies to accommodate different learning styles and cultural patterns.

ABOUT CHOICES

—Give children choices whenever possible. This allows some control over themselves so they do not feel continually dominated by adults and helps them practice self-reliance, self-direction, and self-discipline. "Looks like there is plenty of room at the easels or at the lotto games, Seth. Where would you like to play?"

—Give choices only when you mean for the children to have a choice. Be prepared to accept their answer when a choice is offered. Make sure you present choices to children only when they really have one. "Some of the children are going inside for music now. Would you like to join them?" Do not ask "Would you like to go home now?" when it is not an option.

—Suggest two choices when there is the possibility of resistance. Let children know you expect them to comply with your request, but allow some decision on their part. Do not box them into a corner. "It's time to go home now. Would you like to get your artwork before or after you put on your jacket?"

—Make the choice real and valid. Acknowledge children's growing ability to deal with responsibility and help them practice making reasonable choices. "There are several kinds of nails, Stacey. Try them out to see which ones work best for you."

---

harshly and made to feel they have no ability to control themselves. Shame, disgrace, and embarrassment have no part in good disciplinary procedures.

One of the goals of a good guidance process is to help children achieve self-discipline. This happens only if adults lead in ways that support children's developing ability to control themselves. Teachers who are sensitive to this will decrease the amount of control they exercise. By gradually handing over to children the opportunity to govern their own actions, adults communicate trust. For young children, with their urge to prove themselves, their drive toward initiative, this is an important step to take. With added responsibility and trust comes an added dimension of self-respect and self-confidence. Such children feel capable and worthwhile.[1]

Along with self-respect, the child must taste the freedom that comes with a lessening of adult controls. Children do not learn to handle freedom by being told what to do all the time. Only when they have an opportunity to test themselves, make some decisions on their own, will they know their capabilities. Young children must learn this in safe places, with adults who allow them as much freedom as they can responsibly handle.

Developmentally Appropriate Guidance

Children's growth follows certain patterns (see Chapters 3 and 4). Each developmental stage has shared characteristics, modified, of course, by a child's individual rate of growth. It is as typical, for instance, for 4-year-olds to test limits as it is for toddlers to have a strong sense of ownership about their possessions. To have a developmentally appropriate guidance approach, teachers take this knowledge and understanding of child development principles into consideration as they contemplate how best to respond to a child's behavior.

OUR DIVERSE WORLD OUR DIVERSE WORLD OUR DIVERSE WORLD OUR DIVERSE WORLD OUR DIVERSE WORLD OUR DIVERSE WORLD OUR DIVERSE WORLD OUR DIVERSE WORLD

[1] This is a good reminder for teachers to examine their interactions with all the children in their care. Whom do they encourage to take risks and assume responsibilities? Are there different assumptions for children of different cultures?

BEING POSITIVE

—Tell children what it is you want them to do. Make directions and suggestions in positive statements, not in negative forms. "Walk around the edge of the grass, Hilla, so you won't get hit by the swing," instead of, "Don't get hit!"

—Reinforce what children do right, what you like, and what you want to see repeated. This helps build the relationship on positive grounds. "Good job, Sammy. You worked hard on that puzzle."

—Give indirect suggestions or reminders, emphasizing what you want children to do. Help them refocus on the task without nagging or confrontation. "I know you are excited about the field trip, Mickey. Looks like you are almost finished putting on your jacket so we can go," instead of "Hurry and button that jacket so we can go."

—Use positive redirection whenever possible.

—Use encouragement appropriately, focusing on helping children achieve success and understanding what it is you want them to learn: "Harry, I notice you are being careful about where you put your feet as you climb that tree. It looks to me like you are finding good places to stand," communicates a supportive attitude and tells the child what he is doing well. Global praise, such as 'Great climbing, Harry. Good for you!" may leave children wondering what exactly it is they have been praised for and omits the learning they can derive from the experience.

—Give reasons for your request. Let children know in simple, straight-forward statements the reasons behind your request. Children are more likely to cooperate when they can understand the reason why. "Tom, if you move those chairs, then you and Dee will have more room to dance," instead of "Move the chairs, Tom."

It is useful to identify the behaviors typical to a specific age group, for it provides a context in which to understand the child. Behavior then can be seen as normal and predictable and can be responded to accordingly. Guidance based on a developmental approach would, for instance, help a teacher to know that first and second graders have an ability to consider others' points of view, and so they would choose problem-solving methods that would ask children to think of how their behavior affected others. A developmentally appropriate approach also requires that the teacher consider what is known about the individual child as well as what is typical for the age group. This ensures that the guidance techniques will match the capabilities of the child and that adult expectations will remain reasonable.

The Language of Guidance and Discipline

Guidance has a language all its own.[1] As beginning teachers gain experience in handling problem behaviors, they learn to use that language. The result, in most cases, is a startling **interdependence**: the more practiced teachers become in the language of guidance, the more comfortable they become in developing their own approach to disciplinary problems. And the more comfortable they are in that approach, the more effectively they use language to solve behavior problems.

The language and communication techniques in guidance are both spoken and unspoken. Teachers discover how potent the voice can be; what words will work best and when. They become aware of facial expressions and what a touch or a look will convey to

OUR DIVERSE WORLD OUR DIVERSE WORLD OUR DIVERSE WORLD OUR DIVERSE WORLD OUR DIVERSE WORLD OUR DIVERSE WORLD OUR DIVERSE WORLD OUR DIVERSE WORLD

[1] The language of discipline may differ from culture to culture. Gender differences, which may be cultural, may emerge (e.g., boys are encouraged to "hit back," whereas girls are taught a more passive approach to conflicts).

children. How they use their body reflects a distinct attitude and approach to discipline. New teachers should know how to use these tools in ways that will work best for them and the children.

Voice. Some adults feel that when they are speaking to children they must assume a different voice from the one they normally use. This "teacher voice" often occurs when disciplinary issues are at stake. The teacher's voice becomes tight, high-pitched, the tone increasingly strained. Teaching requires no more than a normal speaking voice. Talk to children in the same way you talk to other people. Learn to control the volume and use good speech patterns for children to imitate. To be heard, get close enough to speak in a normal tone; get down to the child's level. Often, lowering volume and pitch is effective.

Words. Children have torrents of words rained on them in the course of a school day. Teachers fall into the trap of overusing words. Where behavior is concerned and anger or frustration aroused, some adults seem to gain release from a string of words. This works against good guidance practices. Children tend to turn off people who are excessively verbal with them. Their eyes glaze over, they become fidgety or even frightened, and the incident loses significance.

The fewer the words, the better. Simple, clear statements, spoken once, will have more impact. The child will be able to focus on the real issues involved. A brief description of what happened, a word or two about what behavior is acceptable and what isn't, and a suggestion for possible solutions are all that is necessary.

Choose words carefully. They should convey to the child exactly what is expected. "Richy, move the block closer to the truck. Then Sarah won't bump into it again," tells Richy in a positive, concrete way what he can do to protect his block building. If he had been told, "Richy, watch where you are building," he would not know what action to take to solve the problem.

Body Expressions. When working with small children, the teacher must be aware of body height and position. Show children respect for their size by speaking with them face to face. Sit, squat, or kneel—but

Figure 7.8 ● Body height and position are important. Getting down to the child's eye level provides for greater impact and involvement.

get down to their level. It is difficult to communicate warmth, caring, and concern from 2 or 3 feet above a child's head, or by shouting from across the room.

Guidance is founded on a loving, caring relationship between child and adult. To help children gain control over their impulses and monitor their own behavior, teachers must establish a sense of trust and well-being with children. The way teachers use their body invites or rejects close relationship and familiarity. A child will find teachers more approachable if they are seated low, with arms available, rather than standing, with arms folded.

Making full use of the senses can soften the impact of words. A firm grip on the hand of a child who is hitting out, a gentle touch on the shoulder, tells children the adult is there to protect them from themselves and others. Eye contact is essential. Teachers learn to communicate the seriousness of a situation through eye and facial expressions. They also show reassurance, concern, sadness, and affection this way.

Physical presence should convey to the child a message that the teacher is there, available, and interested.

Attitude. This is part of the unspoken language of guiding children. Attitudes are derived from experience.[1] Most adults who take care of children reflect

[1] Attitudes affect expectations. Check to see if you have any assumptions on how children behave depending on their race, gender, or culture.

PLAN AHEAD

—Allow plenty of time for children to respond. Give them an opportunity to decide their course of action.

—Review limits and rules periodically. Modify them as children's growth and maturation indicate. Change them as circumstances change; be flexible.

—Encourage children to talk things over. Be open to their point of view even if you cannot accept it. Let them know you are willing to listen to all sides of the conflict.

—Become aware of the climate in the room or yard. Anticipate the need for a change of pace or a different activity *before* children become bored or troublesome.

—Remember, it takes time and numerous opportunities for changes in behavior to occur. By using consistent guidance techniques, you will help children practice new behavior repeatedly.

how their own parents treated them and how they were disciplined. Some people react against the way they were raised; others tend to follow the model their parents established. Teachers find it useful to look at the way they were disciplined as youngsters and acknowledge their feelings about it. As they begin to inhibit the behavior of the children in their classes, teachers should be aware of their own attitudes. The following questions may help that process:

● Do you accept the fact that all children will have problems, misbehave, and make mistakes?

● Do you believe children are capable of solving their own problems, and do you involve them in the process?

● Do you accept the child's right to independence and actively encourage self-reliance?

● Do you think children misbehave deliberately, to bother the teacher?

● Do you help children accept the responsibility for their own actions without blaming them?

● Are you optimistic that problems can be solved and that you and the child can work them out together?

Guidance Practices

Children's behavior is influenced by more than just their own impulses, needs, or reactions. Factors beyond the scope of childhood can cause misbehavior. There are several areas over which adults have control that may cause problems for children. Three of the most common are the classroom environment, setting limits on children's behavior, and the teacher's role in guidance.

Because the classroom promotes or detracts from positive interactions and appropriate behavior, it is the first place to look for ways to improve guidance and disciplinary techniques.[1] The goals for positive behavior should be reflected in the classroom setting. Too often, good intentions are defeated by the physical environment. The physical setting should tell children clearly and directly how to act in that space. That makes it easier for them to know what is expected and how they should behave.

Through the intentional use of the environment, the teacher indirectly influences behavior in the classroom. The schedule allows for enough time to play and clean up; there are adequate and interesting materials to use; there is a sense of order, and adults are skilled in guidance techniques that work. Use the classroom

 OUR DIVERSE WORLD OUR DIVERSE WORLD OUR DIVERSE WORLD OUR DIVERSE WORLD OUR DIVERSE WORLD OUR DIVERSE WORLD OUR DIVERSE WORLD OUR DIVERSE WORLD

[1] As we educate ourselves about children who are socially and culturally diverse, we need information about child-rearing beliefs that affect how families discipline their children.

ALWAYS AVOID

—Methods that will shame, frighten, or humiliate children.

—Physical abuse.

—Comparisons among the children. Comparisons foster competitiveness and affect self-esteem.

—Carryovers from the incident. Once it is over, leave it behind; do not keep reminding children about it.

—Consequences that are too long, too punitive, or postponed. Children benefit most from immediate, short consequences.

—Lots of rules. Set only enough to ensure a safe environment for all children.

—Making promises you cannot keep.

—Being overly helpful. Let children do as much as they can by themselves, including solving their own conflicts.

—Threatening children with the loss of your affection.

checklist in Figure 7.9 to evaluate how the environment is related to your guidance philosophy and to the behavior of children.

Consider the Limits

To provide a safe and caring environment in which children can play and learn, teachers set limits on certain behavior. **Limits** are the boundaries set up to help children know what will or will not be tolerated. Teachers generally have two reasons for setting limits: (1) to prevent children from injuring themselves or others and (2) to prevent the destruction of property, materials, or equipment.

Limits are a necessary part of any group or society. Every group has its bottom-line rules—rules that must be kept to ensure order and living in accord. The early childhood classroom is no exception; teachers make it clear to children what rules determine the conduct within that group. Teachers plan the curriculum, arrange rooms, and follow good guidance practices so that a great number of rules are not necessary. Frequent exclamations of "Don't do this . . ." or "Don't do that . . ." need not be a part of the early childhood classroom when one understands the nature of setting limits.

Limits are like fences; they are protective structures that help children feel secure. Fences and limits are erected and maintained to help people know how far they can go. Fences—or limits—set up a framework in which everyone knows the rules. When children know where fences are, what limits, what rules apply, they do not have to continually try to find out *if* fences are there and *where* they are. Inside the fences, children are free—and safe—to try out many behaviors.[1]

A natural part of growing up is to stretch those limits and push those fences aside. The womb first holds and protects the growing fetus; the infant is protected in the confines of the crib. The toddler has safe space defined in a playpen. The preschool child plays first in small, protected yards before moving on to the large, open playground in elementary school. Physical limits expand as the child is able to handle more freedom, more space, more responsibility. It is the same with behavioral limits.

Children may not like fences; they may resist attempts to limit their behavior. The beginning teacher must learn to set and maintain limits with confidence and authority. Children respond to how limits are set as much as to the limits themselves. Be sure children help determine limits. Keep in mind that a good guidance

OUR DIVERSE WORLD OUR DIVERSE WORLD OUR DIVERSE WORLD OUR DIVERSE WORLD OUR DIVERSE WORLD OUR DIVERSE WORLD OUR DIVERSE WORLD OUR DIVERSE WORLD

[1] A good way to prepare children to live successfully and productively is to help them become increasingly responsible for their actions and their behavior.

TIME

_____ Does the daily schedule provide enough time for unhurried play?

_____ Are those periods that create tension—transitions from one activity to another—given enough time?

_____ Is cleanup a leisurely process built in at the end of each activity, with children participating?

PROGRAM PLANNING AND CURRICULUM

_____ Is there enough to do so that children have choices and alternatives for play?

_____ Is the curriculum challenging enough to prevent boredom and restlessness?

_____ Is the curriculum age appropriate for the children in the class?

_____ Are there activities to help children release tension? Do the activities allow for body movement, exploration, and manipulation of materials?

_____ Are children included in developing the rules and setting guidelines? How is their inclusion demonstrated?

ORGANIZATION AND ORDER

_____ If children are expected to put things away after use, are the cabinets low, open, and marked in some way?

_____ Are the materials within easy reach of the children, promoting self-selection and independence?

_____ Are there enough materials so that sharing does not become a problem?

_____ Are the areas in which activities take place clearly defined so that children know what happens there?

_____ Does the room arrangement avoid runways and areas with no exits?

_____ Do children have their own private space?

_____ Are children able to use all visible and accessible materials? Are there materials about which children are told, "Don't touch?"

PERSONNEL

_____ Are there enough teachers to give adequate attention to the number of children in the class?

_____ Are the group size and makeup balanced so that children have a variety of playmates?

_____ Are the teachers experienced, and do they seem comfortable in setting limits and guiding children's behavior?

_____ Do teachers use their attention to encourage behavior they want, and do they ignore what they want to discourage?

_____ Do all adults consistently enforce the same rules?

Figure 7.9 ● Classroom checklist. By anticipating children's needs and growth patterns, teachers set up classrooms that foster constructive and purposeful behavior.

process involves children as active participants; this fosters self-discipline. Children also seem less resistant to following rules when they are a part of the limit-setting procedure. Figure 7.10 illustrates positive ways to set limits when working with young children.

For the child, limits are self-protective. Young children have not yet learned the skills to control themselves in all situations. Their behavior easily goes out of bounds. Children are just beginning to exert that inner pressure (self-control) that will help them monitor their own actions. Until then, they need adults to help them learn when and how to apply self-restraint. Limits keep them from going too far. Children can frighten themselves and others with anger, frustration, fear. They need adults who care to stop them from doing physical or emotional harm to themselves. Well-considered limits give the child freedom to try out, test, and explore avenues of self-expression in ways that will promote growth and protect budding autonomy. Children feel more secure with adults who will stop them from going too far and who help them learn to gain control.

Consider the Teacher's Role

A teacher has direct and indirect influence on children's behavior. Some of the ways teachers deal directly with discipline are by what they say and what they do. Indirectly, a teacher's influence is felt just as strongly. Room arrangements and time schedules, attitudes and behavior can work for or against good guidance practices.

Teachers who are well grounded in the developmental process know that problem behaviors are normal and occur in every early childhood setting. They realize that growing children must have a safe, secure place in which to test themselves against the world.

The teacher as a behavior model is an important element in guidance. Children pattern their responses after adult behaviors. They are aware of how teachers respond to anger, frustration, and aggression; how they solve problems and conflicts. Adults must be sure to model the desired behavior around the children they

teach. To be successful models, teachers should be aware of their emotions and feelings; they do not want to compound a problem by their own reaction.

Being consistent is one of the key elements in good guidance practices. If adults want to develop mutual trust, the rules must be clear, fair, and enforced consistently and regularly. At the same time, children need to know what will happen if rules are not followed. Consequences, too, should be consistent.

An emerging issue, as our population becomes more and more diverse, has to do with cultural values and discipline. Teachers may be confronted by parents whose disciplinary practices are contrary to the school's philosophy.[1] Pressure may be exerted on teachers to apply some of those same techniques at school that parents use at home. Teachers want to maintain the school's as well as their own standards *without* communicating to the family that their values are wrong or have children feel that something about their home and family is diminished in the teacher's eyes. Gonzalez-Mena (1993) stresses the teacher's responsibility to learn cross-cultural communication when child-rearing practices are in conflict between home and school and suggests the following strategies:

● Accept that both viewpoints are equally valid.

● Work together to figure out a solution to the situation.

● Resist assigning meaning and values to the behavior of others on the basis of your own culture.

● Remember that your behavior does not necessarily convey your own meaning and values.

● Educate yourself about the different cultures represented in your classroom. Learn how and what is communicated through facial gestures, touch, eye contact, physical closeness, time concepts.

● Observe, ask, and talk about what the differences are; learn from the parents of the children in the classroom what you need to know about their culture.

● Maintain an open attitude that promotes respect and appreciation for each other's views.

OUR DIVERSE WORLD OUR DIVERSE WORLD OUR DIVERSE WORLD OUR DIVERSE WORLD OUR DIVERSE WORLD OUR DIVERSE WORLD OUR DIVERSE WORLD OUR DIVERSE WORLD

[1] There are *professional codes of guidance* versus *family socialization practices*. Parents and teachers may have the same goals for the child, but the teacher is bound by professional standards and codes for behavior, whereas parental guidance has more latitude because of the strong bond of love, security, authority, and loyalty.

When Setting Limits	For Example
1. Make sure that the limit is appropriate to the situation.	"Andrew, I want you to get down from the table. You may finish your snack by sitting in your chair or standing next to me. You may not stand on the table."
2. Fit the limits to the individual child's age, history, and emotional framework.	"Sheila, you've interrupted the story too many times today. Find a place at the puzzle table until we are finished. Remember, I told you earlier that you wouldn't be able to hear the end of the story if you yelled again." "Jamal, I know it's your first day back since you broke your arm, but it is time to listen to the story now. You and Sascha can talk together in a few minutes."
3. See that the limits are consistently applied by all adults.	"I know you want to ride the red bike now but both teachers have said you already had a long turn today."
4. Reinforce the same rules consistently.	"Judy, remember everyone *walks* inside. You can run outside."
5. Follow through; support your words with actions.	"I can't let you tear the books. Since this is the second page this morning, you'll need to make another choice instead of the book corner." If child does not leave, begin to pick up books. Lead child firmly to another activity.
6. Use simple statements; be clear and state limits positively.	"Roger, use a gentle voice indoors. When your voice is too loud, people can't hear one another. You may use your big loud voice outside."
7. Respect the child's feelings and acknowledge them when you can.	"I know you want your mom to stay. She has to go to her job now. I'll stay with you while you feel sad and I'll take care of you until she comes back."
8. Act with authority; be sure of your purpose and be confident.	"I can't let you hurt other people. Put the block down," instead of "I wish you wouldn't do that."
9. Be ready to accept the consequences; have a plan for the next step, if needed. Maintain the limit. Don't avoid the situation or give in if the child threatens to fall apart or create a scene.	"I'm sorry, Sarah. You won't be able to play here any longer. Remember, we agreed earlier that you wouldn't call Gerry 'Fatty' any more because it hurt her feelings. I'm sorry that makes you cry but I can't let you keep making fun of one of our classmates. When you are finished crying you can work in the writing center or go to the art room. Which do you want to do?"
10. Have children help in defining limits.	"We'll be taking a bus to the museum next week. What are some of the rules we should follow so that we can enjoy the trip? Wally, do you have an idea?"

Figure 7.10 ● Guidelines for setting limits. Children feel safe when appropriate limits are set on their behavior.

"I get to be the first because I'm the biggest."

"I want my mommy."

"Gimme that, it's mine."

"Look, I won again, you dummy."

Figure 7.11 ● Good discipline practices involve children as active participants. How would you set limits in these situations?

Cultural Pattern	Child's Behavior	Guidance Strategy
Reside in extended family household	High level of cooperation and responsibility; children do not like being separated	Provide activities that build on cooperation and sharing; have mixed-age groupings
Family members share in decision-making	Learns to negotiate, compromise	Give choices; use problem-solving techniques
One family member makes all the decisions	Expected to be obedient, follow commands, respect authority	Support child in making choices; do not force eye contact
Child considered an infant for first 12 months	Cries when told "no" and slapped on hand; allowed to cry it out	Use simple, short commands at end of first year
Child is considered an infant until 2 years old	Relies on constant contact with mother; has not learned self-help skills	Touch, hold, and carry child often; let child play near or with other children, not alone
Child is considered an infant until 5 years old	Has not been disciplined until now; may still drink from bottle; parents unconcerned about developmental milestones	Allow for separation anxiety; support this with transitional objects from home
Family life includes discrimination, violence, lack of opportunities	Used to being ignored or ridiculed; learns to tolerate inequality	Use firm discipline but delay responses to child; respect parents' need to keep child safe
Strong, closely knit family	Learns that family, not individual, comes first	Understand that school demands will take second place to family needs
Independence	Held infrequently, has own space and toys at home	Allow solitary play with little pressure to share; needs to move around independently
Pride and dignity	Upholds family honor; used to being disciplined for rude behavior and poor manners	Tell parents of child's accomplishments; be sensitive to their pride when discussing discipline problems
Family comes from strong oral tradition	Behavior has been guided by stories with morals	Use songs and stories to model acceptable behavior
Family expresses feelings readily	Crying, screaming, and temper tantrums are common	Support with your presence while gently setting limits
Family does not show feelings	Has been told not to cry; showing feelings is discouraged	Comfort as soon as child cries; remove from group while child is expressing feelings
Discipline is harsh: spanking, threats, humiliation	Understands authority	Begin with firm statements; model desired behavior; praise appropriate behavior
Foster harmony and avoid conflict	Scolded and shamed when misbehaves; humiliated for fighting	Find ways to encourage and praise cooperation; teach problem-solving techniques

Figure 7.12 ● Sample of culturally diverse family patterns that affect guidance and discipline. Knowledge of culturally diverse family patterns and guidance strategies to parallel these child-rearing styles can allow you to begin a dialogue with the children you teach. (Adapted from York, S. [1991]. *Roots and wings: Affirming culture in early childhood programs.* St. Paul, MN: Readleaf Press, and reprinted by permission from Gordon, A., Browne, K.W. [1996]. *Guiding young children in a diverse society.* Boston: Allyn & Bacon.)

Ethical issues involving culture-based differences are discussed in Chapter 5. The anti-bias curriculum, as described in Chapters 5 and 9, suggests some strategies as well. Also see "Child Development and Cultural Diversity" in Chapter 4.

Children have a right to express negative feelings and air their grievances, but what are the considerations if a teacher shows anger? Children are very sensitive to adult emotions. It is best to acknowledge the feeling, label it, and then discuss it together. Once it is identified, it becomes more manageable for both. Adults who express negative feelings to children must proceed carefully, stating their position clearly, honestly, and objectively, and in a low, calm voice.

It bothers me when you call Roberto a dummy.

You don't need to yell at me. I can hear you from right here. Tell me again in a quieter voice.

I'm serious about this—no biting.

Sometimes I get mad when children try to hurt each other.

It makes me sad to see all that food going to waste. Please put just enough on your plate so that you will eat it all.

Remember that children are frightened by strong feelings; do not overwhelm them by your own behavior.

Sometimes teachers have unrealistic expectations for children, either too high or too low. They presume children have abilities and skills they do not yet possess. This may cause children to respond in inappropriate ways. It can be helpful to rehearse with children how they are expected to act. Practice sessions are especially useful when introducing a new topic or plan. One teacher rehearsed the children for their first bus ride. They practiced singing, looking out the windows, having snacks, talking with friends. A large outline of a bus was drawn with chalk on the patio floor. The children pretended to board the bus, walk down the narrow aisle, find a seat, and remember to take big steps getting up and down the steps. When the field trip day arrived, children knew several appropriate ways of behaving while on the long bus trip.

Many times children are asked to do jobs that are too complicated for them. The young child who is just learning to put on jackets and pants or to make a bed is a good example. Children may not be able to accomplish the entire job at first; it is helpful to them if the task is broken down into smaller steps. Straighten the sheet and blanket for Gordon, then let him pull the spread up over the pillow. Little by little have Gordon assume more of the bed-making job as he becomes capable.

Preventing opportunities for children to misbehave is another part of the teacher's role. Good discipline practices call for teachers to be alert to potential problems and situations *before* they result in children's inappropriate behavior. Even then, unpredictable situations occur: a child becomes tired in the middle of snack time; one of the teachers is called out of the room with a sick child; rain forces an activity to move indoors; or a scheduled event gets postponed. At these trying and typical times, a teacher's full range of abilities is called into play. Ways to help children maintain good behavior patterns in these situations include:

● *Recognizing and labeling the problem or situation.* Acknowledge the difficulties it presents to the children. Example: "You seem tired, Gus, and I know you had to wait a long time for your snack. When you have finished your juice and cracker, put your head down on the table and rest for a minute."

● *Asking children for their help.* Get them involved in working out the solutions. Example: "Mr. Gallo had to leave for a while. How can we continue with this cooking project when I need to watch the block area too? Who has an idea? What do you think would work, Henry?"

● *Assigning a job or a task to the children who are most likely to react to the crisis.* Example: "Lorraine and Paul, will you carry the special drums inside, please, while I help the toddlers put the wagons away?"

● *Always being prepared with a story to tell, songs to sing, guessing games to play, or exercises to do.* Help children pass the time in an appropriate way modeled by the teacher. Give a new focus. Example: "Oh, dear. The fire truck hasn't arrived at school yet; we'll have to wait another five minutes. While we are waiting to go and see it, show me how firefighters climb ladders and slide down poles."

● *Saying what you would like to have happen.* Admit what you wish you could do to correct the situation. Example: "Oh, little Riko, I wish I could bring your mommy back right now but I can't. She has to go to work, but I will hold you until your crying stops."

These disciplinary practices apply equally to infants and toddlers, but there are some special considerations that teachers should remember. Infants cry— sometimes a great deal. It is their only means of communication. When they cry they should not be ignored or chastised, but comforted. It is helpful to talk to the baby, no matter how young, and begin to identify the steps you will take to ease the distress. "Oh, Fernando, you are crying and I don't know what's wrong. Let's take a look at your diaper; maybe a change will make you more comfortable. Perhaps you are teething; I know that can hurt. Maybe you are hungry; is it time for your bottle yet?" Those soothing words as a teacher changes diapers, rubs the baby's back, cuddles and rocks, ease this time of stress. Toddlers, too, need adults to use words to express problem situations, and the preceding examples readily apply to working with this active and lively age group. One word of caution, however. Removing infants and toddlers from the group as a means of discipline or confining them to a playpen or crib is not appropriate. Very young children do not understand that kind of isolation. Guidance, to be effective, should be helpful, not punitive.

Teachers can learn a great deal about the effects of their discipline and guidance techniques and when to use them if they are active observers in their own classrooms. When teachers observe, they can time intervention; they do not want to interfere too soon. Observations can be used to show children their actions and the consequences they have for others.

Guidance Techniques

There are a number of guidance and discipline approaches woven throughout the chapter. They have many similar components and fall under the definition of **inductive guidance**. The most effective guidance methods require children to think and reflect on their feelings and their actions and actively involve them in the process of solving the problem. These goals are accomplished by providing choices (see *"About Choices,"* p. 240), asking open-ended questions ("What would happen if you took her book?" "How do you think he would feel if you did that?"), and communicating trust and confidence in children to solve

problems and control their own behavior. These are key elements in the use of inductive guidance, as are the following:

● Guidance is an interactive process and involves children as much as it does adults.

● Children are increasingly held responsible for their actions as they come to understand the impact of their behavior on others.

● Teaching thinking and reasoning skills helps children achieve self-control and the development of a conscience.

These principles are based on the theories of Erikson and Piaget but owe particular credit to Vygotsky. Vygotsky placed the child as a learner in the context of social interactions. The concept of the *zone of proximal distance* (see Chapter 4), for instance, reinforces the reciprocal relationship between adult and child implied in most inductive guidance techniques. Too, Thomas and Chess's *goodness of fit* (1977), where the adult works with the child's unique temperament to determine the best guidance approach to take, is reflected in the following material. Family context as well continues to be a priority when selecting appropriate guidance methods.[1]

At the other end of the guidance spectrum are **power assertive** methods, which are harsh and punitive and rely on children's fear of punishment rather than the use of reason and understanding. Spanking, hitting, calling children names, and otherwise demeaning punishments exclude the opportunity for teaching and learning to take place or to promote problem-solving.

Each of the inductive guidance methods is a valuable tool for teachers. These approaches influence children to change their behavior because they place the responsibility where it belongs: with the child. The adult informs the children of the results of their actions and trusts in their willingness and ability to cooperate in a solution. The child's self-respect is left intact because no one has placed blame. By integrating these methods into a discipline approach, teachers enlarge the child's capacity to become increasingly self-directed and self-reliant.

One thing that becomes apparent when using many of the guidance methods that follow is the aware-

 OUR DIVERSE WORLD OUR DIVERSE WORLD OUR DIVERSE WORLD OUR DIVERSE WORLD OUR DIVERSE WORLD OUR DIVERSE WORLD OUR DIVERSE WORLD OUR DIVERSE WORLD

1 The families in early childhood programs reflect a wide range of discipline and guidance beliefs and practices.

Tantrums As a Teaching Tool
Ways to Help Children Learn
Elizabeth Crary

Marie doesn't want Stephanie to go home.

Josh wants the truck that Eli is playing with—
Right now!

David doesn't want his diaper changed, even though it stinks.

One of your jobs as a parent or teacher is to help children understand and deal with their feelings. There are several things you can do. During the tantrum you can acknowledge children's feelings and help them distinguish between feelings and behavior. *Before* the next tantrum you can begin to teach children ways to deal with their feelings and the situation.

1. Acknowledge children's feelings. You can help do that by helping children develop a feeling vocabulary and by validating their feelings.

- Label children's feelings: *"You're disappointed we can't go to the park today."*
- Share your feelings: *"I feel frustrated when I spill coffee on the floor."*
- Read books that discuss feelings, such as the **Let's Talk about Feelings** series.
- Observe another's feelings: *"I'll bet he's proud of the tower he built."*

Validate children's feelings. Many people have been trained to ignore or suppress their feelings. Girls are often taught that showing anger is unfeminine or not nice. Boys are taught not to cry. You can validate feelings by listening to the child and reflecting the feelings you hear. Listen without judging. Remain separate. Remember, a child's feelings belong to her or him. When you reflect the feeling (*"You are mad that Stephanie has to go home now"*), you are not attempting to solve the problem. Accepting the feeling is the fist step toward dealing with it.

2. Help children distinguish between feelings and actions. All feelings are okay. Actions may or may not be okay depending on the situation. For example, hitting a baseball is fine. Hitting a person is not acceptable. You can clarify the difference by saying, *"It's okay to be mad, but I cannot let you hit Eli."* You can also *model* the difference between feelings and action. You might say, *"This morning someone cut me off on the road. I was so mad I wanted to crash into them. Instead I . . ."*

3. Teach children several ways to calm themselves down. If telling children to *"Use your words"* worked for most kids, grown-ups would have little trouble with children's feelings. Children need a variety of ways to respond—auditory, physical, visual, creative, and self-nurturing. First children need to practice different responses when they are calm. Then when children are familiar with different ways to respond, you may ask them which they would like to try when they are upset.

For example: *"You're real angry. Do you want to feel mad right now or do you want to calm down?"* If you child wants to change her feelings, you could say, *"What could you do? Let's see, you could dance a mad dance, make a card to give to Stephanie, talk about this feeling, or look at your favorite book."* After you've generated ideas, let the child choose what works for her.

4. Offer tools to resolve situations that are hard for them. If Josh wants the truck Eli has, teach him to ask, wait, or trade for it. If Sonja gets frustrated putting puzzles together, teach her how to take breaks or to breathe deeply so she does not get upset. You can use books such as *I Want It, I Can't Wait* or *I Want to Play* to introduce options. Research has found that the more alternatives children have the better their social behavior.

Elizabeth Crary is a parent educator and author of many books and articles on guidance.

If This Is the Behavior	Try This	For Example
Whining	Ignoring	Do and say nothing while whining persists. Pay attention to child when whining stops.
Playing cooperatively	Positive reinforcement	"You two are sure working hard on this garden! What a good team you make."
Refusing to cooperate	Provide a choice	"Reva, do you want to pick up the Legos off the floor or help Charlie empty the water table?"
Restlessness, inattentiveness	Change the activity	"This story seems long today; we'll finish it later. Let's play some music and dance now."
Daydreaming	Indirect suggestion	"As soon as you get your coat, Winona, we'll all be ready to go inside."
Arguing over the ownership of a toy	Active listening	"You really wanted to be the first one to play with the blue truck today, didn't you, Lief?"
Dawdling, late for snacks	Natural consequences	"Sorry, Nate, the snacks have been put away. Maybe tomorrow you'll remember to come inside when the other children leave the yard."
Pushing, crowding, running inside	Change room arrangement	Create larger, more open spaces so children have greater freedom of movement and do not feel crowded together.
Unable to take turns, to wait	Review daily schedule, equipment	Buy duplicates of popular equipment. Allow enough time for free play so children won't feel anxious about getting a turn.
Boisterous play	Positive redirection	"You and Sergio seem to want to wrestle. Let's go set the mats out in the other room. If you wrestle here you disturb the children who are playing quietly."

Figure 7.13 ● Varieties of guidance techniques. The astute teacher selects from the options available and individualizes the responses.

ness that often the adult's behavior must change as well, if the child is to achieve some measure of self-control. Look at the various strategies in the discussion that follows and note how many of them require the adult to alter a response or attitude before the child can be expected to alter behavior. Figure 7.13 illustrates how some of these disciplinary techniques may be used to the best advantage.

Active Listening and "I" Messages

Parents and teachers can learn the art of **active listening** to respond to a child's feelings as well as words. The technique encourages sensitive, atuned

hearing—checking on the accuracy of what is being said. To do this, teachers or parents listen carefully, trying to understand what the child is saying beyond the words being used. Then they reflect back in their own words what it is they think the child has said. The child has an opportunity to correct any misinterpretations. Further dialogue helps to clarify what it was the child meant. An example is:

Rita: I hate school!

Teacher: Sounds as if you are really disappointed you didn't get a turn cooking today.

Rita: I *really* wanted to help make pancakes.

Figure 7.14 ● "They won't let me play with them." A sensitive teacher will move in and help redirect a child's behavior before it becomes a problem. What would you do in this situation?

"I" messages are an adult's way of reflecting back to children how their actions have affected others.

Parent: When you scream indoors, it really hurts my ears.

Parent: I feel sad when you tell me you don't like me.

"I" messages are honest, nonjudgmental statements that place no blame on the child but that state an observation of the behavior and its results. They avoid accusing statements, such as "You made me . . ." and call for a framework that allows adults to state their feelings to that child (Gordon, 1970).

Natural and Logical Consequences

Natural and logical consequences enhance children's ability to take responsibility for themselves. As implied, this approach lets children experience the *natural consequences* of their actions. This approach, designed by Rudolf Dreikurs, emphasizes the opportunity children have to learn from the way their environment functions:

> If Libby does not eat her dinner, she can expect to be hungry later.

> If Kara puts her hand on a hot stove, she is likely to get burned.

> If Tony grabs the book away from Ben, Ben may hit him.

This method allows adults to define the situation for children without making judgments and lets children know what to expect. The consequences are a natural result of the child's own actions. *Logical* consequences, on the other hand, are a function of what adults impose. A logical consequence of disrupting group time is removal from the group. For the adult, this means a commitment to follow through; consequences, once stated, must be enforced. It is important to give children an opportunity to choose a course of action for themselves once they have some understanding of what is likely to happen. Four main areas of Focus when guiding children who need extra support in managing their behavior are presented in Figure 17.15.

Behavior Modification

Behavior modification is an organized approach based on the premise that behavior is learned through **positive and negative reinforcement** or rewards. The belief is that children will tend to repeat behavior for which they get the desired results (positive reinforcement) and are likely to avoid doing things that have undesirable consequences (negative reinforcement). Positive reinforcement is used to teach new and different behaviors to a child and to help the child maintain the change. Negative reinforcement may simply involve ignoring or withdrawing attention when the child acts inappropriately. Initially, the reinforcement (or reward) must be swift and consistently applied, as often as the behavior occurs. If the desired behavior, for instance, is for Janie to always hang her coat on the hook, praise and appreciate the effort each time Janie hangs up her wraps. Once this is a well-established routine, the reinforcement (praise) becomes less intense.

Reinforcers, or rewards, must be individualized to meet the needs of the child and the situation. Social reinforcers, such as smiling, interest and attention, hugging, touching, and talking, are powerful tools with

Area of Focus	What You Can Do
Observations	*Collect information* about the behavior: Identify the components that cause children to lose control. When does Nan throw a temper tantrum? Only before snack time? Just after her mother leaves? What prompts Rudy's resistance? What precedes it? How long does it last? How much attention does Arturo get when he interrupts story time? How many teachers intervene? For how long? How has his attention been sought prior to his disruption? Observe and learn also when these children are behaving appropriately and record what and how much attention they receive from teachers at that time.
Modify the classroom	*Evaluate the classroom* on the basis of the observations you made. Is it orderly and free of clutter? Are there legitimate opportunities to move about and use large muscles? Can children select their own activities and make choices about where they will work and play? Is the curriculum challenging and appropriate to the age level? Is there advanced warning when activities will change? Is there an established routine that children can count on? Is there a cleanup time when the children help restore the play areas? *Examples:* Materials should be stored in low, open, easy to reach shelves that are labeled (scissors, crayons) and placed in containers that children can handle. Remove puzzles if they are crowded on a shelf, leaving only a few. Rotate them frequently. Display blocks and block accessories (trucks, people, etc.) clearly. Block sizes and shapes on the shelves give children the necessary cues to assist them with cleanup. Provide protected area for block building, away from quieter activities. Check to see if the dividers between the activity centers are low enough for ease of supervision.
Teacher attention and language	*Give minimum attention* to child during aggressive episode, taking care of any injured party first. Use short, direct sentences, without judgment and without lecturing. *Look at and speak to child at eye level.* Do not shame, ridicule, or use physical punishment. *Good Example:* "No. I can't let you hurt children." *Poor Example:* "It's not nice to hit other children. They don't like you when you are mean. Why can't you play nice like they do? I'm gonna have to tell your momma you were bad when she comes. Can you promise me you won't hit anybody else today? Now tell Tomi you are sorry." *Pay attention* to disruptive, nonattentive, aggressive children *when they are behaving appropriately.* Talk over with them alternatives to their nonappropriate behavior. *Examples:* "Next time, tell someone you are angry instead of hitting." "When you are finished playing with the blocks, call me and I will help you find another place to play." "If you don't want to hear the story, what else could you do that wouldn't bother other people who want to listen?"

(continued)

Figure 7.15 ● Managing aggressive, disruptive, high-energy behavior. (Adapted from Allen, K.E. [1992]. *The exceptional child: Mainstreaming in early childhood education.* Albany, NY: Delmar. Used with permission. Taken from Gordon, A., & Browne, K.W. [1996]. *Guiding young children in a diverse society.* Boston: Allyn & Bacon.)

Follow through. Help child return to play, giving choices when possible, with activities that require energy (clay, woodworking, climbing) or those that are more calming (water play, painting), depending on what the child seems to need at the time. Support the child's involvement with relevant comments, interest, and suitable challenges.

> *Examples:* "Let's decide where you want to play now, Faisal. There's room for you at the water table or pounding the clay. I'll help you get started." (Later) "You look as if you are having a good time with that clay, Faisal. I bet you can squeeze it so hard it oozes out your fingers! I'll watch while you try."

Interacting with children

Start with a child's known interests. Through observations, determine which activities consistently hold the child's attention so that you can reinforce positive behavior while the child is engaged. This technique also helps to increase attention span.

> *Example:* "You sure have been having fun at the water table, Jessica. Here are some funnels and tubes. What could you do with them?"

Help child plan where to go next and assist in getting started, if necessary. This is effective if the child's activity is changed before he loses interest or before he loses control.

> *Example:* "Jay, it is nearly cleanup time and I know that sometimes it is a hard time for you when we stop playing. How about your helping me organize the children who want to move the tables. Could you be my assistant today and show everyone where to put the tables?"

Give time for response; take time to teach. Children need adequate time to respond to requests without being nagged and may need assistance in learning a skill or getting started with what was requested. Make the task manageable. If, after a reasonable time has passed and Shaquille still hasn't put his jacket on, the teacher restates the request and offers assistance.

> *Example:* "You may go outside as soon as your jacket is on, Shaquille. If you put the jacket down on the floor like this, and slip your arms in here, you can pull it over your head."

Help children focus their attention. Get down to their eye level, call them by name, look at them, and speak directly to them. Give advance warning, clear, simple directions, and choices when possible. Do not overwhelm with rules and instructions.

> *Example:* "Coretta, it will soon be time to go home. When you finish writing your story, you may choose to come over to the rug to sing songs or you may find a favorite book and look at it in the book corner."

Point out the consequences of their actions to help them understand others' feelings and become responsible for what they do.

> *Examples:* "Linda is sad because you won't let her play with you."
> "Other children won't be able to use the paint when you mix the colors in the paint jar."

Remind children of the rules and expectations. Rehearse them in remembering appropriate behavior. Use positive phrases.

> *Example:* "Before you go to the block area, remember how much space you need for the roads you like to build. Look around and see who else is playing and find a safe place for your road."

Figure 7.15 ● Continued.

young children. Food, tokens, and money are also used as reinforcers in home and school settings. The goal is that inner satisfaction will become its own reward, no matter the type of reinforcer one might use initially.

To succeed, the adult will focus on only one behavior change at a time. If parents want to use behavior modification methods to help their children arrive at the dinner table on time, then Dad does not nag about homework or Mom about a messy room. The behavior that is targeted for change becomes the primary concern until it is successfully altered.

Parents and teachers often take for granted the positive, desirable behavior in children and may forget to acknowledge these behaviors frequently. Behavior modification helps to correct that oversight. Whenever adults focus on a negative aspect of a child's behavior and make an attempt to change it, they also look at the positive qualities the child possesses and reinforce them. This keeps a balanced perspective while working on a problem.

Behavior modification enables adults to invite children to be part of the process, giving them an active part in monitoring their own behavior. Children are capable of keeping a chart of how many times they finished their plate, made the bed, or fed the dog. This chart serves as a natural reinforcer.

Ignoring Behavior

When misbehavior is of a less serious nature—for instance, when a child whines constantly—it may be best to ignore it. This kind of behavior, although mildly annoying, is not harmful. To use the technique successfully, the adult chooses not to respond to the child in any way and may even become occupied elsewhere while the behavior persists. This method is based on the learning theory that negative reinforcement (the adult ignoring the child) will eventually cause the child to stop the undesirable behavior. At first there might be an increase in the misbehavior as the child tests to see whether the adult will truly ignore the action. Once the child sees there is nothing to gain, the behavior disappears.

Redirecting the Activity

Sometimes the adult will want to change the activity in which the child is engaged to one that is more acceptable. For example, if Pat and Elena are throwing books off the reading loft, the teacher will want to redirect them and may suggest throwing soft foam balls into a makeshift basket. This technique calls for the adult to make an accurate assessment of what the children really want to do. In this case, it appears they enjoy throwing from a height. Now the teacher can consider alternatives that permit the desired activity while changing the expression or form it takes: "It looks as if you two are enjoying dropping things from up there. Let's figure out a way you can do that so that books won't be damaged."

The substitute activity must be a valid one, acceptable to the adults and fulfilling to the children. In most cases children are not being deliberately malicious or destructive. More than likely they are expressing curiosity, imagination, and the need to explore. Positive redirection satisfies these needs in a way that enhances children's self-concept and self-control.

Distraction

When the adult helps focus the child's attention elsewhere, some problems may be avoided. Very young children, especially infants and toddlers, can easily be distracted from undesirable actions. Consider the example at the beginning of the chapter in which Kim grabs at one of the necklaces Shawnsey has. A fast-thinking teacher could present Kim with another attractive one. This method calls for well-timed intervention.

Time Out

Removing a child from the play area is particularly appropriate when, owing to anger, hurt, or frustration, the child is out of control. Taking children away from the scene of intensity and emotion to allow them time to cool off and settle down is sometimes the only way to help them. The teacher is firm and consistent as the child is quietly removed from play. It is important that this discipline technique be used with a positive attitude and approach, not as punishment for misbehavior.

The time-out period is very much like that used in athletic events: a brief respite and a chance to stop all activity and regroup. The teacher's role is to help the child talk about the incident—the feelings involved as well as the need for self-control—and to give the child

Figure 7.16 ● Young children should not be isolated for misbehavior in ways that damage their self-esteem.

an opportunity to gain self-control before resuming play. Children can monitor themselves and choose when they are ready to return to classroom activity. Noah, who persists in knocking down other children's block structures, might be told, "You may come back to the block area when you think you are ready to play without knocking over other children's work." Noah can then assume some responsibility for how he will behave and when he is ready to return to play.

Use this technique lightly; it can be misused too easily by adults who leave the child with a sense of rejection. As with other good disciplinary techniques, it should be appropriate to the misbehavior and should help the child toward self-discipline.

Active Problem-Solving

The principle in active problem-solving is to actively engage children in confronting their differences and working together to solve their problems. The adult has a sensitive role to play: that of guiding children toward solutions but not solving problems for them. Posing open-ended questions helps the adult stay focused:

"What could you do _____"

"How might she feel when _____"

"What might happen if _____"

"How can you _____"

The point is to encourage children to come up with alternative solutions. This requires an accepting attitude on the part of the teacher; all of the children's suggestions must be acknowledged seriously, even if they seem unreasonable. Young children are likely to start the discussion by suggesting extreme solutions. In the case of Malcolm, for instance (see the second example at the beginning of this chapter), they might initially suggest a radical alternative: "Don't let Malcolm come to this school anymore." These suggestions will become tempered as other children respond; fair and reasonable solutions will eventually emerge: "Anyone who knocks over somebody else's blocks has to help them build it back up again."

Rather than assessing blame, teachers help children think through a number of alternatives, including the consequences of what they suggest: "If we close the block area, what will happen when you want to play with your favorite trucks this afternoon?" By assisting them in anticipating the results of what they suggest, teachers can help children understand how their behavior influences and affects others. This is an early lesson in a lifelong quest to become responsible for one's own behavior.

Conflict resolution should become part of the child's daily life. Teachers can help children solve disagreements nonviolently and explore alternative ways to reach their goals. Figure 7.17 outlines a process for active problem-solving and conflict resolution (see also Figure 7.13). It is useful for resolving differences through group discussion, as noted above, or when one or more children become embroiled in conflict. By following such a process, children learn to respect others' opinions, to express their own feelings in appropriate ways, and to learn tolerance for doing things in a different way.[1] The process also suggests an important principle in guidance and discipline: the adult role is to intervene as little as possible, allowing children the opportunity to come up with an acceptable solution.

When children help create a solution, they come away with a sense of commitment to it. This process also gives children a sense of power and control, a sense of independence, and a feeling of self-worth.

Summary

The early childhood educator provides opportunities for children to express their feelings in appropriate ways and to solve their social problems constructively. Children are incapable of controlling their own impulses all the time, so caring adults are needed to guide them toward self-control. Teachers base their methods and guidance principles on an understanding of why children misbehave and what factors influence behavior.

Most guidance techniques begin by accepting the feelings the child expresses and verbalizing them. Then the adult sets limits on what form the behavior may take, guiding the action as needed and following through to conclusion.

The most effective methods of guidance are clear, consistent, and fair rules that are enforced in consistent, humane ways. Children should be aware of the consequences if the rules are broken.

Good guidance practices emphasize the positive aspects of a child's behavior, not just the problem behaviors. Guidance measures have greater meaning to children if they are encouraged to take responsibility for their own actions and are part of the problem-solving process.

OUR DIVERSE WORLD OUR DIVERSE WORLD OUR DIVERSE WORLD OUR DIVERSE WORLD OUR DIVERSE WORLD OUR DIVERSE WORLD OUR DIVERSE WORLD OUR DIVERSE WORLD

[1] Children should come to know schools as places large enough and diverse enough to hold an infinite variety of people whose backgrounds and experience are respected and understood.

The Six-Step Approach to Problem-Solving

SCENARIO: Two children run outdoors to get the available wagon. They reach it simultaneously and start pulling on the handle, yelling "Mine!" One child starts shoving the other child out of the way.

Step 1: **Approach (Initiate Mediation)**
— Approach the conflict, signaling your awareness and availability.
— Get close enough to intervene if necessary; stop aggressive behavior or neutralize the object of conflict by holding it yourself.

Step 2: **Make a Statement**
— *Describe the scene.*
— Reflect what the children have said.
— *Offer no judgments, values, solutions.*
"It looks as if you both want the wagon."
"I see you are yelling at each other."

Step 3: **Ask Questions (Gather Data, Define the Problem)**
— Don't direct questions toward pinpointing blame.
— Draw out details; define problems.
— Help kids communicate versus slugging it out.
"How did this happen?"
"What do you want to tell her?"
"How could you solve this problem?"
"How could you use it without fighting?"

Step 4: **Generate Alternative Solutions**
— Give children the job of thinking and figuring it out.
— Suggestions may be offered by disputants or observers.
— Ask questions: "Who has an idea of how we could solve . . .?"
"You could take turns."
"You could both use it together."
"You could both do something else."
"No one could use it."
— Common mistake: rushing this stage; give it the time it deserves.

Step 5: **Agree on Solution**
— When both children accept a solution, rephrase it. ("So, you both say that she will be the driver?")
— If any solution seems unsafe or grossly unfair, you must tell the children. ("It is too dangerous for you both to stand up and ride downhill together. What is another way you can agree?")

Step 6: **Follow Through**
— Monitor to make sure agreement is going according to plan: if the decision is turn-taking, you may need to be a clock-watcher.
— Tell the players and the group:
"Looks as if you solved your problem!"
— Use the power of language to:
● Reinforce the solvability of the problem
● Note the ability of the players to do so
● Point out the positive environment to be successful

Figure 7.17 ● Using these guidelines to help children solve problems, teachers listen more than talk, allow children the time to make mistakes and figure out solutions, and point out that diversity of viewpoints is natural, normal, and workable.

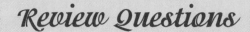

Review Questions

1. What are some of the goals of children's misbehavior? What techniques can adults use to deal with children who exhibit these goals?

2. What developmental factors affect children's behavior? What environmental factors? How does a child's individual style affect behavior? What do developmental and learning theories (see Chapter 4) add to the discussion?

3. Why is it important to understand the child's family culture as you guide and direct behavior?

4. What is your own definition of discipline?

5. Why do teachers have to set limits on children's behavior? How does setting limits help the child?

6. Describe ways children differ in temperament.

7. Discuss in small groups the appropriate uses of time out. Describe those ways in which this technique can be harmful to young children.

8. In what ways might the guidance techniques on pp. 251–261 be considered culturally insensitive to a particular family? What technique might be more appropriate?

Learning Activities

1. Your 3-year-old daughter always interrupts when you talk on the telephone. She cries for you to play with her, hits her brothers, and crawls into cupboards. What is she doing and why? What is your reaction? How will you solve the problem?

2. List activities that channel aggressive feelings into acceptable ways to play. After each, note the emotion or feeling the specific activity might release.
Example: Clay—anger, frustration

3. Finish this sentence: "When I was four years old, the worst thing I ever did was . . ." How did the adults around you react? What would you do if you were the adult in charge? Discuss and compare responses with a classmate.

4. Children's literature helps us focus on disciplinary and behavior problems. Select a book from the following list. Define the problem behavior and the person creating the problem. Do you agree with the author's way of handling the situation? Suggest alternatives. When and with whom might you use this story?

Suggested books: *Peter's Chair*/Ezra Jack Keats
Annie and the Old One/Miska Miles
Jamaica's Find/Juanita Havill
Momma, Do You Love Me?/Barbara M. Joosse
Tree of Cranes/Allen Say
Shy Charles/Rosemary Wells
Bread and Jam for Frances/Russell and Lillian Hoban
Where the Wild Things Are/Maurice Sendak

5. Observe a group of young children during play. See whether you can identify an example of a child who might be described as an easy child, a difficult child, and a slow-to-warm-up child. What disciplinary techniques do the teachers use with each child? Are they the same? If they are different, describe the differences. How successful are the disciplinary techniques that are being used? What might you do differently?

6. How do you feel about spanking children? Were you spanked when you were a child? If so, what precipitated the spankings? Can you think of any other forms of behavior control that might have worked instead of spanking? Compare your thoughts and insights with those of another member of this class.

7. What can you find out about a technique known as "Assertive Discipline," and why do some early childhood educators consider it inappropriate for young children? Report your findings to this class.

Bibliography

American Academy of Pediatrics. (1997). *A guide to your child's symptoms* (p. 35). Elk Grove Village, IL: Author.

America's immigrant challenge. (1993, Fall). *Time*, Special Issue.

Berk, L. E. (1994). *Infants and children*. Boston: Allyn & Bacon.

Brazelton, T. B. (1992). *Touchpoints: Your child's emotional and behavioral development*. Reading, MA: Addison-Wesley.

Galinsky, E., & David, J. (1991). *The preschool years*. New York: Ballantine Books.

Gonzalez-Mena, J. (1993). *Multicultural issues in child care*. Menlo Park, CA: Mayfield.

Gordon, A., & Browne, K. W. (1996). *Guiding young children in a diverse society*. Boston: Allyn & Bacon.

Gordon, T. (1970). *Parent effectiveness training*. New York: Peter H. Wyden.

Honig, A. S., & Wittmer, D. S. (1992). *Prosocial development in children: Caring, sharing and cooperating: A bibliographic resource guide*. New York: Garland Press.

Likona, T. (1991). *Educating for character*. New York: Bantam Books.

Nelson, J., Erwin, C., & Duffy, R. (1995). *Positive discipline for preschoolers*. Rocklin, CA: Prima Publishing.

Nelson, J., & Glenn, H. S. (1992). *Time out: Abuses and effective uses*. Fair Oaks, CA: Sunrise Press.

Thomas, A., & Chess, S. (1977). *Temperament and development*. New York: Brunner/Mazel.

Wichert, Susanne. (1989). *Keeping the peace*. Philadelphia: New Society Publishers.

York, S. (1991). *Roots and wings: Affirming culture in early childhood programs*. St. Paul, MN: Redleaf Press.

Parents and Teachers: Partners in Education

CHAPTER 8

Questions for Thought

Why is it important to have good working relationships with parents?

What are the benefits of an effective parent–teacher partnership?

How do parents get interested and involved in the classroom?

What are the ingredients for a good parent program?

What are the components for a successful parent–teacher conference?

What is the teacher's role in providing a supportive atmosphere for parents?

What are some major concerns of parents?

How has the American family changed in recent years?

HISTORICAL PERSPECTIVE

Working with parents can be one of the teacher's most satisfying responsibilities, or it can be one of the most frustrating. It is usually both.[1] The potential is clearly present for a dynamic partnership between the most important adults in a child's life. The common goal is obvious: the welfare of the child. Each has knowledge, skills, and a sense of caring to bring to that relationship. Each has a need for the other. Partnerships usually begin with such a need. So, parents and teachers become coworkers, colleagues in a joint effort to help the child develop fully.

There is a historical **precedent** for the partnership between parents and teachers. Pestalozzi and Froebel, early 18th-century educators, detailed many of their procedures for home use. The involvement of the mother in the education of the child was considered important even then. When kindergartens were organized in the United States, classes for parents and mothers' clubs were also started. The National Congress of Mothers evolved from that movement. Today it is the National Parents and Teachers Association. This well-known organization is an integral part of most school systems and continues to promote a union between school and home, teachers and parents.

At times during the 1930s parental involvement in education was actively discouraged. Teachers were seen as experts who wanted to be left alone to do their job. In many cases, teachers felt they did little but remedy parental mistakes. Parents in or near the classroom were barely tolerated. That trend ended in the 1940s when the need for parent support and encouragement was recognized. Closer relationships between teachers and parents were established. This view of a need for closer ties between teacher and parents, now over 50 years old, stands today as a commonly accepted principle.

Teacher training curricula began to reflect the change. Teachers were exposed to courses that would help them appreciate and use parents as coworkers in the child's development. By the 1960s, Head Start programs required parental involvement and set about developing parent education and parent training programs. Their commitment to children included a commitment to the parents of those children.

Parent involvement and education were largely ignored in the education reform movement of the 1990s, and the typical parent education prevalent in early childhood programs is also being reassessed. That omission is now being addressed in elementary, middle, and high schools throughout the country, a fact that reinforces the need for parents and teachers of preschool children to become full and equal partners and set the stage for future relationships. Further discussion of the parent support movement follows.

At no other level of education is the responsiveness to the needs of parents so high. Yet, today, there is a renewed effort to extend the role of parents in their children's educational process. There is now a broader emphasis from serving only children to serving children and their families. Also, there is a move from parents' role as volunteers to one of family support and a deepening of parent involvement. There is general agreement among early childhood teachers that at no other age is such a relationship more important than in the early years of a child's schooling, for children's needs are so interwoven with those of their parents. Strong parent–school relationships have always been a part of the early childhood educators' portfolio in ways that have not been understood or developed by teachers of other age groups.

Note: Throughout this chapter, the terms *parents* and *parenthood* are meant to include mothers and fathers as well as other extended family members who have the responsibility for raising a child.[2]

[1] Ellen Galinsky coined the word *parentist*. Just as educators must heighten their awareness of their sexist and racist bias, they must also be aware of individual bias toward particular "types" of parents.

[2] As one works in OUR DIVERSE WORLD it is important to be mindful that many children are being parented by people other than their biologic or adoptive parents (e.g., grandparents, or foster parents, or aunts and uncles, or legal guardians, or an adult living with the parent).

PARTNERSHIP IN EDUCATION

What Parents Contribute

Parents have a unique contribution to make in the child's schooling. They have different knowledge about the child from what the teacher has. They know the child's history: physical, medical, social, and intellectual. They know the child as a member of a family and the role that child plays in the total family group. Through parents, teachers learn about the home life of the children in their classes: who they live with, in what kind of family situation, and what their life-style is like. Parents bring with them a sense of continuity about the child: they provide the context with which the teacher can view the whole child. As the teacher will soon learn, the parents already know what makes their children happy or sad or how they react to changes in routines. Thus, parents have a wealth of intimate knowledge about their children that the teacher is only just beginning to discover.

What Teachers Contribute

Teachers bring to the partnership another perspective. As child development professionals, they see the child in relation to what they know are normal milestones and appropriate behaviors. They notice how each child plays with other children in the group, what seems to challenge Elizabeth and when Patrick is likely to fall apart. Unlike parents, teachers see individual children from a perspective that is balanced by the numerous other children they have taught. They observe how the child behaves with a variety of adults, sensing children's ability to trust other adults through interactions with them at school. When parents need help for themselves or for their child, teachers become resources. They may work with the parents to find psychologists, hearing and speech specialists, or other educational programs, if warranted.

A true partnership begins with recognizing the strengths that each party brings and must be a basic premise in parent–teacher relationships. By pooling their knowledge of a child, both parents and teachers gain a more complete picture of the whole child. By becoming aware of the role each plays in the life of the child, teachers and parents grow in their understanding of one another. They can respect each other's unique contribution. As they recognize their need to share their strengths, they can learn from one another.

The Value of Working Together

The very first contact between parents and teachers is likely to take place within the early childhood education setting, be it a child care center, nursery school, or with a family child care provider. If parents feel welcome and important, the stage is set for ongoing involvement in their child's education. By working closely with parents, teachers establish a pattern that can be repeated as the child grows. Parents should be involved in the school life of their child at all grade levels. Their introduction to this world of schools and teachers, then, is important.

The majority of parents today want to learn the best way to raise their children and want to improve their child-rearing skills. There are numerous opportunities for the early childhood teacher to work with parents. Figure 8.2 cites a multitude of ways to begin to fulfill these needs.

What Parents Gain

One of the greatest values of a strong parent program is the opportunity for parents to meet each other. They find that they share similar problems and frustrations and that they can support one another in finding solutions. Friendships based on mutual interests and concerns about their children blossom.

Through close home–school relationships, parents can find ways to become more effective as parents and as teachers of their children. They can observe modeling techniques that teachers find successful in dealing with children and can learn what behaviors are appropriate at certain ages. By observing how their children relate to other adults and children, parents can come to know them better as social beings. They may become more aware of school and community resources that are available to them and, in the person of the teacher, they now have access to a consultant who knows and understands their child and can help them when they need it.

Parents are the child's teachers too. They teach by word, by example, by all they do and say. Through closer home–school relationships, parents can be helped to see that their everyday experiences with their children provide teachable moments, opportunities for educating their children. Teachers can support parents in their roles as teachers of their children by keeping them informed about each stage of the child's development, by showing them how to encourage language

Figure 8.1 ● A true partnership happens when parents and teachers share their strengths with one another for the benefit of the children they care for and love.

and thinking skills, by educating them to children's social needs at any given age, by providing lists of books and toys that encourage children's thinking and creative abilities as they provide the joy of reading. Teachers should make sure parents have copies of children's favorite songs, recipes that are popular at school, and information, in a bilingual format as needed, on how to teach health and safety habits at home.[1] Parents need not teach a curriculum; they do need to use common household routines and experiences to encourage children's total growth. The teaching staff has a strong role to play in helping parents learn how to do this. In Figure 8.3 a noted author and family counselor lists 10 of the most important things parents can teach their children.

A family-centered approach to parent–school relationships supports the growth of the family as well as the child. When parents have a meaningful partnership with their children's teachers, it raises their sense of importance and diminishes some of the isolation and anxiety of child rearing. By empowering parents in a critical area of their children's lives, allowing them

to participate in decisions affecting their children's education, teachers can help parents can see themselves as part of the solution.

What Teachers and the School Gain

Active parents involvement benefits the teacher and school, too. Parents are an untapped resource in most schools. The skills and talents in a group of parents multiply the people resources available for children.[2] Some parents will want to work directly in the classroom with children, others may volunteer to help in the office, the schoolyard, or the kitchen. Parents can sometimes arrange to take some time off their job to accompany a class on a field trip. Some parents are willing to work at home, either sewing, typing, mending, building, or painting; others are available for a variety of fund-raising activities. In an equal partnership, however, the parent level of involvement must go beyond volunteer participation in school activities to parent participation in decision-making roles, such as serving on school boards, parent

[1] It is important to remember that fewer than half of the children under the age of 5 are being brought up in two-parent, middle-class, English-speaking, stay-at-home-mom, households. Do parent–teacher policies reflect changing demographics?

[2] Parents are an excellent resource for bringing experiences of diversity into a classroom (e.g., a dad cooking an ethnic favorite with children).

A Checklist for Making Your School "Parent Friendly"

☐ Hold an orientation for parents at a convenient time

☐ Provide a place for parents to gather

☐ Create a parent bulletin board

☐ Give annual parent awards for involvement

☐ Create a parent advisory committee

☐ Allow parents to help develop school policies and procedures

☐ Schedule events on evenings and weekends

☐ Provide child care for meetings

☐ Establish a book or toy lending library

☐ Make informal calls to parents, especially to share child's successes

☐ Provide transportation for parents who need it

☐ Provide translators for parents who need them

☐ Send appropriate duplicate mailings to noncustodial parents

☐ Survey parents for issues of interest and need

☐ Develop links to health and social support services

☐ Provide resource and referral lists

☐ Publish school newsletter on regular basis

☐ Provide multilingual written communications as needed

☐ Hire teachers with strong commitment to supporting families and parents

☐ Provide in-service training for teachers in working with parents

☐ Hire teachers who are respectful of social, ethnic, and religious backgrounds of parents

☐ Hire staff reflective of the cultural background of students and parents

☐ Encourage regularly scheduled conferences between parents and teachers

☐ Offer variety of family support programs

☐ Provide many opportunities for parents to volunteer

☐ Provide frequent opportunities for parents to air their concerns

☐ Encourage parents to ask questions, to visit, to call

☐ Encourage parents to know what goes on in the classroom

☐ Encourage parents to report back on what works well

☐ Encourage parents to attend social events

☐ Encourage teachers to make home visits

Figure 8.2 ● A checklist for a family-oriented approach to meet children's needs.[1]

OUR DIVERSE WORLD OUR DIVERSE WORLD OUR DIVERSE WORLD OUR DIVERSE WORLD OUR DIVERSE WORLD OUR DIVERSE WORLD OUR DIVERSE WORLD OUR DIVERSE WORLD

[1] Many of the items on this list demonstrate an awareness of life in OUR DIVERSE WORLD. Can you think of others to add to make your school "parent friendly" in a diverse world?

The Ten Most Important Things Parents Can Teach Their Children
1. To love themselves
2. To read behavior
3. To communicate with words
4. To understand the difference between thoughts and actions
5. To wonder and ask why
6. To understand that complicated questions do not have simple answers
7. To risk failure as a necessary part of growing up
8. To trust grownups
9. To have a mind of their own
10. To know when to lean on adults

Figure 8.3 ● A list of important basics that children can learn at home. (Adapted from LeShan, E. [1992]. *When your child drives you crazy.* New York: St. Martin's Press.)

advisory committees, and other groups that advocate for children's educational needs.

Some parents may be unable to participate because of work schedules, small children to care for at home, lack of transportation, or inability to speak English.[1] If a school is serious about strengthening the family, these issues must be addressed and solutions must be found to involve all parents.

What Children Gain

The children whose parents choose to take an active part in the school reap the rewards of such involvement. Decades of research show the positive effects on achievement when children's parents are involved in their education. The family is the primary source from which the child develops and grows. It is needed to reinforce the learning, the attitudes, and the motivation if children are to succeed. Parent visibility is especially important for low-income and minority children; their parents' presence can heighten a sense

of belonging. Children gain, and parent impact is increased when parents are able to monitor their children's progress and reinforce the mission of the school at home.

Guidelines for Working with Parents

Supporting and encouraging parents in their role are part of a teacher's responsibility. Good teachers are sensitive to parent concerns and understand their needs, similar to those expressed in the Focus Box on p. 270, written by a parent to her child's caregiver. To ensure good parent–teacher relationships, review the following guidelines:

Prepare parents for what they can expect from their child's school experience. School polices and a yearly calendar should be clearly stated and thoroughly reviewed with parents as the child enters school. Then parents will know what their responsibilities are, where the school can be of assistance to them, and what expectations the school has of the parents.

Protect the parent–child relationship. Enhance the pride children naturally feel about their mothers and fathers. Tell Maggie her eyes are just like her Dad's, or mention to Kevin that his Mom will be pleased to hear he slid down the big slide. Reinforce that unique place families have in children's lives. This is particularly critical for children who spend long hours in child care centers away from their parents. Parents need teachers to support them in raising their children, and they like to hear when they have done well. They take pride in doing their best and appreciate teachers who acknowledge their efforts.

Contact parents frequently and on a regular basis. Keep the lines of communication open and flowing between school and home. Be sure to know the parents by name. Take advantage of the daily contact as they bring their child to and from school. It may be brief and breezy, but it is a good way to stay in touch. Be sure to find ways to touch base with those parents who do not come to school every day, by telephone, note, or home visit.

OUR DIVERSE WORLD OUR DIVERSE WORLD OUR DIVERSE WORLD OUR DIVERSE WORLD OUR DIVERSE WORLD OUR DIVERSE WORLD OUR DIVERSE WORLD OUR DIVERSE WORLD

[1] It is important to help all parents feel welcome, wanted, and involved.

How You Can Help—From a Parent Perspective

Yvonne Ricketts

Dear Caregiver:

I bravely smile as I reluctantly allow you to take my infant into your arms. I know in my mind that I can trust you, as I quickly go over all of your carefully chosen qualities. I know that I am doing the right thing by returning to work. But I also know that if I linger much longer my tears will take over and I will grab my baby, run to Tasmania, and go into hiding. All of my early childhood education training and experience didn't prepare me for this first separation. So, as a parent experiencing the intensity of a parent–child bond, I would like to offer some suggestions for helping to ease the separation transition:

1. Take the time to visit with me in advance of my child's first day. Show me around, let me see where my child will eat, sleep, play, and keep his belongings. Find out what our daily routine is and share yours with me.
2. Encourage me to visit with my child before his first day.
3. Help me feel relaxed and comfortable. Be empathic and listen to me. If I am uncomfortable, my child will be, too.
4. Reassure me of how you will help my child cope while I am gone. Will he be stimulated with developmentally appropriate activities? Will he have a special "buddy" looking out for him, helping him learn the new routine? If he cries, how will you handle this?
5. When we arrive, greet me with a smile, and a hug or a touch for my child on his level. Ask

about his night. Help him get settled, put away his belongings.
6. If I am lingering too long, help me leave. I may feel awkward and uncomfortable and need your firm but reassuring push out the door.
7. If I am rushing out the door, remind me to say goodbye to my child, and tell him when I will return in concrete ways he can understand (e.g., "after snack").
8. If my child is having a hard time allowing me to leave, let me see you comfort him and help him with your kind words and reassuring touch.
9. Acknowledge that my child may miss me and that I may miss him. Let my child wave good-bye to me.
10. Allow me to call or visit my child during the day during convenient times for you and me.
11. When I pick up my child, tell me something specific about his day—something positive.

Try not to take it personally if I seem nontrusting, overly concerned, and ask a lot of questions. Remember, I'm a new parent and I'm leaving someone precious in my life with you. I need your reassurance just as you need my trust. Helping me positively separate will help my child. Together we are creating great beginnings for my child.

Thank You!

Yvonne Ricketts is a former children's center director who is now a child advocate and the parent of two children, Casey and Delaney.

Figure 8.4 ● A parent's participation in his child's school life can heighten his child's sense of belonging.

 Respect parents for the difficult job they have, the role they play, and the persons they are. Respect their religious, cultural, social, and ethnic backgrounds and heritage.[1] Respect their privacy. Do not allow one parent to seek information about another. Respect the right of the parent to disagree. Above all, respect the unparalleled part they play in the growth and development of their child.

Listen to parents. Hear them out. They, too, have accumulated experiences to share, and their views are valid. Learn to listen to them with a degree of understanding; try to hear it from their point of view. Listen to parents without judging them or jumping to conclusions; this is the basis for open communication.

Becoming Full and Equal Partners

Families and schools are natural allies; together they claim the primary responsibility in educating and socializing children. They can and should be equal partners in that effort.

Family-Support Movement

Early childhood educators have long recognized the importance of providing parents with child-rearing information and support. Today, the task of raising children has become increasingly difficult, and the type of parent education and participation is changing to meet current parents' needs. What is termed a "family-support" or "parent-support" movement is evolving where the primary goal is to strengthen families to meet the challenges of parenting in the years ahead.

Parent education has often been achieved through lectures on discipline and guidance or age-appropriate characteristics. Parent participation in school activities has been through fund raising, volunteering to help out in the classroom, and driving on field trips. Resource and referrals for children's special needs have defined parent support. These are certainly important aspects of building good relationships between parents and schools, but they are no longer enough for today's parents.

"Children influence and are influenced by a social network: family, school, and community" (Kagan, 1991). Many programs today offer a more comprehensive approach to the parent–school partnership out of a growing recognition of the "ecology of the family" (see Chapter 15 for further discussion). Programs with a strong family orientation create parent centers that offer counseling, cultural events, support groups, weekend family activities, and links to health and social service agencies. Factors that increase the need of a more family-centered approach are: increase in the divorce rate, the growing number of single-parent families and families where both parents work, and increasing numbers of immigrant families. (See the following section, "Today's Parent," and Chapter 15 for examples and discussion). Long-held school perceptions of what constitutes a family may no longer correspond to the reality of today's definition of a family. Family support takes on new meaning when the differences in family styles are acknowledged and supported.[2]

 OUR DIVERSE WORLD OUR DIVERSE WORLD OUR DIVERSE WORLD OUR DIVERSE WORLD OUR DIVERSE WORLD OUR DIVERSE WORLD OUR DIVERSE WORLD OUR DIVERSE WORLD

[1] To demonstrate respect, be supportive of dietary restrictions, special holidays, or customs that parents choose to share.
[2] The more information the school has about the families of the children enrolled (preferred language, work schedules, particular challenges and areas of expertise, etc.) the higher the likelihood of successful home–school relationships.

Figure 8.5 ● Visits and participation in classroom activities are opportunities for parents and teachers to support a family-centered view of the child.

Government Recognition

A growing awareness of the need for a family-centered approach to parent education has been recognized by several government agencies. From its beginning in 1965, Head Start mandated parent involvement as necessary for the health and welfare of many young children. More recently, the Education of the Handicapped Amendments (PL 99-457) in 1986 required early intervention services aimed at the family, not just the child. PL 99-457 includes parents as members of a team of professionals who develop an individualized plan related to the child and family's needs. Two states, Minnesota and Missouri, have developed comprehensive, family-centered early childhood programs funded through local school districts.

Developing a Strong Partnership

Powell (1989) has defined four components of a high-quality parent program that promote the family's contribution to their children's education and growth as well as a more equal and meaningful partnership,

1. **Parents and teacher collaborate** to ensure that parent program goals, methods, and content are responsive to parents needs. The needs, concerns, and interests of parents will vary according to the population the school serves. Parents have many needs in common, but they do not all have the same needs at the same time. A good program for parent involvement reflects those needs in the number, type, and kinds of opportunities it provides. An assessment of parent needs is critical, as is parent involvement in planning the program.

2. At the same time the **parents' social services and community support networks are strengthened,** care must be taken not to overshadow the needs of the child. The interconnectedness of the child, the family, and the community must be recognized without disturbing the balance between meeting children's needs and parents' needs. Teachers have a dual role of caring for and educating children while being sensitive and responsive to their parents. As parents and teachers develop a partnership, they should keep in mind that the children's best interests are the common goal of a good parent program.

3. **Programs must be tailored to the needs and characteristics of the specific parent population**, responding to cultural characteristics and values of ethnic populations. To build on the family's strength and promote the family's contribution to their children's education, some programs will serve a targeted audience. Support groups for teenage parents, non-English-speaking parents, and parents who are working on their high school equivalency tests may be developed alongside the usual parenting classes and workshops.[1]

4. **Frequent discussion groups** in which parents are free to share their experiences and insights with one another are critical to parent–teacher growth in the partnership. Parents will grow in self-confidence and security only if teachers will respect their knowledge and instincts about their own children. A good parent program is based on mutual respect; parents have the freedom to accept what is useful, and they can reject what they cannot in good conscience adopt for themselves.

Two considerations must be emphasized to strengthen and reinforce the role of the family as the most important influence in the child's life. First, teachers must be trained to work with parents from many ethnic, religious, and cultural backgrounds. They must be willing to listen to and respect parents as well as demonstrate their commitment to an equal partnership.[2]

Second, high-quality parent programs show they are serious about the partnership when they give parents a greater say in school decision-making. Parent involvement will be limited unless there are decisions parents can make that have meaning for their children (Levin, 1990). Empowering parents to be change agents in their children's educational process results in greater parent commitment and involvement.

Reggio Emilia: An Exemplary Partnership

One of the best examples of school–parent partnerships that bears witness to Powell's criteria for high-quality programs are the schools of Reggio Emilia,

Italy (see discussions in Chapters 1 and 2). A fundamental principle is an assumption of strong and active parent involvement at every level of school functioning. This is not surprising, since the schools were originally founded as parent cooperatives; part of the guiding philosophy continues to uphold a model of equal and extended partnership. Malaguzzi (Edwards, Gandini & Forman, 1993) refers to this balanced responsibility of teachers, parents, and children as a "triad at the center of education"; who, in turn, count on the rest of the community to provide a cultural context for children's learning.

School-based management fosters meaningful participation of parents. All of the discussions and decisions are made by the teachers and parents within each school setting, including cooks and other adults who work within that particular school. No area seems the exclusive property of either parents or teachers. Curriculum planning, for instance, depends on the family's involvement, interest, and contributions. Parents are the core of the individual school boards, and their numbers are well represented on the city-wide school board; they are an integral part of the decision-making process that determines their children's education. Frequent parent meetings are held to inform parents of the school's program and to bring them up to date on what their children are doing. Other meetings may be focused on a topic of interest or an opportunity for parents to explore and debate, or an expert may lecture on a topic regarding their children's development. Smaller groups of parents meet throughout the year with the teachers to talk about their children and the program; individual parent–teacher conferences, which either can request, are held to deal with specific concerns.

There are opportunities as well to be actively involved in the daily life of the school. Parents, teachers, and town residents build furnishings and maintain materials for the classrooms and the schoolyard and rearrange the space to accommodate program needs. In sessions with teachers and **pedagogistas**, parents learn various educational techniques necessary to the program, such as photography and puppet making, and they use these new skills in the classroom with

OUR DIVERSE WORLD OUR DIVERSE WORLD OUR DIVERSE WORLD OUR DIVERSE WORLD OUR DIVERSE WORLD OUR DIVERSE WORLD OUR DIVERSE WORLD OUR DIVERSE WORLD

[1] As American families continue to change, programs for young children will need to create linkages between family and school environments.

[2] Many early childhood educators choose the profession because of their interest in children only to realize that a large focus of their work needs to be on adult development as it relates to families in a multicultural world.

their children. Using the whole town as a backdrop, parents participate in many of the field trips to city landmarks, or as small groups visiting a child's home. Recording and transcribing children's activities and projects are often a parent's responsibility (see Chapter 11).

The meaning of family is communicated to the children of Reggio Emilia throughout their school environment. In classroom dramatic play areas and in the school's own kitchen there are displays of foods, materials, and utensils common to the region and found in the children's homes. Children are encouraged to bring special objects from home, and these are accorded special and beautifully arranged display space.[1] Photographs of children and families abound. These elements are the vehicles used to ensure a rich flow of communication between the school and the homes of the children of Reggio Emilia.

The schools of Reggio Emilia seem to have a unique reciprocal relationship with the families they serve. Parents have influence and help effect change; in turn, the schools influence and change parents. Each becomes a stronger voice for what is in the best interest of the child, whose needs are foremost.

Figure 8.6 ● Because half of the women with children younger than age 6 work outside the home, fathers often bring children to child care.

TODAY'S PARENT

There is little preparation for the job of being a parent, and most mothers and fathers feel inadequate in their role. Parents are pretty much alone as they strike out in unfamiliar territory. Due to our increasingly mobile society, most couples do not live around the corner from grandparents or other family members. There is often no extended family to teach new mothers and fathers some of the traditional, time-honored child-rearing skills. There is no one with whom parents can share their worries, frustrations, and concerns. So the *pediatrician's* phone number is etched in their minds, and they proceed to become the best parents they can.

Recently, an important change has taken place within young families. Raising children as a shared experience is becoming a commonly accepted way of life. Young men, influenced by changing values and attitudes toward traditional sex roles, are taking an active part in raising their families. Fathers seem aware

of the critical role they play in the child's life and are making appropriate changes to see that they have the time to be with their children. Child rearing is no longer just the mother's responsibility, according to a new generation of fathers.

Stages of Parent Development

The role of parent is not a static one; parents grow and change as their children do. The cycle of stages parents experience is only recently being recognized and studied. Identifiable stages of parental growth are described in a manner similar to the stages of growth that occur as all humans develop and as teachers develop (Galinsky, 1987).

According to Galinsky, there are six stages of parenthood. Because parents may have children of different ages, they may be going through several stages at once. Growth can occur at any time and during any stage. The tasks and issues at each stage vary as shown in Figure 8.7.

[1] Diversity will be found and reflected through each child and family.

SIX STAGES OF PARENTHOOD

Stage	Parent Task	Age of Child(ren)
1. Image-making stage	Parents draw on their memories and fantasies of what kind of parent they want to be, prepare for changes in themselves and with other important adults.	Occurs during gestation
2. Nurturing stage	Parents confront the demands of attachment, compare their images with their actual experiences.	From birth until child says "No," around 18–24 months
3. Authority stage	Parents define the rules of the family system and their roles in it; they decide what kind of authority to be.	From 18 months to 5 years of age
4. Interpretive stage	Parents decide how to interpret the world to their child and are concerned with how they interpret themselves to their children, how they are developing the children's self-concepts, and what kind of values, knowledge, and skills to promote.	From late preschool years until the beginning of adolescence
5. Interdependent stage	Parents renegotiate the rules with their teenagers; issues of stage 3 (authority) reappear; parents form a new relationship with their almost-grown children.	The teenage years
6. Departure stage	Parents evaluate their sense of success or failure—whether they have achieved the parent–child relationship they want—and redefine these new relationships.	When children leave home

Figure 8.7 ● The role of a parent changes in various ways as parent and child grow older together. (Adapted from Galinsky, E. [1987]. *Between generations*. Reading, MA: Addison-Wesley.)

The advent of the first baby brings with it life-altering changes and implications. For many parents who were raised to believe that having children is fun, that children will keep a marriage together, or that every married couple must have children, the myths do not match the reality of the experience.

As they gain confidence in themselves, as more children are added to the family, and as each family member matures, parents continually change. The issues they face with only one child are altered considerably when a second or third baby is born. As each of the children grows, develops, and progresses through stages, parents are required to adapt. As parents adjust their own ideas about child rearing to the realities they experience, they grow as parents. Changing their own behavior is a sign of growth. In other words, parents do not have a consistent or permanent pattern of child rearing over the years (Bee, 1997).

Patterns of Child Rearing

One notable study of how parents behave with preschool children was published by Baumrind in 1972. Of the three types of parental styles identified (authoritative, authoritarian, and permissive), authoritative parents were associated with the highest levels of self-esteem, self-reliance, independence, and curiosity in children. *Authoritative* parents provided a warm, loving atmosphere with clear limits and high expectations. In a follow-up study done when the children were 8 or 9, Baumrind's findings persisted.

In contrast, *authoritarian* child-rearing patterns reflect high control and maturity demands combined with relatively low communication and nurturance. Authoritarian parents are dictatorial; they expect and demand obedience yet lack warmth and affection. *Permissive* patterns are essentially the reverse of authoritarian child-rearing styles. There is a high level of warmth and affection but little control. Clear standards and rules are not set, nor are they reinforced consistently.

This research points out clearly how children are affected by the way their parents treat them. The role of the teacher becomes clear also—to help parents learn appropriate and effective ways to raise their children.

Incidentally, it has been noted that in lists defining characteristics of unusually effective schools, the qualities cited sound similar to those of the authoritative child-rearing style. The effective parent and the effective school each establish "clear goals and rules, good control, good communication, and high nurturance" (Bee, 1997).

The Changing American Family

The American family as a whole is experiencing significant alterations. Statistics gathered almost 30 years apart show a dramatic picture of the changing family.

Since 1970, the number of

● Divorced persons has more than tripled

● Children living with only one parent has more than doubled

● Children living in female-headed families has doubled (Children's Defense Fund)

● Births to unmarried mothers has more than doubled

● Children who are poor has increased from 14% to more than 20%

● Mothers with children under age 6 who are in the work force rose from 30% to 65%

● Mothers with school-age children who are in the work force rose from 50% to 77% (U.S. Bureau of the Census, 1997; Children's Defense Fund, 1998)

Since the 1970s the United States has experienced a significant demographic transformation, with non-European cultural groups playing a more dominant role in American society. A new pluralistic environment is being created, one that requires teachers and caregivers to respond to the cultural needs of children and their families. Data on the ethnic distribution of the school population enlarge the story. According to the U.S. Department of Education (1996), students in elementary and secondary schools were represented in the mid-1990s as follows: whites make up 68%, African Americans 16%, Hispanics 13%, and other minorities 3%. The U.S. Bureau of the Census projects that in the 21st century, Hispanics will be the fastest-growing population and will surpass African Americans as the largest minority in the country. During the same time, the non-Hispanic white population will decline and the number of Native Americans will double (Robles de Melendez & Ostertag, 1997). That means that one out of three children in 2010 in the United States will be a non-European American (U.S. Bureau of the Census, 1992). These population dynamics will require a multicultural mindset, and teachers and caregivers will lead the way in helping children learn that diversity is not just tolerated, but valued. The challenge for the teacher is to be prepared to understand families in their various forms and to be part of a family support system.[1]

Parents with Unique Needs

Parents are parents the world over and have mutual problems and pleasures as they go about bringing up their young. Their shared experiences create an automatic bond whenever parents meet. Today, there are some families, however, who face additional challenges in child rearing and who may need added teacher support. These are:

● Parents of children with developmental delays and disabilities

OUR DIVERSE WORLD OUR DIVERSE WORLD OUR DIVERSE WORLD OUR DIVERSE WORLD OUR DIVERSE WORLD OUR DIVERSE WORLD OUR DIVERSE WORLD OUR DIVERSE WORLD

[1] Teachers and caregivers should be familiar with the characteristics and issues that affect the families they serve and should be able to suspend any judgments based on their own ethnocentric views.

- Single parents

- Adoptive and foster parents

- Parents who both work outside the home

- Divorced parents

- Gay/lesbian parents

- Homeless parents

- Teenage parents

- Grandparents raising grandchildren

- Parents who are raising their children in a culture not their own

- Parents who do not speak English and whose child is in a setting where English is the predominant language

- Multiracial families

- First-time parents

Many of these family characteristics place parents in situations where they do not have access to an extended family support system. Any one or combination of these situations can create complex challenges for parents. A teacher should become aware of the forces at work within these families and be sensitive to their needs. Teachers should treat these parents with the same respect as they do any other. It is not necessary to single them out, and, indeed, such an effort may be resented. For the most part, teachers can help these parents by focusing on the many interests and concerns they share with all other parents.[1] In some cases, additional support for these parents is needed.

- Help parents locate community resources to assist them.

- Put them in touch with other parents who have similar parenting circumstances.

- Assist them in exploring school settings for the future.

- See that they are included in all school functions.

- Learn about their special needs.

- Seek their help and advice.

- Help them establish contact with other parents who may be willing to assist in translating, transporting, babysitting, and sharing friendship.

Needs of Single Parents

1970   Single parents made up 5% of all U.S. households.

1995   Single parents made up 9% of all U.S. households.

In their eagerness to do right by their child, some parents grab for help whenever and however it is offered: how-to books, television talk shows, magazine articles. They seem willing to listen to anyone, to try anything. That is surely some measure of how lonely and frightened parents must feel at times.

These feelings may be particularly acute for single parents—men and women who are raising children without a partner. One in every four children today lives in a single-parent household (Children's Defense Fund, 1998). If current trends continue, 60% of all children will live in a single-parent household sometime in their lives (Wanat, 1991).

Faced with the economic necessity to work, single parents must cope not only with raising children alone, but also with child care arrangements and costs. Particularly hard hit are women who head single-parent households. They are more likely than men to live below the poverty level, to never have married, not to have finished high school, and to be members of a minority population.

Single parents need the early childhood professional to be part of a support system for them and their children. To best serve the interests of children, educators must be sensitive to the unique aspects of raising children alone. This means reexamining school policies and attitudes that ignore the needs of single parents.[2] Overburdened child care professionals, some of whom are single parents themselves, need to be flexible in exploring new avenues of home–school collaboration. They need to ask:

OUR DIVERSE WORLD OUR DIVERSE WORLD OUR DIVERSE WORLD OUR DIVERSE WORLD OUR DIVERSE WORLD OUR DIVERSE WORLD OUR DIVERSE WORLD OUR DIVERSE WORLD

[1] Many of the challenges and joys of parenting young children are universal—crossing the lines of the child's family structure, culture, ability, social class, and so on.

[2] School policies can seem hostile or insensitive to the challenges faced by single-parent families (e.g., policies that require parent conferences during workday hours).

- What kind of involvement in a child's classroom is *possible* for a working single parent?

- How can teachers help parents feel connected even if they are unable to be at the center?

- What is appropriate support for single parents?

- How do teachers maintain the role of the professional, offering support, without getting involved with inappropriate friendships?

- How judgmental are teachers about single parents? About single mothers?

- How do teachers help parents and children deal with the absent parent?

- What are some of the best strategies for helping children cope with the transitions when visiting one parent or the other?

These and other similar questions must become an agenda of staff meetings, in-services for teachers, and parent-group meetings.

Needs of Immigrant Parents

1970   4.8% of the U.S. population was born outside of the United States.

1994   8.7% of the U.S. population was born outside of the United States.

The U.S. Bureau of the Census (1995) highlights the extensive changes in immigration over the last 30 years. The origin of immigrants has also undergone a significant shift, from a largely European base to one dominated by Latin America and Asia. Mexico and Russia are the two origin countries where the largest immigrant groups have come from. About 43% of recent immigrants are of Hispanic origin, less than two thirds are white, nearly 25% are Asian or Pacific Islander, and only 7% are African American. In Texas and Florida, for instance, 70% and 61%, respectively, of all recent immigrants are of Hispanic origin; in California and New Jersey, Asian immigrants account for 28% and 25%, respectively, of recent immigrants (U.S. Bureau of the Census, 1995). These data, added to existing ethnic populations already present in the United States, challenge the early childhood teacher to a multicultural sensitivity not yet realized. These data also challenge the profession to aggressively recruit and train early childhood professionals within these cultures. A willingness to learn various cultural norms

and a knowledge of languages will be helpful for teachers to communicate with children and parents whose primary language is not English. Because some studies suggest that teacher's stereotypes of social and racial subgroups influence their attitudes about a parent's ability and competence, teachers will want to examine their own biases (Powell, 1989). See the appropriate sections in Chapters 5, 9, and 11 for discussion of teacher bias, anti-bias curricula, and anti-bias environments.

Miscommunication may be a problem when teaching a classroom of diverse children. When cultural perspectives of the family and the school differ markedly, teachers can easily misread a child's attitude and abilities because of different styles of languages and behaviors. Also, teachers use classroom practices that are at odds with a child's cultural norms. For example, in some preschool settings, children are encouraged to call their teachers by the teacher's first name. This informal style of addressing authority figures may make some parents uncomfortable. How adults and children interact with children, their teaching language, and the strategies they use to guide children's behavior are areas in which immigrant parents can help teachers learn the cultural differences that cause difficulties for children.

The Teacher's Role

The child care specialist is often one of the first people, outside the home, to whom parents turn for help. Parents come to the center looking for teachers who know about children and who will work with them. They arrive at school confused and discouraged; being a mommy or daddy is not at all like they thought it was going to be. Helping parents with their child-rearing problems is part of a teacher's role. The way in which teachers define that role and their response to parental concerns should be carefully thought through. The following are guidelines to consider in establishing a supportive atmosphere for parents:

Do not confuse the role of teacher and parent. Although committed to meeting the needs of the individual children in the class, remember that teachers are not and cannot be **surrogate** parents. Allow parents to do their part of the job to the best of their ability, and teachers their part without infringing on that relationship.

Support all parents, even those with differing opinions. Find ways to acknowledge them and what they are trying to do even though you may be at odds with some of their child-rearing philosophies. There is a greater chance to discuss differences and affect change if there are areas where teachers and parents find agreement.[1] Children are sensitive to adult feelings, whether they are spoken or not. A teacher should not overtly disagree with a child's parents. Differences of opinions should be discussed out of the child's hearing, and teachers should do nothing that would undermine that parent in the eyes of his or her child.

Respect the values of families. Social, cultural, and religious differences and a variety of life-styles, child-rearing methods, and educational philosophies are reflected in every classroom. It is important that parents feel accepted. Focus on the similarities among parents and develop an anti-bias approach to teaching.

Be friendly with parents, but do not be their friends. Keep a professional distance. The temptation to move into a social relationship with some families in your class is one that every teacher faces. When a teacher develops close relationships with one family or another, this can complicate the teacher role. It makes a teacher feel good to know that friendship is desired, but it can be confusing to parents and children. The teacher maintains a more realistic, objective picture of the child if there is some detachment. The child and the family will probably benefit most if a close relationship is postponed until the child moves on to another class.

Ask parents instead of telling them. A teacher-tell approach should be used sparingly. Teachers are most helpful when they begin with the parents' concerns. Suggestions will be received more favorably if teachers avoid telling parents what to do. A teacher's role is one of helping parents clarify their own goals for their children and identifying the trouble spots. Teachers then encourage and support parents as they work together to solve the problem. Parents will feel overwhelmed and inadequate if they think they must change their whole child-rearing style. The sensitive teacher will observe parents and move toward reasonable solutions.

A little support goes a long way. Everyone likes to be reinforced for doing a good job. Parents respond positively to a comment, a phone call, or any brief acknowledgment of their efforts. As Alex's parents enter or leave school, the teacher could mention how Alex has relaxed since they began to insist on a reasonable bedtime. A quick note, sent home with Juanita, that commends her parents for getting her to school on time would be appreciated.

Help parents support each other. Any group of parents represents a multitude of resources. Each parent has accumulated experiences that might prove helpful to someone else. Parents have common concerns and a lot to share with one another. The teacher can provide an arena in which sharing happens. Introduce two families to each other by suggesting that their children play together outside of school. Parent meetings, work parties, and potluck dinners are methods for getting parents involved with each other. The teacher's role can be one of providing the setting, encouraging introductions, and then letting it happen.

Enhance parents' perception of their child. Parents want teachers who know their child, enjoy their child, and are an advocate for their child. That means acknowledging the child's strengths and those personality traits that are particularly pleasing. Help parents to recognize the joys of parenthood, rather than focusing on the burdens.

Focus on the parent–child relationship. Help parents learn the "how-to's" of their relationship with their child rather than the "how-to's" of developing academic skills. Concentrate on the nature of the parent–child interaction—how they get along with each other and how they interact as a family. A major concern of parents may be how to get Rhoda to stop biting her nails; how to set limits that Joel will keep; how to stop Richard and Monica from fighting at the dinner table; how to get Timmy to stop wetting his bed; how to get Allie to take care of the puppy; or how to get Frannie to clean up her room. These issues are the heart and soul of parent–child relationships. Teachers have a role to play in enhancing the quality of those relationships by helping parents focus on their child's uniqueness.

Accept parents for what they are. Their feelings get aroused by teachers, schools, children's behavior,

1 Early childhood professionals must be willing to enter into a dialogue with parents that exposes cultural assumptions and allows for differing perspectives.

being judged, being criticized, feeling inadequate, and being told what to do. Meantime, teachers have to face their feelings about parents. The important thing to keep in mind is that parents just want to be accepted for who and what they are. As teachers accept the individuality of each child, they must accept each parent as a unique combination of traits, personalities, strengths, problems, and concerns.[1] Parents and teachers seem frightened of one another. This is especially true of inexperienced teachers and first-time parents. Each has anxieties about what the other does—or does not do. They must work at putting the other at ease and come to some understanding and respect. Teachers who have a clear understanding of that role can help parents relax and set aside some of their fears.

TEACHER–PARENT INTERACTIONS

The Separation Process

When parents leave a child at school, it may be a time of stress for all concerned. Each time this process occurs, the child, parents, and teachers are entering into a new and unpredictable relationship.

The Child's Perspective

Each year, as school begins, a child enters a classroom and says good-bye to a parent. Each year this is, in some ways, a new experience for that child, no matter how long he or she might have been enrolled in school. Even children returning to the same classroom will find some changes with which they must cope. There may be new teachers and new children together with some familiar faces. The room arrangement might be different enough to cause some anxiety. For most, school is a new and alien place. Each child will react differently to the situation, and it is difficult to predict how a child will respond. Some children will have had previous group experience to draw on; others will never have been a part of a group of children before.

Here are some scenes of children entering school for the first time:

Paul, clinging to his Dad's trouser legs, hides his face from view. All efforts to talk with him are met with further withdrawal behind his father.

Sherry bounces in, runs from her mother over to the blocks area and begins to play there. Her mother is left standing alone, just inside the classroom.

Taryn clutches a stuffed animal as she enters school with her grandmother. She smiles when the teacher addresses her by name and looks surprised when the teacher asks to meet the rabbit she is holding. Taryn lets go of her grandmother's hand and moves forward to show the teacher her favorite toy. After a few moments, the grandmother tells Taryn good-bye, leaving her in conversation with the teacher.

The wide range of behavior these children exhibit is normal, predictable, and age appropriate. Each child has a natural way of dealing with the anxieties of coming to school. Their behavior will be as varied as they are themselves.[2]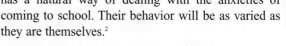

The Teacher's Perspective

The **separation process** is one instance in which the teacher's role is to help the parents as much as the child. Parents and teachers must be especially clear with one another during this time. It is helpful to have written school policies and procedures so the teacher can go over the process step by step, on an individual basis, as each child enrolls, or at a general parent meeting held before the opening of school.

In some schools, teachers arrange to make a home visit to each child enrolled in the class before school begins. This helps the teacher know more about students before they enter school and gives children a chance to become acquainted with a teacher on their home ground.

OUR DIVERSE WORLD OUR DIVERSE WORLD OUR DIVERSE WORLD OUR DIVERSE WORLD OUR DIVERSE WORLD OUR DIVERSE WORLD OUR DIVERSE WORLD OUR DIVERSE WORLD

[1] Every cultural group interprets life events, such as child rearing, birth, and marriage, according to its own cultural framework.
[2] Early childhood educators are reminded regularly that there is not one right way, rather many right ways.

Figure 8.8 ● Good communication is enhanced when parents and teachers leave notes for one another about important changes in the child's daily routine.

The Parent's Perspective

Most parents want their children to make a smooth transition from home to school. Adjustment is a gradual process; parents need encouragement and guidance as their child moves toward independence. When parents are reassured their child is acting normally, and their own anxieties are common, they relax and begin to help the child feel more comfortable.

Parents encourage their child's participation in the program by asking questions and talking together about school activities. They communicate their interest in ways to help their child meet the challenge with a minimum of stress and a maximum of enjoyment.

The Partnership

In giving support and encouragement to both the parent and the child, the teacher helps them achieve independence from one another. Together, parents and teachers make a plan, going over the guidelines and

ground rules. The teacher takes the lead, encouraging the child to move out from the parent. The teacher is there to make the decisions regarding the time of actual separation. The parent and teacher prepare children and tell them when it is time. The teacher supports the parents' exit and stands by the child, ready to give comfort, if needed. This is a time when a teacher needs to act with conviction. Parents appreciate firmness and confidence at a time when their own feelings may be *ambiguous*. Children are reassured by teachers whose attitudes express a belief in what they are doing.

Some parent–child attachment relationships are difficult to assess, and it is not always easy or obvious for the teacher to know what to do. Figure 4.12 may be helpful as a reminder of how patterns of attachment affect the separation process. For most children, the separation process is a struggle between their natural desire to explore the world and their equally natural resistance to leaving what is "safe". It is during these years that children are learning to move about under their own power and to trust themselves. Coming to school can provide each child with the opportunity to grow, starting with the separation from parents. Through careful planning, close communication, and sensitivity to one another, parents and teachers will assure the child mastery of this task.

Parent Education and Involvement

Almost any contact between the teacher and the parent can be perceived as parent education. Teachers interpret children's behavior to their parents, suggest alternative ways for dealing with problems, show them toys and games that are appropriate, hold workshops on parenting skills, mention books and articles of interest to parents, and reinforce parent interest and attention to their children's education. All of these activities are considered parent education. Some are planned, some are spontaneous. Parent education happens frequently, whether in a class on positive discipline or in an informal chat about car seat safety.

Parental involvement in children's education has a wide variety of options, as discussed earlier in this chapter. The concept of parent education and involvement in early childhood programs is broadening to include any number of family support programs based on the needs of parents and their children. Parent education and involvement are at the core of the family–school relationship and go a long way to

Figure 8.9 ● Young children become intensely involved when parents participate in classroom activities. Here, a mother helps them understand more about her baby's feeding needs.

promote a true partnership between parents and teachers.

Communicating with Parents

There are many ways for parents and teachers to increase their communication with one another.[1] In doing so, teachers demonstrate that they value the role parents play in their children's lives. Parents are made aware of what their children are doing in school. Five of the most common ways teachers can involve and inform parents are:

1. *Newsletters from the classroom*. They give a general idea of what the children are doing and any special events taking place in class, personal information about new babies, vacations, or other important events in the lives of the children. Be sure the newsletter is written in the language of the parents in this class.

2. *Bulletin boards*. Posted where parents can see them, these boards contain notices about parent meetings, guest speakers, community resources, child care, babysitting, clothing and furniture exchanges, and library story hours. Information regarding health

OUR DIVERSE WORLD OUR DIVERSE WORLD OUR DIVERSE WORLD OUR DIVERSE WORLD OUR DIVERSE WORLD OUR DIVERSE WORLD OUR DIVERSE WORLD OUR DIVERSE WORLD

1 Parents can be an invaluable source of information, support, and affirmation to the teacher and the school.

programs, automobile and toy safety, and immunization clinics are also publicized. Post information on cultural events appropriate to the ethnic makeup of the school community.

3. *A place for parents.* Providing an area or room at the school set aside for parent use can be an important step in letting parents know they are wanted and needed. Some schools provide space for a parent lounge, complete with a library of resource books on child rearing. If there is no available space, set up a coffee bar in the office or hall. The smallest amount of space—even a countertop with magazines—is a start.

4. *Informal contacts are the easiest and most useful lines of communication with parents.* All it takes is a phone call, a brief note, or a brief talk on a daily basis. For parents who have difficulty attending meetings or who do not accompany their child to and from school, teachers can send home a note along with a sample of artwork, or a story the child has dictated, or a photograph of the child with friends.

5. *Home visits.* Depending on its purpose, a home visit can be used to enhance communications. The visit might be set up to focus only on the relationship between the teacher and the child. Or the visit might have a purely social function—a way for teachers to meet the whole family and for them to get acquainted with the teachers. In any event, the teacher can use this as a bridge to build a pleasant, casual beginning with this family.

Parent–Teacher Conferences

Parent conferences are the backbone of any good parent–teacher relationship. They provide a way of coming together to focus on the needs of the individual child. Conferencing can be a mutually supportive link established between the adults who are most concerned about an individual child, with the purpose of helping the child reach the fullest potential possible.

Conferences between parents and teachers are held for many reasons. The initial conference, when the child first enrolls in school, may focus on the

Figure 8.10 ● There are many avenues for parent-teacher communication. This bilingual bulletin board, located just outside the classroom door, holds newsletters, notices, and even children's art.

family. Important information to share includes a brief overview of the child's development, daily habits, and interests, as well as the parents' view of the child and what the parents expect of the school. The teacher will want to assure parents that they are free to call at any time if they have questions about the school or their child. Farther into the school year, both parents and teachers will want an up-to-date assessment of the child's progress, noting especially the strengths of the child and areas where improvement is needed. Several formats to help focus the discussion are cited in Chapter 10.

A conference may be called at any time by either a parent or a teacher if there are concerns to discuss. A written outline listing the goals of the conference will help guide the discussion and direct it to problem areas. Every occasion when parents and teachers get together to talk about a child is a step toward building trusting relationships between home and school.

Too often, teachers are left to figure out for themselves how to have a conference that is satisfying and productive to both parties.[1] Experience is the best teacher is an old saying that certainly has merit. The more new teachers work with parents and hold regular

[1] All parents want their children to do well yet may feel uncertain when dealing with a language and culture that is not their own.

Figure 8.12 ● A good parent information program can inform parents of the need for greater child advocacy

conferences, the more effective they become. The chart in Figure 8.11 might help the beginning teacher hold fulfilling parent conferences.

Maintaining Privacy and Confidentiality

The more involved parents are in the workings of the school, the more important it is to establish guidelines for protecting the privacy of all the families enrolled. Parents who volunteer in the office, the classroom, or on a field trip must understand they cannot carry tales out of school about any of the children, the teachers, the administration, or other parents. The school must be clear about its expectations for ensuring such privacy and communicate policies to parents. Parents who work on advisory boards, planning committees, or other activities that allow them access to the school office should be sensitive to the confidentiality issue and respect the privacy of every family enrolled in the school.

Summary

The partnership in education between parent and teacher has a long and varied history, with each partner recognizing the unique part he or she plays in the child's life. The value of sharing the information they have about the child highlights their separate but important functions.

In current practice, there is a movement to integrate parent education and parent participation toward a more highly developed family-centered approach. An equal partnership, based on mutual respect for the strengths that both parents and teachers bring to the relationship, requires a deepening of parent involvement, particularly in the decision-making process.

One of the first and most intensive ways parents and teacher work together is through the separation process that takes place when the child enters school. There are other basic skills teachers must have to work successfully with parents. Frequent and open communication, comfort with diversity, and planning for varied parent education activities are but a few. Conferencing is a critical part of the parent–teacher partnership.

Building Home and School Relationships through Effective Parent Conferences

1. *Schedule conferences on a regular basis.* Parents and teachers should share some of the positive aspects of child growth and development and not meet only in crisis. This promotes better feelings about one another, not to mention the child, if meetings are at times other than when a problem occurs.

2. *Be prepared.* Discuss with the staff ahead of time any points they want to include. Gather any materials, notes, and samples of the child's work that might illustrate a point.

3. *Select a quiet place, free from interruption.* If necessary, sign up for use of a conference room. Make sure that someone is available to intercept phone calls and other appointments.

4. *Have a clear purpose.* Use a written format as a guide to keep focused on the intent of the conference. This gives a brief reminder of points to be covered and serves to keep parents on the track.

5. *Put parents at ease right away.* Offer them a cup of coffee or share an amusing anecdote that just took place in the classroom. Acknowledge the important part they played in the school fair. These light, positive comments will help relax both teacher and parent.

6. *Use up-to-date information and data.* Cite examples, from teacher's observations, that occurred that morning or a few days ago. Include examples of situations that occurred when they were present. "Timmy is very empathic for a 3-year-old, isn't he? That was so clear from the way you two were talking as you came through the door today."

7. *Give them a place to shine.* Tell them what they do well—their success with car-pool crowds or in mediating fights in the yard. If they have a special talent they have shared with the class, comment on its impact on the children.

8. *Ask—don't tell.* Get them talking by asking open-ended questions. "How is that new bedtime arrangement working?" "Tell me more about Katie's eating habits." Teachers will relate these to their own knowledge and experiences with the child and then share what has worked in school, but acknowledge the difference between school and home, teacher and parent. Learn how to listen. Concentrate on what the parents are saying. Don't listen with half an ear while planning an appropriate response or comment.

9. *Avoid blaming parents.* Keep the conversation based on mutual concerns and how to help each other. Look at some alternatives together and make a plan of action. Discuss ways to check in with each other or provide for follow-through at school or home. This way the parent will have a feeling of working together rather than of being blamed.

10. *Know where and how to secure community resources and referrals.* Many parents do not know where to get a child's speech tested, or what an IQ test is, or where to secure family therapy. They may be unaware of play groups, gymnastic schools, library story hours, or children's museums. Be sure the school can provide this information for parents who need it.

11. *Take time to write a brief report after the conference.* Make special note of who attended and who requested the conference, what important issues were raised by either the parents or the teacher, what solutions and strategies were discussed, and what time was agreed upon for checking in with each other regarding progress.

12. *Find a good role model.* Ask experienced teachers to share their ingredients for success. When possible, attend a parent conference with one of them. Observe what works for them and learn from their experience. Ask them to critique your own performance after a conference.

Figure 8.11 ● One of the most important responsibilities of the teacher is the parent conference. A good parent-teacher conference is focused and strengthens the relationship between home and school. (See Chapter 10.)

Review Questions

1. What do you consider to be the most important reasons for teachers and parents to have good relationships? Why should parents be involved in their child's schooling? If you were a parent, how would you balance this involvement with your career and family responsibilities?

2. Describe three ways you would encourage parents to participate in your classroom. Cite the advantages for the (a) children, (b) parents, and (c) teacher. Are there any disadvantages?

3. What are some of your own "Myths about Parenthood"? Make two lists, one headed "Myths Teachers Have about Parents" and another headed "Myths Parents Have about Teachers." Compare the two and then discuss them with both a parent and a teacher.

4. What are some of the key elements in a successful parent–child separation? What is the role of the teacher?

5. What would you do to help immigrant families feel welcome in your classroom? What are the difficulties you might have to overcome? What are the benefits to the class? To the family?

6. Describe the critical components of a high-quality parent education program. Give examples.

7. What is the value of a family-centered parent education program?

8. Outline what you would do in a parent conference that was (1) a routine get-together to discuss the child's progress, (2) to inform parents of recently observed behavioral problems, and (3) to recommend further assessment of a child's developmental delays in motor development.

Learning Activities

1. Discuss the following in small groups, then share your responses with the rest of your classmates. Finish the sentences:

   a.) "For me, the most difficult part of being a parent today is or would be . . ."

   b.) "When I have children, I plan to (work/stay at home/do both) because . . ."

   c.) "As a single parent, I will . . ."

   d.) "When I have children, I will raise them (just as my parents raised me/the opposite of the way I was raised) because . . ."

2. Look at the five "Guidelines for Working with Parents." Give an example of how you would apply each of the five principles in your classroom. Do you see any examples of ways these guidelines are not being met? What would you do to change that?

3. Are there ethnic minorities in your school setting? How are these parents supported or not supported by school practices and policies? What changes would you make?

4. The last step in Figure 8.11 suggests that you find a good role model. Look around at the teachers you know and select one. Go through the steps suggested in number 12 and write up your impressions.

5. Interview a parent or parents of (1) a 6-month-old baby, (2) two or more children, and (3) children with a wide age range. Using the "Six Stages of Parenthood," (Figure 8.7) identify where each parent is. Discuss.

6. Interview several single parents, both men and women. What do they say are the most critical issues they face? How do they see their children's schools supporting them? Where is there a need for improvement? How will this information influence your work with children and families?

Bibliography

Armstrong, L. S. (1991, March 20). Census confirms remarkable shifts in ethnic makeup. *Education Week*.

Balaban, N. (1985). *Starting school: From separation to independence*. New York: Teachers College Press.

Baumrind, D. (1972). Socialization and instrumental competence in young children. In W. W. Hartrup (Ed.), *The young child: Review of research* (Vol. 2). Washington, DC: National Association for the Education of Young Children.

Bee, H. (1997). *The developing child*. Menlo Park, CA: Addison-Wesley.

Children's Defense Fund. (1998). *The state of America's children*. Washington, DC: Author.

Delpit, L. (1995). *Other people's children: Cultural conflict in the classroom*. New York: The New Press.

Edwards, C., Gandini, L., & Forman, G. (1993). *The hundred languages of children: The Reggio Emilia approach to early childhood education*. Norwood, NJ: Ablex.

Galinsky, E. (1987). *Between generations*. Reading, MA: Addison-Wesley.

Gollnic, D. M., & Chin, P. C. (1998). *Multicultural education in a pluralistic society*. Bellevue, WA: Merrill.

Grant, C. A. (Ed.), (1995). *Educating for diversity: An anthology of multicultural voices*. Boston: Allyn & Bacon.

Igoa, C. (1995). *The inner world of the immigrant child*. New York: St. Martin's Press.

Kagan, S. L. (1991, January 18). Family-support programs and the schools. *Education Week*.

Lee, L. (1997, July). Working with non-English-speaking families. *Child Care Information Exchange*, pp. 57–58.

LeShan, E. (1992). *When your child drives you crazy*. New York: St. Martin's Press.

Levin, H. M. (1990, August 1). As quoted in L. Jennings. Parents as partners. *Education Week*.

Powell, D. R. (1989). *Families and early childhood programs*. Washington, DC: National Association for the Education of Young Children.

Robles de Melendez, W., & Ostertag, V. (1997). *Teaching young children in multicultural classrooms: Issues, concepts, and strategies*. Albany, NY: Delmar.

US Bureau of the Census (1991). *Marital status and living arrangements, March 1990*. Current Population Reports. Series P-20, No. 450. Washington, DC: US Government Printing Office.

US Bureau of the Census. (1991). *Household and family characteristics: March 1990 and 1989*. Washington, DC: US Government Printing Office.

US Bureau of the Census. (1992, 1995, 1997). Census reports. Washington, DC: US Government Printing Office.

US Bureau of the Census. (1995, August). *Characteristics of the foreign-born population*. Washington, DC: US Government Printing Office.

US Department of Education, Office of Educational Research and Improvement. (1996). *Youth indicators 1991*. Washington, DC: US Government Printing Office.

US Department of Education (1996). National Center for Educational Statistics. Washington, DC: US Government Printing Office.

Wanat, C. L. (1991, May 8). Of schools, single parents, and surrogates. *Education Week*.

What Is the Setting?

Guest Editorial   PLACES FOR CHILDHOODS

Jim Greenman

Children and the Environment

Children and adults inhabit different worlds. Adults dwell far more in the world of mind and function. Children respond to the sensory and motor message of the space, whereas adults are more utilitarian. "Is it clean?" "Safe?" "What is it for?" We are not drawn to the hot sunny spot on the floor attractive to cats and children, or the mud, or to chipping away and enlarging the hole in the plaster. We do not view the world as puddle-rich, or full of tight angular spaces to squeeze ourselves into. Except perhaps responding to an atavistic urge to shout in tunnels or trail our fingers along a picket fence, we rarely allow space to command our bodies. Corridors do not impel us to run, nor does a trellis or stack of chairs say "climb."

A Place Not A Space

It is important to think as children's centers as "places," with character, rather than mere stage settings where the character and charm all have to come from the people and activities. Many of us spend much of our time in spaces that never become places. Places are spaces charged with meaning. We attach to places through endearing objects and people, but also the sensibility of the place: the sounds, smells, lighting, texture, and the actions that the space invites.

Quality in early education and care is an accumulation of small transactions, between child and adult, child and child, child and the objects and the physical environment. It is in the laps and conversations, the side-by-side work and play, and the shared bouts of silliness and sadness that a child learns that he or she is somebody important. It is the bursts of energetic noises and the interludes of silence that punctuate reflection. The sunlight, and breezes and frost on the window and the shadows descending on a corner of the room give daily life its fullness and sensuality. The three Rs are present as well in the exuberant exploration of the world, if the awareness of the value of language and number infuse every experience. The sifting, kneading, and mixing on the table and the digging and splashing are necessary precursors to laboratories of beakers and archeological expeditions. The rhythm of the rain and the pendulum of the swing are both mathematical and musical experiences. Gazing at the crack on the ceiling that had the habit of looking like a rabbit, the row of dandelions at attention like an army of golden soldiers, and the flashing color from the angelfish or the canary enriches our sensibilities and informs our artistic vision.

A Good Place to Be

Security: a safe, warm place that fits me; that I understand, and own.

Competence: a place scaled for me so I can feel competent and in control of my daily needs.

Different places to be: places that look, sound, smell, and feel different. Remember your childhood places, under the piano, behind the couch, on the stairs, beside the tree.

Seclusion and privacy: "places to pause" when the world moves too fast or I'm out of sorts or need to concentrate.

Autonomy: children invent the spaces they need, if we let them.

Room to grow: ample space is essential for mobility, learning, privacy, and social life.

A Good Place to Learn

Children don't learn in a predictable, linear fashion. They swallow experience in sips and gulps as well as measured doses. Their investigations often do not fit into tidy spaces and neat time slots. Movement is as necessary to their learning as air and light, and their sounds and silences punctuate discoveries. They are generous and selfish and social and solitary at will.

Young children are active, messy scientists: exploring with their senses and bodies. A child seeking a good learning environment might ask (if he or she could):

Can I be messy?
Can I be noisy?
Can I be alone?
Can I get some quiet?
Can I move?
Can I be still?
Who can I talk to?
Who will listen?

Can I spread out over space and time?

Where's the stuff, the loose parts: the raw material of discovery?

A developmentally appropriate learning environment is designed for INDIVIDUAL children to be messy, noisy and quiet, alone and social, and active and quiet. It is designed to accommodate much STUFF—loose parts: the raw material of discovery by active hands and minds. Therefore, it is designed for individual, independent learning and easy set up and "take down" so that the teacher can really focus on the children.

Jim Greenman is the author of Caring Spaces, Learning Places: Children's Environments That Work *(Exchange Press). Material for this editorial originated in his columns in the* Child Care Information Exchange.

Creating Environments

CHAPTER 9

Questions for Thought

What does the term *environment* mean?

What criteria are used in planning the optimum environment?

What is a *self-help* environment?

How do teachers create an *anti-bias* environment?

What is involved in an *inclusive* environment?

What health and safety measures must be considered when planning the total environment?

What are basic materials for a classroom, and how are they selected?

What are adults' needs in a children's environment?

In building the physical environment, what are basic areas and materials for a classroom and yard?

In planning a temporal environment, what kinds of daily schedules should teachers consider?

In creating an interpersonal environment, how does the teacher create an atmosphere for learning?

WHAT IS THE ENVIRONMENT?

What does it mean to create an environment appropriate for young children? What makes up the environment? The **environment** is the stage on which childen play out the themes of childhood: their interests, triumphs, problems, and concerns. An environment for children, therefore, includes all of the conditions that affect their surroundings and the people in it.

Each environment is unique. There is no such thing as a single model or ideal setting for all children. Each school has goals that reflect the values of its own program. When the goals and the setting mesh, the individual atmosphere of the school is created.

But just what does environment mean? What do teachers mean when they say they want to create:

- ● Environments for learning?
- ● Optimal-growth environments?
- ● Positive-learning environments?
- ● Child-centered environments?
- ● Favorable classroom environments?

Definition

The *environment* is the sum total of the physical and human qualities that combine to create a space in which children and adults work and play together. Environment is the *content* teachers arrange; it is an *atmosphere* they create; it is a *feeling* they communicate. Environment is the total picture—from the traffic flow to the daily schedule, from the numbers of chairs at a table to the placement of the guinea pig cage. It is a means to an end. The choices teachers make

Figure 9.1 ● Each environment is unique, and children respond to whatever is offered. Does this equipment challenge the physical skills of young children? Is it safe for youngsters? Can it be properly supervised? For what age range would the playground be most appropriate?

concerning the **physical** setting (the equipment and materials, the room arrangement, the playground and the facilities available), the **temporal** setting (timing for transitions, routines, activities), and the **interpresonal** setting (number and nature of teachers, ages and numbers of children, types and style of interactions among them) combine to support the program goals. The environments adults create for children have a powerful effect on their behavior. Research shows that children's play is strongly influenced by settings and materials (Phyfe-Perkins & Shoemaker, 1986). Individual cubbies and children's art on the walls say "You belong here"; materials on low shelves tell children "You can do things on your own." Social interaction, independence, or imaginary play may all be fostered—or discouraged—by the ways the indoor and outdoor spaces are designed and used. The environments teachers create should be safe, effective, challenging, and in concert with the theoretical framework of the early childhood program.

CRITERIA FOR CREATING ENVIRONMENTS

All settings for the care and education of young children have the same basic environmental components and the same basic goals—meeting the needs of children—despite the fact that programs vary widely in the size of the group, age of children, length of day, program focus, and number of staff.

Such variation on this common educational theme is one of the reasons why our field is so diverse and interesting. Caution must be exercised, however, to ensure a *quality* experience for all children. For instance, size does matter. Research conducted over 25 years ago (Prescott, Jones, & Kritschevsky, 1972) and corroborated more recently (Fowler, 1992) found that when a center gets too large, rules and routine guidance are emphasized, outdoor areas often have little variety, and children are often less enthusiastically involved and more often wandering. On the other

Figure 9.2 ● The environment includes not only physical space and materials but also aspects of time and interpersonal relationships.

Recommended Staff–Child Ratios within Group Size*

Age of children	Group size 6	8	10	12	14	16	18	20	22	24	28
Infants (birth to 12 mo)	1:3	1:4									
Toddlers (12–24 mos)	1:3	1:4	1:5	1:4							
2-year-olds (24–30 mos)		1:4	1:5	1:6							
2½-year-olds (30–36 mos)			1:5	1:6	1:7						
3-year-olds					1:7	1:8	1:9	1:10			
4-year-olds						1:8	1:9	1:10			
5-year-olds						1:8	1:9	1:10			
6–8 year-olds								1:10	1:11	1:12	
9–12-year-olds										1:12	1:14

*Smaller group sizes and lower staff–child ratios have been found to be strong predictors of compliance with indicators of quality such as positive interactions among staff and children and developmentally appropriate curriculum.

Figure 9.3 ● Group size and staff-child ratio are two aspects of the environment that affect the quality of children's educational experience. (from Bredekamp, S. [1991]. Accreditation and criteria procedures [Rev. ed.] Washington, DC: National Association for the Education of Young Children.)

extreme, too many of us know the problems associated with crowding and cramped conditions, little rooms that become "child care in a closet for ten hours a day" (Greenman, 1994). As the National Association for the Education of Young Children (NAEYC) continues its work with accreditation of programs (see Chapter 10) and developmentally appropriate practices (DAP, see Chapters 2, 6, 9 and 10), we continue the efforts to articulate what is *quality* for children in early childhood settings. Figure 9.3 gives recommended standards for group size and adult–child ratios. Although there are endless variations in planning for children, certain common elements must be considered: (1) the physical plant, (2) available resources, and (3) program goals.

Physical Plant

Before creating an environment for children, the early childhood teacher must analyze the physical plant. The building that is inviting and beautiful beckons children to enter; a space with color and light encourages children to play with both. Many settings use space designed for other purposes, such as a family home, a church basement, or an empty elemen-

tary school classroom. The size and shape of the designated space determine how to plan for safe and appropriate use. To rescale the space, teachers shift from an adult perspective to a child's scale. Getting on one's knees provides a glimpse of the environment from the child's point of view; child space is measured from the floor and playground up. A child's stature determines what is available to and noticed by that child. For crawling infants, space consists primarily of the floor, whereas school-aged children can use and learn from the space up to about 5 feet, roughly their own height. It is this perspective that teachers must remember as they plan the physical space for children (see the planning section in this chapter for details).

Resources

In planning the environment, the teacher must know what kinds of resources are available. Rarely do teachers have unlimited dollars: "This year we can only afford . . ." determines many of the decisions made about the environment. Priority is usually given to teacher salaries and benefits, equipment and materials for the school, and other related services (maintenance, office help, bus service). Despite budget constraints, teachers must beware of operating on too low a materials budget. Lack of necessary materials can create increasingly passive, angry, and unhappy children out of sheer boredom. Only by knowing the extent of the fiscal boundaries and budget limits can a teacher plan a complete environment.

There are ways to stretch that budget, however. Good environmental principles do not depend on numerous or expensive equipment, materials, or buildings. A creative child-centered environment can happen in any setting, regardless of the lack of financial resources. Some equipment can be made, borrowed, or purchased second-hand. In church-based schools, annual rummage sales at the church provide a wealth of dress-up clothes, books, toys, and some appliances. Resource books are filled with ideas for recycling materials into usable equipment for young children. Parents and others can provide computer paper, wood scraps, or office supplies for dramatic play kits. Community sources, such as the public library storyteller or a senior citizens group, may be available for extended experiences for the children. Effective fund raising provides an added source of revenue in many schools and centers.

The human resources must also be identified. Adults do their best with children when their abilities, experience, and availability are matched with what is expected of them. Volunteers, for instance, will feel satisfied if their time is organized and spent in ways meaningful to them. A first-year teacher's resources are best expended in the classroom rather than on administrative projects. A master teacher is ready to be challenged in other ways, such as orienting parents or evaluating curriculum materials. When the entire community values its children, as in the case of Reggio Emilia, the school is a showcase, sending a strong message of how important children are in the life of its citizens. Just as we try to match children's developing skills to the tasks at hand, so, too, should we consider individual people as part of an environment's resources.

Program Goals

The program must be defined in relationship to the physical space because the goals and objectives of the program are expressed directly in the arrangement of the environment. Teachers of young children ask themselves: What sorts of goals should there be for children and families in our care? Harms (Harms & Clifford, 1989) names three general goals in designing environments: to plan soft and responsive settings that avoid behavior problems, to set up predictable environments that encourage independence, and to create a stimulating space for active learning. The physical space and materials should tell the children exactly what is going to happen and how they are to go about their work. In every program, consideration of what children are to accomplish puts goals and environments together.

The goals of an early childhood program will vary widely because early childhood settings contain such a wide range of age and experience. Some programs are housed in large centers, others in homes; children may attend all day or for part of the day and for educational, recreational, or even custodial reasons. The important point is that good environments for children must reflect clear and reasonable program goals. Once we know what we wish to do, and why we want to do it, we can create space, timing, and an atmosphere in which to meet those goals.

Reflecting Goals in the Environment

In creating an environment, teachers plan a program directed toward their goals:

1. They take care to arrange the daily schedule in ways that provide the time blocks needed to teach content when and how they want to teach it.

2. The room and yard are arranged to give maximum exposure to the materials and equipment they want children to use.

3. They see that a warm relationship exists among the teachers and in their interactions with children.

It is essential that teachers have a clear idea of their program goals before they begin to arrange the environment for children. When they invite children in to work, play, and learn, teachers must be sure that the way they have expressed goals through room arrangements, daily schedules, and personal styles matches what they believe. Blending all the factors that create an environment for children uses the environment to its fullest and demonstrates a belief in how and what children need for learning to occur.

If a goal of the program is to have children practice cognitive and fine-motor skills, games using prereading and writing materials should be prominent. Puzzles and table toys should have a central place in the classroom. Enough tables and chairs should be provided to accommodate all the children. Larger amounts of time should be made available for children to work on these activities every day, and teachers should be available to reinforce and encourage children as they play. Research on children's behavior in preschool settings (Moore, 1983) indicates that social participation and child involvement in activities can be influenced by equipment and materials placement, as well as by the teacher's interactive style.

When children walk into a classroom, the environment should communicate how they are to live and work in that setting. Children should receive clear messages about what they can and cannot do there as well as cues that tell them:

- Where they are free to move to and where they cannot go
- How they will be treated
- Who will be there with them
- What material and equipment they can use
- How long they have to play
- That they are safe there
- What is expected of them

Teachers communicate these messages in many ways. Figure 9.4 describes how teachers use the environment to tell children what is important there. For instance, when it is time to go outside, the doors are opened. If children need to stay off a piece of equipment, it is marked by dividers or a flag, and a teacher stationed nearby explains the instruction. Children know that they matter when they are welcomed each day, and they know their time is valued when teachers tell them how long they have to complete a project or play sequence and when that time is nearly up.

The teacher is the key element in making a creative environment. It is not the facility itself that counts, as much as the teacher's understanding of the use of all the environmental factors and how they are related to one another. The indicators of quality in a program, such as the adult–child ratio, the stability, education, and experience of the caregiver, and group size all contribute to an environment that meets its goals for children. Chapter 2 details these indicators, and Chapter 10 describes their place in program and teacher evaluation.

A room is just a room and a yard is just a yard until a teacher makes them environments for learning.

The teachers themselves are the most responsive part of the environment; it is they who converse, hug, appreciate, give information, and see the individuality of each child. They are the ones who create the space, the time, and the atmosphere that will engage children's curiosity and involvement. Figure 9.4 summarizes these environmental goals.

The Self-Help Environment

One common goal in most early education programs can be demonstrated through the careful use of environmental factors. Promoting self-help and independent behavior in children is a widespread practice. In planning the environments, teachers attempt to create situations and settings where this is likely to happen.

A self-help environment has as one of its fundamental goals the development of children's own skills—fostering their mastery of basic abilities that will allow them to become responsible for their own personal care, their own learning, their own emotional controls, their own problem-solving, and their own choices and decisions. A self-help environment gives children the feeling that they are capable, competent, and successful. It allows children to do for themselves, to meet the challenge of growing up. A self-help environment reflects the belief that autonomy and independence are the birthright of every child.

Nothing renders people more helpless than not being able to maintain their own needs or to take care of themselves in basic ways. Children are still in the process of learning about what they can and cannot do. They need many different kinds of experiences to help them learn the extent of their capabilities. Most of all, they need adults who understand their tremendous drive to become self-reliant, adults who will not only encourage their abilities and provide the time for them to practice skills, but adults who understand that it is the nature of the child to develop this way.

Self-concept is based on what we know about ourselves, which includes the ability to take care of our own needs. To care for oneself, to feel capable of learning, to solve problems, are all related to feelings of self-esteem. Self-esteem is the value we place on ourselves; how much we like or dislike who we are. Helping children achieve a positive self-concept and self-esteem is the most important part of teaching. The development of a strong sense of self-esteem is a lifelong process; its origins are in the early years.

Children Need to . . .	So the Environment Should . . .
Be treated as individuals, with unique strengths and developmental goals.	Ensure that the teacher–child ratio supports one-to-one interactions. Provide private as well as public spaces so children can experience group and solitary play. Ensure that children have ready access to teachers and materials. Be staffed by teachers who will set goals for each child on the basis of observation and assessment. Be equipped with materials that will match the developmental level of the group. Provide a balance of quiet and active times.
See themselves and their family culture represented positively in the environment; be exposed to cultural diversity in meaningful ways.	Include pictures, books, dolls, dramatic play materials, activities, and people that reflect many cultures and life experiences.
Have an opportunity to make choices and participate in independent learning.	Be arranged to encourage free exploration and a clear view of what is available. Offer a variety of activity centers so children can explore, manipulate, probe. Allow large blocks of time for child-initiated free play so children can make more than one choice. Provide an adequate number of trained teachers to support self-discovery.
Learn to be part of a group.	Be set up for group play with three to five chairs around the tables, easels adjacent to one another, more than one telephone, carriage, wagon. Facilitate regular scheduling of small and large group times, which children are encouraged to attend and participate in. Include trained staff who select developmentally appropriate group activities for the group. Allow children to use each other as resources. Provide activities that will stress cooperation and social interaction.
Become responsible for the setting and take care of the equipment and materials.	Schedule cleanup times as part of the daily routine. Include teachers and children working together to restore order. Allow time for children to be instructed in the proper use of materials and be made aware of their general care.
Be aware of the behavioral limits of the school setting.	Ensure that the teachers and the daily schedule reflect the important rules of behavior. Include teachers who deal with behavior problems in a fair and consistent way. Allow plenty of time during transitions so that children can move from one activity to another without stress. Be arranged to avoid runways and dead ends created by furniture.
Be with adults who will supervise and facilitate play and encourage learning throughout the day.	Be set up before children arrive so teachers are free to greet them. Encourage teacher–child interactions through the use of small groups and a time schedule that allows for in-depth interactions.

Figure 9.4 ● The environment mirrors the goals of the program.

For all of these reasons, teachers establish settings that promote self-help. They want children to feel good about themselves and they want to foster that growing sense of self-esteem. This happens in classrooms that allow children to do what they are capable of doing. For the teacher, the reward comes from each child who says, "I can do it all by myself."

Planning an environment designed to promote self-help skills is the teachers' responsibility. Every aspect of the environment, from the room arrangement to the attitudes of the teachers, supports children in doing all they can for themselves. Each activity is designed to foster self-reliance, thereby building self-esteem. The supermarket is a good example of an environment created for maximum self-reliance. Shelves are accessible and the products are clearly marked and attractively displayed. It takes that kind of thoughtful preparation to create space that says to children, "Do me. Master me. You are capable." Teachers want to communicate to children that they value self-help skills as much as they appreciate an art project or science experiment. The utlimate goal is for children to see self-reliance as valuable. If Claudia feels that learning to tie her shoes is worth doing just because of the pleasure it gives her to manipulate the strings, weave them through the holes, and bring them together in a knot, then that becomes her reward. She becomes capable of reinforcing herself and leaves the way open for adults to praise her for other important learnings.

The Anti-Bias Environment

Among the core values (see Appendix B, and the section on professional ethics in Chapter 5) in any good early childhood program is the recognition of each child as unique, as deserving of respect, and as a part of a family.[1] Each child has the right to achieve full potential and to develop a positive self-esteem. Each family deserves support for the unique role it plays. Part of the commitment of the early childhood teacher is to help children learn to value one another's uniqueness, the differences as well as the similarities. Teachers do this, in part, by expressing such inclusive attitudes.

The **anti-bias** curriculum, developed at Pacific Oaks College, encourages children and adults.

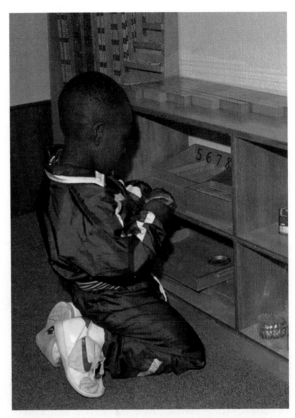

Figure 9.5 ● "I can do this myself!" Through self-help environments, children become independent.

1. To explore the differences and similarities that make up our individual and group identities, and

2. To develop skills for identifying and countering the hurtful impact of bias on themselves and their peers (Derman-Sparks & the ABC Task Force, 1989).

The physical and interpersonal environment can be used to help children see that culture consists of the various ways people do similar activities. This approach is different from the "tourist curriculum," which provides only superficial information that is often detached from the child's own life. It is also different from an approach that is based only on the interests of the class and gender, racial, and cultural groups represented therein. The anti-bias environment incorporates the positive aspects of a multicultural

OUR DIVERSE WORLD OUR DIVERSE WORLD OUR DIVERSE WORLD OUR DIVERSE WORLD OUR DIVERSE WORLD OUR DIVERSE WORLD OUR DIVERSE WORLD OUR DIVERSE WORLD

[1] The anti-bias and inclusive environments encourage children to learn tolerance and acceptance of the diversity in our world.

Figure 9.6 ● The anti-bias environment encourages girls and boys to play together, respecting differences and including others in new ways.

curriculum and uses some of the activities that high-light other cultures, but it provides a more inclusive, ongoing approach. This approach avoids patronizing or emphasizing trivial, isolated, exotic differences (Derman-Sparks et al., 1989). There is an inherent feeling of fairness to self and others in the anti-bias approach, as children explore the many ways people do the basic human tasks of everyday life. Think of the diverse cultures expressed in how babies and things are carried from place to place in different parts of the world. How many ways do people eat? Cook? Shop for food?

A value common to all early childhood programs is expressed in this anti-bias curriculum: that every person is valuable and so diversity is valuable, and peaceful and just cooperation among all is possible. The key here is the belief that "unity is the completed puzzle, diversity the pieces of the puzzle" (Hernandez, 1991). In this curriculum, the environment and the activities are derived from three sources: the children and their activities, the teachers' awareness of the developmental needs and learning styles of the group, and societal events. Teachers, of course, make general selections of what children are to learn and arrange the environment for learning to begin. Then, the environment, which includes the children themselves, begins to change. If children are especially interested in making things, perhaps the theme "All people live in homes" emerges, with activities that focus on how

people build things, what they use the buildings for, and how they work to get something built.

Lessons about children's identity and budding attitudes concerning race, gender, disability, and age are learned early in life. With the prevalence of stereo-typing in society, and the impact of bias on children's development (Cross, 1985; Gutierrez, 1982; Kutner, 1984), early childhood educators have a responsbility to find ways to prevent, even counter, the damage done by such stereotyping. Teachers do this by arranging an anti-bias physical environment, as well as creating an atmosphere of problem-solving and learning in the day-to-day conflicts and interactions that arise natural-ly. Think about how teachers provide the materials and encourage an atmosphere of trust and time for conflict resolution in these examples:

A kindergarten teacher shows the children a magazine picture entitled "Brides of America." All of the women pictured are Caucasian. She asks, "What do you think of this picture?" Sophia responds, "That's a silly picture. My mom was a bride, and she's Mexican" (Derman-Sparks et al., 1989).

A toddler teacher sets up the water play table for washing babies. Choosing dolls that represent several racial and ethnic groups, she invites the children to soap and rinse them. One 2-year-old begins to wash the teacher's arm, then scrubs it hard. "Do you wonder if my color will wash off?" the teacher asks. The child nods, and several others look up. "Does it? Go ahead and try. . . . See, a person's color is her own and stays with her. Try yours, too. That's one way people look different: we all have skin, and yet we each have our own color" (Gutierrez, personal communication, 1987).

The anti-bias approach to creating environments has its roots in the theories of Maslow, Piaget, and Erikson (see Chapter 4). Research data reveal that children begin to notice and construct classifications and evaluative categories very early; indeed, 2-year-olds begin to notice gender and racial differences and may even notice physical disabilities (Froschl, Rubin, & Sprung, 1984; Honig, 1983). Early childhood programs must develop a child's basic sense of trust and mastery so that children can learn to understand themselves and become tolerant and compassionate toward others. Figure 9.7 is a multicultural classroom environment checklist that can help teachers evaluate their environment.

The anti-bias approach to a classroom goes hand in hand with self-help principles that foster:

● *Positive self-concept.* Curiosity and creativity stem from being able to affect the environment and what is in it. When Jamal says his baby's hair is fuzzy like his, his smile tells how good he feels about it.

● *Awareness.* All people have interests and feelings, both about themselves and about others. Yoko notices that her classmate Julie runs and throws her arms around her dad, but she prefers a less demonstrative greeting.

● *Respect for diversity.* This stems from the ability to classify similarities and differences and then to appreciate both. For example, when the children create self-portraits for their class books, some choose different colors of paper for drawing faces, but all of them use the same markers to draw in their features.

● *Skills in communication and problem-solving.* Learning how to express thoughts and feelings includes being able to hear others and finding peaceful ways to resolve conflicts. Jim and LaNell are quick to tell Eben he can't play, but they find out that telling him he is "too little" does not work. He does not

accept that simply being 3 years old is enough reason to leave him out, and they must either try to include him or make a claim for privacy.

Both the self-help approach and the anti-bias curriculum differ from traditional educational practices often seen in classrooms for older children in that the self-help, anti-bias environment is pluralistic and developmental. As Elizabeth Jones (personal notes, 1984) stated:

> The pluralistic view assumes that (1) people are different from each other and (2) differences are valuable; they add to the richness of everyone's experiences. The task of the worker with children, then, is to acknowledge and appreciate differences. The developmental view assumes that growth and learning are spontaneously motivated. The task of the teacher is to provide a supportive environment that frees each individual to grow and learn—to empower children so that they will assert their needs and develop thoughtful strategies for meeting them.

The Inclusive Environment

In 1975, the Education for All Handicapped Children Act (P.L.94–142) called for an end to segregation for disabled students from kindergarten through high school. This policy filtered down to preschools and child care centers, and in 1986 an amendment made to this bill (P.L.99–457) mandated that preschoolers with special needs be placed in the *least restrictive environment.* First called **mainstreaming**, the practice of placing children with disabilities in the same classroom as children without disabilities is now known as *full* **inclusion** (see Chapters 3, 8, and 10). The Americans with Disabilities Act of 1990 prohibits child care centers from denying admission to a child simply because the child has a disability. Together, these federal laws form part of the rationale for early childhood centers to become more inclusive environments.

Children with disabilities need the same things in their environment as other children. They need an environment that is safe, secure, and predictable and one that provides a balance of the familiar and novel, so that there are materials and activities that provide for their development. "When a child with disabilities

Overall Environment

1. In general is the classroom hospitable?

2. What is hanging on the walls?
   If there is work done by children, does it all look alike? For example, are there bunnies or other animals that you have cut out and the children colored or is the art *genuinely* done by the children?
   Yes _____ No _____
   Are the pictures of people hanging on walls or bulletin boards representative of a multicultural community?
   Yes _____ No _____
   Even if pictures *do* represent a diverse population, are they stereotypic in any way? For example, is there an alphabet chart that uses "Indian" to symbolize the letter "I" or a calendar that features little girls wearing dresses watching little boys involved in activities? Are there Hawaiians in grass skirts or people from South America sparsely clothed and with spears and painted faces?
   Yes _____ No _____

3. Are all of the pictures for children and the art hung *at children's eye level?*
   Yes _____ No _____

4. Are parents and/or family members involved in creating a hospitable classroom environment?
   Yes _____ No _____
   If yes, how do you include them? How might you make them feel even more a part of their children's school lives?

Blocks

1. Are the accessories in the block area representative of various cultural groups and family configurations?
   Yes _____ No _____
   List them below to be sure that no major cultural group or family configuration is missing.

2. Are the people block accessories stereotypic in terms of sex roles?
   Yes _____ No _____
   If yes, how will you change them?

Social Studies

1. Does the curriculum as a whole help the children increase their understanding and acceptance of attitudes, values, and life-styles that are unfamiliar to them?
   Yes _____ No _____
   If yes, how?
   If no, what will you do to change your current curriculum so that it reflects a diversity of values?

2. Are materials and games racially or sex-role stereotypic—for example, black people shooting dice or boys playing war games? Are women depicted only as caregivers while men do lots of exciting jobs?
   Yes _____ No _____
   If yes, what will you weed from your current collection?
   What materials and games can you add that decrease stereotypes?

Dramatic Play

1. Is there a wide variety of clothes, including garments from various cultural groups, in the dramatic-play area?
   Yes _____ No _____
   If yes, what are they?
   If no, what do you need to add?

2. Are the pictures on the walls and the props in the dramatic-play area representative of a diversity of cultures?
   Yes _____ No _____
   If yes, what is included?
   If no, what do you need to add?

3. Are the dolls in the dramatic-play area representative of a broad variety of racial groups?
   Yes _____ No _____
   If no, what do you need to add?

4. Are the dolls of color just white dolls whose skin color has been changed?
   Yes _____ No _____
   If so, which ones need replacing?

Figure 9.7 ● A multicultural environment checklist provides questions for teachers to evaluate and monitor progress toward an anti-bias environment for children. (Adapted from Kendall, F. [1996]. *Diversity in the classroom* [2nd ed.]. New York: Teachers College Press.)

Language Arts

1. Does the classroom have a wide variety of age-appropriate and culturally diverse books and language-arts materials?

   Yes _____ No _____

   What are the strengths of the collection in general? Where are there gaps?

2. Are there stories about a variety of people from each of the following groups in the book corner?

   _____ Native American cultures

   _____ Asian American cultures

   _____ Black cultures

   _____ White ethnic cultures

   _____ Spanish-speaking cultures

   _____ Biracial or multiracial people

   _____ Family configurations, including biracial and multiracial families and gay and lesbian families

3. Are there any books that speak of people of diverse cultures in stereotypical or derogatory terms (e.g., describing Latinos as "lazy" or Japanese as always taking photographs)?

   Yes _____ No _____

   If yes, what are they? What new titles can you replace them with?

Music and Games

1. Do the music experiences in the curriculum reinforce the children's affirmation of cultural diversity?

   Yes _____ No _____

   If so, how?

2. Are fingerplays, games, and songs from various cultural groups used in the classroom?

   Yes _____ No _____

3. Are there many varieties of musical instruments, including ones made by children, in the classroom?

   Yes _____ No _____

Cooking

1. Do the cooking experiences in the classroom encourage the children to experiment with foods other than those with which they are familiar?

   Yes _____ No _____

2. Are the cooking experiences designed to give young children a general notion of the connections between cultural heritage and the process of preparing, cooking, and eating food?

   Yes _____ No _____

   If so, how?

   If not, what can you do differently to help children make those connections?

Figure 9.7 ● Continued.

has different developmental needs than other children of the same age, adaptations must be made" (Youcha & Wood, 1997). These may require either adding something to the environment that is not already there or using something in the environment in a different way.

Adaptations are changes that make the environment fit the child better, so they will vary with the children. Children with motor disabilities need different adaptations than those with hearing or language disabilities or with visual impairments. Physical changes may be necessary, modifications in the schedule may be recommended, or individualizing activities may be best. Parents will be the best source of information about the child, and other reading or specialists can be further guides. Three key concepts

are helpful to remember: access, usability, and maximizing learning.

● Can the child get where she needs to be in the classroom to learn something?

● Once the child is in that location, can she use the materials and equipment and participate in the activity as independently as possible to learn something?

● Are the learning activities arranged and scheduled to meet the individual learning needs of the children, including the child with disabilities? (Youcha & Wood, 1997)

Figure 9.8 is an abbreviated checklist for adaptations to create an inclusive environment.

Checklist for an Inclusive Environment

Physical Environment

Questions to think about:

- How do different children use their bodies or the space around them for learning?
- How can we enhance or adapt the physical environment for children who have difficulty moving (or who move too much)?
- How can we capitalize on the physical environment for children who learn by moving?

Accessing the environment safely:

❑ Are doorway widths in compliance with local building codes?
❑ Ramps in addition to or instead of stairs?
❑ Low, wide stairs where possible (including playground equipment)?
❑ Hand rails on *both* sides to stairs?
❑ Easy handles on doors, drawers, etc.
❑ At least some kids' chairs with armrests?
  - "Cube" chairs are great!
  - Often a footrest and/or seat strap will provide enough stability for a child to do fine-motor activities
❑ When adapting seating, mobility, and/or gross-motor activities for a specific child with physical disabilities, consult a physical therapist.

Learning through the environment:

❑ Do the environment and equipment reflect variety?
  - Surfaces, heights (textured, smooth, low, high, etc.).
  - Space for gross-motor activity (open spaces, climbing structures, floor mats).
  - Quiet/comfort spaces (small spaces, carpet, pillows).
  - Social spaces (dramatic play area, groups of chairs or pillows, etc.).
❑ Are toys and equipment physically accessible?
  - Glue magnets to backs of puzzle pieces and attribute blocks and use on a steel cookie tray.
  - Attach large knobs or levers to toys with lids, movable parts.
  - Attach tabs to book pages for easier turning.
❑ An occupational therapist can provide specific suggestions for adapting materials and activities so a child with physical disabilities can participate.

Visual Environment

Questions to think about:

- How do different children use their vision for learning?
- How can we enhance the visual environment for a child with low or no vision?
- How can we capitalize on the visual environment for children who learn by seeing?

Accessing the environment safely:

❑ Are contrasting colors used on edges and when surfaces change (e.g., tile to carpet, beginning of stairs, etc.)?
❑ Can windows be shaded to avoid high glare?
  - Also consider darker nonglossy floors and tabletops.
  - Some children's behavior and learning may improve dramatically once a strong glare is eliminated.
❑ Is visual clutter avoided on walls, shelves, etc.?
  - Visual clutter can interfere with learning, predictability, and safety.
❑ Is "spot lighting" (e.g., swing arm lamp) in a dimmer room available?
  - Spot lamps help some children pay attention and work better on table tasks.
❑ Orientation and mobility specialists help children with visual impairments learn to navigate the environment.

Learning through the environment:

❑ Are objects and places in the environment labeled ("door," "chair," etc.)?
❑ Are the size and contrast of pictures and letters adequate for the children with visual impairments in your program?
❑ Are visual displays at the children's eye level?
❑ Are large-print materials, textured materials, and auditory materials available (e.g., big books, sandpaper letters, books on tape)?

(continued)

Figure 9.8 ● When designing an inclusive environment, keep in mind that the environment needs to be safe and to help everyone participate, learn, and communicate. (Adapted from Haugen, K. [1997, March]. Using your senses to adapt environments: Checklist for an accessible environment: Beginnings workshop. *Child Care Information Exchange.*)

❑ Is the daily schedule represented in words and pictures?
  • A Velcro schedule that allows children to post the schedule and then remove items as activities are completed can help children to stay focused and make the transition more easily from one activity to the next.
❑ Are children with low vision seated close to the center of activity and away from high glare?
❑ Teachers for the visually impaired assist in selecting and adapting materials for children with low vision.
❑ Children who are blind may need a "running commentary" of events, places, etc. Pictures in books and food on plates, for example, should be described.

Auditory Environment
Questions to think about:
• How do different children use their hearing for learning?
• How can we enhance the auditory environment for a child who is deaf, hearing impaired, or has poor auditory discrimination skills?
• How can we capitalize on the auditory environment for auditory learners?

Accessing the environment safely:
❑ Does background noise (from indoor or outdoor sources) filter into the area?
❑ Is there a way to eliminate or dampen background noise (using carpeting, closing windows and doors, etc.)?
  • Some kids are unable to do the automatic filtering out of background noises.
❑ Is "auditory competition" avoided?
  • Raising one's voice to compete with a roomful of noisy children is rarely as effective as "silent signals" such as holding up a peace sign and encouraging children who notice to do the same until the room is full of quiet children holding up peace signs!
❑ Are nonauditory signals needed to alert a child with a hearing impairment?
  • Turning the lights on and off is a common strategy.
  • Ask the child's parents what strategies are used at home.

Learning through the environment:
❑ Are auditory messages paired with visual ones (e.g., simple sign language, flannel boards, picture schedules)?
❑ Are children with hearing impairments seated so they can see others' faces and actions?
❑ Teachers for the hearing impaired can provide strategies for modifying activities for children with hearing impairments.
❑ A child who is deaf and communicates through sign language will need a teacher or aide who uses sign language.

Social Environment
Questions to think about:
• How do different children use social cues for learning?
• How can we adapt the social environment for children with impulsive behavior, attention deficits, or behavior problems?
• How can we capitalize on the social environment for children who learn by relating to others?

Accessing the environment safely:
❑ Is the schedule predictable? Are children informed of schedule changes?
❑ Does the schedule provide a range of activity level (e.g., adequate opportunities for physical activity)?
❑ School psychologists and behavior specialists can help analyze misbehavior and modify the environment or schedule to minimize problems for children with attention deficits or behavior problems.

Learning through the environment:
❑ Does the environment have a positive impact on self-esteem?
  • Allows all children to feel safe?
  • Invites all children to participate?
  • Maximizes all children's opportunities for independence?
❑ Do learning materials and toys include representations of all kinds of people, including children and adults with disabilities?
  • People with disabilities should be represented in active and leadership roles, not just as passive observers.
❑ Does the schedule include opportunities for a variety of groupings (pairs, small groups, whole class) as well as quiet time or time alone?
  • Pairing or grouping children with complementary abilities eases the demands on the teacher and enables children to help one another.
  • When given a chance, peers often come up with the most creative ways for children with disabilities to participate.
  • Creative use of staffing may be needed to provide additiional support for some children during some activities.
❑ Does the schedule provide both structured and open activity times?
  • Children who have difficulty with a particular type of activity may need extra support at those times.

Figure 9.8 ● *Continued.*

How Can This Process Come Together for a Child?

Consider Andrew (Rogers, 1994), who, at 5 years of age had a motor/muscle disability with some speech difficulties. His cognitive skills were very strong and his social skills very weak. Andrew's mother talked to everyone during class about Andrew's needs and fears. If he fell down, he had a hard time righting himself. He needed help sitting and standing. He was afraid of getting bumped because he couldn't catch himself before falling very hard and then could not get up. The children all agreed to be careful about **roughhousing** around him. *The setting for success was being created.*

Because Andrew did not have much control of his fine-motor skills, we provided him with painting and playdough. We kept up the crafts table; soon he was gluing pictures on paper, with or without order, and was very proud of his accomplishments. He even started using scissors on simple patterns. *The physical environment was responding to his needs.*

He was a wonderful puzzle builder, and the other children asked for his help often when they were struck. It was wonderful to watch how they included him in many things. They accepted his differences right from the beginning and treated him just like all the rest—except they were careful when running and playing around him. His fear was apparent, and they respected it. *Thus the interpersonal environment was emerging.*

We had a regular P.E. time each day in the big room. We jumped rope, played "Simon Says," played "Red Light, Green Light," and ran obstacle courses. At first Andrew sat on the sidelines and watched. He cheered and looked interested, so I started asking him if he'd be my partner because I was a little afraid. At first he refused and told me to use someone else. I kept asking but would drop it as soon as he gave me his answer; then one day he said, "OK." We ran and jumped over the snake (rope), and all the kids laughed. We hugged, and that was the beginning. *When given the time that is needed (the temporal environment), the child triumphs.*

Principles of Successful Environments

● *Give children ways to identify their own space.* Label their cubbies with their names, a photo, or a familiar picture so that they can see where to put

Figure 9.9 ● Children develop a sense of self when they have their own space, labeled with a photo or other visual clue so that they can easily identify it as their own.

up their wraps, artwork, and other personal belongings.

● *Give children an opportunity to make choices.* Both indoors and out, children should be given an abundance of materials and a range of activities from which to choose so that they will decide how they spend their time. Choosing to play with the hamster rather than in the block corner helps children practice self-direction. Children should also be able to decide with whom they would like to play and with which teachers they would like to establish close relationships.

● *See that children are responsible for caring for the equipment and materials.* Establish a cleanup time in the daily schedule and allow children time to help restore the room and yard. Label shelves and cupboards with pictures or symbols of what is stored there so that children can readily find where things belong. Outlining block cabinets with the specific shape of the blocks that are stored on each shelf will help develop children's self-help skills. Outdoor areas, clearly marked for wheel toys, help children function independently. A drying rack with large clothespins that is accessible to children tells children that they are expected to care for their own artwork.

Involve children in the process of planning and setting up the environment. Let the children help decide what they want to learn by developing areas and units around what they bring into class. For instance, if a child's pet has babies, encourage a visit and then send a newsletter asking for other pets, arranging a field trip to a pet store, and organizing a dramatic-play corner as a pet hospital or pet shop. When furniture or outdoor equipment needs moving, include the children in planning what the changes will be and then assist them in moving the pieces themselves. Make the yard more interesting by encouraging the children to rearrange climbing boards. Let them choose what game from the shed will be used that day. And the class feast is made more exciting when the children themselves move all the tables together or plan the menu!

Provide children with enough time. One of the ways children learn is to repeat an activity over and over again. They explore, manipulate, experiment, and come to master an 18-piece puzzle, a lump of clay, or how to brush their teeth. Large blocks of time in the daily schedule—especially for routines—let children proceed to learn at an unhurried pace.

Allow children to solve their own problems without adult **intervention** *whenever possible.* See how far a child can go in discovering how to manipulate a pin so that it will close or to work out with another child who will use the red paint first. In solving social or mechanical problems, young children can begin to find out for themselves what is or is not successful. One mark of a good teacher is a person who can let a child struggle sufficiently with a problem before stepping in to help.

Accept children's efforts. To support children in their quest for independence, the adult must be satisfied with children's efforts and be ready to accept the way that Tom made his sandwich or that Shelley put her boots on the wrong feet.

Communicate expectations. Let children know what they are expected to do. Tell them in both verbal and nonverbal ways. "You don't have to hurry; we have plenty of time for cleanup" lets children know they can do a job without pressure. Prompt children by giving them clues that indicate how to proceed: "If you pull up your underpants first, it will be easier to get your trousers up," can be said to

Figure 9.10 ● Allowing children to solve their own problems without interference is one principle of successful educational environments.

Raymond who is waiting for an adult to dress him. Give him feedback on what is working. "Good. You've got the back up. Now reach around the front." Focus on how Raymond is succeeding and communicate your confidence in his ability to finish the task.

Be sure staff expectations are consistent. The teaching team should set common goals for each child and reinforce them consistently. Janice will become confused if one teacher tells her to get her cot ready for nap and another teacher does it for her.

Consider the developmental level of the child. Recognize that there are many things young children will not be able to do for themselves, but allow them the chance to do all they can. Be developmentally aware—know what children in the class are capable of, where they are now in their development, and what the next step should be. Perhaps 3-year-old Sophie can only zip her jacket now. Soon she will be able to put the zipper in the housing by herself. Recognize her readiness for taking the next step.

Make it safe to make a mistake. Children learn from their own actions and their own experiences. Let them know it is perfectly acceptable, indeed inevitable, that they will at times make mistakes. Children need to be accepted for who and what they are, and this includes when they are in error. Help them deal with the consequences of their mistakes. Adults in the preschool can provide models for children in coping with unexpected results and how to bring forth a positive resolution. When Chelo spills her juice, she is encouraged to find a sponge and clean up the table. The teacher reinforces Chelo's efforts and comments on her scrubbing ability or her swift action in preventing the juice from going on the floor.

Give credit where it is due. Provide feedback so that children will know when they have been successful. Compliment Chaz on the length of time he took sorting through the nails to find the one he wanted. Tell Ellen she worked hard at opening her own Thermos bottle. Let children take some credit for their own accomplishments.

Be sure children have access to enough toys and materials. Help children imagine and live in alternative worlds, in communities and homes where things are different. Show children respect by giving them the option to take care of themselves. Make sure that supplies are stored in such a way that adults do not have to hand them to children each time they will be used. Equipment placed at a child's height on open, low shelving permits children to proceed at their own pace and to select materials without depending on adults to serve them.

Let children teach one another. Encourage children to share the skills they have mastered with their peers. Actively seek out each child's way of doing things; support a diversity of approaches. Those who can tie shoes enjoy helping their friends with stubborn laces or slippery knots. Whether reading or telling stories to one another, or showing a friend a fast way to put on a jacket, children benefit from helping each other.

Adults who work with children should remember to interact with children in ways that will help them grow toward independence. To perceive children as helpless is to rob them of the satisfaction of achievement. A well-planned environment opens up infinite possibilities for children to achieve a feeling of self-

Figure 9.11 ● Children learn through play, and the outdoor play environment stimulates motor development, thinking skills, and social interaction.

satisfaction while they explore the boundaries of their own beings. Chapters 1 and 5 expand on educational ethics that serve as guidelines in working with children; Chapter 10 gives suggestions for how to evaluate children, teachers, and programs to check that these goals are met.

PLANNING FOR THE ENVIRONMENT

Who Is in the Environment?

Many people live and work in the early childhood environment. Cooks, bus drivers, office personnel, yard and building maintenance people are but a few. Each of these persons has special demands on the environment to do the job they are hired to do.

Teachers, parents, and children have the greatest influence on the early childhood environment; their needs are outlined below.

Children

Children's needs are met through the environment. The physical, social, emotional, and intellectual requirements of children suggest the type of building,

The Role of the Environment in Reggio Emilia

Rebecca S. New

Historians have long noted that one index of the value of children is the extent to which they are visible and differentiated in the physical elements of a society. School environments can also reveal much about the values, beliefs, and goals of the adults who are responsible for children's education. Yet traditional images of schools often fail to make children visible. School environments themselves are often nothing more than containers for educational enterprises and convey little of the actual pursuits of the adults and children who spend their days in school.

In contrast, early childhood educators in Reggio Emilia assign significant credit to the role of the environment in their work with young children. Their discussions of its critical importance remind me of anthropological interpretations of sociocultural contexts within which young children learn and develop. In Reggio Emilia, the school environment not only reflects what it is that children are learning; it plays an active role in nurturing and stimulating that learning and development. Such an interpretation of the environment includes not only the physical elements associated with schooling—tables, books, paints, blocks, paper—but the social, intellectual, and ideological elements as well.

Thus, teachers in Reggio Emilia arrange the environment to promote children's relationships—with one another as well as with adults. The drilling of small peepholes in the divider between the blocks and the dramatic-play area, the installation of real telephones between classrooms, the visibility of the kitchen and the accessibility of the central "piazza"—all are designed to contribute to the aim of schooling based on relationships.

Reggio Emilia teachers' interpretation of their own roles as *provocateurs* in children's learning is extended to the environments as well. Classrooms and hallways are designed with the intent to surprise, inform, and inspire. Children reflect on their images and their actions in the many mirrored surfaces to be found on the floors and walls. Play areas modified with the addition of draped fabric invite children to reconceptualize old patterns of play. Juxtapositions of children's work in various media highlight the common themes in their experiences, as well as the rich possibilities inherent in diverse forms of self-expression.

Perhaps most important, the environments in Reggio Emilia convey an image of children who are "rich in potential, strong, powerful, competent, and most of all, connected to adults and other children" (Malaguzzi, 1993, p. 10). Documentation panels portray children's knowledge—of shadows, the rain—as well as their need to grapple with profound concerns in contemporary society—gender, war, friendship.

When Reggio Emilia teachers describe the environment as a "third teacher," they are acknowledging a professional role that goes far beyond that of providing a safe and stimulating setting for children's learning. In Reggio Emilia, the environment serves an advocacy role on behalf of young children, inspiring adults—parents and community members as well as teachers—to work together to realize the potentials

307

of children. The effectiveness of such advocacy is apparent in the quality of care and commitment on behalf of young children that has characterized Reggio Emilia's efforts over the past three decades.

Rebecca S. New is Assistant Professor, Department of Education, University of New Hampshire, Durham. She has studied extensively in Reggio Emilia and has led numerous study tours to the Reggio Emilia schools.

the size of the furniture, the choice of equipment, the size and age range of the group, the number of teachers who lead and supervise, and the budget allocations. Guided by child development principles, teachers match the setting to the children who will learn and play there. The individuality of a particular group of children, of a school, and of its philosophy is expressed by the arrangement of the environmental factors. First and foremost, though, are the questions Who are the children who will use this space? What are their needs? How can those needs be met in this particular setting?

Routines. What is meant by a **routine**? Routines are the framework of programs for young children. A routine is a constant; each day, certain events are repeated, providing continuity and a sense of order to the schedule. Routines are the pegs on which to hang the daily calendar. When should children eat? Sleep? Play? Be alone? Be together? These questions are answered by the placement of routines. The rest of the curriculum—art activities, field trips, woodworking—works around them. Routines in an early childhood environment setting include:

● Self-care (eating, rest/sleeping, dressing, toileting)

● Transitions between activities

● Group times

● Beginning and ending the day or session

● Making choices

● Task completion

● Room cleanup and yard restoration

Most routines are very personal and individual rituals in children's daily lives. Children bring to school a history firmly established around routines, one that is deeply embedded in their family and culture. Routines are reassuring to children, and they take pride in mastering them; they are also a highly emotional issue for some.

The self-care tasks—eating, sleeping, dressing, and toileting—can be difficult issues between adult and child, virtually from the moment of birth. Everyone can recall vivid memories associated with at least one routine. They seem to become battlegrounds on which children and adults often struggle. Many times this is where children choose to take their first stand on the road to independence.

The early childhood teacher must be able to deal with the issue of self-care routines in sensitive and understanding ways. Children adjust to routines when they are regularly scheduled in the daily program and when there are clear expectations.

Routines are an integral part of creating a good environment for children. All three environmental factors are influenced by routines:

1. *Physical:* Child-sized bathroom and eating facilities; storage of cots, blankets, and sleeping accessories; equipment for food storage and preparation.

2. *Temporal:* Amount of time in daily schedule for eating, resting, toileting, cleanup.

3. *Interpersonal:* Attitudes toward body functions; willingness to plan for self-care tasks; interactions during activities and transitions; expectations of staff, parents, and children.

As teachers plan for children's basic needs, they are aware of the learning potential of ordinary, everyday routines. Figure 9.13 illustrates how self-care routines teach the young child important skills and habits. In the four curriculum chapters of the next section ("What Is Being Taught?," Chapters 11–14), there is specific planning for routines, transitions, and group times. It is these times that provide a sense of security for children. Beyond the planning for indoor and outdoor activities, careful teachers realize that helping children with the routines of daily living provides a solid underpinning so other learning can take place.

Teachers

What has been done to meet the needs of the teachers? Do they have an office? A teachers' room? A place to hold conferences? Where do they keep their personal belongings or the materials they bring to use at school? Do they have a place to park? All teachers need room to create curriculum materials, to evaluate their programs, to review other educational materials, to meet with their peers. Recent research (Whitebrook, 1996) indicates that the working environment of caregivers (including the general context of the setting, opportunities for professional development, status, and wages) are important predictors of the quality of care children receive. How well teachers are provided for helps to determine the atmosphere they will establish in their classrooms.

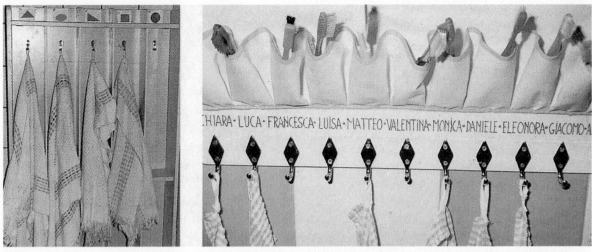

Figure 9.12 ● Self-help is an international goal. Toothbrushes and towels are accessible so that children in the Reggio Emilia centers in Italy can help themselves. On the left, towels are color coded in easily recognizable shapes in a Russian child care center. (Courtesy of the city of Reggio Emilia, Italy.)

Parents

The needs of parents will differ, depending on whom the program serves. Parents who bring their children to child care or school need adequate and safe parking facilities. In settings where parents are free to stay, a reading room, resource library, or a comfortable place to talk with other parents is desirable. Parents who participate in the class are welcomed by a teacher, shown a place to put their belongings, and given a name tag and task card.

There are many reasons parents may need to contact the school or center. Are there ways for parents to reach teachers and children in emergencies? How welcoming is the environment to parents as they enter the building? The office? The classroom? What does the environment say about parent involvement and interest?

To meet parents' needs, the teacher can make the school environment accessible and welcoming in several ways. Posting telephone numbers at which school authorities and teachers can be reached when the school is closed assures parents that teachers are available whenever needed. A bulletin board for community notices and for parent use can be put up along with mail pockets. Written communication can go between parents and teachers and among families. Working with parents is vital to creating both an anti-bias and a self-help focus in children's education and care. Teaching from these perspectives is more likely to create positive changes in children's lives

when parents are included in the process. The classroom that offers parents both an authoritative teacher and other useful resources helps them feel that their children are important.

Health and Safety in the Environment

Regardless of how many children are in the setting and for how long, the first priority is to provide for their health and safety. Health, safety, and nutrition are closely related because the quality of one affects the quality of the others (Marotz, Rush, & Cross, 1993). Therefore, programs for children must establish policies that provide for the protection, service, and education of child health and safety at all times. Government regulations and professional recommendations vary, but all establish some kind of standards to ensure good health and safety practices. For instance, here are several key documents for teachers:

● *Keeping Healthy: Parents, Teachers, and Children* (NAEYC, 1995)

● *Healthy Young Children: A Manual for Programs* (NAEYC, 1994)

● *Stepping Stones to Caring for Our Children* (National Resource Center, 1997)

● *Serving Children with HIV Infection in Child Day Care* (Pressma & Emery, 1991)

● *The ABCs of Safe and Healthy Child Care* (Centers for Disease Control and Prevention, 1997)

● **Eating Teaches Health:**
Introduction to new and different foods, good nutritional habits

● **Eating Teaches Social Skills:**
How to manage oneself in a group eating situation, focusing on eating *and* conversing; acceptable mealtime behavior and manners

● **Eating Teaches Fine-Motor Skills:**
Pouring; handling spoons, forks; serving self; drinking, eating without spilling

● **Eating Teachers Independence Skills:**
Finding and setting one's place, serving self, making choices, cleaning up at snack and lunch times

● **Eating Teaches Individual Differences:**
Likes and dislikes; choices of food; pace of eating

● **Resting and Sleeping Teach Health:**
Personal care skills; relaxation habits; internal balance and change of pace; alternating activity to allow body to rest

● **Resting and Sleeping Teach Independence Skills:**
Preparing own rest place; selecting book or toy; clearing bed things after rest

● **Dressing Teaches Independence Skills:**
Self-awareness: size of clothes, comparisons between clothes for girls and boys, younger and older, larger and smaller children, and children in and out of diapers or training pants
Self-esteem: caring for one's own body; choosing one's own clothes

● **Dressing Teaches Fine-Motor Skills:**
How to manage snaps, buttons, zippers; handling all garments; maneuvering in and out of a snowsuit or jacket; matching hands and feet with mittens and boots or shoes

● **Toileting Teaches Emotional Skills:**
Self-awareness: body functions, learning the names and physical sensations that go with body functions
Self-identity: comparisons between girls and boys (sit versus stand)
Self-esteem: caring for one's own body without guilt, fear, shame
Human sexuality: in a natural setting, promotes healthy attitudes toward the body and its functions; that adults can be accepting, open, and reassuring about the body and its care

FIGURE 9.13 ● Every routine can be used as a vehicle for learning within the environment.

Keeping Children Healthy

Sanitation. When groups of people live in close quarters, proper sanitary conditions are imperative to prevent the spread of disease. For an early childhood center, the physical plant must have adequate washing and toileting facilities for both children and adults. The number and size of toilets and wash basins are usually prescribed by local health or other regulatory agencies. Children don't realize their role in spreading germs, especially as their moist and warm hands touch and handle everything. Through gentle reminders and role modeling, teachers help children learn the *habit* of washing their hands at important times such as before snack and mealtimes.

The classrooms require daily cleaning, and equipment that is used regularly should be sanitized on a periodic basis. Nontoxic paint must be used in all circumstances, including an outdoor equipment, cribs, and for art activities with children. Classroom dress-up clothing, pillows, nap blankets, and cuddle toys all need regular laundering, either at school or at home.

The nature of preventive health care in educational settings has expanded in the last decade. Knowledge of how disease is spread and concern over infectious diseases such as hepatitis B and infection by the human immunodeficiency virus (HIV) have increased awareness of the kinds of practices teachers must engage in on a daily basis. These include *handwashing* (the number 1 way to prevent unnecessary spread of germs) and an approach known as *Universal*, or *Standard, Precautions.*

Because we cannot be guaranteed of the infectious state of an individual, it is very important to always follow universal safety procedures with all children. The steps that keep a barrier between persons and blood can apply to more than blood-borne infections. All programs should be equipped with sets of latex gloves and plastic bags to properly handle and dispose of anything with blood or fecal material. Because intact skin is a natural barrier against disease, it may not always be necessary or possible to use gloves, but it is essential that hands be washed immediately after any toileting activity. All areas for eating, diapering, and toileting must be cleaned and sanitized, using a bleach solution after cleaning away visible soiling.

Temperature, Ventilation, and Lighting. Heating and ventilaton should be comfortable for the activity level of the children and should change when weather conditions do. Adequate, nonglare lighting is a neces-

sity. Studies indicate that uniform, fluorescent lighting may not be the best environment for children; therefore, a mixture of lighting such as is in homes is preferable (Alexander, 1995). Rooms should have some means of controlling light (shades, blinds). Cross-ventilation is necessary in all rooms where children eat, sleep, or play. Proper heating and insulation are important.

Communicable Disease. This is an important issue when dealing with young children in group care. Some people question the advisability of early group care on the grounds that it exposes children to too much illness. Others claim that such exposure at an early age helps children build up resistance and that they are actually stronger and healtier by the time they enter primary grades. In the largest U.S. study to date on children's health, the Centers for Disease Control and Prevention concluded that, although infants and toddlers face a higher risk of colds and viruses, day care was not seen as increasing children's illnesses at older ages and not a risk overall (CDC, 1997).

Parents should be notified when normal childhood diseases (such as chickenpox) or common problems (such as head lice) occur in the classroom. Infections of special concern to adults include chickenpox, hepatitis A, and cytomegalovirus (CMV). A description of the symptoms and the dates of exposure and incubation period may be helpful to parents. They can then assist the school in controlling the spread of the disease in question.

In group care, children can contract a fair number of colds and viruses, especially when they are eating and sleeping close to each other. Figure 9.14 summarizes the 10 most common health problems in school, with tips for dealing with them. The school and its staff have responsibility to ensure that good health standards are instituted and maintained to keep illness to a minimum.

Health Assessment and School Policies. Every early childhood center should establish clear health policies and make them known to parents. A daily inspection of each child will help adults spot nasal discharge, inflamed eyes, and throat and skin conditions of a questionable nature. This daily check will screen out more serious cases of children too ill to remain at school and may be done by a teacher, nurse, or administrator. Educating parents about the warning signs of illness will encourage sick children to be cared for at home.

Condition	Tips
1. Allergies and asthma	Post a list of all children with chronic conditions; check ingredient lists on foods; watch what triggers reactions.
2. Scrapes and cuts	Reassure and sympathize with child; supervise child's washing with soaped pad and caring comments; use packs of ice or frozen peas in towel for swelling.
3. Bumps on the head	Notify parents of any loss of consciousness and watch for signs for 2–3 days.
4. Sand in eyes	Remind child "Do not rub!"; have child wash hands and cover eye with tissue; normal eye-tearing will bring sand to inside corner of eye, remove with clean tissue.
5. Splinters	Clean area with alcohol and remove with tweezers or cover with adhesive strip and let parent remove.
6. Conjunctivitis	"Pinkeye" is highly contagious; watch for excess eye rubbing and red eyes; have child wash hands; isolate with washable toys until parent takes child home and gets treatment.
7. Head lice	Distressing but not dangerous; wash shared clothing, stuffed animals, bedding; vacuum rugs and furniture; remove hats, combs and brushes from dramatic-play area; send notices home and inspect children's hair for 2–3 weeks.
8. Chickenpox	Isolate child until parents pick up; alert all parents about contagious period; watch for signs on all children for 3 weeks after exposure.
9. Strep throat	Send home notices; wash all equipment that might carry germs.
10. Lingering coughs	At onset, send child home until evaluated; frequent drinks will soothe; coughs may last up to 2 weeks; if longer, may suggest infection or allergy.

Figure 9.14 ⬤ Teachers need to be trained in first aid and cardiopulmonary resuscitation (CPR); in addition, a working knowledge of common health problems in school helps the teacher care for children. (Adapted from Needlman R., & Needlman, G. [1995, November/December]. 10 most common health problems in school. *Scholastic Early Childhood Today.*)

It is very important for the school to inform parents about what happens when children are refused admittance or become ill during the school day. Every school should provide a place for sick children where they can be isolated from others, kept under supervision, and be made comfortable until they are picked up. For their part, parents must arrange to have sick children cared for elsewhere if they are unable to take them home. School policies on these issues must be *explicit* and upheld consistently and compassionately, for the sake of all the children.

Teachers must be sensitive to parents' feelings and situations when sending a sick child home. This situation often produces guilt feelings in parents and work-related stress. Working parents may need school assistance in locating alternatives for care of a sick child.

Most schools require, under state or local laws, a doctor's examination and permission to participate in an early childhood education program before a child can enter the program. This includes a record of immunizations and the child's general health. Parents, too, should submit a history of the child, highlighting eating, sleeping, and elimination habits. It is critical to note any dietary restrictions or allergies and then post them in the classrooms for a reminder.

Nutrition. What children eat is also important for proper health. Places where food is prepared and stored must be kept especially clean. The child who has regular, nutritious meals and snacks will likely be healthier and less susceptible to disease. Many children do not have the benefits of healthy meals and snacks. Some do not receive adequate food at home; others are used to sugar-laden treats and "fast foods." Education about nutrition becomes the responsibility of a school that is concerned with children's health and physical development. The need for educating parents regarding child nutrition exists in virtually all early childhood programs, regardless of social or economic status. Some centers establish food regulations in an attempt to ensure that nutritionally sound meals are served to children. Most schools attempt to provide a relaxed atmosphere at meal and snack time. Children are asked to sit and eat, sharing conversation as well as food. Because lifelong eating patterns are established early in life, teachers of young children have a responsibility to understand the critical role nutrition plays in the child's total development.

Clothing. The health and safety of children are affected by the clothing they wear. A simple way to be sure children stay healthy is to encourage them to dress properly for play and for varying weather conditions. Children need clothing in which they can be active—clothing that is not binding and is easy to remove and easy to clean. To promote a self-help environment, parents and teachers should provide clothes the children can manage themselves (elastic waistbands, Velcro ties, large zippers). Pants are a good choice for both boys and girls; long dresses can become a hazard when climbing, running, or going up and down stairs. The safest shoes for active play should have composition or rubber soles. Whenever possible, it helps to keep changes of clothes at school.

Health of the Staff. A responsible early childhood center is one that supports and maintains a healthy staff. Teachers should be in good physical and mental health to be at their best with children. It is wise to check the health regulations and benefits of the individual school when employed there. Many states

Figure 9.15 ● Children need clothing in which they can be active, playful, and messy!

require annual chest x-rays as a condition of employment. Sick leave policies should be clearly stated in print.

Early childhood education is an intense job involving close interpersonal contact. Most teachers work long hours, often with low wages and few health benefits, and with clients in various stages of health. Such working conditions produce fatigue and stress, which can lead to illness or other stress-related problems.

Guarding Children's Safety

Beyond the continual supervision of indoor and outdoor space, everything is planned with the children's safety in mind. Creating a hazard-free environment that still allows for risk and challenge for children takes careful observation and attention to detail. A quick walk around the room and yard will reveal potential problems:

● Are there any sharp corners at children's height?

● Are rug edges snagged or loose?

● Are absorbent surfaces used wherever there is water? Are mops and towels available for spillage?

● Is hot water out of the reach of children?

● Are children allowed to run inside?

- Are there rules governing the children's use of scissors, hammers, and knives?

- Are safety rules explained to children and upheld by adults?

- Are electrical outlets covered when not in use?

- Do open stairwells have gates?

- Do adults monitor the use of extension cords and appliances?

- Is broken equipment removed promptly?

- Are fences high enough to protect and safe to touch?

- Are there areas where wheel toys can move freely without fear of collision?

- Are swings placed away from traffic areas and set apart by bushes or fences?

- Can a child's foot or ankle be caught on equipment; under a chain-link fence?

- Does playground traffic flow easily?

- Are the toys safe for children's use?

In addition, with an estimated 12 to 15 million children participating in organized sports each year (Nelson & Raymond, 1989), safety issues are paramount for school-aged children. The adults serve as the link between children and sports and are the chief means of prevention of injuries and accidents.

Figure 9.18 is a safety checklist for the indoor areas; Figure 12.9 shows how to make playgrounds safe.

First Aid. Every school should establish procedures for dealing with children who are injured on the property. First aid instructions should be required of all teachers and made available as part of their in-service training. Teachers should know how to treat bumps and bruises, minor cuts and abrasions, bleeding, splinters, bites and stings, seizures, sprains, broken bones, and minor burns.[1] Each classroom should be equipped with two first-aid kits. One is for use in the classroom and yard; the other should be suitable for taking on field

Figure 9.16 ⬤ Be sure that swings are placed away from the traffic area and set apart so that other children can keep at a safe distance.

trips. Each kit should be readily available to adults, but out of children's reach, and supplies should be replenished regularly.

Emergency numbers to be posted near the telephone in each room include those of the ambulance squad, fire department, police, health department, nearest hospital, and a consulting physician (if any). All families enrolled at the school should be aware of school policy regarding injuries at school and should provide the school with emergency information for each child: the name of their physician, how to locate the parents, and who else might be responsible for the injured child if the parents cannot be reached. The school in turn must make sure they notify parents of any injuries the child has incurred during the school day.

Natural Disaster. Most adults are familiar with the most common disaster preparation, the fire drill. Most local fire regulations require that fire extinguishers be

 OUR DIVERSE WORLD OUR DIVERSE WORLD OUR DIVERSE WORLD OUR DIVERSE WORLD OUR DIVERSE WORLD OUR DIVERSE WORLD OUR DIVERSE WORLD OUR DIVERSE WORLD

[1] All teachers should receive training in using universal health precautions with all children. Teachers should not make assumptions about who is at risk and who is not for HIV infection or hepatitis.

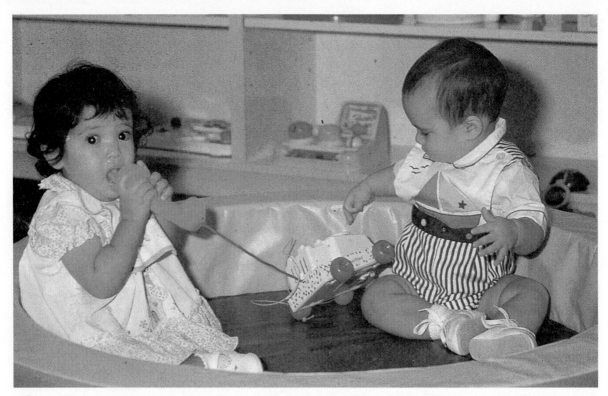

Figure 9.17 ● When planning for infants and toddlers, the teacher must check toys carefully, because children explore them with all their senses.

in working order and placed in all classrooms and the kitchen area. Fire exits, fire alarms, and fire escapes should be well marked and functioning properly. Children and teachers should participate in fire drills regularly. Other natural disasters vary by geographical location; helping children prepare for earthquakes, tornadoes, hurricanes, floods, and snowstorms will include participating in drills for those disasters. Proper preparedness will include eliminating potential hazards (e.g., bolting down bookcases), establishing a coordinated response plan (a "Code Blue!" emergency plan should involve children, parents, all staff, and local emergency agencies), and, in some areas of the country, conducting regular earthquake and tornado drills. These experiences can reinforce in parents the need for establishing similar procedures at home.

Automobile Safety. Automobile safety is a related concern when considering potential hazards for preschool children. The use of approved car seats and restraints for children riding in automobiles has received national attention in recent years. Some states have passed legislation requiring the use of specific devices to ensure safer travel for young children. Whether or not they walk to school, children should also be aware of basic rules for crossing streets. The school parking lot can be a source of danger unless the school articulates policies to parents regarding the safety needs of children. There are potential risks when cars and children occupy the same space. Children should not be left unattended in parking lots.

Maintaining Children's Well-Being

The overall environment for children takes into consideration many factors. To provide for children's *health and safety*, teachers look at the physical environment carefully—its materials, the equipment, and their arrangement and presentation (see Figure 9.18). Another factor in children's care and education is their *well-being*. Young children are growing up in a world threatened by violence abroad and at home, drug abuse, unresolved conflicts among adults, and constant bombardment of television and other media.

SAFETY LIST FOR INDOOR ENVIRONMENTS

_____ Person monitoring children (at entrances, indoors, outdoors)

_____ First aid and emergency:
   _____ Materials readily available to adults, out of children's reach, and regularly stocked and updated
   _____ Adults trained in first aid and CPR regularly and familiar with emergency routines

_____ Safety plugs on all outlets

_____ Cords:
   _____ Electrical cords out of children's reach; avoid using extension cords
   _____ Curtain and window cords, window pulls and poles out of children's reach

_____ Floormat and carpet tacked down to avoid slippage

_____ Doors:
   _____ Made to open and close slowly
   _____ All clear access, marked exits, and not blocked

_____ Cubbies and storage cabinets:
   _____ Bolted to walls (or back-to-back together)
   _____ Cabinets equipped with child-proof latches
   _____ Any dangerous materials in locked area

_____ Toys:
   _____ In good repair; no splinters or sharp, broken edges
   _____ Check for size with younger children (purchase safety sizing gadget or estimate to keep at the size of a child's fist)
   _____ Check for peeling paint

_____ Plants and animals:
   _____ Nonpoisonous plants _only_
   _____ Check animal cages regularly
   _____ Supervise animal handling carefully
   _____ Store animal food away from children's reach

_____ Adult materials:
   _____ Keep adult purses, bags, and so on, away from children
   _____ Avoid having hot beverages around children
   _____ No smoking in children's areas

_____ Kitchen and Storage:
   _____ Children allowed in _only_ with adult supervision
   _____ Poisonous or hazardous materials stored in a locked area

Figure 9.18 ● Children's safety is of primary importance to teachers and caregivers. Careful evaluation and regular safety checks eliminate dangerous materials and conditions in children's spaces.

This chapter, as well as those on the curriculum, demonstrate the importance of teachers' addressing issues of racism, sexism, and handicappism as well as helping children cope with growing up in a nuclear-war and television age[1] (Carlsson-Paige & Levin, 1990; Derman-Sparks et al., 1989).

The health, safety, and nutritional needs and emotional well-being of the children are of primary and fundamental importance. The National Academy of Early Childhood Programs has established explicit guidelines for health, safety, nutrition, and food service (NAEYC, 1991). When the basic needs of children are protected, the foundation for sound development has been laid.

CREATING THE ENVIRONMENT

The Physical Environment

Every educational setting is organized fundamentally around physical space. This means teachers work with the size and limitations of the facility, both inside and out-of-doors. The building itself may be new and designed specifically for young children. In Reggio Emilia, for example, it is the environment that creates an atmosphere of discovery. As founder Louis Malaguzzi explains (Edwards et al., 1993):

> There is an entrance hall, which informs and documents, and which anticipates the form and organization of the school. This leads into the dinning hall, with the kitchen well in view. The entrance hall leads into the central space, or *piazza*, the place of encounters, friendships, games, and other activities that complete those of the classrooms. The classrooms and utility rooms are placed at a distance from but connected with the center area. Each classroom is divided into two contiguous rooms . . . to allow children either to be with teachers or stay alone. . . . In addition to the classrooms, we have established the *atelier*, the school studio and laboratory, as a place for manipulating or experimenting.

More than likely, however, the space is a converted house or store, a church basement, a parish hall, or an elementary classroom. Sometimes a program will share space with another group so that mobile furniture is moved daily or weekly. Family child care programs are housed in a private home; therefore, adaptations are made in the space both for the children and the family that lives there. There may be a large yard or none at all. Some playgrounds are on the roof of the building, or a park across the street may serve as the only available playground. (See the section on playgrounds in Chapter 12.)

Restraints also come in the form of weather conditions. Outside play—and therefore large-muscle equipment—may be unavailable during the winter, so room for active, vigorous play is needed inside during that time. Hot summer months can make some types of play difficult if there is little or no shade outdoors. Weather conditions must be considered when planning programs for children.

Early childhood programs have specific needs that must be met by the buildings they occupy. Although the choice of building is generally determined by what is available, at a minimum the setting should provide facilities for:

Playing/working	Food preparation
Eating	Storage
Washing/toileting	Office/teacher work space
Sleeping/resting	Clothing and wraps

Ideally, the setting should have enough space to house these various activities separately. In practice, however, rooms are multipurpose, and more than one event takes place in the same space. A playroom doubles as an eating area because both require the use of tables and chairs. When a school room serves many functions (playing, eating, sleeping), convenient and adequate storage space is a necessity. Harms and Clifford (1989) list as important environmental supports for each of these areas:

1. Personal care routines
2. Appropriate furnishings and display space
3. Language and reasoning experiences
4. Fine- and gross-motor activities
5. Creative activities
6. Social development experiences
7. Personal and professional needs of the adults in the program

[1] The skilled early childhood educator is well informed in a wide area of topics challenging our society.

Figure 9.19 ● Early childhood programs provide for children's playing and working alone and together, with friends and teachers, indoors and out.

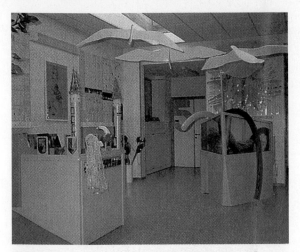

Figure 9.20 ● Even the hallways serve a function in the Reggio Emilia Schools in Italy. (Courtesy of the city of Reggio Emilia, Italy.)

The amount of teacher time needed to prepare the room for each change of activity is worth consideration when planning the daily schedule.

General Requirements

Ground-floor classrooms are preferable for young children to ensure that they can enter and leave with relative ease and safety. For noise reduction, the walls and ceilings should be sound-proofed. Carpeting, draperies, and other fireproof fabrics in the room will help absorb sound. Floors must be durable, sanitary, and easily cleaned. They should be free from drafts. Rugs should be vacuumed each day. Room size should be sufficient to allow for freedom of movement and the opportunity to play without interference. Some licensing agencies may suggest minimum room and yard size standards.

Many local and state agencies have regulations regarding the use of space for children in group care settings. The fire marshall, health department, and similar agencies must be consulted and their regulations observed. It is wise to consider their requirements when arranging space.

The National Academy of Early Childhood Programs (NAEYC, 1991) has developed guidelines for indoor and outdoor facilities that promote optimal growth. Besides floor and play space (minimum 35 square feet indoors and 75 square feet outdoors), the guidelines suggest how to arrange activity areas to accommodate children and what kinds of activities and materials are safe, clean, and attractive. Harms and Clifford (1989) have developed environmental rating scales that are used widely. The sections "Materials and Equipment" and "Organizing Space" in this chapter draw on these two exemplary works, which are cited in the chapter bibliography.

Bathrooms

Bathrooms should be adjacent to the play and sleeping areas and easily reached from outdoors. Child-sized toilets and wash basins are preferable, but if unavailable, a step or platform may be built. In most early childhood settings, the bathrooms are without doors, for ease of supervision. Toileting facilities for children should be light, airy, attractive, and large enough to serve several children at a time. An exhaust fan is desirable. Paper towel holders should be at child height and waste baskets placed nearby.

If diapering is part of the program, areas for this purpose should be clearly defined and close to hand-washing facilities. Handwashing regulations for the staff should be posted, and an area should be provided for recording children's toileting and elimination patterns. Closed cans and germicidal spray must be used, and diapering materials should be plentiful and handy.

Room to Rest

Schools that provide nap and sleeping facilities require adequate storage space for cots and bedding. Movable screens, low enough for teacher supervision, allow for privacy and help reduce the noise level.

Cots or cribs should be labeled with children's names and washed regularly. They should be placed consistently and in such a way that children feel familiar, cozy, and private—not in the center of the room or in rows. Teachers can develop a "nap map" that places children so they can get the rest or sleep they need while still feeling part of the group.

Out of Doors

The traditional playgrounds—typically on a flat, barren area with steel structures such as swings, climbers, a slide, perhaps a merry-go-round or see-saws, fixed in concrete and arranged in one row—are poor places for children's play from both safety and

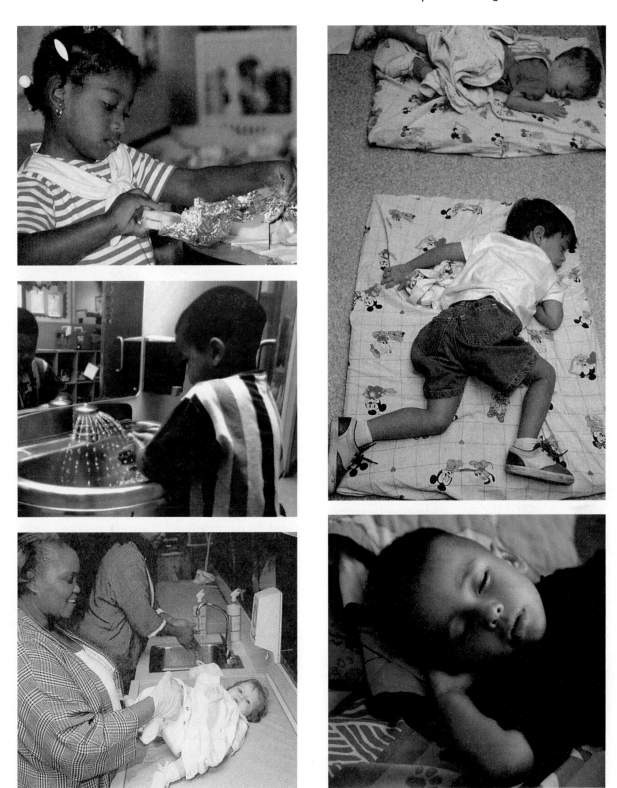

Figure 9.21 ● Every routine—eating, resting, handwashing, sleeping, and diapering—has a place in the early childhood classroom.

developmental perspectives (Frost, 1986). Children as young as toddlers and through the primary years much prefer the adventure or creative playground, spaces that have a variety of fixed and movable equipment (Campbell & Frost, 1985). Raw materials, such as sand, water, tires, spools, sawhorses, bowls, or pans, in combination with larger superstructures or open-air "houses" with some flexible parts, stimulate a wide variety of both social and cognitive play (including constructive, dramatic, and games play).

A wide porch or covered patio is ideal for rainy days or days when the sun is too severe. Many activities can be extended to the outside area with this type of protection. The physical plant should include adequate playground space adjacent to the building. A variety of playground surfaces makes for more interesting play and provides suitable covering for outdoor activities. Tanbark can be used in the swing area, cement for wheel toys, and grass for under climbers. Sand is used for play in a large area and also in a sensory table. No matter what the surface, the yard should be constructed with a good drainage system. Trees, bushes, and other plantings will allow for both sunshine and shade. Fences are *mandatory*. They must be durable, an appropriate height, with no opportunity for a child to gain a foothold.

Because there are no mandatory standards for the manufacture of play equipment, adults who work with children must assume responsibility for playground design. Teachers can familiarize themselves with the literature, visit high-quality playgrounds, and consult with child development specialists when selecting equipment. Given the importance that young children attach to the outdoors, teachers are well-advised to concentrate their efforts in a similar fashion. Chapter 12 discusses playgrounds in detail.

Food Service

All schools for young children serve some sort of refreshment during the daily session. In an infant program, storing formula and milk is a necessity. Whether involved in a light snack or full meal program, the center must adhere to the most rigid standards of health protection and safety provisions. Every precaution must be taken to ensure maximum hygienic food service. Daily cleaning of equipment,

Figure 9.22 ● No matter what age the child is, snacks are a favorite part of the day.

counters, floors, and appliances is a necessity. Proper disinfecting of highchairs and tables requires half a cup of bleach to one gallon of water; bottles of this solution can be stored away from children's reach yet handy for teachers.

Local school districts, Coordinated Community Child Care (4Cs), or affiliates of the NAEYC may be consulted for guidelines on serving nutritional foods and may even offer financial subsidies. For infant and toddler programs and in many full-day programs, space for recording feeding information must be designated, and enough highchairs or low tables must be provided to prevent an unreasonable wait for eating. Each age has its unique food service needs.[1] Infants will need to be held or seated near an adult. Toddlers should not be fed popcorn, nuts, or raw carrots because of the hazard of choking. All children must be served food on disposable dishes or on dishes cleaned in a dishwasher with a sanitation cycle. Lunches brought from home by school-age and full-day children must be checked for spoilage. Information about eating patterns, proportions, and nutritional needs should be regularly shared with parents.

[1] Food preferences and customs, as well as toys and materials, need to reflect the cultures served.

Materials and Equipment

Selection of materials and equipment is based on a number of criteria. Out of necessity, most school budgets limit the amount of money available for such purchases. To make every dollar count, teachers select materials that:

● Are age and developmentally appropriate

● Are related to the school's philosophy and curriculum

● Reflect quality design and workmanship

● Are durable

● Offer flexibility and versatility in their uses

● Have safety features (e.g., nontoxic paints, rounded corners)

● Are aesthetically attractive and appealing to children (and adults)

● Are easy to maintain and repair

● Reflect the cultural makeup of the group and the diversity of the culture overall

● Are nonsexist, nonstereotypical, and anti-bias

Materials should be appropriate for a wide range of skills because children within the same age group develop at individual rates (Figure 9.23). Selecting equipment and toys to support development is important; because young children typically will try to play with everything in their environment, the selection of play materials involves many decisions (Bronson, 1995). Many of the materials can be open-ended; that is, they can be used in their most basic form or they can be developed in a variety of ways. Unit blocks, clay, and Legos® are examples of materials that children can use in a simple fashion; as skills develop these materials can be manipulated in a more complex manner.

 Toys and materials need to reflect the diversity of the class, the families, and the community.[1] From a self-help viewpoint, dressing frames and plenty of workable doll clothes will help children learn those

self-care tasks. Children's books that demonstrate social values and attitudes that expand gender roles and family life-styles show a value for an anti-bias environment. Modifications in the environment that promote inclusiveness might include ramp access for wheelchairs and materials to highlight tactile, auditory, and olfactory experiences for children with visual impairments. Classroom practices that encourage sociodramatic play involving interaction (restaurant, grocery store, and so on) help children learn about peaceful means to negotiate and solve problems, demonstrating a peace education perspective.

Recall the Walfdorf Schools of the 1980s and 1990s discussed in Chapter 1. Because Steiner believed the classroom is an extension of the family experience and was to be as free as possible from the intrusions of the "modern world," a Waldorf kindergarten might look like this (Waldorf, 1995):

> The feeling of warmth and security is largely created by using only natural materials: woods, cotton, wool in the construction of the decor and toys. The curtains transmit a warm glow in the room. Ideally, the walls and floor of the room are of natural wood. In this warm environment are placed toys which the children can use to imitate and transform the activities that belong to everyday adult life. In one corner stands a wooden scale and baskets for children to pretend they are grocery shopping; a pile of timber stands ready to be constructed into a playhouse, a boat, or a train; a rocking horse invites a child to become a rider; homemade dolls lie in wooden cradles surrounded by wooden frames and cloths the children can use to create a pretend family and play house. Pinecones and flowers are artistically dispersed. Lovely watercolors adorn the walls. The effect of this beautiful arrangement of decorations and toys is the feeling of stepping out of the business and clutter of modern life into a sanctuary where one can breathe easily, relax, and play according to the impulses of one's heart.

 OUR DIVERSE WORLD OUR DIVERSE WORLD OUR DIVERSE WORLD OUR DIVERSE WORLD OUR DIVERSE WORLD OUR DIVERSE WORLD OUR DIVERSE WORLD OUR DIVERSE WORLD

[1] Numerous resources are available to help the teacher select books, dolls, puzzles, and posters that will expose children in a positive way to people who are ethnically different, people with disabilities, and people who have different work and play habits from their own.

Basic Materials in an Early Childhood Classroom

Art Supplies
Easels, paints, watercolors
Plastic dough, clay
Pens, pencils, brushes
Scissors, holepunches
Glue, paste
Collage materials
Assorted paper

Infants/toddlers: Limit materials.
   Use open shelves with few choices.

School age: Have self-help table and
   teacher-guided projects.

Discovery and Science
Nature materials
Textured materials
Water/sensory table and materials
Magnifying glasses, mirrors
Scales
Small pets

Infants/toddlers: Simplify, watch for
   safety. Aquarium.

School age: Display to read, computer.

Dramatic Play
Safety Mirrors
Furniture: child-sized, versatile
Clothing: variety, nonstereotyped
Dolls: variety, and accessories
Cooking utensils
Food items
Purses, suitcases, briefcases,
   backpacks

Infants/toddlers: Limit the choice, add
   hats or dolls that can get wet.

School age: Varied units such as
   prehistoric cave, moonscape

Blocks and Manipulatives
Unit blocks
Block accessories: people, animals,
   vehicles
Puzzles
Construction toys: Legos®, Tinkertoys®
Stringing beads, dressing frames

Infants/toddlers: Push-pull toys, nesting
   toys, soft blocks

School age: Diversify accessories,
   increase complexity, add math
   materials.

Language and Books
Books
Flannel board, accessories
Photos
Lotto games
Records, tapes
Writing center: typewriter, pads, and
   pencils

Infants/toddlers: Cardboard books; use
   others with adults only.

School age: Readers, listening post

Outdoors
Large building blocks
Sand/water toys
Wheel toys
Dramatic-play props
Balls and game materials
Workbench materials
Dancing materials

Infants/toddlers: Omit workbench;
   simplify choices.

School age: Team-games equipment.
   Sequence projects, such as building
   bird feeders, piñatas.

Figure 9.23 ● A sample materials and equipment list for an early childhood program. Although not comprehensive, this list starts to organize the environment for a variety of play. Note the adjustments that must be made to accommodate different ages. See Figure 9.7 for ideas about culturally diverse materials and Figure 9.8 to adapt environments for children with special needs.

Children are active learners, and their materials should provide them with ways to explore, manipulate, and become involed. Teachers encourage the use of fine- and gross-motor skills by providing equipment that involves their use. Children learn through all their senses, so the materials should be appealing to many of the senses. Children need opportunities for quiet, private time and space as well; particularly for children in care for long hours or in large group sizes, a cozy corner is essential.

Organizing Space

There are many different ways to arrange and organize the living space in an early childhood setting; the final result expresses the diversity of the program. Most early childhood centers are arranged by **interest areas, learning centers,** or **activity areas.** Dodge and Colker's *Creative Curriculum* (1992) outlines six environmental areas as being art, blocks, table toys, house corner, library, and outdoors; we elaborate on them to give you a broader view: These will most likely include:

Indoors	*Outdoors*
Blocks	Sand
Manipulatives/table toys	Water play/sensory play
Art	Woodworking
Discovery: Science/ nature/cooking	Wheel toys
	Climbers
Music	Swings
Math	Balls/games
Dramatic play	Art
Books/language/listening	Science/nature
Quiet/private place	Dramatic play
Water play/sensory play	
Housekeeping	

Figure 9.24 shows an environmental plan for optimizing learning and interaction for 3- to 5-year-olds; Figure 9.25 shows indoor alternatives for toddlers and school-age children.

The room arrangement and the choice of activity centers show what is being emphasized in the program.

The amount of space devoted to any one activity says a great deal about its value to the staff. A housekeeping area with plenty of space encourages active use by a number of children. Social play is promoted when two or more items are available. Four telephones, three doll buggies, or two easels can be tools for social interaction. At the same time, the environment must be flexible to respond to the developing needs and interests of the children. For instance, one class may have great interest in block-building, and thus need to expand that area for several weeks. As interests change, so do the room and yard—someone brings in a hamster and the discovery area blossoms, or family camping brings out tents around the grassy outdoor areas.

Because the physial environment is such a powerful influence on children, it is worthwhile to consider several key dimensions that affect their experiences. Prescott (1994) names five in Figure 9.26.

Room arrangement and choice of materials play such an important role in children's educational experience. The environment says, "You can do things on your own and be independent" when there are materials on shelves for children to reach. A job chart that outlines children's responsibilities is a *self-help* environment. Teachers who evaluate their materials so that they reflect all children and adults in nonstereotyped activities are committed to an *anti-bias* environment. A program that has, for instance, prop boxes with materials for their children with visual or auditory disabilities is one that is making real strides to be an *inclusive* environment.

The placement of the interest centers is important. Balance the number of noisy and quiet activities, both indoors and out. Some activities are noiser than others, so place the noisier centers together and cluster the quieter ones together. Quieter activities, such as puzzles, language games, and story telling, take place in areas away from blocks, water play, or dramatic play, because the last three tend to kindle animated, active, and sometimes noisy behavior.

Environments must be arranged so that there are enough play spaces for the number of children in the group. When the number of play opportunities in school settings, both indoors and out, is analyzed, areas and activities can be assigned a value (Prescott et al., 1972). A simple area (swings, climbers) counts as one play space, a complex area (housekeeping/dramatic play) counts as four play spaces, and a super area (sand and water play combined) counts as eight play spaces. The value assigned an area generally coincides with

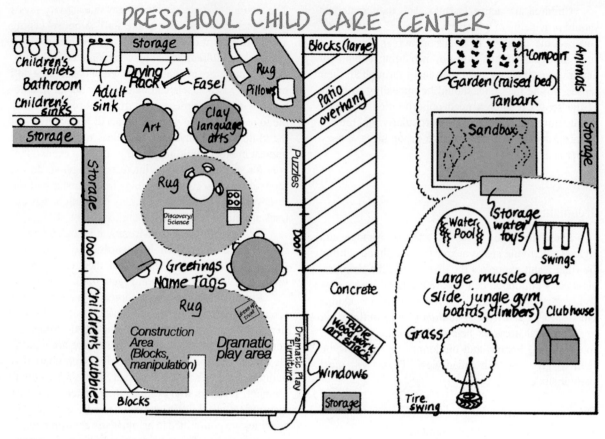

Figure 9.24 ● Layout for a preschool child care environment, ages 3 to 5. For a group of 18 to 20 children, teachers plan indoor and outdoor environments that are challenging and uncrowded.

the number of children who might be accommodated in that space. When the total for the space is figured, it is matched against the actual number of children in the group to see if there is a place for everyone to play.

Adult needs also should be met through proper organization of classroom and yard. How can the teachers supervise all areas while ensuring cozy spots for children's privacy? Are the teachers deployed evenly throughout all the space? Is storage integrated so that equipment is located near the place where it will be used? Is the space arranged for cooperation and communication among the adults as well as the children? In other words, is this a workplace that is accepting, inviting, and challenging to all?

Clearly defined boundaries and obvious pathways make it easy for children to live and work in the space.

There should be enough space for larger groups to gather together as well as small groups.

A good environment for children reflects the teachers' knowledge of how children play, what skills they possess, what they know, and what they need to learn. The settings are arranged to promote those aspects of child growth and development. They also reflect the teachers' values. A self-help perspective will have spaces and materials arranged for the children's access and use without undue teacher permission or help; Figures 9.4, 9.24, and 9.25 demonstrate such environments. With an anti-bias viewpoint, the environment would reflect images in abundance of all the children, families, and staff of that program as well as of the major racial and ethnic groups of the community and nation, with a balance of men and women as well as the elderly

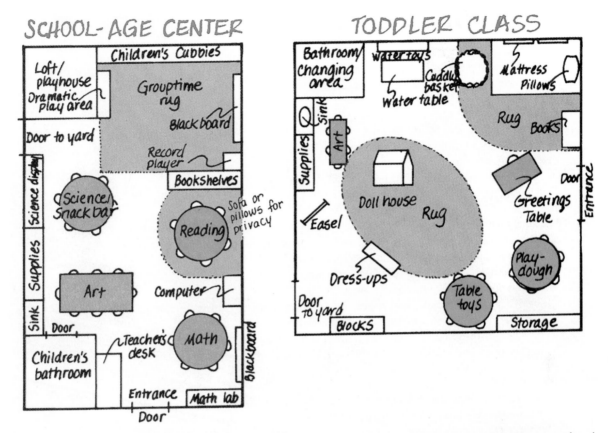

Figure 9.25 ● Room layouts for school-age and toddler groups differ according to the developmental and individual needs of the groups. These plans accommodate up to 20 school-age children and 12 toddlers.

 and disabled doing many jobs typical of daily life.[1] An inclusive environment could be reflected in the addition of cube chairs, easy handles on the doors, and puzzles whose pieces have magnets on the backs and are put together on a steel cookie tray. With peace education in mind, teachers provide materials to expand children's concepts, including those of similarity and difference, and help them develop a strong sense of self and the ability to cooperate and resolve conflicts peaceably.

One place in particular reflects the community's value of creativity and self-expression. On entering one of the community preschools in Reggio Emilia, one sees (New, 1990)

the work of children (drawings, paintings, sculptures) and their teachers (photographs and displays of projects in progress), often with the dramatic use of graphics....Everywhere you turn, there is something else to ponder. Art supplies, including paints and clay as well as recycled or naturally found materials (leaves, bottle caps, fabric scraps) are pleasingly arranged, often by color, on shelves within children's reach. Groupings of found objects, including flower petals and plastic bags filled with "memories" from field trips, are carefully displayed so as to acknowledge the importance children attribute to the objects as well as the aesthetic qualities (shape, color, texture) of the objects themselves.

In summary, the physical environment should be organized for children according to these criteria:

OUR DIVERSE WORLD OUR DIVERSE WORLD OUR DIVERSE WORLD OUR DIVERSE WORLD OUR DIVERSE WORLD OUR DIVERSE WORLD OUR DIVERSE WORLD OUR DIVERSE WORLD

[1] See the anti-bias curriculum resources listed in the bibliography.

1. **Softness/Hardness**
   Soft: rugs, pillows, playdough, finger paints, grass, sand, swings
   Hard: tile floor, wooden furniture, asphalt, cement

2. **Open/Closed**
   Open (no one right way to use it): sand and water, dress-up, collage materials, painting
   Closed (manipulated only one way to come out right): puzzles, many board games, most Montessori equipment
   In-between: many manipulatives such as Legos®, TinkerToys®, blocks, balls

3. **Simple/Complex**
   "Play equipment can differ in its holding power; i.e., the capacity to sustain attention.... A simple unit has one manipulable aspect, a complex unit has two different kinds of materials combined, and a super unit has three different kinds of materials that go together."
   Simple: swings, climbers, sand pile with no toys
   Complex: dramatic play with only a kitchen
   Super: Climbers with slides and ropes, playhouse with kitchen, dress-up clothes, dolls, and/or playdough; sand area with equipment and/or water
   As you add more features to a unit, you increase its complexity and the children's interest in it. To simple playdough, add cookie cutters, then add toothpicks or a garlic press and it becomes a super unit.

4. **Intrusion/Seclusion**
   Intrusion: places where children can enter or go through easily; blocks, housekeeping, even the entire environment are often highly intrusive areas
   Seclusion: places where children can be alone or with only one child or adult; cubbies, a fort, or under a table become secret places

5. **High mobility/Low mobility**
   High: whole-body places and activities; outdoors, climbers, trike lanes, gym mats
   Low: sitting-still places and activities; puzzles and games, story and group times, naptime
   In-between: dramatic play, block corner, woodworking

Figure 9.26 ● Key dimensions when considering an early childhood environment. (From Prescott, E. [1994, November]. The physical environment—A powerful regulator of experience. *Exchange Magazine.*)

● *Availability:* open, low shelving with visual cues for placement of toys, equipment—aids in cleanup and room setup

● *Consistency in organization:* neat, systematic, in logical order

● *Compatibility:* noisy activities are grouped away from quiet ones; art needs natural light when possible; water play near a bathroom or kitchen; messy projects on washable floors

● *Definition:* clearly defined boundaries indicating available space and what is to take place; obvious pathways outlined in class and yard; ways to get in and out of an area without disrupting activity in progress; no dead ends or runways

● *Spacing:* interest areas with enough space to hold the children who will play there; one-third to one-half of the surface should remain uncovered; materials stored near space where they are used; storage and activity spaces have visual cues

● *Communicability:* tells children what to do instead of relying on adult to monitor activities; communicates to children what behavior is expected; arrangement suggests numbers of children, levels of activity.

The Temporal Environment

Daily Schedule: Time to Learn

The daily schedule defines the structure of each program. It creates the format for how children will experience the events of the day—in what order and for what length of time.

No two schedules are alike because each reflects the program it represents. The amount of time devoted to specific activities communicates clearly what value the school places on them. The amount of time given to certain aspects of the curriculum, the variety of events, and the flexibility tell children and adults what is important in this particular setting. Figure 9.27 and Chapter 11 expand on this issue of time.

In developing a schedule by which to function on a daily basis, teachers first decide what is important for children to learn, how that learning should take place, and how much time to allow in the daily program. If small-group work and individual attention are program goals, enough time will have to be set aside to ensure their success. More time is needed to allow children a number of curriculum choices than if they had only one or two activities from which to select. Three-year-olds need more time for toileting activities than do 5-year-olds, who are considerably more self-sufficient.

The golden rule for child care is to treat children as we want them to treat us. Australian educator Anne Stonehouse (1990) notes that the children in child care today are the adults of tomorrow who will be taking care of us in our old age. Remembering that, it helps to think of how often children are asked to do and finish their tasks on others' schedules, to ask permission to do what they wish, to be required to participate in activities of someone else's choice. A children's program must be *for* children, on *their* timetable as much as possible. Stonehouse's recommendations for a program's schedule reflect this respect:

1. Suitable choices are built in as much of the time as possible, avoiding the expectation that everyone should do the same thing at the same time. Flexibility . . . makes for a more humane environment.

2. The need for a sensitive and flexible settling-in period is taken into account. This starts with respect for the client and the client's family and the recog-

nition that different people cope with change and new experiences in different ways.

3. Meaningless and sometimes mindless activities that simply "fill up the day," "help pass the time," or that have no intrinsic value are avoided.

4. A healthy balance between an individual's need for autonomy, freedom, and independence, on the one hand, and the need for rules that help us get along together, on the other, is strived for.

5. Staff balance the need for a routine, for the comfort and reassurance of the familiar, with the need for variety and novelty for change.

The physical plant itself may dictate a portion of the daily schedule. If toilet facilities are not located adjacent to the classroom, then more time must be scheduled to travel to and from the bathrooms. If the building or space is shared with other groups, some portion of the program may be modified. Many schools housed in church buildings schedule field trips during the annual church rummage sale to free up the space for the church's use.

The daily schedule is important for everyone in the setting. When the time sequence is clear to all, then everyone can go about the business of learning and teaching. Children are more secure in a place that has a consistent schedule; they can begin to anticipate the regularity of what comes next and count on it. In that way they are then free to move, explore, and learn without hesitation. Children can freely involve themselves without fear of being interrupted. Adults, too, enjoy the predictability of a daily schedule. By knowing the sequence of events, they are then free to flex the timing when unforeseen circumstances arise.

And it is the unforeseen that often does happen. Amidst the noise of children at work, the play is likely to be interrupted by a number of things that can affect the "best laid plans" of all teachers. For instance, a child unexpectedly decides that he doesn't want Dad to go—just as the teacher was helping someone onto the toilet for the first time. Or chaos breaks out in the block corner—at the moment a teacher was leaving with a group of children for the kitchen with several cookie sheets full of carefully constructed gingerbread people. A visitor is coming in the door—just as two children collide and bump heads. A parent is walking in the door with a special group-time activity—and this time a child refuses to clean up her playdough creation.

The plans and routines of a program do provide the security of the known; at the same time, spontaneous happenings of the day always occur and are often moments of intense learning. Good teachers prepare children for upcoming transitions, using a song or strumming of an instrument and the words, "Get ready to clean up soon." And they are also prepared for children's perceptions of time, immediacy, and closure to collide with the schedule. So if Chad doesn't want his dad to go, perhaps Shana's getting on the toilet will have to wait, or Dad can read him another story until Shana's "all done now!" has happened. The gingerbread sheets can be held momentarily so the quarrel can be resolved, or some of the "fighters" could be invited to be door-openers and help march the group to the kitchen. Perhaps Marisa could keep working on her masterpiece while the rest of the class joins the parent on the rug (at least, just this once?).

These examples all illustrate the common clash of "adult timetables and children's quest for engagement" (Ambery, 1997). Programs need to be designed to allow for both consistency and **flexibility**. Consistency brings security and closure, allowing for teacher authority and expertise to assert themselves; flexibility invites sensitivity to individuals and respectful agreements to be reached. As teachers work with schedules, they continually balance the needs of individuals with those of the group.

Developmentally Appropriate Schedules

Just as the arrangement of space should reflect the group of children within, so does the daily schedule allow for appropriate growth at the developmental level of the group. There are common factors to consider for all children in the early years, as well as some developmental distinctions at the various ages.

There are common elements in all schedules, whether they are designed for toddler groups or 5-year-olds, all-day programs or half-day nurseries. Sound child development principles provide the framework on which the daily schedule is structured. The individual schools then adapt these requirements to their own philosophy as they work out their individual daily schedule. All schedules must:

● Include time for **routines** (to eat, rest, wash, toilet) as well as time for **transitions** (what happens when there is a change from one activity to another) and **group times** (circle time to begin the day, songtime for announcements, or storytime as closure).

● Alternate quiet and active play and work to help children pace themselves.

● Provide opportunities for both inside and outside play.

● Allow children to participate in structured activities as well as those of their own choosing.

● Make it possible for children to work individually, in small groups, or in larger ones.

● Gear the time to the age and developmental levels of the group.

● Provide for flexibility so that children's interests can be maintained and emergencies met.

● Have a beginning and an end. Some provisions must be made for children to be met and greeted when they enter. The day is brought to closure with a review of the day's activities and a daily class anticipation of what will come tomorrow. Allow time for dismissal or transition to extended care.

● Involve the adults in daily planning and review; include a regular meeting time for more substantial discussion of children, long-range planning, and evaluation.

● Include time for cleanup and room restoration.

● Incorporate the teachers' roles and assignments so that they will know their area of responsibility.

● Be posted in an obvious place in the classroom for all to see.

All schedules have a great deal in common, but certain age-related differences can be seen. Figure 9.27 outlines three typical daily schedules for a half-day toddler class, a full day for preschoolers, and a kindergarten. (See also Figures 2.1 and 2.3.) There are several important differences in schedules for the various age groups:

● More *choices* are available to children as they grow.

  Example: Two-year-olds could be overstimulated by the selection of materials that is appropriate for school-aged children.

● *Transitions* can be handled differently in the various age groups.

Half-Day Toddler Program

9:00–9:30	Greet children
	Inside activities
	● playdough and art/easel
	● home living
	● blocks and manipulatives
	● books
9:30	Door to outdoors opens
9:45–10:20	Outdoor play
	● large motor
	● social play
10:20	Music/movement outdoors
10:30	Snack/"Here We Are Together" song
	● washing hands
	● eating/pouring/cleanup
10:45–11:45	Outside
11:15	"Time to Put Our Toys Away" song
	● all encouraged to participate in cleanup
11:20	Closure (indoors)
	● parent–child together
	● story or flannel board

Full-Day Program for Preschoolers

7:00	Arrival, breakfast
7:30	Inside free play
	● arts/easels
	● table toys/games/blocks
	● dramatic-play center; house, grocery store, etc.
9:00	Cleanup
9:15	Group time: songs/fingerplays and small group choices
9:30	Choice time/small groups
	● discovery/math lab/science activity
	● cooking for morning or afternoon snack
	● language art/prereading choice
10:00	Snack (at outside tables/cloths on warm days) or snack center during free play
10:15	Outside free play
	● climbing, swinging; sand and water, wheel toys, group games
12:00	Handwash and lunch

12:45	Get ready: toileting, handwashing, toothbrushing, prepare beds
1:15	Bedtime story
1:30	Rest time
2:30	Outdoors for those awake
3:30	Cleanup outdoors and singing time
4:00	Snacktime
4:15	Learning centers; some outdoor/indoor choices, field trips, story teller
5:30	Cleanup and read books until going home

Half-Day Kindergarten Plan

8:15–8:30	Arrival
	Getting ready to start
	● checking in library books, lunch money, etc.
8:30	Newstelling
	● "anything you want to tell for news"
	● newsletter written weekly
9:00	Work assignment
	● write a story about your news *or*
	● make a page in your book (topic assigned) *or*
	● work in math lab
9:30–10:15	Choice of indoors (paints, blocks, computer, table toys) or second-grade tutors read books to children
	● when finished, play in loft *or* read books until recess
10:15	Snack
10:30	Recess
10:45	Language: chapter in novel read *or* other language activity
11:15	Dance *or* game *or* visitor and snack
11:45	Ending: getting ready to leave
	● check out library books
	● gather art and other projects
12:00–1:30	for part of group each day
	Lunch, then:
	● field trips
	● writing lesson
	● math or science lab

Figure 9.27 ● Daily schedules reflect the children's needs and ages while meeting the program's goals. The time and timing of the school day show what is valued in the program.

Example: Older children can move through some transitions as a group, such as changing from one activity area to another or going out with a specialist in pairs or even in a single file. This is difficult for younger children, who would push or wander away. For them, the door to the yard opens quietly, allowing children to go out slowly.

Example: A child care class of 3- and 4-year-olds is dismissed from songtime to snack by the color of people's shirts, or the first letter of their names, rather than as one whole group. Figure 9.28 gives examples of handling transitions for all ages.

● The *structure* of the day changes with age.

Example: The balance of free-play and teacher-directed activities shifts from relatively few directed activities for younger children to some more for the nursery school and child care ages. The kindergarten schedule provides more structure both in individual work projects and teacher-focused time. A first-grade schedule with some whole-group teacher instruction times is developmentally appropriate for those older children.

● The *content of group activities* changes with age.

Example: In the toddler class, group times are simple: a short fingerplay, story with a flannel board or puppets, or a song to dismiss is adequate. Preschool group times include several songs, a dramatization of a favorite fingerplay, and a short story. By kindergarten, groups can last 15 to 20 minutes, with announcement and weather board, children's "newstelling," longer dramas, and even chapter stories.

The temporal environment thus mirrors the children's age and individual interests. In this regard it is useful to note that many programs divide the day into relatively small segments of time. This is done because adults believe that young children, particularly preschoolers, have such short attention spans that they cannot remain at an activity for long. However, we know that children can stay focused for long periods of time on activities of their choice or interest. Although they may last only a short time in teacher-planned, structured activities, children need and thrive with more time to get their own creative juices flowing. Children can spend hours with blocks, Legos®, sand, water, and dramatic play. Consult Figure 9.27 to see how the temporal environment allots time for such endeavors.

The Interpersonal Environment

A child responds to everything in school: the color of the room, the way the furniture is arranged, how much time there is to play, and how people treat one another. To the child, everything is a stimulus. The *feeling* in a room is as real as the blocks or the books. Thus, the interpersonal or social aspects of an early childhood setting are powerful components of the environment.

Children are the most important people in the setting; they should feel safe and comfortable. A warm, interpersonal environment invites children to participate and to learn. When children feel secure with one another and with the setting, they will be able to engage more fully in the total program.

Parents matter in the life of school, especially in the early years. The way people feel about each other and how they express their feelings have an impact on children. Teachers have to see children within their family and social context, and to do so, they must invite families into the schooling process, as in these situations:

> You can't believe it; no matter how many times you tell Kai's Chinese grandfather that school starts at 9 AM, he continues to bring him between 9:30 and 10 . . . until you find out that in China, old people are often late and the people respect their habits. *Now you may need to flex your schedule to allow for this late arrival and support this family custom.*

> Elena's father is large and speaks with such an accent you can hardly understand him. You'd like to just avoid talking with him, but then you'd connect only when there's a problem . . . and you discover that, in his Central American culture, teachers' ideas are to be solicited for parents to be seen as "good parents." *Now you may need to overcome your discomfort and ask him respectfully to repeat what he is saying a bit more slowly.*

> Every day Maryam brings her lunch, and it is so difficult to manage. These Iranian foods are not the same as the other children's, and there is often teasing that you have to keep redirecting. You wonder if you should simply tell her auntie to send her with a sandwich . . . only you realize that everyone wants to eat familiar foods, and

TRANSITION TIMES MADE EASIER

Questions for Planning

● Who is involved in the transition time (child, parents, teachers, other children, visitors, etc.)?
● What kind of activity has preceded the transition time and what will follow?
● What will the children be asked to *do* during transition?
● What will the teachers be doing *during* transition?
● How will the children be told or find out what to do during the transition?
● What do you know about child development and this particular child(ren) that can help with these questions?

Teaching Strategies

Arrival

● Greet each child with a smile and welcome child and parent with what activities are available.
● Make name cards and/or an attendance sheet that child and parent can participate in as a starting point.
● Plan with parents, and alert the child, a simple and clear way for them to say goodbye and for the parents to leave (see Chapter 8 for details).

Cleanup Materials

● Give the children a 5-minute "warning" to alert them to upcoming changes.
● Have a consistent and calm signal to start putting away toys.
● Use music as background and/or sing during cleanup.
● Consider having necklaces or cards of specific areas for children, or make teams.
● Construct the environment so that it is clear where things go and children can do the majority of it themselves.
● Occasionally thank the children publicly for cleaning up, noting individual efforts and specific chores done well.

Preparing Children to Attend

● Make a chart that shows the choices available.
● Sing a song or familiar fingerplay to get everyone's attention and participation.
● Ask the children to put on "elephant ears" (rabbit, etc.) or lock their lips and put the key in their pockets.

Ready to Rest/Naptime

● Prepare the environment ahead of time to be restful—darkened room, soft blanket/cuddlies nearby, quiet music, teachers whispering and available to walk children to their places and stay with them.
● Read a story to the group in one place before they are to lie quietly, or split larger groups into small subgroups with a teacher reading to each.

Moving to Another Place/Building

● Gather the group and tell them exactly what will be happening.
● Ask for ideas of how to behave ("What will we need to remember? How can we stay safe and have fun together?") and reinforce with a few concrete rules.
● Have the children be a train, with adults as the engine and caboose, or a dragon with head and tail.
● Have the children choose a partner to stay with and hold hands.
● Ask preschoolers and early primary children to remember the "B" words ("beside or behind") in staying near adults.

Waiting for Others to Finish

● Prepare a part of the room for children to move to, such as a book corner or listening post, having an adult in that space with more than two children.
● Make an apron or hanging with several pockets filled with activity cards or small manipulatives for children to use alone.
● Plan a special table with folders or large envelopes with activities.
● Have a "waiting box" with special small items for these times only.

Figure 9.28 ● Transitions are a regular part of children's routines and should be learning times that are as well planned as other parts of the day.

letting Maryam eat what her parents want her to should also be coupled with having the other children learn some tolerance, too. *Now you might use the lunchtime situation to help everyone become curious and interested in new foods.*

The interpersonal connection between parent and teacher can bolster what happens to the child within the classroom and can offer the child a smooth transition between school and home. Learning is enhanced when parents and teachers come to communicate in supportive, nonthreatening ways.

Because it is understood that the single most important factor in determining the quality of a program is the teacher (see Chapter 5), it follows that teachers will be the key ingredient in determining the interpersonal "flavor" of a class. The first component of the National Academy's criteria for high-quality early childhood programs is the interactions among the staff and children (see Chapter 10). The human component, the connections among the people in a center or home, makes all the difference to young children, for they are the barometers of interpersonal tension or openness and freedom.

Just how important is the interpersonal environment? Although most experts agree that the relationship between teacher and child is important, extensive research has only recently begun to document exactly how teacher–child interactions occur and how variations in such interactions might be related to behaviors or other results in children. Quality in a program does seem to be determined by the interactions between children and adults and the relationships that such interactions develop. In fact, "researchers demonstrate a pattern of positive relationships between children's sensitive, involved interactions with teachers and children's enhanced development. The impacts of these types of interactions are likely to be seen in children's cognitive, socioemotional, and language development" (Kontos & Wilcox-Herzog, 1997). Such research confirms the findings of recent brain-based research and theories of Erikson, Bandura, and Vygotsky (see

Chapter 4) and confirms our belief that how teachers interact with children is at the heart of early childhood education.

Young children develop best through close, affectionate relationships with people, particularly adults. Although this is true for all young children, it is particularly important for children under 3 and those without facility in the dominant language spoken in the class. "The interpersonal aspect of environment is the central element affecting the quality of toddler play, more important than elaborateness of physical setting," declares Zeavin (1997). "Toddlers cannot talk about what is going on inside them. It is through their play that they externalize troubling feelings, work out emotional conflicts, and gain control of their world. . . . Every issue is a relationship issue." In a human and humane environment, people are respected, and the focus of the staff is on children's strengths and capabilities; limitations are seen as needs rather than liabilities. Teachers observe and engage children in interactions that include smiling, touching, listening, asking questions, and speaking on eye level. The language and tone of voice used are respectful and friendly, with children treated equally across lines of race, culture, language, ability, and sex.[1] Staff use positive guidance rather than punitive discipline techniques (see Chapter 7) and develop warm relationships with parents (see Chapter 8). What teachers do—and how they do it—determines what learning takes place in the class and how each child and family will respond.

The attitudes and behaviors of teachers affect children's behaviors. Questions teachers can ask themselves as they evaluate the quality of the environment are:

● Is there a feeling of mutual respect between children and adults?

● Do teachers pick up on nonverbal and verbal expressions of both girls and boys? Of children with varying abilities? Of children of color?

1 The first challenge is to recognize biases; the next is to restructure and expand perceptions; and the greatest challenge is the part that children are most likely to notice—how one speaks, truly feels, and behaves.

Figure 9.30 ● The teacher's posture and facial expressions show her respect for children and their learning pace and style.

- How do children treat one another?

- Do teachers model cooperative behavior with other adults and children? Do they show by example how to work through a disagreement or problem?

- Does the physical setup allow the teacher to focus on the children?

- Do housekeeping details keep teachers disconnected from children?

- Do teachers encourage children to use one another as resources?

- Do teachers take time to show children how to accomplish a task by themselves?

- Are girls complimented only on appearance and boys just for achievement? Are all children helped to appreciate similarities and differences?

- Do teachers use reasoning and follow-through?

- How and when do teachers interact with children?

- What are the teacher's posture and facial expression when involved in a problem situation?

- If I were a child, would I like to come to school here?

The answers to these questions provide teachers with a barometer of how well they are maintaining an atmosphere of positive social interaction. The most important thing to remember is that the way people feel about each other and how they express their feelings have an impact on children. Teachers must focus as much attention on the interpersonal part of the environment as they do on buying equipment or arranging the room. Chapter 11, on play, and Chapter 14, on social and emotional skills, will emphasize the interpersonal aspects of the environment further.

Summary

A good environment for young children is a combination of many factors. Teachers must consider the needs of the children, teachers, and parents as well as the program goals and objectives.

The physical environment includes the buildings and yard, the equipment and materials, and the way the space is organized and used. The setting is organized to support the program's goals and must meet necessary health and safety standards.

The daily schedule outlines the timetable of events. Time blocks are arranged around the daily routines of food, rest, and toileting. The temporal environment is balanced so that children alternate indoor and outdoor play, quiet and active play, and self-selected activities with teacher-directed learning. Good interactions between children and staff are characterized by warmth, personal respect, and responsiveness. It is the interpersonal relationships that set the tone in each environment. The size of the group, the number of teachers per child, and the quality of relationships affect the interpersonal environment.

It is essential to have a clear idea of program goals before arranging the environment. The environment mirrors those goals in the way the room is arranged, teachers are deployed, and the time schedule is framed. In early childhood settings where children's independence and self-reliance are valued, the environment is created to enhance the child's budding sense of autonomy. Anti-bias environments value individual differences in race, ethnicity, ability, and gender to help children develop positive identities. Inclusive environments help children and teachers alike see every child, regardless of ability, as competent and every place as adaptable for all. Such environments build attitudes and institutions that support social justice. A peace education framework encourages children to learn to cooperate and resolve conflicts peaceably, as well as increase an understanding of war and peace. All environments reflect the goals through careful application of many factors.

Creating good environments for young children does not require great sums of money or newly designed buildings. In most settings, teachers can adapt general principles of environments to create challenging, safe, and effective group settings for children.

Review Questions

1. Why is there no standard or ideal environment for early childhood schools? How would you describe a good environment for 1-year-olds? For 3-year-olds? For 6-year-olds? Why?

2. What are the three aspects of environments to consider when planning programs for children? What do you think of first and why?

3. Why is self-help a common goal in most early childhood settings? How can teachers support self-help in infants? In toddlers? In nursery schoolers? In school-aged children?

4. Discuss three school health and safety policies that help keep illness and injury to a minimum. Include how you would explain these guidelines to parents and how you would handle a problem.

5. Why might educators want to create an anti-bias environment? How might that look in a multiethnic community? In a homogeneous setting?

6. Look at the daily schedule of an early childhood program. What transitions occur in the daily schedule, and how are they handled?

7. What kinds of adaptations might be needed to provide an inclusive environment for children with motor disabilities? With visual impairments?

Learning Activities

1. Hunch down on your knees and look at a classroom from the child's perspective. Describe what you see in terms of the principles of successful environments.

2. Examine a daily schedule from an early childhood center. What do you think are the program goals of the school? How can you tell? Compare this with a daily schedule of a family day care home. How are they alike? How are they different?

3. Below are listed some common problems that can be remedied by changing the environment. List at least one solution for each problem.

   a. Too many children crowding into one area

   b. Overcrowded shelves

   c. Grabbing or arguments over the same toy

   d. Hoarding of materials

   e. Lack of cooperation during cleanup

   f. Wheel toy collisions

   g. Children crying when others' parents leave

4. Visit a toddler program, a 4-year-old program, and a kindergarten. How are the learning centers defined? Name the centers of interest and indicate which of them are for quiet play and which are for active play and work.

5. Check a classroom for diversity. Using the checklist below (de Melendez & Ostertag, 1997), enter a checkmark whenever you find something in the classroom that complies with the element of diversity.

Checking the classroom environment for diversity

	ELEMENT OF DIVERSITY				
	Ethnicity	**Gender**	**Social class**	**Disability**	**Age**
Pictures/posters					
Books					
Housekeeping Items					
Manipulatives					
Art materials					
Dramatic area					
Music					

Comments:

• Things I need to change:

• Things I need to add:

Bibliography

Alexander, N. P. (1995, September). Turning on the light: Thinking about lighting issues in child care. *Exchange*.

Ambery, M. E. (1997, May). Time for Franklin. *Young Children, 52.*

Aronson, S. (1995). *Keeping healthy: Parents, teachers, and children.* Washington, DC: National Association for the Education of Young Children.

Bredekamp, S. (Ed.). (1986–87). *Developmentally appropriate practice in early childhood programs serving children from birth through age 8* (Expanded ed.). Washington, DC: National Association for the Education of Young Children.

Bredekamp, S. (Ed.). (1991). *Accreditation and criteria procedures* (Rev. ed.). Washington, DC: National Association for the Education of Young Children.

Bredekamp, S., & Willer, B. (Eds.), (1996). *NAEYC accreditation: A decade of learning and the years ahead.* Washington, DC: National Association for the Education of Young Children.

Bronson, M. B. (1995). *The right stuff for children birth to 8.* Washington, DC: National Association for the Education of Young Children.

Campbell, S., & Frost, J. (1985). The effects of playground type on the cognitive and social play behavior of grade two children. In J. P. Frost, & R. A. Sutherlin (Eds.), *When children play.* Wheaton, MD: Association for Childhood Education International.

Carlsson-Paige, N., & Levin, D. (1990). *Peace, war, and the nuclear threat.* Washington, DC: National Association for the Education of Young Children.

Centers for Disease Control and Prevention (1997). *The ABCs of safe and healthy child care.* Atlanta, GA: Author.

Copeland, M. L. (1996, January). Code blue! Establishing a child care emergency plan. *Exchange*.

Cross, W. E. (1985). Black identity: Rediscovering the distinctions between personal identity and reference group orientations. In Spencer, Brookins, & Allen (Eds.). *Beginnings: The social and affective development of black children.* Hillsdale, NJ: Erlbaum.

De Melendez, W. R., & Ostertag, V. (1997). *Teaching young children in multicultural classrooms: Issues, concepts, and strategies.* Albany, NY: Delmar.

Derman-Sparks, L., & the ABC Task Force. (1989). *Anti-bias curriculum: Tools for empowering young children.* Washington, DC: National Association for the Education of Young Children.

Dodge, D. T., & Colker, L. J. (1992). *The creative curriculum* (3rd ed.). Washington, DC: Teaching Strategies.

Edwards, C., Gandini, L, & Forman, G. (1993). *The hundred languages of children.* Norwood, NJ: Ablex Press.

Fowler, W. J. (1992). *What do we know about school size? What should we know?* Washington, DC: Office of Educational Research and Improvement.

Froschl, M., Rubin, E., & Sprung, B. (1984). *Including all of us: An early childhood curriculum about disabilities.* New York: Educational Equity Concepts.

Frost, J. L. (1986). Children's playgrounds: Research and practice. In G. Fein & M. Rivkin (Eds.), *The young child at play: Review of research* (Vol. 4). Washington, DC: National Association for the Education of Young Children.

Greenman, J. (1988). *Caring spaces, learning places.* Redmond, WA: Exchange Press.

Greenman, J. (1994, March). It seemed to make sense at the time. *Exchange*.

Gutierrez, M. E. (1982). *Chicano parents' perceptions of their children's racial/cultural awareness.* Unpublished master's thesis, Pacific Oaks College, Pasadena, CA.

Harms, T., & Clifford, R. M. (1989). *Early childhood environmental rating scale, family day care, and infant-toddler environmental rating scales.* New York: Teachers College.

Haugen, K. (1997, March). Using your senses to adapt environments: Checklist for an accessible environment: Beginnings workshop. *Child Care Information Exchange.*

Hernandez, A. (1991, July 8). What do we have in common? *Time.*

Honig, A. S. (1983). Sex role socialization in early childhood. *Young Children, 38*(6), 57–90.

Kendall, F. (1996). *Diversity in the classroom* (2nd ed.). New York: Teachers College Press.

Kendrick, A. S., Kaufmann, R., & Messenger, K. P. (Eds.). *Healthy young children: A manual for programs.* Washington DC: National Association for the Education of Young Children.

Kontos, S., & Wilcox-Herzog, A. (1997, January). Research in review: Teachers' interactions with children: Why are they so important? *Young Children, 52.*

Kutner, B. (1984). Patterns of mental functioning associated with prejudice in children. *Psychological Monographs, 72,* pp. 406.

Malaguzzi, L. (1993, November). For an education based on relationships. *Young Children,* pp. 9–12.

Marotz, L., Rush, J. M., & Cross, M. Z. (1993). *Health, safety, and nutrition for the young child* (3rd ed.). Albany, NY: Delmar.

Moore, G. T. (1983). *The role of the socio-physical environment in cognitive development.* Milwaukee, WI: University of Wisconsin.

Moore, G. T. (1996, June, September, November; 1997, January, March). Child care facility design. *Exchange.*

National Association for the Education of Young Children. (1991). *Accreditation criteria and procedures of the National Academy of Early Childhood Programs* (Rev. ed.). Washington, DC: Author.

National Association for the Education of Young Children. (1995). *Keeping healthy: Parents, teachers, and children.* Washington, DC: Author.

National Resource Center for Health and Safety in Child Care. (1997). *Stepping stones to caring for our children.* Washington, DC: U.S. Department of Health and Human Services.

Needlman, R., & Needlman, G. (1995, November/December). 10 most common health problems in school. *Scholastic Early Childhood Today.*

Nelson, M. A., & Raymond, B. (1989, September). Sports, kids, fun, & safety. *Good Housekeeping,* pp. 4, 52.

New, R. (1990, September). Excellent early education: A city in Italy has it. *Young Children.*

Phyfe-Perkins, E., & Shoemaker, J. (1986). Indoor play environments: Research and design implication. In G. Fein & M. Rivkin (Eds.), *The young child at play: Reviews of research* (Vol. 4). Washington, DC: National Association for the Education of Young Children.

Prescott, E. (1994, November). The physical environment—A powerful regulator of experience. *Exchange Magazine.*

Prescott, E., Jones, E., & Kritschevsky, S. (1972). *Group care as a child-rearing environment.* Washington, DC: National Association for the Education of Young Children.

Pressma, D., & Emery, J. (1991). *Serving children with HIV infection in child day care.* Washington, DC: Child Welfare League of America.

Rogers, C. (1994, Spring). Mainstreaming: Special needs—Special experiences. Unpublished paper.

Sprung, B. (1975). *Non-sexist education for young children.* New York: Citation Press.

Stonehouse, A. (1990, November/December). The Golden Rule for child care. *Exchange.*

Waldorf School (author unknown). (1995, January). *What is a Waldorf kindergarten?* Los Altos, CA: Author.

Whitebrook, M. (1996). NAEYC accreditation as an indicator of quality: What research tells us. In S. Bredekamp & B. Willer (Eds.), *NAEYC accreditation: A decade of learning and the years ahead.* Washington, DC: National Association for the Education of Young Children.

Youcha, V., & Wood, K. (1997, March). Enhancing the environment for ALL children: Beginnings workshop. *Exchange.*

Zeavin, C. (1997, March). Toddlers at play: Environments at work. *Young Children, 52*(4).

ACKNOWLEDGMENT

Special thanks to Cañada College students Laura Colker, Ingrid Hernandez, and Kim Payne.

Evaluating for Effectiveness

CHAPTER 10

Questions for Thought

What is evaluation?

Why is evaluation important?

What are the components of good evaluations?

What are some common problems?

What is important to know about standardized testing and developmental and readiness screening?

How can children be assessed?

What are critical issues in teacher evaluation?

How can evaluating programs help children and teachers?

EVALUATION

Evaluations are a part of everyday life. We look out the window and assess the weather situation, then decide if we want to carry an umbrella. Before making a purchase, we read the label on the box of crackers. We size up a person we have just met. We check the newspapers to find out where our favorite football team is ranked.

We are constantly evaluating, judging, and rating. In education, we evaluate:

● *Curriculum.* Will this language game help develop the listening skills of 3-year-olds?

● *Materials and equipment.* If we order the terrarium, will there be enough money for the math lab?

● *The environment.* Should the children begin school with free play or a group time? Where can we store the nap cots? Do the cubbies create a hazard out in the hallway?

● *Children's behavior.* Evan and Francie interrupt each other too much. Should they be placed in separate work groups?

● *Teacher effectiveness.* Sandra has a knack for making parents comfortable in her classroom. Audrey finds leading large groups difficult. Karl supervises student teachers with great skill. How can each be challenged supportively? How can each learn from the other?

What Is Evaluation?

Definition

Evaluation is a process. It is at once a definition, an assessment, and a plan. Defining the kind of weather outside helps a person evaluate what to wear. Assessing a person's manner and style determines whether or not to talk with that person at a party. Planning a meal involves evaluating who will be eating and what their food preferences may be. Evaluation involves making decisions, choices, and selections.

In its simplest form, evaluation is a process of appraisal. Think of the first time you ate at a new restaurant. What did you look for—the service, setting, range of menu, or costs? Were the portions related to the price? Were the clerks helpful or friendly? Would you go back or recommend it to a friend? We evaluate things on a daily basis, to understand and assess our lives and experiences. Making priorities about the relative importance of the menu or atmosphere of a restaurant is similar to planning how much space in the classroom will be given to blocks and art or how long a period will be devoted to free play or group times. Deciding whether to revisit a restaurant is akin to deciding if a certain activity is worth repeating with a classroom of children or whether to ask a teacher candidate for a second interview.

In educational circles, evaluations involve materials, people, and processes. Programs may be evaluated by taking an inventory of a school's curriculum and educational materials. Classroom organization may require mapping the environment, counting the number of play spaces in a room or yard, and evaluating the daily schedule. Observing and recording children's behavior could effectively evaluate behavior management techniques. Assessing teacher effectiveness requires gathering information about what teachers do and how they work. Feedback about performance is based on specific information concerning teacher behavior. Program evaluation might involve analyzing children, teachers, parents, and administration and how they all work together to meet the goals of the program.

Figure 10.1 ● Evaluations are part of everyday life in an early childhood setting. How are these children learning to listen? To relate to the teacher?

Premises

All evaluation procedures are based on three important premises:

1. *Evaluation must be part of the goal-setting process.* Without evaluation, goals are meaningless. Evaluation helps shape a goal into a meaningful plan of action. For instance, a family who wants to go weekend camping will have to decide what they need to pack their suitcases. In the classroom, teachers decide what they want their children to learn before ordering equipment for the program.

2. *Goals are based on expectations.* Everyone has standards for themselves and others. Standards are used to anticipate performance and behavior. Should the office buy a block of tickets to the upcoming soccer match? Many people would consider the team ranking and likelihood of a victory before making the decision. Teachers think about how 2-year-olds will use puppets or what use the 4-year-olds will make of wheel toys before purchasing equipment.

   In every early childhood setting, more than one set of expectations is at work. The director has job expectations of all the teachers. Teachers have standards of performance for themselves, the children, and parents. Parents have some expectations about what their children will do in school and about the role of the teachers. Children develop expectations regarding themselves, their parents, teachers, and the school.

3. *Evaluations determine the degree to which expectations are met.* By evaluating, people check to see if their goals have been realized. This can be as simple as listening for the doorbell after hearing a car stop outside. It can be as complex as changing the curriculum to match the group as its needs and interests emerge during a school year or as complex as analyzing questionnaires returned by parents. A good evaluation tool outlines clearly and specifically how expectations have been met. Evaluation is a system of mutual accountability. It is a way of stating expectations and defining how they are being met.

Why Evaluate?

In early childhood education, evaluations are used for several reasons. Teachers are aware that *evaluation* and *education* must be linked when creating good programs for children. To evaluate is to test the quality of the educational endeavor. Teachers are becoming more sophisticated in informal and formal assessments, in combining their daily observations with high-quality instruments that give a rich and full picture of each child or of the class as a whole. *Evaluation monitors growth, progress, and planning.*

Evaluation is a way to look at where and how improvements can be made, to challenge methods, assumptions, and purposes. Teachers and children are rated for their level of development and areas of growth. Environments are assessed to see if they foster behavior and learning according to their stated goals. Total programs are evaluated to see if they accomplish their objectives. In fact, *evaluations provide information* by which to rate performance, define areas of difficulty, and look for possible solutions.

Setting goals is a third reason for evaluating. To be useful, an evaluation must include suggestions for improving the performance or behavior. The assessment tool that only describes a situation is an unfinished evaluation; goals for improvement must be established.

Components of a Good Evaluation

Certain elements are common to all evaluations. The following criteria serve as a guideline to good evaluations:

1. *Select who or what will be evaluated.* Decide how often and under what circumstances the evaluation will take place.

2. *Have a clear purpose or motive.* Know the reasons you are making an evaluation and consider who or what will benefit from the process. State what you expect to gain from it.

3. *Decide how the data will be collected.* Have a good understanding of the process or format that will be used. For a report, discover what tools you might need and what is available to you. Outline who will collect the data and make the report. If more than one person is reporting, check for consistency among the evaluators. Sample tools for data collection may be found in Chapter 6 as well as later in this chapter.

4. *Know what use will be made of the evaluation.* Be aware of what decisions will be made from the

Figure 10.2 ● Know the reasons for making an evaluation. Evaluations should avoid unfair comparisons, acknowledge individual differences and uniqueness, and not look at children in a competitive manner.

results. Know who receives this information and how they will interpret it.

5. *State goals clearly.* Make sure goals and objectives are outlined in ways that can be measured and observed easily. State behavioral goals in terms of what the person will do.

6. *Make a plan.* Be prepared to act. Use the results to motivate people to put into action what they learned from the evaluation. Set new goals. Continue the process for another stated period of time. Set up a timetable to check progress on a regular basis.

Evaluations are deliberate and systematic ways to judge effectiveness. Because they are based on goals and expectations, all evaluations need some kind of **feedback loop** to recycle what is perceived (Steps 1–4) into action for improvement (Steps 5 and 6). Figure 10.21 illustrates how a feedback loop works for

teacher evaluation. The important point to remember is that evaluation should be a continuous process, for without follow-through, long-lasting improvement is unlikely to occur.

Concerns

Of all the functions performed by teachers, probably none calls for more energy, time, and skill than evaluation. Be it of children, teaching, or the overall program, evaluation is challenging, sometimes one of the more difficult tasks teachers must perform. Anyone involved in evaluation should avoid:[1]

1. *Unfair comparisons.* Evaluations should be used to identify and understand the person or program involved, not to compare one with another in a competitive manner.

 OUR DIVERSE WORLD OUR DIVERSE WORLD OUR DIVERSE WORLD OUR DIVERSE WORLD OUR DIVERSE WORLD OUR DIVERSE WORLD OUR DIVERSE WORLD OUR DIVERSE WORLD

[1] Numbers 1–6 are directly related to working in our diverse world.

2. *Bias*. Evaluations can label unfairly or prematurely the very people they are intended to help. Typecasting will not produce a useful assessment. Insufficient data and overemphasis on the results are two areas that need close monitoring. Evaluation tools should be free of language bias or other cultural bias.[1] For instance, an evaluation of children should not include experiences not familiar to the cultural group being assessed.

3. *Overemphasis on norms*. Most evaluation tools imply some level of normal behavior or performance, acceptable levels of interaction, or quantities of materials and space. People involved in an evaluation must remember to individualize the process rather than try to fit a person or program into the mold created by the assessment tool.[2]

4. *Interpretation*. There is sometimes a tendency to overinterpret or misinterpret results. Whether the evaluation assesses a child's skill, a teacher's performance, or an educational program, it must be clear *what* is being evaluated and *how* the information will be used. It is particularly important to be sensitive to the feelings of those being evaluated when communicating the results of the assessment. Parents and teachers need to interpret evaluations clearly and carefully if they are to understand the findings and feel comfortable with them.

5. *Too narrow a perspective*. An evaluation tool may focus too much on one area and not enough on others. Moreover, no single occasion or instrument will tell teachers all they need to know about a child's abilities, a teacher's performance, or a program's effectiveness. It is essential that information be gathered in many ways and on several occasions. Using a single yardstick to assess program effectiveness, for example, would ignore the comprehensive nature of the goals that most early childhood programs are designed to attain. These goals may encompass all areas of development while providing services for children and their parents that affect the health and well-being of the whole family. Sampling only children's skills as the single measure would lead to conclusions that were neither reliable nor valid. An imbalanced assessment gives an incomplete picture.

6. *Too wide a range*. An evaluation should be designed for a single level or age group and not cover too wide a range. It is appropriate to measure a child's ability to print at age 6 but not at age 2. A teacher's aide should not be evaluated by the same standards used to rate head or supervising teachers. What is expected of the person or task should be taken into account and the evaluation method modified accordingly.

7. *Too little or too much time*. The amount of time necessary to complete an evaluation must be weighed. The evaluation that is too lengthy loses its effectiveness in the time it takes. Time for interpretation and reflection must be included in the overall process.

For evaluations to be most productive, teachers must use caution in selecting an assessment method. Often, they will rework a common technique to meet their needs better. For instance, a testing tool could be used to describe children's skills, but the averages that accompany the test could be discarded. In this way, teachers would avoid overemphasizing norms (Caution 3), making unfair comparisons (Caution 1), or typecasting the children according to the results (Caution 2).

Sometimes a staff or administrator will design an instrument rather than using one already devised. Individualizing the evaluation process can thus balance an assessment, giving a perspective that is more in tune with the individual or program in a particular setting (Caution 5). Periodic evaluation checks give more than one set of results so that early childhood personnel are less likely to misinterpret or overemphasize the data (Caution 4). A comprehensive evaluation done semiannually is more time efficient than a lengthy, detailed one done only once every year or so (Caution 7). In all evaluations, it is important to keep in mind that children and teachers are at various stages of development and skill; an assessment that is individualized or one in which a range of scores is acceptable allows for these variations (Caution 6).

OUR DIVERSE WORLD OUR DIVERSE WORLD OUR DIVERSE WORLD OUR DIVERSE WORLD OUR DIVERSE WORLD OUR DIVERSE WORLD OUR DIVERSE WORLD OUR DIVERSE WORLD
[1,2] As we become aware of those we teach, we must adjust our evaluation systems to avoid bias and to reflect reality accurately.

Evaluations in the Early Childhood Setting

In the educational setting, the process of evaluation is separate from the teaching or instructing process even when it is based on the teaching or learning as it happens. Judging an activity, a child's growth, or a teacher's performance is something "extra," apart from the everyday routine of the class. Yet it need not always be so. Teaching and evaluating are closely integrated. As teachers examine how they work, they also look at the effect this has on the children, the curriculum, parent relationships, and themselves.

Evaluation is a very broad concept, often confused with testing and measurement. Formal testing or separated assessment is only one way of measurement. To be truly accurate, evaluations of children, teachers, and programs must be done in a multitude of ways, with a combination of informal and formal methods.

The teacher plays a critical role in the evaluation process. Through evaluation, teachers link specific goals to larger, more encompassing objectives, such as those illustrated in Figure 10.4. These goals focus on the relationship between teaching in the classroom and the overriding educational objectives. The teacher sees the broad picture and keeps a perspective on education that includes the children, the program, and the teaching staff.

The three areas of evaluations we discuss in this chapter are (1) evaluating children, (2) evaluating teachers, and (3) evaluating programs. The purposes

Figure 10.3 ● Evaluations in programs with a wide age range may need to be individualized to adequately record children's skills.

Educational Aims	Behavioral Goals
To achieve independence and autonomy.	Children separate from their parents successfully; can manage their own clothing needs; initiate own activities.
To become a functional part of a larger society.	Children participate actively in small and large groups.
To learn to live effectively with others.	Children develop social skills with peers and adults, show tolerance of differences.
To learn basic tools for acquiring knowledge.	Children show signs of curiosity, memory, and symbol recognition.

Figure 10.4 ● Teachers relate what happens in the classroom (behavioral goals) to traditional educational goals.

underlying each type of evaluation will be examined, followed by specific techniques for effective evaluations.[1]

EVALUATING CHILDREN

How do we evaluate children? What do we look for? How do we document growth and difficulties? How do we communicate our findings to parents? These questions focus our attention on children's issues and the evaluation process.

Why Evaluate?

Children are evaluated because teachers and parents want to know what the children are learning. Evaluations set the tone for a child's overall educational experience. Highlighting children's strengths builds a foundation from which to address their limitations or needs. The process of evaluating children attempts to answer several questions: Are children gaining appropriate skills and behaviors? In what activities does learning take place? What part of the program supports specific learning? Is the school philosophy being met? Are educational goals being met?

Hills (1993) and others identify clear purposes for assessing children:

1. Educational planning and communicating with parents

2. Identifying children with special needs

3. Program evaluation and accountability

In other words, evaluation processes can help teachers discover who children are, what they can (and cannot) do, and how we can help children grow and learn.[2]

In evaluating children, teachers first decide *what it is they want to know about each child, and why.* With an understanding of children in general, teachers then concentrate on individual children and their unique development. Goals for children stem from program objectives. For instance, if the school philosophy is, "Our program is designed to help children grow toward increasing physical, social, and intellectual competencies," an evaluation will measure children's progress in those three areas. One that claims to teach specific language skills will want to assess how speaking and listening are being accomplished.

Evaluations provide teachers with an opportunity to distance themselves from the daily contact with children and look at them in a more detached, professional way. Teachers can use the results to share their opinions and concerns about children with each other and with parents. For instance, an infant and toddler center might schedule parent conferences around a sequence of child evaluations: the first, a few weeks after the registration of the child; the second, 6 months after the child's admission into the program; and the third, just before the move up to an older age group (such as moving from the infant to the toddler class), which would include the parents and two teachers, the current and the receiving one. This concentrated effort expands everyone's vision of who and what the child can be, highlights patterns of the child's behavior, and helps in understanding the meaning of that behavior. It gives teachers the chance to chart growth and acknowledge progress and, in doing so, sets the child apart as an individual and unique human being. Evaluations are a reminder to all that they work with individuals and not just a group.

Of course, evaluations contain varying degrees of subjectivity and opinion. For an evaluation to be reliable and valid, multiple sources of information should be used. Chapter 6 contains specific tools for direct observation of children, and Chapter 8 discusses parent interviews, both of which are useful in assessing children (Cryan, 1986; Meisels, 1989). Observing young children in action is the key to early childhood assessment, and readers will notice that most of the child evaluation instruments described in this chapter are based on what children do spontaneously or in their familiar, natural settings. As Schweinhart (1993) puts it, "the challenge of early childhood assessment is to apply the methods of the assessment field to the goals of the early childhood field." A proper evaluation of a child documents a child's growth over time (e.g., keeping a portfolio of the child's creations, dictations, teacher observations—anecdotes of behavior or snips of conversations overheard). The Focus Box by Nancy

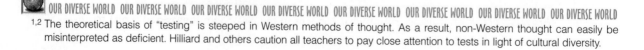

[1,2] The theoretical basis of "testing" is steeped in Western methods of thought. As a result, non-Western thought can easily be misinterpreted as deficient. Hilliard and others caution all teachers to pay close attention to tests in light of cultural diversity.

Barbour offers some key ideas about child assessment in a portfolio format.

In general, evaluations are made to:

1. Establish a baseline of information about each child by which to judge future progress.

2. Monitor the growth of individual children.

3. Have a systematic plan for intervention and guidance.

4. Plan the curriculum.

5. Provide parents with updated information on their child.

6. Provide information for making administrative decisions.

To Establish a Baseline

One purpose of evaluating children is to establish a starting point of their skills and behavior. This is the beginning of a collection over a period of time of important information on each child. Through this cumulative record, teachers learn a great deal about the children: whom they play with, how they spend their time, how they handle problems, what fears and stress they show. In other words, they learn a lot about how children live their lives.

A **baseline** is a picture of the status of each child; an overview of individual development. It shows where the child is in relation to the school's objectives because the child is being measured according to program expectations. Baseline data give a realistic picture of a child at that moment in time, but there is a presumption that the picture will change.

A Baseline Tool. The beginning of the school term is an obvious time to start collecting information. Records of a child are established in the context of the child's history and family background. Parents frequently submit this information with an application to the school. Teachers can gather the data by visiting the child at home or holding a parent conference and speaking directly with the parents about the child's development.

An **entry-level** *assessment* made during the first few weeks of school can be informative, particularly when added to the child's family history. The evaluation itself should be done informally, with teachers collecting information as children engage naturally

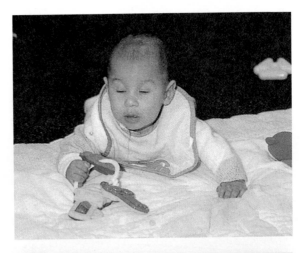
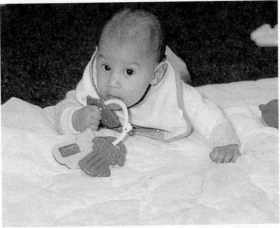

Figure 10.5 ● A baseline is a picture of a child framed at a particular moment. Infants' use of materials, fine-muscle control, and task persistence can all be seen in these assessments.

Assessment

Nancy Barbour

Journal Entry 4-2-99

Today three children spent the entire morning wrapping and unwrapping "presents" for me. All they needed were small objects, tape, scissors, and paper. They took great delight in my surprise as I opened each present and found lovely objects. So what are these 3-year-olds thinking as they work so diligently? I listened to them from a distance as they chatted: "This is the best surprise. . . . Susan won't know where we got this pretty necklace for her."

"You're not putting enough tape on that; let me tape it more."

"When we buy presents for my grandma, we find things she likes and doesn't have . . . then we give the store person a plastic card and then we go home and wrap it up for her . . . she cries when she opens presents."

"Susan didn't cry when she opened this. . . . do you think she liked it?"

"Maybe Susan doesn't like to cry at school."

They seem to be thinking about what presents mean and maybe what it means to give someone something they really want. How can I extend their play, go beyond the repetitive activity and explore something that makes them think more deeply?

Susan's journal entry has much to tell us about the activity of three children in her classroom. She has written this entry as a way of processing what she sees happening in her classroom, as a way of examining what she sees as the children's interests, and as a way of reflecting on where she wants to go

with the interests demonstrated. Her journal entry has information about the children's fine-motor skills, their language ability, and their awareness of family and others' feeling.

Nora, another teacher, has been collecting data about their children in other ways. She has completed a child development checklist, written anecdotal records on each child at least once a week, collected examples of their artwork, taken photos of their constructive play, and had each family complete a survey. She is using all of this information to develop an individual portfolio for each child. Every week she scans the children's portfolios and determines her curriculum plan for the next week. She considers what interests are evident in the portfolios, what skills are still emerging for some, and what social levels of play she hopes to facilitate among children who are not seeking others for play partners.

Both teachers are doing careful observation of young children to address the needs and interests in their respective classrooms. They are engaged in assessment. What is assessment, and what purpose does it serve?

Assessment in early childhood is the quantitative and qualitative study of children's work, activity, and interactions for the purposes of planning curriculum and instruction, reporting progress toward goals, and conveying accountability to families, communities, and institutions. All teachers have some repsonsibility to assess so that they know who their children are, what they know, and how they will best respond to instruction. Their choices revolve around how, what, when, and where assessment occurs.

Authentic assessment, in particular, fits best with the overall goal of developmentally appropriate practice because it focuses on the whole child within the context of family, community, and society. Assessment is authentic when it occurs in the child's natural setting while the child is performing real tasks. Assessment is authentic when the information is used to make decisions relating to curriculum and instruction. Assessment is authentic when data are collected and organized over time, from multiple sources, and using a variety of methods. And, assessment is authentic when it is viewed as a process rather than a place or end. Portfolio assessment is often the form of choice when doing authentic assessment. It represents children's learning and development in a meaningful and systematic way.

The process of assessment is second nature to those teachers who view children in a holistic manner. For these teachers, the classroom is a dynamic, ever-changing community to be observed, documented, constructed, and re-constructed. Assessment, for them, is an integral part of what they do every day.

Susan and Nora are each performing the vital task of assessment in different yet meaningful ways. They have the power to share important information with children, parents, schools, and the community. And they are promoting the expectation in children that such documentation is essential in their lives.

Dr. Nancy Barbour is a faculty member of the College of Education at Kent State University. Her research and writing have focused on prekindergarten education, early childhood teacher preparation, history of child development laboratory schools, and portfolio assessment.

ENTRY-LEVEL ASSESSMENT

1. Child's name_____ Teacher_____
   Age_____ Sex_____
   Primary language_____ Fluency in English?_____
   Any previous school experiences?_____
   Siblings/others in household_____
   Family situation (one/two parents, other adults, etc.)_____

2. Separation from parent:
   Smooth_____ Some anxiety_____ Mild difficulty_____ Unable to separate_____
   Did parent have trouble separating?_____
   Comments: _____

3. How does child come to and leave from school?
   Parent_____ Car pool_____ Babysitter_____ Bus_____

4. Physical appearance:
   General health _____
   Expression _____
   Nonrestrictive clothing _____
   Body posture _____

5. Self-care:
   Dressing: Alone_____ Needs assistance _____
   Toileting: By self_____ Needs help _____
   Eating: _____
   Toothbrushing: _____
   Sleeping/resting: _____
   Allergies/other health-related problems: _____

6. Child's Interests:
   Indoors:
   Clay_____ Books_____ Puzzles_____ Water play_____ Easels_____ Language_____
   Table/rug toys_____ Sensory choices_____ Art_____ Science_____ Blocks_____
   Outdoors:
   Swings_____ Climbers_____ Sandbox_____ Water play_____
   Wheel toys_____ Animals_____ Group games_____ Woodworking_____
   Group times (level of participation): _____

7. Social-emotional development:
   a. Initiates activities_____ Plays alone_____ Seems happy_____ Has to be invited_____
      Brings security object_____ Seems tense_____
   b. Plays mostly with children of: Same age_____ Younger_____ Older_____
   c. Moves into environment: Easily_____ Hesitantly_____ Not at all_____ Wanders_____
   d. Special friends: _____
   e. Does the child follow teachers?_____ Anyone in particular?_____

8. Cognitive development:
   Use of language: Follows directions_____ Clear pronunciation_____ Memory_____
   Curiosity_____ Holds conversations_____ Words/Phrases_____

9. Physical development
   Climbs safely_____ Uses scissors_____ Hand preference_____ Runs smoothly_____
   Uses pens, brushes_____ Foot preference_____ Handles body well_____

10. Goals/Points to remember: _____
    _____
    _____

Figure 10.6 ● Entry-level assessments collect baseline information. Once teachers and children have had some time together, these first impressions can be documented.

with materials and each other. A few notes jotted during the first month of school can serve as a beginning collection of pertinent data about the child. Or the format can be more structured, such as in Figure 10.6.

Application. Teachers then use this information to understand children and their various levels of development. They can see children's strengths and weaknesses and where future growth is likely to occur. When the information is shared with parents, they feel more relaxed about their child and even laugh when they recall those first few days of school. One must remember, however, that the entry assessment is only a first impression. Care must be taken to avoid creating a self-fulfilling prophesy by labeling children so that they become shaped into those beginning patterns. Again, teachers must be mindful of the cautions associated with all assessments as they document children's early behaviors. Still, so much happens in that short period of time; the rich information we gain from documenting this growth is invaluable.

Goals and Plans. Teachers use baseline data to set realistic goals for individual children. They tailor the curriculum to the needs and interests they have observed. An entry-level assessment is a vehicle for watching children's growth throughout the year. For instance, after setting a baseline of Mariko's language ability in English, teachers plan activities to increase her understanding and use of language. Then, they make periodic checks on her increased vocabulary as the school year progresses.

To Monitor Children's Progress

Teachers use evaluations to document children's growth. Data collected provide evidence of children's growth or lack of progress. A careful evaluation of each child furnishes the teaching staff with the necessary foundation from which they can plan the next steps.

Hita has mastered the brushes at the easel. Now we can encourage her to try the smaller brushes in table painting.

Enrico has been asking how to spell simple words. Let's see that he gets some time away from the blocks to work at the writing center.

All the children seem able to separate from their parents and say good-bye comfortably. How can we celebrate this progress with the group?

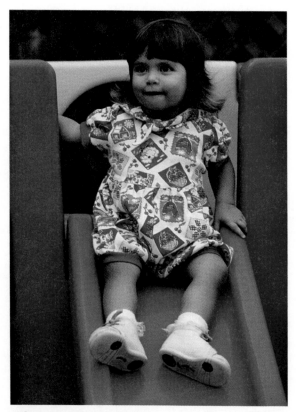

Figure 10.7 ● On her own! An evaluation can capture children's development in all skill areas, including self-concept.

A Progress Tool. Figure 10.8 is a sample *midyear evaluation*. Criteria for each area of development are included to build a profile of the whole child. Teachers note the intervention and guidance steps they plan, where appropriate. Although a general form is outlined here, early education teachers individualize their assessments to specify the skills of their group; an infant and toddler group would have different age-appropriate skills than would a preschool or primary-age class. Such a revised form should include what the child will do to show a suitable level of behavior in each developmental stage.

Application. Information about a child will be used to assess growth and change. How often this happens can vary. Although many changes occur in rapid succession in these early years, it takes time for a child to integrate life experiences and for teachers to see them expressed as a permanent part of behavior. Evaluating too frequently does not reveal sufficient change to make it worthwhile and places an added burden on the teaching staff as well.

A TOOL FOR MONITORING CHILDREN'S PROGRESS

Check one of the evaluations below for each skill area; for those that need work, document with specific examples.

Developmental Area	Age Appropriate	Highly Skilled	Needs Work
Self-Management			
Personal care	Can feed, dress, toilet self well		
Making choices	Prefers indoors to outside		
Following routines	Does fine in routines		
Physical/Motor			
1. Fine Motor	Uses easels—brushes good grasp, pens also		
Art materials	Likes blocks, table toys		
Woodworking tools	Hasn't chosen woodworking, but watches often		
Manipulatives			
		Very cautious, seems fearful	
2. Gross Motor		Won't swing, slide, use climber	
Ball handling		Wanders outdoors, sometimes does music	
Balancing		Runs away when wheel toys	
Jump/hop/skip		are rolled down hill	
Communication and Language			
Vocabulary		Exceptionally strong	
Articulation		Converses with adults daily	
Comprehension		Responds to children but rarely initiates talk	
English as a second language		Outstanding at grouptime—lots of ideas	
Converses with children		Talks around fears, but fears seem to keep him from trying	
Converses with adults			
Listens			
Expresses self (needs, ideas, feelings)			
Cognitive Development			
Sees cause and effect			
Processes and uses information			
Solves problems with:		Dylan has so much information to share, and lots of interest in	
objects		problem-solving with indoor materials and interactions with teachers.	
peers		We wish he could extend these skills into work with children and	
adults		open up at a bit more.	
Premath (sequencing, measuring, numbers)			
Prereading concepts (size, colors, shapes, letters, position)			
Social-Emotional			
Independence/initiative			
Positive self-concept	Does well on own, gets around		Seems hesitant/fearful outdoors
Recognizes/accepts own feelings	Is comfortable and confident		Is more solitary or onlooker; is
Deals with frustration	around adults		this self-esteem or just fear?
Flexibility			Don't know about leadership yet;
Leadership			have seen little because of lack
Initiates social contacts			of interaction with children
Prosocial behaviors (friendly, sharing, inclusive, cooperative, empathic)			
Child–child interactions			
Child–adult interactions			

OVERALL STRENGTHS: GOALS

Figure 10.8 ● A midyear evaluation is a more detailed description of the child. It highlights areas of concern and progress. (Developed by Bing Nursery School, Stanford University, 1975 to 1990.)

Figure 10.9 ● What do children need from a program? Evaluation assesses each individual's needs for guidance or help, such as learning to feed herself.

Once the initial baseline data have been gathered, a progress evaluation approximately every 3 months seems reasonable. In a normal school year, this would mean establishing a baseline in the fall and checking progress in the winter and the spring. For centers operating on a year-round basis, a brief summer report would be in order. These need not be time consuming. Many evaluations take the form of a checklist and can be accomplished while the class is in session.

Goals and Plans. Goals are established for children as a result of an assessment. These goals are changed as growth takes place. A good assessment tool monitors progress in each developmental area so that plans can be made to challenge the child physically, socially, emotionally, creatively, and intellectually.

At the same time, theory reminds us that the child develops as a whole, with each area of growth influencing and being influenced by what changes take place in other areas. Evaluations that document growth include information so that all teachers see the interrelationships among areas of development. By assessing growth in individual areas, teachers relate that development to the child's collective abilities, as in this example:

Dylan's midyear report shows that he lacks dexterity in running and climbing and that he is exceptionally strong in verbal and listening skills. This influences his development in the following areas:

Emotionally. He appears to lack self-confidence, and his self-esteem deteriorates the longer he feels inept at physical skills. He may even be afraid to master the art of climbing and running for fear he will fail.

Socially. Children tease Dylan because he often cannot keep up with them while playing outside. He often ends up playing alone or watching the other children in more active pursuits.

Intellectually. There is a lack of risk taking in Dylan's whole approach to play. Because of his slow physical development, he seems unlikely to challenge himself in other ways.

Dylan's progress report thus sets a primary goal in physical/motor skills, with the knowledge that such growth can positively affect learning in other areas. Teachers also plan the strategy of helping him talk about what he likes and dislikes about the outdoors and collecting some stories that depict characters persisting to master difficulties (such as *The Little Engine That Could*), using his strength as a springboard for growth.

To Plan for Guidance and Intervention

A third purpose for evaluation is to help teachers determine guidance procedures. These are based on insights and perceptions brought into focus through the evaluation. This process serves as a primary tool on which guidance and planning are based. When teachers see a problem behavior or are concerned about a child, they plan for further assessment (see Chapter 7). If a developmental screening is done to assess if a child has a learning problem or needs special services, teachers will either refer the family to a proper specialist or agency or administer the screening themselves. Developmental screening tests will be discussed further in this chapter.

A Guidance Tool. Evaluations help in behavior management. Once a need has been pinpointed, the teaching staff decides how to proceed. Individual

CHILDREN GUIDANCE FORM

Presentation of Problems (In behavioral terms)

What behaviors are causing the staff concern? Be specific. Limit to three problems or concerns.

1.

2.

3.

Family History (Information from family, medical info if needed)

School History (Child's relations to adults, children, materials, activities)

Intervention (What procedures have and have not worked? What strengths does the child bring to this issue?)

Future Plans (What is going to happen as a result?)

1. In classroom

2. With parents

3. Date for reviewing results

Figure 10.10 ● One purpose of evaluating children is to plan for behavior management. A good evaluation form will include how to follow through on the plans made for intervention. (Adapted from K. McLaughin and S. Sugarman, personal communications, 1982.)

problems are highlighted when teachers make a point of concentrating on the child's behavior. Figure 10.10 illustrates a form used to determine intervention. Used at a team meeting, this form demonstrates what steps are to be taken in addressing the concern directly. It also helps teachers clarify how to talk to parents in a concerned and supportive manner.

Application. The following case studies demonstrate how information from evaluations is used for guidance and intervention:

Elizabeth's recent evaluation revealed an increase in the number of toilet accidents she has had. The staff noted a higher incidence during midmorning snacks but came to no conclusion as to the cause. They agreed to continue to treat her behavior in a relaxed manner and have one teacher remind Elizabeth to use the toilet before she washes her hands for snack. At the same time,

they made plans to contact the parents for further information and insights. They will confer again afterward and agree on an approach.

Trevor's parents report that he says he has no friends at school. At their staff meeting, the teachers make plans to suggest that Trevor's parents invite Ryan and Brooke to play with Trevor at home. Teachers have seen both children approach him, but he didn't seem to know how to respond. At school, the teachers will give Trevor verbal cues when children make attempts to play with him.

Goals and Plans. An evaluation tool, such as the *child guidance form* in Figure 10.10, helps teachers set goals for children. Narrowing the focus to include only those behaviors that concern the staff enables the staff to quickly review the needs of many children.

Summary of Development/Fall Progress Reports (see forms for details)
Developmental Area: + = fine; – = needs work; ? = don't know

Child	Physical	Language	Cognitive	Social	Emotional	Creative
Greg	–	+	+	+	–	?
Anwar	?	–	+	–	–	+
San-Joo	+	?	?	–	+	+
Reva	+	+	+	+	+	+
Katy	–	+	?	?	?	–

Group Goals for Winter:
• Emphasize social and emotional areas of curriculum.
• Plan physical games (indoor games because of weather).
Individual Goals for Winter:
Greg: Encourage some creative arts, games. Observe creativity in intellectual activities.
Anwar: Needs to be helped to feel confident and express himself; don't push too hard on physical risks yet.
San-Joo: Need assessment of language and cognitive skills; observe use of table toys, receptive language at group time.
Reva: What is the next step? Is she ready for helping the others? Involve her with 100-piece puzzles and the computer.
Katy: Need to focus on her overall development; too many unknowns—is she getting enough individual attention?

Figure 10.11 ● A group chart. Teachers can use individual assessment tools to plan for the entire group and for each child in the class.

To Plan Curriculum

Teachers plan the curriculum the basis of on children's evaluations. Translating the assessment to actual classroom practice is an important part of the teacher's role. A thorough evaluation helps teachers plan appropriate activities to meet children's needs.

Planning Tools. All three of the previous evaluation tools can be used to plan curriculum. The entry-level assessment and midyear report are often summarized in a group chart, as in Figure 10.11. One such chart, made at the end of the first semester of a prekindergarten class, revealed this pattern:

At least one third of the class was having trouble listening at group time, as evidenced by the group chart that identified "Group Time" and "Language Listening Skills" as areas for growth for nearly half the children. The staff centered their attention on the group time content. It was concluded that a story made the group times too long;

the children were restless throughout most of the reading. It was agreed to move storytime to just before nap and shorten the group time temporarily.

Evaluation also applies to daily events, such as individual projects and the day as a whole. One tool for curriculum evaluation reviews the results of a specific activity. Figure 10.12 is a sample of that kind of curriculum assessment. Chapter 11 discusses the planning of curriculum in further details.

Application. Evaluation results assist teachers in seeing more clearly the strengths and abilities of each child in the class. Curriculum activities are then planned that will continue to enhance the growth of that child. Also, areas of difficulty will be identified:

Jolene has trouble mastering even the simplest puzzle. Provide her with common shapes found in attribute blocks (small plastic shapes of varying color, thickness, size) and do some matching exercises with her.

Activity _____

How many children participated? _____ Did any avoid the activity? _____

How involved did children become? Very _____ Briefly _____ Watched only _____

What were children's reactions? Describe what they said and did. _____

_____
_____
_____
_____

What did you do to attract children? To maintain their interest? _____

_____
_____
_____
_____

How would you rate the success of this activity? Poor _____
Adequate _____ Good _____ Great _____ Why? _____

What skills/abilities were needed? Did the children exhibit the skills? _____

_____
_____

What parts of the activity were most successful? Why? _____

_____
_____

Describe any difficulty you encountered. Give reasons and tell how you would handle it if it happened again. _____

_____
_____
_____

If you did this activity again, what would you change? _____

_____

In light of your evaluation, what would you plan for a follow-up activity? _____

_____

How did this activity compare with your goals and expectations? _____

_____

Figure 10.12 ● Evaluating daily activities lets teachers use assessment as a planning tool. Although not every activity will need this scrutiny on a daily basis, careful planning and evaluation create effective classrooms. (Adapted from Vassar College Nursery School.)

The younger children in the class are reluctant to try the climbing structures designed by the older ones. Build an obstacle course with the youngest children, beginning with very simple challenges and involving the children in the actual planning and building as well as rehearsing climbing techniques with them.

Goals and Plans. Each of the previous case studies demonstrates how evaluation tools can be used to plan

curriculum. By analyzing both group and individual skills through periodic assessment, teachers maintain a secure and challenging environment.

To Communicate with Parents

Plans for evaluating children should include the means by which parents are to be informed of the results. Once the teachers have identified a child's needs and capabilities, parents are entitled to hear the conclusions. The teaching staff has an obligation to provide a realistic overview of the child's progress and alert the parents to any possible concerns. (See Chapter 8 for details about parents and teachers working together.)

Using the child guidance form (see Figure 10.10), teachers define problem behavior for a child and work closely with the parents to reach a solution:

> Yum-Tong refuses to let his mother leave. The teachers agree that there are two issues: (1) Y.-T.'s screaming and crying as his mother leaves and (2) his inability to focus on an activity while she attempts to go (though she stays as soon as he starts screaming). The family has told them that their other two children had separation problems as preschoolers. The previous school asked the parents to stay until the children stopped protesting, although the parents report that this took nearly 6 months and so was a hardship for them in their workplaces.[1]

> The teachers choose to intervene by asking Yum-Tong's mother to plan ahead with Y.-T., deciding before school how they will spend 5 minutes together each morning. After playing and helping him to settle in, she will then say good-bye and leave Y.-T. with Pete, his favorite teacher. Pete will be prepared to be with him at the departure and stay with him until he calms down. They also plan to have a conference date after 2 weeks of this intervention plan to follow through and review how it is working for everyone.

A Tool with Parents. Teachers and parents need to talk together, especially when problems are revealed by the evaluation. As parents and teachers share knowledge and insights, a fuller picture of the child emerges for both. Each can then assume a role in the resolution of the problem. The role of the teacher will be defined in the context of the parents' role, and the parents will be guided by the teacher's attitudes and actions.

Evaluation tools can help parents target areas in which their child may need special help. A child guidance form (see Figure 10.10) is an effective tool for parent–teacher conferences and as a method for forming intervention plans. Chapter 8 discusses the parent–teacher relationship and offers guides for effective parent–teacher conferences. The tool that works best is one that summarizes the school's concerns and solicits high parent involvement.

Application. Aside from identifying normal behavior problems, evaluations may raise questions concerning a child's physical development, hearing and visual acuity, or language problems. Potentially serious problems may emerge from the evaluation, and parents can be encouraged to seek further professional guidance.

Goals and Plans. Because evaluation is an ongoing process, reevaluation and goal setting are done regularly. Communicating to parents both progress and new goals is critical for the *feedback loop* of an evaluation form to be effective, as shown in Figure 10.21 on page 369.

To Make Administrative Decisions

Evaluation results can help a school make administrative decisions. They can lead to changes in the overall program or in the school's philosophy. For example, a child care component might be added to the half-day program after learning that most children are enrolled in another child care situation after nursery school. Or an evaluation might conclude that there is too little emphasis on developing gross-motor skills and coordination. To invite more active play, the administration might decide to remodel the play yard and purchase new equipment.

In the early childhood setting, both **informal** and **formal methods** are used for evaluating children. *Informal* and *homemade methods* such as those in Chapter 6 and Figures 10.6, 10.8, 10.10, 10.11, and 10.12 include observation, note taking, self-assessments, parent interviews and surveys, samples

[1] Teachers need to examine theories of child development and practice for ethnocentricity (e.g., in Western-European and American culture it may be seen as the sign of a secure attachment if a parent and child separate comfortably and quietly, whereas in another culture a secure attachment may be demonstrated by a passionate and emotion-laden farewell).

Figure 10.13 ● Assessing the group is one reason to evaluate children. How can you tell if these children are ready for more engaging and challenging group-time activities?

of children's work, and teacher-designed forms. More *formal* kinds of *evaluations* are used also, although somewhat less frequently in the early years. These include standardized tests and various "screening" instruments. The yearly tests taken in elementary and secondary school, using a Number 2 pencil, are an example of such procedures. Those and other standardized forms are examples of formal methods of evaluation. Commercially developed, these tests usually compare the individual child's performance with a predetermined norm. There are problems associated with testing and screening of young children (see section "Testing and Screening" later in this chapter).

It is important to choose assessment tools and techniques that are appropriate for the group or the child under consideration. Informal observations can be made more systematic (see Chapter 6) or comprehensive to gain more information about a specific problem. Formal, commercially developed instruments need to be used more carefully if at all.

An Administrative Tool. Many kindergartens and some nursery schools use various kinds of "screening" tests before children begin school in the fall.[1] The usual purpose of these evaluations is to determine readiness: that is, to verify that the child will be able to cope with and succeed in school. These tools are best devised with the individual child in mind. Their purposes are positive: to highlight the skills the child has and to identify the areas in which the child may need help in the next class. Figure 10.14 shows a homemade screening evaluation that was developed for individual 4- to 5-year-old preschoolers who were

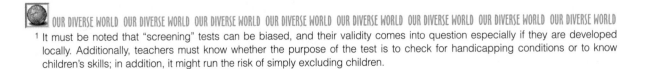

OUR DIVERSE WORLD OUR DIVERSE WORLD OUR DIVERSE WORLD OUR DIVERSE WORLD OUR DIVERSE WORLD OUR DIVERSE WORLD OUR DIVERSE WORLD OUR DIVERSE WORLD

[1] It must be noted that "screening" tests can be biased, and their validity comes into question especially if they are developed locally. Additionally, teachers must know whether the purpose of the test is to check for handicapping conditions or to know children's skills; in addition, it might run the risk of simply excluding children.

leaving for kindergarten. The activity uses a one-to-one, gamelike approach in which a child and a favorite teacher can explore both strengths and difficulties in a safe, supportive setting.

Some teachers conclude the year with a summary report. This evaluation serves as an overview of what a child has accomplished, what areas of strength are present, and what future growth might occur. These records are useful to parents as a summary of their child's learning experiences. Teachers may use them as references should they ever be consulted by another school about the child. Again, it is critical to administer these assessments in a sensitive and accepting manner, to keep the time period as brief as possible, and to communicate the results in the same tone. If this is not done, the child's self-esteem may be damaged and the parents' trust may be lost. The disadvantages of these tools parallel those of standardized tests (see next section).

Application. Making administrative decisions based on evaluation results is a sound idea. Assessments give administrators specific and verifiable information on which to base decisions.

The issue of readiness or placement of children is difficult and complex. The next section describes the potential problems and misapplications of tests in this regard. Whether or not a child is ready to succeed in a program affects parents and children personally. Having a good evaluation tool helps in making such decisions equitably and in communicating results in a clear and kind manner.

Goals and Plans. The evaluation tool that gives a specific profile of a child's skills will allow an administrator to share information with a family clearly and honestly. By carefully choosing a tool, administrators give the parents information they can use to plan for the child's development.

SKILLS INVENTORY

Teacher _____

Child _____ Age_____ Date _____

Task	**Teacher Comments**
Cognitive Skills	
1. Can you say the alphabet?	1. Sequence correct? Yes ___ No ___ Length:
2. Can you tell me what these letters are?	2. Number of letters correct ___ Comment:
3. Can you count for me?	3. Note how far: Sequence correct how far? ___
4. Please point to the number.	4. 3-1-6-4-8-2-9-7-5 How many correct? ___
5. Can you put these in order from smallest to biggest? Which is the largest? Smallest? First? Last?	5. Three sizes of triangles. Comments:
6. What color is this? If child cannot name the color, then ask to "Point to the red one," etc.	6. Point to red, blue, yellow, black, green, orange, brown, purple. Comments:
7. What shapes are these? If child cannot name the shape, then ask to "Point to the circle," etc.	7. Point to circle, square, triangle, rectangle. Comments?
8. Can you find your shoulders? Elbow? Thumb? Neck? Lips?	8. Comments:
9. Name all the animals you can think of	9. Comments: *Continued*

Figure 10.14 ● By creating effective tools for assessment, we are able to evaluate children's developing skills and their readiness for the next educational step. (Developed by Bing Nursery School, Stanford University, 1975 to 1990.)

Task	Teacher Comments
10. Please put these animals into two groups. One has the animals that live in water, and the other the ones that live on the land.	10. Giraffe, deer, cat, frog, alligator, shark, goldfish
11. Here are a bear and a cube. Put the cube on top of the bear. Under the bear. Behind the bear. Beside the bear.	11. Check correct responses:
12. Here are three pictures. Can you put them in order so that they tell a story?	12. Tree with green leaves. Tree with orange or red leaves, falling. Bare tree. Comments:

Auditory-Perceptual Listening Skills

Task	Teacher Comments

1. Please repeat these numbers after I say them (Practice with 6-3-1-4):
    5-3-8-2
    2-7-9-3
	1. Sequence correct? Numbers correct?

2. Tell me the sentence in the same order as I say. (Practice with "The dog ran to the park.") The mother pointed to the airplane in the sky.	2. Sequence correct? Words correct?
3. Listen to what I say, and then do what my words tell you. (Practice with "Put your hands on your head.") Stand up, go to the door, and walk back to me.	3. Comments:

Fine-Motor Skills

Task	Teacher Comments
1. Print your name.	1. Note grasp, hand preference.
2. Draw a circle, square, triangle, rectangle.	2. Comments:
3. Write the letters: O E P A J	3. Comments:
4. Write the numbers: 1 3 7 2 5	4. Comments:
5. Cut out a circle.	5. Note scissor grasp, hand preference.
6. Draw the best person that you can. Have you left anything out?	6. Comments:

Gross-Motor Skills

Task	Teacher Comments
1. Jump on two feet from A to B.	1. Note balance.
2. Hop on one foot from B to A.	2. Note balance.
3. Skip from A to B.	3. Comments:
4. Walk backward from B to A.	4. Comments:
5. Stand on one foot while I count to three.	5. Note balance.
6. Walk across this balance board.	6. Note balance.
7. Can you jump over these poles with your feet together?	7. Comments:
8. How high can you climb our climber? Go up our slide?	8. Comments:
9. Now run from the climber to the fence and back to me as fast as you can!	9. Note gait and balance.
10. Please throw the ball to me. Catch it. Kick it.	10. Comments:

Figure 10.14 ● Continued.

Figure 10.15 ● Fine-motor skills are one indicator of an ability to succeed in school and should be assessed as regularly as cognitive or socioemotional abilities.

Testing and Screening

The practice of testing and **screening** for readiness and retention has increased dramatically in the last decade. With the passage of Public Law 94–142 (Education for All Handicapped Children Act) and the early childhood amendment to the law (P.L. 99–457), states now have the responsibility to establish specific procedures and policies to identify, evaluate, and provide services to all children with learning problems. Moreover, testing for admittance to kindergarten or promotion to first grade has become more common. The results are that more children are being denied entrance to a school system, being put in extra-year or pull-out programs, or being placed in kindergarten twice. Such practices raise some practical and serious philosophical issues.

● Young children do not function well in common test situations, nor do the test results necessarily reflect children's true knowledge or skills.

● These practices (often based on inappropriate uses of readiness or screening tests) disregard the potential, documented long-term negative effects

of retention on children's self-esteem and the fact that such practices disproportionately affect low-income and minority children (NAEYC, 1988).

● Although the most needed and appropriate tests (teacher-made) are the hardest to create, the standardized ones are frequently misused and misunderstood by teachers and parents (Meisels, 1989).

● Teachers are pressured into running programs that overemphasize the testing situation and test items (Kamii, 1990).

● Most tests focus on cognitive and language skills; such a narrow focus ignores other areas of development.

The practice of standardized testing has caused early childhood curricula to become increasingly academic. Early childhood educators and parents are alarmed that:

Many kindergartens are now structured, "watered-down" first grades, emphasizing workbooks and other paper-and-pencil activities that are inappropriate for 5-year-olds. The trend further trickles down to preschool and child care programs that feel that their mission is to get children "ready" for kindergarten. Too many school systems, expecting children to conform to an inappropriate curriculum and finding large numbers of "unready" children, react to the problem by raising the entrance age for kindergarten and/or labeling the children as failures (NAEYC, 1988).

The implications of such testing further erode the curriculum when teachers, wanting their classes to do well on the test, alter activities to conform to what will be tested. They then begin teaching children to learn "right" answers rather than to engage in active, critical thinking. Rather than making teachers more accountable, "the overuse (and misuse) of standardized testing has led to the adoption of inappropriate teaching practices as well as admission and retention policies that are not in the best interests of individual children or the nation as a whole" (NAEYC, 1988).

Teachers and schools are beginning to respond to the overuse and inappropriate use of tests. The National Association of Elementary School Principals now urges limited use of formal tests and retention.

The Texas Board of Education has barred retention before first grade, and in New York State a coalition of groups is urging a ban on mass standardized testing of children before grade three.

Testing does have appropriate uses, such as using valid screening tests to "identify children who, because of the risk of possible learning problems or a handicapping condition, should proceed to a more intensive level of diagnostic assessment" (Meisels, 1989). The nonstandardized instruments in this section demonstrated can be used to plan programs that respond to the individual children in them. NAEYC has adopted specific guidelines for the use of standardized testing that include using only reliable and valid instruments and interpreting the test results accurately and cautiously to parents and others (NAEYC, 1988; Bredekamp & Rosegrant, 1992).

Perhaps most important is the reminder to all teachers that tests have no special magic. Evaluation is *more* than testing. A standardized test, a homemade tool (see Figure 10.14), or a screening instrument should be only one of several measures used to determine a child's skills, abilities, or readiness. Any test result should be part of a multitude of information, such as direct observation (see Chapter 6), parental report, and children's actual work. Above all, keep the testing to a minimum, thus guarding against "pulling up the plants to look at them before the roots take hold" (Cryan, 1986).

EVALUATING TEACHERS

It is understood that teachers are the *single most important* factor in determining program quality. What makes "the effective teacher" has no one simple answer. Section 3, especially Chapter 5, describes the role of the teacher. Somehow we need to define and describe "Caregivers of Quality" (Cartwright, 1998) in such a way that these qualities can be assessed:

Good physical health is a prerequisite . . . **emotional maturity,** "a person so secure within herself that she can function with principles rather than prescriptions . . . matured and perceptive **kindness** . . . keenly aware of emotional and physical safety for each child . . . **courage,** a strong and upbeat will to work through whatever odds for what one cares about . . . **integrity** . . . **self-awareness** . . . a theoretical

ground . . . warm **respect** for and courtesy for children . . . **trust** in each child to find his own way . . . discretion . . . **intuition**, a non-reasoning, often quite sudden, insight . . . professional detachment . . . don't forget **laughter**.

How these can be assessed is complicated, but assessing them is necessary. There are ways to evaluate teachers that guide them toward more effective teaching, in their work with children, coworkers, parents, and administrators.

Think of teachers as conductors of a symphony orchestra. They do not compose the music. They do not design or build the instruments, nor do they decide which ones will be played in the orchestra pit. They may even have limited choice of the music that will be played. Yet it is their job to lead a group of musicians through a medley of songs, bringing out the best in each musician. And all under the intense scrutiny of a critical audience. Teachers must do this with care and expertise under the watchful eyes of parents, boards, and funding agencies.

Many teachers do this well, often with little training except direct experience. As teachers' effectiveness is measured, they can learn better techniques for working with children, for planning environments and programs. The process for establishing and meeting these goals is evaluation. Teacher evaluation forms in this chapter can be adapted for use with student teachers and aides.

Why Evaluate?

Teachers are evaluated for several reasons. The end result of an assessment may be setting guidelines for what kinds of teaching are expected. Or the intent of an evaluation might be to set clear goals for job improvement. The first part of any effective evaluation procedure is a statement of purpose.

To Describe Job Responsibilities

It is essential for teachers to understand their job to do it well. A good job description outlines what is expected. One purpose of an evaluation is to see how those expectations are being met.

In an infant and toddler center, for example, teachers try to help children learn to separate comfortably from their parents. Evaluation in this setting could focus on the exact skills needed to implement this goal.

Figure 10.16 ● Evaluating teachers can help set professional growth goals and clarify a teacher's strengths and areas of improvement.

How does a teacher help a parent separate from a young child? What environmental cues does the teacher prepare? How is the child in distress comforted? What teaching strategies are important?

Evaluation for specifying job responsibilities is a part of one's professional self-definition as well as a clarification of actual duties. Studying ourselves helps us know who we are and what we do. Assessing job responsibilities aids in this process.

To Monitor Job Effectiveness

Once clear guidelines are set for teaching expectations, a method is needed to monitor actual teaching. Most evaluation systems attempt to check teacher effectiveness. It is important to establish a process for analyzing how teachers are doing their job.

This process may vary from school to school. In some schools, teaching effectiveness is measured, in part, by child achievement, such as how children score on tests. Other centers may solicit parent opinion. A teacher's coworkers may be part of an assessment team. For the most part, an evaluation for job effectiveness

will include an observation of teaching time with children.

To Clarify Strengths and Weaknesses

An evaluation procedure preferred by many teachers is one that identifies specific areas of strength and weakness. Feedback about actual teaching and other job responsibilities is helpful to all teachers, whether beginners or experienced personnel. As assessment that offers teachers information about how to perform their job better contributes to job competence and satisfaction. By recognizing strengths, teachers receive positive feedback for high-quality work.[1] By identifying weaknesses, they can begin to set realistic goals for improvement.

To Set Professional Growth Goals

One function of teacher evaluation is to foster professional development. Teachers do not become "good" and then stay that way for life. Regardless of their stage of development, teachers need goals in order to continually improve.

Regular feedback to staff can help in setting goals for continual professional growth. Beginning teachers will need to work on skills that apply their educational training or background to the classroom and children. A professional with 15 years of experience might need to polish skills acquired a decade or more ago or to try another educational challenge, such as developing curriculum or planning a workshop.

To Determine Employment

An evaluation can also be used to decide whether teachers should be retained, promoted, or released. Assessment procedures are an administrator's most valuable tools in making that decision. A clear and effective evaluation tool enables the administrator to monitor performance and target specific areas for improvement. The administrator then has a fair and equitable way to determine the promotional status of each employee.

[1] Teacher expectations can have a substantial effect on children's behavior and self-esteem. Check yourself for biases: how you interact with children is key to your effectiveness, and discriminatory interactions must be noted and remedied.

Figure 10.17 ● Teacher evaluations monitor job effectiveness as teachers work with people in several dimensions. This teacher demonstrates skill with groups as well as with individual children and adults.

Critical Issues in Teacher Evaluation

How to evaluate is an important issue in teacher assessment. A system for evaluating employees can be one of trust and mutual respect or of anxiety and tension. The method often determines how successful the entire evaluation will be.

Preliminary Steps

To begin with, a school follows the same guidelines for developing a teacher evaluation as for child assessment. That is, the process includes determining a purpose, establishing who will collect the data and how, and clarifying how the evaluation will be used.

In the assessment of teachers, the important components are: purpose (as described earlier in the chapter), evaluators, process, and follow-through.

Evaluators

Several models have been developed around the issue of who will assess teacher performance.

Self-Evaluation. This can be an effective starting point. Self-assessment is used in the Child Development Associate's evaluation system, for these reasons (Ward & CDA staff, 1976):

● The candidate is a valid source of information for use in assessment. Certain information is available only from the candidate's perspective.

● The candidate is able to clarify information on his or her performance, thereby adding to the assessment team's evidence for a valid decision.

● The candidate is better able to identify strengths and weaknesses and to receive recommendations for continued professional growth.

Figure 10.18 illustrates one type of systematic self-assessment. Another self-assessment technique, somewhat less formal, is to ask questions about yourself and your job, such as:

● What aspects of my work give me the greatest sense of satisfaction and achievement?

● What changes in my work assignment would increase my contribution to the school and my own personal satisfaction?

● What additional development activities would help me do a more effective job or prepare me for the next step on my career path?

● What would improve the effectiveness and quality of my relationship with my supervisor? (Young-Holt, Spitz, & Heffron, 1983).

The answers to these few questions can provide a solid base for discussion between teacher and supervisor or assessment team.

One drawback of self-assessment is its subjectivity. We see ourselves too closely, too personally, to be able to be entirely objective about our teaching. Therefore, self-assessment must be accompanied by other evaluating feedback.

SAMPLE SELF-EVALUATION

Rate the following items on the scale below, on the basis of your performance in the classroom. (Note: This form allows for a yes/no response if desired. Supervisors may use this same form to rate the student after the self-evaluation.)

Superior Perf.	**Acceptable Perf.**	**Unacceptable Perf.**	**Not Applicable**
3	2	1	0

Relationship to Children

_____ I am able to understand and accept a child as he/she is and recognize individual needs.

_____ I use knowledge and understanding of child development principles to understand children.

_____ I use information regarding home, family, and sociocultural background to understand children.

_____ I am able to modify situations to forestall negative behavior.

_____ I use positive suggestions and choices to redirect behavior.

_____ I use prescribed limits and follow-through.

_____ I adapt methods of guidance to the individual and adjust guidance measures to fit the situation.

_____ I avoid the use of threats.

_____ I express positive reinforcement when appropriate.

_____ I can verbalize my own feelings in an honest, open, and humane manner when interacting with children.

_____ I avoid using baby talk.

_____ I relate to individual children.

_____ I relate to children in small groups.

_____ I relate to children in large groups.

Developing the Program

_____ I permit the children to explore materials in a variety of ways.

_____ I recognize and use spontaneous happenings to help children's learning.

_____ I make use of child development principles to plan curriculum for children.

_____ I offer a wide range of experiences so children can make choices according to their interests and needs.

_____ I allow for various levels of ability among children.

_____ I utilize a variety of media when developing instructional materials.

_____ I use a note-taking system to assist in planning and evaluating experiences for children.

_____ I maintain equipment and materials in good order and consider health and safety factors.

Relating to Parents

_____ I recognize parents by name.

_____ I converse with parents at appropriate times.

_____ I incorporate the cultural backgrounds of families into the program.

_____ I facilitate a free flow of information between staff and parents.

_____ I communicate concerns to parents in both written and verbal forms.

_____ I recognize and appreciate parental values and priorities for their children.

_____ I communicate children's school experiences to parents.

Administration and Professional Development

_____ I recognize and use policies and procedures of the program.

_____ I attend and participate in staff meetings.

_____ I inform the administrative staff correctly of illness, time off, vacation, etc.

_____ I am a member of at least one professional organization in the field of early childhood.

_____ I attend meetings conducted by professional groups.

_____ I make use of professional resources and contacts.

_____ I maintain professional confidentiality and discretion.   *Continued*

Figure 10.18 ● Self-evaluation can be an insightful and useful process. (Adapted from Young-Holt C., Spitz, G., & Hefron, M. C. [1983]. A model for staff evaluation, validation, and growth. Palo Alto, CA: Center for the Study of Self-Esteem.)

Working with Other Staff Members

_____ I show positive attitudes toward other staff members.

_____ I give directions carefully.

_____ I take directions from others.

_____ I participate as a team member.

_____ I coordinate my efforts with those of my coworkers.

_____ I share my time, interest, and resources with other staff members.

_____ I listen and hear staff feedback regarding my teaching.

_____ I act on suggestions.

_____ I communicate my perceptions of my teaching in an honest and clear manner.

Figure 10.18 ● *Continued.*

Supervisory Evaluation. Supervisors, or head teachers, are usually part of the evaluation process. Job performance is an administrator's responsibility; therefore, teachers can expect their supervisors to be involved in their evaluation. Supervisors often use a single form combining a teacher's self-assessment and the supervisor's evaluation. This kind of form simplies the paperwork and assures both teacher and supervisor that both are using the same criteria for evaluation. They may, however, develop a different kind of form, such as the one in Figure 10.19.

Coevaluation. Evaluation by others associated with the teachers is a welcome addition to the evaluation process. Often a system includes more than a teacher's supervisor. Possible combinations are:

● Teacher (self-evaluation) and supervisor

● Teacher, supervisor, and parent

● Teacher, supervisor, and another team member (coteacher, aide, student teacher)

A team evaluation is a more collaborative approach. More information is collected on the teacher's performance. A team approach may be more valid and balanced because a decision about teaching will be made by consensus and discussion rather than individual, perhaps arbitrary, methods. And the evaluation will have a wider perspective, evaluating a teacher's job performance from several viewpoints.

Coevaluation does have its disadvantages, however. It is a time-consuming process because more than one person is asked to evaluate a teacher. Feedback may be contradictory; what one evaluator sees as a strength, another may view as a shortcoming. The system can be complicated to implement. For instance,

how do teachers work in a classroom and evaluate another team member at the same time? Can funds be found to bring in substitutes? Do fellow teachers have the time to devote to evaluating each other? How and when does a parent evaluate a teacher? Clearly, a school must weigh these issues carefully as evaluation systems are devised.

The Process

The evaluation tools used determine how and how valid the information gathered will be. Informal techniques often use information that is gathered sporadically, and conclusions may be unreliable or based on opinions. A process that is formalized and systematic has a greater chance of success. Such evaluations will be based on observable, specific information on what the teacher actually does. This is known as **performance-based assessment**. Figure 10.20 is an example of performance-based assessment in regard to a teacher's work with children. When paired with specific goals and expectations, this system is known as competency-based assessment.

Competency-based assessments outline exactly what teachers must do to demonstrate their competency, or skill, in their job assignment. Criteria are set as a teacher begins working (or a student starts a class or teacher education program). Areas are targeted that pinpoint what knowledge, skills, and behaviors the teacher must acquire.

Follow-Through

What happens after evaluation is critical to the overall success of an evaluation system. For instance, after gathering information for an evaluation session,

Teacher Evaluation Form

Instructions: This form is designed to be used by the center director for evaluating teachers. To the left of each characteristic listed below write an **E** if the teacher's performance in this area is **excellent, S** if it is **satisfactory**, and **N** if it **needs improvement**. Make any explanatory notes to the right.

Name of Teacher: _____   **Classroom:** _____

___ 1. Friendly, with ability to relate positively to people.
___ 2. Enjoys the egocentricity of children.
___ 3. Speaks clearly, distinctly, and grammatically.
___ 4. Demonstrates tact, compassion, empathic concern for children and families.
___ 5. Tolerant and considerate of differences in children and adults.
___ 6. Understands humor, humorous incidents, and jokes of children.
___ 7. Displays a sense of humor with children and enjoys laughing with them.
___ 8. Smiles and shows enjoyment often.
___ 9. Is dependable and energetic.
___ 10. Makes real effort to become very involved in the program.
___ 11. Enthusiastic and excited about teaching.
___ 12. Indicates a desire to keep up in the field of ECE.
___ 13. Grows in ability to critically evaluate self.
___ 14. Can follow directions.
___ 15. Accepts and uses suggestions to improve teaching.
___ 16. Accepts share of responsibility for classroom preparation, gathering of materials, and other tasks assigned.
___ 17. Accepts individual differences.
___ 18. Uses a positive approach with all children.
___ 19. Alert to total group of children even when dealing with an individual child or small group.
___ 20. Remains controlled in startling or difficult situations.
___ 21. Assists children in gaining self-confidence and in becoming communicative.
___ 22. Makes an effort to joyously participate with children in small groups or 1:1 basis, indoors and outdoors.
___ 23. Displays a general positive attitude toward other adults in place of a negative, criticizing attitude.
___ 24. Responds well to adults.
___ 25. Respects the rights and teaching techniques of others in the group.
___ 26. Welcomes new ideas and demonstrates flexibility with willingness to consider new ideas.
___ 27. Realizes that situations cannot always be handled at home as they are at school.
___ 28. Evidences growth and potential for teaching young children.
___ 29. Demonstrates knowledge about growth and development of young children.
___ 30. Demonstrates knowledge about the meaning of specific activities for children.
___ 31. Is positive and supportive of parents as partners in ECE.

Signed: _____   Date: _____

Figure 10.19 ● A teacher may be evaluated by the center director or supervisor using an evaluation tool such as this form. (From Murphy, C. [1986, September]. Teacher evaluation forms. *Child Care Information Exchange*, No. 51.)

Teacher Goal	Example
To help each child develop a positive self-concept	I greet each child with a smile and a personal comment.
To help each child develop socially, emotionally, cognitively, and physically	I have goals for each child in each developmental area, Fall and Spring.
To help provide many opportunities for each child to be successful	My parent conference sheets have examples; for instance, Charlie didn't want to come to group time, so I had him pick the story and help me read it—he comes every day now!
To encourage creativity, questioning, and problem-solving	This is my weak point. I tend to talk too much and tell them what to do.
To foster enjoyment for learning in each child	I do great group times and give everyone turns.
To facilitate children's development of a healthy identity and inclusive social skills.	I participated in our center's self-study and am taking an anti-bias curriculum class.

Figure 10.20 ● Performance-based assessment ties the goals of the program to a teacher's work. This example asks the teacher to do a self-assessment; a director, parent, or peer could observe and make a second assessment.

a supervisor and teacher might discuss and evaluate concrete examples and live performance. Together they can establish goals for changing what may be ineffective or problematic.

Follow-through is the final part of a continuous *feedback loop* in a good evaluation system. Data are collected on teacher behavior and given to the teacher in person. Goals are set to improve teaching. A follow-up check is done periodically, to see how—and if—goals are being met. Teaching improves as recommendations are put into practice. Follow-through makes the *feedback loop* complete as information about improvement is communicated. Figure 10.21 illustrates this cycle.

Evaluation takes hard work, time, and dedication to a higher quality of teaching. It is also a shared responsibility. The supervisor must be explicit about a teacher's performance and be able to identify for the teacher what is effective and what is problematic. The teacher is responsible for participating in the evaluation.

Techniques for Productive Evaluation Sessions

Teachers must value the process itself. Evaluations emphasize how valuable the work of professional teachers is, and the benefits of producive evaluation sessions are clear. They range from improved self-esteem, higher levels of job effectiveness, and less absenteeism and turnover to assessment-related salary raises and other job benefits. Teachers need to analyze and take seriously the substance of the evaluation and understand its implications for their teaching. To further their professional growth, they must use this opportunity to improve the tools of their trade.

Certain techniques help make evaluation sessions productive for teachers:

1. Become involved from the beginning as the evaluation procedure is established. Know what is expected and how you will be evaluated.

2. Set a specific meeting time for your evaluation. Ask your supervisor for a time that works for you both.

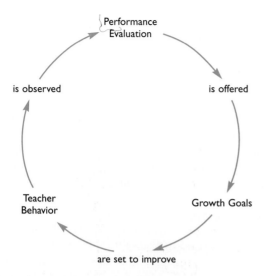

Figure 10.21 ● A feedback loop is a continuous cycle in which teacher behavior is observed for a performance evaluation. The evaluation is offered through growth goals, which are set in order to affect teacher behavior. Thus, the circle is continuous, with each part helping the next.

3. Set some goals for yourself before meeting with your supervisor. If you know what you want to work on, you are more likely to get help achieving your goals.

4. Develop a plan for action. Be prepared to set a timeline for when and how you will work on your goals.

5. Establish a feedback loop. Make a follow-up date and make copies of your goal sheet for both you and your supervisor.

6. Approach the meeting with a sense of trust, respect, and openness. Planning ahead promotes these attitudes.

What results from productive feedback sessions are better teaching and continued professional growth. Teacher evaluations help recognize strengths and build on them. They identify areas where growth is needed.

They individualize the process itself. No two teachers are identical; each evaluation must be interpreted in terms of the behavior and stage of development of the individual person.[1] As teachers become more effective in their work with children, the quality of the entire program is improved.

EVALUATING PROGRAMS

Why Evaluate?

To Gain an Overview

Evaluating a program gives an overview of how all the various components function together. This assessment asks the larger questions. Returning to the restaurant example earlier in the chapter, one might ask, "Would you ever go back and eat there again? Would you take a friend there?" In educational terms, the fundamental questions are, "Is this a good place for children? Would you want your child to be here? What is a high-quality program for young children?" See Chapters 2 and 9 for additional information.

Looking at children, teachers, and the total environment, a program evaluation reveals the entire environment as an integrated whole. These assessments add an awareness of how one area is related to another and how the parts mesh in a particular setting. Such evaluations, then, are the standards of quality and include:

● Children's progress

● Teacher performance

● Curriculum development

● The financial structure

● Parents' involvement

● The community at large

● The governing organization of the school

In program evaluations, each of these is assessed for how it functions alone and how each works in concert with the others.

[1] What teachers know about understanding and respecting diversity in children and families needs to be translated into working with colleagues.

To Establish Accountability

Besides providing an overview, a program evaluation establishes **accountability**. This refers to a program's being answerable to a controlling group or agency, for instance the school board or the government office or to parents and the community in which you work. These groups want to know how their funds are being spent and how their philosophy is being expressed through the overall program. Just as a teacher's evaluation is sometimes linked to salary increases, a program evaluation may be related to future funding. This can add stress to the evaluation process since teachers and administrators must justify their worth in dollars and cents.

To Make Improvements

A third purpose of a program evaluation is to determine where and how improvements can be made. Program evaluations are an opportunity to take an objective look at how the goals of the school are being met. A good evaluation will support the strengths of the existing program and suggest where changes might improve overall effectiveness. An in-depth assessment increases the likelihood that program goals and visions will be realized. The evaluation helps determine the direction the program may take in the future.

To Acquire Accreditation

Finally, evaluations are a necessary step for some schools who wish to be approved for certification or accreditation by various organizations or government agencies. Such groups require that a school meet certain evaluation standards before the necessary permits are issued or membership is granted. Agencies, such as a state department of social services or department of education, often license family day care homes, and private schools may need to follow certain criteria to be affiliated with a larger organization (such as the American Montessori Society).

To improve the quality of schools, begin with children and place them in the center of program evaluation. In seeing the children's perspective, teachers and parents must be part of program evaluation, for they are the ones closest to the children. One particular system established by early childhood professionals is noteworthy. The National Academy of Early Childhood Programs, a division of NAEYC, has established an accreditation system for improving the quality of life for young children and their families. The Focus Box by Sue Bredekamp describes this system.

Attempting to define a high-quality early childhood program, the accreditation system articulates what promotes the physical, social, emotional, and cognitive development of children in group care. The Academy established goals for schools around several component areas, which include curriculum goals, adult–child interactions, health, safety, nutrition, relations between the home and program, developmental evaluation of children, and qualifications and on-going staff development of teachers.

For children to have positive experiences, Bredekamp (1992) identifies several *predictors of quality:*

● Teachers who are specially trained in child development and early education

● Enough adults to respond to individual children, adequate ratios of adults to children, reasonable group sizes

● Regular communication with parents, who are welcome visitors at all times

● Many, varied age-appropriate materials in a well-arranged, accessible environment both indoors and outdoors

● Nutritious meals and snacks

● Effective administration, including clear, written policies and procedures to facilitate communication, that meets the needs of adults as well as children

● Systematic, ongoing evaluation of how well the program is meeting its goals for children and families

A key dimension of quality is program evaluation. The NAEYC accreditation process is the first attempt by the national early childhood profession to articulate what is meant by a "good" program for young children. As such, it is based on observing children in the United States and has some of the dominant culture's values embedded in it. Therefore, in the last decade there has been an ongoing critique of this initial model.

Improving Program Quality through National Accreditation

Sue Bredekamp

Parents want the best for their children. Teachers want to work in programs that provide good quality care and education for children. Program administrators want to provide a high-quality service to their clients. Program funders want to know that their investment is sound.

Parents, teachers, administrators, and funders involved in early childhood programs now have a system for helping ensure that their programs are of the highest quality. That system is the National Academy of Early Childhood Programs, a division of the National Association for the Education of Young Children (NAEYC). The academy administers a national, voluntary accreditation system for child care centers and preschools. This system, initiated in 1985, is designed for any full-day or part-day group program serving children from birth through age 5 and school-age children in before- and after-school care. Accredited programs represent the diversity of the field of early childhood education—church-housed and church-sponsored; private, for-profit; community-based, nonprofit; employer-sponsored; university-sponsored; parent cooperatives; Head Start programs; and public school prekindergarten and kindergarten.

The goal of NAEYC's accreditation system is to *improve* the quality of care and education provided for young children in group programs. The accreditation system achieves its goal by establishing high standards

of quality for programs and recognizing programs that achieve substantial compliance with the criteria. The criteria for accreditation were developed over a three-year period with input from thousands of early childhood professionals.

How does the academy define a high-quality early childhood program? A high-quality program provides a safe and nurturing environment while promoting the physical, social, emotional, and intellectual development of young children. In accredited programs, you will see: positive, warm interactions among adults and children; age-appropriate activities; specially trained teachers; adequate ratios of staff to children; healthy and safe environment; nutritious meals or snacks; regular communication with parents; effective administration; and systematic and ongoing program evaluation.

Early childhood educators often stress process over product. The same is true of the accreditation system. The criteria form the basis for the system, but the accreditation process is what accomplishes the goal of program improvement. The three-step accreditation system is designed to bring about real and lasting improvements in the program. The first step is a thorough *self-study*. Using an observation form and questionnaires provided by the academy, the teachers, director, and parents evaluate how well the program is meeting the criteria and set goals for improvement. After improvements have been made, the director reports the results of the self-study by completing a rating form, called the Program Description. During step two, the accuracy of the program description is verified during an on-site visit by trained early childhood professionals, called validators. The verified program description is then reviewed by a three-person commission that makes the accreditation decision on the basis of professional judgment. The accreditation decision considers all the criteria but weighs most heavily the criteria that directly affect children such as the quality of interactions with adults, the appropriateness of the curriculum, and the safety of the environment.

The accreditation system benefits the early childhood profession in many ways. It establishes professional consensus regarding program standards. It provides a goal that programs can use in working toward improvement. It provides tools for self-evaluation by administrators and teachers as well as overall program evaluation. It provides a mechanism for identifying programs that exceed the minimum requirements for operation and strive toward achieving professional standards. It provides additional assurance for parents as they make important decisions about the care and education of their children.

Although accreditation is a relatively new concept for the field of early childhood education, accreditation is a well-known and trusted concept in other professions. Most of us would not want to send our child to a nonaccredited college, nor would we want to be treated in a nonaccredited hospital. The implementation of a national accreditation system indicates that the early childhood profession, like other professions, is willing to establish standards for practice and to monitor the quality of services offered on behalf of children. Thus, accreditation is one of several recent trends that enhance the professional image and status of early childhood educators.

The major benefactors of accreditation are the children. Directors and teachers whose programs participate in the accreditation process report that it works! It improves the quality of care they provide for children. And after all, all children deserve the best.

Dr. Sue Bredekamp is director of the National Academy of Early Childhood Programs at NAEYC.

Those who are familiar with the wide diversity of cultures in America are looking critically at adapting this process.[1] "The accreditation criteria themselves have been criticized for reflecting a bias toward white, middle-class childrearing practices and values" (Bredekamp & Rosegrant, 1995). Professionals working hard to develop high-quality programs feel the challenge of the question "Is the Academy accreditation culturally appropriate for . . . all children?" Proponents of Vygotsky's ideas argue that, because adults teach children skills that are socially valued by the particular family or ethnic group, no single document could ever describe practices of all subcultures in American society. Additionally, because the NAEYC accreditation process has been "normed" on U.S. programs and populations, there may well be other interpretations of "good" programs for young children. In other words, we need to consider that developmentally appropriate practices might look different in different cultures.

At the same time, one might ask the question differently, as Cunningham (1996) does here:

> Is there a Black or African American early childhood tradition? Are there aspects of what we call developmentally appropriate practice that are not appropriate for Black children? . . . In more than 20 years of work in early childhood education, I have not become aware of Black early childhood programming, and I am unable to identify any developmentally appropriate criteria that are inappropriate for Black children.

It may (or may not) be a matter of degree. Certainly the accreditation process must be flexible enough to see many ways of determining what constitutes an appropriately multicultural, anti-bias environment and teaching practices. Clearly much more thinking and observing must be done to help resolve this issue.

A part of the problem is definitely *economics*. High-quality programs require well-trained staff, which takes time, materials, and financial support to implement. In addition to the cost of training staff, there are monies required to set up and maintain well-equipped classrooms and playgrounds. Most centers nationwide are not accredited, and many do not complete the initial self-study part of the process because

of lack of time or staff turnover and program instability (Talley, 1997). Support for ongoing expenses to maintain high-quality programs often disappears after accreditation has been achieved. Finally, staff stability (read: turnover) affects the quality of a program. The NAEYC accreditation system will need to address concerns related to staffing (Whitebrook, 1996), and the field as a whole needs to acknowledge and act on the issue of compensation. See Chapter 15 for a further discussion of *cost* as it is related to *quality*.

Some adaptations are already apparent; for instance, the American Montessori Institute has worked with the Academy on some of the component parts that need adjusting to fit the Montessori model of good education.

Now that a tool has been developed, the Academy has revised this initial document (Bredekamp & Copple, 1997). Clearly, both the Academy's accreditation and the concepts of developmentally appropriate practices will evolve as our awareness of culture and education increases.

Guidelines for Program Evaluation

Defining the Objectives

A program evaluaton begins with a definition of the program's objectives. Knowing why a program is to be evaluated indicates how to tailor the procedure to the needs and characteristics of an individual school. With the objectives defined, the choice of evaluation instrument becomes clear. If, for example, a program objective is to provide a healthy environment for children, the evaluation tool used must address the issues of health, safety, and nutrition.

Choosing a Tool

Evaluation instruments vary with the purpose of the program evaluation. Moreover, a survey of various program evaluations shows that many are designed to be program-specific; that is, the evaluation itself is devised to examine one program only. Individualized assessments are difficult to generalize. However, it appears that most program evaluations assess several, if not all, of the following areas:

[1] Keeping an open mind and critical eye is important for teachers who are trying to assess and be equitable.

The Physical Environment

Are the facilities clean, comfortable, safe?

Are room arrangements orderly and attractive?

Are materials and equipment in good repair and maintained?

Is there a variety of materials, appropriate to age levels?

Are activity areas well defined?

Are cleanup and room restoration a part of the daily schedule?

Are samples of children's work on display?

Is play space adequate, both inside and out?

Is personal space (e.g., cubby) provided for each child?

The Staff

Are there enough teachers for the number of children? How is this determined?

Are the teachers qualified? What criteria are used?

Is the staff evaluated periodically? By whom and how?

Does the school provide/encourage in-service training and continuing education?

Do the teachers encourage the children to be independent and self-sufficient?

Are the teachers genuinely interested in children?

Are teachers aware of children's individual abilities and limitations?

What guidance and disciplinary techniques are used?

Do teachers observe, record, and write reports on children's progress?

Are teachers skilled in working with individual children, small groups, and large groups?

Does the teaching staff give the children a feeling of stability and belonging?

Do teachers provide curriculum that is age-appropriate and challenging?

How would you describe the teachers' relationships with other adults in the setting? Who does this include, and how?

Can the teaching staff articulate good early education principles and relate them to their teaching?

Parent Relationships

How does the classroom include parents?

Are parents welcome to observe, discuss policies, make suggestions, help in the class?

Are different needs of parents taken into account?

Where and how do parents have a voice in the school?

Are parent–teacher conferences scheduled?

Does the school attempt to use community resources and social service agencies in meeting parents' needs?

The Organization and Administration

Does the school maintain and keep records?

Are there scholarships or subsidies available?

What socioeconomic, cultural, religious groups does the school serve?

What is the funding agency, and what role does it play?

Is there a school board, and how is it chosen?

Does the school serve children with special needs or handicaps?

Are the classroom groups homo- or heterogeneous?

What hours is the school open?

What age range is served?

Are there both full- and part-day options?

Is after-school care available?

Does the school conduct research or train teachers?

What is the teacher-child ratio?

The Overall Program

Does the school have a written, stated educational philosophy?

Are there developmental goals for the children's physical, social, intellectual, and emotional growth?

Are the children evaluated periodically?

Is the program capable of being individualized to fit the needs of all the children?

Does the program include time for a variety of free, spontaneous activities?

Is the curriculum varied to include music, art, science, nature, math, language, social studies, motor skills, etc.?

Are there ample opportunities to learn through a variety of media and types of equipment and materials?

Is there ample outdoor activity?

Is there a daily provision for routines: eating, sleeping, toileting, play?

Is the major emphasis in activities on concrete experiences?

Are the materials and equipment capable of stimulating and sustaining interest?

Are field trips offered?

Do children have a chance to be alone? In small groups?

In large groups?

Cultural Responsiveness

Are multicultural perspectives already incorporated throughout the school, classroom curriculum, and classroom environment?

Do my attitudes (and those of all staff) indicate a willingness to accept and respect cultural diversity? How is this demonstrated?

Do classroom materials recognize the value of cultural diversity, gender, and social class equity?

Do curricular activities and methods provide children opportunities to work and play together cooperatively? In mixed groups of their choice and the teacher direction?

Do schoolwide activities reflect cultural diversity? How is this noticed?

Does the program planning reflect the reality (views and opinions) of families and the community?

Does the curriculum include planning for language diversity? For full inclusion? (Adapted from Baruth & Manning, 1992, and de Melendez & Ostertag, 1997.)

 Tools for program evaluation are woven together to give a more comprehensive look at the total program.[1]

Developmentally Appropriate Practices

Educational reform to improve the quality of programs for young children in the last several years has been spearheaded by a movement toward what is now called "developmentally appropriate practice" (Bredekamp, 1987; Elkind, 1989; NAEYC, 1991). It is essential that all early childhood educators understand the terms and issues. Knowing what is meant by the phrase "developmentally appropriate practice" helps the dedicated teacher to be able to plan programs that are of high quality and integrity and to articulate what is important for children to their parents and the greater community.

Developmentally appropriate practice (DAP) describes teaching and learning from a developmental perspective—children are seen as learners with *developing* abilities, with differing rates of growth, and with individual differences (i.e., temperament, family history, ethnic background, gender, and so on). Teaching content is tied to who the learners are; thus, programs change to reflect the children in them. Teachers prepare environments and ask questions that stimulate individual thinking processes. An evaluation of a developmentally appropriate program includes the environ-

ment, the quality of adult–child interaction, work with parents, and so on.

Think of DAP with a three-part definition. First, a good program is *age appropriate*; it is planned with the typical behaviors, skills, and capabilities of the age range in mind. Second, it is *individually appropriate*; the needs, characteristics, and concerns of each individual child are held in high regard and are responded to in the program. Third, it is *culturally responsive*; the particular family, ethnic, and community cultures are considered as the program develops.

In contrast, **psychometric** philosophy is a view more commonly held in primary education. From this standpoint, children are seen as having *finite quantities of abilities*. Individual differences in performance are seen as reflecting differences in the amount of a given ability. In such classrooms, the teacher's job is to match children of similar abilities, and the curriculum will likely follow a traditional content. Such programs will be evaluated with assessments such as tests. Then, getting children to know correct information (thus high test scores) often becomes too important.

There are clear differences in these two viewpoints. Teachers of *young* children usually base their programs more on developmentally appropriate (rather than psychometric) practices, because much of the philosophy of early childhood education is based on child development theories of Piaget and Erikson rather than on the behaviorist and psychometric models (see Chapter 4). Because the theoretical underpinnings are different, early childhood programs differ from most elementary school programs. Consequently, teachers and parents find themselves with two contrasting systems of teaching and evaluation.

The debate over how to plan and evaluate programs for young children continues today, and it is useful for those who work with young children to understand the issues. Our task is to create "developmentally appropriate evaluation." As the concept of DAP expands to include cultural, ethnic, and inclusive aspects of children's lives, the concept of appropriate assessments becomes especially important.[2] Martin (1994) has identified key components of developmen-

---

 OUR DIVERSE WORLD OUR DIVERSE WORLD OUR DIVERSE WORLD OUR DIVERSE WORLD OUR DIVERSE WORLD OUR DIVERSE WORLD OUR DIVERSE WORLD OUR DIVERSE WORLD

[1] Principles of quality care in a diverse society must include building on the cultures of families and promoting respect (Chang et al., 1996).

[2] Any evaluation process must factor in all the components of the child's experience if it is to be appropriate. . . . Without an acknowledgment of the child's context, behavior cannot be understood" (Martin, 1994).

Figure 10.22 ● Program evaluations should represent the diversity of the field of early childhood education, from family day care for infants to after-school programs for primary schoolchildren.

tally appropriate evaluation of children. Adapted to include teachers and programs, they are:

● An objective recording of actual behavior, actions, or situations

● The selection of appropriate methods of recording, collecting information, and analyzing the information

● A recognition of personal biases of the observer, and a thorough check for inferences in the data collected

● An emphasis on the process of individual patterns of development for children and teachers

● The necessity for ensuring that evaluation is based on objective data rather than casual perceptions

● The belief that in the observation of real behavior and actions we reach the best understanding of individual development—whether child or adult—and a realistic view of programs.

NAEYC has developed an extensive list of publications that provide guidance in establishing and operating programs of quality and that explain in detail what is meant by developmentally appropriate programs for young children. Teachers and administrators should become familiar with these documents and use them as standards for program excellence. Chapters 11 through 14 are based on materials with these guidelines.

HOW EVALUATIONS AFFECT AN EARLY CHILDHOOD SETTING

A useful assessment encourages positive change. It is easy to continue the same program, the same teaching techniques, even the same assessment techniques, year after year when a school is operating smoothly. Sometimes it is not clear what—or how—improvements could be made. A regular evaluation keeps a system alive and fresh.

Evaluations help give meaning and perspective to children, teachers, and programs. An assessment that helps clarify these processes brings renewed dedication and inspiration.

Assessments of children, teachers, and programs can blend together for positive results. Children and program evaluations often work in tandem, as program goals must be defined in terms of children and their growth. How well the children are doing is a measure of program success.

Teacher evaluations may be related to program assessment when they include an **upward evaluation**,

Figure 10.23 ● A program evaluation can determine how the class includes parents. The presence of parent volunteers shows that the school welcomes parent involvement.

or teacher evaluation of administrators. The program effectiveness is checked by the people who are responsible for its implementation. In the case of family child care providers, there are no immediate supervisors to provide feedback on job performance or the program effectiveness. In this case, the provider may devise a system of self-evaluation (Cundiff-Smith, 1996) that will include client feedback—the parents (usually in the form of anonymous questionnaires) and the children (enthusiasm, laughs, and hugs are good indicators!).

A teacher's effectiveness is evaluated every day by how the children respond to the environment, the schedule, teaching techniques and relationships, and each other. No more effective test exists than the dynamics of the children at work and play in a class. In that sense, we can look at program evaluation through the eyes of a child. In adding the child's viewpoint to program evaluation, we bring the assessment of quality back to its starting point: the children. Whether by videotaping, direct observation, or reflective questioning, teachers can discover what it is like to be a child in a program. Such "bottom-up" perspective (Barclay & Benelli, 1996) might be gained in these questions:

Do I usually feel welcome, rather than captured?

Do I usually feel accepted, understood and protected, rather than scolded or neglected by the adults?

Do I find most activities meaningful, rather than mindless or trivial?

Am I usually glad to be here, rather than eager to leave?

As teachers, we learn to accept evaluation as a process, rather than a series of static end points. In doing so, we see that there can be continuity and consistency in how evaluations of the people and programs in early childhood education work together to enhance learning and growth at all levels. If high quality is to be maintained, program evaluation must be ongoing and systematic. Centers must be willing to spend money on quality and to invest time in the single most important determinant of quality: the adults with whom the children interact every day. Quality begins with us.

Summary

Evaluation is a way of taking stock; it is an opportunity to look at how things are going. We can assess where we are now and where we want to be. A good evaluation instrument may even suggest ways to achieve our goals. A good evaluation process includes a clear purpose, knowing who and what will be evaluated, and what use will be made of the results.

Any program designed to meet the needs of children must be evaluated on a regular basis. Teachers, children, and the program must be assessed individually and then evaluated as a whole. Each supports and depends on the other; an evaluation is a way to look at how those relationships are working. It can identify specific concerns and determine the areas of growth and potential development.

Setting goals is an important part of the evaluation process. Evaluating goals is a measure of success or lack of it. We judge whether we have met our goals effectively and whether the goals are reflective of the program.

Evaluations serve many purposes. Assessing individual children highlights their growth and potential more clearly. One method, standardized testing, is being used extensively in early childhood settings and can be misapplied and inappropriately used. Evaluation gives teachers information about their own performance and suggests ways to strengthen their teaching style. Examining the total program reveals a better picture of how all its aspects work in unison. The National Academy of Early Childhood Programs has established an accreditation system that encourages developmentally appropriate practices in settings for children from birth to 8 years of age.

The process of evaluation can be positive and can encourage growth for all involved. The choice of evaluation instruments is important, as is the use made of the data collected. Programs will keep pace with their children and professional teachers if evaluation is considered an integral part of the program structure.

Review Questions

1. List three reasons for evaluation in the early childhood setting. Which do you think would be the hardest? Why?

2. What are the components of all good evaluations? What are the problems? Include some suggestions for solutions.

3. What are the reasons for assessing children's progress? How can you communicate both strengths and weaknesses to parents?

4. Describe some of the problems with testing or screening of young children. How can you address these problems if you are required to administer a standardized test to your class?

5. Who can be involved in evaluating teachers? Who would you prefer? Why?

6. How can teachers help make their evaluation sessions productive?

7. Name three purposes of program evaluations.

8. What is the National Academy's accreditation, and how does it attempt to improve program quality?

Learning Activities

1. Does your own setting have an evaluation plan? Is it for child assessment, teacher evaluation, or program quality? Analyze the goals of your plan and how the tools or implementation meet (or do not meet) those goals.

2. Develop an informal assessment tool to evaluate children's skills in a toddler class. Discuss how this would differ from one for a preschool and one for a school-age child care program.

3. Try to establish goals for your own growth as a professional in the following areas:

	Goal	Objectives/Implementation	Timeline
Programmatic			
Administrative			
Staff Relations			
Professional Growth			

Ask your supervisor or a colleague to help you make a realistic timeline for each goal.

4. Locate a copy of "Developmentally Appropriate Practices." Using the categories it outlines, make an informal assessment of the program in which you work. Share your results with another teacher or a supervisor.

Bibliography

Barclay, K., & Benelli, C. (1995/96, Winter). Program evaluation through the eyes of a child. *Childhood Education.*

Baruth, L. G., & Manning, M. L. (1992). *Multicultural education of children and adolescents.* Needham Heights, MA: Allyn & Bacon.

Bredekamp, S. (1987, 1991, 1997). *Developmentally appropriate practice in early childhood programs serving children from birth through age 8* (Expanded ed.). Washington, DC: National Association for the Education of Young Children.

Bredekamp, S. (1992). Evaluating for effectiveness. In A. Gordon & K. Browne (Eds.), *Beginnings and beyond* (3rd ed.). Albany, NY: Delmar.

Bredekamp, S., & Coople, C. (1997). *Developmentally appropriate practices in early childhood programs.* Washington, DC: National Association for the Education of Yong Children.

Bredekamp, S., & Rosegrant, T. (Eds.). (1992, 1995). *Reaching potentials* (Vols. 1 & 2). Washington, DC: National Association for the Education of Young Children.

Cartwright, S. (1998, March). Caregivers of quality. *Exchange.*

Chang, H. M., Muckelroy, A., Pulido-Tobiassen, D., Dowell, C., & Edwards, J. O. (1996). *Looking in, looking out: Refining child care in a diverse society.* San Francisco: California Tomorrow.

Cryan, J. R. (1986, May/June). Evaluation: Plague or promise? *Childhood Education, 62*(5).

Cundiff-Smith, D. (1996, May/June). Evaluating your program. *Scholastic Early Childhood Today.*

Cunningham, G. (1996). The challenge of responding to individual and cultural differences and meeting the needs of all communities. In S. Bredekamp & B. A. Willer (Eds.), *NAEYC accreditation: A decade of learning and the years ahead.* Washington, DC: National Association for the Education of Young Children.

De Melendez, W. R., & Ostertag, V. (1997). *Teaching young children in multicultural classrooms.* Albany, NY: Delmar.

Dunn, L., & Kontos, S. (1997, July). Research in review: What have we learned about developmentally appropriate practice? *Young Children, 52*(5).

Elkind, D. (1989, October). Developmentally appropriate practice: Philosophical and practical implications. *Phi Delta Kappa.*

Helm, J. H., Beneke, S., & Steinheimer, K. (1997). *Windows on learning: Documenting young children's work.* New York: Teachers College Press.

Hilliard, A. G., & Vaughn-Scott, M. (1982). The quest for the "minority" child. In S. G. Moore & C. R. Cooper (Eds.), *The young child? Reviews of research* (Vol. 3). Washington, DC: National Association for the Education of Young Children.

Hills, T. W. (1993, July). Assessment in context—Teachers and children at work. *Young Children, 48*(5).

Kamii, C. (Ed.). (1990). *Achievement testing in the early grades: The games grown-ups play.* Washington, DC: National Association for the Education of Young Children.

Kerman, S., & Martin, M. (1980). Teacher expectations and student achievement. *Phi Delta Kappa.*

Kostelnik, M. (1993, March). Recognizing the essentials of developmentally appropriate practice. *Exchange.*

Martin, S. (1994, April). Developmentally appropriate evaluation. *Educational Resources Information Clearinghouse, ED 391 601.*

McAfee, O., & Leong, D. (1997). *Assessing and guiding young children's development and learning* (Rev. ed.). Needham Heights, MA: Allyn & Bacon.

Meisels, S. J. (1989). *Developmental screening in early childhood: A guide* (3rd ed.). Washington, DC: National Association for the Education of Young Children.

Murphy, C. (1986, September). Teacher evaluation forms. *Child Care Information Exchange,* No. 51.

National Academy of Early Childhood Programs. (1991, July). *Accreditation criteria and procedures.* Washington, DC: National Association for the Education of Young Children.

National Association for the Education of Young Children. (1988, March). Position statement on standardized testing of young children 3 through 8 years of age. *Young Children, 43*(3).

Schweinhart, L. J. (1993, July). Observing young children in action: The key to early childhood assessment. *Young Children, 45*(5).

Talley, K. (1997, March). National accreditation: Why do some programs stall in self-study? *Young Children, 52*(3).

Ward, E. H., & CDA Staff. (1976, May). The Child Development Association Consortium's assessment system. *Young Children,* pp. 244–255.

Whitebrook, M. (1996). NAEYC accreditation as an indicator of program quality: What research tells us. In S. Bredekamp & B. A. Willer (Eds.), *NAEYC accreditation: A decade of learning and the years ahead.* Washington, DC: National Association for the Education of Young Children.

Young-Holt, C., Spitz, G., & Heffron, M. C. (1983). *A model for staff evaluation, validation, and growth.* Palo Alto, CA: Center for the Study of Self-Esteem.

Zeece, P. D. (1995, March). Quality begins with us. *Exchange.*

SECTION Five

What Is Being Taught?

Guest Editorial | **THE ESSENCE OF OUR MISSION**

Louise Derman-Sparks _____

Alice Walker's advice to "Keep in mind always the present you are constructing; it should be the future you want" speaks to the essence of our mission as educators.[1] Early childhood educators and parents share a profound responsibility for helping children lay a strong foundation for productive and ethical existence in a complex, diverse nation and world. Integral to this work is understanding how children develop as individuals, as members of groups and of a society.

Learning how young children develop their identity and attitudes toward others is a key component of our professional education. A growing body of research tells us that infants as early as 6 months of age begin to notice human differences. By 18 months they begin to identify who is like them and to develop preferences. By 4 they begin to internalize socially prevailing beliefs, positive and negative, about their own and others' group identities. Considerable research also reveals the serious damage that prejudice has on young children's budding awareness and feelings about themselves and others. It appears that we have a sensitive period between ages 6 months and 9 years when we can most effectively work to nurture healthy self and group identity and prevent or reduce prejudice.

To thrive, even to survive in the 21st century, children need environments in which they are "free to publicly affirm their own racial, ethnic, cultural, gender identification; able to transcend their own cultural borders and reach beyond them; and free to participate in action to make our society more democratic and free."[2] Our knowledge about children's development suggests that quality caregiving and education environments must include:

- Fostering of individual development within a child's own cultural group,

- Supporting every child's learning and experiencing the value of diversity, and

- Exposing every child to experiences that counteract bias and stereotypes.[3]

Becoming an excellent teacher requires learning how to effectively infuse these three dimensions in all aspects of early childhood education. Some adults prefer to deny that young children notice differences or that they are

[1] Walker, A. (1989). *The temple of my familiar* (p. 236). New York: Harcourt Brace Jovanovich.
[2] Dr. James Banks. California Association for Young Children Conference, 3/12/95, Long Beach.
[3] From: Phillips, C. B. (1991). *Essentials for child development associates working with young children.* Washington, DC: Council for Early Childhood Professional Recognition.

aware of and hurt by the various forms of prejudice prevalent in our society. This denial usually reflects the adult's own discomfort with these issues. However, avoidance doesn't give children the guidance and support they need. Becoming an effective professional challenges us to face and change the myths and stereotypes based on gender, race, ethnicity, class, disabilities, different family formats that we have learned. By so doing we free ourselves to teach children the most current wisdom the field of early childhood offers. Then we can truly build the future we want in the present we are creating.

Dr. Louise Derman-Sparks is a faculty member of Pacific Oaks College, the author of the well-known Anti-Bias Curriculum (1989), and an advocate for diversity in education.

11

Planning for Play: Curriculum Basics

Questions for Thought

What is curriculum in the early childhood setting?

What is developmentally appropriate curriculum?

What is the process of developing emergent curriculum for young children?

What is the value of play?

How are play and curriculum related?

How do children learn through play?

Why is dramatic play important to the young child?

What is the role of the teacher?

How do teachers support the play process?

How is curriculum culturally sensitive?

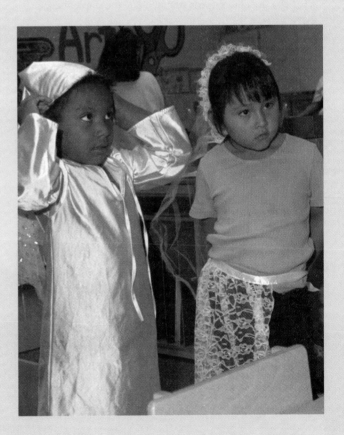

CURRICULUM

What Is Curriculum?

Ira, a 2-year-old, is more interested in the process of pouring milk (especially what happens after the cup is filled) than in eating and conversing at snack time.

In an early childhood setting, the curriculum consists of the art activity and language game; it is also the spontaneous investigation of liquids at snack time, the song that accompanies digging in the sand, and the teacher's explanation of why the hamster died. It can become, literally, everything that happens in the course of a school day.

The curriculum is the planned and the unplanned.

Kindergartners Bert and Leo become absorbed in watching a snail make its way across the sidewalk, ignoring for the moment the lesson on running relays.

Young children are like sponges; they absorb everything going on about them. Because they are young, the whole world is new and fresh. Therefore, children do not discriminate between what is prepared and structured for them to learn and whatever else happens to them at school. It is *all* learning.

Creating a good curriculum for young children is not simply a matter of practicing curriculum planning. It is a matter of understanding the process: how children interact with people and materials to learn. It is the sum of a teacher's knowledge about children's needs, materials, and equipment and what happens when they meet.

Planning the curriculum is the process of translating theories of education into practice. It is spontaneous, yet organized; it is planned, yet it emerges; it is based on the children's interests tempered by adult awareness of children's needs. Four areas of focus are (Bredekamp & Rosegrant, 1995):

● The content is *what* is being taught—the subject matter or the theme—and stems primarily from children's interests. Teacher and parent observa-

Figure 11.1 ● Curriculum happens when child meets materials. (Courtesy of Centro Infantil & de Reabilitacao de A-Da-Beja, Lisbon, Portugal.)

tions and evaluations will ensure that the content reflects the interests, needs, and experiences of the child as well as addresses what children should learn.

● The process is *how* and *when* learning takes place, the choice of activities or projects and how they are integrated with one another, and the time frame within the daily schedule or yearly calendar. The process enhances children's involvement in their own learning through a hands-on, exploratory approach with a variety of open-ended materials. Play is the medium for the process.

● The teacher is the person *who* creates the curriculum, planning and providing for activities and materials in relation to the age range of the group and observing and evaluating children's growth. Teachers are grounded in child development theory, have an understanding of how children learn, and are aware of the need to individualize to meet children's special needs.

● The context is *why* certain projects and activities are chosen and is based on the program's philosophy and goals, the cultural backgrounds of the children, and their family and community values and influences. To provide meaningful learning experiences, the curriculum should mirror the life of the local community.

 The relevance of curriculum is important to note.[1] Head Start classes on Indian reservations in the Southwest will develop curricula that utilize the history and traditions of the various Native American tribes the students represent. Relevant curriculum for a suburban preschool in Seattle may include field trips to the Pike Street Market to see the recent salmon catch, while a transportation unit for inner city Chicago preschoolers may include subway and train rides. Curriculum planning that takes children beyond their own community fosters the learning of new skills and concepts. Urban children may make new discoveries about the food they eat when they visit a dairy farm. One of the factors most critical to the success of the schools of Reggio Emilia, as noted in earlier chapters, is the overlay of the child's cultural history in the curriculum. Their town becomes the classroom as they investigate a project on light and shadow among the many columns of the local buildings. The city's rich architecture becomes a means of learning about art, science, math, and history. The theories of Erikson and Vygotsky are evident in this approach to curriculum, especially Vygotsky's belief in the influences of family and culture on the child's learning.

Curriculum is both integrated and individualized. **Individualized curriculum** is tailored to meet the needs and interests of a single child rather than those of a group. Teachers individualize curriculum to help foster specific skills and knowledge in a particular child, such as learning to cut with scissors or how to find playmates. **Integrated curriculum** coordinates many subject areas and utilizes a wholistic approach to learning. See Figure 11.5 on page 390 for an example.

Open Education Revisited

The characteristics of curriculum just described may bring to mind the open schools (see Chapters 1 and 2) of the British infant school model. The emphasis in an open classroom is on the integration of the total curriculum, rather than on the separate subject matter. Academic skills—reading, writing, number concepts—are a natural part of all learning. Music can include math and counting; science discussions develop language arts; and dramatic play can spur writing. The stress is on the learning process—what happens when child and materials meet. Through play, children explore, manipulate, and construct; classroom space encourages them. Activity areas, or centers of interest, are set up throughout the room. Children select where and with whom they want to spend their time, be it with clay, at woodworking, or at one of the table games. The relationship between an open school curriculum and children's learning is also discussed in Chapter 4 in the section regarding the application of cognitive theory.

Teachers facilitate, or guide, setting up the environment to promote independence and self-sufficiency so that they are free to interact with children. Team teaching is ideal for the open classroom; several teachers can provide the amount of supervision, organization, and planning necessary for success.

 OUR DIVERSE WORLD OUR DIVERSE WORLD OUR DIVERSE WORLD OUR DIVERSE WORLD OUR DIVERSE WORLD OUR DIVERSE WORLD OUR DIVERSE WORLD OUR DIVERSE WORLD

[1] Skilled teachers plan a curriculum that strikes a balance between being based on the backgrounds and interests of individual members of the class and the surrounding community while exposing children to experiences from the culture beyond the immediate area.

Figure 11.2 ● Children enjoy and get involved with developmentally appropriate materials. Building with blocks is a fun and popular activity.

Although informally structured classrooms may prove challenging and stimulating to some children, others may find the lack of structure difficult. More traditional programs offer clear goals that are measured by evaluation and testing. The open school's approach includes the children in the planning and evaluation of some of the learning that takes place. If the experiences in an open classroom are not integrated into the total curriculum and the learnings are not related in some meaningful way, they remain merely good—but isolated—experiences for the child.[1] "Done well," says Elkind, "open education can be a model of truly humanistic education; done poorly, it can be a disaster" (Elkind, 1993).

Emergent Curriculum

There are many ways to plan curriculum. One of the most common in early childhood settings is based on the premise that the curriculum is everything that happens throughout the course of a day; it is all of the children's experiences as they interact with people and materials. The emphasis is on children's interests and involvement in their learning and in their ability to make constructive choices. Teachers set up the room and the yard, sometimes planning one or two activities each day that will invite children to participate. For the most part, teachers respond by watching and evaluating what children do and support what use children make of their experience. This is a process-oriented approach; curriculum content is apparent, but an end product or result is not the major focus. It is known as emergent curriculum (Jones & Nimmo, 1994). Figure 11.3 is an example of curriculum planning based on the emergent curriculum approach.

High/Scope and Reggio Emilia schools are programs that seem to typify the rationale for emergent curriculum. Based on the principles of Erikson, Piaget, and Vygotsky, they epitomize a philosophy that says that children are active, curious, powerful learners, capable of taking the initiative and constructing their knowledge through experience. Children are encouraged to use whatever style of learning is most natural to them (Gardner, 1983), making use of the variety of materials in their own way. A materials-rich environment where play is valued forms the setting for such programs.

Emergent curriculum is a process approach to curriculum that calls for collaboration on the part of teachers with children and with other adults. The accent is on mutual learning for both children and adults. Teachers and children think, plan, and critique together. Curriculum emerges from dialogue and reflection among the teaching staff (Jones & Nimmo, 1994) as much as it draws from the interactions between children and teachers. In the Reggio Emilia schools, teachers are seen as collaborators and guides who create curriculum as they take their cues from children's interests and assist them in serious investigation of a topic (see "Webbing" on p. 396 and "The Project Approach" on p. 402; for examples of how teachers' collaboration evolves into curriculum). Emergent curriculum seems to capture the spontaneous nature of children's play and blend it with the necessary planning and organization.

A number of sources feed into emergent curriculum: children's interests, teachers' interests, developmental tasks of the age group, the physical environment, the natural environment, people, curriculum resource books, unexpected events, everyday life experiences and routines, and the values expressed by the school, the parents, and the community (Jones & Nimmo, 1994). As teachers observe, discuss, and

plan, the focus is always on the child, not on the activity.

Developmentally Appropriate Curriculum

Appropriate early childhood curriculum is based on the theory, research, and experience of knowing how young children develop and learn. An infant curriculum meets the basic needs of young babies; a toddler curriculum considers the emerging independence and mobility of toddlers. Four-year-olds require different materials and teaching techniques, as do 5- or 8-year-olds. Each age level deserves special consideration when curriculum is being planned.

What is meant by developmentally appropriate programs, curricula, or practices has been defined by NAEYC (Bredekamp & Copple, 1997) as follows:

● *Appropriateness:* Programs and practices are based on knowledge of normal child development within a given age span.

● *Individual appropriateness:* Programs and practices are based on respect for the individual child, the individual rate of growth, and the unique learning style.

● *Social and cultural appropriateness:* Programs and practices provide meaningful and relevant learning experiences that are respectful of the backgrounds of the children and families in the group.[1]

In her Focus Box in this chapter, Sue Bredekamp discusses some of the factors that determine development appropriateness and notes specifically those components that will most likely result in high-quality experiences and programs.

Developmentally appropriate curriculum takes into account a knowledge of child development theory, research, and practice, including various related disciplines; cultural values; parental desires and concerns; community context; individual children; teachers' knowledge and experience; and it is related to overall program goals.[2] This implies a theoretical framework about how, when, and what children learn. The foundation for developmentally appropriate practices and

[1] DAP is CAC, Developmentally appropriate curriculum is culturally appropriate curriculum.
[2] There is no one "recipe" for developmentally appropriate practice; rather, sound practice is related to the individual children, families, and the community in which one teaches.

Lesson Plan For A Week in February

AREA	GOALS OF ACTIVITY	LEARNING OPPORTUNITY	EMERGENT CURRICULUM	NOTES
INSIDE				
blocks	to use structure for play to build cooperatively to use different cuts for different purposes	unit blocks; scissors, paper, tape for embellishment	Tues.—add batteries. switches, light bulbs to illuminate structures	
dramatic play	to sustain play in groups of 3+ to play a variety of roles	post office; envelopes, mail boxes, individual mail boxes, stamps, bags for letter carrying	Wed.—add walking trip to post office for a tour	
writing table	to write some upper and lower case letters to dictate compositions for transcription	markers, pencils, blank books, paper, class dictionary		work with Nora on writing name indep.
sensory	to use site for exploration to explore physical properties of sand to construct knowledge of conservation	sand table; funnels, scoops, graduated measures		
manipulatives	to strength fine motor control to sort and classify over two variables	mosaic boards; colored pegs: cylinders, rectangles, triangles	Thur.—add pattern cards	make available materials to copy own patterns onto cards
cooking	to wait to take turns to follow a sequence to explore physical properties	fruit shakes; bananas, strawberries, yogurt, honey, butter knives, blender; cups, straws, recipe cards		vary fruit
book rug	to follow sequence of a story read aloud to relate story in own words after hearing	books about the beach, cooking, post office, mail, letters		include books of diversity—nongender-specific roles, ethnicity[1]
OUTSIDE				
climbing	to climb w/alternating feet and hands to develop upper body strength	boards and boxes, play scape, tree house		
riding	to pedal, steer with skill to use for dramatic play	tricycles—traditional and low-slung styles		help Miguel with steering tricycle
sensory	to use site for exploration to use site for constructing replicas of environment	sand box; scoops, buckets trucks, cardboard piping	Tues.—add water	
dramatic play	to role play with 3+ children to incorporate many elements into play to make own props	play houses; scarves, wraps, housekeeping props, wagons	Wed.—add doll carriages	Petero's new baby to visit

Figure 11.3 ● This plan, created by Kelly Welch, a teacher at the Connecticut College Children's School, is built on the interests and abilities of the group as well as the individual needs of the children. It is a good example of emergent curriculum in a written format.

OUR DIVERSE WORLD OUR DIVERSE WORLD OUR DIVERSE WORLD OUR DIVERSE WORLD OUR DIVERSE WORLD OUR DIVERSE WORLD OUR DIVERSE WORLD OUR DIVERSE WORLD

[1] Children need books that are relevant to their social and cultural reality and that are expressive of the multiethnic world in which they live.

GUIDELINES FOR DEVELOPMENTALLY APPROPRIATE CURRICULUM

NAEYC and the National Association of Early Childhood Specialists in State Departments of Education jointly developed guidelines to ensure developmentally appropriate curriculum. Each of the guidelines is in the form of a question to which teachers developing curriculum for young children should be able to answer "yes."

1. Does it promote interactive learning and encourage the child's construction of knowledge?

2. Does it help achieve social, emotional, physical, and cognitive goals?

3. Does it encourage development of positive feelings and dispositions toward learning while leading to acquisition of knowledge and skills?

4. Is it meaningful for these children? Is it relevant to the children's lives? Can it be made more relevant by relating it to a personal experience children have had or can they easily gain direct experience with it?

5. Are the expectations realistic and attainable at this time, or could the children more easily and efficiently acquire the knowledge or skills later on?

6. Is it of interest to children and to the teacher?

7. Is is sensitive to and respectful of cultural and linguistic diversity? Does it expect, allow, and appreciate individual differences? Does it promote positive relationships with families?

8. Does it build on and elaborate children's current knowledge and abilities?

9. Does it lead to conceptual understanding by helping children construct their own understanding in meaningful contexts?

10. Does it facilitate integration of content across traditional subject matter areas?

11. Is the information presented accurate and credible according to the recognized standards of the relevant discipline?

12. Is this content worth knowing? Can it be learned by these children efficiently and effectively now?

13. Does it encourage active learning and allow children to make meaningful choices?

14. Does it foster children's exploration and inquiry, rather than focusing on "right" answers or "right" ways to complete a task?

15. Does it promote the development of higher order abilities such as thinking, reasoning, problem solving, and decision making?

16. Does it promote and encourage social interaction among children and adults?

17. Does it respect children's physiological needs for activity, sensory stimulation, fresh air, rest, and nourishment/elimination?

18. Does it promote feelings of psychological safety, security, and belonging?

19. Does it provide experiences that promote feelings of success, competence, and enjoyment of learning?

20. Does it permit flexibility for children and teachers?

Figure 11.4 ● (Adapted from Bredekamp, S., & Rosegrant, T. [1995]. *Reaching potentials: transforming early childhood curriculum and assessment* [Vol. 2]. Washington, DC: National Association for the Education of Young Children.)

In music: Singing "Five Little Pumpkins"

In routines: Waiting for a turn because "too many" are brushing teeth already

In books: *Inch by Inch* by Lionni, *Millions of Cats* by Gag

In block play: Observing and using the fractions and wholes that make up a set of unit blocks

In physical development: Playing hopscotch

In cooking: Measuring and counting items in the recipe

In dramatic play: Noting there are only four hoses but five firefighters

In science: Counting number of rainy/sunny/snowy days; recording temperatures (thermometers); time (clocks and calendars); and seasons (charts)

In art: Numbers: learning one-to-one correspondence by counting brushes, crayons, Magic Markers, and colors

Figure 11.5 ● Young children learn best from an integrated approach to curriculum. Mathematical concepts are reflected throughout the classroom in a variety of activities.

curriculum content is historically rooted in John Dewey's vision that schools prepare students to think and reason in order to participate in a democratic society (see Chapter 1). Figure 11.4 lists 20 guidelines jointly endorsed by the National Association for the Education of Young Children and the National Association of Early Childhood Specialists in State Departments of Education to ensure developmentally appropriate curriculum. It can be used as a checklist as you move through the next three chapters, which focus on curriculum.

Developmentally appropriate curriculum is integrated curriculum; that is, it is woven across many subject areas. Figure 11.5 shows how mathematical principles are fostered as an integral part of the child's day. Other illustrations in this and the following three chapters demonstrate an integrated curriculum.

The NAEYC's recent position statements and guidelines on appropriate program practices and curriculum for early childhood settings can be used as a basis for sound curriculum planning. These materials cover the age span of birth through age 8; develop-

mental characteristics unique to each age group (infants, toddlers, preschoolers, and primary ages) form the basis for determining appropriate practices. A resource of this kind should be consulted before curriculum plans are developed.

Culturally Appropriate Curriculum

Throughout this text the rationale for multicultural education is underscored, from demographics to anti-bias practices. Vygotsky's sociocultural theory adds further endorsement. If meaningful learning is derived from a social and cultural context, then multiculturalism must permeate the environment and become totally integrated into the curriculum. A multicultural atmosphere must be created where awareness and concern for true diversity (including ethnicity, gender, and abilities) "permeates the ongoing program of teaching and learning" (King, Chipman, & Cruz-Janzen, 1994). Creating a truly multicultural classroom calls into question the familiar ways of doing things and provides new insights and ways of thinking about culture. Multicultural education is about "modifying the total school environment so that students from diverse ethnic and cultural groups will experience equal educational opportunities (Banks, 1994). Figure 11.6 highlights the difference by comparing common characteristics of a dominant culture with an approach that would offer more perspectives from other cultures.

Culturally appropriate curriculum is also developmentally appropriate curriculum. The challenge is to develop a curriculum that reflects the plurality of contemporary American society in general and the individual classroom, in particular, and present them in sensitive, relevant ways. This does not necessarily mean creating a whole new curriculum. Banks (1992) suggests the **infusion** of multicultural content within the current practices as a way to begin to develop a multicultural curriculum. This is a continual, ongoing process of integrating the learning environment with the "inclusion of the pluralistic nature of our society in all aspects of the curriculum" (King et al., 1994).

Infusion, according to Banks (1994), allows the teacher to continue using a developmentally appropriate curriculum while incorporating many perspectives, frames of reference, and content from various groups that will extend a child's understanding of today's society. This principle is demonstrated in Figure 11.7, in which the theme of "All About Me" is used for a dual purpose: to help children recognize

Characteristics of a Multicultural Curriculum

Common Practices of Dominant Culture	For a Multicultural Approach
Focuses on isolated aspects of the histories and cultures of ethnic groups	Describes the history and cultures of ethnic groups holistically
Trivializes the histories and cultures of ethnic groups	Describes the cultures of ethnic groups as dynamic wholes
Presents events, issues, and concepts primarily from Anglocentric and mainstream perspectives	Presents events, issues, concepts from the perspectives of diverse racial and ethnic groups
Is Eurocentric—shows the development of the United States primarily as an extension of Europe into the Americas	Is multidimensional and geocultural—shows how many peoples and cultures came to the United States from many parts of the world, including Asia and Africa, and the important roles they played in the development of U.S. society
Content about ethnic groups is an appendage to regular curriculum	Content about ethnic groups is an integral part of regular curriculum
Ethnic minority cultures are described as deprived or dysfunctional	Ethnic minority cultures are described as different from mainstream Anglo culture but as rich and functional
Focuses on ethnic heroes, holidays, and factual information	Focuses on concepts, generalizations, and theories
Emphasizes the mastery of knowledge and cognitive outcomes	Emphasizes knowledge formation and decision-making
Encourages acceptance of existing ethnic, class, and racial stratification	Focuses on social criticism and social change

Figure 11.6 ● A comparison of two different approaches to multicultural curriculum, one from a Eurocentric point of view, the other from a culturally sensitive perspective. (Adapted from Banks, J. A. [1994]. *Dominant and desirable characteristics of multiethnic studies* [p. 185]. Boston: Allyn & Bacon. Used with permission.)

their own unique self and to foster pride in their cultural diversity. This is a good example of using a common early childhood curriculum theme and and infusing other cultural perspectives into it.

The infusion approach calls into question the common practice in many early childhood programs of cooking ethnic foods or celebrating ethnic or cultural holidays as isolated experiences, which often trivialize or stereotype groups of people.[1] Folk tales, songs, food,

and dress are symbols and expressions of a culture, not the culture itself. For children to gain any meaningful knowledge, the content must contribute to a fuller understanding of human diversity, not just a special-occasion topic. On the other hand, using music from various cultures for movement and dance activities throughout the curriculum throughout the year incorporates the perspective of a pluralistic society into the established routines and rituals of the classroom.

OUR DIVERSE WORLD OUR DIVERSE WORLD OUR DIVERSE WORLD OUR DIVERSE WORLD OUR DIVERSE WORLD OUR DIVERSE WORLD OUR DIVERSE WORLD OUR DIVERSE WORLD

1 This is often referred to as the tourist approach to diversity.

Planning for Quality: The Basics

Sue Bredekamp

In the early 1980s, the National Association for the Education of Young Children (NAEYC) developed a voluntary accreditation system for early childhood centers and schools. The development of the system began with the question "What is a high-quality early childhood program?" NAEYC defines a high-quality early childhood program as "one that meets the needs of and promotes the physical, social, emotional and cognitive development of the children and adults—parents, staff, and administrators—who are involved in the program."

The accreditation criteria address several components of an early childhood program and define standards for each. But "quality" is more than the sum of a program's parts. Our accreditation experience has taught us that what happens to children in classrooms—the nature of the interactions, the appropriateness of the curriculum, and the provisions for health and safety—is the real quality.

But in order for children to have these positive experiences on a daily basis, many other things must be in place.

These other things, the *predictors of quality*, are specially trained teachers, adequate ratios of adults to children, regular communication with parents, age-appropriate materials, accessible indoor and outdoor environments, nutritious snacks and meals, effective administration, and systematic ongoing evaluation.

These predictors of quality grew out of NAEYC's continuing efforts to define what is "developmentally appropriate practice" (DAP) for teaching children, in order to provide young children with a positive educational experience. It is important to remember that many factors enter into providing a high-quality program; key factors are staff who are positive and supportive of individual children and a curriculum that is appropriate for the age, the individual, and the cultures of the children.

Another important dimension of the basics of high-quality education for young children is understanding the interrelatedness of the various components of a program. Research tends to show that "good things" happen together and influence each other. Well-trained teachers do a better job if they work with small groups of children and have adequate materials; a well-planned, age-appropriate curriculum; a supportive administrator; and involved parents.

Dr. Sue Bredekamp was the Director of Professional Development at NAEYC and is now at the Council for Early Childhood Professional Recognition in Washington, D.C.

De Melendez & Ostertag (1997) offer some helpful perspectives in this regard through Figure 11.7 and the following suggestions on how to begin the process of infusion:

1. List the topics/themes/units from your current curriculum guide or lesson plans.

2. With your class list in hand, look for the traits that are descriptive of cultural diversity of the students in your class (ethnicities, religion, languages, social class, exceptionality/abilities).

3. Circle on the list of topics/themes/units those areas that lend themselves to infusion of diversity. Begin by incorporating those characteristics found in your own classroom, then consider those of others.

4. Brainstorm how you could incorporate diversity into the selected topics. Ask yourself what other views could help children expand their understanding of this topic? Write down all responses.

5. Refine the list of ideas and topics/themes/units including the additional perspectives. Put into action.

6. Assess the results. Keep notes on children's responses and reactions. Revise your plan according to what you have learned.

Curriculum materials and activities need to be evaluated to ensure fair and sensitive portrayals of various cultures. When choosing a topic for curriculum infusion, make sure it is consistent with the philosophy and goals of the school as expressed in the current curriculum, and it should contribute to the understanding of life in our diverse society, according to de Melendez & Ostertag (1997). Those authors propose asking the following questions as a way of assessing the choice of a topic for infusion. Does the topic:

● Present, elaborate and/or expand concepts of diversity?

● Fit logically into the child's learning and experience, giving a sense of real, not unimportant, learning?

● Include the perspectives of how the people with diverse cultural views would behave or react to it?

All About Me

Topics
- I am like you but I'm different, too
- Things I can do
- Stories I like
- Stories my friends like
- Where do I come from? (community, state, country)
- Things my friends and I enjoy doing
- Things I do at home
- Things I do in the classroom
- My favorite game
- Clothes I like to wear
- My favorite words
- Things I like to eat
- My favorite song

Possible Activities
- Visit local grocery store to pick favorite fruits, vegetables
- Learn games from other countries
- Invite parents to tell us about their favorite games and songs
- Read stories from other countries, learn about the authors
- Prepare a graph about the physical characteristics of children in the class
- Learn words in other languages (greetings, names of food)
- Look at the pictures of children from Haiti or India to see how they dress. Compare with how we dress in the United States

Perspective on Diversity
- Learning about what children in other states and countries do (e.g., India, Haiti)*
- Learning about the communities of other countries
- Stories children like in other countries
- Games from other countries
- Activities children do in other countries
- Clothes children use in, for example, Haiti and Venezuela
- Learning basic words in other languages
- Typical snacks and food in other places
- Music children sing in other countries

*Emphasis on what is current in those countries or cultures.

Figure 11.7 ● An example of curriculum infusion. (From de Melendez, R. W., & Ostertag, V. [1997]. *Teaching young children in multicultural classrooms.* Albany, NY: Delmar. Used with permission.)

PLANNING AN ACTIVITY

Purpose of Activity: Think about how children will learn
    Concepts
    To discriminate
    Vocabulary
    Social skills
    Motor skills
    Feelings of competence and confidence
    Method or process of the activity

Presentation: Think about
    What antecedents are necessary for this activity?
    To whom will you present it—individual, group—and what ages?
    Where are you going to present it—in/outdoors? What area?
    Materials/props you will need—how will you use them?
    What words will you use to introduce and carry through the activity?
    What are the cleanup provisions? Will children be involved? How?

Results: Ask yourself
    What was the children's response to the activity?
    Did you achieve what you wanted?
    What are the implications for other activities?
    Were there any problems, and how did you solve them?

Figure 11.8 ● Good planning takes time and thought. These questions can help the teacher focus on the important aspects of planning an activity for young children.

● Reflect issues that are common to the children in the classroom or the community?

● Offer opportunities to present other positions that expose the children to divergent views?

● Serve as a link to discuss emotions and feelings as perceived by the children?

● Facilitate clarification of stereotypes and biases? How?

To gain a greater sense of what multicultural curriculum can be in the early years, keep these questions in mind as you read through the rest of this chapter. Refer to the sections in Chapter 9 on anti-bias environments and inclusive environments and to the multicultural environment checklist (Figure 9.7) as well.

Planning Curriculum

Written Plans

In the development of curriculum, written plans are helpful, especially for the beginning teacher. A written plan is an organized agenda, an outline to follow, a framework for the curriculum. It may include a list of activities, goals for children's learning experiences, the process or method of instruction, the teacher's responsibilities, the time of day, and other special notations. A curriculum may be developed for a day, a week, a month, or a specific unit or theme. The questions in Figure 11.8 should be asked when planning a curriculum activity for young children. Figure 11.3 illustrates a weekly curriculum, and Figure 11.20 illustrates a curriculum for toddlers. This and the next

PLANNING BY OBJECTIVES

Activity	Teaching Objectives	Behavioral Objectives/Child Will:
Painting with corn cobs	Tactile stimulation; awareness of textural design; fine-motor coordination; observational skills	Describe how it feels and looks; grasp, manipulate, and examine cob; use thumb and forefinger to hold cob while painting; compare with other textures
Outdoor obstacle	Spatial awareness; balance; gross-motor development; building confidence	Walk across 6′ board at 2″ and 4″ heights; crawl through tunnel; jump from height of 2½′ without assistance; call for others to watch; repeat the course on own

Figure 11.9 ● Learning objectives define the goals and describe the desired behavior or outcome. (For guidelines in observation, see Chapter 6.)

three chapters contain many examples of written lesson plans.

Planning by Objectives

Another approach to curriculum development requires more formal, organized planning. Comprehensive lesson plans are developed, sometimes for the whole year, and usually include *objectives*, the stated concepts that children will learn through this experience. These are commonly called *behavioral objectives*. The lesson plans include specific, stated, observable behaviors that children will be able to demonstrate to show that the teaching objective has been met. In other words, a behavioral objective states clearly what children will actually *do* (be able to hold scissors properly; grasp a pencil between thumb and first two fingers). If the behavioral objective is to improve fine-motor skills, the lesson plan includes activities and events that foster children's use of their fine-motor skills. Several objectives may apply to a given activity. It is then important to order the objectives so that the purposes of the lesson remain in focus. To plan successfully, the teacher needs to know developmental and behavioral theory (Chapter 4), to have good observational strategies (Chapter 6), and to possess tools to assess whether the objective was accomplished (Chapter 10).

Figure 11.9 reflects the planning approach with the use of behavioral objectives. A more developed plan found in early childhood classrooms would include activities for the full range of curriculum areas, such as art, motor activities, and dramatic play, for each of the objectives.

If too much attention is focused on an isolated skill (Elkind, 1987), the objectives and goal become the curriculum itself. Too little planning can result in a curriculum free-for-all where integration of learning never takes place. A balance must be achieved between excess planning and go-with-the-flow curriculum to ensure that children's needs and interests are being met and to guarantee children a sense of organization and intentionality about what they learn.

Two important factors in developing curriculum objectives are (1) how much knowledge and understanding children have and (2) what children are interested in. The most effective curriculum grows out of the child's interests and experiences. As they play, children reveal their levels of experience and information as well as their misconceptions and confusions, providing the clues from which teachers can develop curriculum that is meaningful.[1]

 OUR DIVERSE WORLD OUR DIVERSE WORLD OUR DIVERSE WORLD OUR DIVERSE WORLD OUR DIVERSE WORLD OUR DIVERSE WORLD OUR DIVERSE WORLD OUR DIVERSE WORLD
1 Adults who are culturally sensitive can use this information to plan activities that deal with racism, sexism, and disabilities bias.

Webbing

According to Katz and Chard (1989), **webbing** is the process through which teachers develop a diagram based on a particular topic or theme, highlighting key ideas and concepts. Ideas generated from brainstorming sessions flesh out the topic with many subheadings and lists of curriculum possibilities. Figure 11.10 illustrates a curriculum or topic web.

Webbing is a planning tool that provides depth to a topic and creates a map of possible activities and projects. A web may be organized around a theme (water), into curriculum areas (language arts, music), or around program goals (problem-solving, cooperation). By their very nature, webs foster an integrated curriculum approach and help teachers extend children's learning and experiences.

Creating a web can be fun, allowing teachers to use their imaginations and calling into play their knowledge, resources, and experience. Katz and Chard (1989) suggest the following process to develop a web, using examples from Figure 11.10:

1. *Brainstorming*. Using small slips of paper, teachers write down theme or topic ideas—each idea on a separate piece of paper. For the topic "Things that happen in fall and winter," for instance, the slips would contain ideas such as "cut jack-o-lanterns" or "rake leaves."

2. *Grouping*. The slips of paper are organized into groups of similar ideas, and, on a colored piece of paper, a heading is given to each group. "Canning and preserving" and "seasonal recipes" fall under the heading of "Cooking." Subgroups can be created, if necessary.

3. *Sharing*. Teachers can share their ideas with one another, rearranging the headings and subheadings as they share skills, resources, and information with one another.

4. *Drawing*. The ideas can be transferred to a piece of paper, placing the topic or theme in the center and drawing lines radiating out to the headings (group time, manipulatives, dramatic play). This creates a visual record of the relationships between and among the ideas and becomes what Workman and Anziano (1993) call "a living, growing resource."

Jones and Nimmo (1994) emphasize the organic nature of a web. First created as a response to children's ideas, it creates a picture in which ideas emerge and connect in any number of ways. It is, of course, a tentative plan, for what happens next depends on the children's responses. The web creates a flexible plan that can be altered and adapted as teachers observe children and evaluate their interest.

Advantages of Written Plans

Setting lesson plans to paper has many advantages. Doing so:

● Helps teachers focus on the nature of the children they teach—their interests, their needs, their capabilities, their potential.

● Encourages thorough, in-depth planning of curriculum in a logical progression; provides a direction.

● Helps teachers clarify thoughts and articulate a rationale for what they do.

● Stimulates teamwork when teachers plan together, sharing their ideas and resources.

● Allows everyone to know what is happening; in case of absences, a substitute teacher can carry out the plans.

● Gives a foundation from which changes can be made; allows for flexibility, adaptation, and on-the-spot decisions.

● Allows for time to prepare materials, to see what is needed and what resources to gather or contact.

● Provides a concrete format from which evaluation and assessment can be made.

● Serves as a communication tool for the teaching staff, for parents, and for the governing agency.

● Teachers see how much they have offered children, and the program's worth is communicated to others.

Written plans may or may not include all of the other activities normally available in the interest centers all week. Blocks, manipulatives, and dramatic play, as well as science, math, and language materials remain available for children to choose, but some teachers include only planned learning experiences and teacher-directed activities in their written plans. Certain activities are part of the everyday routine. The

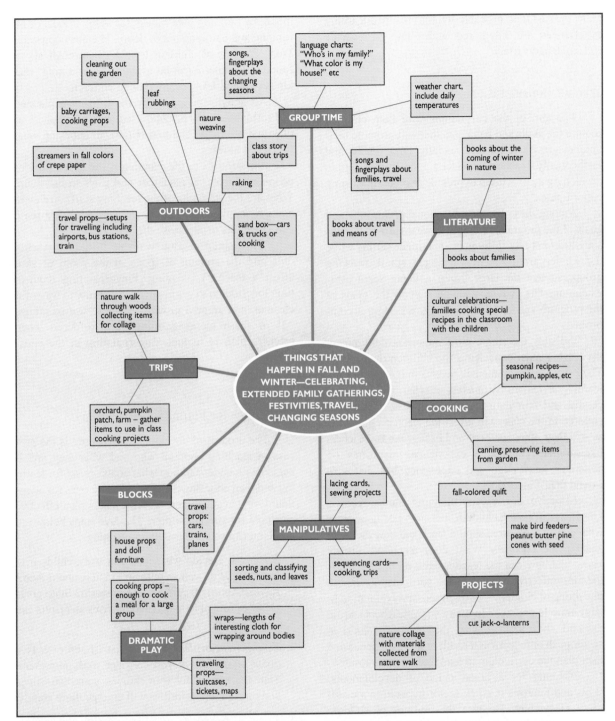

Figure 11.10 ● Using a theme based on children's interests and ideas, the web provides an avenue to foster relationships between ideas and events and helps extend children's knowledge and experience.[1] (Thanks to Kelly Welch of Connecticut College Children's School for this example.)

OUR DIVERSE WORLD OUR DIVERSE WORLD OUR DIVERSE WORLD OUR DIVERSE WORLD OUR DIVERSE WORLD OUR DIVERSE WORLD OUR DIVERSE WORLD OUR DIVERSE WORLD

[1] This chart represents a multicultural point of view, particularly in the way fall and winter holidays are expressed.

more focused (and probably written) planned learning experiences are integrated with them to provide challenge and variety.

Teacher Considerations

The aim of the curriculum is to help children acquire the skills and behaviors that will promote their optimal growth physically, socially, emotionally, and intellectually. Teachers consider a number of factors in developing a curriculum to provide maximum learning opportunities.

Among these are the educational philosophy and goals of the program. A family day care provider plans activities for a few children in an intimate setting while the kindergarten teacher arranges small working groups so that the large group will not seem overwhelming. The activities should support the goals of the program and result in those goals's being accomplished.

Probably the single most important determinant the teacher must consider is the children themselves. Their ages, developmental levels, individuality, and learning styles are barometers of what will be a successful and stimulating curriculum. The number of children in the class will affect the teacher's planning, as will their ethnic and cultural backgrounds. Teachers like to plan curriculum experiences that draw on children's knowledge and experience but that also extend their thinking.

Effective curriculum planning stems from a knowledge of young children. Teachers ask themselves what concepts children should learn and how they will teach those concepts. What does the child already know, and how can the teacher build on that? What is the most effective way to teach a particular concept to this group of children—through sensory exploration or large-muscle practice? In many ways, teachers start at the end: they look at what they want the child to accomplish or to learn as a result of this experience and then plan the curriculum to lead toward those results.

Planning for a broad range of developmental skills and interests is a key factor in creating a classroom curriculum. Because the abilities of children even of the same age vary, activities must be open-ended and flexible enough to be used by a number of children with varieties of skills. Remember, too, that some children may not be interested in formal or organized art projects or science experiences. These children may learn more easily through self-selected play: by wearing a space helmet and fantasizing a trip to the moon, by building with blocks for long periods, or by running and climbing out of doors. The developmental Word Pictures of children from birth through age 8 found in Chapter 3 can be useful in determining what kinds of activities appeal to young children.

All activities—especially those that are planned and formal—should be conducted in an atmosphere of play that offers the children options in choosing what they need to learn.

A *prerequisite* for planning is the availability of people and material resources and ways to use them. What are the strengths of the teaching staff? Are there enough supplies and equipment available? Are there enough adults to supervise the activities?

The amount of time available in the daily schedule and the amount of space in the room or yard affect a teacher's planning. Fingerpainting requires time for children to get involved, proximity to water for cleanup, and an area in which to store wet paintings. All of these elements must be considered when teachers plan to include fingerpainting in the curriculum.

Guidelines for Planning Curriculum

The process of developing curriculum is the process of teaching children who and what they are. It begins with understanding what goals are set for learning and then choosing the most pressing ones for attention. Using available resources, teachers plan effective curricula for young children. The five steps below are guidelines to sound curriculum planning.

1. *Set goals.* Decide what it is you want children to learn. What do you want them to know about themselves? About others? About the world? State goals clearly, preferably in behavioral terms so results can be measured.

2. *Establish priorities.* Make a list of three to five goals or objectives you consider most important. State the reasons for your choices; your own values and educational priorities will emerge more clearly.

3. *Know the resources.* A rich, successful, and creative curriculum relies on a vast number of resources. To create a health clinic in the dramatic play area, for instance, you might need the following resources:

● *Materials:* Props, such as stethoscopes, x-ray machines, tongue depressors, adhesive strips, medical gowns, and masks.

● *People:* Parents and/or community people in the health care professions to visit the class.[1]

● *Community:* Field trips to nearby clinic, hospital, dentist's office.

4. *Plan ahead.* Set aside a regular time to meet for curriculum planning. This may be on a weekly, monthly, or seasonal basis. Discuss the curriculum activities as well as the daily routines in order to integrate the two.

5. *Evaluate.* Reflect on the outcome of your planning. Consider what worked and what did not, why it was successful or not. Look at the part of the experience that did not work as well as you would have liked. How can it be improved? What can you change about it? An evaluation should be immediate, precise, and supportive. Teachers need feedback about their planning and implementing skills. The needs of children are best served when the curriculum is refined and improved.

Curriculum Focus

Curriculum, as defined here, is all-encompassing. Teachers select from all the possibilities that afford the potential for learning and focus on projects and activities in a balanced, integrated way. Three common approaches are to look at (1) the activity or learning centers in the classroom, (2) the skills of the children, and (3) themes.

Classroom Activity Centers

The activity centers in most early childhood programs consist of:

Indoors	Outdoors
Creative arts	Climbing equipment
Blocks	Swings
Table toys/manipulatives	Sand/mud/water
Science/discovery	Wheel toys
Dramatic play	Woodworking
Language arts/books	Hollow blocks
Math	Music
Music	Nature/science

All of these centers offer activities and materials for children to choose from during free play time—the greatest portion of their school day. (See typical daily schedules in Chapter 2.) Paints are in the easel trays, puzzles on the tables, dress-up clothes and props in the housekeeping/dramatic play center, blocks and accessories in the block corner, and books and tapes in the language area. Teachers plan the resources and materials and place them so that children readily see the alternatives available to them. Some of these activities might be teacher-directed on occasion: cooking snacks in the housekeeping area, fingerpainting in art, creating castles with blocks. For the most part, however, these activities will be self-initiating and child-directed. At all times, the emphasis will be on providing a child-centered curriculum.

Whatever the area, it needs attention and planning. Wherever children are present, learning and playing will take place. Because each play space will make a contribution to children's experiences, teachers should develop appropriate curriculum for that learning area. The web in Figure 11.10 demonstrates curriculum potential, both indoors and out.

Go back and review what Chapter 9 offers as some of the important principles in creating environments that reflect curriculum goals and what Chapter 2 offers for daily schedules.

Children's Skills

Just as curriculum can be developed by focusing on the activity or learning centers, so, too, can an early childhood program be planned around the skill levels of the children in the class.

The first decision teachers must make concerns what particular skill they wish to help children develop. The skill can be in the area of physical, cognitive, language, creative, social, or emotional development. The nature of the individual class and the program philosophy will help teachers establish priorities for these skills. Teachers then select the activities and materials that will enhance the development of any one or more of those particular skills. Figure 11.12 shows how the cognitive skill of classification can be implemented in the classroom, making it the focus of the entire curriculum.

 OUR DIVERSE WORLD OUR DIVERSE WORLD OUR DIVERSE WORLD OUR DIVERSE WORLD OUR DIVERSE WORLD OUR DIVERSE WORLD OUR DIVERSE WORLD OUR DIVERSE WORLD

[1] Involving parents in their work or professional role is a supportive and meaningful way to help them become involved in their child's learning.

Figure 11.11 ● Teachers of toddlers encourage touching and feeling, simple problem-solving, and choosing play materials. They remain patient as children explore the environment.

Themes

A common method of developing curriculum is to focus on themes, also known as units. Though used interchangeably, themes are generally a smaller part of a unit, allowing for a more specific focus. For example, a unit on the body may have "What I can do with my hands" as one theme. This mode of planning is used in many early childhood and elementary settings; it is often a way to emphasize holidays. Focusing on themes, however, can and should be much more than that.

Themes that are of great interest to young children are those that directly concern themselves. The body as a theme suggests many avenues for development; body parts may be emphasized; exploration using the senses may be stressed; measuring and weighing children may be used to demonstrate growth of the body. Another subject to which children readily respond is that of home and family. Animals, especially pets, are appealing to young children and can lead into

further curriculum areas of wild animals, prehistoric animals, and so on.

The more in touch with children the teachers are, the more their classroom themes should reflect the children's interests and abilities. Children who live in Silicon Valley in California, in Houston, Texas, or in Central Florida may have a local interest in space shuttles and computers.[1] The urban child of New York, Detroit, or Washington, D.C., will relate more readily to themes about subways, taxis, and tall buildings. Children's interests often focus on, but are not necessarily limited to, what they have experienced. By choosing themes that coincide with children's daily lives, teachers promote connected and relevant learning.

Television, travel, and older brothers and sisters enlarge a child's vision so that the themes a teacher chooses do not have to reflect only the world in which the child lives. With appropriate visual aids and manipulative materials, a child in the sunbelt can experience snow and ice *vicariously* or enjoy learning a song and dance from Spain.

Some themes in an early childhood setting can address children's own issues. All young children share similar fears and curiosity about the world they do not know but imagine so vividly. The cues children give, particularly about their concerns, suggest to the observant teacher some important themes of childhood. During Halloween, for example, it can be helpful and reassuring to children if the theme of masks is developed. Select some masks that have a function, such as hospital masks, ski masks, safety glasses, sun glasses, snorkel masks, or wrestling and football helmets. Children can try them on and become comfortable with the way their appearance changes. They can laugh with friends as they look in the mirror to see how a mask changes the appearance but does not change the person.

Prehistoric animals is another theme that calls attention to the natural world and deals with issues of monsters. Learning about sea animals and the ocean can give young children an opportunity to talk about the wild and noisy waves, sharks, and just getting their faces wet in salty water.

[1] A good multicultural curriculum should make maximum use of experiential learning, especially using local community resources.

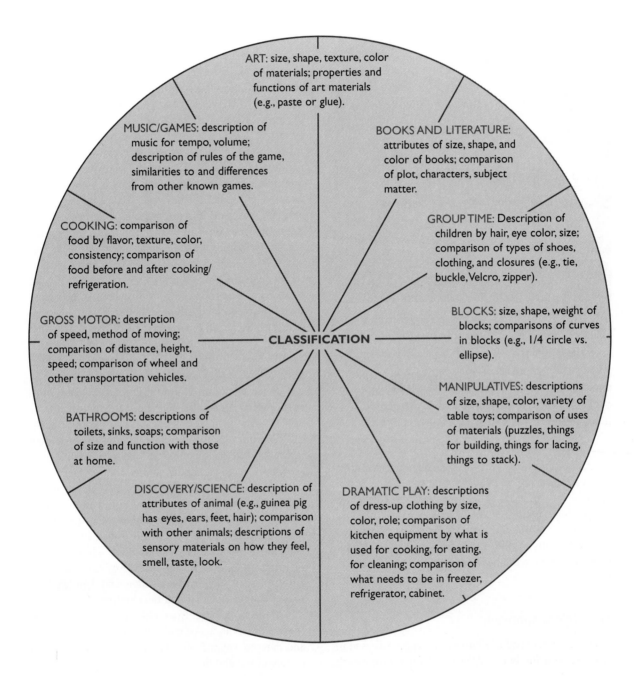

ART: size, shape, texture, color of materials; properties and functions of art materials (e.g., paste or glue).

MUSIC/GAMES: description of music for tempo, volume; description of rules of the game, similarities to and differences from other known games.

BOOKS AND LITERATURE: attributes of size, shape, and color of books; comparison of plot, characters, subject matter.

COOKING: comparison of food by flavor, texture, color, consistency; comparison of food before and after cooking/refrigeration.

GROUP TIME: Description of children by hair, eye color, size; comparison of types of shoes, clothing, and closures (e.g., tie, buckle, Velcro, zipper).

GROSS MOTOR: description of speed, method of moving; comparison of distance, height, speed; comparison of wheel and other transportation vehicles.

CLASSIFICATION

BLOCKS: size, shape, weight of blocks; comparisons of curves in blocks (e.g., 1/4 circle vs. ellipse).

MANIPULATIVES: descriptions of size, shape, color, variety of table toys; comparison of uses of materials (puzzles, things for building, things for lacing, things to stack).

BATHROOMS: descriptions of toilets, sinks, soaps; comparison of size and function with those at home.

DISCOVERY/SCIENCE: description of attributes of animal (e.g., guinea pig has eyes, ears, feet, hair); comparison with other animals; descriptions of sensory materials on how they feel, smell, taste, look.

DRAMATIC PLAY: descriptions of dress-up clothing by size, color, role; comparison of kitchen equipment by what is used for cooking, for eating, for cleaning; comparison of what needs to be in freezer, refrigerator, cabinet.

Figure 11.12 ● Curriculum can be developed with a focus on a particular skill. Classification skills can be enhanced throughout the curriculum and in activity centers. NOTE: This is a graphic way to demonstrate an integrated curriculum, not an example of a format on how to write curriculum plans.

Figure 11.13 ● A project emerged from the need for a new table. Children in Reggio Emilia, Italy, used their feet as a measuring device and drew up plans for the carpenter. Active exploration of the problem and art as a natural medium for children of all ages give the project approach meaning. (Courtesy of the city of Reggio Emilia, Italy.)

Through holiday themes, teachers can reinforce the multicultural nature of the curriculum. Ethnic, national, and religious holidays from all over the world help children celebrate the differences and similarities in people and their heritage. Themes relating to children's cultural and ethnic backgrounds and their neighborhood environments also provide rich curriculum potential.[1]

The Project Approach

A recent revival of a curriculum approach used in progressive schools (see Dewey, Chapter 1) is worth noting here. In *Engaging Children's Minds: The Project Approach* (1989), authors Katz and Chard describe how to go beyond themes and units for an in-depth study of a particular topic by one or more children. Based on the belief that "children's minds should be engaged in ways that deepen their understanding of their own experiences and environment" (Katz & Chard, 1989), the *project approach* consists of exploring a theme or topic (such as babies, dinosaurs, riding the school bus) over a period of days or weeks. Investigations of the theme and preplanning by the children and teachers is the first step: they observe, question, estimate, experiment, and research items and events related to the topic. Together they make dramatic play and display materials they need. When fully engaged, dramatic play becomes the primary vehicle by which children enact the roles related to the project theme. Children work in small groups throughout the process and have the opportunity to make numerous choices about their level of participation. Project work has different levels of complexity so it meets the needs of children of different ages and abilities.

In the small town of Reggio Emilia in northern Italy, a similar approach to curriculum has received worldwide attention. The project approach is used in even greater depth as it permeates the entire curriculum and school environment.

Four keys elements create the unique curriculum of Reggio Emilia and enhance the project approach to learning: (1) teachers believe that children learn best when they actively explore problems; (2) the art media, as natural forms of expression and exploration, provide the vehicle by which children can express themselves, their understanding of the world, and their learning; (3) the entire community is a resource—from a statue in a park to an observatory outside of town to senior citizens; and (4) the teachers understand their teaching role as co-constructors with the children.

Projects emerge from children's own interests, teacher observations of children's needs and interests, and parents' suggestions. The topics reflect the local culture of the children.[2]

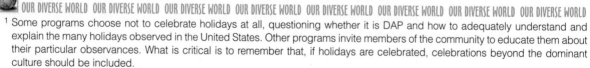
OUR DIVERSE WORLD OUR DIVERSE WORLD OUR DIVERSE WORLD OUR DIVERSE WORLD OUR DIVERSE WORLD OUR DIVERSE WORLD OUR DIVERSE WORLD OUR DIVERSE WORLD

[1] Some programs choose not to celebrate holidays at all, questioning whether it is DAP and how to adequately understand and explain the many holidays observed in the United States. Other programs invite members of the community to educate them about their particular observances. What is critical is to remember that, if holidays are celebrated, celebrations beyond the dominant culture should be included.

[2] The project approach provides the opportunity to avoid a "tourist approach" (emphasizing superficial facts or "foreign" customs) and provides children and teachers with an in-depth understanding of a particular culture and its traditions.

Art supplies range from fabrics and natural materials to pieces of wire and plastics and are artfully arranged and accessible to children. A special room in each school, the *atelier*, is used by every class for long-term projects. Sculptures, drawings, collages, and paintings throughout the school serve as reminders of numerous projects.

To achieve outstanding results, children work in small groups so they are able to discuss and analyze problems and negotiate solutions. The teacher records the activity on tape and with photographs.

The planning process is crucial to the success of the project approach as is the underlying philosophy that children can be co-constructors of their own education. This approach has much in common with the approaches of both Dewey and Summerhill (see Chapter 1). The teacher helps children explore what they already know about the topic, what they might need to know, and how they can represent that knowledge through various media, reinforcing Vygotsky's theory that interaction and direct teaching are important aspects of intellectual development. Teachers pose questions for children that lead them to suggest a hypothesis: What might happen if you do that? What do you think you could do to make that work? Children are encouraged to evaluate their own work and learn to defend and explain their creations to others.

A project approach has the potential to "provide a context in which all aspects of children's minds can be engaged, challenged, and enriched" (Katz & Chard, 1989).

Figure 11.14 ● Planning for physical skills is part of good curriculum development, especially in urban areas where space is at a minimum.

CURRICULUM EXPRESSED THROUGH PLAY

What Is Play?

Play! What a wonderful word! It calls up images from the past, those childhood years when playing was the focus of our waking hours. "Will you play with me?" is one of the most expressive, expectant questions known. It carries with it hope and anticipation about a world of fun and make-believe, a world of adventure and exploration, a world of the young child.

City streets, parks and fields, tenements, huts, empty rooms, and backyards are all settings for play. Play is a way of life for children; it is their natural response. It is what children *do* and it is serious business to them. Any activity children choose to engage in is play; it is never ending.

Play is the essence of creativity in children throughout the world. Play is universal and knows "no national or cultural boundaries" (Frost & Sunderlin, 1985).[1] Educators and psychologists have called play a reflection of the child's growth, the

 OUR DIVERSE WORLD OUR DIVERSE WORLD OUR DIVERSE WORLD OUR DIVERSE WORLD OUR DIVERSE WORLD OUR DIVERSE WORLD OUR DIVERSE WORLD OUR DIVERSE WORLD

[1] Play allows the early childhood educator to focus on universal characteristics that are the same for children the world over, yet we must also remember that play is an expression of a child's family and ethnic culture.

Figure 11.15 ● Play: the essence of childhood.

essence of the child's life, a window into the child's world. It is a self-satisfying activity through which children gain control and come to understand life. Play teaches children about themselves; they learn how tall—or short—they are, what words to use to get a turn on the swing, and where to put their hands when climbing a ladder. Through play, children learn about the world: what the color purple is, how to make matzoh balls, and how to be a friend. Play helps children define who they are.

Play takes many forms. Children play when they sing, dig in the mud, build a block tower, or dress up. Play can be purely physical (running, climbing, ball throwing) or highly intellectual (solving an intricate puzzle, remembering the words to a song). Play is creative when crayons, clay, and fingerpaint are used. Its emotional form is expressed when children pretend to be mommies, daddies, or babies. Skipping rope with

a friend, playing jacks, and sharing a book are examples of the social side of play.

Types of Play

There is a general sequence to the development of social play. Babies and toddlers have a clearly defined social self. Infant play begins with patterns established at birth: babies gaze, smile, and make sociable sounds in response to the quality and frequency of attention from a parent or caregiver. Socialization of infants occurs through interaction. By the end of their first year, infants smile at and touch one another and vocalize in a sociable effort (Berk, 1996). Toddlers play well on their own *(solitary play)* or with adults. They begin solitary pretend play around 1 year of age. During the toddler years, as children become more aware of one another, they begin to play side by side, without interacting *(parallel play)*. They are aware of and pleased about, but not directly involved with the other person. It is during this second year that toddlers begin some form of *coordinated play*, doing something with another child. This is similar to the preschooler's *associative play*. The preschool years bring many changes for children in relation to social development. The number and quality of relationships outside the home increase as does the ability to play with other children. At first, this is accomplished just by a child's presence in a group: playing at the water table with four other children or joining a circle for fingerplays *(associative play)*. When children join forces with one another in an active way, when they verbalize, plan, and carry out play, *cooperative play* is established. This is the most common type of peer interaction during these preschool years. Figure 11.16 shows a timeline of social play development.

Yet developmentally and culturally appropriate practice would remind us that our understanding and knowledge about play have been based on Euro-American cultural patterns.[1] The way in which we interpret children's development through play differs from culture to culture. Children's play always portrays their own social values and family ethnic practices (Hyun, 1998), and wise early childhood practitioners will incorporate this perspective into their work with children.

OUR DIVERSE WORLD OUR DIVERSE WORLD OUR DIVERSE WORLD OUR DIVERSE WORLD OUR DIVERSE WORLD OUR DIVERSE WORLD OUR DIVERSE WORLD OUR DIVERSE WORLD

[1] Children's play is culturally grounded.

Associative play—fun to do together.

Solitary play.

Parallel play—side by side.

Joining forces in cooperative play.

Figure 11.16 ● A timeline of social play.

Most play is unstructured and happens naturally when the curriculum is designed for play. **Spontaneous play** is the unplanned, self-selected activity in which children freely participate. Children's natural inclinations are toward play materials and experiences that are developmentally appropriate. Therefore, when they are allowed to make choices in a free play situation, children will choose activities that express their individual interests, needs, and readiness levels.

Dramatic play—or imaginative or pretend play—is a common form of spontaneous play. Three- and 4-year-olds are at the peak of their interest in this type of activity. In dramatic play, children assume the roles of different characters, both animate and inanimate. Children identify themselves with another person or thing, playing out situations that interest or frighten them. Dramatic play reveals children's attitudes and concepts toward people and things in their environment. Much of the play is wishful thinking, pretending great strength and deeds. This is the way children cope with their smallness or lack of strength. **Superhero** play is appealing because it so readily addresses a child's sense of helplessness and inferiority. Pretending to be Wonder Woman makes it easier to understand and accept the limitations of the real world. Dramatic play provides the means for children to work out their difficulties by themselves. By doing so, they become free to pursue other tasks and more formal learning. For all these reasons, play is invaluable for young children.

Sociodramatic play happens when at least two children cooperate in dramatic play. Both types of play involve two basic elements: imitation and make-believe (Smilansky, 1990). Sociodramatic play is, according to Frost (1996), "the most highly developed form of symbolic play," and its importance to social and intellectual development cannot be exaggerated.

Vygotsky takes that one step further, according to Berk (1996), by naming play as "the preeminent educational activity of early childhood." His view of pretend play is that the *zone of proximal development* (see Chapters 4 and 7) allows children to raise themselves to higher levels of behavior. Play assists the child in creating imaginary situations that are governed by

rules. Pretending to be a firefighter, Sherry grabs a piece of rope and runs toward the playhouse, saying "shhshhshshshshsh" while pretending to squirt water on the fire. She shouts to her playmates, "Over here! Come over here! The fire is on this side."

Sherry's make-believe scenario and her ability to follow the rules of behavior common to firefighters (grabbing hoses, calling for help) are the two critical factors from Vygotsky's point of view: that firefighting scene supports his theory that cognitive skills develop through social interactions. Sherry examplifies a child moving from concrete to abstract thought because she did not require realistic objects (a hose and water) but imagined them with a rope and her ability to create the sound of water. This ability to separate thoughts from actions and objects will stand Sherry in good stead when she studies math concepts. Rules that children follow in make-believe play teach them to make choices, to think and plan about what they will do, and to show a willingness toward self-restraint, as children learn to follow the social rules of pretend play.[1] This is important preparation for real-life situations. Vygotsky, more than anyone else, has made that critical connection between social and intellectual development.

Elizabeth Jones's Guest Editorial in Section 3 and Laura Berk's Focus Box in Chapter 4 illuminate Vygotsky's principles in differing but complementary ways.

Gender Differences

Teachers and parents, as well as researchers, have observed that boys and girls seem to show distinct differences in their play choices, play behavior, and toy selection from an early age. In fact, gender differences are first noticeable in children around 1 year of age and quite obvious by the later preschool years. Although biology certainly plays a part, it would seem that parents and society exert powerful influences[2] (Frost, 1996). The toys parents and teachers choose (dolls for girls, trucks for boys), the predominance of females in early childhood settings, television shows and advertising, and toy store displays combine to communicate a

OUR DIVERSE WORLD OUR DIVERSE WORLD OUR DIVERSE WORLD OUR DIVERSE WORLD OUR DIVERSE WORLD OUR DIVERSE WORLD OUR DIVERSE WORLD OUR DIVERSE WORLD

[1] Curriculum should foster children's decision-making abilities and their social participation skills. Effective interpersonal skills are necessary for interactions across cultures, gender, and abilities.

[2] Early childhood educators need to be constantly vigilant in noticing their personal gender biases, along with staying current with research in gender differences.

Play

J. Ronald Lally

Of all the issues of early childhood education, play is often the most misunderstood. There is the tendency of many educators to see play as "only fun," something into which "appropriate learning experiences" need to be channeled. Other educators treat play as something sacred, an activity that should be "free" and not altered by adults. Both of these views are limiting because they fail to capture the changing contexts of play and the variations in play.

In child care, it is almost always the adult who sets the context for play. Materials are made available, the size of the group and ages of the children in the group are decided on, general rules are laid down (no hitting, no destruction of property, and so on), and the area where play takes place is circumscribed (e.g., environments are designed and fences are built). All this is done by knowledgeable adults who set the stage for play. It is on this stage that children play. *Free play*, then, is a relative rather than an absolute term. Play is always structured by the early childhood educator in some way. It is how these structures are decided on and implemented that is key.

I have found it useful when thinking about the adult role in play with all children to take my guidance from infants. If you watch infants closely, you will see that they clearly do not differentiate between work and play, and amusement and learning. You will see that in almost every waking moment they are occupied with thoughts and actions of discovery and accomplishment. They seem to have an agenda. They are busy in what some might call play, others work, others amusement, and others learning. In fact, they are busy with all of these things at once. What they are doing defies accepted definitions. The Funk and Wagnalls dictionary of the English language defines play as: (1) To engage in sport or diversion; amuse oneself; frolic; gambol; (2) To take part in a game of chance; gamble; (3) To act in a way which is not to be taken seriously.

Infants have taught me that play should be taken very seriously. Their type of play is something that should be respected, supported, encouraged, and assisted. It is different from what adults have come to understand as play. It is exploration, experimentation, imitation, and adaptation. Although preschooler play seems to be more social in nature than the play of infants, their play too is serious business. One of the worst things that an early childhood educator can do in the name of teaching is to interrupt play activity to do something he thinks is more important. But one of the best things an early childhood educator can do is facilitate and participate in play. My experience has shown me that often the most interesting part of a child's play can be the participation and sharing of that play with an interested and "in tune" adult.

Unfortunately, knowing when to join in, when to hold back, when to help, and when to watch is not easy. These decisions are part of the art of good care, an art based on a respect for and a study of the developing child.

Dr. J. Ronald Lally is director of the Center for Child and Family Studies, Far West Laboratory for Educational Research and Development, San Francisco, CA.

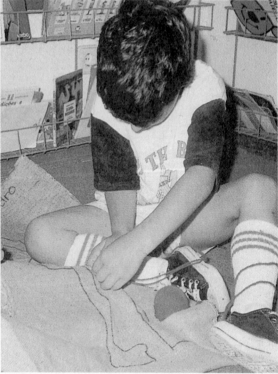

Figure 11.17 ● With encouragement, boys can learn to enjoy activities, such as drawing and sewing, that are often associated with girls. (Courtesy of Centro Infantil & de Reabilitacao de A-Da-Beja, Lisbon, Portugal.)

very strong reinforcement of traditional sex-role expectations, Figure 11.17. Further discussion of gender issues can be found in Chapters 4, 12, and 15.

Values of Play

For the first half of this century, interest in children's play focused on emotional causes and effects (Bowman, 1990). The main theme was the emotional release play provided children. Play is a suitable outlet for expressing negative feelings, hostility, and aggression. Clay can be pounded, balls can be kicked and thrown, dolls can be spanked. Young children give free expression to a wide range of emotions, playing them out and releasing tension.

But play is more than an avenue for emotional release. Rubin, Fein, and Vandenberg (1983) cite three common factors that emerge from the many definitions of play: (1) children's feelings and motivations, (2) how children behave when they play, and (3) the environment that supports play and where play occurs. The early childhood curriculum is developed with all three aspects of play in mind.

Why do children play? Why is play so universal to childhood experiences? One answer may be that play is intrinsically motivated; that is, it is naturally satisfying to children. Rubin and associates suggest other reasons as well:

● Play is relatively free of rules except for what children will impose themselves.

● Play is controlled and dominated by the children.

● Play is carried out as if the activity were real life.

● Play focuses on the activity—the doing—rather than on the end result or product.

● Play requires the interaction and involvement of the children.

Play promotes learning for the whole child as well. A wide range of learning opportunities is inherent in any single play activity. Water play is a popular activity in most early childhood settings. Figure 11.18 highlights some of the learning that is likely to occur as children play with water. All play activity holds this potential for growth and learning. Blocks, easel painting, woodworking, and clay could also be analyzed for how they contribute to the development of the child as a whole. Figure 11.19 demonstrates further the learning possibilities in all play activity.

Water Play Promotes:	By Teaching Children:
Emotional growth	The soothing effect of water; the pleasure of playing with a messy, sometimes forbidden medium; sensory pleasure in splashing, trickling, swirling water through fingers, hands, and feet.
Language development	Play with words of alliteration (swish, swirl, splish, splash); new words: funnel, eyedropper, siphon, float.
Creativity	New ways to store, move, and pour water.
Social growth	To share space at a water table as well as to share some of the equipment; to be next to or across from a friend; to have fun with others; to wait for a turn.
Cognitive development	Problem-solving with tubes, sieves, pipes; experimenting with measurement, float and sink properties, volume, quantity, fractions, weight, comparisons, numbers, temperature.
Physical coordination	Eye-hand coordination; fine-motor control in learning to pour, squeeze, balance.

Figure 11.18 ● Water play is fun and promotes learning.

Play As a Cornerstone of Learning

Outside of child development circles, there has been little appreciation in the U.S. culture for the value and importance of play for young children (Frost, 1996). Early childhood educators continually search for ways to answer, "Don't they do anything but play?" In many settings, parental pressure and teacher uncertainty have led to curricula with more table tasks and less active play periods in the daily schedule.

Jones (in her Guest Editorial in Section 3) states the case aptly: "But if children are just playing, how will they learn? Each child learns by asking his or her own next questions and trying out the answers. Often both the questions and the answers take the form of actions rather than words. Children learn by doing."

In summing up, Jones adds, "In play, children are autonomous; they're independent. They make decisions, solve the problems, deal with the consequences."

Early childhood specialists must become adept at speaking out on the value of play and its relationship to what children learn. Figure 11.19 highlights this relationship.

Play, Work, and Learning

For some years, theorists have stated that play is the child's work. This statement is confusing, for as any adult knows, work is work even though it may sometimes have some characteristics of play. This theory has fostered the misconception that all young children do in an early childhood setting is play. By extension, their

COGNITIVE/LANGUAGE

Distinguishes between reality and fantasy
Encourages creative thought and curiosity
Allows for problem-solving
Encourages thinking, planning
Develops memory, perceptual skills, and concept
　formation
Learns to try on other roles
Acquires knowledge and integrates learning
Learns communication skills
Develops listening and oral language skills

CREATIVE

Fosters use of imagination and make-believe
Encourages flexible thinking and problem-solving
Provides opportunity to act upon original ideas
Supports taking risks
Learns to use senses to explore
Recreates images in buildings and art media
Sharpens observational skills
Provides variety of experiences
Learns to express self in art, music, and dance
Develops abilities to create images and use
　symbols
Acquires other perspectives

SOCIAL

Tries on other personalities, roles
Learns cooperation and taking turns
Learns to lead, follow
Builds a repertoire of social language
Learns to verbalize needs
Reflects own culture, heritage, values
Learns society's rules and group responsibility
Shows respect for others' property, rights
Teaches an awareness of others
Learns how to join a group
Builds awareness of self as member of a group
Gives sense of identification
Promotes self-image, self-esteem
Experiences joy, fun

PHYSICAL

Releases energy
Builds fine- and gross-motor skills
Gains control over body
Provides challenges
Requires active use of body
Allows for repetition and practice
Refines eye–hand coordination
Develops self-awareness
Encourages health and fitness

EMOTIONAL

Develops self-confidence and self-esteem
Learns to take a different viewpoint
Resolves inner fears, conflicts
Builds trust in self and others
Reveals child's personality
Encourages autonomy
Learns to take risks
Acts out anger, hostility, frustration, joy
Gains self-control
Becomes competent in several areas
Takes initiative

Figure 11.19 ● Play is the cornerstone of learning.

teachers are erroneously thought of as simply baby-sitters who watch children play all day. To reclaim play as a special activity crucial to children's development and growth, we should look at play and work as equally important developmentally appropriate activities for young children (Frost, 1996).

Play is the cornerstone of learning, the foundation from which children venture forth to investigate, to test out. Curriculum takes on expression through play; teachers plan curriculum that uses play as the medium for learning. As they mature, children integrate and assimilate their play experiences. What started out as play—the sheer fun of it—is transformed into learning experiences. Curiosity about magnets at age 5 nourishes a scientific attitude for the later years, as well as a foundation for studying gravity, planetary movements, and the like. Feeling free to sing out at group time at age 3 can prepare a child to be an active participant in the kindergarten classroom at age 6.

Teachers want children to learn about *themselves,* to learn about the *world around them,* and to learn how to *solve problems.* A childhood filled with play opportunities should culminate in these three types of learning.

1. *Learning about themselves* includes developing a positive self-image and a sense of competence. Children should know and feel good about themselves as learners. They should develop a sense of independence, a measure of self-discipline, and knowledge based on full use of their sensory skills.

2. *To learn about others and the world around them* means developing an awareness of other people. Teachers want children to perfect their communication and social skills so that they will be more sensitive participants in the world in which they live. This means that children learn and appreciate the values of their parents, the community, and society at large. When children become aware of the demands of living in today's society, that awareness can help them become more responsible citizens. The emphasis on social interaction and group relationships in the early childhood setting underscores this goal.

3. *To learn to solve problems,* children need to be accomplished in observation and investigation.

When exploring a puzzle, for example, children need to know how to manipulate it, take it apart, and put it back together, to see how other people solve puzzles, and to know how to get help when the pieces just do not seem to fit together. They should know how to predict and experiment. What will happen, wonders a kindergartner, when a glass is placed over a glowing candle? How will that change if the glass is large or small? What is the effect if the glass is left over the candle for a long time or for a second? Young children also need to learn how to negotiate, discuss, compromise, and stand their ground, particularly when they encounter and solve problems socially. "I want the red cart and someone already has it," thinks the preschooler. "Now what? How can I get it? What if the other person says no? Will the plan that works with my best friend work with someone else? When do I ask for help? Will crying make a difference?" To be effective problem-solvers, children must know and experience themselves and others.

Teacher Considerations

Play is a window to the child's world, and the adult who knows the value of play is committed to learning about children while they play. The vast knowledge of human development and behavior comes from researchers who spent countless hours observing and recording children playing. Classroom teachers continue to learn about children by listening to and observing spontaneous play activity and planning curriculum that encourages play. They discover each child's individual personality, learning style, and preferred mode of play.[1]

Genuine interest is one way teachers show their approval of the play process. Creating a safe environment where children feel physically and emotionally secure is another. To establish play as an important part of the curriculum, teachers must:

● *Understand,* appreciate, and value play experiences for young children.

● *Focus* on the process of learning rather than on the process of teaching.

[1] Observing children while at play helps a teacher understand how each child is unique *and* how all children are the same in OUR DIVERSE WORLD.

● *Reflect* on their observations in order to know what activities, concepts, or learning should be encouraged or extended.

Frost (1996) reminds us of the excellent advice from one of the most able contributors to the field of human development:

Erikson advises that play has a very personal meaning for each individual.[1] Perhaps the best thing that we as adults can do to discover this meaning is to go out and play; to reflect upon our own childhood play; to once again look at play through the eyes of the child.

Teachers have two major roles in promoting spontaneous play environments. (1) They are facilitators or supervisors of play, and (2) they set the stage and create an atmosphere for play.

The Teacher As Facilitator

One of the most difficult tasks teachers face is knowing when to join children at play and when to remain outside the activity. They must ask themselves whether their presence will support what is happening or whether it will *inhibit* the play. Sometimes teachers are tempted to correct children's misconceptions during play. Abby and Salina, deeply involved in their grocery store drama, are making change incorrectly. A teacher must judge whether to explain the difference between nickels and quarters at that time or to create an opportunity at a later date. Teachers must be aware of what happens if they interrupt the flow of play and how they influence the direction it takes. If Abby and Salina begin to talk about their coins, showing an interest in learning how to compute their change, the teacher can move into the discussion without seeming to interfere.

Many adults enjoy playing with the children in their class; others feel more comfortable as active observers. But every teaching situation will demand the teacher's involvement at some level. The hesitant child may need help entering a play situation; children may become too embroiled in an argument to settle it alone; play may become inappropriate, exploitative, or dominated by a particular child.

Vygotsky gives us other reasons to be involved with children as they play, particularly in relation to the interpersonal nature of teaching (see Chapter 4). The belief that learning is interpersonal and collaborative is exemplified by the teachers of Reggio Emilia (see Chapters 2 and 5), who guide and support children's learning by engaging in play and knowing what strategy will best help an individual child reach the next level of skill (zone of proximal development). The Reggio Emilia approach to curriculum finds an appropriate and appealing blend of Vygotsky's concern for individual exploration and assisted discovery. The teacher's role is a balance between facilitating children's development and taking advantage of those teachable moments in which further learning is enhanced.

The following guidelines are ways teachers facilitate play. A good teacher:

● Guides the play, but does not direct or dominate the situation or overwhelm children by participation.

● Capitalizes on the children's thoughts and ideas; does not enforce a point of view on them.

● Models play when necessary. Shows children how a specific character might act, how to ask for a turn, how to hold a hammer when hammering. Models ways to solve problems that involve children interacting on their own behalf.

● Ask questions; clarifies with children what is happening.

● Helps children start, end, and begin again. Gives them verbal cues to enable them to follow through on an idea.

● Focuses the children's attention on one another. Encourages them to interact with each other.

● Interprets children's behavior aloud, when necessary; helps them verbalize their feelings as they work through conflicts.

● Expands the play potential by making statements and asking questions that lead to discovery and exploration.

[1] Curriculum should provide all children with continuous opportunities to develop a better sense of self.

Curriculum through Play for the 1½-Year-Old

Sensory Stimulation

Objective: To help toddlers begin to explore and understand the five senses

	Activity	Small-Group Focus	Optional Activities
Monday	Soap painting	Guessing game: textures. Distinguish soft from hard using familiar objects.	Play hide-and-seek with two or three.
Tuesday	Water table play	Guessing game: smells. Identity familiar scents in jars.	Blow bubbles.
Wednesday	Fingerpainting	Guessing game: weights. Distinguish heavy/not heavy using familiar objects such as book or doll.	Take walk to collect collage materials of different textures.
Thursday	Making collages of textures collected day before	Guessing game: shapes. Use puzzles of shapes and shape-sorting boxes.	Have a parade of sounds from many musical instruments.
Friday	Playdough	Food fest of finger foods: Try different textures, sizes, shapes, and flavors.	Make foot or hand prints on large mural paper.

Figure 11.20 ● Example of teacher-directed activities to help toddlers explore their sensory skills.

Creating the Environment for Play

To structure the environment for play, teachers include uninterrupted time blocks in the daily schedule (at least 45 minutes to an hour) for free-play time. This allows children to explore many avenues of the curriculum free from time restraints. It is frustrating to young children to have their play cut off just as they are getting deeply involved.

A variety of activity areas and learning centers set up with specific play and learning materials provides children with choices for play. There should be enough to do so that each child has a choice between at least two play options. Established routines in the schedule add to the framework of a day planned for play. The raw materials of play—toys, games, equipment—are changed periodically so that new ones may be introduced for further challenge.

In choosing materials, teachers select dress-up clothes and accessories that appeal to all children's needs, interests, and emotions. Props are required for a variety of roles[1]: men, women, babies, doctors, nurses, grocers, mail carriers, teachers, and firefighters. Hats for many occupations help a child establish the role of an airline pilot, tractor driver, construction worker, police officer, or baseball player. Large purses are used for carrying mail and babies' diapers; they also double as a briefcase or luggage. Simple jackets or capes

OUR DIVERSE WORLD OUR DIVERSE WORLD OUR DIVERSE WORLD OUR DIVERSE WORLD OUR DIVERSE WORLD OUR DIVERSE WORLD OUR DIVERSE WORLD OUR DIVERSE WORLD

[1] Choosing materials to place in a classroom should be done with an awareness of exposing children to images of diversity (e.g., male nurses, female construction workers, African American physicians, etc.) rather than fostering and reinforcing existing stereotypes. These materials are available to purchase or you can make your own photo albums and posters.

Play Materials to Enhance Cultural Diversity and Inclusivity

Curriculum Area	Materials and Equipment
Music	Rainstick (Chile), marimba (Zulu), balaphon (West Africa), ankle bells (Native American), maracas (Latin America), Den-den (Japan), Shakeree (Nigeria), drums (many cultures), ocarina (Peru), songs of many cultures
Literature	Books on family life of many cultures, stories of children from far and near, legends and folktales from many countries, stories with common childhood themes from many lands, favorite books in several languages, wordless books, sign language, Braille books
Blocks and accessories	Variety of accessories depicting many ethnic people, aging people, community workers of both sexes in nonstereotyped roles and with various disabilities; Russian nesting dolls, Pueblo storytellers,[1] animals from around the world
Art	Paints, crayons, markers, and construction paper in variety of skin tone colors, child-size mirrors
Dramatic play	Anatomically correct dolls representing many ethnic groups, doll accessories, including glasses, wheelchairs, crutches, walkers, leg braces, and hearing aids; doll clothes, including cultural costumes and dress-up clothing from many cultures, cooking utensils, such as a wok, tortilla press, cutlery, chopsticks
Games	Language lotto, dreidle game, lotto of faces of people from around the world, Black history playing cards, world globe
Outdoors	Elevated sand and water tables and ramps for wheelchair access, lowered basketball hoops, sensory-rich materials.
Classrooms	Carp banners (Japan), paper cuttings from Mexico and China, photographs and magazine pictures of daily life from many cultures, artwork by artists from a variety of ethnic backgrounds, pictures of children from many ethnic backgrounds and cultures

Figure 11.21 ● A child's family and culture can be brought into the classroom through a variety of curriculum materials; so, too, can children with disabilities feel included.

transform a child for many roles. Things that represent aspects of the child's daily life are important; children need many opportunities to act out their life stories.

For younger children, teachers make sure there are duplicates of popular materials. Group play is more likely to occur with three telephones, four carriages, eight hats, and five wagons. Social interaction is enhanced when three space shuttle drivers can be at the controls.

Play is further enlarged by materials that are **open-ended**. These are materials that will expand the children's learning opportunities because they can be used in more than one way. Blocks, a staple of the early childhood curriculum, are a case in point. Children explore and manipulate blocks in many ways. The youngest children carry and stack blocks and also enjoy wheeling them around in wagons or trucks. They also enjoy the repetitious action of making small

OUR DIVERSE WORLD OUR DIVERSE WORLD OUR DIVERSE WORLD OUR DIVERSE WORLD OUR DIVERSE WORLD OUR DIVERSE WORLD OUR DIVERSE WORLD OUR DIVERSE WORLD

[1] When using artifacts from other cultures, take care to avoid using materials or items that may have sacred or privileged status in that culture.

A future banker.

A future artist.

An inspired chef.

A future doctor scrubbing up.

A future zoologist.

Figure 11.22 ● As they play, children learn. They may even be practicing for the future.

columns of blocks. As children learn to make enclosures, they add animals, people, and transportation toys to their block play. Older preschoolers build multi-storied structures as part of their dramatic play—offices, firehouses, garages, and the like.

Cultural Diversity and Inclusivity

Positive attitudes toward self and others emerge when children know they are valued for their individuality and appreciated as members of a family and a culture. The school environment can reflect this in a number of ways. Figure 11.21 lists ways in which an early childhood program can use culturally diverse materials in activities and learning centers on a daily basis to foster the relationship between home culture and school.

Children with special needs are often able to use most of the curriculum materials typically found in early childhood classrooms. They, too, need their life mirrored in the school setting with dolls, books, and play accessories that signify acceptance and belonging. Figure 11.21 has a number of suggestions for inclusive materials for children with special needs.

CURRICULUM PERSPECTIVES CONTINUE

A sound curriculum is the linchpin of a quality program for children. Curriculum planning and development is a creative act, one that is rewarding for teachers. In the next three chapters, curriculum implementations will be explored from another perspective, that of the major areas of development in the child's growth. In Chapter 12, the focus will be on how curriculum affects the growing body. Chapter 13 will emphasize the curricular role in developing the mind, and Chapter 14 will explore the curricular issues surrounding social and emotional growth.

Summary

Curriculum encompasses the planned and unplanned events children experience in group settings. Curriculum can include whatever happens to a child while in school or day care, or it can be a syllabus with detailed lesson plans.

Developing curriculum includes setting goals, establishing priorities, knowing what resources are available, planning ahead, and then evaluating the process. As teachers develop their curriculum plans, they may focus on the classroom activity or learning centers, the skills of the children, or a particular theme. All three lend themselves to a basis for curriculum planning, and all are important vehicles for creative and effective curriculum for young children.

Play is the way curriculum is expressed in the early childhood setting. The function of play in the life of a young child is more than sheer enjoyment. Play provides an avenue for growth in social, emotional, intellectual, and physical development. Teachers, aware of play as a foundation for learning, provide an atmosphere that supports the play process. They provide a setting in which play is recognized as the curriculum of the child, the primary process through which children learn. Curriculum comes alive as children discover and take pleasure in learning.

Teachers demonstrate their appreciation of diversity by carefully selecting materials and planning experiences that are culturally responsive and inclusive.

Review Questions

1. Define developmentally appropriate curriculum for early childhood programs. What two principles determine whether a curriculum is "appropriate"? Describe the difference between an infant/toddler and a preschool curriculum.

2. Name five guidelines for developing curriculum for young children.

3. Observe several early childhood programs (e.g., a family child care home, a child care center, and an after-school program for primary-age students) for examples of multicultural infusion in the curriculum. Describe the way the content does or does not expand the children's understanding of diversity.

4. What is emergent curriculum, and why is it appropriate for early childhood teachers?

5. How is play beneficial to the child's development?

6. Define the common stages of play, and state at what chronological age each is likely to appear.

7. What learning occurs when children (a) play in the sand area; (b) play with easel paint; (c) play on the climbers; (d) engage in dramatic play?

8. Describe the project approach to curriculum development, including how it can be incorporated into the curriculum. Be sure to show how it can affect every major curriculum area.

Learning Activities

1. Create a curriculum web with several classmates following the process described on page 396.

2. Develop a curriculum for a week-long celebration: (a) for 3-year-olds in a half-day nursery school; (b) for 6-year-olds in an after-school extended-day program; (c) for a family day care home. Use a nonholiday theme.

3. What do you think of superhero play in the preschool years? Research recent articles on the subject and prepare to present an argument for or against this type of play. Ask a classmate to prepare an opposing viewpoint.

4. Observe teachers as children play. What is the difference in the play when (1) a teacher interacts with children in their play and (2) a teacher intervenes? What happens to the play immediately after teacher contact is made? How long does the play last? What is your conclusion?

5. Develop a dramatic play kit for your school. Select a theme and collect appropriate props and accessories. Describe why you chose this theme and what you expect children to gain from this experience.

6. Write a defense of play as a hallmark of early childhood philosophy and curriculum. How would you adapt the paper for parents? For a student of early childhood education? For teachers?

7. Research holidays and festivals (other than Christmas and Hanukkah) that some cultures use to celebrate childhood. How would you integrate these into a curriculum? Why did you choose each of the specific festivals? How are your choices related to the children in your classroom?

Bibliography

Banks, J. A. (1992, November/December). Reducing prejudice in children: Guidelines from research. *Social Education*, pp. 3–5.

Banks, J. A. (1994). *Multiethnic education: Theory and practice*. Boston: Allyn & Bacon.

Berk, L. E. (1996). *Infants and children*. Boston: Allyn & Bacon.

Berk, L. E. (1994, November). Vygotsky's theory: The importance of make-believe. *Young Children*, pp. 30–39.

Bowman, B. (1990). Play in teacher education: The United States perspective. In E. Klugman & S. Smilansky (Eds.), *Children's play and learning*. New York: Teachers College Press.

Bredekamp, S., & Copple, C. (1997). *Developmentally appropriate practices in early childhood programs*. Washington, DC: National Association for the Education of Young Children.

Bredekamp, S., & Rosegrant, T. (Eds.). (1995). *Reaching potential: Transforming early childhood curriculum and assessment* (Vol. 2). Washington, DC: National Association for the Education of Young Children.

de Melendez, R. W., & Ostertag, V. (1997). *Teaching young children in multicultural classrooms*. Albany, NY: Delmar.

Derman-Sparks, L., & the ABC Task Force. (1989). *Anti-bias curriculum: Tools for empowering young children*. Washington, DC: National Association for the Education of Young Children.

Elkind, D. (1987). *Miseducation: Preschoolers at risk*. New York: Knopf.

Elkind, D. (1993). *Images of the young child*. Washington, DC: National Association for the Education of Young Children.

Frost, J. L. (1996). *Play and playscapes*. Albany, NY: Delmar.

Frost, J. L., & Sunderlin, S. (Eds.). (1985). *When children play*. Wheaton, MD: Association for Childhood Education International.

Gardner, H. (1983). *Frames of mind: The theory of multiple intelligences*. New York: Basic Books.

Grant, C. A. (Ed.). (1995). *Educating for diversity. An anthology of multicultural voices*. Boston: Allyn & Bacon.

Guidelines for appropriate curriculum content and assessment in programs serving children ages 3 through 8. (1991, March). A position statement of the National Association for the Education of Young Children and the National Association of Early Childhood Specialists in State Departments of Education. *Young Children*, pp. 21–38.

Hyun, E. (1998). *Making sense of developmentally and culturally appropriate practice (DCAP) in early childhood education*. New York: Peter Lang Publishing.

Jones, E., & Nimmo, J. (1994). *Emergent curriculum*. Washington, DC: National Association for the Education of Young Children.

Jones, E., & Reynolds, G. (1992). *The play's the thing*. New York: Teachers College Press.

Katz, L., & Chard, S. (1989). *Engaging children's minds: The project approach*. Norwood, NJ: Ablex.

King, E. W., Chipman, M., & Cruz-Janzen, M. (1994). *Educating young children in a diverse society*. Boston: Allyn & Bacon.

Malaguzzi, L. (1987). *The hundred languages of children*. Reggio Emilia, Italy: Department of Education.

Rubin, K. H., Fein, G. G., & Vandenberg, B. (1983). Play. In E. M. Heatherington (Ed.), *Handbook of child psychology* (Vol. 4, Socialization, personality and social development). New York: Wiley.

Smilansky, S. (1990). Sociodramatic play: Its relevance to behavior and achievement in school. In E. Klugman & S. Smilansky (Eds.), *Children's play and learning*. New York: Teachers College Press.

Vgotsky, L. S. (1978). *Mind in society: The development of higher psychological processes.* Cambridge: Harvard University Press.

Vgotsky, L. S. (1987). *Thinking and speech* (N. Minick, trans.). New York: Plenum.

Workman, S., & Anziano, M. C. (1993, January). Curriculum webs: Weaving connections from children to teachers. *Young Children*, pp. 4–9.

York, S. (1991). *Roots and wings: Affirming culture in early childhood programs.* St. Paul, MN: Redleaf Press.

Planning for the Body: Physical/Motor Development

CHAPTER 12

Questions for Thought

What is physical/motor development?

Does physical growth differ from motor development in young children?

What are the physical and motor skills children learn in an early childhood setting?

How can teachers encourage physical development?

What should the teacher of young children consider when planning for physical/motor development?

In what ways can physical/motor curriculum be developed?

Why are outdoor and playground play important?

Figure 12.1 ● Children are the picture of movement, spending the greatest portion of their day in physical activity.

INTRODUCTION

Teachers often characterize children through their movements. Movements are one of the most notable features of young children's behavior. Pregnant mothers are aware of fetal motions and often assign personality traits to their children by these movements. What is striking about newborns is the extent of their full-bodied, random movements when they cry, roll over, follow, and reach for a crib mobile. Learning to walk is a major milestone in a child's development. Holding a pencil, cutting with scissors, tying a shoe are further illustrations of how motor development signifies growth. Motor skills are a good indication of how the child is progressing.

Basic motor skills develop in the early childhood years and form the foundation for movement and motor proficiency. If children do not develop them during the early years, these skills often remain unlearned. The early years form a foundation for movement and motor proficiency and are recognized as the critical time for mastering fundamental movement skills. Many environmental factors, such as opportunity, practice, encouragement, instruction, and environment play an important role in the acquisition of movement skills (Gallahue, 1996).

Learning through Movement

Motor abilities affect other areas of development. Malina (1982) reinforces the notion that motor development greatly affects "the child's cognitive development, the child's own self-discovery, and the child's ability to communicate." There is evidence of such interrelationships in children.

Tim is reluctant to climb outside. He is easily frightened when he—or anyone else—is up in a tree or on any climber. Because he cannot risk using his body in space, he stops himself from playing with anyone who invites him to try these activities. Thus, Tim's lack of gross-motor development is affecting his social skills.

Samantha loves to draw and cut. She chooses the art area every day she attends the 2-year-old class. Not only are her fine-motor skills well developed for her age; she takes great pride in her creations. Her motor skills enhance her self-confidence in school. In turn, she receives praise and attention from others as she communicates with both adults and children through her work.

The greatest portion of the young child's day is spent in physical activity. Quality early childhood programs recognize this, providing for a full range of physical and motor experiences. Indoors, children use puzzles, scissors, and dressing frames as they practice fine-motor skills. They dance with scarves and streamers to music. **Perceptual motor development**, as with body awareness, occurs when children learn songs and games ("Head and Shoulders, Knees and Toes" or "Mother May I Take Two Giant Steps?") or while fingerpainting. Outdoors, gross-motor skills are refined by the use of climbers, swings, hopscotch, and ring-toss.

Throughout the program, physical/motor development is emphasized as an important part of children's learning. Children will need time as well as equipment and activities to practice their skills. The value teachers place on physical and motor development is directly related to the time allotted in the daily schedule for children to pursue them.

For years, early childhood programs have made an outdoor environment available to children, assuming a great need for physical activity and that children will find ways to fill that need themselves. However, many school outdoor areas contain few challenges, perhaps only a blacktop for bouncing balls and a small metal climber for hanging and climbing. Moreover, American children are exposed to a value system in which physical/motor fitness is not always a high priority. Children live with adults whose primary sport is as spectators only, and they are often encouraged toward *sedentary* activities themselves at an early age, such as watching television and using computers.

Physical/motor development is the central focus of the needs and interests of young children; it should play a central role in planning the curriculum. Teachers must recognize that children have different needs from adults; they are growing, developing, emerging beings with a set of physical needs and interests that are quite different. Too often, adults try to develop miniathletes without first developing the child's fundamental movement activities.

PHYSICAL GROWTH/MOTOR DEVELOPMENT

Physical Growth

According to Bee (1997), an understanding of physical development is important to teachers and parents for a number of reasons. For example:

● New behavior is made possible through physical change; a toddler can be toilet-trained once anal sphincter muscles develop.

● Growth determines the child's experiences: observe the new vistas that open up to the brand new walker.

● Growth changes the way people respond to the child: the mobility of crawlers and toddlers leads to more restrictions from parents.

● Self-concepts are profoundly related to physical development: an obese kindergartner avoids the running and chasing games during recess.

Early childhood is the time of most rapid growth, though development does not occur at an even pace, but in starts and spurts. A child will tend to grow rapidly in infancy and as a toddler, with the growth rate beginning to taper off during preschool and middle childhood years. Although there are individual differences in the rate of maturation among children, growth follows a sequential pattern.

Figure 12.2 ● Growth follows a predictable pattern: large muscles develop before smaller ones.

Development seems to follow a directional pattern as well. Large muscles develop before smaller ones—one reason why most preschoolers are more proficient at running than at cutting with scissors. Growth also starts at the center of the body and moves outward. Watch a toddler walk using whole-leg action and compare that with a 5-year-old whose knees and ankles are involved in a more developed response. Children also tend to develop in a head-to-toe pattern. Infants move their eyes, head, and hands long before they learn to creep or crawl. See also Chapter 3 for an overview of developmental norms.

It is important to remember, however, that though growth is sequential and directional, it does not occur in a smooth and unbroken pattern.

Tremendous growth occurs just within the first 2 years of life, slows through the preschool and

Age	Weight	Height	Proportion	Teeth
Newborn	7 lb	20 in.	Head = ¼ of length	None
Infancy (up to 18 mo)	Gains 15 lb (now 20–25 lb)	Adds 8 in. (now 28–29 in.)	About the same	6
Toddler (18 mo to 2½ y)	Gains 5 lb (now 28–30 lb)	Adds another inch or two (now 29–33 in.)	Legs = 34% of body	20
Preschool (2½–5 y)	About 5 pounds/y (now 30–40 lb)	Adds 14–15 in. from birth; at age 2 = ½ of adult height (now 35–40 in.)	Head growth slows; legs at age 5 = 44% of body	20
Early-middle childhood (5–8 y)	Doubles before adolescence; (age 6 = 45–50 lb)	Adds 9–10 in. (age 6 = 44–48 in.)	Continues to move slowly toward adult proportions	Begins to lose baby teeth; replaced by permanent teeth (age 6 = 20–24)

Figure 12.3 ● An overview of growth shows how rapid physical growth is in childhood.

elementary-school years, and increases rapidly again during the adolescent growth spurt. Figure 12.3 shows an overview of these dramatic changes for children up to age 8.

Growth is influenced by a variety of factors. Genetic makeup, disease, and injury all play a part in how children grow. Environmental influences, such as nutrition and experience, have their greatest effect during the early years.[1]

Gender and Cultural Differences

There are gender differences as well. Boys have a larger proportion of muscle tissue than girls, and, from the beginning, girls have more fat tissue than boys. Each of these differences becomes more obvious in adolescence. In regard to physical development, girls mature earlier than boys and their growth is more regular and predictable. In motor skills, preschool girls have an edge in fine-motor skills, such as writing and drawing, and gross-motor skills, such as hopping and skipping. By age 5, boys can jump slightly farther, run slightly faster, and throw a ball about 5 feet farther than girls. These gender differences remain small until adolescence (Berk, 1996). See Chapter 15 for further discussion on gender-related issues.

There is some indication that physical development differs among ethnic groups. African American infants and toddlers seem to walk earlier and as a group are taller than Euro-Americans. Asian children also seem to develop physically earlier than Euro-American babies but are smaller and shorter overall (Bee, 1997). Some researchers suggest that because African American children have longer limbs, they have better leverage, which accounts for their superior performance in running and jumping (Berk, 1996).

Always, while looking at general growth patterns of children, parents and teachers must keep in mind the wide individual differences in the rates at which children grow and in the timing of each change. As a general rule, the pattern within individuals is consistent; that is, a child who is early, average, or late in one

OUR DIVERSE WORLD OUR DIVERSE WORLD OUR DIVERSE WORLD OUR DIVERSE WORLD OUR DIVERSE WORLD OUR DIVERSE WORLD OUR DIVERSE WORLD OUR DIVERSE WORLD
[1] Early childhood educators need to be aware of each child's early experiences before coming to the program. Early experiences vary and have a direct impact on who the child is.

aspect of physical development will be so in all aspects. There are sex differences as well in rate and patterns of physical growth. The most obvious of these is that girls generally begin puberty 2 years ahead of boys (Bee, 1997). Bee also found that as a group, poor children grow more slowly and are shorter than middle-class children, a finding attributed to diet. Even though the *rate* of physical development may differ, however, the *sequence* of development remains the same. This holds true even for children who are physically or mentally disabled.[1]

Including Children with Special Needs

Every classroom is likely to have children who have special needs that must be met. It has already been established (see Chapters 3 and 9) that inclusion of children with special needs in early childhood programs is not only appropriate but is mandated by law. Physical eduction is the only subject area cited in the definition of an "appropriate education" in Public Law 94-142 (Gallahue, 1996), providing an opportunity for children to grow and develop through movement and physical activities.

Children with physical, cognitive, emotional, or learning disabilities are faced with a variety of challenges, many of which may be met by adapting the environment and planning for activities that help children function within their range of abilities. "The Inclusive Environment" and Figure 9.8 in Chapter 9 offer a number of ways for teachers and caregivers to individualize the setting for a variety of needs. In Chapter 3 many types of disabilities are discussed.

Gallahue (1996) suggests a number of teaching strategies that can enhance the participation of children with special needs in regular classroom activities:

● *For Children with Learning Disabilities*

Help children gain a better understanding of their body, the space it occupies, and how it can move.

Structure personalized activities that work within the child's present level of abilities.

Progress from simple to more complex activities in small increments.

Make frequent use of rhythmic activities, stressing the rhythmical elements to movement.

● *For Children Who Are Visually Impaired*

Use many auditory cues to help children gain a sense of space and distances.

Include strenuous, big-muscle activities.

Modify activities that require quick directional changes.

● *For Children with Cognitive Disabilities*

Stress gross-motor activities.

Focus on fundamental stability, locomotor, and manipulative skills.

Allow children to repeat their successes to enjoy the accomplishment.

Avoid activities in which participants are eliminated from the game.

These brief examples make it clear that including children with special needs takes some careful thought about what kinds of movement experiences and physical development activities are within their abilities. Many of the suggestions are appropriate for all children, reminding us that the needs and interests of all children are essentially the same.

Motor Development

Motor development "is the process of change in motor behavior brought about by interaction between heredity and environment" (Gallahue, 1996). It is a lifelong process of continuous change based on the interaction of (1) *maturation* (i.e., the genetically controlled rate of growth); (2) *prior experiences*; and (3) *new motor activities*. Like physical growth, motor development is a sequence of stages that is universal but still allows for individual differences.[2] Each stage is different from, yet grows out of, the preceding level.

[1] Variations in growth patterns are influenced by environment and genetic make up. This holds true for all children.

[2] One is reminded of the definition of developmentally appropriate practice—some characteristics of development are universal and sequential and other characteristics are highly individual.

roller-skating/bicycling (5–8 years)
running faster (5 years and up)
skipping (5–6 years)
hopping on one foot (3–5 years)
up/downstairs with continuous movement (4 years)
jumping on two feet (3–5 years)
running (2–3 years)
walks up/downstairs alone (3 years)
toddling (18–24 months)
standing/walking alone (12–15 months)
climbing stairs (13 months)
walking when led (11–12 months)
creeping/crawling (8–10 months)
standing holding onto something/someone (8–10 months)
sitting and supporting self (6–8 months)
infant on belly, with chest up (2 months)

Figure 12.4 ● Motor development follows a developmental sequence. (Adapted from Allen K. E., & Marotz, L. [1999]. *Developmental profiles: Prebirth through eight.* Albany: NY, Delmar.)

Figure 12.4 charts motor development through the early years.

Gross-Motor Development

Gross-motor activity involves movements of the entire body, or large parts of the body. Using various large muscle groups, children try to creep, crawl, roll, bounce, throw, or hop. Activities that include balance, agility, coordination, flexibility, strength, speed, and endurance foster gross-motor development.

Fine-Motor Development

Fine-motor activity uses the small muscles of the body and its extremities (the hands and feet). Such movement requires dexterity, precision, and manipulative skill. Grasping, reaching, holding, banging, pushing, spinning, and turning are all activities that refine these skills.

Perceptual-Motor Development

Perceptual-motor development is a process in which the child develops the skill and ability to take in and interpret information from the environment and respond to it with movement. Children obtain data and impressions primarily through their senses. How often have you seen babies, for instance, mimic a parent's or

caregiver's mouth movements—taking in visually the various expressions, then physically responding in kind.

In a sense, every moment is perceptual-motor activity because the body and mind must work together to complete all motor tasks. The perceptual task is to process information; the motor response activates what is received in a physical way although perceptual and motor abilities do not necessarily develop at the same time or the same rate (Gallahue, 1996). The complex nature of perceptual-motor development can be seen when examining the three basic categories of spatial, temporal, and sensory awareness, which also include perceptual-motor concepts of body and directional, visual, and auditory awareness.

Spatial Awareness. For children, **spatial** awareness means a sense of body awareness and the body's relationship to space, as well as a knowledge of what the body parts can do. For the toddler, concepts of spatial relationships are developed through motor activity: dropping objects from a highchair or forcing a large stuffed animal into a small box. Their definition of space is related to the action and movement involved in specific activities. A sense of relationship to less immediate things and places (knowing a specific route to school and home, making simple maps) develops in the preschool years. Not until ages 6 to 8 do children develop the more abstract spatial ability of distinguishing left from right on their own bodies and others'.

Figure 12.5 ● Gross-motor activity uses the various large-muscle groups so that children can move their entire bodies.

Figure 12.6 ● Fine-motor activity requires using the small muscles of the body with dexterity and precision.

Specifically, directional awareness refers to left and right, up and down, front and behind, over and under. To illustrate, let us look at 2½-year-old Tamara. She demonstrates her awareness of spatial relationships as she moves herself up to a table (without bumping into it), reaches to her left to pick up a ball of clay, and turns around behind her to choose a rolling pin.

Temporal Awareness. Temporal awareness is the child's inner clock, a time structure that lets the child coordinate body parts. Dancing to a rhythmic beat, speeding up and slowing down, develops this kind of skill. It is also a force that helps children predict time. For instance, 7-year-old Luis and Aref ask if it is time to clean up as they finish their game of soccer. The after-school center has sports time for about an hour before getting ready for snack; the children have an inner sense of time that parallels their knowledge of the daily schedule.

Sensory Awareness. Sensory awareness refers to use of the senses. It is another way the body gives the mind information. Vision is the dominant sense for young children. *Visual awareness* is the ability to mimic demonstrated movements and to discriminate faces, emotions, sizes, shapes, and colors. It is the ability in 3-month-old babies to recognize their mothers.

Auditory awareness includes the ability to understand and carry out verbal directions and to discriminate among a variety of sounds ("Is this loud? fast? soft?" "Is that Josie or Dominick who called you?"). Auditory skills help children process information about language. From infancy, children seem to be able to combine visual and auditory awareness. Further sensory awareness develops through touch. Babies seem to put everything in their mouth to learn. When 4-year-old Stephanie picks up each object at the display table, she is using her sense of touch to discover size, shape, and volume.

PHYSICAL/MOTOR SKILLS IN EARLY CHILDHOOD

Types of Movement

Physical/motor skills involve three basic types of movement: *locomotor, nonlocomotor,* and *manipulative.*

● Locomotor abilities involve a change of location of the body (Gallahue, 1996) and include the skills of walking, running, leaping, jumping, climbing, hopping, skipping, galloping, sliding, and tricycling.

● Nonlocomotor abilities (sometimes referred to as balancing or stabilizing) are any movements that require some degree of balancing (Gallahue, 1996). These skills are turning, twisting, pushing, bending, stretching, pulling, swinging, rolling, dodging, and balancing.

● Manipulative abilities include the operation and control of limited and precise movements of the small muscles, especially those in the hands and feet. Manipulative skills include throwing, catching, reaching, bouncing, striking, kicking (gross-motor manipulation) and holding, grasping, cutting, sewing (fine-motor manipulation).

These three basic movements are necessarily combined when children are active in physical play:

With doll buggy: Holding onto buggy—
　　　　Manipulative
　　Pushing buggy—Nonlocomotor
　　Walking with buggy—Locomotor

Playing ball: Bending down for the ball—
　　　　Non-locomotor
　　Throwing the ball—Manipulative
　　Running to base—Locomotor

Jumping rope: Holding and turning the rope—
　　　　Manipulative
　　Jumping—Locomotor
　　Balancing self after jump—
　　　　Nonlocomotor

Breaking a piñata: Holding the bat—Manipulative
　　Swinging the bat—Nonlocomotor
　　Running to get the prize—
　　　　Locomotor

Figure 12.16 on page 439 shows age-appropriate toys and games that foster the development of the three types of basic motor skills.

Learning Motor Skills

Children must use their bodies to learn motor skills. They acquire these skills by making comparisons between their past experience and new actions. Such comparisons use memory and experience.

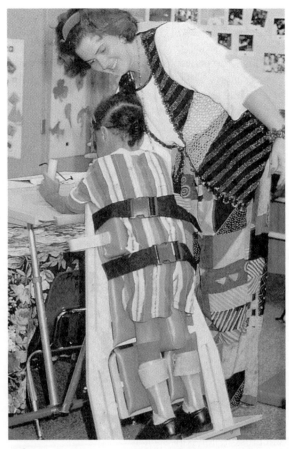

Figure 12.7 ● To learn a motor skill, children must combine memory with experience, taking advantage of opportunities to try something new and to practice what has already been learned.[1]

Memory and Experience

Memory plays an important part in learning motor movements because children need to recall what they just did to make corrections or refinements. In the short term, the ball that does not reach the basket is tossed farther on the next shot. To get the puzzle piece to fit, a child remembers other ways to manipulate the pieces. A long-term memory of movement is one that may go unrehearsed for long periods of time. The experience of swimming, for example, may be recalled only in the summer. Whether using short-term or long-

OUR DIVERSE WORLD OUR DIVERSE WORLD OUR DIVERSE WORLD OUR DIVERSE WORLD OUR DIVERSE WORLD OUR DIVERSE WORLD OUR DIVERSE WORLD OUR DIVERSE WORLD

[1] Children with physical limitations can experience many daily activities if the environment is appropriately adapted.

term memory, children learn motor skills by remembering what they have already learned and by practice.

The experiences children have and the ability to recall those experiences are necessary to the process of gaining motor skill. Rehearsal is as important to the young child as it is to the actors in a play. "Overt practice, repeating a specific movement over and over again, provides a motor rehearsal young children display every day" (Clark in Ridenour, 1978). Growth will depend on a variety of experiential factors, including opportunities for practice, encouragement, and instruction in an environment that is conducive to learning (Gallahue & Ozmun, 1995).

Practicing Basic Skills

A child's typical day, at home or at school, provides numerous opportunities to practice motor skills. Through *play*, the child can practice fine-motor skills such as:

● Holding a paintbrush, scissors, or rattle

● Tiptoeing to music

● Grasping a bottle, a hand, a toy

● Threading a bead or a wide needle

and gross-motor skills such as:

● Pumping on a swing

● Climbing a tree

● Digging a garden

● Balancing on a board, on one foot

Through *self-help activities* the child can practice fine-motor skills such as:

● Buttoning a coat or doll's clothes

● Brushing teeth, hair

● Turning a faucet handle or doorknob

● Feeding self with utensils

Gross-motor practice includes:

● Moving a nap cot or table

● Kicking covers off

● Walking, holding onto furniture

● Climbing into crib, bed

Children learning motor skills need experience in basic skills; they must learn simple skills before combining them into complex activities. To gain mastery over a skill, there must be an opportunity for practice. Children must have time to try, refine, and try again.

Feedback

Children modify and improve their motor skills as they receive information about their movements, both **intrinsic** (the paintbrush makes marks when it is pushed across the paper) and **extrinsic** ("I notice that your legs are very far apart as you try to somersault; how about holding them together as you roll next time?").

A Range of Developmental Levels

Any group of young children will have various levels of motor growth and physical development. An individual child may have different abilities and skills in gross-, fine-, and perceptual-motor areas; activities should, therefore, be offered on several developmental levels. Play materials and equipment, such as balls, climbers, and ladders, should accommodate a variety of skill levels, particularly if children with physical disabilities are in the class. Climbing boards put on several levels and puzzles ranging from 6 to 60 pieces are two examples of how teachers can meet the need for success and challenge.[1]

ROLE OF THE TEACHER

Considerations

As teachers plan programs for physical/motor development, they reflect on several important issues. One often overlooked area is that of gross-motor development as an everyday occurrence. Teachers sometimes take for granted children's progress as they walk

OUR DIVERSE WORLD OUR DIVERSE WORLD OUR DIVERSE WORLD OUR DIVERSE WORLD OUR DIVERSE WORLD OUR DIVERSE WORLD OUR DIVERSE WORLD OUR DIVERSE WORLD
[1] When planning the environment, curriculum, and activities, teachers need to be ever mindful of OUR DIVERSE WORLD.

Figure 12.8 ● Teachers provide many opportunities to practice motor skills through fingerplay, games, and songs.[1]

up and down stairs, climb on and off platforms and benches, and dance with abandon. Favorite rainy-day activities such as moving around like *Tyrannosaurus rex* or spinning like a top are exercises in physical/motor development using gross-motor skills. Remember that the normal classroom setting can promote physical development every day through established routines and curriculum.

Sex-Role Stereotyping

Is motor behavior different for boys and girls? If so, why? Research indicates that there are differences between girls and boys in these areas. For example, behavioral differences in motor development are apparent in early life: 1-year-old girls already spend more time in fine-motor tasks, while baby boys are more engaged in gross-motor activity. Around the age of 2, children begin to identify people by their gender. Preschoolers often characterize many toys, articles of clothing, occupations, and behaviors with one sex or the other (Huston, 1983; Picariello, Greenberg, & Pillemer, 1990). Girls of this age increasingly seek out other girls to play with in quieter pursuits, while boys seem to prefer more active, aggressive play (Bennenson, 1993; Maccoby & Jacklin, 1987).

Why does this happen? Probably some sex differences are the result of genetics. At the same time, sex-role expectations profoundly affect the motor and physical development of young children. This is the crucial issue for teachers, for their attitudes can either encourage or discourage children from developing to their fullest potential.[2] Teachers must acknowledge the differences that exist, and then ask themselves:

 OUR DIVERSE WORLD OUR DIVERSE WORLD OUR DIVERSE WORLD OUR DIVERSE WORLD OUR DIVERSE WORLD OUR DIVERSE WORLD OUR DIVERSE WORLD OUR DIVERSE WORLD

[1] Having many cultures in the classroom provides an opportunity to learn songs, dances, and fingerplays in several languages.
[2] When planning the environment, curriculum, and activities, teachers need to be ever mindful of OUR DIVERSE WORLD.

● What messages do I give children about physical activity? Do I value it for myself? For children? Do I value physical expression for girls as well as boys?

● Do I emphasize sports as a way to have fun? A way to be healthy? Do I only praise the "winner"?

● Can I provide male and female role models for physical activities using parents, grandparents, older siblings, staff, visitors, and guests?

 ● Do I encourage children to wear clothing that allows them the freedom to run, climb, tumble?[1] What do I do when girls arrive in long dresses and party shoes? What should I wear?

● Are all physical/motor activities made equally available and attractive to boys and girls? What should I do if some children dominate these activities, while others never choose them?

● How do I actively engage all children in every form of physical activity? Do I let them know I think it is important?

A Safe and Challenging Environment

First and foremost, teachers ensure the safety of the children. To maintain a safe physical environment, they see to it that materials and equipment are in usable condition and that overall traffic patterns are free of hazards. For example, to make a gymnastic activity safe, teachers would provide mats and make sure that only one child is tumbling at a time.

Psychological safety requires an even finer sensitivity on the part of the teaching staff. Fear is a learned response, and teachers must be careful not to discourage children from using their full range of abilities, creating overly anxious and fearful children. The new teacher is often concerned about children's safety, particularly when they are climbing. It helps to remember that children generally climb to heights that are comfortable for them; in other words, they set their own limits.

The practice of picking children up and placing them on equipment, often at their own request, is questionable. If teachers comply with children's wishes to be lifted and set somewhere high, they are placing those children in situations outside of their natural limits. The children may see this as saying, "You are incapable of climbing up there yourself," or "It is too dangerous for you to try that alone." Also, this does not allow children to gain experience in basic skills first, but puts them in a situation that calls for skills more complex than they have at the time. This denies the child the opportunity to practice those skills. Children learn their capabilities by being held responsible for what they do. When they must seek solutions to getting up, out, in, or down, they learn to handle realistically their current level of physical and motor development. Teachers lend encouragement and confidence to children by saying, "I can't put you up there, but I will help you try." Making playgrounds safe is a good way to promote physical growth and sets the stage for learning through motor development (Figure 12.9).

Playground Enrichment

The playground is the natural arena for optimal physical development and the ideal environment to promote physical fitness. On the playground, all motor skills are called into play.

Carmine *grabs* a scarf and begins to dance, *twirling* and *whirling, hopping* and *bending* in time to the music. Following the teacher's lead, Carmine *balances* on his toes and *waves* his scarf high over his head.

Tina *walks* to the climber, *grasps* the highest rung she can *reach, pulls* herself up by *lifting* one leg and then the other until she *stretches* vertically full-length along the climber bars. Satisfied, she *pushes* off with her feet and *jumps* backward to the ground. She *bends* her knees as she lands, *balances* herself to an upright position, and *runs* off.

Ramon *toddles* over to *pick* up the large red ball. Momentarily overwhelmed by its size, he *falls* backward to *sit* on the grass. As a teacher approaches him, he *rolls* the ball toward her. She *throws* it back to him and Ramon imitates her movements. Soon they are involved in *kicking* and *tossing* the ball to each other.

 OUR DIVERSE WORLD OUR DIVERSE WORLD OUR DIVERSE WORLD OUR DIVERSE WORLD OUR DIVERSE WORLD OUR DIVERSE WORLD OUR DIVERSE WORLD OUR DIVERSE WORLD OUR DIVERSE WORLD

[1] Be sensitive to family or cultural influences about gender typing.

MAKING PLAYGROUNDS SAFE

Safety in the yard means:
● Enough room for the number and age of children who will use it
● Adequate empty space
● Availability of both hard and soft surfaces
● Soft surfaces under any equipment from which a child might fall
● Shady areas alternating with sunny spots
● No standing water—good drainage
● No poisonous or thorny plants, or litter or debris
● Areas of play clearly defined and differentiated from one another
● Sand area protected at night from animals
● Fences high enough and in good repair
● Gates secure with latches out of children's reach

Equipment is:
● Well maintained—no exposed nails, screws, sharp edges, chipped paint
● Chosen with children's ages in mind in regard to height and complexity
● Stable and securely anchored
● Repaired immediately or removed if damaged
● Varied to allow for wide range of skills
● Not crowded
● Smooth where children's hands are likely to be placed
● Checked frequently
● Placed appropriately: slides facing north, swings away from other structures and busy areas
● Scaled to age level: steps and other openings are 4 inches or less apart *or* 8 to 10 inches apart
● Modified for age levels: swings have soft seats

Teachers:
● Reinforce safe practices
● Wear appropriate outdoor clothing
● Check frequently *where* children are playing
● Involve children in safety checks of yard, equipment, and grounds
● Provide continual, adequate supervision
● Avoid congregating to talk
● Get involved with children
● Provide enough activities and challenges
● Watch for sun exposure, especially with toddlers
● Assist children when they want to rearrange movable equipment

Figure 12.9 ● Before children are allowed to use a playground, teachers should use a checklist such as this to ensure that safety standards are met. A safe playground stimulates physical development, social interaction, and full exploration of the materials and environment.

Figure 12.10 ● Playground equipment should be challenging and should provide a variety of movement experiences and a significant amount of physical activity.

Using both small and large muscles, children gain control over their bodies as they run and play. The playground provides open space where full-bodied action takes place, providing many opportunities to develop balance and coordination.

Physical skills, however, are not the only benefit of outdoor play. Social and cognitive skills are enhanced as well. On the playground, children must negotiate turns with the wagons, ask for a push on the swing, and wait in line going up the slide. Some of the most intricate and involved dramatic play takes place outdoors. Problems get solved when two trikes collide. Science experiences are all around—finding a bird's nest or planting a garden. According to Frost (1992), "good playgrounds increase the intensity of play and the range of play behavior."

On the playground no one says "Be quiet!" or "Quit wriggling!" It is a place of motion and space, filled with the special sensations found only outdoors.

When creating and maintaining a challenging environment, teachers consider both variety and level of challenge. A choice of surfaces encourages a variety of movements. Cement may be appropriate for transportation toys, but tanbark and rubber mats are better for climbing, hanging, and dropping. Varying the equipment also stimulates motor activity. Equipment that is mobile allows for greater range of uses and allows children to manipulate their own environment. By creating their own physical challenges with wooden crates, children make platforms, caves, and houses to crawl in, over, and through. Another way to provide variety is to focus on the less-developed skills, such as catching and throwing, rolling, latching, snapping, or zipping. When children are encouraged to discover their own physical potential, they learn to solve problems of movement defined by the limits of their own abilities rather than by performance. This kind of learning encourages self-confidence as children find success through their own challenges.

The importance of playgrounds, and outdoor play is underscored by Paula Carreiro's Focus Box.

Child's Play—Outdoors

Paula J. Carreiro

Madeline, smiling her Cheshire cat smile, sits atop the climbing structure. Her long brown hair is blowing in the wind as she surveys the activity below.

Similarly, from a less scenic vantage point, her teacher takes stock of events beginning to unfold. As an early childhood professional, she recognizes the importance of this time for her students. Just as the indoor classroom has been carefully prepared, so, too, is the outdoor environment planned, maintained, and supervised. A quick look around the area reveals many reasons for the success of this experience for these young children.

An initial planning session led to the creation of an outdoor space that is, first and foremost, safe for this age group. Careful and frequent maintenance assures that the play area will remain hazard free. The adults moving around the playground provide the same pupil-teacher ratio that exists in the indoor environment. They are carefully observing behavior and giving assistance when needed. Today there is much to behold. The large sand play area is the site for a major dig. The young explorers are assisted by buckets, shovels, measuring containers, and water. Another area is ripe for dramatic play, with a boat containing moving parts for an authentic adventure. There is an outdoor storage area where the trikes are kept only to be rediscovered every day by drivers who are anxious to hit the highway—a paved path around the playground. A well-designed slide moves children safely along in any kind of weather, and a huge tree stump attracts the more serious scientist in search of the ultimate insect.

In one corner of the playground the older students have planted a colonial garden that all the children help maintain. Another area has been left open as a nature center with plants, flowers, and bird feeders for the children's discoveries and exploration.

The attention given to the development of the large body muscles in the arms and legs is not limited to the climbing equipment. In addition, there are swings and other structures to aid in this development. Other important features of the playground include a hard surface for bouncing balls, a balance of sunny and shaded areas, easels for outdoor painting, an area for building with large blocks, and plenty of open-ended materials such as boxes and barrels for children to use in their own creative ways.

It is little wonder that a significant portion of the day is spent here. The playground not only provides important physical development opportunities; it is here that children also experience true joy in learning.

Paula J. Carreiro is the head of Beauvoir School in Washington, D.C., which serves children from preschool through third grade.

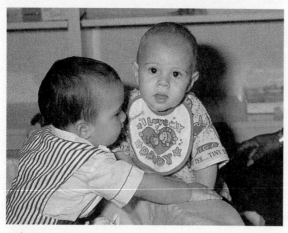

Figure 12.11 ● Parents and teachers encourage physical play from early infancy.

A Child's Self-Concept

The image of physical self is an important part of self-concept. How people feel about themselves is rooted in the way they feel about their bodies and what they can or cannot do with them. Attitudes about the body and its abilities directly affect the types of activities children will try. Studies show that skill in games appears to be tied to peer-group acceptance (Gallahue, 1996). Psychologists and teachers often notice a link between learning problems and clumsiness. Children with problems seem to have motor difficulties more often than those who do well in the classroom (Cratty, 1986).[1]

Physical activity, then, contributes to a child's self-concept. With practice comes a sense of competence. Children can learn to relax as they gain experience in physical activities, and thus reduce the stress of anticipating failure. Competence breeds self-confidence and a willingness to try greater challenges. As children try new activities, they learn more about themselves. And physical activity increases awareness of what fun it is to move—to run through a field or pump a swing just for the sheer joy of it!

Teachers support positive self-concept through physical and motor development in several ways. They let children discover their own physical limits, rather than warning or stopping them from trying out an activity for themselves. "I'm stuck!" a child shouts across the yard. Rather than rushing to lift down the child, the teacher might reply, "Where can you put your foot next? How can you find a way to get across?" To the child afraid to climb, the teacher might stand close by, responding to the fear by saying, "I'll stand close to the climbing ropes so you will feel safe." Using positive reinforcement encourages children in physical and motor endeavors. Teachers notice children who try something new: "Greg, it's good to see you cutting out the pumpkin yourself." They congratulate efforts for the achievements they really are: "Your hands reached the top this time, Shannon! I'll bet you are feeling proud of yourself." Children who stand on the sidelines observing others may need some encouragement from the teacher to take the first step in mastering the climbing frame or slide. "Here's a good place for you to put your foot, Arturo. I'll hold onto your hand until you tell me to let go."

It is often not so much what teachers say to children that influences their feelings about themselves as it is the way in which children are treated. Children value themselves to the degree they are valued by others. The way teachers show how they feel about children actually builds their self-confidence and sense of self-worth. Children create a picture of themselves from the words, attitudes, body language, and judgment of those around them.

Encouraging Physical Play

The vital role of physical activity is best fulfilled when teachers:

● Create time in the daily schedule for periods of physical activity, preferably, but not limited to, outdoors.

● Actively participate while supervising and encouraging *all* children to become involved in strenuous activity.

● Set goals for children's motor development and physical fitness.

OUR DIVERSE WORLD OUR DIVERSE WORLD OUR DIVERSE WORLD OUR DIVERSE WORLD OUR DIVERSE WORLD OUR DIVERSE WORLD OUR DIVERSE WORLD OUR DIVERSE WORLD

[1] A skilled early childhood educator carefully observes children, documents observations, and makes a referral if an assessment is needed for an individual child, attempting to include children with a variety of abilities.

● Use a variety of activities including science, art, and music to stimulate physical development.

● Select age-appropriate equipment and materials, providing a variety of props to enhance their use.

● Give children opportunities to repeat, practice, and refine the skills they learn.

 When children develop their physical and motor skills under this kind of encouragement, their confidence and sense of competence grow.[1]

Observing children while they play outdoors allows teachers an opportunity to assess potential problems in motor development. The checklist in Figure 12.12 indicates some areas to observe.

Curriculum Planning for Physical/Motor Development

Teachers plan activities that promote physical/motor skills in the areas of gross-motor, fine-motor, and perceptual-motor development. They look at the environment, both indoors and out, to see that all three areas of physical growth are encouraged.

In the Classroom Setting

When thinking of physical/motor development in the classroom and yard, teachers tend to focus on the fine-motor (or small-muscle) tasks for the classroom and on gross-motor (or large-muscle) tasks for the outdoor play space. The indoor area lends itself more readily to activities with less movement, and the outdoor area encourages whole-body play. Yet children can have a wider variety of activities if teachers remember that both gross-motor and fine-motor projects can happen everywhere in the environment.

Indoor Areas. Indoors, the art area is stocked with pens, crayons, scissors, and hole punches that develop the fine-motor skills. Add large brushes or rollers to the easel, or plan fingerpainting, and the art area now includes gross-motor development. When children use templates to trace both inside and outside spaces, they practice perceptual-motor skill. In the science area, getting "just a pinch" of fish food is a fine-motor

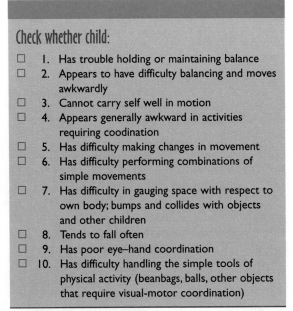

Check whether child:

☐ 1. Has trouble holding or maintaining balance
☐ 2. Appears to have difficulty balancing and moves awkwardly
☐ 3. Cannot carry self well in motion
☐ 4. Appears generally awkward in activities requiring coodination
☐ 5. Has difficulty making changes in movement
☐ 6. Has difficulty performing combinations of simple movements
☐ 7. Has difficulty in gauging space with respect to own body; bumps and collides with objects and other children
☐ 8. Tends to fall often
☐ 9. Has poor eye–hand coordination
☐ 10. Has difficulty handling the simple tools of physical activity (beanbags, balls, other objects that require visual-motor coordination)

Figure 12.12 ● A checklist of possible problems in physical/motor development serves as a guideline when devising a developmentally specific profile for spotting problems.

activity; cleaning out the turtle house requires larger muscles to move rocks and sand. Perceptual-motor development occurs as children use pitchers to fill the fish tank or turtle tub and learn about water levels. At the manipulative table, when a child puts a peg into a pegboard, fine-motor skills are used. Removing puzzles from a shelf and carrying them to a table brings in gross-motor skills. Add nuts and bolts, and the child's perceptual-motor skills are called into play. The block area has endless possibilities, from lifting and carrying (gross-motor), to balancing and stacking (fine-motor), to building a space so that an animal or car will fit through (perceptual-motor). The language and library areas are places for turning pages or looking at words and pictures (fine-motor). They also involve taking books off shelves and replacing them and trying out the movements and activities read about in books. For instance, Tana Hoban's *Is It Hard? Is It Easy?* encourages children to act out the scenes pictured in the story, all gross-motor tasks. With a listening post nearby,

 OUR DIVERSE WORLD OUR DIVERSE WORLD OUR DIVERSE WORLD OUR DIVERSE WORLD OUR DIVERSE WORLD OUR DIVERSE WORLD OUR DIVERSE WORLD OUR DIVERSE WORLD

[1] For all children, a sense of personal worth is at the core of their existence.

Figure 12.13 ● The outdoor area has great potential for developing gross-motor skills (climbing, bending, sliding), fine-motor skills (grasping, reaching, holding), and perceptual-motor skills (eye–hand coordination, directionality, tempo).

children listen for the "beep" and coordinate what they hear (perceptual) with turning the pages (motor).

Outdoor Areas. Outdoors, children develop motor skills of all kinds. In the sand, children dig, a gross-motor activity. As they judge how big a hole is, or how much water will fill it, they are practicing and improving their perceptual-motor skills. Turning on a faucet, planting seeds, and making mudpies are for fine-motor development.

Wheel toys offer children opportunities in all motor areas. Pushing someone in a wagon develops arm and leg strength—gross-motor development. Guiding tricycles and carts on a path and around obstacles requires perceptual-motor skill. Trying to "repair" or "paint" a wheel toy with tools or with large brushes, tying wagons together, or weaving streamers through the spokes of a bicycle all use fine-motor skills. By looking at the classroom and yard with one eye to physical and motor development, teachers

can plan activities that support growth in all skill areas.

Transitions and Group Times. Every part of the daily schedule can be planned to use all physical/motor skills. For instance, getting in and out of coats and snowsuits is a large-muscle activity. Children learn perceptual-motor skills as they try to get their arms in the correct sleeves. Buttoning, zipping, and tying are fine-motor activities. As children get ready for group time, often a difficult transition, they might practice drawing faces in the air or making their bodies into the shapes of letters, both perceptual-motor tasks.

Group times also include activities for motor development. When there are balloons, scarves, or a parachute at music time, children practice gross-motor skills. Fingerplays at group time are a fine-motor task. Activities for developing the senses of hearing and sight are two areas of sensory growth that can be utilized as content for group times.

PLANNING INCLUSIVELY FOR CHILDREN WITH SPECIAL NEEDS

(*Nathan* is a short-statured 4-year-old, approximately 2/3 as tall as his peers. His legs are short in proportion to his body size and he loses his balance easily. *Ana's* physical development is normal, but she is quite shy and prefers to watch others rather than participate in activities. A step-by-step process that builds on children's strengths and skills helps teachers plan meaningful activities for each child.)

1. Ascertain child's strengths
   Nathan—imaginative, agile, healthy, outgoing, demonstrates positive self-image
   Ana—persevering, patient, compliant, methodical, each small success is evident in her expression

2. Ascertain child's needs
   Nathan—to prove that he is as competent as his peers, despite short stature; to improve poor balance due to disproportionately short legs
   Ana—to improve large-motor skills; to gain confidence in joining groups

3. Set goals
   Nathan—to gain better balance and to be offered the chance to feel tall and big
   Ana—to become a bit more adventurous, more sociable, and more comfortable with her body in space

4. Brainstorm: What group activities are suitable?
   Nathan—physical activities that require stretching and balancing
   Ana—noncompetitive experiences that require different kinds of motor planning and that allow her to proceed at her own pace while participating with her peers

5. Select an activity (e.g., an outdoor obstacle course)

6. Plan the activity (see "Planning an Outdoor Obstacle Course")

7. Implement the activity (see "Building an Obstacle Course")

8. Evaluate the activity
   Nathan—Was he able to stretch sufficiently to climb the rungs and reach across the empty spaces between obstacles? Did he work on his balancing skills?
   Ana—Was she willing and able to work through the course? Did she need a teacher's hand throughout? Did she interact with her peers?
   Both—Did they do the whole course, or did they skip some obstacles? Did they return to a favorite spot? Did they voluntarily repeat the whole course?
   All—Did everybody have fun?

9. Refine the activity—and try again!

Figure 12.14 ● Planning inclusively for children with special needs. (Adapted with permission from Kranowitz, C. S. [1992]. Obstacle courses are for every body. In B. Neugebauer [Ed.], *Alike and different: Exploring our humanity with young children* [p. 23]. Washington, DC: National Association for the Education of Young Children. © by NAEYC.)

Focus on Skills

The physical/motor skills include those that use large and small muscles and that coordinate perception and motor response. Teachers planning activities for children can focus on any one of these as a basis for curriculum planning. For example, the skills of eye–hand coordination (perceptual-motor) and of walking on a balance beam (gross-motor) are elabo-rated below. They show how teachers can focus on a single skill and develop a rich curriculum for children. Figure 12.14 outlines a process for developing activities to meet the needs of children with a wide variety of skills and considers each child's strengths and needs.

Eye–Hand Coordination. Developing stitchery skills uses the perceptual-motor skill of eye–hand coordina-

Figure 12.15 ⬤ At an early age, children take pride in their physical accomplishments. Feeling strong or capable enhances self-confidence.

tion. A series of activities can be planned to help children learn these skills. This learning begins in infancy, when the baby first begins to manipulate and examine on object, learns to grasp with thumb and forefinger *(pincer grasp),* and shows a hand preference. Stringing large wooden beads is a first step and leads to using pieces of straw and punched paper, with somewhat smaller holes. Macaroni can be strung on shoelaces or on stiff string, then onto yarn, which is softer and more challenging. Sewing cards made by punching holes in polystyrene trays can be introduced as the next activity. Large, plastic needles can be used with the lacing cards or with the trays; large embroidery needles with big eyes can be used for stitching yarn onto burlap. Children may be ready to use embroidery hoops with which they can make a design on burlap first and then stitch over the outlines. Buttons can be sewn on burlap or other fabric. Popcorn or packing material can be strung using a needle. A final project might be to make a group wall hanging, with squares of children's stitchery sewn together. Simple backpacks and coin purses might be made, with the children sewing most of it themselves.

Walking on a Balance Beam. Teachers might want to focus on the skill of walking on a balance beam, a gross-motor and perceptual-motor activity. Using any kind of beam requires more balance and slower movements than regular walking. Teachers place tape on the floor and ask children to walk forward and backward on it. Use a rope on the floor and everyone can pretend to be a tightrope walker. Place a wide board flat on the floor, then substitute a narrow one (still on the floor itself) after children have mastered the first board. Next, place the wide board at a minimal height (perhaps 2 inches off the ground). Once children have successfully walked on this board, they are ready to try a narrower board at the same height. Set some boards at a slant, from the ground level up, providing a challenge that allows children to move their bodies off the ground as gradually as they wish. By planning activities for walking on wide and narrow boards of various heights, teachers help children of all levels acqure the gross-motor skills necessary to master these tasks. Figure 12.16 shows age-appropriate equipment that fosters the development of motor skills.

Type of Motor Skill	Infants 0–1½ y	Toddlers 1½–3 y	Preschoolers 3–5 y	Early School Years 6–8 y
Locomotor: Walking Running Jumping Hopping Skipping Leaping Climbing Galloping Sliding	Safe areas to explore body movements Balls to roll Hanging jumpseats Walkers on wheels Simple obstacle course	Walker wagons Pull/push toys Dancing Wide balance board Toddler gym—stairs and slide Ring Around the Rosey	Hippity-hop balls Sled Beginning skis Trampoline Roller skates Jump rope Balance beam Climber Dancing	Jump rope Roller skates Ice skates Climbing rope Tumbling mats Hopscotch
Nonlocomotor: Pushing Pulling Bending Balancing Stretching Rolling Turning Twisting	Large, safe areas for exploration Parent/caregiver play: holding, pushing arms, legs, sturdy push toys Soft obstacle course of pillows	Pounding board Simple, low rocking horse Ride-on toys Toddler-type swing Large Legos® Sturdy doll buggy Wagon Fabric tunnels Blocks Cars, trucks to push	Shopping cart/doll carriage Wheelbarrow Pedal toys, trike Rakes, shovels Slide Swing Punching bag	Scooter Two-wheel bike Sled, toboggan Exercise mat Acrobatics Diving mask for swimming Doorway gym bar
Manipulative: Grasping Throwing Catching Kicking Receiving/ moving objects Bouncing	Mobile attached to crib—kicking feet moves it Rattles, teething rings Crib activity board Soft foam blocks Snap beads Floating bath toys	Variety of balls Stacking, nesting toys Activity box—on floor Shape sorters Large, fat crayons Large pegs and board Water/sand table	Crayons, markers Clay, dough Bowling games Puzzles Woodworking tools Balls Lacing board Water/sand table	Baseball glove/bat Ring toss game Full-size balls Oversize bat Frisbee "Miss Mary Mack"

Figure 12.16 ● Toys and games help develop specific motor skills in young children.

Use of Themes

When beginning teachers plan activities, they often have a theme or unit as their focus. Themes can be used to encourage physical and motor involvement. A unit of "Outerspace" involves gross-motor skills (jumping around on the moon, taking a space walk, getting in and out of the rocketship, building a space-ship with large blocks). Fine-motor skills are needed to manipulate knobs on the instrument panel, to draw maps of the stars or to write out a countdown on a chalkboard. Perceptual-motor skills are needed to work out how to get ready for a trip to Mars, what happens on the trip, and when and how to get back to Earth. Use the sample forms in Chapter 11 to develop an outer-space unit as well as other appropriate themes to encourage motor skills.

Once teachers realize which physical/motor skills the children possess and what the group is ready to learn, they can plan activities around a classroom unit.[1]

 OUR DIVERSE WORLD OUR DIVERSE WORLD OUR DIVERSE WORLD OUR DIVERSE WORLD OUR DIVERSE WORLD OUR DIVERSE WORLD OUR DIVERSE WORLD OUR DIVERSE WORLD

1 Parents are an excellent source of ideas for ensuring that themes will reflect a true multicultural experience.

APPRECIATING CULTURAL DIVERSITY THROUGH MOTOR DEVELOPMENT

For Indoor and Outdoor Play

Activity	Motor Skill Practice	Culture
Lion or dragon dance	Gross-motor	Chinese (New Year)
Making and flying carp kites	Fine- and gross-motor	Japanese
Dodgeball	Gross-motor	Euro-American
Chinese jump rope	Gross-motor	Chinese
Breaking the piñata	Gross-motor	Latino
Spinning like a dreidel	Gross-motor	Jewish (Hannukah)
Origami art	Fine-motor	Japanese
Weaving	Fine-motor	Native American
Country/Western dance step	Gross-motor	Euro-American
Make mariachi instruments	Fine-motor	Latino
Dancing to mariachi band music	Gross-motor	Latino
Hokey pokey	Gross-motor	Euro-American
Make and twirl a grager	Fine-motor	Jewish (Purim)
Cooking: stir-fried rice	Fine-motor	Chinese
Making fry bread	Fine-motor	Native American
Kick the can	Gross-motor	Euro-American
Making and beating drums	Fine-motor	Native American

Figure 12.17 ● A variety of activities that reflect many cultures can be integrated into the curriculum for motor and physical development. These activities are, at best, an approximation of traditional cultural expressions and not authentic presentations, yet they can enlarge the child's world view through physical play.

Curriculum planning for motor and movement skills requires teachers to know principles of physical growth and motor development. They then can use this knowledge to plan activities that encourage children to master their own movements and to learn other skills through movement. In the early childhood setting, curriculum can be planned by concentrating on activity areas, focusing on a specific motor skill, or using a classroom theme.

Summary

Children are in motion virtually from conception and develop their abilities to move their bodies as they grow. Young children spend most of the day in physical activity; therefore, the development of physical and motor skills must take a high priority in early childhood programs. Physical growth, that which pertains to the body, is for teachers an issue of fitness and health. They need to have an overview of growth to help children develop functional and flexible bodies. Motor development means learning to move with control and efficiency. Development involves maturation and experience. Teachers must know the sequence of development and what part they play in providing physical and motor experiences for the young child.

Muscular development can be categorized as gross-motor, fine-motor, and perceptual-motor. Gross-motor movements use the entire body or large parts of it, such as the legs for running or the arms and torso for throwing. Fine-motor movements, such as manipulating objects, are those that use smaller muscles and that require precision and dexterity. Perceptual-motor movements are those that combine what is perceived with a body movement. Spatial, temporal, and sensory awareness all play an important part in the development of perceptual-motor skills.

In the early childhood years, children need exposure to many motor activities. They need a chance to practice, to get feedback, and to have a broad range of experiences of variety and challenge. Because children acquire motor skills through short- and long-term memory, rehearsal plays an important role as well.

When planning curriculum, teachers must have an awareness of sex-role stereotyping and must consider safety as well as challenge. A child's self-concept is linked with the concept of physical self and skill, so teachers keep in mind which behaviors should be encouraged and which behaviors may indicate potential problems. As they plan activities for children, teachers use classroom and yard areas, focus on a specific skill, or use a theme to develop curriculum for physical/motor skills.

Review Questions

1. How does physical growth differ from motor development in young children?

2. What factors influence motor development in young children?

3. What physical/motor skills are appropriate for young children to develop?

4. How can the teacher of young children support motor development in classroom areas?

5. How can the teacher support acquisition of specific motor skills in young children?

6. Follow (a) an infant or toddler; (b) a 3½-year-old, and (c) a 6- to 8-year-old during a typical play period at school or at home. Try to observe for 1 hour. Does the child exhibit all three basic types of movement (locomotor, nonlocomotor, and manipulative)? Describe the action of each, including any toys or materials the child uses.

7. How would you present the activities in Figure 12.14 to visually impaired children?

8. Have you observed gender differences in the physical development of young children? If so, what implications are there for teachers planning motor activities?

Learning Activities

1. Map the classroom in which you are currently working. List at least one activity in each area that develops physical motor skills. Add one more activity of your own that widens such development.

2. In what ways does a school program you know reinforce sex-role stereotyping in motor activities? What could be done to change this?

3. Try to develop the theme of "at the beach" or "camping" in your setting in such a way that physical/motor skills are used. Be sure to include gross-motor, fine-motor, and perceptual-motor activities. List at least six other themes around which you could build a similar curriculum.

Bibliography

Allen, K. E., & Marotz, L. (1999). *Development profiles: Prebirth through eight*. Albany, NY: Delmar.

Bee, H. (1997). *The developing child*. Menlo Park, CA: Addison-Wesley.

Bennenson, J. F. (1993). Greater preference among females than males for dyadic interaction in early childhood. *Child Development, 64*, 544–555.

Berk, L. E. (1996). *Infants and children*. Boston: Allyn & Bacon.

Berk, L. E. (1997). *Child development*. Boston: Allyn & Bacon.

Cratty, B. J. (1986). *Perceptual and motor development in infants and children*. Englewood Cliffs, NJ: Prentice-Hall.

Elkind, D. (1994). *A sympathetic understanding of the child*. Boston: Allyn & Bacon.

Frost, J. L. (1992). *Play and playscapes*. Albany, NY: Delmar.

Frost, J. L., & Sunderlin, S. (Eds.). (1985). *When children play*. Wheaton, MD: Association for Childhood Education International.

Gallahue, D. L. (1996). *Developmental physical education for today's children*. Madison, WI: Brown and Benchmark.

Gallahue, D. L. & Ozmun, J. (1995). *Understanding motor development: Infants, children, adolescents*. Madison, WI: Brown and Benchmark.

Harris, J. R., & Liebert, R. M. (1992). *Infant and child*. Englewood Cliffs, NJ: Prentice Hall.

Hoyenga, K. B., & Hoyenga, K. T. (1993). *Gender-related differences*. Boston: MA: Allyn & Bacon.

Huston, A. C. (1993). Sex typing. In E. M. Heatherington (Ed.), *Handbook of child psychology* (Vol. 4, pp. 387–467, *Socialization, personality, and social development*). New York: Wiley.

Kranowitz, C. S. (1992). Obstacle courses are for every body. In B. Neugebauer (Ed.), *Alike and different: exploring our humanity with young children*. Washington, DC: National Association for the Education of Young Children.

Maccoby, E. E., & Jacklin, C. N. (1987). Gender segregation in childhood. In E. H. Reese (Ed.), *Advances in child development and behavior* (Vol. 20, pp. 239–287). New York: Academic Press.

Malina, R. M. (1982). Motor development in the early years. In S. G. Moore & C. R. Cooper (Eds.), *The young child: Reviews of research* (Vol. 3). Washington, DC: National Association for the Education of Young Children.

Picariello, M. L., Greenberg, D. N., & Pillemer, D. B. (1990). Children's sex-related stereotyping of colors. *Child Development, 61*, 1453–1460.

Ridenour, M. V. (Ed.). (Contributing authors: Clark, Herkowitz, Roberton, Teeple). (1978). *Motor development: Issues and applications*. Princeton, NJ: Princeton Book Company.

Planning for the Mind: Cognitive and Language Development

Questions for Thought

How are language and thought connected?

What do the theories of constructivism and multiple intelligences, sociocultural theory, and brain-based research offer to curriculum development?

What are the cognitive skills of early childhood?

How can the teacher support cognitive development?

What language skills are developed in an early childhood setting?

What is the teacher's role in supporting and extending language development in young children?

How does the teacher introduce and develop reading and writing in the early childhood setting?

What can children's literature offer young children?

How might computers be used with young children?

Portions of this chapter were developed with the assistance of Gay Spitz, Salinas Adult School, Salinas, CA.

PREFACE

What is the mind? How do children think, communicate, and then act on the world? How does knowledge about language and thought dictate planning activities for children's development?

To begin, the relationship between language and thought must be emphasized. Thoughts are produced when people internalize what they experience. Language is what turns these experiences, such as actions and events, into thought. Language also shapes the way thoughts are produced and stored, bringing a semblance of order to the thought process. The two are intertwined: according to Bruner, language is "a logical and analytical tool in thinking" (Vygotsky, 1962).

Think of language as a tool. People are influenced by the kinds of tools they use. Farmers who work the land develop tools that till the soil and, in turn, learn more about that soil by using those tools. Mechanics begin to see the world in terms of the nuts and bolts of the vehicles they see every day. Tribes who are snowbound develop tools to deal with snow and ice; small wonder, then, that their language reflects more than a dozen ways to describe frozen water conditions. Language and thought are the instruments people use to make sense of and interact with the world.

For these reasons, this chapter contains curriculum planning units for both cognition and language rather than treating them in separate chapters. Inclusion in the same chapter emphasizes their close relationships. A third unit addresses the special topics of graphic language (reading and writing), children's literature, and computers as vehicles for language and intellectual development in the young child.

INTRODUCTION

Ah, to be a child again! The world is a place of wonder and promise. There are worlds and people to discover, explore, and understand. Childhood is a time:

● Of self . . . a baby plays with his hands and feet for hours and rolls over just for the sake of doing it.

● Of things everywhere . . . a toddler invades the kitchen cabinets to see what treasures can be found.

● Of people . . . a preschooler learns the teachers' names and then makes a first "friend."

● Of faraway places . . . a kindergartner packs for the first "sleepover."

The amount of learning that takes place in early childhood is staggering. How do children manage to absorb the sheer quantity of information and experience they accumulate in their first few years of life?

Every child accompanies this mighty feat by *thinking*. Early theories about cognition have been based on the idea that intelligence is a general capacity or potential that can be measured by standardized tests (such as IQ tests) and, therefore, that cognition can be developed by a specific, rather narrow, set of teaching techniques. During the last half of the 20th century, however, new ideas began to emerge. All of the recent theories revolve around the same fascinating question: What accounts for the remarkable changes in thinking, language, and problem-solving in young children? Jean Piaget's theories (see Chapter 4) are an important part of early childhood educational philosophy. Recent research on information-processing, plus the theories of Vygotsky (see Chapter 4) and Gardner, have broadened our notions of thinking and intelligence.

Cognition is the mental process or faculty that children use to acquire knowledge. To think is to be able to acquire and apply knowledge. By using conscious thought and memory, children think about themselves, the world, and others. Educating the thinking child is a critical function of parents and teachers. Curriculum in the early years must address the thinking, or cognitive, skills.

Language is the primary form of expression through which people communicate their knowledge and thoughts. A baby does not start life with language, but always communicates. In fact, oral language begins early, as infants learn to express themselves with sounds if not words. The growing child communicates needs, thoughts, and feelings through meaningful language. Thus, language and thought are intertwined.

Yet, the two are also separate. Cognition can occur without the language to express it. For example, an infant's laughter during a game of peek-a-boo indicates the child's knowledge that the hidden face will reappear. Conversely, the use of language can occur without cognition (i.e., without knowing the meaning). A child's counting from 1 to 20 (". . . 11, 13, 17, 19, 20!") is a case in point.

Figure 13.1 ● As children investigate the world of people and places, they ask themselves and others what they want to know.

Cognition and language generally become more interdependent as development progresses. Children expand their knowledge base through language. They listen, question, tell. The child with good language skills can thus apply them to widen the horizons of knowledge.

Cognition and language are related not only to the developing mind but also to all areas of the child's growth. Young thinkers are at work no matter what they are doing. For example, physical/motor development is also a cognitive process. Learning to roller skate involves skinned knees and learning to balance (motor tasks), along with analyzing, predicting, generalizing, evaluating, and practicing the art of locomotion on wheels (cognitive skills). When trying to enter into group play (a social task), children will think of strategies for how to get started (cognitive skill).

Children use language in developing emotionally. They listen, label, describe, elaborate, and question (language skills) as they learn to tell themselves and others how they feel (emotional tasks). And anyone who has heard a child mumbling instructions on how to get down from a tree knows that language can be of great help in using physical skills.

This chapter explores in depth the framework for planning curriculum for the mind. Chapter 3 describes cognitive and language development in early childhood. This chapter elaborates the development of both cognition and language in the early years, describes the skills acquired by children from birth to age 8, and gives specific curriculum content appropriate to their development. For the purposes of clarity, cognition and language will be separated into units. However, teachers must remember that these work together constantly in the minds and lives of young children. Planned programs for early childhood will be more successful if that link is recognized.

● UNIT 13-1   Cognition

THE DEVELOPMENT OF COGNITION: A PERSPECTIVE

An Eclectic Point of View

In trying to enhance cognitive development, early childhood educators draw on developmental and learning theories and their direct experiences with children.[1,2] By combining theoretical and practical viewpoints, teachers take a blended, or *eclectic*, perspective on the development of the thinking process. They work with children to encourage their ability to formulate ideas and to think rationally and logically.

Most important, the early childhood professional works toward helping children acquire skills that will lead to the development of:

Concepts: labeling or naming an idea, moving from the specific to the abstract

"What is a grape?"

Relationships: What is the association between two or more things? How are they similar or different? What are their functions, characteristics, attributes?

"How many colors of grapes are there? Do all of them have seeds? Are they different sizes? Do they taste alike?"

Generalizations: Drawing conclusions from relationships and concepts/ideas. This means grouping into classes and finding common elements.

"Are grapes a fruit or meat? How do grapes grow?"

A Piagetian Perspective

Developmental psychology, particularly through the works of Jean Piaget, has provided a deeper understanding of cognitive development. Piaget's view of cognition is twofold. First, *leaning is a process of discovery*, of finding out what one needs to know to solve a particular problem. Second, *knowledge results from active thought*, from making mental connections among objects, from constructing a meaningful reality for understanding.

For Piaget, knowledge is "an interpretation of reality that the learner actively and internally constructs by interacting with it" (Labinowict, 1980). Piaget divided knowledge into three types: physical, logical mathematical, and social. **Physical knowledge** is what children learn through external sensory experiences. Watching leaves blow in the wind, grabbing a ball, sniffing a fresh slice of bread are all instances of children learning about different physical objects and how they feel, taste, smell, move, and so on. The basic cognitive process involved in the development of physical knowledge is *discrimination*. For example, by touching magnets to paper clips, puzzles, and paper dolls, children learn first-hand about magnetism. They learn to discriminate between those objects that "stick" to the magnet and those that do not.

Logical mathematical knowledge derives from coordinating physical actions into some kind of order, or logic. This is not to be confused with formal mathematics; rather it is the kind of mathematical thinking children use in making connections about what they see, such as an infant's lifting the blanket to find a hidden toy. The logic of the young child is seen in the coordination of actions to make an **inference**. Think back to the magnets example. If a child deliberately takes a magnet to the metal drawer pulls and metal climbing bars, we can see the logical knowledge used: the child has made the inference that it is the *metal* things that "stick" on the magnet.

Social knowledge comes from our culture, the rules of the game, the right vocabulary, the moral

---

● OUR DIVERSE WORLD OUR DIVERSE WORLD OUR DIVERSE WORLD OUR DIVERSE WORLD OUR DIVERSE WORLD OUR DIVERSE WORLD OUR DIVERSE WORLD OUR DIVERSE WORLD

[1] Teachers must blend what they know about theory and concepts with what they learn about individual children and culture; see Chapter 3 for descriptions by Janice Hale and Louise Derman-Sparks about how children develop attitudes regarding race, gender, and ability.

[2] The role of culture in cognition is one of several major diversity areas in this chapter. Piaget's constructivism informs educators about how they should teach; because children construct knowledge from their own personal experiences, their culture will have a major impact on how they come to know.

codes. It includes learning vocabulary and being taught or told things, as well as knowledge about the social aspects of life. Value-laden and often arbitrary, it can rarely be constructed logically but is learned through life. With the aforementioned magnets, social knowledge would need to be used to decide who gets to play with the magnets, or when it is somebody else's turn.

In developing cognitive curriculum, teachers plan experiences that enhance those types of knowledge. They can teach using different forms of knowledge. Rote knowledge is information given with no particular meaning to the learner—that which could be learned meaningfully but is not. A teacher talking about magnets or telling children what attracts or repels gives children rote knowledge. Meaningful knowledge is what children learn gradually and within the context of what they already know and want to find out—like the example of letting the children handle the magnets themselves if they choose, and answering their questions as they arise. Both telling (rote) and asking or allowing (meaningful) can be useful; the question for the children is the balance between the two in everyday educational encounters.

As you may recall from Chapter 4, a special topic of Piaget's theory of cognitive development was *constructivist theory*. How does this theory apply to curriculum? The constructivist classrooms will vary greatly in their organization and activities, but the following characteristics are likely to be consistent (adapted from Roberts & Spitz, 1998):

● *Choice:* It is crucial to practice life in a democracy and to learn to evaluate choices and decisions from a variety of materials or activities so they can focus on formulating their own real questions and learn how to find genuine answers.

● *Play:* Through play experiences children will develop their own thinking because it will allow for self-selection and create situations where children must exchange views and solve problems.

● *Materials and Activities:* Concepts will be developed through interactions and experimentation with real objects, materials, and people and thus will need an environment that provides materials both appropriate and interesting as well as many activities that stimulate interaction with peers.

● *Time:* Each day will allow long blocks of uninterrupted time for child-initiated activities.

● *Teacher:* The teacher's role is to facilitate and to impart information and social knowledge, along with providing an emotionally safe and intellectually stimulating environment.

● *Curriculum Content:* The content arises from the issues of the students' real lives, their interests, family, and events so that learning is in the context of meaning for each child.

Gardner's Multiple Intelligences

Research in cognition documents that children possess different *kinds of minds* and therefore understand, learn, remember, and perform in different ways (Gardner, 1991). Most experts agree that intelligence is complex and that traditional tests do not measure the entire host of skills or abilities involved. This alternative view is expressed by Howard Gardner (1983, 1991).[1] Gardner, a Harvard University psychologist, suggests that there are eight "frames of mind":

1. Linguistic (language ability)

2. Musical (the earliest talent to emerge)

3. Logical (ability to manipulate, order, and assess quantity and quality)

4. Spatial (capacity to perceive visual world, change perceptions, recreate aspects of what one sees without its being in view)

5. Body-kinesthetic (ability to control body motions and handle objects)

6. Intrapersonal (understanding self, access to own feelings, and range of emotions)

7. Interpersonal (social understanding)

8. Naturalistic (ability to recognize and classify plants, minerals, animals, artifacts, etc.)

Multiple intelligences theory acknowledges that people learn and use knowledge in different ways. The implications for teachers are enormous: if the ways in which children represent what they know are varied,

OUR DIVERSE WORLD OUR DIVERSE WORLD OUR DIVERSE WORLD OUR DIVERSE WORLD OUR DIVERSE WORLD OUR DIVERSE WORLD OUR DIVERSE WORLD OUR DIVERSE WORLD

[1] Considering intelligence beyond standard IQ testing provides the opportunity to consider the diverse forms individual children's intelligence may take.

then we are faced with which knowledge we value and how we can address all areas of intelligence to help each child succeed.

In other words, we will need to vary both what and how we teach. In too many schools, people are taught the same things in the same way, asserts Gardner. Such uniformity cannot continue as we learn of the many ways children are "smart." This is good news for most early childhood teachers. "Gardner's theory is a dream come true for teachers," says Nelson (1995), "because it means many intelligences can be nurtured. And with that in mind, I [can] reinvent my curriculum and the way I teach it so that it meets the needs of a wider range." By asking questions such as "In what ways does this child demonstrate intelligence?" (Hatch, 1997), teachers begin to expand curriculum to fit the child.

This does not mean that teachers must develop every activity to all eight intelligences. Rather, teachers learn about each individual child and then tailor their curriculum to build on their children's strengths. Organizing interest centers applies multiple intelligences theory well, as does the notion of "going with the flow" of a child's or group's spontaneous interests. Even the creators of the television show *Sesame Street* are using the works of Gardner and Armstrong to help develop shows for young children (Blumenthal, 1995). The New City School (1995) gives these suggestions for center activities for the letter "F":

● Linguistic
Story/words—sort objects that begin with the letter F, make an "F" chant, with every word starting with "F"
Listening—listen to "Frog Went A Courtin'"
Computer—play "Fun on the Farm"

● Logical Mathematical
Manipulatives—measure by the foot
Language—learn about feelings; talk about feeling frustrated

● Spatial
Art—paint fancy feet or face painting
Clay—make the letter "F" out of playdough

● Musical
Dramatic play—listen to "Fantasia" while you play in playhouse
Music—listen and sing in French; make rhythms with your feet

● Bodily Kinesthetic
Outdoors—bounce balls around a giant letter "F"
Group time—draw imaginary letters ("F") on each other's back
Sensory—use funnels

● Intrapersonal
Manipulatives—a "one-only" game with sandpaper letters ("F")
"Me place"—a beanbag chair for one only

● Interpersonal
"Social table" or "help-yourself" table—"F" templates with markers and paper; "F" lacing cards
Small group time—partners find all the "F's" in sheet of letters

● Naturalistic
Group time—How many dinosaurs can we think of that start with the letter "F"?
Discovery/science table—start a "flora" and "fauna" mural

Vygotsky, Thinking, and Culture

Focusing on how our values and beliefs affect what we transmit to the next generation, Vygotsky's sociocultural theory claims that much of children's development and knowledge is culturally specific (see Chapter 4). Because children learn from more knowledgeable members of the community, they come to know those skills that are socially valued. In today's America, the most salient sources of knowledge are family members, the media, and the school. The psychological tools children need to learn higher mental functions, such as symbolic thought, memory, attention, and reasoning, need the mediation of someone who knows the tools of that particular society.

Vygotsky adds an important element to our understanding of thinking.[1] If knowledge is connected

OUR DIVERSE WORLD OUR DIVERSE WORLD OUR DIVERSE WORLD OUR DIVERSE WORLD OUR DIVERSE WORLD OUR DIVERSE WORLD OUR DIVERSE WORLD OUR DIVERSE WORLD

[1] Vygotsky's approach to development recognizes the social origins of an individual's thinking functioning: for instance, taking into account children's home langauge experiences can turn passive learners into lively participants (Berk & Winsler, 1995).

to what a culture values, then learning must be done in a collaborative style. Teachers and parents must have some agreement about what is important to teach children, and the best way of teaching is a kind of assisted learning, or apprenticeship. This kind of teaching-learning situation allows for *scaffolding*, a natural learning technique known as "apprenticeship." It occurs when a more experienced person "supports the efforts of a less experienced learner through careful, individualized instruction of a new skill" (Elicker, 1995). Such learning can occur via physical or verbal interaction and as long as both the learner and the teacher are motivated (one to learn and other to assist). An older child or adult serves as a guide who is responsive to what the child is ready to learn.

The implications for teaching include a strong case for mixed-age groupings so that young children can learn from older ones. Indeed, of all the strategies used to deal with reading problems in primary grades (which have devastating effects on children), the "most effective by far for preventing early reading failure are approaches incorporating one-to-one tutoring of at-risk first graders" (Slavin, Karweit, & Wasik, 1994). Play is a valuable way for children to work with the symbols and other higher forms of thinking. With other people alongside, the child practices what is to be expected and valued in society. The teacher is both observer and participant: for instance, if a child builds with blocks, the adult might sketch the building and then encourage a joint effort to make a map or use measurement tools.

Research from cognitive-developmentalists such as Flavell (1993) and brain research (Caine & Caine, 1997) support these alternative findings. Already preschoolers know about thinking: they can distinguish thinking from other psychological activities; 3-year-olds know that thinking is not seeing or talking, and 4- and 5-year-olds can often tell that there is a difference between thinking and knowing. The biologic evidence strongly suggests that there are sequences in children's thinking, that there are at least multiple expressions of intelligence, and that the context of learning affects what children know. These theories all attempt to describe some of the incredible diversity of human cognitive ability.

Brain-Based Research

New research on the brain development of young children (see Chapter 4) has important implications for early education and care. Indications are strong that children's brains need to be stimulated for the network of connections to grow and be protected from being discarded. "Brain connections that have been reinforced by repeated experience tend to remain while those that are not are discarded" (Galinsky, 1997). Thus, a child's early experiences help to shape the brain and will affect to some extent how one thinks, feels, and behaves.

Applying brain research to the early childhood classroom is a new challenge for teachers, and much more needs to be learned about how the brain functions. Teachers will need to understand several key ideas as well as translate these ideas into actual curriculum:

● *The brain is strongly run by patterns rather than facts.* Children learn best with curriculum developed around themes, integrated learning, whole experiences.

Conclusion: Develop meaningful themes for activity planning. Uninteresting or abstract pieces of information (e.g., drilling young children on alphabet letters) will not provide understanding. Plan some kinds of "immersion experiences" that encourage children to go deeply into their play and work.

● *Stress and threat affect the brain in many ways.* Emotions run the brain, and bad emotions reduce the capacity for memory and understanding as well as reducing higher order thinking skills. Good emotions create excitement and love of learning.

Conclusion: Make a positive, personal connection with each child, and avoid threats by loss of approval, hurried schedules, or implying children are helpless or bad. A secure environment counteracts the **downshifting** children do when feeling defensive and therefore less flexible and open to new information and ideas.

● *The brain runs better when food intake is steady.* Insulin levels stay more even, cortisol levels are lower, and glucose tolerance is better.

Conclusion: Snacks are good! Regular snack times may lead to better cognitive functioning, fewer discipline problems, and an enhanced sense of well-being.

● *All learning is mind-body.* A child's physical state, posture, and breathing affect learning. Our brain is designed for cycles and rhythms.

Conclusion: Keep track of and teach to children's bodily functions and body states and how long they are expected to sit or nap. Plan a daily schedule with both variety and balance, and work in regular routines and productive rituals.

Curriculum ideas based on brain research are shown throughout the chapter. In general, teachers of children can keep these ideas in mind:

● *Birth to age 4*: Provide for healthy sensory stimulation. This means all the senses need to be included in a child's exploration of the world. "There is a very important time in a child's life, beginning at birth, when he should be living in an enriched environment—visual, auditory, language, and so on—because that lays the foundation for development later in life" (Weisel in Caine & Caine, 1997).

● *Age 4 to 8*: The brain is eagerly searching for stimulation; "schooling from kindergarten through fifth grade, therefore, must be richly stimulating with activities that reward the brain's insatiable appetite for meaning" (Kotulak in Phipps, 1998). Give children plenty of opportunities to use stories, explore ideas, and master tasks rather than use worksheets or other repetitive tasks that kill enthusiasm for learning.

● *All ages*: Develop curriculum that emphasizes choices. Create opportunities for "collaboration" and cooperation, both among children and between children and teachers. "Exercise and positive social contacts, such as hugging, music, and the supportive comments of friends, can elevate endorphin levels and thus make us feel good about ourselves and our social environment" (Leventhal in Sylwester, 1995).

COGNITIVE SKILLS IN EARLY CHILDHOOD

The actual skills children acquire as they learn to think are considerable. A basic skill is defined by two fundamental qualities:

● A skill is basic if it is **transcurricular**: that is, if the child can use it in a variety of situations and activities throughout the school day. For example, children who can express feelings and opinions clearly—who can let adults know when they are having difficulties with a particular task or social situation—have acquired a skill that is useful anywhere.

● A skill is also basic if it has **dynamic** consequences: that is, if it leads to other worthwhile responses. For instance, children who are articulate tend to elicit more verbal responses from adults. Consequently, they are exposed to more verbal stimulation, which in turn strengthens their verbal abilities, and so on. Thus, having this skill leads to major dynamic consequences in a favorable direction, whereas *not* having the skill leads to dynamic consequences in an unfavorable direction.

Most skills fall into the nine categories below. The list, though long, is comprehensive; what children learn in the thinking realm of their development will fall into one of these categories. The teacher plans activities for all cognitive skills to ensure challenging children's thinking.

Skills of Inquiry

Young children are curious, watching the world carefully. Through exploration and examination, they increase their attention span. Inquisitive children begin to organize what they see, analyzing and identifying confusions or obstacles for themselves. The next step is communication; the child asks questions, listens, gets ideas, and makes suggestions. This includes interpreting what others communicate. Then children are ready to use resources, seeking assistance from other people and materials.

Piaget called these skills of inquiry; some of Gardner's spatial intelligence would also be included. Organizing and finding patterns, reasoning, and problem-solving are also inquiry skills. As children examine alternatives, they choose a course of action, revising their plans as needed. Young children thrill in making educated guesses, then checking their **hypotheses** by experimenting and taking risks. In doing so, they learn to evaluate, to use judgments and opinions, and to distinguish between fact and opinion, reality and fantasy. These basic skills of inquiry are the foundation for thinking; as such, they are far more important to develop than simple prereading or number skills.

Knowledge of the Physical World

How do children learn about the physical world? First, they use objects, spending plenty of time explor-

Figure 13.2 ● Being able to explore actual materials and objects encourages children to assimilate and use new knowledge.

ing, manipulating, choosing, and using toys and natural materials. Babies search for something to suck; they begin to grasp objects and let them go. Toddlers will pick up and throw things or drop objects from a highchair to see what happens. Children observe reactions, discover relationships, and try to predict what will happen. Six-year-olds with balloons and water explore how to fill, roll, throw, and burst the balloons. This knowledge is part of Gardner's logical-mathematical intelligence, for knowledge of the physical world is essential to making order of it. As they learn the properties of objects, children gain a better understanding of the concept of cause and effect.

Knowledge of the Social World

Learning about others is hard work because the social world is not concrete and is often illogical. The child needs an awareness of self before developing an awareness of others and how to interact socially. To Gardner, this kind of knowledge requires two types of intelligence. The first is *intrapersonal*, having access to one's own feelings and a range of emotions, and the second is *interpersonal*, being able to notice others, making distinctions among individuals, particularly their moods and motivations. Infants begin by distinguishing friends from strangers. Toddlers learn to use "mine" and then to use others' names as well. The next step is to expand their knowledge of roles to include those of family, school, and the community. Four- and 5-year-olds are provided with daily opportunities to cooperate, to help, and to negotiate with others about their needs and wishes. According to Vygotsky, preschoolers learn appropriate actions by playing with older children. Also, makebelieve is a major means through which children extend their cognitive skills.

In the best of circumstances, children are encouraged to notice both similarities and differences in people and then are led to develop tolerance for both. "Contextual intelligence" describes the ability to understand and manipulate the environment to suit oneself.[1] School-aged children seek small-group teamwork and moments of private time with a close friend. Children in the primary grades experience the development of conscience and learn rules for social living. In these ways children learn what is appropriate conduct in various situations—indoors or out, happy or sad, at the grocery store or at the dinner table.

Classification

Knowledge of the physical world teaches children to have different responses to different objects. *Classifying* this knowledge is a lengthy process. Classification is a basic process that children use to develop logical and mathematical reasoning abilities (see Gardner in Chapter 4). As children develop, they initially classify by sorting groups of completely different objects, using a logic that only the child understands. During the preschool years, they begin to sort objects using consistent criteria. Once they develop language proficiency, they can name and classify objects. Gradually, and with help from adults who stimulate describing and manipulating, they learn that objects have more than one attribute and can be classified in more than one class (Micklo, 1995). To clarify this process, consider how 2-year-old Tisa learns to classify:

OUR DIVERSE WORLD OUR DIVERSE WORLD OUR DIVERSE WORLD OUR DIVERSE WORLD OUR DIVERSE WORLD OUR DIVERSE WORLD OUR DIVERSE WORLD OUR DIVERSE WORLD OUR DIVERSE WORLD
[1] Social knowledge is a critical factor in children's development, enabling them to function in OUR DIVERSE WORLD.

What can Tisa do to the stuffed bear *and* the pet dog? What can she do with one and *not* the other? Which are her toys? Which are Rover's? Which ones have fur? What is different about them?

Tisa learns the *attributes* of the objects by exploring, learning the class names of "toy" and "pet." Tisa makes collections, sorting by similarity those that are Rover's toys and those that are her own. She uses class relationships to understand that both animals have fur, but she can tug on only one animal's ears without encountering a problem.

Seriation

How do children learn to seriate, or to arrange items according to a graduated scale? Like classification, **seriation** can appear confusing at first glance. To illustrate its development, look at some of the materials designed by Montessori. These toys were developed to make clear to children exactly what seriation is and how it can be learned. Many of these toys distinguish grades of intensity by size, color, weight, number. Children build pyramid towers, fit nesting blocks together, and use the counting rods. By noting differences, often through trial and error, children learn seriation systematically. For instance, the pyramid tower is ordered from largest piece to smallest as it is built. Boxes are nested, one inside the other, by their graduated size or volume. The counting rods can be put into a staircase array, the units building on each other from one to ten. Children can arrange several things in order and fit one ordered set of objects to another. Gardner's category of musical intelligence requires seriation, as well as the skill of inquiry ("How do I make noise? Rhythm? Musical song?") and a knowledge of the social world ("How can we make music together? A real band?").

Numbers

Understanding the concept of *number* means learning about quantity: that is, understanding amount, degree, and position. Once infants develop an understanding of *object permanence* (that an object exists whether or not it can be seen), they are ready to learn about quantity as they compare objects—for example, by stacking rings on a stick. Toddlers and twos can sort by groups (large versus small, hard versus soft) and

Figure 13.3 ● Cognition in action! The concepts of the world come to life through Montessori materials.

start noticing what is "more." To learn about the names of numbers, one begins with their sound. Settings for children under 5 have plenty of songs, chants, and fingerplays that include numbers ("One Potato, Two" or "Five Speckled Frogs"). Once children comprehend numbers, they are ready to use mathematical terms and forms of expression. For instance, after singing about the frog that jumped into the pool in the song "Five Speckled Frogs," Chantel can begin to understand that four is one less than five.

But a knowledge of number is neither complete nor meaningful unless children have direct experience with materials and objects. Learning about quantity also means comparing amounts (as when children work with table toys, blocks, sensory materials, and the like) and arranging two sets of objects in one-to-one correspondence ("Each person needs one and only one napkin for snack, Tyler"). Children can also count objects and begin computation ("Parvin, you have three shovels. Here is one more; now how many do you have?"). With countless experiences such as these, children in kindergarten through third grade will be ready and excited to learn more mathematical skills.

Symbols

A symbol stands for something else; it is not what it appears to be! Young children have to think hard and long to symbolize. It is a task of some skill to imitate or use one object to represent something else.

Children begin by using their bodies. Infants and toddlers love to play peek-a-boo, reacting to "Boo!" with full-bodied excitement each time it is said. Preschoolers revel in playing favorite characters. Primary school children make up plays and puppet shows. Make-believe helps in the process of symbolizing, as does making sound to represent objects ("Choo-choo" is a train, for example). Using and making two- and three-dimensional models are other ways children symbolize, when they transfer what they see to the easel or to the clay table. Children are also symbolizing when they dress up in costumes and uniforms. Teachers add to the symbolizing process when they use descriptive words. Description games encourage children to do the same. For example, "It is round and red and you eat it. What is it?" (An apple!) After all these skills have been mastered, children are ready for written symbols, when they can use the written word to label, take dictation, or write notes. Using Gardner's and Vygotsky's ways of thinking, educational environments for school-age children might take the form of a discovery center, or kind of museum, where apprentice-groups with children of different ages would help children with numerical and computer skills.

Spatial Relationships

Spatial relationships develop early. Infants visually track what they see, trying to reach and grasp. As they experience one object's position in relation to another, they begin to have a mental picture of spatial relationships. Toddlers find this out as they learn to steer themselves around tables and seat themselves on the potty. The concept of "close" (the chair) and "far away" (the quesadilla cooling on the counter) give clues to length and distance. ("How far do I have to reach to get one?"). As spatial skills develop, children learn to fit things together and take them apart. They rearrange and shape objects. They observe and describe things from different spatial viewpoints. This perspective is learned only through experience. The child under 5 needs to describe and then try out the notion that what one sees from the side of the hill is *not* what can be seen from the top.

Adults help children learn such skills by letting them locate things at home, in the classroom, in the department store. Both Piaget and Gardner would agree that body and kinesthetic knowledge are used in this type of activity. In Reggio Emilia, for instance, mirrors are placed around corners, found at the school

entrance, and embedded in the floors, giving children a sense of self in space in a number of ways. Teachers encourage children to represent such spatial relationships in their drawings, with pictures, and in photographs.

Time

Understanding time is a complicated affair because time is composed of at least three dimensions: time as the present, time as a continuum, and time as a sequence of events. Children must learn each of these to fully understand the concept of time. In some settings, children learn to stop and start an activity on a signal (when the teacher strikes a chord on the piano for cleanup time). They try to move their bodies at different speeds, indoors and out. Older children begin to observe that clocks and calendars are used to mark the passage of time. Specifically, children come to know the sequencing of events in time: which comes first, next, last? Having an order of events through a consistent daily schedule helps children learn this aspect of time. They also benefit from anticipating future events and making the appropriate preparations. Planning a course of action and completing that plan give meaning to the idea of time.

What children learn intellectually in the early years is massive in quantity and quality. Yet young children are ready—eager, in fact—to engage themselves with the world around them to acquire these cognitive skills. By remaining aware of how much is to be learned, educators keep a realistic—and humble—appreciation for the "work" of children.

THE TEACHER'S ROLE

Considerations

When considering children's intellectual development, teachers should keep in mind:

● *Education is exploration.* The process of education is more than its products. Teachers enhance learning by allowing children to interact with the environment. The teacher is a source of information and support rather than one who gives answers or commands. A project approach, based on the belief that children's minds should be engaged in ways that deepen their understanding of their own experiences and environment, may be used.

Figure 13.4 ● When considering intellectual development, teachers should keep in mind that, to children, education is exploration. Let children use their imagination to use materials in new and different ways. (Courtesy of the city of Reggio Emilia, Italy.)

Consisting of exploring a theme or topic (such as shadows, houses, building a table) over a period of weeks, this approach reflects Dewey's progressive education and the British Open Schools (see Chapter 1) and is implemented regularly in the Reggio Emilia schools. The goal is to have children ask their own questions and create their own challenges.

● *Children do not think like adults.* Children think and perceive in their own ways, as Piaget believed. They think in sensory and concrete terms and come to conclusions based on what they see and touch.

● *Children's thinking is legitimate and should be valued.* Their thought processes and perceptions are as valid as adults'. Teachers support those processes by asking questions to stimulate further thought and by providing materials for exploration, as seen in Figure 13.15.

● *The language of the teacher should support cognitive development.* Throughout their interactions with children, teachers help children use words, terms, and concepts correctly:

> Mariko (at water table): I need that suckup.
>
> Teacher: The baster really does suck up water, doesn't it?

Teachers' questions are open-ended; they are not to be answered with a simple yes or no. As teachers in

Reggio Emilia question children (more often than not in small groups of three or four), they explore together what the children are doing, how they are going to solve a problem, or what they would like to do next. They may even tape record the interchange so that, later, the child can play it back and evaluate the approach in greater depth. For example, Tony asks his kindergartners what will happen if they do not count the cups of flour while making bread. What he is really asking them to do is to predict what will happen and consider the results. The goal is to use language to help children *think*.

Sometimes teachers use their own language skills to define a problem, help children figure out what they are doing, and decide what they need to do next. They leave the child with something to ponder.

> Teacher: I wonder why the turtle's head went back in its shell when you put your finger close by.

> Teacher: If you want to play with José, how can you let him know?

> Teacher: What *do* we need from the wood-working shelf to make a spaceship?

Figure 13.5 shows further how teachers' use of language helps children think and develop cognitive skills as part of their early childhood experience.

The Focus Box by Larry Schweinhart describes two issues concerning curriculum development.

The teacher must consider, include, and plan for children with learning disabilities and other varied learning "styles." Each type of learning disability (see Chapter 3) has its own description and treatment. Teachers must develop a wide range of techniques to address such disabilities. After the identification and assessment phases, teachers and families need to work with specialists and devise options (an individualized education plan, or IEP) that include the child and establish reasonable learning goals.

Curriculum Planning for Cognitive Development

In the Environment

Teachers can plan cognitive curriculum for their children by considering the class setting, both indoors and out, throughout the daily schedule. Each activity

Skill	Teachers Can:
Inquiry	● Ask questions so children make statements about their conversations.
	Example: "What do you notice about the guinea pig?"
	● Try to be more specific if such questions seem overwhelming or if they elicit little response.
	Example: "What sounds do you hear? What can you find out by touching her?"
	● Ask how children arrived at their answers.
	Example: "How did you know that the marble wouldn't roll *up* the ramp?"
	● Ask questions that expand the process.
	Example: "Can you tell me anything else about your doll?"
Social Knowledge	● Try not to respond to unstated needs.
	Example: "Do you want something? Can I help you?"
	● Help children define what they want or need, so that they learn how to ask for it.
	Example: Marie: I wonder who is going to tie my shoes?
	Teacher: So do I. When you want someone to tie your shoe, you can say, "Would you tie my shoe?"
	Marie: Would you tie my shoe?
	Teacher: I'd be glad to.
Classification	● Ask questions that will help children focus on objects and see differences and details.
	Example: While cooking, ask
	Which things on the table do we put in the bowl? Which are made of plastic? Which go in the oven?
	What on the table is used for measuring? How do you know?
	Now look carefully—what do you see on the measuring cup?
	What do those little red lines mean?
Spatial Relationships	● Ask for the precise location of an object the child asks for or is interested in:
	Examples: "Where did you say you saw the bird's nest?"
	"You can find another stapler in the cabinet underneath the fish tank."
Concept of Time	● Use accurate time sequences with children.
	Example: Teacher: Just a minute.
	Milo: Is this a real minute, or a "wait a minute"?
	Teacher: You're right. I'm with Phoebe now. I'll help you next.

Figure 13.5 ● Teachers' use of language affects how children develop cognitive skills. The more children are allowed and encouraged to think for themselves, the more their cognitive skills will develop.

center can be used to encourage intellectual development with a variety of curriculum materials and methods (see High/Scope in Chapter 2). The environment and methods required to help children think include challenging situations, enriching materials, and supportive adults. Young children have special ways of thinking (see Chapter 4) that expand with age. Some children under age 3 have a limited attention span and can be overstimulated unless the environment is kept simple. Three- to 5-year-olds can absorb more and in finer detail as they have more developed motor and perceptual skills. Older preschoolers and kindergartners learn best trying to solve real problems, and the 6- to 8-year-old still benefits in discovery-oriented, "learn by doing" situations. Figure 13.6 shows how one activity (which can be done with nearly all ages) contributes to the development of children's thought processes.

What's an Early Childhood Teacher to Do?

Larry Schweinhart

You want to be an early childhood teacher because you love young children, but reading this book has helped you realize that love of young children is just the beginning. To be a good early childhood teacher, you must also master a body of knowledge and skills and make basic decisions about your early childhood curriculum goals and practices.

The first curriculum issue you must resolve for yourself is whether to equate early childhood education with direct instruction in academic lessons or with supporting child-initiated learning activities. The appeal of direct academic instruction is that it gets down to business about academically preparing young children for school, zeroing in on the basic skills of reading, writing, and arithmetic. The appeal of an approach based on child-initiated learning activities is that it focuses on all aspects of children's development—social, physical, and intellectual, including the basic academic skills.

Since 1967, we have been conducting the High/Scope Preschool Curriculum Study, a comparison of the effects of preschool programs based on either scripted academic instruction (Direct Instruction) or two child-initiated-learning-activities approaches—High/Scope and traditional Nursery School (Schweinhart & Weikart, 1997). All three approaches helped prepare children for school intellectually, but only the approaches based on child-initiated learning activities contributed to their long-term social development:

- Only 6% of either the High/Scope or the Nursery School group needed treatment for emotional impairment or disturbance during their schooling, as compared with 47% of the Direct Instruction group.

- Only 10% of the High/Scope group had been arrested for a serious crime by age 23, as compared with 39% of the Direct Instruction group.

Such findings make a strong case for basing your curriculum approach on child-initiated learning activities rather than on direct academic instruction.

A second curriculum issue you must resolve for yourself is whether to take a documented curriculum approach, such as the Montessori method (Montessori, 1967) or the High/Scope Curriculum (Hohmann & Weikart, 1995). The alternative is to invent your own approach, borrowing from the approaches and practices of others. In fact, even if you take a documented curriculum approach, you have to exercise intelligent judgment about when and how to use various teaching practices. But be careful—your own invented approach may lack consistency on curriculum issues and surely lacks evidence of its effectiveness. A documented, validated curriculum approach gives you a thought-out, consistent position, with proof of the approach's effectiveness. For example, the evidence shows that adults born in poverty who had High/Scope Curriculum preschool experience had significantly greater educational and financial success and half the crime rate they would have had otherwise (Schweinhart, Barnes, & Weikart, 1993). If you study, train in, and use this approach, you can expect similar results.

No matter what approach you take, be sure it is a thoughtful and consistent one. In this way, you can take full advantage of the extraordinary opportunity you have to positively influence the children you serve for the rest of their lives.

Larry Schweinhart is research division chairman of the High/Scope Educational Research Foundation in Ypsilanti, Michigan. With David Weikart, he directs the High/Scope Perry Preschool Study and the High/Scope Preschool Curriculum Study.

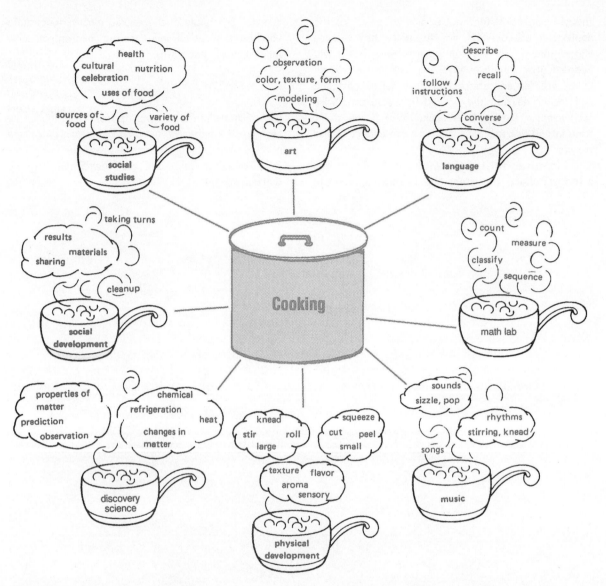

Figure 13.6 ● Each activity, such as cooking, can enhance cognitive development throughout the curriculum. A trip to the market can be an experience in classification and calculation. (For further reading, see Dahl, 1998).

Throughout the environment, teachers remember to notice and appreciate *efforts* as well as children's projects. Too often only the take-home pieces of a day, such as preschool art projects or primary written assignments, are noted. Teachers can record examples of children's thinking by photographing or sketching creations made with blocks and manipulatives and can take notes about incidences in drama and social interactions. A specific example of their child's reasoning

or problem-solving tells parents of the tremendous cognitive work in children's play.

Indoor Areas. The indoor environments described in Chapter 9 include the basic ingredients of a stimulating cognitive environment. The indoor areas might have some of the following materials and activities:

Art: Include a shelf for self-chosen projects. A variety of paper, drawing implements, and tools encourages children to re-create their own reality, using representational art forms that show how children see the physical and social worlds.

Blocks: Have paper models of each block shape to help children with classification by shape and size. Accessories, such as animals and homemade trees and lakes, help children symbolize. As they experiment with blocks, they learn about physical laws and reality and have experiences in cooperative learning and living, all of which are cognitive tasks (Cuffaro et al., 1995). Counting blocks, which builds on one-to-one correspondence rather than rote memorization, contributes to genuine understanding (Unglaub, 1997).

Discovery/science: Rotate a display of "touch me" materials. This gives children firsthand experience with plants, seeds, animals, magnets, sea shells, foods, and so on. Help children formulate questions and then experiment or observe to seek the answers. School-age children can find out which plants grow in saltwater or freshwater by setting up plants in each environment and watching daily ("Today something has changed!" wrote a 7-year-old. "The duckweed is not relly grren anymore. A scnd root is hanging."). If you can, have a computer available with developmentally appropriate software (see the *Special Topics* section of this chapter for details).

Dramatic play: Stock this area with materials for role playing, puppet making, and acting out of adult activities. Have anatomically correct boy and girl dolls of a variety of races and some with disabilities. Include clothing for all types of work, equipment for carrying things and babies, that reflect the homes of all the children in the group but also extend the play to include new ways of dressing, eating, and playing.[1] Children learn to understand the world of people as they pretend to be adults with adult occupations and responsibilities.

Language/library: Choose books that focus on both the physical and social worlds. Children's interests in numbers, symbols, and time can also be extended by selecting literature that reflects their level of understanding. Look for the message in children's books and choose good stories that reflect diversity, such as *Helping Out* (Ancona) and *George the Babysitter* (Hughes). Be sure to listen to the group's interests, and make a point to place books that respond to those interests in the library. (See the *Special Topics* section of this chapter.)

Manipulatives (table toys): The manipulatives area is an ideal place for materials that encourage cognitive development; highlight this area with both favorites (Legos® or Crystal Climbers®) and new items (Construx® or sewing cards). Counting cubes aid in classification and seriation, while puzzles or nesting blocks focus on spatial relationships. Information-processing theory emphasizes the importance of experiences that develop children's working memory and familiarity. Manipulative materials (including beads, tiddley winks, and so on) and games give children hands-on experiences with counting, sorting, and organizing that are both meaningful and socially natural. Homemade lotto games or puzzles with the children's photos encourage self-esteem and group identity as well as cognitive and motor development.

Outdoor Areas. The outdoor area provides opportunities for children to plan and organize their own thoughts. Toddlers can classify what they find as they look for balls, sand buckets, and toy trucks hidden around the yard. Kindergartners playing tag need inquiry skills. Preschoolers in the sand pit predict how water will affect the sand, using their growing knowledge of the physical world. Children learn to classify water table and wheel toys; they learn seriation when they select sand buckets by size. Counting shovels to see that there are enough to go around, building with large, hollow blocks, and watching the seasons change are all cognitive skills children gain as they play outside.

Physical- and logical-mathematical activities are thus easily incorporated into the curriculum outdoors. A Piagetian approach of asking "I wonder why . . .?" or "What would happen if . . .?" inspires experimenting and reasoning in young children. The water table outdoors could have a large block of ice, a variety of materials such as wood, cotton balls, straws, and cardboard, or containers of colored water and eyedroppers. Balancing activities might mean hollow blocks, milk cartons, or beanbags (or all three). A hillside or long plank can become a site for predicting and trying out rolling, using different sizes of balls or even bodies.

OUR DIVERSE WORLD OUR DIVERSE WORLD OUR DIVERSE WORLD OUR DIVERSE WORLD OUR DIVERSE WORLD OUR DIVERSE WORLD OUR DIVERSE WORLD OUR DIVERSE WORLD

[1] Children's learning environments should be rich with images of diversity. This diversity adds to the complexity of their thinking!

Routines, Transitions, and Groups

Groups, transitions, and routines all play a part in developing children's knowledge of the social world. As children learn to conduct themselves in school, they learn:

● To enter a class and start to play (transition).

● To take care of their own belongings and those of their school (routines).

● To concentrate on an activity with others around (group times).

● To interact with others while at the same time paying attention to a leader or task (group times).

● To end an activity, an interaction, a school day (transition).

Teachers plan environments, activities, and grouping of children to give the class experience in all these cognitive challenges. Look back at Figure 9.24 in Chapter 9. It describes strategies for helping children learn concrete and comfortable ways to think and live with transitions. Teachers use signs, their own words, and helpful tips that illuminate for children what is happening, what is expected of them, and how they can express themselves in all three of these daily segments.

Moreover, many routine activities offer wonderful opportunities for cognitive learning. For example, consider the snack table. Incorporating math concepts into snack time will engender enthusiasm and skill development. Whether as a part of free-choice time or a time period on its own, snack time becomes "think time" as children:

● Fill out and use menu cards

● Learn the concept of sets ("*everyone* needs five of *everything*, huh?")

● Work with the concept of uniform units ("are the ham and cheese pieces the same?")

● Understand the concepts of equal, less, and more

● Learn how to count "wet stuff" and to count by the spoonful or handful

● See geometry and fractions at work (circles for raisins, triangles for sandwiches, "break the graham cracker in pieces for everyone . . . fair!") (adapted from Meriwether, 1997)

Focus on Skills

How can teachers help children develop specific cognitive skills? After observing the children carefully, teachers identify a particular skill and then list those processes, concepts, and vocabulary involved. For instance, the skill of *inquiry* can be encouraged in every part of the curriculum by *asking questions* (see Figures 13.14 and 13.15). Teachers model curiosity by observing and asking questions about what they see and what children may be thinking. This stimulates children to look, wonder, and interact:

Teacher: I wonder which piece of wood you'll choose to glue on your board next?

Teacher: What part do you want to play in our grocery store?

Teacher: How can we find out how long your road of blocks is?

Figure 13.7 illustrates the kinds of questions teachers ask children that help children think and learn.

When children see that it is all right to ask "Why?" they feel encouraged to ask questions themselves. Brainstorming is a technique that helps children get ideas and use resources to find out how many ways there are to make a kite or build a castle.

Outdoors, inquisitive children explore their environment. Children ask questions: "Can we turn on the water? What if we bury all of the toy bears in the gravel?! Could we use the ladder to see over the fence? Let's all hide from the teacher?!" The way teachers handle inquiries from children about what they want to do sends a message that supports—or discourages—this cognitive skill. When there is no harm in *asking* (though the answer may be "No"), children are encouraged to develop further the skill of inquiry. Figure 13.8 illustrates exactly how the cognitive skills of reasoning and problem-solving could serve as the basis for curriculum development around the entire classroom.

Use of Themes

A specific theme can be chosen for cognitive development. Units based on things in the physical world (season changes, pets, the garden), on unexpected or current events (a new load of sand, a community fair, road work nearby), or the special interests

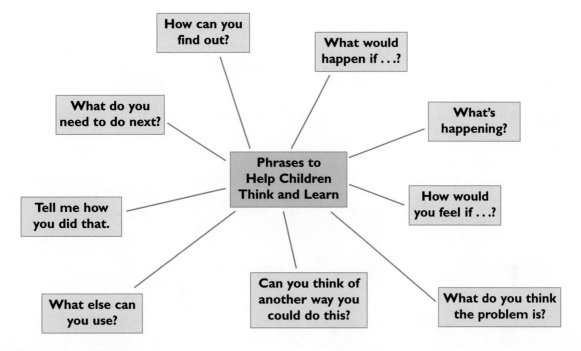

Figure 13.7 ● Teachers encourage children's thinking when they ask questions. Posted in the classroom or given to students and parents, this chart serves as a reminder that to TEACH is to ASK more often than to TELL.

of the children (sharing the African mask or spacesuits, using the puppet stage, studying reptiles) are all appealing. Figure 13.9 illustrates a dinosaur theme.

Current events must be chosen carefully because young children may have only passing knowledge or interest in most of them. Meaningful events might be a space shuttle mission or a solar eclipse. More likely, the event will be a local one, such as a children's fair or someone's new baby. Units based on these happenings might be named "Space and Travel" or "Our Beginnings As Babies." Events such as the discovery of ants on the playground have a high level of interest and are worth pursuing; see Figure 13.10 on page 464 for an example.

Themes can change with the seasons. Fall is the time for a unit on "Harvest Time," "Corn," or "Masks and Hats." Winter may mean a unit on "Water, Water Everywhere," since snow, sleet, hail, and rain are a regular part of winter in most of the United States. Spring is a time for green and growing things, and a unit could focus on the physical world of growing plants from seeds, hatching chicks, visiting a farm. Summer weather on the coasts sends everyone to "The Seashore," or at least the local lake or river.

The theme of "Friendship" during Valentine's month expands children's knowledge of the social world, as they increase their awareness of others through the giving and receiving of letters and cards. Cooperation and group conflict resolution expand the friendship theme. A unit can also focus on symbolizing through use of names, letters on a "post box," or the numbers and location of people's houses and apartments.

Throughout the year, teachers observe the interests of the particular group and notice what is relevant to their lives. For a group interested in the passage of time, "Watches and Calendars" could be a theme, with timepieces from hourglasses to digital watches and clanging timers and calendars from around the world. Having children build ramps from cardboard tubes in the block corner, for instance, stimulates a discussion about slides and ramps that expands into a unit on "Push, Pull, Toss & Tilt" (Marxen, 1995). Using a calendar means involving the children in the process of construction, including events that the children look forward to (including birthdays, community events, field trips), and making it accessible so that the children can interact and "own" it.

The Concepts:
Selecting a course of action
Making educated guesses
Making and revising a plan
Risking and evaluating the results

The Vocabulary:
Guess
Plan
Problem
Solution/solve
What? why? how?

The Process:

Activity area	Process question
Art	How many ways can you use the brush (pen, squirt bottle) to make a mark on the paper? Why is it dripping? How can you stop it when you're ready?
Bathrooms/cubbies	You found Paul's sweater. . . . How can you find where it goes? Where did the water come from? How can you clean it up?
Blocks	What makes the tower of blocks fall over? How can a block be used to connect two others?
Cooking	How do we mix these ingredients together? What will happen when it is put in the oven?
Discovery/science	Why did the magnet pick up the nail and not the pen? What is the difference between the rabbit and the guinea pig? How are they alike?
Dramatic play	Who will be the dad? What happens when these other children want to play? How can you get to wear the costume you want?
Language/library	What happens next in the story? Why do you think so? Why did the child feel unhappy at first? Then what happened?
Large group	Why can't you see/hear the leader? What can you do about feeling too crowded? What can you do when your friend keeps whispering to you during storytime?
Gross-motor	How do you jump rope? What do you use to pump yourself on a swing? How will you find a ball?
Manipulatives	How do you figure out what puzzle piece fits? Do you see a pattern on the peg board? What is it?
Sensory	How do you get the water from the large pitcher to the small cup? How will you get the wet sand through the funnel?

Figure 13.8 ● Children want to know how to solve problems, such as, "How much milk will a bowl of this size hold?"

Theme: Dinosaurs

Area	Cognitive Skill(s)	Activity
Indoors		
Art	Organization	Papier mâché model of a dinosaur, make a "dinosaur world" mural.
Blocks	Seriation	Use blocks to compare relative sizes of dinosaurs.
Cooking	Relationships	Prepare vegetarian snack (herbivores), then meatballs for the carnivores.
Discovery	Observation	Get fossils, other skeletons.
		Collect books on how scientists learn about dinosaurs.
		Compare relationships (size, stature, etc.) of prehistoric to common animals.
		Hide bones in the sand table to dig up and role play paleontologist.
Dramatic play	Symbols	Dinosaur puppets.
		Masks of dinosaurs.
Library	Label/recall; use of resources	Provide books about dinosaurs.
		Make dinosaur books with stamps and children's words.
Manipulatives	Reasoning; problem solving	Individual and floor dinosaur puzzles.
		Templates to trace and cut.
Outdoors		
Sensory	Symbols	Rubber dinosaurs in pebbles; dinosaur cookie cutters in clay/playdough.
Gross-motor	Symbols	Measure children's bodies with a rope the length of various dinosaurs.
Sand	Symbols	Act out digging up dinosaur bones.
Games	Social world	"Tyrannosaurus, May I?" game, naming and taking steps of various dinosaurs.
Groups		
Large	Label/recall; educated guessing	"Who Am I?", verbally describing dinosaur.
		Mystery Pictures, showing parts of dinosaurs and having children guess.
Music	Symbols	Acting out dinosaurs to a record, or to music of various tones.
Small	Label/communicate	Draw your favorite dinosaur, dictate what you like about it and what you know.
		Dinosaur sheet, folded in quarters, with a sentence to fill in and space to draw: The dinosaurs laid . . .
		Some dinosaurs lived . . .
		Dinosaurs ate . . .
		Dinosaurs died because . . .

Figure 13.9 ● Using a theme of special interest, such as dinosaurs, teachers can develop children's cognitive skills in many classroom areas.

Discovery Learning about Ants:
Curriculum Planning for Primary Cognitive Development

The Setting:
- ● The playground after a rain and in the sidewalk cracks
- ● The classroom, especially around the wastebasket

The Discovery:
Ants everywhere!
Children: "Let's smash them!"
Teacher: "Wait—let's get to know them."

The Process:
Asking what you want to know about ants (RESEARCH QUESTION)
1. What do ants eat?
2. Why do they go into an anthill?
3. Do ants sleep?
4. Where do ants go when it rains?
5. What does an ant's body look like?
6. What is inside an anthill?

Finding out about these things (METHODOLOGY, PROCEDURE)
1. Consult experts (a library visit, checking at home, asking parents, looking at class copies of *Ranger Rick*, and so on)
2. Observe them (watch ants, collect them, put them in containers)
3. Collect information (write journals, do group stories and reports)
4. Do experiments on ants ("Do ants hear?" try blowing a trumpet; "Can ants swim"? put them in a bowl of water; "How strong are they?" give them various sizes of bread and see what they can carry)

Telling what you know (RESULTS, CONCLUSIONS, NEXT STEPS)
1. Write reports.
2. Make a drama or play and act it out.
3. Take photos or draw pictures.
4. Make a book.

Figure 13.10 ● A lesson that uses the discovery method engages the children in scientific thinking and is related directly to their own thinking. Children's innate curiosity, the foundation for scientific thinking, is thus extended into the primary years. (Special thanks to Amelia Klein, *Young Children*, July, 1991.)

Young children, particularly those under age 5, use themselves as a starting point. Working their way into the world from there, they are often interested in their bodies, and a loosely formed theme of "Our Bodies, Ourselves" allows for learning about racial, physical, and gender similarities and differences as well as differences in physical abilities.[1] Expanding this unit to family and community is a natural process that builds on a solid base. Another way to plan curriculum is to focus on the children's developmental level. Infants and toddlers have less need for a theme curriculum; curriculum ideas for them concentrate on cognitive stimulation at their particular level of development, as in Figure 13.11.

OUR DIVERSE WORLD OUR DIVERSE WORLD OUR DIVERSE WORLD OUR DIVERSE WORLD OUR DIVERSE WORLD OUR DIVERSE WORLD OUR DIVERSE WORLD OUR DIVERSE WORLD

[1] What better time to deal with the potential of children's misconceptions and pre-prejudice attitudes and create an understanding and celebration of diversity!

Curriculum Planning for Cognitive Development with Infants and Toddlers

The Environment

● Contains soft items (such as pillows) and hard elements (such as mirrors) to see, taste, and touch.
● Has contrasts of color and design.
● Changes periodically, from the floor to strollers to swing.
● Is decorated with pictures of people's faces, animals, families.

The Skills

● Include self-help activities of eating, toileting/changing, and dressing.
● Highlight language and thinking as the adults label objects, describe events, and reflect feelings in a simplified, conversational manner.
● Encourage listening to a person, a story, a flannelboard song, fingerplay.
● Use appropriate art media to explore and manipulate, not to produce a finished product.

The Themes

● Are loosely defined and flexible, as is the schedule.
● Are of family and belonging, of self and bodies, of babies.
● Are dictated more by children's needs than by adults'.

Figure 13.11 ● Planning for infants and toddlers involves understanding specific development and intimate knowledge of the individual child. Consistent caregiving and flexibility are as important to effective planning for children under 2 years of age as are the actual activities offered.

● UNIT 13-1 Checkpoint

Cognition is the ability to learn, remember, and think abstractly. Children's cognitive development is related to learning in all other skill areas. Early childhood educators see cognitive development from an eclectic point of view and draw heavily from the works of Jean Piaget.

Cognitive skills in the early years can be put into several categories. The teacher's role is to understand how cognition develops in children and to put that knowledge to work in the classroom. While creating curriculum, teachers keep certain attitudes and ideas in mind. Then, they set about planning for their programs.

The methods of developing children's cognition skills are as varied and creative as the teachers—and children—can be. By focusing on the class setting, a specific skill, or a theme, teachers help children acquire and use the skills of thinking to understand themselves and the world around them.

Ask yourself:

● What perspective do early childhood teachers have on the development of cognition?

● What are nine cognitive skills of the early years?

● What should teachers consider when defining their role in cognitive development?

● How can cognitive curriculum be developed in the class setting?

● What skills could be the focus for curriculum planning?

● What are three themes that encourage the development of cognitive skills?

● UNIT 13-2 Language

Alexis:	Laleña, will you help me full this pitcher up?
Laleña:	No, because my ponytail is keeping me in bothers.
Veronique:	Hey, come here! I accidentally dropped a piece of bread and the birds yummed it right up!
Abhi:	I know, that's what the tooth fairy did to my tooth.
Marty:	I'm going to keep *all* my baby teeth in a jar and the next time a baby comes along, I'll give him my baby teeth.

Language is the aspect of human behavior that involves the use of sounds in meaningful patterns. This includes the corresponding symbols that are used to form, express, and communicate thoughts and feelings. Any system of signs used for communication is language. For the developing child, language is the ability to express oneself. Language is both receptive—listening, understanding, and responding—and expressive—pronunciation, vocabulary, and grammar. In other words, as illustrated above, language has meaning.

THE DEVELOPMENT OF LANGUAGE

Language seems to be an innate characteristic of humankind. Wherever people live together, language of some form develops. Languages worldwide vary remarkably in their sounds, words, and grammatical structure. Nonetheless, young children around the world acquire language.

What Research Tells Us

Research into language development and expression reveals several interesting characteristics. First, the language of children is different from adult language (deVilliers & Jill, 1981). Children's language deals with the present and is egocentric, taking into account only the child's own knowledge. There appears to be a lack of awareness on the child's part of language form. Preschool children do show awareness of language structure (for instance, "feets" to mark the plural form) but do not seem to know the parts of speech. In other words, children use language to communicate but seem to have no understanding of language as an entity itself.

Language is not learned simply by imitating adult speech (Beck, 1979). Child language is not garbled adult language, but rather is unique to the child's age and linguistic level. Gardner lists language ability as one form of cognition (linguistic intelligence), and most language development theorists agree that there seems to be an innate human tendency toward language (Chomsky, 1993). Children are not just trying to imitate others and making mistakes but are trying to come to terms with language themselves. A child will try out theories about language in attempts to understand its patterns. In language, as in so many areas of cognition, children are involved as active participants in their own learning. The use of speech is not merely imitative but productive and creative.

Moreover, language development is a process of maturation.[1] Just as in the development of cognitive skills, there are stages of language growth that follow a specific sequence. There are also variations in timing that are important to remember.

Stages of Language Development

Children follow a six-step sequence in language development, one that seems *invariable* regardless of what language is being learned.

[1] Teachers must be aware of the children they teach and alert for a diversity of language issues and skills, particularly in the area of bilingualism, speech or language disorders, and dialects (see later in this chapter).

1. *Infant's Response to Language.* Babies begin by attending to speech, changes in sound, rhythm, and intonation. These are the **precursors** of speech, and young infants are especially sensitive to some sound differences. Infants need to hear speech, and plenty of it, to develop the foundations of sound.

2. *Vocalization.* By 3 to 4 months of age, infants begin cooing and babbling. Babbling increases with age and seems to peak around 9 to 12 months. This is a matter of physical maturation, not just experience; children who are deaf or hearing impaired do it at the same time as those whose hearing is normal. Furthermore, similar patterns are seen among different languages.

3. *Word Development.* According to deVilliers and Jill (1981), the child must first separate the noises heard into speech and nonspeech. The speech noises must be further separated into words and the sounds that form them. The growing infant starts to shift from practice to playing with sounds. The end result is planned, controlled speech.

   Children begin playing with sounds around 10 to 15 months of age. From this point, the development of speech is determined as much by control of motor movements as by the ability to match sounds with objects.

   Most children can understand and respond to a number of words before they can produce any. Their first words include names of objects and events in their world (people, food, toys, animals). Then the child begins to overextend words, perhaps using "doggy" to refer to all animals. Finally, single words can be used as sentences: "Bye-bye" can refer to someone leaving, a meal the child thinks is finished, the child's going away, a door closing.

4. *Sentences.* Children's sentences usually begin with two words, describing an action ("Me go"), a possession ("My ball"), or a location ("Baby outside"). These sentences get expanded by adding adjectives ("My big ball"), changing the verb tense ("Me jumped down"), or using negatives ("No go outside"). Children learn grammar not by being taught the rules, but as they listen to others' speech and put together the regularities they hear.

   Child language, though not identical to that of adults, does draw on language heard to build a language base. Children incorporate and imitate what they hear to refine their own language structures.

5. *Elaboration.* Vocabulary begins to increase at an amazing rate. Sentences get longer, and communication begins to work into social interaction. In the hospital corner of a nursery school, this conversation takes place:

   Chip: I'm a nurse.

   Brooke: I'm going to try to get some patients for you.

   Megan: Do I need an operation?

   Chip: Yeah, if you don't want to be sick anymore.

6. *Graphic Representation.* By 5 or 6 years of age, reading and writing emerge as children become aware of language as an entity itself and of the written word as a way of documenting what is spoken. Awareness of print and emerging literacy are the outgrowth of this last stage of development. These areas are developed in the elementary school years, yet teachers can begin this process with preschool children in an interesting and child-oriented fashion. The *Special Topic* units on "Reading and Writing," and "Children's Literature" address the issue of language and literacy. Additionally, several professional associations that serve as advocates for literacy standards have issued a joint statement of concerns about practices in pre-first grade reading instruction. Prepared by the Early Childhood and Literacy Development Committee of the International Reading Association, it articulates objectives for a pre-first grade reading program, what children know about language, concerns, and recommendations. Figure 13.12 is a sample of a child's developing language skills.

LANGUAGE SKILLS IN EARLY CHILDHOOD

Teachers translate language development theory into practice as they work with children. Language skills in the early childhood setting include articulation, receptive language, expressive language, graphic language, and enjoyment. Children's conversations, their ways of talking, some children's lack of expres-

Stage	Age (approx.)	Sample
1. Response	0–6 months	Smiles, gazes when hearing voices
2. Vocalization	6–10 months	Babbles all types of sounds, creating babble-sentences Uses vocal signals other than crying to get help
3. Word Development	10–18 months	Mama, Dada, Doggie Bye-bye, No-no
4. Sentences	18 months–3 years	Me want chok-quit (I want chocolate) She goed in the gark (She went in the dark)
5. Elaboration	3–5 or 6 years	You're my best Mommy, you can hold my Turtle at bet-bis (breakfast) (Cough) That was just a sneeze in my mouth.
6. Graphic Representation	5+–8 years	

Figure 13.12 ● Children's language skills develop with both age and experience.

sive language, and their ways of asking questions all offer glimpses into children's language skills (Wolf et al., 1996).

Articulation

Articulation is how children actually say the sounds and words. Children's ability to produce sound is a critical link in their connecting the sounds to form speech. Mispronunciation is common and normal, especially in children under 5 years of age. The preschool teacher can expect to hear "Thally" for Sally, "wope" for rope, and "buh-sketty" for spaghetti. As children talk, teachers listen for their ability to hear and reproduce sounds in daily conversation. Can they hear and produce sounds that differ widely, such as "sit" and "blocks"? Can they produce sounds that differ in small ways, such as in "man" and "mat"?

Receptive Language

Receptive language is what children acquire when they learn to listen and understand. It is what they hear. With this skill children are able to understand directions, to answer a question, and to follow a sequence of events. They can understand relationships and begin to predict the outcome of their behavior and that of others. They develop some mental pictures as they listen.

Children begin early and can become experts in reacting to words, voice, emphasis, and inflection. How many times does the child understand by the *way* the words are spoken?

"You finally *finished* your lunch." (Hooray for you!)

"You *finally* finished your lunch?" (You slow-poke.)

Children learn to listen for enjoyment, for the way the wind sounds in the trees, the rhythm of a storytelling, or the sound of the car as it brings Mom or Dad home.

Expressive Language

Expressive language in the early years includes words, grammar, and elaboration.

Words

Expressive language is the spoken word. Children's first words are of what is most important to them (Mama, Da-Da). Adults help children extend their knowledge and vocabulary by using the names of objects and words of action (walk, run, jump) and feelings (happy, sad, mad). By describing objects in greater and greater detail, teachers give children new words that increase their skills. Children are then ready to learn that some words have more than one meaning (the word "orange," for example, is both a color and a fruit) and that different words can have the same meaning (such as "ship" and "boat" as similar objects, or *muñeca* and "doll" as the same word in different languages).

Grammar

Basic grammatical structure is learned as children generalize what they hear. They listen to adult speech patterns and use these patterns to organize their own language. It helps to hear simple sentences at a young age, with the words in the correct order. Next, children can grasp past tense as well as present, plural nouns along with the singular. Finally, the use of more complex structures is understood (prepositions, comparatives, various conjugations of verbs).

Elaboration of Language

Elaboration of language takes many, many forms. It is the act of expanding the language. Through description, narration, explanation, and communication, adults elaborate their own speech to encourage children to do the same. For instance, communication for children includes talking to oneself and others. When a teacher verbalizes a process aloud, children see how language helps them work through a problem. ("I am trying to get the plant out of its pot, but when I turn it upside-down, it doesn't fall out by itself. Now I'll use this trowel to loosen the dirt from the sides of the pot, and hope that helps.") Communicating with others involves giving and following directions. ("It's time to make a choice for cleanup time. You find something to do and I'll watch you.") It means asking and answering questions. ("How do you feel when she says she won't play with you? What can you say? What can you do?") Sticking to the subject keeps communication flowing: "I know you want to play kickball, but first let's solve this problem between you and Conor about the wagon." Children are encouraged to communicate verbally with others as they see teachers using speech to get involved in play themselves. ("What a great house you have built. How do you get inside? Do you need any dishes?")

Graphic Language

"Talk written down" is the essence of graphic language. The child now learns that there is a way to record, copy, and send to another person one's thoughts. Learning to put language into a symbolic form is the gist of the reading and writing process. Children learn about print when they are read to regularly, when they see adults reading and writing, and when they are surrounded with a print-rich environment. Because words and letters are simply "lines and dots and scribbles" to young children, the teacher and parent must demonstrate how meaningful graphic language can be. Moreover, the translation of talk into print is a cognitive task (that of symbols, see previous section), so children's intellectual development as well as their language abilities are at play when learning about the printed word. This area is developed further in the *Special Topics* section of this chapter.

Enjoyment

To encourage language is to promote enjoyment in using it. Teachers converse with children, parents, and other adults, modeling for children how useful and fun language can be. Knowing the power and pleasures of language gives children the motivation for the harder work of learning to read and write. Children learn to enjoy language by participating in group discussion and being encouraged to ask questions. Reading and listening to stories and poems every day

Figure 13.13 ● Teachers and children can share intimate moments when they enjoy using language together.

is an essential part of any program. The program should also include children's literature and stories children dictate or write themselves.

Word play and rhyming are fun as well as educational. Group language games are useful, such as asking the question "Did you ever see a bat with a hat? a bun having fun? a bee with . . .?" and letting the children add the rest. Begin a song, for instance, "Do You Know the Muffin Man?", and add the children's names. Whatever contributes to the enjoyment of language supports its growth, from varying voice and tone to fit the situation (in storytelling, dramatic play, and ordinary activity periods) to spontaneous rhyming songs.

THE TEACHER'S ROLE

Considerations

When considering how to work with young children in language development, teachers should keep several things in mind.

Children Must Use Language to Learn It. Adults often spend much of their time with children *talking*— to, at, for, or about them. Yet, to learn language, chil-

dren must be doing the talking. Children need time, a place, and the support for practicing language. Children's conversations with each other are important in learning the basics of how to take turns and keep to one topic and of saying what they mean, getting their ideas and themselves heard and accepted. Time with peers and adults, in both structured (group times) and nonstructured (free play) situations, allows children to practice and refine language skills.

The Most Verbal Children Tend to Monopolize Language Interactions. Research shows that teachers interact verbally with the children who are most skilled verbally. Seek out and support language development in those with fewer skills, generally by drawing them out individually through (1) reading the unspoken (body) language that communicates their ideas, needs, and feelings and (2) helping them express verbally those ideas, needs, and feelings.

Adults Should Know the Individual Child. Consistency in adult–child relationships may be as important for language as for effective development during the early years. If so, teachers must have a meaningful relationship with each child. This includes knowing the parents and how they communicate with their child.

Bilingualism. In early childhood terms, bilingualism is the acquisition of two languages during the first years of life. The bilingual child must learn to comprehend and produce aspects of each language and then develop two systems of communication. Bilingualism in early childhood also occurs under these general conditions:

1. Children can comprehend and produce some aspects of both languages.

2. Through natural exposure, such as in a classroom, children get experience in both languages.

3. The two languages are developed at the same time (Garcia, 1986).

With more bilingual/bicultural children in early childhood classrooms, it helps to understand how children learn a second language and how to apply this research in practical ways. Hedy Chang's Focus Box describes the benefits of supporting bilingualism, and the chapter bibliography offers several current resources. Research (Diaz-Soto, 1991) shows that the process of learning a second language in childhood

Bilingualism: An Untapped Resource

Hedy Nai-Lin Chang

Although English is the dominant language of the United States, this nation is home to many families and communities whose members also speak other languages. Nationwide, at least one of every 25 children comes from a home where a language other than English is spoken. Unfortunately, this country has often not taken advantage of the tremendous resource offered by our language diversity, which is an invaluable asset for creating opportunities for children to become bilingual.

Being bilingual offers many benefits. It offers children and adults greater appreciation and insight into people of other cultural and linguistic backgrounds and can promote greater mental flexibility. Bilingualism is certainly an invaluable job skill.

Achieving bilingualism, however, can require different strategies. In English-speaking families, promoting bilingualism involves finding opportunities for children to interact with speakers of other languages. Languages are best learned naturally through meaningful relationships with other people.

For children whose families speak a language other than English, bilingualism can be supported by nurturing the continued development of their home language while creating conditions for them to acquire English as well. Unfortunately, children who speak a language other than English are at a tremendous risk for losing their home language. Children are surrounded by English whether they hear it at school or while watching television. Children quickly internalize the fact that people who cannot express themselves easily in English are often treated with disdain. Many eventually refuse to speak their home language out of embarrassment or shame.

What happens in early care and education settings can play an important role in promoting bilingualism. Children notice whether different languages are spoken or affirmed by their caretakers and through classroom activities. Children are more likely to feel proud of their home language as well as gain an interest in learning the languages of others if all those languages are used and valued in the care setting.

Hedy Nai-Lin Chang is Co-Director of California Tomorrow, a nonprofit organization working to help build a strong and fair multiracial, multicultural, multilingual society that is equitable for everyone.

depends, in part, on the individual child. Cognitive, social, and linguistic skills are all at work in acquiring a second language. Moreover, the child's culture, unique temperament, and learning style play a part as well. For instance, Tjarko is of Swiss-German ancestry, so is it any wonder he pronounces an English "v" like an "f," as in "Can I *haff* one of those?" Sachiko, who has moved from Japan within the year, complains, "My *neck* hurts when I drink," and disagrees that it is a sore throat, since "neck" is the word she knows.

Adults often mistakenly assume that young children learn a new language quickly and easily and that the younger the child, the more quickly a second language is acquired. Some studies (Diaz-Soto, 1991) indicate the contrary: several reports favor adults in rate of language acquisition, and there appears to be no critical period for second language learning.

Putting aside those misconceptions, teachers need guidance in educating language-minority children, both in helping the child and family become part of the educational process and in supporting children's culture and language while aiding in the process of English language acquisition. Alvarado Kuster (see Chapter 5) suggests trying to become fluent in the child's first language and focusing on the family's child-rearing practices, as well as learning about your own culture and personal biases. The following recommendations serve as guidelines for teachers of children who speak other languages:

1. *Accept individual differences* with regard to both the style and the time frame of language learning. Don't insist that a child speak, but do invite and try to include the child in classroom activities. Assume developmental equivalence: that is, that the children, although different, are normal. For example, Maria Elena just will not come and sit at group time. Allow her to watch from a distance and believe that she is learning, rather than be worried or irritated that she isn't with the group yet.

2. *Support children's attempts* to communicate. The learning process of a second language is not unlike that of the first; that is, encouraging children's communication bids rather than correcting them will help children try to learn. Teachers recognize developmentally equivalent patterns. For instance, Kidah may not *say* the word "car" but can *show* it to you when you ask. There are a number of equally good ways to show development, as well as to teach skills.

3. *Maintain an additive philosophy* by recognizing that children are acquiring more and new language skills, not simply replacing their primary linguistic skills. Asking Giau and his family about their words, foods, and customs allows teachers to use a style and content that are familiar to the Vietnamese, thus smoothing the transition and adding onto an already rich base of knowledge.

4. *Provide a stimulating, active, and diverse environment* with many opportunities for language in meaningful social interactions and responsive experiences with all children. Learning in a self-help environment with an anti-bias curriculum gives children a developmentally and linguistically appropriate education. For example, learning the origin and meaning of each person's name (*Mweli* is Swahili for "moon," and *Anna* in Hebrew means "graceful one") highlights each person's uniqueness and binds the children together as people with names.

5. *Use informal observations* to guide the planning of activities and the spontaneous interactions for speakers of other languages. A day in the life of a center or children's group has a tremendous number of teachable moments. For instance, seeing a group of girls building a zoo with blocks, a teacher gives a basket of wild animals to Midori. Walking with her to the block corner, she offers to stock the zoo and then helps all the girls make animal signs in Japanese and English. Thus does Midori enter the play in a positive and strong way.

6. *Find out about the family*, and establish ties between home and school. "School learning is most likely to occur when family values reinforce school expectations" (Bowman, 1989). Parents and teachers do not have to do the same things, but they must have a mutual understanding and respect for each other and goals for children. For example, Honwyma's parents and his teacher talk together about what of the Hopi language and culture can be brought into the classroom. Where there are differences between the Hopi patterns and those of the school, teachers deal with them directly and in an interested manner.

7. *Provide an accepting classroom climate* that values culturally and linguistically diverse young children. Teachers must come to grips with their own cultural ethnocentricity and learn about the languages, dialects, and cultures beyond their own. It is critical

to value all ways of achieving developmental milestones, not just those of the teacher's culture or educational experience.

The challenge to young children and their teachers is enormous. With informed, open-minded teaching, children can learn a second language without undue stress and alienation. As of this date we can conclude that:

● Children can and do learn two languages at an early age, though the process and time vary with the individual child.

● Two languages can be learned at the same time in a parallel manner. The depth of knowledge of one language may be different from that of the other, or the two may develop equally.

● The acquisition of languages may mean a "mixing" of the two, as heard in children's speech when they use words or a sentence structure of both languages.

● Learning two languages does not hurt the acquisition of either language in the long run.

Teachers must understand the increased workload bilingualism creates, and they must keep in mind that learning another language affects cognitive and social development.

Dialect Differences. Teachers may encounter differences in the way words are pronounced or grammar is used, even among English-speaking children. These differences reflect a **dialect**, or variation of speech patterns within a language. When we travel to New York, for example, our ear is attuned to the unique pronunciation of "goyl" (girl), and when we move north we hear "habah" (harbor). Southern speakers are easy to identify with elongated vowel sounds such as "Haiiiii, yaaw'll!" In addition to regional dialects, there are also social dialects that are shared by people of the same cultural group or social class. Inner city children may express their enthusiasm for reading with a statement such as "I been done knowed how to read!"

Italian, Russian, and numerous other languages have regional and social dialects. Linguists, the scholars who study languages, argue that there is no such thing as a good or a bad language. Each language and dialect is a legitimate system of speech rules that governs communication in that language. Some dialects, however, are not viewed favorably within the larger society and often carry a social or economic stigma. In the United States the dialect that has received the most attention and controversy is **Ebonics**, or black English.

The unique linguistic characteristics of African American children have been studied for decades (Thomas, 1983). The name "Ebonics" is made up of the words ebony and phonics. "It has a West African base with English vocabulary superimposed on top," says Hoover (1997). "It's based on the grammar of West African languages." Elementary schools have traditionally grappled with the dual missions of doing everything within their power to help all students succeed and, at the same time, respect the cultural and linguistic backgrounds of everyone. One way to respond to this is to improve the instructional strategies for those whose linguistic background is not standard English. Such programs for African American students were developed individually in largely urban schools (Ross & Steele, 1997).

The debate over the significance of Ebonics was thrust into the public spotlight in 1997 when the Oakland, California, school district voted to view Ebonics as a separate language and adopt it to help improve student learning. Critics cite educators who claim the dialect will interfere with reading achievement, whereas supporters insist that the real barrier to academic success is teachers' low expectations of dialect speakers (Cecil, 1988; Goodman & Buck, 1997). As of this printing, the National Head Start Association (see Appendix D) has spoken out against Ebonics, emphasizing that all children must be taught to use language in ways to increase their power, not to segregate.

Often cited in the argument is the concern for how nonstandard speakers will fare in our future high-tech society. Negative views of black English or any nonstandard dialect held by prospective employers have been documented (Atkins, 1993) and are of concern to parents who want better opportunities for their children. Certainly there is much in our early childhood education history and in our current work on developmentally appropriate practices that points in the direction of respecting and welcoming children's individual dialects while also addressing any linguistic differences that limit children. As the controversies over the role of dialect in education wax and wane, the early childhood educator would be prudent to develop the goal of "communicative competence" (Cazden, 1996) or "language power" (Saxton, 1998) for all students. This goal would strive to empower each child to be a comfortable and capable speaker in any situation demanding "standard" English or the language of his own "speech community."[1]

Speech and Language Disorders. Early childhood professionals should have knowledge of speech and language disorders. Disorders of both receptive and expressive language can be detected early. The perceptive teacher does a great service to children and parents by discovering potential problems. Additionally, the preschool years are an ideal time not only to learn a second spoken language but also to introduce children to sign language (Reynolds, 1995). Children love and learn well with multisensory learning experiences, and sign language can enhance language development by using all modalities (Good et al., 1994). Teachers also need to be well-versed in any language or speech disorders of children in their care; for instance, although all children experience disfluencies (disruptions in the flow of speech), prolonged stuttering challenges the teacher to work with the child (and the group) in special ways (Swan, 1993). Special needs are normal and common, and Chapter 3 elaborates how these are dealt with in early childhood settings.

The Language of the Teacher. What teachers say—and how they say it—is important. Moreover, it is often what they do *not* say that communicates the most to children in their struggle to gain mastery of the language. For instance, when a child is tumbling over a word or phrase, teachers must give the child the time to work through the difficulty, rather than correcting or "helping" by finishing the sentence themselves. Teachers provide a rich environment and a high quality of interaction with the child that encourages articulation, receptive language, expressive language, and graphic language (the written word).

To *articulate* means to speak distinctly and with moderate speed. Teachers reinforce clear speech by giving frequent opportunities for children to practice speech.

Receptive language can be developed by using several strategies.

1. Give clear directions: "Please go and sit on the rug next to the chairs," instead of "Go sit over there."

2. Let children ask questions, and give them acceptable answers. For example, repeat a phrase from the child's last sentence that asks the child to try again: "You want *what*?" or "You ate *what*?" Or cast the question back to a child by changing the phrase "Where did you put it?" into "You put it *where*?"

3. Give instructions in a sequence: "Put your lunch on your desk, then wash your hands. Then you are ready to go to lunch." It often helps to ask the children what they think they are to do: "How do you get ready for lunch? What comes first? Next?"

4. Try to understand what the child means, regardless of the actual language. Look for the purpose and intent beyond what the child may have said. This is particularly important with toddlers, non-English speakers, and newcomers.

5. Ask children to state their thoughts out loud. "Tell me what you think is going to happen to the eggs in the incubator. Why do you think some might hatch and some might not?"

6. Use literature, poetry, and your own descriptions to give children an idea of how words can be used to paint verbal and mental pictures. Ask questions about children's own images and dreams. To older children read aloud from books without pictures.

Expressive language is encouraged when teachers focus on the spoken word. They use short, concise sentences to frame or highlight a word. If a child says, "Look at that!", teachers reply, "That's a butterfly," or "I see; do you think it's a butterfly or a bee?"

One way children gain a greater awareness of themselves is by describing their own actions in words. To make sure that all children experience the art of conversation, be sure to provide plenty of opportunities for them to converse with adults as well as peers to help them learn the reciprocal nature of communication. Ask them to say what they are doing. Make a statement describing the child's behavior or actions. This is particularly helpful when dealing with feelings, such as the statement "It looks as if you are feeling angry" (when confronted with a frown and clenched fists).

OUR DIVERSE WORLD OUR DIVERSE WORLD OUR DIVERSE WORLD OUR DIVERSE WORLD OUR DIVERSE WORLD OUR DIVERSE WORLD OUR DIVERSE WORLD OUR DIVERSE WORLD

[1] By helping children learn communicative competence while still keeping their own community speech patterns, teachers can educate more children effectively. Special thanks to Dr. Ruth Saxton for her contributions to this issue.

Curriculum Planning for Language Development: The Teacher Talks

Description

● Use nouns for people, places, events: "We are going to visit Grandma now. That means we need to get dressed and walk to her apartment."

● Use modifiers: "That is your uncle's truck outside" or "Can you find your sister's teddy bear?"

● Use relational terms: "You are taller than the chair, the wagon is wider than the bed."

● Try more differentiated words to express differences: Instead of just "big/little," try "fat/thin" and "tall/short."

Narration

● Describe simple relationships of time: "Yesterday you stayed at home. Today is a school day. Tomorrow is Saturday, a stay-home day."

● Clarify a sequence of events: "When you come to school, first you put your things in your cubby, then you make an inside choice."

● Use words to describe repetition, continuation, and completion: "We are going to the store again, to buy food for dinner" or "I see that you and Juana are still playing together today" or "You finished building the box last time; now you are ready to paint it."

Explanation

● Point out similarities and differences: "Both Cathi and I have brown hair, but what is different about us? Yes, she has on shorts and I am wearing overalls."

● Try classifying what you see as well as asking children to do so: "I notice that all these shells have ridges on the outside; what do you see that is different about them?"

Figure 13.14 ● Several aspects of language development affect how teachers speak to children in the early years.

Teachers help children by directing their attention to objects, events, and relationships.

Michelle: I have something to show you.

Teacher: Can you give us some clues?

Michelle: It's not a record and it's not a book, and you can't play with it.

Teacher: Can you hold it in your hand?

Michelle: No, silly, it's a kiss!

Give children opportunities to describe what they are going to do and what they have done. Through this, teachers discover what is meaningful to children and what they remember, and it gives them the chance to plan and review. When the class celebrates a birthday, children will want to discuss when their birthday is, what they will do, or how they feel. The answers may range from "July thirty-last" to "We're going to the moon" to "On my birthday my heart is filling me with lightening." Figures 13.14 and 13.15 demonstrate the adept teacher at work on language development.

Developing communication skills with others is particularly important for children in the early years. Encouraging active listening and repeating one child's words to another ("Bahrain, did you hear what Joanna said about the sandtruck?") give children support. Expressing thoughts and feelings in words offers a

The Question: A Teaching Strategy

A 2½-year-old looking at a picture of families

T: What do you see in this picture?

C: A mommy and a daddy and a baby!

T: Good for you—you see a family. Look again.

C: A baby just like me . . . more babies!

T: There is more than one child. How many children are there?

C: One-two-three . . . is that a children (pointing to a teenager)?

T: Yes, that is a child, but older—we call them teenagers.

C: I like the boy the best.

T: You like the boy—and he is just about your age, huh?

A teacher at grouptime with 3–5 year olds

T: Who has on short-sleeved shirts today?

Children (some): I do! I do!

T: Some children say they do—can you all find them and ask them to stand up?

Children (all): Johan, get up. Françoise, you, too. Here's Patrick!

T: Now all the short-sleevers are standing. What do you notice about them?

Children (various ones): They are all different colors; two are plain, one has pictures; they all have buttons, they are different sizes.

T: Good for you, you've noticed a lot. I have written all your ideas here. If Patrick's is the smallest, whose comes next?

A 6½-year-old looking at a picture of a field of flowers

T: What do you see in the photograph?

C: Flowers . . . a buncha flowers.

T: Good observation. About how many flowers would you say there are?

C: I dunno. About a hundred.

T: Do you think there are only a hundred? Look again.

C: Maybe, probably there's more.

T: Well, how many do you think?

C: About a thousand.

T: A thousand is a lot more than a hundred. That's more accurate, since there is such a difference between a hundred and a thousand.

Figure 13.15 ● Questions are the building blocks of teaching. The adept teacher asks questions that stimulate language, thinking, and interacting between a child and teacher and among children.

model. By telling a child what works for you ("I like it when you listen to my words"), a teacher provides a good example of how to communicate. Helping children stick to the subject shows that there is a topic at hand: "Stevie, now we're talking about our field trip to the track. You can tell us about your new dog next."

Graphic language can be developed in hundreds of ways. What is now called "emergent literacy" is a broad view of reading and writing as developing, or emerging, out of language development as a whole. Rather than a simple set of skills, early literacy involves a set of attitudes and behaviors related to written language. Teachers use their own language as a way to direct children in a variety of symbol-using activities, such as making grocery lists for a dramatic play corner or the zoo signs in the previous example of bilingual education. The *Special Topics* that follow this unit elaborate on graphic language.

Curriculum Planning for Language Development

Teachers who plan curriculum for language skills, just as for cognitive development, focus on the class setting, specific skills, and themes. They organize the environment and activities to help children acquire linguistic skills of their own.

In the Environment

Indoors. Teachers arrange space so that children will practice speaking and listening and, in programs for older children, reading and writing. Indoor areas can be arranged to enhance language development as follows:

Art

- Offer templates for tracing letters.
- Have signs and pictures that show where things are kept.
- Ask children to describe the materials they use.

Blocks

- Ask children to give each other directions for where blocks go and what they are used for.
- Label block shelves with shapes and words.
- Sketch children's structures and then write their word descriptions.

Cooking

- Label utensils.
- Describe actions (pour, measure, stir).
- Use recipe cards with both pictures and words.

Discovery/Science

- Label all materials
- Ask questions about what is displayed.
- Encourage children's displays, with their dictated words nearby.
- Graph growth and changes of plants, animals, children, and experiments.

Language

- Label the bookshelf, record player, other equipment.
- Help children make their own books that involve description (My family is . . .), narration (It is winter when . . .), and recall (Yesterday I . . .).
- Have children "write" notes, lists, or letters to one another, the teachers, and their families.
- Develop a writing center with a typewriter, office supplies, and so on.

Manipulatives

- Recognize this area as a place for self-communication, as children talk and sing to themselves while they work.
- Explain similarities and differences of materials and structures.

There are other ways to develop language along with cognitive and socioemotional skills. One is to build a "Talkalot Kit" (Jones, 1988). These collections of materials with something in common stimulate conversation as well as classification and dramatic play. Kits could be made of buttons, gloves, shoes, brushes, face coverings, containers: use your imagination!

Another idea for programs of older children is a "Writer's Briefcase" (Wrobleski, 1990). This is a take-home briefcase filled with stationery items such as paper, blank books, pens or crayons, envelopes, paper clips and brads, scissors and stapler, even stickers. Attached is a note to parents explaining the reading-writing connections and a little about emergent literacy and scribbling/invented spelling. Children check it out overnight, and their creation can be shared at school. An alternative to this is "A Friend's Sleepover": a favorite toy, such as Curious George, takes turns going home in a bag with a journal. Parents are encouraged to take down their children's dictation of their adventures with George, to be read in school.

Outdoors. Outdoors, motor skills can be described and pointed out by teachers and children, as both use words of action and of feeling. For example, what actions does it take to get a wagon up the hill? How does a child's face feel when swinging up high? How do people sit? move? carry things?

Theme: Babies

Art: Limit the art materials to just what toddlers and infants can use.

Cooking: Make baby food.

Discovery/science: Display baby materials, then bring in baby animals.

Dramatic play area: "The Baby Corner" with dolls, cribs, diapers.

Manipulatives: Bring in several infant and toddler toys.

Gross-motor/games: Make a "crawling route," an obstacle course that requires crawling *only*.

Field trip/guest: A parent brings a baby to school to dress, bathe, or feed.

Large group time: Sing lullabies ("Rock-a-Bye-Baby").

Small/large group: Children discuss "What can babies do?"

   Joshua: Babies sleep in cribs. They wear diapers. Babies can't talk.

   Becky: They sometimes suck their thumbs. Babies cry when they are hungry.

   Dennis: Babies go pee in their diapers.

   Stevie: Babies sit in highchairs. Babies eat baby food that looks like squished bananas.

   Corey: Babies sleep in a basinette. Then they crawl and bite your finger.

Figure 13.16 ● Teachers plan a unit to promote the skills they are focusing on in the class. A "babies" theme brings out the expert in all children and encourages language.

Routines, Transitions, and Groups

Transitions and routines are more manageable if the children understand what is happening and exactly what they are to do. Teacher language helps talk children through the process so that they can internalize what they are asked to do. A teacher can write a note to "Please save" for the child who does not have time to finish a project, or they can write children's dictated notes to parents.

Group times, with fingerplays, songs, and stories, are language-intensive activities. Children's articulation skills are strengthened, as is receptive language through listening to others. Group times are also opportunities for children to express themselves. When children discuss daily news and important events, brainstorm ideas about a subject, or report on what they did earlier in the day, they gain experience in listening and speaking. Children can also dramatize familiar stories and fingerplays.

Using visual aids or name cards gives children experience in graphic language. These might include having felt letters for the song "B-I-N-G-O," numbers for the fingerplay "One, Two, Buckle My Shoe," or name cards for the activity "I'm Thinking of Someone. . . ." And children enjoy the cadence and rhythm of language spoken or chanted.

Focus on Skills

Language development involves five different skills. Teachers can plan a curriculum focusing on a single skill, be it articulation, receptive, expressive, or graphic language, or the enjoyment of language. After choosing one of the skills, they look at the environment to see how that skill can be developed.

To emphasize expressive language, teachers allow children to express themselves by practicing words and grammatical structure and by elaborating on their own expressions. A teacher asks 3-year-old Ceva to describe what she is doing with the art materials. "I'm dripping my paint," she replies. Outdoors, 2-year-old Hadar describes her actions: "Teacher, look at me! I'm taller than you!" The teacher responds "You climbed up the ladder to the top of the tunnel. Now, when you stand up, your head is above mine." At group time, the kindergarten class makes a group story about "The Mystery of Space." Then they separate into small groups with second-grade helpers to write their own books in story form, complete with illustrations.

To help children talk and learn, teachers find ways of talking that is respectful of children. Listening carefully promotes expression; writing a child's words or story encourages interest; laughing along with a joke stimulates enjoyment. At the same time, when adults speak to children they are also transmitting values and attitudes. A focus on the skills of language development sends the message that language and communication are important tools of human endeavor.

Use of Themes

How could using themes for curriculum planning be used to develop language skills? One unit with universal appeal is "Babies," charted in Figure 13.16. Other units that elicit an extensive use of language are:

● *Harvest.* Activity area: Ask preschool and kindergarten children to bring food from home for a "feast corner." Make a display of food from a harvest feast in the past or change the housekeeping corner into a "feast for all" area.

Group time: Begin a group story using the sentence "I am thankful for . . ."

Special project: Plan a feast, with the children creating the menu and preparing both the food and the table for their families at the school.

● *Summertime.* Activity area: Toddler and preschool children bring a piece of summer clothing for a display and "try-on" corner.

Group time: Children respond to the phrase "One summer morning . . ." with stories and pictures.

Special project: A trip to the beach or a treasure hunt for buried shells in the sand area outside.

● *The Earth Is Our Home.* Activity area: Kindergarten and primary children can make a large circle in a shade of blue, sketching the continents. Provide brown, green, and blue paint in pie tins and let children make a hand print on the ocean or land. Next, have the children bring from home the names of the countries of their family's ancestry.[1] Help them locate those areas and attach their names to those parts of the world.

Group time: Sing *The Earth Is Our Home* (Greg & Steve) and *One Light, One Sun* (Raffi). Read *Just a Dream* (Van Allsburg) and *Where the Forest Meets the Sea* (J. Baker).

Special project: Help make a class recycling area or compost heap. Take a field trip to recycle the materials, or visit a garden that uses compost. Young children can learn about endangered species through Burningham's *Hey! Get Off Our Train*; older children can do research on an animal and make its natural habitat in a shoebox.

● *Favorite Foods.* Activity area: Make a salad from everyone's favorite vegetable, or follow the storyline of *Stone Soup.*

Group time: Discussion topic: "My favorite fruit is . . ." (Example: "An apple because it is crunchy and is big enough to share.")

Special project: Make recipe cards to send home. (Example: Chicken—"First you get seven pounds of skin. Then you get flat pieces of roast chicken. Then you put some bones in. Then you get one pound of pickle seeds and put them on the chicken. Then cook it in the oven for about five hours!")

Any theme can be developed, so long as it brings out oral and graphic language experiences.

Although, preschool and school-age children are challenged by specific themes, curriculum development for infants and toddlers does not always need this kind of focus. Rather, these classes look to the developmental level of the group to encourage language growth for the very young. Figure 13.17

[1] Be sensitive to the fact that some families do not have a strong attachment to a national heritage or ancestry beyond the United States.

Curriculum for Language Development of Infants and Toddlers

The Environment
- Is gentle and supportive, with adults who listen and respond to sounds made and who let the children initiate language.
- Is explained simply, such as what the caregiver is doing during clothing or diaper changing.
- Is responsive, as adults respond quickly to crying and redirect what the children can do and express.

The Skills
- Adults expand on the children's own words. Toddler: "The shoe." Adult: "Oh, that's your shoe you are holding."
- Adults model for children the words to say. Adult: "Elenoa, I want the puppet now."
- Children listen in small groups of two or three, on laps or next to adults, and are allowed wide variation in their participation.

The Themes
- Revolve around the children's individual interests.
- Include favorite stories presented in several ways: reading *The Three Bears*, doing a flannelboard story, singing a fingerplay, having bear puppets and stuffed animals.

Figure 13.17 ● Language experiences for infants and toddlers consider the developmental milestones and the individual child's level of self-expression.

describes curriculum ideas for language development in an infant/toddler class.

● UNIT 13-2 Checkpoint

Children develop language in their own ways, following patterns consistent over different cultures and countries. In the early years, language consists of several skills. The teacher's role is one of knowing how language develops and what skills to encourage in a class setting.

Then, teachers plan curriculum for language development. They organize the environment and schedule by focusing on the various areas and activities, a specific skill, or a unit.

Ask yourself

- What does research tell us about child language and its development?

- What are the six stages of language development?

- What are the five language skills in early childhood education?

- What are six teacher considerations in planning for language development?

- How can teachers plan a curriculum that uses language skills?

- What themes promote language skill in the classroom?

● UNIT 13-3 Special Topics in Cognition and Language

READING AND WRITING

As mentioned earlier in the chapter, *graphic language* is the written word. For the young child, what once looked like dots and lines become letters and words. How does the early childhood teacher help children in this process?

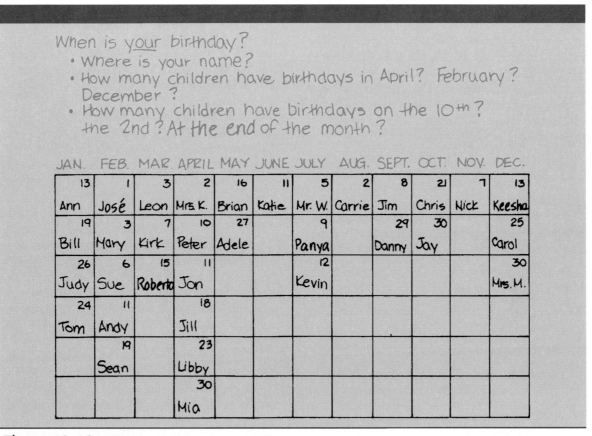

Figure 13.18 ● A language experience chart involves children through the subject matter and the way in which information is displayed.

The ability to read and write does not just happen when children reach a certain age. Their readiness for graphic language must be nurtured. A child's language proficiency will determine readiness for reading. Teachers identify this readiness by knowing how well a child understands the structure and vocabulary of the language. Therefore, a program to encourage beginning reading will offer experiences in oral language. Research shows that successful readers see a relationship between spoken language and the written word. They are aware that sounds are how language is put together. So teachers plan activities that make connections between what is said and what is written.

There is an important role for teachers of young children in the early stages of reading and writing. Teachers can influence positive attitudes toward reading and writing. Supporting children's interest in learning to read and write is a part of this role. Teachers encourage children to talk and converse with others about what they see and do; this gives them increasing

experience in using and attaching experiences to words. Taking the time to write down what children say and then reading it back gives a sense of importance to children's language and their ability to express themselves. In these ways, teachers can help children get involved with print in natural and unpressured ways.

Children and Reading

The role of the adult is one of engaging children with print in ways that make sense to them. By creating an environment that provides rich opportunities to use the printed word, teachers help motivate children toward reading. Research tells us that children who are successful readers in elementary school are typically those who have a history of successful reading in their early years (Schickedanz, York, Stewart, & White, 1983).

Adults and even children often have a stereotypical concept of reading. They think the ability to read is only the literal translation of signs and symbols on a printed page (called **decoding**). In actuality, learning to read is not merely decoding the symbols. It is attaching experiences and knowledge to those words and understanding the use of the written word in their daily lives. Many parents and teachers believe that reading instruction begins in elementary school, so little is done to expand a child's simplified concept of reading before first or second grade.

Emergent Literacy

In the last several years, early childhood professionals have begun to articulate the processes involved in helping children learn graphic language. Freeman and Hatch (1989) report research findings that indicate:

1. Young children begin the process of literacy development before they enter [elementary] school.

2. Reading and writing develop concurrently and in an interrelated manner.

3. Literacy develops in everyday activities.

4. Children learn about literacy through interaction with their world. Furthermore, literacy development is part of the total communication process that includes listening, speaking, reading, and writing.

We need to change our definition of reading from a *technical skill* (translating print to spoken language) to the conception of a different mode of *language use*. In the years before elementary school, this is known as **emergent literacy**. Children's emergent reading skills follow stages, which overlap (Early Childhood Resources, 1995):

● *Stage One:* Children learn that print is a form of language. They find that books are filled with magic, messages, and mystery (prereading).

● *Stage Two:* Children hear stories, poems, chants, and songs many times. They rehearse by chanting, singing, resaying, and "reading along" as we read to them (prereading).

● *Stage Three:* Children learn to recognize words. They read and know the text, and they use some phonics to discover which words say what (beginning reading).

● *Stage Four:* Children are readers. Now the task is to make them better readers (reading).

Teachers of young children will find the concepts and activities familiar, as it has been common early childhood practice for years. Figure 13.19 illustrates some of these activities.

In the early childhood setting, there is an opportunity to teach a broader concept of reading that goes beyond decoding and permeates children's lives. To do this, teachers should not teach reading as "basal reading" but instead should treat it as part of a child's immediate and ongoing life. This can help create positive attitudes about reading before the decoding process begins.

It is up to adults to provide children with opportunities that will enlarge their concepts of the power of the written word. Teachers and parents can wield a great deal of influence in communicating positive feelings about reading. One way to do this is by providing real and valid prereading experiences (Sawyer & Sawyer, 1993).

Children can learn to recognize, read, and write their names when given interesting ways to do it. A popular technique in many early childhood centers is to use a waiting list for highly desirable activities. By learning to read or print their names, children receive a tangible benefit: they can sign up for the activities they want and check the list to see where their names are. Some computer programs now allow children to manipulate letters for making their names, then print them (see computer section in this chapter). Through these experiential activities in reading and writing, children learn that words are useful and can be fun.

In her book *Teacher*, Sylvia Ashton-Warner describes another technique for introducing printed language to young children. A kindergarten teacher who believed strongly in children's innate creativity and curiosity, Ashton-Warner developed a system of "organic reading" in which the students themselves build a key vocabulary of words they wish to learn to read and write. This method was effective for her classes of native Maori children in New Zealand, for whom the British basal readers held little meaning. Ashton-Warner's personal, culturally relevant teaching works well, because it flows naturally from the child's own life and interests.[1]

 OUR DIVERSE WORLD OUR DIVERSE WORLD OUR DIVERSE WORLD OUR DIVERSE WORLD OUR DIVERSE WORLD OUR DIVERSE WORLD OUR DIVERSE WORLD OUR DIVERSE WORLD

[1] Years later, Ashton-Warner's technique is just as relevant in America.

Reading Readiness Is	Teachers
1. Oral vocabulary	1. Encourage talking, learning new words and phrases, singing, finger-plays, remembering and reflecting verbally.
2. Curiosity about/for reading	2. Provide a separate area for books (and are available to read to children), language games (lotto), dictation from children ("If I could fly I would . . ."), notes about children that the children deliver themselves to other adults.
3. Auditory discrimination (the ability to detect sound differences)	3. Create sound discrimination boxes in the science area, a "listen-to-the-sound" walk, guessing games with musical instruments, activities that teach letter sounds by using the children's names.
4. Visual discrimination	4. Support directionality: left and right (in the "Hokey-Pokey" dance and labeled on shoes and mittens), up and down, top and bottom, likenesses and differences.
5. Awareness of print	5. Help the children name and label the classroom (door, tables, book corner), with bilingual signs as appropriate. Bring children's native language into print by asking parents for the names of common objects, numbers, and so on for use around the classroom and in song and fingerplay charts. Encourage children to help print their own names on creative works. Write group newsletters to send home. Make flannelboard letters for free play and for use in songs, such as "Bingo."

Figure 13.19 ● Children gain reading readiness skills through activities for oral vocabulary, curiosity about reading, and auditory and visual discrimination.

The child's readiness to read is related to the development of certain skills (see Figure 13.19). Readiness skills can be acquired through planned experiences in the school program that:

● Promote meaningful interaction with words.

Example: Writing children's names on their drawings; labeling cubbies with children's names and pictures.

● Are age-level appropriate.

Example: For 2½-year-olds, play lotto games using pictures of familiar objects; for 4-year-olds, use animal pictures; for 6-year-olds, use alphabet letters.

● Are fun and enjoyable for children.

Example: Creating a class newspaper to take home.

● Take a gradual approach through the use of non-reading materials.

Example: Label toy storage boxes with pictures. Later in the year, add the words alongside the pictures.

● Acknowledge the child's ability to read the environment, to read events, to read other people.

Example: Clark, looking out the window at the darkening sky, says, "Looks like it's gonna rain." Margo "reads" her painting as she describes the vivid monster to the teacher.

● Involve the use of children's senses.

Example: Display baskets of vegetables and foods along with the book *Stone Soup*.

The school will have many activities in the area of "reading readiness." An early childhood program promotes an awareness of the graphic aspects of language by:

1. Developing children's speaking and listening proficiencies through the use of conversation, descriptive language, oral feedback, and meaningful listening comprehension activities.

2. Helping children hear phonemes (language sounds) through oral language activities such as rhyming, initial consonant substitution, and the use of alliterations in jingles and language play.

3. Providing many opportunities for children to make the connection between spoken and written language.

4. Emphasizing children's own language in beginning reading activities.

5. Filling the environment with printed words and phrases, so children become familiar with meaningful print.

6. Highlighting the language used in beginning reading instructions; for example, use the terms "letter," "sound," "word," and "sentence."

Whole Language

The concept of "whole language" has many familiar and exciting elements from the early childhood tradition. An approach that has become popular since the early 1980s, whole language (Cruikshank, 1993)

is different in both theory and practice from the traditional basal approach. Because it is child-centered rather than teacher-dominated, curriculum activities arise from children's current interests, needs, and developmental levels. Making connections is emphasized, and it is through meaningful integrative themes that students acquire knowledge and skills. Children are also encouraged to share ideas and work with others, as socialization is valued. Evaluation focuses on the child's growth over time, and both pupil portfolios and anecdotal reporting are common assessment tools.

Goodman (1986) sets out key principles of the whole language approach, which will be of interest to all teachers and a special focus for those students who teach kindergarten and primary school. Generally, whole language is a way of viewing language, learning, and people (children, teachers, parents) in a *holistic, integrated* way. All the language arts are related to each other. For instance, a teacher might read a story to

the children, then ask them to make up their own endings. The class would be *listening* (to the story), *speaking* (telling their ideas), *writing* (trying their hand at spelling and handwriting), and *reading* (their creations to a friend or the class at the end of the lesson).

This integrated lesson also illustrates another principle, that of *meaningful* content. Children use language in a purposeful way, developing naturally through a need to communicate. The young child who is read stories and engaged in conversations from infancy is then led smoothly to reading and writing as another extension of language use. Because children can use language before they learn the correct form, whole language encourages this extension of *function into form*; that is, children's own mastery of oral language and unique interests are drawn on in teaching the "rules" of sounds, letters, and words. Figure 13.20 charts some sample "whole language" activities.

One note: Critics of whole language argue that this approach leaves out teaching the decoding skills, which the traditional phonics approach emphasizes. Current knowledge concludes that to learn, children need both specific phonics instruction and a rich background in literature (such as being read stories). Current thinking leans toward an active role of early phonics instruction in the teaching of reading (Manzo, 1997) while at the same time stressing the importance of balance (Diegmueller, 1996). Learning graphic language is a creative process that involves both an "art" (literature, rhyming songs, invented spelling) and a "science" (the nuts and bolts of decoding). It is the teacher's job to be the master craftsperson in helping children put the two together.

Children and Writing

Children learn about words in print much the same as they learn about reading and other aspects of language: that is, by seeing it used and having plenty of opportunities to use it themselves. Writing can be as natural for children as walking and talking. Children begin to write when they first take a pencil in hand and start to scribble. Later, they can write a story by drawing pictures or by dictating the words and having someone else write them down.

The early childhood classroom heightens an interest in writing through a writing center. It can be part of a language area or a self-help art center. Wherever it is located, this center will include a variety

Whole Language in the Classroom

● Have a cozy library corner, giving children lots of time to explore and read all kinds of books.

● Make a writing corner with different kinds of supplies, using this area to develop grouptime activities (children's stories), meaningful themes (post office), and connected learning (writing and sending letters).

● Take field trips, pointing out print as they find it (street signs, store shelves, bumper stickers) and writing about it afterward.

● Use large charts for poems, fingerplays, and songs as well as for listing choices available and for group dictation.

● Plan activities that incorporate print: read recipes for cooking projects, make menus for lunch and snack, follow directions in using a new manipulative toy, write sales tickets for dramatic play units, bring books into science displays.

● Use written notes regularly, sending a regular newspaper home that the children have written or dictated, writing notes to other team teachers that children deliver, encouraging children to send notes to each other.

Figure 13.20 ● Whole language in the primary classroom means integrating graphic language activities in a natural, meaningful way.

of things to write with, to write on, and "writing helpers." Children write with pencils (fat and thin, with and without erasers), colored pencils, narrow and wide marking pens, and crayons. They enjoy having many kinds of paper products, including computer paper, old calendars, data-punch cards, and colored paper. Children also enjoy simple books, a few blank pages stapled together. Carbon paper, dittos, and lined paper will add variety. "Writing helpers" might be a picture dictionary, a set of alphabet letters, a print set, an alphabet chart, a chalkboard, or a magnetic letter board. All of these serve to help children practice writing skills.

Children's first attempts at writing will likely include drawing or scribbling. Because drawing helps children plan and organize their thoughts (and, thus, their text), teachers encourage children to tell them about their stories and can ask for a child's help in "reading" these writings. As children begin to work with words themselves, adults can help them sound out words or spell words for them. Spelling development is similar to learning to speak: adults support the efforts, not correct the mistakes, and allow children to invent

their own spelling of words. Picture dictionaries and lists of popular words help children use resources for writing. Figure 13.21 is a sample of **invented spelling** in a kindergarten.

Writing materials can be available throughout the room and yard. Paper and pencils come in handy in the dramatic play area. Menus, shopping lists, prescriptions, and money are but a few uses children will find for writing equipment. The block corner may need traffic signs; the computer, a waiting list. Outdoors, pictures can label the location of the vegetables in the garden; markers indicate where children have hidden "treasures" or where the dead bird is buried.

The "language experience" approach involves taking dictation, writing down and reading back to children their own spoken language. It is important to use the child's exact words so they can make the connection between their speech and the letters on the page. This is true for group stories, for children's self-made books, or for descriptions of their own paintings. A useful technique in taking dictation is to say the words while writing them, allowing the child to watch the letters and words being formed. When the content

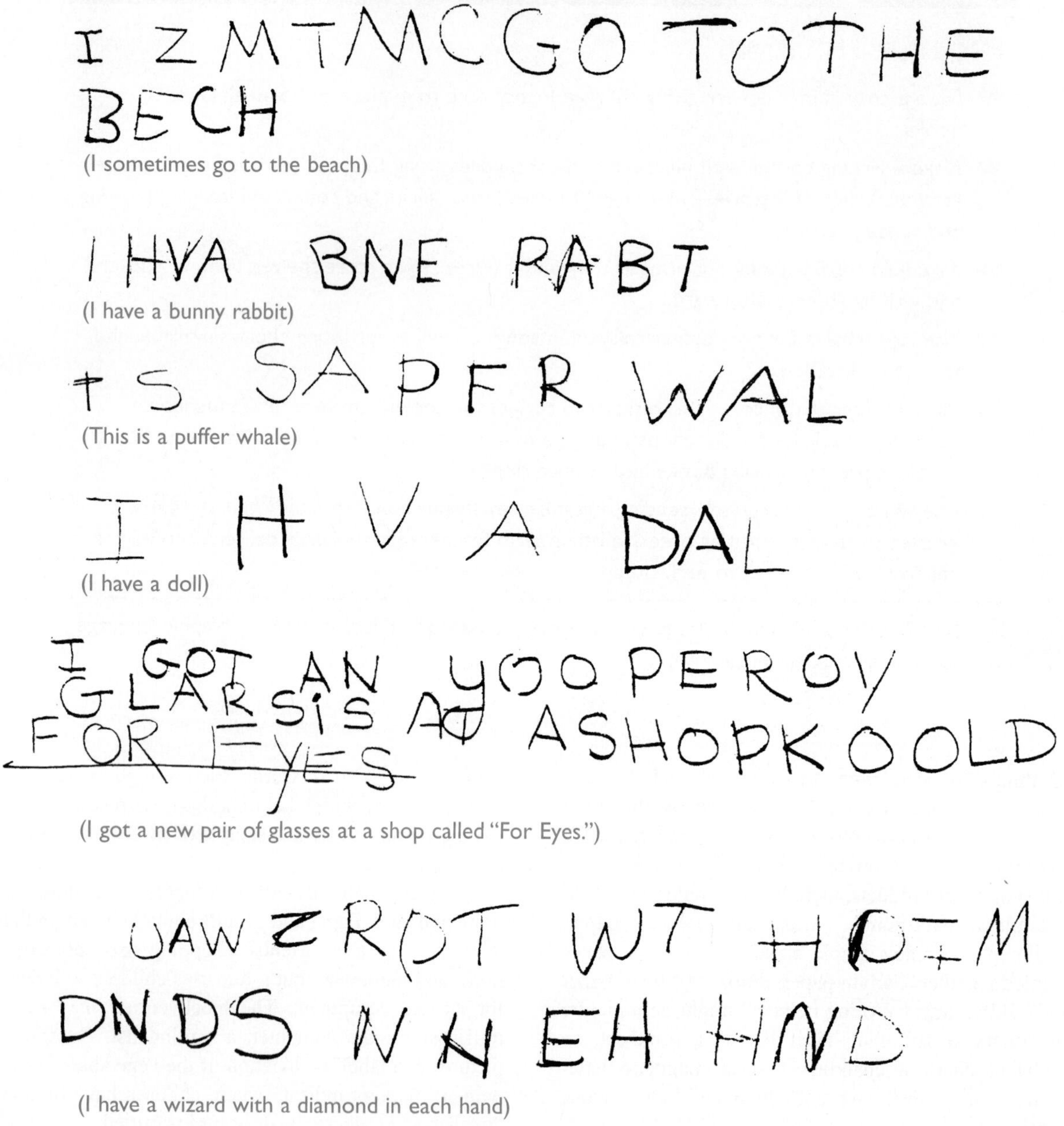

I ZMTMCGO TOTHE
BECH

(I sometimes go to the beach)

I HVA   BNE   RABT

(I have a bunny rabbit)

tS   SAPFR WAL

(This is a puffer whale)

I   H V A   DAL

(I have a doll)

I GOT AN YOOPEROY
G LARSIS AT ASHOPKOOLD
FOR EYES

(I got a new pair of glasses at a shop called "For Eyes.")

UAW ZRPT WT HOM
DNDS NH EH HND

(I have a wizard with a diamond in each hand)

Figure 13.21 ● Early writing usually involves children's attempts at words of their own invention. Invented spelling can be treated with respect for the efforts and as a foundation for successful writing experiences. (Courtesy of Kim Saxe.)

The Language Experience Approach

1. **Start with a leading sentence.**

   If I were a musical instrument . . .

   Michelle: I would be a piano with strings and lots of sparklies on top. And you could play me even if you were blind.

   Janette: I would be a drum. I would be hit and I wouldn't be happy because they would make me hurt.

   Dennis: I would be a violin. Someone would play me with a bow and I would make a beautiful sound.

2. **Take dictation on topics and pictures of their making.**

   "On our Halloween Nights"

   Ehsan: There was a witch and skeleton and ghost in my room on Halloween night.

   Lionel: Costume night. A cow jumping over the moon. The little rabbit sleeping.

   Martine: There was a big pumpkin and a big bat and a bear and a pirate. There was a jack-o-lantern and the light glowed.

   Andrew: There was a smiley monster and Aka-Zam!

   Luke: We went to my church for hot dogs and cider.

3. **Ask for stories of their own.**

   Once upon a time there's a boy named Timothy and he punched all the bad guys dead. And he was very strong and he can punch anything down. And he can do anything he likes to. And he makes all the things at winter. And he was so strong he could break out anything else. And he had to do very hard work all day long and all day night. And he had to sleep but he couldn't. And he had a very small house and cup. And then he did everything he want to all day long. The End. Tim (signed)

4. **Make a group book (including illustrations).**

   All By Myself (our version of the book by Mercer Mayer)

   "I can put on my overalls all by myself." (Stephanie)

   "I can brush my hair all by myself." (Lindsey)

   "I can make pictures all by myself." (Jessica)

   "I can buckle my jeans all by myself." (Megan)

   "I can make a drill truck with the blocks all by myself." (Lionel)

   "I can jump in the pool all by myself." (Andrew)

Figure 13.22 ● The language experience approach takes many creative forms in a classroom. (Special thanks to Gay Spitz for example 1 and to Ann Zondor and Lynne Conly Hoffman and the children of the Children's Center of the Stanford Community for several of the examples in 2 and 4.)

is read back, the child has a sense of completion. Figure 13.22 is an example of these kinds of language experiences in classrooms of 3-, 5- and 6-year-olds.

The early childhood setting encourages an awareness of and interest in writing by having the printed word displayed regularly. Storage units are labeled with pictures and words of what belongs where (scissors, turtle food, blocks). Areas of the room are named, and stories, poems, or familiar fingerplays are hung on charts. Written signs remind children of the rules, such as "Inside Voices Here" in the book corner or "Wear an Apron" near the easels. Primary classes may add calendars and helper charts, visual cues for children to read and prepare for the next event. Story maps help children see the parts and sequencing of the writing process. Depicted as a body, the head serves as the beginning (with facial features called "topic," "characters," and "setting"), the body as the middle, and the legs as the end ("Finally . . .") A primary child can write in the various parts of the story and read it from the map or continue to elaborate with full sentences in a more traditional manner. In these ways, teachers help raise awareness of the use and enjoyment of the printed word.

CHILDREN'S LITERATURE

Children's books bring us back to ourselves, young and new in the world. "Our bones may lengthen and our skin stretch, but we are the same soul in the making. . . . Children's books are such powerful transformers because they speak, in the words of the Quakers, to one's condition, often unrecognized at the time, and remain as maps for the future. . . . In children's books we preserve the wild rose, the song of the robin, the budding leaf. In secret gardens we know the same stab of joy, at whatever age of reading, in the thorny paradise around us (Lundin, 1991).

Literature does indeed have an important place in the curriculum today. It is especially valuable as a vehicle for cognitive and language development. Books help to acquaint children with new words, ideas, facts, and adventures. Planned and spontaneous reading experiences are a vital part of the young child's day.

Reading books to children introduces them to the reading concept, to a different form of communication from spoken language. It is a symbol system with which they will become familiar as they learn that words and pictures have meaning.

Literature and Cognitive Development

Literature can perform several functions in aiding cognitive development. Through the use of good books, teachers can help children broaden their interests and concepts. Books that are primarily used

for transmitting information expand the child's knowledge base. Thoughtful books that draw on children's everyday experiences widen their understanding of themselves and others. Through books, children can learn to see things in an endless variety of ways. Five different books will describe and illustrate the behavior of cats in five different ways. Exposure to *Millions of Cats* (Gag), *Angus and the Cats* (Flack), and *The Cat in the Hat* (Dr. Seuss), as well as to the cats portrayed in *Peter Rabbit* (Potter) or *Frog Went A-Courtin'* (Langstaff), will enlarge the child's concepts of cats. Different cultures are also represented in any number of children's books, teaching a greater awareness of all of humankind.[1]

Teachers have an opportunity to encourage divergent thinking through the use of children's literature. Children gain more than facts from books; they learn all matter of things, providing they can interpret the story rather than just hear the individual words. Quizzing children about whether the dinosaur was a meat- or plant-eater will bring about responses that are predictable and pat, but comprehension does not have to be joyless. Zingy questions will provide not only thought but also interest. "Would a brontosaurus fit in your living room?" will get children to think about *Danny and the Dinosaur* (Hoff) or Kent's *There's No Such Thing as a Dragon* or Most's *If the Dinosaurs Came Back* in a new way. "Is the troll bigger or smaller than your brother?" might be a point of discussion after reading *The Three Billy Goats Gruff*. The point is not to have children feed back straight factual information but to get them involved in the story.

Selection of books obviously plays a part in using literature to stimulate thought and conversation about what was read. The wise teacher will choose books that invite participation. Everyone can "roar a terrible roar, gnash their terrible teeth, and show their terrible claws" during a rendition of *Where the Wild Things Are* (Sendak). Meaning for children lies more in action than in words. Children will be more apt to talk about stories that have in some way touched them and stimulated their involvement.

Questions for thought and children's participation must be related to children's experiences and knowledge yet lead them toward discovery. Books provide a pleasurable avenue for this type of intellectual growth.

OUR DIVERSE WORLD OUR DIVERSE WORLD OUR DIVERSE WORLD OUR DIVERSE WORLD OUR DIVERSE WORLD OUR DIVERSE WORLD OUR DIVERSE WORLD OUR DIVERSE WORLD

[1] Children's literature provides a window and a mirror to OUR DIVERSE WORLD.

Literature and Language Development

A great many language skills are learned when children are exposed to good literature in the classroom. Whether the child is 8 years or 8 months old, book-reading experiences contribute to children's language development (Soundy, 1997). The value lies in the use of language by the author and the use the teacher makes of the language potential.

If language development is the goal, auditory appeal is one of the best reasons for choosing a book. The actual sounds of the words catch children's attention and imagination. Familiar sounds of animals or objects reinforce and provide new ways to express thoughts. "Buzz" and "humm" are playful words that have a great appeal to children. Sensory words, such as cold, soft, and slippery, capture children's attention.

Building and extending vocabulary is another function of literature in the language arts curriculum. Old familiar words take on new meaning as they reflect the content of each different story. Children love new words, especially big ones, and they do not necessarily need them defined. If used correctly in the context of the storyline, the words will be self-explanatory. Many children memorize phrases from favorite books, sometimes unaware of their meaning, but fitting the rhythm and pattern into their play.

When Andrea was struggling to find the words to describe a large amount, Mitra began to recite: "Hundreds of cats, thousands of cats, millions and billions and trillions of cats!" (*Millions of Cats*, Gag)

Riding home in the car after school one day, Parker chanted: "Tik-ki tik-ki tem-bo no sa rembo, chari bari ru-chi, pip peri pembo." (*Tikki Tikki Tembo*, Mosel)

Derek and Shigeo were playing grocery store. To attract customers they called out: "Caps for sale! Fifty cents a cap." (*Caps for Sale*, Slobodkina)

Language—and vocabulary—come alive with such repetition, as children integrate the words into their play. Their using the words demonstrates another benefit of books and literature in language development: that of learning the skill of listening. As Trelease (1982) puts it, "If our first problem is not reading enough to children, our second problem is stopping too soon." Whether 1- or 10-years-old, children need and

thrive on being read aloud to regularly. Teachers could ask for no better activity to promote good listening habits than a wealth of good children's books.

Creating a Rich Literary Environment

The comics of yesterday are far outdistanced by the television and video games of today. How can teachers give children experiences in literature in the face of such competition?

The field of children's literature is rich in its variety, including both great classic stories and those of present-day situations and concerns. Fiction and informational books, children's magazines, and poetry add balance to the literary curriculum. Every classroom should contain representative works from each of these areas.

Provide plenty of time for using books and other materials. Children need time to browse, to flip through a book at their own pace, to let their thoughts wander as they reflect on the storyline. They also enjoy retelling the tale to others. Be sure to plan enough time for children to be read to every day.

Make a space that is quiet and comfortable. In addition to soft pillows or seats, locate the reading area where there is privacy. Crashing blocks and messy fingerpainting will intrude on the book reader. A place to sprawl or cuddle up with a friend is preferable.

Have plenty of books and supporting materials. The language arts center might contain a listening post, with headsets for a record or tape player. Perhaps there is even a place where books can be created, a place supplied with paper and crayons. There may even be a typewriter, puppet stage, or flannel board nearby so that stories can be created in new ways.

Display children's literary creations. The efforts of children's stories and bookmaking should be honored by establishing a place in the room where they can be seen and read. Children then see how adults value the process of literary creation and the final product.

Teachers must model how to care for a book and keep classroom books in good repair. Children can come to realize that a book is like a good friend and should be given the same kind of care and consideration.

Fostering children's reading at home is one of the important contributions a teacher can make to the reading process. Attitudes about reading are communicated to children from the important people in their lives. Because teachers do not have a direct influence on the home environment, their route to the home is through the children. A child who is enthusiastic about books and carries them home is likely to involve parents in the quest for good books and stories. Teachers encourage this enthusiasm in a number of ways. Encourage parents to read good-quality literature by making "book bags," large plastic bags that the children can use to hold a book borrowed from the classroom to read overnight and return the next day. Posting the local library hours, establishing a lending library, and providing parents with lists of favorites will reinforce the child's interest in literature.

Use books around the room. Don't confine them to just the book corner or the book shelf. Demonstrate their adaptability to all curriculum areas by displaying a variety of books in the activity centers. Ask children to help you retell or emphasize parts of a story (see the storytelling section), and ask them questions informally afterward: "How many bowls of porridge were on the kitchen table? Which one did Goldilocks like best? How did you know?" Figure 13.23 shows how books can enhance play and learning throughout the school room.

Extending Literary Experiences

Good literature comes in many forms and can be presented in a variety of ways. A creative teacher uses books and literature to develop other curriculum materials. Translating words from a book into an activity helps a child remember them. Books and stories can be adapted to the flannel board, storytelling, dramatizations, puppets, book games, and audiovisual resources. One particularly useful resource to expand children's book experiences is *Story Stretchers* (Raines & Canady, 1989).

Storytelling

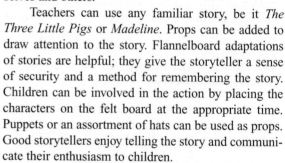

Storytelling is as old as humanity. The first time a human being returned to the cave with an adventure to tell, the story was born. Storytelling is the means by which cultural heritage is passed down from one generation to another.[1] Children's involvement with a story that is being told is almost instantaneous. The storyteller is the medium through which a story comes to life, adding a unique flavor through voice, choice of words, body language, and pacing.

Stories that have a few characters, plenty of repetition, and a clear sequence of events make for easy listening for young children. Fairy tales have all these elements and contain important truths for children. These tales are fascinating, since, in a child's words, "they think about what I think about" (Howarth, 1989). Fairy tales answer basic questions such as "Who Am I? What will happen to me, and how should I act?" Moreover, these stories assure the child of a positive outcome while allowing them to experience some of the hard and scary aspects of life. Critics of fairy tales argue that many are stereotyped; others (Jung and Bettelheim, for instance) assert that the characteristics embodied in fairy tale roles are about the good and bad in us all, and that the teacher who uses fairy tales—particularly from many cultures—will find that children learn the results of kindness and evil in themselves and others.[2]

Teachers can use any familiar story, be it *The Three Little Pigs* or *Madeline*. Props can be added to draw attention to the story. Flannelboard adaptations of stories are helpful; they give the storyteller a sense of security and a method for remembering the story. Children can be involved in the action by placing the characters on the felt board at the appropriate time. Puppets or an assortment of hats can be used as props. Good storytellers enjoy telling the story and communicate their enthusiasm to children.

Dramatizing Stories

Acting out characters from a favorite story has universal appeal. Young preschoolers are introduced to this activity as they act out the motions to fingerplays and songs. "The Eensy-Weensy Spider" and its accompanying motions is the precursor for dramatization. Story reenactment helps children learn to work together so that their *social development* is enhanced, as is the cognitive ability to engage in *collective representation*. As an extension of Steiner's theories, Waldorf kindergartens include fairy and morality tales.

OUR DIVERSE WORLD OUR DIVERSE WORLD OUR DIVERSE WORLD OUR DIVERSE WORLD OUR DIVERSE WORLD OUR DIVERSE WORLD OUR DIVERSE WORLD OUR DIVERSE WORLD OUR DIVERSE WORLD

[1] In many cultures, other than Western European-American culture, there is a high value placed on learning through oral storytelling and rhyming and chanting; a higher value than on learning based on playing with objects.

[2] A single standard of beauty, for example, "fair-haired and fair-skinned," is often depicted in European-based fairy tales.

Living Together: Reflecting Diversity
Knots on a Counting Rope (Martin, Jr. & Archambault)
The Legend of Bluebonnet (de Paola)
The Quilt (Jones)
The River That Gave Gifts (Humphrey)
The Big Orange Splot (Pinkwater)
Mei Li (Handforth)
Gilberto and the Wind (Ets)
Stories for Free Children (Pogrebin)

Creating Art
Black Is Brown Is Tan (Adoff)
Start with a Dot (Roberts)
Little Blue and Little Yellow (Lionni)
My Very First Book of Colors (Carle)

Building Blocks
Changes Changes (Hutchins)
The Big Builders (Dreany)
Who Built the Bridge? (Bate)
Boxes (Craig)

Dramatic Play: On Our Heads!
Martin's Hats (Blos)
Caps for Sale (Slobodkina)
Hats Hats Hats (Morris)

Families
When You Were a Baby (Jonas)
All Kinds of Families (Simon)
Whose Mouse Are You? (Kraus)
Five Minutes Peace (Murphy)

Discovery/Science: Grow, Growing, Growest!
Growing Vegetable Soup (Ehlert)
The Carrot Seed (Krauss)
From Seed to Pear (Migutsch)
Here Are My Hands (Martin, Jr., and Archambault)
Window into an Egg (Flanagan)

Math Lab: 1,2,3, Count with Me!
How Much Is a Million? (Schwartz)
Roll Over! A Counting Song (Peek)
Ten, Nine, Eight (Bang)
Have You Seen My Duckling? (Tafuri)
The Doorbell Rang (Hutchins)

Making Music
Hush Little Baby (Aliki)
Ben's Trumpet (Isadora)
One Wide River to Cross (Emberley)
Over in the Meadow (Wadsworth)
I Know an Old Lady (Bonne)

Having Friends
Friends (Heime)
George and Martha (Marshall)
Best Friends (Cohen)
Frog and Toad Are Friends (Hoban)
I'll Build My Friend a Mountain (Katz)

Books for Under Threes
Goodnight Moon (Brown)
Brown Bear, Brown Bear (Martin, Jr.)
The Baby's Catalogue (Ahlberg)
Truck, Train, Boats, Airplanes (Barton)
How Do I Put It On? (Watanabe)
Spot (Hill)

Books for Early Primary
Charlotte's Web (White)
The Box Car Children (Warner)
Ramona (Cleary)
The Stories Julian Tells (Cameron)
Like Jake and Me (Jukes)

Figure 13.23 ● When literature is a natural part of the environment, children learn to appreciate and use it. (See also Ramirez & Ramirez, 1994.)

"Fairy tales are told to the children on successive days for up to 2 weeks, culminating in the tale as a puppet show offered to the children by the teacher or as a play with costumes acted out by the children with the teacher narrating (Waldorf Staff, 1994). Whether the child is an observer, walk-on, mime, or actor, the learning is real in each step of the continuum.

Stories such as *Caps for Sale* (Slobodkina) and *Swimmy* (Lionni), as well as fairy tales, are popular choices for reenactment by 4- and 5-year-olds. They need plenty of time to rehearse, and simple props help them focus on their role. A red scarf helps Jeannada become *Little Red Riding Hood*; an old pair of sunglasses transforms Joaquin into a character from *Goggles* (Keats).

Older children may choose to write (or dictate) parts or scripts; it is appropriate for 6- to 8-year-olds to have their playmates act out original stories. Once the "right" story has been chosen, the teacher helps the children to retell the story together, set the stage, and let the play begin.

Puppet Shows

Puppet shows can involve a large number of children as participants and audience. Children of all ages enjoy watching and putting on a puppet show. Because puppets are people to young children, they become confidants and special friends. Children will confide in and protect a puppet, engaging in a dialogue with one or more puppets that is often revealing of the child's inner struggles and concerns. Teachers can support their efforts by helping them to take turns, suggesting questions and dialogue to them, and involving the audience. The project of puppet making can be quite elaborate and very engaging for older children.

Book Games

Book games are a good way to extend the literary experience. Buy two copies of an inexpensive book with readable pictures, such as *The Carrot Seed* (Krauss). Tear out the pages, and cover each page with clear plastic. Children must then read the pictures to put the book into proper sequence. A book of rhymes, *Did You Ever See?* (Einsel), lends itself to rhyming games. Children can act out the rhymes from the storyline or match rhyming phrasing from cards the teacher has made.

Audiovisual Resources

Records, cassettes, and filmstrips enlarge the child's experience with books. The auditory and the visual media reinforce one another. Music brings literature alive; besides tapping into the musical aspect of intelligence, it appeals to all children to move and express themselves and thus enjoy literature and books even more. The pictures can show children new aspects of the words; sometimes the music or the voices bring the book to life. Often both happen. Hundreds of children's stories—classics and modern-day—have been translated to these media.

COMPUTERS IN THE CLASSROOM

A computer can be as nonthreatening as a watercolor brush. In the hands of a child it can be a tool for experiencing the world. Early childhood classrooms are arranged so that children learn about the world directly, by piling blocks, molding sand and clay, bouncing a ball. Through these experiences, children gradually form concepts about how the world works and how they can affect it. As children touch the keys of a computer, they are challenged to explore and discover in ways never before possible.

"There are two reasons why every classroom or child care center should have a computer—children love them and they can provide a positive learning experience for even the most hard-to-work-with child" (Buckleitner, 1995).

Discovery-oriented experiences with computers enhance children's learning, especially in stimulating their cognitive thought processes.[1] Children form new knowledge as they interact with computer-based programs to form what is described as "microworlds"

OUR DIVERSE WORLD OUR DIVERSE WORLD OUR DIVERSE WORLD OUR DIVERSE WORLD OUR DIVERSE WORLD OUR DIVERSE WORLD OUR DIVERSE WORLD OUR DIVERSE WORLD

[1] Unlike a teacher or a playmate, computers can wait patiently for a child in a nonjudgmental way; thus computers can provide another avenue for learning and teaching to a diversity of children, even adjusting automatically to a child's abilities.

Figure 13.24 ● Using the computer in a classroom can help individualize a child's educational experience.

(Papert, 1980). Children design and control places and things of their own choosing, such as a house, the seashore, or a face. Then they create events that challenge them to think through consequences of their actions. Moreover, computer programs can be "process highlighters" for children (Haugland & Shade, 1988). That is, the program can speed up or detail hidden processes and cause-and-effect relationships that are more difficult to observe, such as a plant growing, a face changing expression on command, or a dance put together with a special sequence of steps.

Developmentally Appropriate Software

Along with blocks and paints, the computer can become an expressive medium that encourages skills in a variety of ways. It is important that the computer be used in addition to other concrete experiences, not instead of them. For instance, children need to have *real* materials on the art and manipulatives tables, and they can also manipulate *images* of those same kinds of materials at the computer table. Children need to have many experiences with *concrete* items such as paint, crayons, and markers. They are then ready to try their creative hand at computer graphics (see bibliography for books that offer for specific suggestions for computer software for young children).

To use computers appropriately in the classroom, teachers must first be *comfortable* with the computer themselves. A computer area is in a quiet spot of the classroom (such as in or near the library/listening spot), against a wall to minimize damage to the equipment or cords. To introduce the computer, the teacher shows small groups of children the basic care and handling of the computer and disks. The computer can be one of many choices offered during free play, or it can be a more limited choice with a waiting list. Interaction between children can be encouraged by including space for two or more at the computer. Sometimes the teacher will assign turns to a pair or small group of children, particularly if the computer seems to be dominated by a few. As always, the alert teacher watches to ensure that no one becomes "stuck" at the computer or any other area, helping develop children's interests and skills in many activities.

Just a few years ago, computers were seen as a wave of the future. Now computers have become firmly established in early childhood classrooms, particularly in kindergarten and primary grades but also in many preschools. One reason is that the *hardware*, or actual machinery, has become less expensive while being sturdy and workable for busy teachers and young children alike. The most dramatic change, however, has been in the proliferation of *software*, the computer programs themselves.

It is in the area of software that teachers of young children have a multitude of choices. These choices must be carefully made. Not every program intended for children is developmentally appropriate, and teachers must pay thoughtful attention to the program and to what they know about their own group of children. Teachers must know what to look for and how to choose programs that will be useful and appropriate for the specific age of the group. Haugland and Shade (1990) have developed 10 criteria for evaluating computer programs. Not all software will meet all the criteria, but it is important to view the criteria as a continuum for considering computer programs for young children. Computer software should:

1. Be age appropriate.

2. Allow children to control it (children setting the pace and being active participants).

3. Include clear instructions.

4. Have expanding complexity.

5. Support independent exploration.

6. Be "process oriented" (having the software program so engaging that the product of using it is secondary).

7. Include real-world representation.

8. Have high-quality technical features (colorful, uncluttered, and realistic).

9. Provide trial-and-error opportunities.

10. Have visible transformations (being able to affect the software, for example, by transposing objects).

When Child Meets Computer

Specific methods have been devised for teaching young children to work successfully with computers. For instance, a child must be able to maneuver a joystick or mouse, find the keys on the keyboard, and insert a disk into the computer correctly. Because very young children cannot read, they will need help getting started. Teachers must be able to help children learn by setting up their classrooms with a computer positioned in a safe yet accessible place, structuring activities and the daily schedule to give children plenty of time to manipulate the machinery and programs, and

choosing specific hardware and software that work with the class.

Integrating the Computer into Learning

One of the most exciting aspects of computers in the classroom is their ability to support other learning. Teachers who use the computer effectively as an educational tool integrate their program goals to use the computer with individual children. What happens at the keyboard matches each child's individual needs. Davidson (1989) suggests using computers to support a classroom unit on three levels:

1. Specific software can provide unit-related information. For instance, the program "Dinosaurs" can be in place while developing a theme such as the one in Figure 13.9.

2. Tool software—such as graphics or writing programs—can be used for creating unit-related products. For example, a program such as "Explore-a-Story" can help primary-age children write stories about their own interests and responses to whatever unit is being studied. With a younger group, the teacher could help the class make a group story to send home.

3. Computer-related activities can be designed to support the unit theme. One idea is using the program "Name-Jumping," which asks children to jump around a floor-sized keyboard. Both computer concepts and the words of a unit or theme are reinforced using children's full-body involvement.

● UNIT 13-3 Checkpoint

The special topics on cognition and language include reading, writing, and computers. Each offers a unique extension to children's learning in the classroom. Clearly, language and thought are learned both at home and in school and can be connected in meaningful ways.

Children and books belong together. Good literature gives insight into human behavior. Books teach children less important though exciting things such as how to play peek-a-boo or escape a hungry lion. But they also teach matters of substance and character such as how to go to sleep, make a friend, be brave. The early years should lay a foundation in literature upon which children can build throughout their lives.

> Books are no substitute for living, but they can add immeasurably to its richness. When life is absorbing, books can enhance our sense of its significance. When life is difficult, they can give a momentary relief from trouble, afford a new insight into our problems or those of others, or provide the rest and refreshment we need. Books have always been a source of information, comfort, and pleasure for people who know how to use them. This is as true for children as for adults (Arbuthnot & Sutherland, 1972).

The computer is a 20th-century creation, yet it can stimulate the timeless, innate characteristics of curiosity, creativity, and discovery. A major challenge for teachers is to provide a curriculum that will develop these "dispositions," or habits of the mind (Katz, 1985), so that children will be willing as well as able to develop skills. As a teacher, ask yourself:

● How do teachers help children become ready to read?

● What should a writing center in an early education classroom look like?

● How does literature support cognitive development? Language development?

● What literacy software could be used that would entice the reluctant school-aged child?

● What language activities would be appropriate with toddlers?

● What are the guidelines for creating a rich literary environment?

● What are five ways to extend literary experiences?

Summary

People entering early childhood education as a profession are challenged to develop children's minds and language. This chapter began with the premise that intellectual development and language are interrelated. As teachers help children learn how to think, they learn about children's thinking processes by listening to what they say and observing how they respond to others' words, thoughts, and actions.

Much of cognitive development theory has its roots in the work of Jean Piaget. Cognitive development includes the areas of inquiry, knowledge of the physical and social worlds, classification, seriation, numbers, symbols, spatial relationships, and time. Language development, on the other hand, considers how children learn articulation, receptive and expressive language, graphic representation, and enjoyment of language.

Teachers plan curriculum to develop these skills in several ways. Many class settings offer children an opportunity to refine cognitive and language skills. At times, teachers focus on a specific skill, such as reasoning or conversation, and adapt the curriculum to emphasize that area.

The teacher's role also requires an understanding of bilingualism, dialect differences, and a working knowledge of speech and language disorders. Early childhood teachers use their own language abilities to stress and support the language development of their students.

Reading and writing are part of the language and thought processes. Adults in early childhood education seek ways to involve children with the printed word in ways that have here-and-now meaning in the children's lives. Literature and computers further the development of reading and writing skills and provide enjoyable tools for the enhancement of cognition and language.

Review Questions

1. How are cognition and language related?

2. Match the cognitive skill with the appropriate activity:

inquiry	being aware of others
physical world	learning to locate things
social knowledge	pretending to be a puppet
classification	asking questions
seriation	sequencing events
numbers	using nesting blocks
symbols	expressing amounts
spatial relationships	sorting objects
time	manipulating materials

3. How does the teacher's use of language affect how children develop cognitive skills? Give several examples of what discourages such growth; counter that with how what a teacher says encourages skills.

4. How does the teacher help children develop speech and language skills in planning curriculum? How is curriculum planning affected in a class with children whose primary language is not English?

5. The way teachers use language is critical in encouraging children's own language. Name the four areas of language and what a teacher can say to encourage growth in those areas.

6. What are some of the criteria for evaluating computer software for early childhood? What traps are to be avoided?

7. Describe some curriculum activities for cognition and language development. Simplify them for infants/toddlers/twos and elaborate for the primary-aged youngsters.

Learning Activities

1. Look at the program in which you now teach, or recall your own first classrooms. Find at least one example of rote knowledge, social knowledge, and meaningful knowledge.

2. Take one cognitive skill and trace how it could be developed in each curriculum area of the program you used in activity 1.

3. Observe block play at your school. Make a chart, as in Figure 13.6, that describes the learning processes involved.

4. Choose a child in your care whose primary language is not English. How is that child processing language? What are you doing to foster the child's emerging English skills? How is that child's first language being supported in your program? What can you do to involve the family?

5. Make a list of the classroom areas. Beside each, name one activity that would foster cognitive development and one that calls for language skills.

6. One theme often used in early childhood programs is that of the changing season in the fall. How can that theme develop language and thinking skills in preschoolers?

7. Teaching reading readiness involves trying to develop oral language and listening skills. What could a teacher of toddlers plan for each? A kindergarten teacher?

8. Describe three ways children's books and literature help to develop intellectual skills and language proficiency. Through what techniques can literary experiences be extended in the curriculum?

9. Consider the use of a computer in the following classrooms:

    toddler day care program

    preschool half-day program

    kindergarten

    after-school primary program

    Is a computer appropriate in each of them? Why and how? What guidelines, if any, would be needed in each setting? What would be the adult's role in each?

10. Select four or five books from a bibliography of multicultural children's books. What themes are addressed? How does the vocabulary or speech style of the story characters teach children about diversity?

Bibliography

General

Bredekamp, S. (Ed.). (1995). *Developmentally appropriate practice in early childhood programs serving children from birth through age 8* (Expanded ed.). Washington, DC: National Association for the Education of Young Children.

Derman-Sparks, L. (1989). *Anti-bias curriculum*. Washington, DC: National Association for the Education of Young Children.

Cognition

General

Dahl, K. (1998, January). Why cooking in the classroom? *Young Children, 53*(1).

Hohmann, M., & Weikart, D. P. (1995). *Educating young children: Active learning practices for preschool and child care programs*. Ypsilanti, MI: High/Scope Press.

Klein, A. (1991, July). All about ants: Discovery learning in the primary grades. *Young Children, 46*(5).

Marxen, C. D. (1995, Summer). Push, pull, toss, tilt, swing: Physics for young children. *Childhood Education.*

Meriwether, L. (1997, July). Math at the snack table. *Young Children, 52*(5).

Micklo, S. (1995, Fall). Developing young children's classification and logical thinking skills. *Childhood Education.*

Montessori, M. (1967). *The Montessori method* (A. E. George, trans.). Cambridge, MA:

Schweinhart, L. J., Barnes, H. V., & Weikart, D. P. (1993). *Significant benefits: The High/Scope Perry Preschool Study through age 27* (Monographs of the High/Scope Educational Research Foundation, Vol. 10). Ypsilanti, MI: High/Scope Press.

Schweinhart, L. J., & Weikart, D. P. (1997). *Lasting differences: The High/Scope Preschool Curriculum Comparison Study through age 23* (Monographs of the High/Scope Educational Research Foundation, Vol. 10). Ypsilanti, MI: High/Scope Press.

Slavin, R. E. (Ed.), Karweit, N. L., & Wasik, B. A. (1994). Preventing early school failure: Research policy and practice. *Educational Leadership, 50,* 10–18.

Unglaub, K. W. (1997, May). What counts in learning to count? *Young Children, 52*(4).

Wingert, P., & Kantrowitz, B. (1997, October 27). Why Andy couldn't read. *Newsweek.*

Piagetian/Constructivist

De Vries, R. (1987, March). What will happen if . . .? Using a Piagetian approach to inspire reasoning. *Pre-K Today.*

Flavell, J. (1993). *What preschoolers know about thinking.* Paper presented at Stanford University: Center for Youth and Family Studies.

Kamii, C., & Ewing, J. K. (1996). Basing teaching on Piaget's constructivism. *Childhood Education.* Annual Theme.

Labinowitz, E. (1980). *The Piaget primer: Thinking, learning, teaching.* Menlo Park, CA: Addison-Wesley.

Piaget, J. (1969). *The language and thought of the child.* Cleveland: World Publishing.

Roberts, J. M., & Spitz, G. (1998). *What does a constructivist class look like?* Unpublished paper developed with the Advisory Board of "Under Construction." Monterey, CA.

Multiple Intelligences

Blumenthal, R. (1995, November, 19). Curriculum update for "Sesame Street." *New York Times.*

Checkley, K. (1997, September). The first seven . . . and the eight. *Educational Leadership.*

Gardner, H. (1983). *Frames of mind.* New York. Basic Books.

Gardner, H. (1985) *Multiple intelligences: Theory into practice.* New York: Basic Books.

Gardner, H. (1991). *The unschooled mind.* New York: Basic Books.

Gardner, H. (1995, May). *Myths & messages: Reflections on multiple intelligences.* Project Zero, Harvard Graduate School of Education.

Hatch, T. (1997, March). Getting specific about multiple intelligences. *Educational Leadership.*

Hohmann, M. Banet, B., & Weikart, D. P. (1979). *Young children in action.* Ypsilanti, MI: High/Scope Press.

Nelson, K. (1995, July/August). Nurturing kids: Seven ways of being smart. *Instructor.*

New City School Faculty. (1995). *Multiple intelligences: Teaching for success.* St. Louis: The New City School.

Vygotsky and Sociocultural Theory

Berk, L. E., & Winsler, A. (1995). *Scaffolding children's learning: Vygotsky and early childhood education.* Washington, DC: National Association for the Education of Young Children.

Elicker, J. (1995, Fall). A knitting tale: Reflections on scaffolding. *Childhood Education.*

Vygotsky, L. S. (1962). *Thought and language.* New York: MIT Press and John Wiley & Sons.

Brain-Based Learning

Caine, R. N., & Caine, G. (1997). *Unleasing the power of perceptual change: The potential of brain-based teaching.* Alexandria, VA: Association for Supervision and Curriculum Development.

Cuffaro, H., et al. (1995, May). Beginnings workshop: Block play. *Child Care Information Exchange*.

Galinsky, E. (1997, Winter). New research on the brain development of young children. *CAEYC Connections*.

Phipps, P. A. (1998). *Applying brain research to the early childhood classroom*. NY: McGraw-Hill Learning Materials.

Sylwester, R. (1995). *A celebration of neurons: An educator's guide to the human brain*. Alexandria, VA: Association for Supervision and Curriculum Development.

Language

General

Beck, M. S. (1979). *Baby talk: How your child learns to speak*. New York: New American Library.

Chomsky, N. (1993). *Language and thought*. Wakefield, RI: Moyer Bell.

DeVilliers, P. A., & Jill, G. (1981). *Early language*. Washington, DC: National Association for the Education of Young Children.

Diegmueller, K. (1996, March 20). A delicate balance. *Education Week*.

Early Childhood Resources. (1995). *Implementing developmentally appropriate practice kindergarten through grade 2*. Corte Madera, CA.

Good, L. A., et al. (1993/94, Winter). Let your fingers do the talking. *Childhood Education*.

Manzo, K. K. (1997, March 12). Study stresses role of early phonics instruction. *Education Week*.

Reynolds, K. E. (1995, Fall). Sign language and preschoolers: An ideal match. *Childhood Education*.

Schnaiberg, L. (1997, March 5). Research: The politics of language. *Education Week*.

Sholtys, K. C. (1989, March). A new language, a new life. *Young Children, 44*(3).

Soundy, C. S. (1997, Spring). Nuturing literacy with infants and toddlers in group settings. *Childhood Education*.

Swan, A. (1993, Spring). Helping children who stutter. *Childhood Education*.

Wasserman, S. (1991, Summer). The art of the questions. *Childhood Education, 67*(4).

Wolf, D., et al. (1996, July). Beginnings workshop: Talking. *Child Care Information Exchange*.

Wrobleski, L. (1990, March). The writer's briefcase. *Young Children, 45*(3).

Bilingual Education

Barrera, R., et al. (1996, January). Beginnings workshop: Bilingual education. *Child Care Information Exchange*.

Bowman, B. T. (1989, October). Educating language-minority children: Challenges and opportunities. *Phi Delta Kappan*.

Diaz-Soto, L. (1991, January), Research in review: Understanding bilingual/bicultural young children. *Young Children, 46*(2).

Garcia, E. (1986). Bilingual development and the education of bilingual children during early childhood. *American Journal of Education, 11*.

Halford, J. M. (1996, March). *InfoBrief: Bilingual education*. Alexandria, VA: Association for Supervision and Curriculum Development.

Dialect Differences

Applebome, P. (1997, March 1). Dispute over Ebonics reflects a volatile mix that roils urban education. *New York Times*.

Atkins, C. P. (1993, September). Do employment recruiters discriminate on the basis of nonstandard dialect? *Journal of Employment Counseling, 30*(3), 4 (bibliography).

Cazden, C. B. (1996, March). *Communicative competence, 1966–1996*. Paper presented at the annual meeting of the American Association for Applied Linguistics (ERIC No. ED 399764), Chicago.

Cecil, N. L. (1998, September). Black dialect and academic success: A study of teacher expectations. *Reading Improvement, 25*(1).

Goodman, K. S., & Buck, C. (1997, March). Dialect barriers to reading comprehension revisited. *Reading Teacher 50*(6).

Hoover, M. (1997, March/April). Ebonics insider. *Stanford Magazine.*

Ross, R., & Steele, S. (1997, January 29). Beyond Ebonics. *Education Week.*

Sanchez, R. (1996, December 20). Oakland school system recognizes 'black English' as a second language. *Washington Post.*

Saxton, R. R. (1998, July). Different dialects. Personal communication.

Thomas, G. T. (1983). The deficit, difference, and bicultural theories of black dialect and nonstandard English. *Urban Review, 15*(2).

Special Topics

Reading and Writing

Anonymous. (1998). Joint position paper on helping children to read and write. Washington, DC: National Association for the Education of Young Children and International Reading Association.

Anonymous. (1998). Raising a reader, raising a writer (Brochure No. 530). Washington, DC: National Association for the Education of Young Children.

Cruikshank, S. (1993). Whole language: A developmentally appropriate alternative. In A. Gordon & K. B. Browne (Eds.), *Beginnings and beyond* (3rd ed.). Albany, NY: Delmar.

Freeman, E. B., & Hatch, J. A. (1989, Fall). Emergent literacy: Reconceptualizing kindergarten practice. *Childhood Education, 66*(1).

Goodman, K. (1986). *What's whole in whole language.* Portsmouth, NH: Heinemann Educational Books.

Herr, J., & Libby, Y. (1994). *Early childhood writing centers.* Fort Worth, TX: Harcourt & Brace.

Jones, E. (Ed.). (1988). *Reading, writing, and talking with four, five and six year olds.* Pasadena, CA: Pacific Oaks.

Schickedanz, J. A., York, M. E., Stewart, I. D., & White, D. A. (1983). *Strategies for teaching young children* (2nd ed.). Englewood Cliffs, NJ: Prentice-Hall.

Children's Literature

Arbuthnot, M. H., & Sutherland, Z. (1972). *Children and books* (4th ed.). London: Scott, Foresman.

Ashton-Warner, S. (1963). *Teacher.* New York: Bantam Books.

Bisson, J., & Carter, M. (1995, Winter). The good books: Children's books that deal with unfairness, stereotypes, tolerance, and activism. *CAEYC Connections.*

Carter, M. (1997, January). Developing a storytelling culture in our programs. *Exchange.*

Hildebrand, J. M., & Miller, S. (1995–98). Books for children. *Childhood Education.*

Howarth, M. (1989, November). Rediscovering the power of fairy tales. *Young Children, 45*(1).

Jalongo, M. R. (1988). *Young children and picture books.* Washington, DC: National Association for the Education of Young Children.

Kranowitz, C. S., et al. (1992, July). Beginnings workshop: The value of fairy and folk tales. *Exchange.*

Lundin, A. (1991, Summer). Secret gardens: The literature of childhood. *Childhood Education, 67*(4).

Munsch, R., et al. (1994, July). Beginnings workshop: Storytelling. *Exchange.*

Raines, S. C., & Canady, R. J. (1989). *Story stretchers.* Mt. Rainier, WA: Gryphon House.

Ramirez, G., Jr., & Ramirez, J. L. (1994). *Multiethnic children's literature.* Albany, NY: Delmar.

Sawyer, W. E., & Sawyer, J. C. (1993). *Integrated language arts for emerging literacy.* Albany, NY: Delmar.

Sutherland, Z. (1991). *Literature for children,* and *The best in children's books.* Chicago IL: World Book Encyclopedia.

Trelease, J. (1982). *The read-aloud handbook.* New York: Penguin Books.

Tubbs, J. (1984, Winter). Talking with and through puppets. *Beginnings.*

Turner, T. N., & Oaks, T. (1997, Spring). Stories on the spot. *Childhood Education.*

Waldorf Staff of Los Altos, CA. (1994). *Understanding the Waldorf curriculum.* Pamphlet for parents.

Computers

Ballenger, M. (1993–98). Software for the classroom and technology review. *Childhood Education*.

Buckleitner, W. (1995, January). Getting started with computers and children. *Exchange*.

Buckleitner, W. (1996, May). No fail software. *Exchange*.

Davidson, J. I. (1989). *Children and computers together in the early childhood classroom*. Albany, NY: Delmar.

Haugland, S. W., & Shade, D. D. (1988, May). Developmentally appropriate software for young children. *Young Children, 43*(4).

Haugland, S. W., & Shade, D. D. (1990). *Developmental evaluations of software for young children*. Albany, NY: Delmar.

Katz, L. (1985). Fostering communicative competence in young children. *ERIC/EECE Newsletter, 18*(2).

Papert, S. (1980). *Mindstorms: Children, computers, and powerful ideas*. New York: Basic Books.

Samaras, A. (1996, Spring). Children's computers. *Childhood Education*.

Scharf, P., & Chattin-McNichols, J. (1986). *Understanding the computer age*. Hasbrouck Heights, NJ: Hayden.

Trotter, A. (1996, December 11). Software for preschoolers makes market inroads. *Education Week*.

Wright, J. L, & Sade, D. D. (Eds.). (1994). *Young children: Active learners in a technological age*. Washington, DC: National Association for the Education of Young Children.

Acknowledgment

Special thanks to students Sandie Goodwin, Dale Hu, and Sharon Murphy for their contributions of children's language samples.

Planning for the Heart and Soul: Emotional, Social, and Creative Growth

CHAPTER 14

Questions for Thought

What is the connection between a child's *well-being* and emotional, social, and creative development?

What are the components of self-esteem?

What is emotional growth in the early childhood years?

How do teachers handle the expression of feelings in the class setting?

What is social growth in the early childhood years?

What social skills are developed in young children?

What is creativity?

How is creativity expressed in the early years?

Portions of this chapter were developed with the assistance of Gay Spitz, Salinas Adult School, Salinas, CA.

PREFACE

The heart and soul of any good program for young children is a commitment to help children as they struggle with (1) the reality of emotions, (2) the awareness of the need for social skills, and (3) the creative urge as well as acknowledgment of the spiritual. The foundation must be laid in these early years for children to understand themselves and others.

Emotional, social, and creative development are related to the child's self-concept and self-esteem; the child must have an understanding of self before seeing that self in relation to others. It is primarily through emotional, social, and creative growth that children learn who they are, and they must have self-confidence to experience and learn the necessary skills.

This chapter contains three separate units. Each area—emotional, social, and creative growth—is explored individually to give a greater understanding of its importance to the developing child. An overview of development is followed by a discussion of the skills children learn in the preschool years. The crucial role of the teacher is emphasized next, followed by curriculum planning to reinforce each developmental area. At the end of each unit, a checkpoint and review serve as a short summary.

INTRODUCTION

The first thing one notices on entering an early childhood classroom is the children at play. A quick survey of the area shows who is playing together, whether there is crying or fighting, and how happy or sad the children look. This overview gives an immediate sense of the emotional, social, and creative climate in that early childhood setting.

● *Emotional*: Toddler Abier giggles as she runs her hands across the water table, then cries after she splashes soap suds in her eyes and needs to be comforted.

● *Social*: Preschooler Danny wants his favorite red wagon so Pat, the student teacher, helps him negotiate a turn with Christa.

● *Creative*: Kindergartners Fabio, Erika, and Benjy work steadily to build a tall, intricate block structure. When it is finished, the three children stand back and marvel at their creation.

Together these three factors—emotional mood, social dynamics, and creative tone—define the overall atmosphere in which children play and work.

Emotional, social, and creative well-being are woven together in the developing child. Children who are sensitive to their own feelings and moods are able to begin understanding other people and thus become more socially effective and successful. Children with experience in many creative endeavors have the self-confidence that comes from having an outlet for self-expression.

These three areas are also linked to other aspects of the child's growth:

● *Creative/Physical*: Physical skills can define and limit children's creative abilities. Two-year-old Andrea, whose physical skills do not yet include balancing objects, plays with blocks by piling them on top of one another, filling her wagon with blocks, and dumping them or lugging them from place to place.

● *Social/Cognitive*: It is hard for 5-year-old Karena to share her best friend Luther with other children. Her intellectual abilities do not yet allow her to consider more than one idea at a time, so she cannot understand that Luther can be her friend and Dana's at the same time.

● *Emotional/Language*: Tyler is upset with his teacher's refusal to let him go outdoors during storytime. "I hate you!" he screams, "and you aren't the boss of me!" Children learn to label and express their emotions through words.

It is difficult to observe and measure the child's growth in creative, social, and emotional areas; it is easier to determine a child's progress in physical, cognitive, and language development. After all, a child counts or doesn't count, is either 40 inches tall or is not, and speaks in full sentences or in short phrases. Emotional, social, and creative expressions are more subtle and subjective. A child usually gets immediate and concrete feedback when playing lotto, calling for a teacher, or riding a tricycle. That does not always happen when children express their feelings, encounter others, or create something important. Talbot may feel rejected and sad if no one greets him as he enters the playhouse. He may mistake the children's busy-ness as an act of exclusion. In reality, the children did not even notice he was there. Teachers can play a critical role in helping children interpret their emotional, social, and creative interactions.

Figure 14.1 ● The emotional, social, and creative growth of children are the heart and soul of any early childhood program.

Traditionally, early childhood educators have concerned themselves with children's *well-being*, knowing that in the early years the foundations must be laid for children to understand themselves and others. Social growth, creative expression, and experience with a wide range of emotional behaviors also help children develop a strong self-concept with positive self-esteem.

What is included in children's well-being? To be in a good overall condition of health and happiness, children need a positive sense of themselves.

Self-esteem is an individual's sense of personal worth and an acceptance of who one is. Children's self-esteem (the way they feel about themselves) is expressed through children's behavior. They make judgments about themselves as they confront the world. To the extent that children feel worthy and capable, they are ready to succeed. If children disapprove of themselves, they may feel like failures and expect to do poorly.

Self-esteem develops as a reflection of experiences: the way people respond to you gives you some indication of your importance or value. Newborn infants have no concept of self and no past experience to judge their own worth. A young child who has positive experiences with others will more likely have a high sense of self-esteem than one who has felt unloved or unnoticed.

There appear to be four components of self-esteem:

1. A sense of one's own identity

2. A sense of belonging (connectedness)

3. A sense of one's uniqueness

4. A sense of self (power)

Early in life, self-esteem is tied to family, friends, and other important people, such as teachers. Figure 14.2 shows how curriculum can develop each of these characteristics.

Planning for children's success builds self-esteem. It includes the following four components, which we call the "Four Is":

● *I:* When children enter the classroom, the message they receive is "I am important and this is my place." The physical environment, the daily schedule, and the curriculum are designed to give all children permission to express themselves.

● *Initiative:* Children are encouraged to initiate their own learning, to make contact with others, to take action, and to make choices.

● *Independence:* Self-management tasks of dressing, eating, toileting are given an important place in the curriculum. Children are assisted in taking care of their own belongings and in developing independent judgment about events and activities.

● *Interaction:* Social interaction has a high priority in the program. The room and yard are busy places, with children moving about and talking among themselves and with adults.[1] Conflicts are ac-

OUR DIVERSE WORLD OUR DIVERSE WORLD OUR DIVERSE WORLD OUR DIVERSE WORLD OUR DIVERSE WORLD OUR DIVERSE WORLD OUR DIVERSE WORLD OUR DIVERSE WORLD

[1] One of the things that we know from the research is that our children, African American children, are highly people-oriented (Burgess, 1993). There tends to be an "object orientation" in European Americans and a "people orientation" in African Americans. Such awareness helps teachers to interact with children in ways that coincide with their cultural orientation and to understand individual children's challenges with social interaction.

Emotional Skill Development	Curriculum Activity (Use of Senses)
Self-Esteem	Use rocks of various sizes with balances, so that children can touch and hear when they move things around.
1. *Identity:* "Look at what I can do, the noise I can make, the weight I can pick up and move!"	
2. *Connectedness:* "I can make the same snakes as you, we can all make cakes."	A malleable material such as playdough can be used first alone, then with tools.
3. *Uniqueness:* "I'm pouring mine; you're dripping yours, and she is squeezing her stuff out her fingers!"	Make "oobleck," a mixture of cornstarch and water, in separate tubs for each child. Children can manipulate it in their own ways.
4. *Power:* "I can make this water go anywhere I want; look out for the tidal waves!"	Water play offers the child choices: pour into any of several containers, fill or empty the jug, use a funnel or a baster to squirt the water, make waves or splash hands.
Deal with Feelings	
1. *Identification* (to notice and label): "Does it feel very smooth, slippery, slidy? Is it soft and soothing?"	When fingerpainting, the teacher can describe what it appears the child is feeling. Children can identify their feelings as the teacher describes them while they use the materials.
2. *Mastery* (to accept): "She took your baker's dough and that made you angry. You can tell her you don't like it when she grabs what you are using."	Whether the sensory material is clay, soapy water, or fine sand, the issues of ownership and use of materials arise. Then, teachers reflect children's feelings and help them take responsibility for their own feelings.
3. *Expressing* (to express appropriately): Child: "Tami has all the big pitchers." Teacher: "How can you let her know you want one?" Child: "And she splashed me two times!" Teacher: "If you feel too crowded, you need to tell her so."	As children begin to use the sensory materials, they need to communicate to others. Usually the issues are about wanting more material and personal space.
4. *Feelings* (to deal with others): "Whee! Yuk! Mmm! Ha!"	When children share in a sensory activity, such as a feeling walking through tubs of small pebbles, sand, and soapsuds, they have the delightful experience of enjoying their own feelings with another.

Figure 14.2 ● Sensory materials offer a sensorimotor opportunity to deal with materials in a nonstructured way. Because children relax with open-ended activities, they will often share their feelings as they use sensory materials in a comfortable atmosphere.

cepted as a natural consequence of social life. In the spirit of John Dewey (see Figure 1.6, Chapter 1), democratic group living will encourage children to interact and foster a consciousness of interdependence.

A positive sense of self is critical for young children. Research (Marshall, 1989) shows that low self-image is correlated with poor mental health, poor academic achievement, and delinquency. In contrast, a positive self-concept is correlated with good mental health, academic achievement, and good behavior. Children with a positive self-image are ready to meet life's challenges. They will have the self-confidence to deal with the reality of emotions, the changing nature of social interaction, and the risk of creativity.

Building self-image is "complex, multidimensional, and ever changing. It affects everything we do, and is affected by everything we do" (Wardle, 1993). Crucial to children's self-image is how children interpret the response of the environment to their actions. And much of a self-image is based on the way society views the child. Teachers take an important role as they provide an essential ingredient of self-image: the quality of human interactions.[1]

● UNIT 14-1 Emotional Growth

THE DEVELOPMENT OF EMOTIONS

Emotions are the feelings a person has—joy and sorrow, love and hate, confidence and fear, loneliness and belonging, anger and contentment, frustration and satisfaction. They are responses to events, people, and circumstances. Feelings are an outgrowth of what a person perceives is happening. Emotionally healthy people learn to give expression to their feelings in appropriate ways. They do not allow their feelings to overshadow the rest of their behavior. The optimal time to learn these skills is in the early years.

Early childhood teachers encourage children to identify and express their emotional nature so that they can learn to live with these powerful forces. When a child begins to understand and communicate feelings, the emotions are no longer in control of the child; the child is becoming the master of the emotions. Chapter 7 on guidance and discipline and this chapter's sections on emotional and social curriculum contain teacher strategies for helping children grow in these areas.

Infants respond in agitated emotion whether wet, hungry, hurt, or bored. Gradually, the expression of the emotion becomes more refined and varies with the situation. A toddler's cry of distress is different from the cry of discomfort or hunger. As children get older, their emotional expressions change as they gain control over some of their feelings and learn new ways to express them.

Strong external forces are also at work. Parents, family members, teachers, and friends are social influences, helping the young child learn socially acceptable behavior. Much of what children learn is by example, as Erikson, Bandura, Piaget, and Vygotsky would

all agree. Therefore, children learn more from adult models than from simply being told how to behave.

EMOTIONAL SKILLS IN EARLY CHILDHOOD

The emotional skills children learn in their early years are substantial. Research shows that some emotions—interest, disgust, distress, to name a few—are observable in the newborn, and it is posited that all the basic emotions are present within the first few weeks of life. These include happiness, interest, surprise, fear, anger, sadness, and disgust. The more complex emotions of shame, guilt, envy, and pride emerge later, once children have had the social experiences of observing these emotions in others or have been in situations that might evoke such feelings. These expressions have been observed in a wide range of cultural and ethnic groups.[2]

In early childhood, children learn to respond to new situations and to react and connect with a teacher, both very emotional experiences. Good teachers stimulate an emotional response to themselves and the curriculum that is a balance between interest and overwhelming fear. Creating the "right" emotional conditions is a primary way to gain access to a child's capacity for learning. Young children are not yet limited by social mores and standards of conduct that prevent them from sincere and truthful self-expression. Teachers observe children and learn how youngsters feel about facing their own feelings, the feelings of others, and the range of skills categorized as emotional growth.

Ability to Deal with Feelings

Dealing with feelings involves four steps. Each builds on the other so that they follow a developmental sequence; the learning that takes place at one level affects the development of what follows. Figures 14.2 and 14.9 describe how the early childhood classroom and teacher help children deal effectively with their feelings.

OUR DIVERSE WORLD OUR DIVERSE WORLD OUR DIVERSE WORLD OUR DIVERSE WORLD OUR DIVERSE WORLD OUR DIVERSE WORLD OUR DIVERSE WORLD OUR DIVERSE WORLD

[1] Because a child's self-image begins with where she belongs—family, community, culture—it is critical that early childhood programs support a child's home environment—culture, race, language, life-style, and values (Wardle, 1993).

[2] One is reminded of the universal qualities to be found in each of us in OUR DIVERSE WORLD. The challenge is to notice and celebrate our similarities and our differences—both are gifts.

Curious

Happy

Angry

Scared

Figure 14.3 ● Young children feel their emotions strongly. Learning to read faces and body stance is essential to guiding emotional development and for children to be successful socially.

To Notice and Label Feelings

This is the first step. The sobbing 1- or 2-year-old may have many reasons for feeling in distress. As parents recognize the cries of hunger, hurt, and fear, they name these feelings. The child will learn to notice what the feeling is and recognize it. Teachers know how to "read" children's faces and body language to give them the words for and ways to express those feelings. Chapter 6 has suggestions for becoming a skillful observer. Preschoolers are quite verbal and curious about language and ready to learn words that describe a wider range of feelings. They can learn "lonely," "scared," "silly," "sad," and "happy." Labeling what one feels inside is a critical skill to learn. It is a healthy first-grader who can say, "I have tried to cut this string three times and the scissors aren't working. I am frustrated. I need some help!"

To Accept Feelings

Teachers recognize that children are capable of strong feelings. Children can feel overwhelmed by the very strength and intensity of a feeling, be it one of anger or of love. As children come to accept feelings, they learn how to handle the depth of the feeling and not let it overpower them. The changing nature of feelings is also part of accepting the feeling. It can be a source of comfort and relief for young children to discover that the strong emotion they experience now will pass. Adults who work with young children help them work through those feelings safely. Carlos feels sad as his mother prepares to leave. His teacher walks them to the door, then bends down and puts an arm around him as his mother waves goodbye. Acknowledging that he is sad, the teacher stays with Carlos, reminding him that his mother will return and that the teacher will take care of him while he is at school. Because the child is allowed to feel the sadness that is natural in leave-taking, the tense feelings are over in a few minutes. The teacher smiles and encourages Carlos to find something fun to do. Once he has recovered his composure, the teacher can point out that he's "okay now", and Carlos can feel proud for having lived through and grown from saying good-bye. Acknowledgment of the feeling and his ability to accept it help give Carlos the confidence to move on.

To Express Feelings in an Appropriate Way

Expressing feelings appropriately is a two-part process. First, children must feel free to express their feelings; second, they must learn ways of expression that are suitable to their age and to the situation. Many beginning teachers are uncomfortable because children express themselves so strongly (and often aggressively). Yet the child who is passive and unable to express feelings freely should be of equal concern and should be encouraged in self-expression.

As children grow, they acquire the modes of expression that are developmentally appropriate for their age. Babies and toddlers without language cry to express their feelings; thus this type of crying calls for the same kind of immediate response given to other forms of communication in later years. Two-year-olds express their displeasure by pushes and shoves; 4-year-olds use their verbal power and argue. By 6 or 7, children learn to tell others—clearly and with reasons—what they are feeling. The ability to express feelings is intact, but the methods of expression change as children grow. Expression of feelings also has a cultural dimension. Some cultures are open in their display of emotions, whereas others are reserved.[1]

To Deal with the Feelings of Others

Dealing with the feelings of others is the culminating step in the development of emotional skills. Feelings are the spark of life in people: the flash of anger, the "ah-hah" of discovery, the thrill of accomplishment, the hug of excitement. Because recognizing and expressing emotions are closely interwoven, children who can distinguish among different emotions and have some experience in taking the perspective of others by observing their feelings develop *empathy*. Empathy can happen at a young age. Very young children may cry or gather near the teacher when a playmate is hurt or sad; preschoolers smile at another's laughter; and kindergartners imagine themselves

OUR DIVERSE WORLD OUR DIVERSE WORLD OUR DIVERSE WORLD OUR DIVERSE WORLD OUR DIVERSE WORLD OUR DIVERSE WORLD OUR DIVERSE WORLD OUR DIVERSE WORLD

[1] Being encouraged to act out every emotion is not appropriate, for instance, for African American children. "Living under oppressive conditions mandates learning to handle oppression in ways . . . [such as] to learn where to express feelings and who it is safe to let know your feelings," says Cooper (1992). "Their reluctance to engage should be respected, not viewed as a challenge."

vividly in another's predicament during a story. Like the complex emotions discussed earlier, empathy requires cognitive abilities, such as seeing oneself as separate from other people (see the discussion of Erikson in Chapter 4) and also as connected in some way to others (see the discussion of Vygotsky in Chapters 4 and 13). Two- to 5-year-olds can respond with empathy to the emotions of others. Older children, who are better able to put themselves in another's place (see the discussion of Piaget in Chapters 4 and 13) and who understand a wider range of emotions, can respond to others in distress. However, empathy is affected by early experience (Berk, 1999) and needs nurturing to grow. Helping children to tolerate and appreciate how different people express their emotions leads to understanding and cooperation.

Ability to Deal with Change

Change is inevitable. Many people fear or reject change. Children can learn that change is a constant part of their lives and to cope with the challenges changes present. Fear, insecurity, and uncertainty are some of the emotions felt when people experience changes in their lives or routines. Many times, these feelings arise from not knowing what to expect or how to behave or from not understanding different sets of values.

Inevitably, changes will happen in children's lives, bringing with them a measure of stress. The very act of being born is a change, marking the beginning of a life in which stress is part of the act of developmental achievement. Witness the toddler's numerous falls toward walking, the separation of parent and child at the nursery-school doorway, the concentration and frustrations of the 6-year-old on roller skates. A measure of positive stress encourages a child to strive and achieve, to find out and discover.

Stress can arise from several factors, both internal (severe colic) or external (moving to a new home). Some stresses are acute in a child's life, such as a hospitalization, whereas others are chronic, as living in an alcoholic household. Many variables are associated

Figure 14.4 ● Children learn to appreciate and understand one another as they see each others' feelings. How can these children learn to express hurt and comfort?

with different kinds of stress in children's lives. For instance, age, intellectual capacity, and gender can influence a child's response to a stressful situation; research seems to indicate that male children are more vulnerable than female children (Honig, 1986). Inadequate housing, poverty, and war are ecological stressors (see Chapter 15 for a discussion of violence). Family changes—the birth of a sibling, death or loss of a close family member, marriage problems and divorce—are sources of stress on a personal level.[1,2] Inept parenting practices that neglect or abuse children are especially troublesome as they hurt children and provide them with poor role models for learning how to cope with stress.

Yet stress and coping are part of the ability to deal with change. Much has been researched and written of stress in children's lives (Honig, 1986; Selye, 1982), and stages of dealing with stress have now been identified. Figure 14.5 lists the stages of stress and teacher

OUR DIVERSE WORLD OUR DIVERSE WORLD OUR DIVERSE WORLD OUR DIVERSE WORLD OUR DIVERSE WORLD OUR DIVERSE WORLD OUR DIVERSE WORLD OUR DIVERSE WORLD

[1] In working with children from potentially stress-producing situations, teachers recognize and acknowledge the level of coping and resiliency so many children and their families possess.

[2] Simply living in American society is stressful for many children. For instance, the Native American child lives in "a conflict of cultures. She must 'make it' in the white world to survive, and she must recognize her Indian heritage to affirm her own identity. A teacher must accept the total child and help her function effectively in both worlds" (Sample, 1993).

Stage	Behavior	The Teacher Helps
Alarm	Arousal and fear Confusion Swift mood changes	Notices when child is stressed (sees changes in behavior). Listens. Offers words for child's feelings. Offers age-appropriate explanations. Is accepting of unpredictable behavior. Reassures child of teacher's constant availability. Alerts parents and others of child's state. Takes preventive actions to lessen other stressful events.
Appraisal	Attempts to understand the problem	Listens. Offers age-appropriate explanations. Helps child see situation more positively. May make a simple list of the problem. Reassures that the problem *will* be solved. Alerts other adults to the importance of the child's work.
Search	Looks for coping strategy Selects from what is at hand	Listens. Asks for the child's ideas. Helps child list possible solutions. Tells parents and others of child's solutions. Demonstrates self-control and coping skills her/himself. Encourages and enhances child's self-esteem.
Implementation	Tries out a coping strategy Applies a solution to the problem	Listens. Observes child's implementing a solution. Gives supportive feedback about relative success or failure of the plan. Helps child refine or revise strategy as needed. Encourages child's efforts.

Figure 14.5 ● Stages of and strategies for coping with stress: the teacher is observant of the child throughout, makes regular time to talk individually, and encourages the child to use art, books, and class members as supports.

strategies. Teachers help children to deal with stress by supporting them in working through these stages, as they cope with changes in their lives at school, at home, and in the world at large.

For instance, teachers can help children accept change in several ways. Anticipating changes that are likely to occur and identifying the process for children are very important. "Junko, your mother will be leaving soon. We'll go looking for that favorite puzzle after you say good-bye to her." If the daily routine is altered, children should be notified. "We won't be having snacks inside today; let's use the patio table instead." When children are informed that change is anticipated, accepted, and not necessarily disrupting, they become more relaxed about handling the unpre-

dictable. Teachers become resources for helping children cope in ways that are appropriate to the child and the situation at hand, be this by crying in sadness or fear, ignoring an unpleasant situation, finding a compromise, or accepting comfort.

Ability to Exercise Judgment

The ability to exercise judgment is an important skill, for it helps children to make decisions and figure out what to do in new situations. On entering school, a child faces many decisions: Where shall I play? Who shall I play with? What if my friend wants to do something I know is wrong? Who will I turn to for help

Figure 14.6 ● An awareness of their own power can bring enjoyable rewards to children. This girl enjoys feeding and helping to take care of her baby sister.

when I need it? Judgment is selecting what to do, when to do it, with whom to do it, and when to stop.

Making choices is an essential part of decision-making. Children are bombarded with choices in America—too many choices, some people say. Some children must decide about tissues that, in other times, only adults handled. But children "have difficulty discriminating between big choices and little choices. Every choice is a big one for most children" (Simon, 1994). So, as does any skill, learning to make good choices takes thought, guidance, and lots of practice.[1]

There is no easy way to teach children how to make decisions because each situation must be dealt with on an individual basis. The judgment a child exercises in choosing a friend to play with today may have other factors to consider tomorrow. Instead, teachers help children base their decisions on the best judgment they are capable of in each instance. One

way to encourage decision-making is to provide opportunities for choice (see "Focus on Skills" on p. 518 for specific suggestions). Another aspect of judgment is a child's **self-regulation**. Research (Diaz, 1992) suggests that children can develop the capacity to plan and guide themselves. In contrast to self-control, in which we teach children to respond to an external rule, children's self-regulation is a combination of the cognitive and emotional realms. The teacher can encourage this process by serving as a Vygotsky-like mediator, making children participants in their own learning (thinking), and by supporting children's focus on self-competence (emotional). As they mature, children are able to sort out what judgments might be made here, what factors need to be considered there.

Enjoying One's Self and One's Power

Teachers want children to feel powerful—to know that they can master their lives and feel confident in their own abilities. This feeling of power is particularly important in the early years, when so much of what a child can see is out of reach, both literally and figuratively.

Responsibility and limits, however, go hand in hand with power. The child who is strong enough to hit someone has to learn not to use that strength unnecessarily. The child who shouts with glee also finds out that noise is unacceptable indoors. By holding children responsible for their own actions, teachers can help children enjoy their power and accept its limitations.

One kind of fantasy play most teachers encounter is that of superheroes. Common to children as young as 2, **superhero** play is exciting and rowdy, usually active and loud, playacting of heroic roles that give children powers they lack in everyday life. It is the embodiment of control and strength, even wisdom, and the parts to be played are clear for everyone involved.

Children's natural struggles for mastery and the attraction of rough-and-tumble play collide with teachers' concerns about fighting, aggression, and letting the play get out of hand. Kostelnik, Whiren, and Stein (1986) have described this special type

---

 OUR DIVERSE WORLD OUR DIVERSE WORLD OUR DIVERSE WORLD OUR DIVERSE WORLD OUR DIVERSE WORLD OUR DIVERSE WORLD OUR DIVERSE WORLD OUR DIVERSE WORLD

[1] Teachers can help children with some emotionally difficult choices as they work with issues of bias and stereotyping. Social action (see next section) is one way to teach about choices that benefit others as well as helping children express their feelings and ideas.

Feeling	Behavioral Definition
1. Fear	Pale face, alert eyes, tense mouth, rigid body.
2. Surprise	Wide eyes, eyebrows uplifted, involuntary cry or scream, quick inhale of breath.
3. Anger	Red face, eyes staring, face taut, fists and jaw clenched, voice harsh or yelling, large gestures.
4. Joy	Smiling face, shining eyes, free and easy body movements, laughing.
5. Pride	Head held high, smiling face, jaunty walk or strut, tendency to announce or point out.
6. Embarrassment	Red face, glazed and downcast eyes, tight mouth, tense body, small and jerky movements, soft voice.
7. Sadness	Unsmiling face, downturned mouth, glazed and teary eyes, crying or rubbing eyes, limp body, slow or small movements, soft and trembly voice.
8. Anxiety	Puckered brow, pale face, tight mouth, whiny voice, jerky movements, lack of or difficulty in concentration.
9. Curiosity	Raised brow, shining eyes, perhaps tense body in absorption of the object of curiosity; often hand movements to touch and pick up object; sometimes mouth agape.

Figure 14.7 ● As we observe children's behavior, we understand how their feelings are expressed. Expressions of fear, anger, sadness, disgust, and happiness are universal, and the face can be read and understood long before children understand language.

of dramatic play in detail, offering suggestions for managing it:

- Help children recognize humane characteristics of superheroes.

- Discuss real heroes and heroines.

- Talk about the pretend world of acting.

- Limit the place and time for superhero play.

- Explore related concepts.

- Help children de-escalate rough-and-tumble play.

- Make it clear that aggression is unacceptable.

- Give children control over their lives.

- Praise children's attempts at mastery.

In addition, teachers and parents are rightfully concerned with children's aggression and with their exposure to war and violence, both from the media and at home (Carlsson-Paige & Levin, 1987). **Rough-housing** and aggression have distinctly different patterns of behavior and should be recognized as such. Chapter 15 discusses the concerns of war play and violence in children's lives. Children need guidance to learn how to express themselves appropriately and exercise their growing powers responsibly.

Teachers can help children learn to appreciate and enjoy themselves. Each time a child is acknowledged, a teacher fosters that sense of uniqueness: "Carrie, you have a great sense of humor!" "Freddie, I love the way you sing so clearly." Saying it aloud reinforces in children the feeling that they are enjoyable to themselves and to others.

THE TEACHER'S ROLE

Considerations

The first step in helping children develop healthy emotional patterns is for adults to acquire such good patterns themselves. For instance, are you a person who labels others? Do you have high expectations for children? What happens when a child is difficult, or doesn't meet your expectations? Looking inside, stepping back to think about what we are feeling, is helpful. Coming up with a *positive label* for every child may also help teachers deal better with the emotions and behavior of the children in their care (Greenman, 1991). Another step is to develop and use a "feeling" vocabulary. Words of an emotional nature can be used to label and identify feelings as teachers talk with young children.

There are many ways to develop a list of words related to emotions. Figure 14.7 illustrates one way. Identify some of the feelings children express; then describe how the children look and act when experiencing those emotions. This practice helps to build a vocabulary and an understanding of children's emotional expressions.

 Making the classroom a comfortable place for children is essential to a healthy emotional climate.[1] Teachers can also become more attuned to the emotional climate in the classroom by knowing when and how feelings are expressed. To gain insights, teachers might ask themselves:

● What causes children in the class to become excited? Frightened? Calm? Loud? How does this knowledge guide curriculum planning? How can it help a teacher handle an unplanned event or change in the schedule?

● How do I anticipate children's emotional behavior? How do I follow through?

● What can teachers do to handle children's emotional outbursts and crises?

Figure 14.8 ● What causes children to become withdrawn? What can teachers do to handle children's emotions?

● What happens to the rest of the class when one teacher is occupied in an emotional incident with one or more children?

● What do I do when a child shows emotion? How do I feel when a child displays emotion?

● What types of emotions are most common with the young child?

In the early childhood setting, teachers help children come to grips with their strong feelings by discussing those feelings openly. They take the time to help children find names for feelings, to speak of their own feelings, and to begin to be aware of the feelings of others.

When teachers perceive that children are ready to talk about their feelings, small group discussions or individual conversations can be helpful. Good books that touch on sensitive issues (being excluded, being

OUR DIVERSE WORLD OUR DIVERSE WORLD OUR DIVERSE WORLD OUR DIVERSE WORLD OUR DIVERSE WORLD OUR DIVERSE WORLD OUR DIVERSE WORLD OUR DIVERSE WORLD

[1] To feel they belong, children need to have their culture and some of their family rituals and traditions incorporated into their program. For instance, "the rituals of mealtimes, the greetings and goodbyes, are all distinctly Hispanic. . . . Ask children how to acknowledge persons who come to the door, especially older persons. Children should always greet each other's parents and each other" (Barrera, 1993).

blamed, caring for others) offer possibilities for teachers and children to talk about feelings. Games, joking, and teasing can help children to feel relaxed and to explore feelings in an accepting way. Classroom problems (not sharing materials, pushing on the climbers) offer topics for discussion. The ability to express emotions verbally gives children the power to deal with them without resorting to inappropriate behavior.

Social referencing involves "relying on another person's emotional reaction to form one's own appraisal of an uncertain situation" (Berk, 1999). Making use of others' emotional cues can help infants to deal with stranger anxiety, toddlers to calm themselves after saying goodbye, preschoolers to avoid overreacting to a fall, and school-aged children to begin to recognize that people can feel more than one emotion at a time. Social referencing is a vital strategy in learning how to respond emotionally. The teacher who runs to the rescue after a minor spill can engender "learned helplessness" and overreaction. Conversely, the teacher who fails to respond to children when they express emotions may give children the message that others' distress is to be ignored.

When adults show an understanding of feelings, children come to believe that adults are able to help them with their emotions, and the children become more at ease with their own feelings. When something painful happens to a child, adults can express what the child is feeling. "It really hurts to bend your knees now that you have scraped them." "You look so sad now that Gabi is playing with someone else." Children then become familiar with ways to express how they feel in a variety of emotional situations.

Adults can also help children become aware of the emotional states of others. "Look! Paul is crying. Let's go over and see if we can comfort him." Teachers can encourage children to help care for each other's hurts and needs. A child can ease the pain of a friend by sitting nearby as a wound is cleansed or by giving a hug when an achievement is made. Teachers must be sure to allow children to express their concern and to help them learn ways to respond to the emotional needs of others.

Curriculum Planning for Emotional Growth

In the Environment

Teachers set up their classrooms and yards to promote emotional growth. Materials and activities enhance self-esteem and self-expression. How activities are presented and carried out is also a factor. In the class setting, the "how" is as critical as the "what" in curriculum planning for emotional development. Refer to Figure 14.9 to see how curriculum can be developed to encourage emotional growth.

Indoors. Select materials that enhance self-expression. Indoors, children's inner thoughts and feelings are best expressed through:

● *The Arts.* Clay or dough lets children vent feelings, because it can be pounded, pinched, poked, slapped, and manipulated. Fingerpainting and painting on broad surfaces with large brushes encourage a freedom of movement that permits children to express themselves fully.

● *Blocks/Manipulatives.* Vary the materials regularly to help children adjust to change and to allow them to exercise judgment about playing with different materials. A variety of props—motor vehicles, animals, people, furniture—gives children the opportunity to reenact what they see of the world.

● *Discovery/Science.* Often, science projects are geared toward cognitive and language development. They need not always be; some activities can focus on feelings. Caring for pets, for instance, brings out feelings of nurturing and protectiveness. Making "feeling clocks" can emphasize emotions. Blank clock faces are used as a base upon which children draw or paste pictures of people showing various emotional states. Display these at children's eye level so they can be changed frequently.

● *Dramatic Play.* Home-life materials give children the props they need to express how they see their own world of family, parents, siblings. Mirrors, telephones, and dress-up clothes encourage children to try out their emotional interests on themselves as well as each other.

● *Language/Library.* Stories and books in which characters and situations reflect a wide range of emotions are readily available (see Figure 13.23 and Figure 14.9 for some suggested titles). Children enjoy looking at photographs of people and guessing what the person in the photo is feeling. This activity encourages children to find words that label feelings; their responses can be recorded and posted nearby. Once children seem at ease in using feelings words, the discussion can continue when the teacher poses the question "Why do you think this person is sad/happy/angry?"

● *Music/Movement.* Music of all kinds encourages self-expression and permits an endless variety of movement and feelings to be shown openly and freely. Children can be introduced to classical, ethnic, jazz, or rock music while dancing with scarves or streamers or marching with rhythm sticks, as well as singing and dancing to children's recordings.[1] Because musical knowledge is the earliest of human intellectual competencies (see Chapter 13), music can be part of the curriculum for children as young as toddlers. Pounding on drums and dancing both relieve tension in a socially acceptable manner. More structured activities, such as showing children how to use musical instruments, must be balanced by plenty of freedom for individual musical expression.

Outdoors. The environment itself encourages self-expression. Whether in the sand or on a swing, children seem to open up emotionally as they relax in the physical freedom the out-of-doors fosters. Outdoor games are usually highly emotionally charged. Running, chasing, and the dramatic play of superheroes provide emotional release for children.

The outdoor area is an ideal place for large, noisy, and messy activities. It is ideal for tracing body outlines, for instance. These life-size portraits of each child reinforce self-concepts and encourage a feeling of pride in one's self. Woodworking is an outdoor activity that allows children to vent anger and tension. Nails won't be hurt no matter how hard they are pounded; there is satisfaction in sawing a piece of wood into two pieces. Music offers numerous opportunities for self-expression. Children can dance with scarves or streamers, march through the yard with drums pounding, imitate Wild Things, make a maypole around the tree, and create a Chinese dragon for a parade. A rich musical repertoire of band instruments, phonograph records, tapes, and voices can stimulate children to pretend to be elephants, tigers, and dinosaurs, as well as circus performers and ballet artists. Even a simple project such as water painting becomes an avenue for self-expression as children use paint brushes and buckets of water on trees, cement, and buildings, giving them all a fresh coat of "paint."

Routines, Transitions, and Groups

Routines, transitions, and group times have one thing in common: change. Because they all involve shifts from one kind of activity to another, there is a sense of uncertainty and they are emotionally charged. Children's behavior in these times is most likely to be unfocused. Here you will find the wandering and chasing, even oppositional or withdrawn behavior. Teachers help children best by creating an atmosphere of trust and clarity. Giving a child ideas of what to do ("Each of you can sponge a table now," or "You can sit on my lap while your Dad leaves today.") helps a child feel a sense of confidence in managing through a routine or transition. Specific suggestions for group behavior, including those generated from the class itself, inspire success. Finally, changes require teachers to be alert and flexible. As family caregiver McCormick (1993) puts it:

> Flexibility is the cornerstone of successful home child care, and an essential building block in provider/child relationships. Flexibility allows me to adapt to parents' changing schedules, children's changing sleep patterns, and even to alter the day's activities with the changing weather. By remaining flexible, especially to the children's needs, I have built a deep, personal relationship with each of the children I care for. I find ways to adapt to their schedules as much as possible instead of [always] forcing them into a [rigid] routine of the center.

Acknowledging a child's right to strong emotions and understanding a child's reactions to changes in these daily activities help children become comfortable and competent. Figure 14.9 outlines how specific materials and activities can be developed for emotional growth.

OUR DIVERSE WORLD OUR DIVERSE WORLD OUR DIVERSE WORLD OUR DIVERSE WORLD OUR DIVERSE WORLD OUR DIVERSE WORLD OUR DIVERSE WORLD OUR DIVERSE WORLD

[1] Music provides the perfect way to celebrate OUR DIVERSE WORLD—all cultures have music *and* it is all different. Carefully choose tapes for group times, for nap times, and for background music, with an awareness of and ear for diversity.

Curriculum for Emotional Skill Development

Indoor Activities

Art: Reflect children's expressions and see how they are feeling.
- ⬤ "You look as if you are enjoying yourself."
- ⬤ "Your face tells me that was funny (disappointing, etc.) to you."

Write what children say about their work on their creations, at the bottom of a picture, alongside a sculpture.

Blocks: Be there/be aware/ask them how it feels when:
⬤ You make a structure by yourself	⬤ Someone knocks it over (accidentally and on purpose)
⬤ It falls down	⬤ Someone laughs

Discovery/Science:
- ⬤ Use the words "curious" and "proud" to describe what children do as they experiment with materials.
- ⬤ Use the computer program "Choices, Choices."

Dramatic Play: Give children freedom, variety, and reflection.
- ⬤ Have a full-length mirror.
- ⬤ Provide a variety of role-play materials.
- ⬤ Include wall displays with multicultural, bias-free pictures.

Language/Library:

a. Have books that reflect a variety of feelings and ways to deal with them, such as:

Fear: *There's a Nightmare in My Closet* (Mayer); *Storm in the Night* (Stolz)

Self-Esteem: *The Growing Story* (Krauss); *Ruby* (Glen); *Things I Like* (Browne), *Amazing Grace* (Hoffman)

Loss: *The Maggie B* (Keats); *Amos and Boris* (Steig)

Change: *Changes, Changes* (Hutchins); *Sam Is My Half-Brother* (Boyd)

Friendship: *Two Is a Team* (Bemelman); *That's What Friends Are For* (Kidd); *Big Al* (Clements)

Security: *One Step, Two* (Zolotow); *The Bundle Book* (Zolotow); *Rise and Shine, Mariko-chan* (Tomioka)

Choice: *Best Enemies* (Leverich); *Did You Carry the Flag Today, Charly?* (Claudill)

b. Include books on themes, particularly when a child or group is dealing with an emotional issue:

Death: *Death and Dying* (Stein); *The Dead Bird* (Brown); *Nana Upstairs, Nana Downstairs* (de Paoli)

Divorce: *Two Places to Sleep* (Schuchman)

Doctor/Dentist: *Curious George Goes to the Hospital* (Rey); *Your Turn, Doctor* (Robison & Perez); *My Doctor* (Harlow)

Moving: *Mitchell Is Moving* (Sharmat); *Jamie* (Zolotow); *The Leaving Morning* (Johnson)

New Baby/Adoption: *Baby Sister for Frances* (Hoban); *I Want to Tell You about My Baby* (Banish); *Peter's Chair* (Keats); *The Chosen Baby* (Wasson)

Nightmares: *Where the Wild Things Are* (Sendak); *In the Night Kitchen* (Sendak); *There's a Nightmare in My Closet* (Mayer)

Spending the night: *Ira Sleeps Over* (Waber)

c. When reading stories, stop and ask how a particular character is feeling.

d. Tie in children's lives to books. For example, have children bring a special object or toy to share. A warm cuddly can be tied into the stories of *Goodnight Moon* (Brown) or *Teddy Bear's Picnic* (Kennedy).

Figure 14.9 ⬤ Whether 2 years old or in grade two, children learn about their feelings when teachers plan programs that encourage self-expression.

Outdoor Activities

Movement:

a. "How would you walk if you were glad?" (sad, mad, worried, giggly?)

b. "A Tiger Hunt" (this game is known by many names). Go on a "hunt" with children, using their bodies to describe such movements as opening/shutting a gate, swishing through tall grass, climbing a tree, swimming in water, going through mud, looking in a cave, running home so that the "tiger" doesn't catch us.

Music:

a. Choose several cuts of music that differ in tone and type. Ask children how each makes them feel, then have them show you with their bodies.

b. Write songs or chants about feelings.

Routines and Transitions

1. Respect children's feelings of anticipation.
   - Have a chart of daily activities.
   - Discuss upcoming field trips or visitors ahead of time when possible.
2. When unexpected changes occur, discuss them with individuals and the group.
   - "Andy isn't here today. He has a sore throat, so he is staying home. Esther will be the teacher in his group today."
3. When possible, let the children take responsibility for known sequences.
   - Set their own snack table.
   - Get flowers for the table.
   - Help clean a place for the next children.
4. Provide time for self-help *without unnecessary hurry.*
   - Put on their own name tag.
   - Wash and dry their own hands.
   - Dress themselves—jacket for outdoors, shoes after nap, and so on.
   - Take care of their rest items—blanket and stuffed toy in a labeled pillowcase, books back in a basket or bookshelf, and so on.

Group Times

1. Use children's faces as a focus.
   - Practice facial expressions with mirrors.
   - Call out feelings, having them show you on their faces.
   - Sing "If You're Happy and You Know It, . . ." with a variety of feelings. Ask children what situations have them feel each.
   - Show photographs of children's faces and expressions and ask the group to tell you how that person is feeling, why, and so on. Or do the same with the children's own drawings.
2. Try idea completions.
   - "I feel glad when . . ." (also mad, bad, sad, safe, excited, scared, silly)
   - "I like school when . . ." (also don't like, also my friend, mom, it)
   - "I wish . . .", "The best thing I can do . . ."
3. Use situations to elicit feelings.
   - "Here's a picture of a family. What are they doing? How does each person feel?"
   - "I'm going to cover part of the picture of the face to see if you can guess what expression it's going to be."
   - "These are cards of situations that the teachers have seen happen in our class. Let's read them and then ask ourselves, 'How do I feel? What can I say? What can I do?'"

Figure 14.9 ● Continued.

Focus on Skills

Emotional development is a lifelong process that requires experience with one's own feelings. Each child has a unique emotional foundation, which the knowledgeable teacher assesses. Only after assessment can teachers plan curriculum with realistic goals in mind for the children in that class. The goals teachers set for children will determine which emotional skills will be the focus as they individualize the curriculum. Maggie has difficulty with changes in the routine; Caroline never cries, no matter how she hurts; and Clyde screams when he is frustrated. To help children learn to *express and control their emotions*, teachers plan programs such as those illustrated in Figure 14.9.

Making choices is another worthwhile skill as an emotional focus. As does any skill, it takes thought and practice. To teach children to make choices, Simon (1994) suggests examining the process you use to make your own. "Think about your choice to become a teacher. What influenced your choice? What other options did you consider? What were the pros and cons of each of your options? Did your choice turn out as you expected? Would you make the same choice today? Why or why not?" To help children make choices and decisions, focus on a step-by-step process:

1. Help children define the situation by turning it into a question. (What can we do to fix up our playground?)

2. Make a list of options or alternatives. (Plant flowers, get more bikes, add more sand toys.)

3. Ask the children to think of what might happen for each option. (Flowers would look pretty, but we would have to water them.)

4. Make a choice. (This is the key point!)

5. Check later to see how the choice turned out. (Look how nice the yard is! or Darn, when we forgot to water, they died.)

Figure 7.13 offers a more detailed example of this process in social problem-solving.

Use of Themes

One particular theme, that of "Who Am I?", is useful when developing curriculum for emotional growth. Figure 14.11 outlines how this theme can be incorporated in many ways, both indoors and out. A number of other units can be developed to extend the

Figure 14.10 ● Teachers and children explore emotions together.

theme of "Who Am I?". Some of these are: "My Body," "The Senses," "The Community Where I Live," and so on.

● UNIT 14-1 Checkpoint

Emotional growth is a crucial part of children's development in the early years. Emotions develop as children respond to life experiences with a full range of feelings. An undifferentiated state of emotions during infancy evolves into a more refined array of feelings in childhood. Children gain control of their emotions through maturation and experience.

Emotional skills learned in the early years are: the ability to deal with feelings and with change, to be able to exercise judgment, to know and enjoy one's power. Teachers help children develop these skills by building a vocabulary of feeling words, by an awareness of the emotional climate in the classroom, by talking with children about their feelings, and by helping children sense the emotional framework of others. Self-esteem and self-concepts are enhanced by positive emotional growth.

Curriculum planning for emotional development involves an emphasis on many avenues for self-expression in the class setting, sometimes focusing on one particular emotional skill or theme that emphasizes emotional expression.

THEME: WHO AM I?

1. *Art:* Body outlines
   Facial expressions pictures—variations (a) look in a mirror, (b) have a blank face and you draw in the features, (c) have a face partly done and you complete, (d) magazine cut-outs
   Face painting
   Fingerprinting (hand and foot)
2. *Blocks:* People, furniture, structures people live in
   Pictures of same
3. *Cooking:* Share ethnic dishes (tortillas, pasta, things you like to cook at home)
4. *Discovery/science:* Height–weight charts
   Drawing around hands and feet and comparing sizes
   Doing body outlines of a large group of children, each with a different color, and comparing sizes
   Mapping—where people live, charts of phone numbers
   Put out a globe
   Weather–homes connections
5. *Dramatic play:* Lots of mirrors
   A variety of dress-up play for taking on a variety of roles and seeing how they feel
6. *Language/library:* Have children write books about themselves—variations: (a) use *Is This You?* (Krauss) as model, (b) loose-leaf binder of their own books they can add to themselves, (c) "Where I Live" as title, (d) families
   Books on children and families with diverse backgrounds (*Corduroy* [Freeman] lives in an apt.)
   Where animals live
   Feelings about where children live
7. *Manipulatives:* Puzzles with body parts, with people and clothing
   Self-help skills with dressing frames
   Encourage children to build a structure that things could live in; e.g., Lincoln Logs.
8. *Sand and water play:* Bubble-blowing
   Using your bodies to build—digging with hands and feet, encouraging sensory exploration
   Use body parts to help you: e.g., using your foot on the shovel
9. *Swinging/climbing:* Both of these activities use body parts; teachers help the children become aware of how they do physical activity
10. *Games:* Rolling the barrel, rolling yourself   Hide and Seek and Tag
    Mother May I?   Dramatic play games with family members
11. *Large block-building:* Making house-like structures
    Using vehicles that need your body's force to move
12. *Woodworking:* Using body parts
    Make a map board of school, neighborhood, a city
13. *Routines:* Self-help: Awareness of what you can do by yourself by definition of "Who Am I?" tasks; teachers use verbal and musical reinforcement
14. *Transitions:* Use physical characteristics of children for transitions—"Everyone who has brown eyes/freckles/blue jeans can go outside."
15. *Group times:* "Head and shoulders"
    Description games—describe someone and guess who it is as a game "I'm thinking of someone" or with song "Mary Has a Red Dress"
    "Little Tommy (Tina) Tiddlemouse," voice recognition
    "Good morning little Teddy Bear," with bear going around circle and saying names
16. *Snack time/bedtime:* Mark places with names and pictures, such as beds or placemats
    Try to coordinate the name tag, bed, or placemat with symbol on cubby

Figure 14.11 ● A child's school experience is strongly related to how emotional events are handled.

Ask yourself:

● What are the principles of emotional development? How will the 4 Is of I, independence, initiative, and interaction help in my teaching?

● What emotional skills are learned in early childhood?

● What is the role of the teacher in emotional development?

● What are three ways to plan curriculum that will enhance emotional growth?

● UNIT 14-2   Social Growth

THE DEVELOPMENT OF SOCIALIZATION

Social development is the process through which children learn what behavior is acceptable and expected. A set of standards is imposed on the child at birth that reflects the values of the family and the society in which the child lives.

Theorists from Freud and Piaget to Bandura and Gardner (see Chapters 4 and 13) acknowledge the relationship between social development and learning. Indeed, enhancing social intelligence builds a set of skills that may be among the most essential for life success of many kinds. How is it done?

Social development begins in the crib. Within the first few months of life, the infant smiles, coos, and plays in response to a human voice, face, or physical contact. Young children are influenced from birth by a conscious attempt on the part of adults to guide them in ways that society expects. Parents attempt to transmit behavior patterns that are characteristic of their culture, religion, gender, educational, and ethnic backgrounds.[1] Children imitate what they see; they adapt social expectations to their own personality.

This process—called **socialization**—includes learning appropriate behavior in a number of different settings. Children learn very early to discriminate between the expectations in different environments. At school, free exploration of play materials is encouraged, but in a church pew it is not. Grocery stores, circuses, libraries, and Grandma's home call for a repertoire of fitting behaviors.

In general, the socialization process in a school setting revolves around a child's relationships with other people. During this time of their lives, children work out a separate set of relationships with adults other than their parents. They establish different relationships with adults than they do with other children and, most important, they learn to interact with other children.

Through socialization, the customary roles that boys and girls play are also transmitted. Children come to understand how teachers, mommies, daddies, grandparents, males, and females are expected to act.[2]

Children also learn social attitudes at an early age. They learn to enjoy being with people and participating in social activities. At the same time, young children can also develop attitudes of bias, and it is in these early years that prejudicial behavior often begins (Derman-Sparks, 1989). Be honest about your feelings, for the teacher's role with negative comments, unfair acts, and exclusivity based on race, gender, or ability is crucial in combating this kind of socialization. Favorable attitudes toward people and a strong desire to be part of the social world, to be with others, are established in the early years.

Another important facet of socialization involves the development of a sense of community. Classrooms where children learn to care about each other and about the group have been described in the works of Gilligan (1982) and Noddings (1992, 1994). The classroom emotional climate and teacher's behavior contribute not only to children's sense of personal safety and belonging but also to the value of "a web of relationships that is sustained by a process of communication" (Gilligan, 1982). Moreover, teachers who strive for community awareness and bonding often do so by adhering to an anti-bias philosophy (see Chapter 9, among others) that promotes empathic interaction with people from diverse backgrounds and standing up for self and others in the face of bias (Derman-Sparks, 1994).

 OUR DIVERSE WORLD OUR DIVERSE WORLD OUR DIVERSE WORLD OUR DIVERSE WORLD OUR DIVERSE WORLD OUR DIVERSE WORLD OUR DIVERSE WORLD OUR DIVERSE WORLD

[1] The socialization of children ensures that the values and traditions of the culture are preserved.

[2] Early childhood professionals need to be aware of the difference between a child's developing a gender identity and a child's sex role development. One needs to be able to communicate the difference to parents and to be aware of how different cultures may have differing notions about sex role development.

The child's social development is an integral part of the total growth process. Cognitive and social growth are related. To consider the consequences of one's actions, for instance, one must have a certain level of intellectual understanding. According to Smith (1982), the manner in which children define their appearance influences their attitudes toward themselves and their relationships with others. Emotional development is affected also. When children conform to the behavior expected of them, they have a greater self-acceptance and like themselves better. Language, of course is what allows the socially developing child to communicate with others as part of the social process.

In the early years, children mature socially in discernible developmental stages. From birth to age 3, children's interest in others begins with a mutual gazing and social smile in the early months (birth through 8 months), continues with an exploration of others as well as some anxious behavior around strangers in the crawler and walker stages (8 to 18 months), and develops into an enjoyment of peers and adults along with an awareness of others' rights and feelings as a toddler and 2-year-old (18 months to 3 years) (Lally, Provence, Szanton, & Weissbourd, 1987).

In the preschool years, children learn to "control their aggressive impulses, think about others besides themselves, and resist doing what they shouldn't" (Schickedanz et al., 1993). This learning translates into four basic expectations: (1) that they will show interest in others, (2) that they will learn right from wrong, (3) that they will learn to get along with others, and (4) that they will learn a role for themselves that takes into consideration their own unique self—gender, race, ethnicity, and abilities.

Children of the primary years (5 to 8 years) show an increased interest in peers and social competence, and group rules become important. The development of a social conscience and of fairness rounds out the primary-grade developmental milestones (Bredekamp & Copple, 1997).

It is through play (as discussed in Chapter 11) that children learn much of their social repertoires. Dramatizations, role playing, and dramatic play provide opportunities to act out many roles and help children deal with some of the demands placed on them. In play, the child experiments with options: finding out what it feels like to be the boss, to be the baby, to behave in ways that might otherwise be unacceptable. Carla was the oldest of three children and had many "big girl" expectations placed on her within the family setting. At school, Carla enjoyed being the baby, acting out a helpless infant role whenever she could. Under the guise of play, children, like Carla, rehearse for life without suffering the real-life consequences. Figure 14.12 traces the route of social development from infancy through the primary years.

Peer Relationships

For the young child, social development means the steady movement away from the **egocentric** position of self (and parents) as central points toward a more **sociocentric** viewpoint that involves others— both adults and, especially, children. During the early years, the child learns to socialize outside the family; social contacts outside the home reinforce the enjoyment of social activities and prepare the child for future group activity. The intricacies of peer relationships are detailed in Cary Buzzelli's Focus Box.

Peer interactions, that is, associations with friends of the same age group, become important to the child once infancy and early toddlerhood are past. Through peer interactions, children can identify with models who are like themselves and can learn from each other's behavior. Friends provide models for imitation, for comparison, and for confirmation of themselves, and they are a source of support.

Playing with other children begins with solitary parallel play at around 2 years of age, where two or more children are in the same area with each other but do not initiate social interaction. By the ages of 3 and 4, more interaction takes place: there are conversation and conflict as well as cooperation in playing together.

There are stages in children's friendships. In the early years, friendship starts at an **undifferentiated** level, when children are egocentric and a friend is more of the moment. This gives way to a **unilateral** level; a good friend does what the child wants the friend to do. Toward the end of early childhood, friendship becomes more **reciprocal**, involving some give-and-take in a kind of two-way cooperation. Listen to these children trying out their friendship:

Chris: I'll be the teacher, you be the kid.

Suzanne: NO! I want to be the teacher, too.

Chris: No! No! You can't be the teacher, too, cause then there'd be no kids.

Suzanne: OK. Next time, I get to be the teacher.

SOCIAL DEVELOPMENT TIMELINE

Infant-Toddler	Preschooler	Primary Child
Response to Other's Distress Reacts emotionally by experiencing what the other seems to feel	Begins to make adjustments that reflect the realization that the other person is different and separate from self	Takes other's personality into account and shows concern for other's general condition
Peer Interaction ● First encounters mutual inspection ● First social contacts ● (18 mo) growth in sensitivity to peer play ● (2 yr) able to direct social acts to two children at once (beginning of social interaction)	● Adjustment in behavior to fit age and behavior of other ● (3+ yr) friendship as momentary ● (3–5 yr) beginning of friendship as constant	● Friend as someone who will do what you want ● Beginning of friend as one who embodies admirable, constant characteristics
Social Roles ● (10–20 days) imitation of adults ● (3 mo) gurgle in response to others ● (6 mo) social games based on imitation ● (18 mo) differentiation between reality and pretend play ● (2 yr) make doll do something as if it were alive	● (3 yr) make a doll carry out several roles or activities ● (4–5 yr) act out a social role in dramatic play and integrate that role with others (mom and baby)	● (6 yr) integrate one role with two complementary roles: doctor, nurse, and sick person ● (8 yr) growing understanding that roles can influence behavior (doctor whose daughter is a patient)

Figure 14.12 ● A timetable of social development for the ages of infancy through the primary years. (Special thanks to Gay Spitz.)

Figure 14.13 ● Through play, children learn to get along with one another.

Figure 14.14 ● Socialization involves learning how to solve problems and interact with others, particularly in conflict resolution.

Chris: Maybe! OK, everybody go wash your hands for snack time. Suzanne, you can pass out your very nutritious snack to everybody.

Suzanne: Superfasmic, I'm the boss of snack.

A peer group is important for a number of reasons. Social development is enhanced because a child learns to conform to established social standards outside of his home setting. The expectations of the larger society are reinforced. To become autonomous, the child must also learn to achieve independence from the family, especially parents. Young children must also come to understand themselves as part of society. Their self-concepts are enlarged by a group of peers as they see how others respond to them and treat them.

Making and keeping friends are essential to children's positive social development, so important that children without friends by the primary years are considered at risk for overall school success (Bullock, 1993; Lawhon, 1997). Understanding friendship and social interaction is basic required knowledge of every early childhood teacher, for children's constructed knowledge about how to interact with people is more complicated than that of objects or materials. Adults can promote basic skills, take responsibility for guidance and instruction, model constructive and inclusive interactions, and keep track of each child's developing friendships.[1]

Smith (1982) states that three trends emerge in the way children relate to each other. First, children become more sensitive to their play partners. Second, they begin to use language more effectively in their interactions. Finally, cooperative play increases as parallel play decreases. Children pass through three stages of social understanding in the early years: (1) they shift from a preoccupation with self to an awareness of the thoughts and feelings of another; (2) they shift from the observable, physical qualities of the play partner to an awareness of their friend's less obvious characteristics; and (3) they begin to perceive the friendship as long lasting.

SOCIAL SKILLS IN EARLY CHILDHOOD

Social skills are strategies children learn that enable them to behave appropriately in many environments. They help children learn to initiate or manage social interaction in a variety of settings and with a number of people.

Social cognition plays a part in the development of social skills. It is the application of thinking to personal and social behavior; it is giving meaning to social experience. Nadia used the cognitive skill of memory when she wanted to play with Paul, a very popular 4-year-old. She remembered Paul's interest in the rope swing and challenged him to swing higher than she did. Bruno, on the other hand, is well known throughout the group for his inability to share materials. When Sandy wanted to play with the small fire trucks (Bruno's favorite toys), she used cognitive skills to negotiate the use of one truck. Social cognition requires children to interpret events and make decisions, to consider the impact of their behavior on others, and to consider the cause as well as the consequence of an action. Cognitive skills are necessary when we ask children to seek alternative solutions to social problems: "How else could you ask him for a turn, Pete?" These are all social cognition skills, and they serve as the basis for the acquisition of other skills.

In an early childhood setting, children learn a great deal about social behavior and expectations. They develop many skills as they learn to interact with adults other than their parents and children other than their siblings. Social skills emerge as children learn to function as members of a group and as they come to understand themselves as social beings. The social skills of early childhood, then, are complex and change with the age and experience of the individual child. This section details some of the specific social skills and values young children learn.

 OUR DIVERSE WORLD OUR DIVERSE WORLD OUR DIVERSE WORLD OUR DIVERSE WORLD OUR DIVERSE WORLD OUR DIVERSE WORLD OUR DIVERSE WORLD OUR DIVERSE WORLD

[1] Developing friendships is more than teaching general interpersonal skills and is especially important for children with special needs (Lowenthal, 1996). Facilitating friendship development in inclusive classrooms requires teacher awareness and interaction as well as careful environmental and schedule planning.

Helping Children's Friendships

Cary Buzzelli

Research indicates that children who have positive relations with their peers are more successful in school and are better socially adjusted later in life. But not all children are readily accepted by their peers. Indeed, some children are actively rejected by classmates. What's a teacher to do? Can we "force" children to be included, or "muscle" a group of youngsters to let everybody else play?

Through careful observation, teachers *can* determine appropriate ways to assist rejected children in becoming more socially competent. For example, in one classroom of 4-year-olds, Carlos and Felicia were seldom asked to join in the play by other children. When Carlos approached, the children seemed to ignore him. And when Felicia came near, children often told her to get away. The teachers wondered why both children seemed to be unattractive to their peers, and so watched the two closely.

They discovered that Carlos and Felicia were being rejected for very different reasons. Carlos appeared to lack the skills needed to initiate and maintain play. Whenever anyone did approach him, he would drop his eyes or respond in a negative manner, such as frowning or turning away. Once play was started, he appeared to not know how to "keep it going," he would stand and watch, not adding to the play with his actions or ideas. Felicia, on the other hand, was very actively involved—too much so. She was aggressive during interactions with the other children. Either physically or verbally, she would take over the play, interrupting others with her ideas and grabbing at toys and materials.

The teachers realized that different strategies were necessary to help Carlos and Felicia. Coaching Carlos in positive ways of initiating play with other children would help, such as getting him more comfortable with someone's invitation so that he might respond with a smile instead of a frown. Also, modeling how to keep the play going with ideas or additional materials could help him play cooperatively and for longer periods of time. Felicia could also use a teacher role model, helping her to stay calm in situations that frustrate her or to use her words instead of grabbing to get what she wants. Indeed, a teacher alongside Felicia might help her watch how other children "get their way" and still play together.

Not all children need or even want to be so-called superstars, yet every child needs to gain the confidence and competence to engage in positive relations with peers. Being able to interact with others will greatly enhance young children's social and emotional development.

Cary Buzzelli of Indiana University is a frequent contributor to Young Children *and a long-time researcher in issues of friendship and self-esteem.*

Skills Learned with Adults

In their relationship with adults, children learn:

● They can stay at school without parents.

● They can enjoy adults other than parents and respond to new adults.

● Adults will help in times of trouble or need.

● Adults will help them learn social protocol.

● Adults will keep children from being hurt and from hurting others.

● Adults will help children learn about ethnic differences and similarities, disabilities, gender identity, and language diversity.

● Adults will resist bias and stereotyping and teach children to actively do the same.

● Adults will not always take a side or solve the problem.

● Adults will work with them to solve problems.

● Adults believe that every child has a right to a satisfying social experience at school.

Skills Learned with Peers

In their relationship with other children, children learn:

● There are different approaches to others; some work, some don't.

● Interactive skills, and how to sustain the relationship.

● How to solve conflicts in ways other than retreat or force.

● How to share materials, equipment, other children, friends, teachers, and ideas.

● How to achieve mutually satisfying play.

● Self-defense, and how to assert their rights in socially acceptable ways.

● How to take turns and how to communicate desires.

● Negotiating skills.

Figure 14.16 ● Rejection is a common form of social behavior in young children. In the early years children need to deal with the feelings that arise when they are told, "You can't play with us."

Figure 14.15 ● Peer relationships are a source of pleasure and support. As social understanding develops, children shift from a preoccupation with themselves to an awareness of the thoughts and feelings of their friends.

Figure 14.17 ● Cooperation: "I'll help you, then you'll help me."

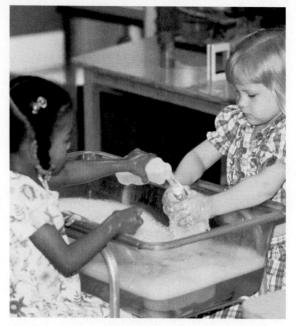

Figure 14.18 ● Friendship: "I'll help you fill that up."

● How to be helpful to peers with tasks, information, and by modeling behavior.

● To anticipate and avoid problems.

● Realistic expectations of how other children behave and respond toward them.

● Ways to deal with socially awkward situations and with socially difficult situations and children.

● How to make, be, share, and lose a friend.

Skills Learned in a Group

In groups, children learn:

● How to take part as a member and not as an individual.

● That there are activities that promote group association (stories, music).

● A group identity (center room class, Mrs. T's group, 4-year-old group).

● To follow a daily schedule and pattern.

● To adapt to school routines.

● School rules and expectations.

● Interaction and participatory skills: how to enter and exit from play.

● To respect the rights, feelings, and property of others.

● To become socially active, especially in the face of unfair or biased behavior and situations.

● How to work together as a group, during cleanup time, in preparation for an event, etc.

● How to deal with delay of gratification: how to wait.

Skills Learned As an Individual

As individuals, children learn:

● To take responsibility for self-help, self-care.

● To initiate their own activities and to make choices.

● To work alone close to other children.

● To notice unfairness and injustice and learn how to handle them.

● To negotiate.

● To cope with rejection, hurt feelings, disappointment.

● To communicate in verbal and nonverbal ways, and when to use communication skills.

● To test limits other people set.

● Their own personal style of peer interaction: degree, intensity, frequency, quality.

● To express strong feelings in socially acceptable ways.

● To manage social freedom.

Specific skills within these four areas include the social and moral aspects of nurturance, kindness, and sharing (Kemple, 1991). As children get older, these skills become more specific, including telling the truth; taking turns, or reciprocity; keeping promises; property rights; and rules (DeVries & Kohlberg, 1987).

Another social skill that has taken hold in the last decade is that of **social action**. In an anti-bias curriculum (see Chapter 9), children can learn how to take social action to make unfair things fair. For instance, preschoolers discover that their adhesive strips are labeled "flesh-colored" but match the skin of only a few children; they take photos and send them to the company (Derman-Sparks, 1989). Promoting activism may not always bring successful results, but the activity and the model are powerful learning experiences.

THE TEACHER'S ROLE

Considerations

A major role for the early childhood teacher is to see that children have enjoyable social contacts and to help motivate children toward a desire to be with others. The early childhood setting affords children numerous learning opportunities for social development.

The teacher has an important role to play as children learn the give-and-take of social interaction. In the role of social organizer, the teacher creates a physical and interpersonal environment that promotes the development of children's social skills.

A first consideration is to *plan and arrange a social environment* to enhance appropriate social behaviors. Child-initiated activities, self-care, and

Figure 14.19 ● Helping: "I'll help clean up."

group responsibility are stimulated by the use of low, open shelves and furniture scaled to size. Group activities, toys, materials, and placement of furniture should be structured in ways that allow children to play alone or with someone. Many areas lend themselves to group play, such as dramatic play corners or blocks. Books, puzzles, and easels, on the other hand, can be a singular experience or can generate associative play. Cooperative play is suggested when there is more than one piece of equipment. The placement of two telephones, three wagons, and eight firefighter hats fosters child–child interactions. The teacher must also allow enough time in the daily schedule for children to get thoroughly involved in playing with one another.

A second part of the teacher's role in social development is to *help children develop trust*. Trusting, in themselves, their peers, and their teachers, is a part of learning about social relationships. Teachers enhance children's social knowledge as they gradually improve their sense of trust. Both professionals and researchers (Buzzelli & File, 1989; Coles, 1991; Derman-Sparks, 1994) recommend specific actions for teachers to take:

1. *Help children recognize their own needs.* Notice children who need to clarify their wishes; ask uninvolved children with whom they'd like to play; help arguing children say how they feel and what they want.

2. *Increase children's awareness of their social goals and the goals of others.* Teachers can aid children by helping them recognize their choices; they can

also meditate so that others can express themselves.

3. *Help children develop effective social skills.* Provide a model for listening, for choosing another place to play, or for going along with another's ideas; help children find ways to stand their ground and also accommodate and learn to use conflict resolution, cooperation, coping, and helping skills (see Figure 7.15 and this chapter's "Focus on Skills" section).

4. *Teach children to recognize others' emotions and intentions.* Children become flooded with their own strong feelings and are not likely to notice someone else's emotions in the heat of the moment; teachers can help children see another's face or hear a tone of voice, thus beginning to "read" another person.

5. *Reflect with children on how their behavior affects others by pointing out what is predictable in their interactions.* Young children do not always "connect the dots" between their behavior and others' reactions. When a teacher makes a statement without disapproval, the child can then understand the effects of her or his behavior on others: "Wow! When you use that loud voice, I see the kids looking scared, and then they tell you not to play here."

6. *Highlight children's success by helping them learn to monitor their own behavior.* It can help children to see their successful social encounters as well as the strategies that didn't work. "When you asked them if you could play, they said, 'No!' But then you went and got shovels for everyone and that worked!"

7. *Avoid telling children who their "friends" are.* Early childhood teachers encourage children to learn about friendship; however, "legislating friendship" often backfires. Telling children "We're all friends here," or "Friends share their things with everyone" denies the distinction between positive, friendly experiences and friendship. *Classmate* and *friend* are not the same word.

8. *Develop a set of strategies to help the socially awkward and troubled in your class.* Although each child is unique, there are certain situations that arise time and again in an early childhood classroom. Children who are socially inept often do not use nonverbal language effectively and are

"out-of-synch" because they miss the signs (Nowicki & Duke, 1992).

9. *Work to provide a caring community in your class.* "In order for children to have the confidence to take the risks inherent in learning . . . they must experience a consistently accepting, inclusive and predictable atmosphere in the classroom" (Maniates & Heath, 1998). Brain research (see Chapter 4) confirms this point, and an anti-bias approach (see Chapters 3 and 9) supports the development of *social action* as an extension of "making right" the classroom and beyond.

10. *Invite parents and families into the process of children's socialization.* Both teachers and families share in the responsibility of helping children develop social skills; neither one can do it alone. There are many ways to make your program family friendly; see Chapter 8 for suggestions.

The teacher's role in social development is also one of *facilitating children's interactions and interpreting their behavior.* To help young children understand each other and to pave the way for continued cooperation, the teacher reports and reflects on what is happening. In the classroom setting, during an active, free-play period, the teacher might:

Reflect the Action:	Say:
Call attention to the effect one child's behavior is having on another.	"Randy, when you scream like that, other children become frightened and are afraid to play with you."
Show approval and reinforce positive social behavior.	"I like the way you carefully stepped over their block building, Dannetta."
Support a child in asserting her rights.	"Chrystal is hanging on to the doll because she isn't finished playing yet, Wilbur."
Support a child's desire to be independent.	"I know you want to help, Keyetta, but Sammy is trying to put his coat on by himself."
Acknowledge and help children establish contact with others.	"Omar would like to play, too. That's why he brought you another bucket of water. Is there a place where he can help?"

Reflect back to a child the depth of his feelings and what form those feelings might take.

"I know George made you very angry when he took your sponge, but I can't let you throw water at him. What can you tell him? What words can you use to say you didn't like what he did?"

Adult responses to children's play are particularly critical in supporting positive social development. The teacher has a powerful, emotional role in children's lives at school. As mentioned earlier, early childhood is a time when children make judgments in error, coming to conclusions about children on the basis of race, gender, native language, or ability. The teacher must intervene, for silence signals tacit approval. How does a teacher engage children in acting on their social environment so that they learn from one another and accept the realities and benefits of living together? In carefully observing and participating with children, the teacher must decide when and how to intervene and tap into children's own belonging social skills and social and moral judgment—without taking over. This is perhaps the most dynamic and challenging part of teachers' jobs, the heart of the profession. Conflicts and their resolution illustrate the interaction between teacher and children and the critical part teachers play in children's lives. Illustrated in Chapter 7 and Figure 7.13, the social problems in early childhood range from possession of toys, to hitting others, to keeping promises. *How* a teacher helps children identify and resolve their own conflicts is often more important than the specific problem or solution.

Curriculum Planning for Social Growth

In the Environment

Teaching social behavior in most classrooms usually occurs in response to spontaneous situations. The teacher's direct involvement in children's social interactions is the most frequent method used. Occasionally, teachers will approach the acquisition of social skills in a more formalized way through planned curriculum activities. The way the environment is arranged has a profound effect on social interaction among children.

Indoors. Most indoor activities are planned and set up to encourage participation by more than one child at a time.

The Arts. At the art table, four or more children will share collage materials, paste, and sponges that have been placed in the center of the table. When easels are placed side by side, conversation occurs spontaneously among children. A small table, placed between the easels, on which a tray of paint cups is placed, also encourages children's interactions. If there is only one of each color, the children will have to negotiate with one another for the color they want to use.

Blocks/Manipulatives. A large space for block cabinets gives children a visual cue that there is plenty of room for more than one child. Puzzle tables set with three or four puzzles also tell children that social interaction is expected. Many times children will talk, play, and plan with one another as they share a large bin full of Legos® or plastic building towers. A floor puzzle always requires a group: some to put the picture together, others to watch and make suggestions. As children build with blocks next to one another, they soon share comments about their work; many times this sharing leads to a mutual effort on a single building.

Discovery/Science. Many science projects can be arranged to involve more than one child. A display of magnets with a tray of assorted objects can become the focus of several children as they decide which objects will be attracted to the magnets. Cooking together, weighing and measuring one another, and caring for classroom pets can be times when teachers reinforce social skills.

Dramatic Play. This area more than any other seems to draw children into contact with one another. Provide an assortment of family life accessories— dress-up clothes, kitchen equipment and utensils— and children have little trouble getting involved. A shoe needs to be tied or a dress zippered up. Someone must come eat the delicious meal just cooked or put the baby to bed. A medical theme in this classroom area also enhances children's social skills. They learn to take each other's temperature, listen to heartbeats, and plan operations, all of which require more than one person.

Language/Library. Children enjoy reading books and stories to one another, whether or not they know the words. Favorite books are often shared by two children who enjoy turning the pages and talking over the story together. Lotto games encourage children to become aware of one another, to look at each person's card in order to identify who has the picture to match. Name songs and games, especially early in the year, help children learn to call each other by name.

- *Music Movement.* Build in regular times for music and movement activities. The entire group can participate in familiar songs; a sense of community is built by everyone's participation. Activities during the free choice times usually involve smaller numbers, where group members can challenge one another to new ways to dance with scarves or use the tumbling mat. Finally, one-to-one experiences encourage new friendships as the intimacy of a shared musical experience brings two children or a teacher and child together.

Outdoors. The outdoor environment can be structured in ways to support group play.

- *Painting or Pasting.* Painting or pasting on murals or drawing chalk designs on the cement are art activities that promote social interaction.

- *Planning and Planting a Garden.* Planning and planting a garden is a long-range project that involves many children. Decisions must be made by the group about what to plant, where to locate the garden, how to prepare the soil, and what the shared responsibilities of caring for the garden will be.

- *Gross-Motor Activities.* Most gross-motor activities stimulate group interactions. Seesaws, jump ropes, and hide-and-seek require at least two people to participate. A-frames, boards, and boxes, as well as other movable equipment, need the cooperative effort of several children in order to be rearranged. Sand play, when accompanied by water, shovels, and other accessories, draws a number of children together to create rivers, dams, and floods. Ball games and relay races also encourage social relationships.

Routines, Transitions, and Groups

Routines and transitions are often social experiences, as they provide children with an opportunity for support and peer interaction. Teachers use these times as an opportunity to build social skills. For instance, the routine of nap preparation can be structured with a "buddy" system so that older children are paired with

the younger ones to set up the cots, choose a cuddly or books, and get tucked in. A cleanup time transition can be made fun and successful if children can wear a necklace to depict the job or area. Another way is to provide a basket of "pick-up" cards; bringing out the basket signals cleanup time and allows children to choose their chores. Children with similar cleanup cards get a sense of teamwork when putting an activity area back in order.

As a directed learning experience, small-group times afford an opportunity to focus on social skills in a more structured way. Small groups provide a setting for children and teachers to participate in more relaxed, uninterrupted dialogue. The intimacy of the small group sets the stage for many social interactions.

Grouptime discussions can focus on problems that children can solve. Too many children crowding the water table, a child's fear of fire drills, or the noise level on a rainy day are subjects children will talk about in small groups. The most relevant situations are ones that occur naturally in the course of a program. Another curriculum idea is to make "Situation Cards" of these and other common incidents. For instance, teachers can create illustrated cards that pose situations such as:

- You tell your friends to "stop it" when they take part of the toy you are using, but they do it again.

- You open your lunch and your mom or dad has packed your favorite foods.

- You come down the slide and your teacher calls "Hooray for you!"

- You promise your friend you'll play with him at recess, but then someone else you like asks you to play with her.

The teacher then guides a discussion around the questions "How do you feel? What can you say? What can you do?" This activity can be simplified or elaborated depending on the individuals and group involved.

Solutions may emerge when the teacher supports active and involved participation. Teachers pose the problem and ask children to respond in several ways: "How does it make you and others feel when that happens? What can you and others do about it? What are some alternatives?" The problems must be real, and they must be about something that is important to children. Figure 14.20 is an example of a sequentially planned curriculum that fosters the development of social skills in small group settings.

Curriculum for Social Skill Development

Time	Skill	Activities
Week 1	Developing a positive self-image	Do thumb print art. Make foot- and handprints. Compare children's baby pictures with current photos. Play with mirrors: make faces, emotional expressions. Dress felt dolls in clothing. Sing name songs: "Mary Wore Her Red Dress." Make a list: "What I like to do best is . . ." Post in classroom. Do a self-portrait in any art medium. Make a silhouette picture of each child.
Week 2	Becoming a member of a group	Take attendance together: Who is missing? Play picture lotto with photographs of children. Play "Farmer in the Dell." Share a favorite toy from home with older children. Tape record children's voices, guess who they are. Have a "friendly feast": each child brings favorite food from home to share.
Week 3	Forming a friendship within the group	Provide one puzzle (toy, game, book) for every two children. Take a "Buddy Walk"; return and tell a story together of what you saw. Play "Telephone Talk": pretend to invite your friend over to play. Play "copy cat": imitate your friend's laugh, walk, cry, words. Practice throwing and catching balls with one another. Form letter together with two children's bodies: A, T, C, K, etc. Play tug-of-war with your friend. Build a house out of blocks together. Make "mirror image" movements with your friend.
Week 4	Working together as a group	Play with a parachute; keep the ball bouncing. Make snacks for the rest of the class. Plan and plant a garden. Make a mural together to decorate the hallways. Play "Follow the Leader." Sing a round: "Row, Row, Row Your Boat."
Week 5	Learning a group identity	Make a map of the town and have children place their house on it. Take a field trip together. Print a newspaper with articles by and about each child. Select and perform a favorite story for the rest of the class. Take a group snapshot. Make a "family tree" of photos of children in group. Learn a group folk dance. Make a mural of handprints joined in a circle.

Figure 14.20 ● Building social skills through small-group experiences, beginning with an understanding of self and moving toward an appreciation of group membership. (See Chapter 11 for specific guidelines to lesson and unit planning.)

Focus on Skills

Social development for the preschool child includes gaining an awareness of the larger community in which the child lives. The early childhood curriculum contains elements of what is often in the later grades called social studies. Visits from police officers, mail carriers, firefighters, and other community helpers are common in many programs. Learning about children from other cultures, exploring the neighborhood around the center, and making maps are other ways children learn social studies skills.[1]

Sharing. Learning to share involves using or enjoying something in common with others. Although sharing may seem simple to adults, it is not a skill that is learned overnight, nor is it easy to orchestrate in young children. Young children understand sharing in different ways at different ages. As a teacher, ask yourself what sharing means to you. Does it mean giving up one's possessions when someone else wants them? Taking turns? Using a timer or the clock? Or dividing everything equally? Moreover, does sharing mean never getting it back, or losing the thread of the play to the intruder? Toddlers and the 2-year-olds are rarely ready to share on their own. Grabbing what they want makes sense to them, and sharing a toy or space feels like giving it up forever. Preschoolers share more readily because of the experiences they have had in "getting it back," and because of the fuss they have seen occur when they do not share. School-age children begin to be aware that some children feel the same as they do and that others may have needs and wishes different from their own. Thus, sharing makes more sense over time. In the classroom, teachers can help by:

● *Understanding child development* and that it is normal not to want to share and to have trouble doing so

● *Explaining in simple terms* what they want the child to do

● *Making sure that children "get back"* what they have shared so that taking turns really works

● *Being an example of sharing* because "Do as I do" is more powerful than "Do it because I told you to."

● *Letting the children experience ownership,* too, because children can't really know what it means to share until they know what it means to own something.

Cooperating. Learning how to cooperate with others is one primary social skill in which young children need plenty of practice. Toddlers and 2-year-olds can begin to see the benefits of cooperation as they become more aware of others' feelings and wishes, and as teachers help all children get what they want through taking turns, dividing materials, looking for another item when it is in demand. Three- to 5-year-olds become more cooperative as they learn more self-help skills (motor development) and can express themselves (language development) as well as remember guidelines and understand reasons for prosocial behavior (cognitive development). School-age children develop an emotional sense of competence (see discussion of Erik Erikson's work in Chapter 4). They do this by acquiring knowledge and skills recognized by our culture as important (e.g., reading and writing in elementary school) and then using them with peers.[2] Children can learn and rehearse their skills in many areas of the classroom (Figure 14.21).

In preschool and primary classrooms, teachers often involve children in "*cooperative learning*" as a strategy that enhances cognitive learning through social interaction. Involving children's participation in small group learning activities, cooperative learning promotes social and academic interaction, increases enthusiasm and motivation, and rewards group participation.

Structured activities that promote cooperation (see Figure 14.21) help children become aware of and learn to work with others and to see viewpoints other than their own. Although most children spontaneously interact in free play periods (thus learning social skills in the process), some children need the structure of a more teacher-directed group activity to promote social development. Moreover, children's

OUR DIVERSE WORLD OUR DIVERSE WORLD OUR DIVERSE WORLD OUR DIVERSE WORLD OUR DIVERSE WORLD OUR DIVERSE WORLD OUR DIVERSE WORLD OUR DIVERSE WORLD OUR DIVERSE WORLD

[1] Notice that these job titles are not gender specific. Try to invite men and women in nontraditional jobs to visit and talk about or demonstrate their work.

[2] Be sure to include skills that are important to each child's culture and family.

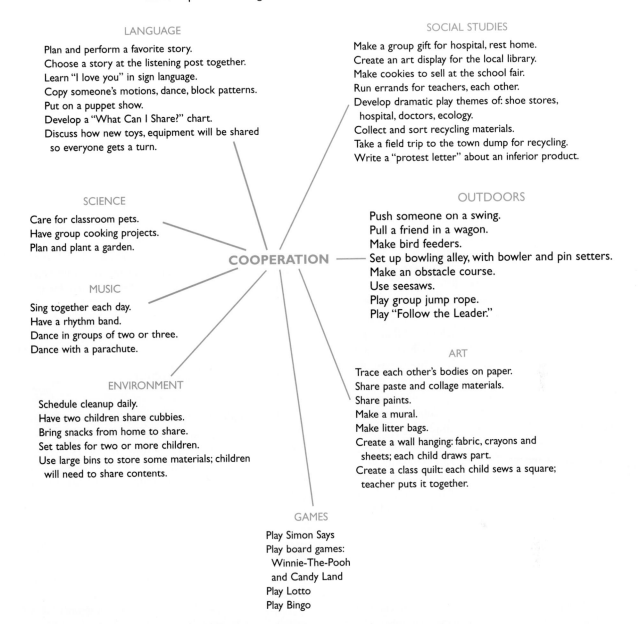

LANGUAGE

Plan and perform a favorite story.
Choose a story at the listening post together.
Learn "I love you" in sign language.
Copy someone's motions, dance, block patterns.
Put on a puppet show.
Develop a "What Can I Share?" chart.
Discuss how new toys, equipment will be shared
  so everyone gets a turn.

SOCIAL STUDIES

Make a group gift for hospital, rest home.
Create an art display for the local library.
Make cookies to sell at the school fair.
Run errands for teachers, each other.
Develop dramatic play themes of: shoe stores,
  hospital, doctors, ecology.
Collect and sort recycling materials.
Take a field trip to the town dump for recycling.
Write a "protest letter" about an inferior product.

SCIENCE

Care for classroom pets.
Have group cooking projects.
Plan and plant a garden.

COOPERATION

OUTDOORS

Push someone on a swing.
Pull a friend in a wagon.
Make bird feeders.
Set up bowling alley, with bowler and pin setters.
Make an obstacle course.
Use seesaws.
Play group jump rope.
Play "Follow the Leader."

MUSIC

Sing together each day.
Have a rhythm band.
Dance in groups of two or three.
Dance with a parachute.

ENVIRONMENT

Schedule cleanup daily.
Have two children share cubbies.
Bring snacks from home to share.
Set tables for two or more children.
Use large bins to store some materials; children
  will need to share contents.

ART

Trace each other's bodies on paper.
Share paste and collage materials.
Share paints.
Make a mural.
Make litter bags.
Create a wall hanging: fabric, crayons and
  sheets; each child draws part.
Create a class quilt: each child sews a square;
  teacher puts it together.

GAMES

Play Simon Says
Play board games:
  Winnie-The-Pooh
  and Candy Land
Play Lotto
Play Bingo

Figure 14.21 ● The social skill of cooperation can be fostered throughout the curriculum. (How to plan a lesson and build a unit are discussed in Chapter 11.)

friendships can be expanded by the guided affiliation determined by a teacher and a project.

Successful implementation of cooperative learning activities in both older preschoolers and early elementary children usually needs a clear focus of project or activity (such as eating a snack, writing a newsletter, building a model, or catching a hamster on the loose). The group size and, often, members are determined by the teacher, who also needs to make the expectations for group behavior known. The teacher then monitors the interaction, providing assistance, clarification, or problem-solving as needed. Evaluation is based on observation, and the group is rewarded for its success.

Being Included. Young children get involved in a variety of interpersonal situations that are beyond their capacities to handle with grace. An overly aggressive child, one who withdraws or stays apart from social opportunities, someone who chronically interrupts or disrupts the play, children who deliberately leave another out—all may end up becoming rejected by their peers. These socially awkward or troubled children need special help to learn the strategies for being included that *all* children have to learn. Developing a conflict resolution curriculum will help all children learn the communication and coping skills necessary for being included (Carlsson-Paige et al., 1992; Dodge, 1991; Gordon & Browne, 1996; Miller, 1998; Porro, 1996). Children who learn good observation and body language skills can then be helped to participate successfully in situations that require prosocial behaviors. In addition, children will need guidance and practice in deciding how to include others whose appearance, interests, age, or behavior differs from their own (Paley, 1992). Chapter 7 has additional suggestions.

Helping. One area of social development that is sometimes not emphasized in an individualistic society or classroom is that of *helping others*. In the past, it was thought that children's egocentric thinking prevented them from developing empathy or helping one another in a genuine way until later in childhood. Good early education programs, however, emphasize cooperation (see earlier section in this chapter) and find that children spontaneously offer help and sympathy to those in need. Curriculum can be developed from the classroom ("What can we do when someone's sad to say goodbye to Mom?") and the larger world ("Some children have noticed a lot of trash in the park next door.") to enhance children's helping skills.[1]

Use of Themes

A popular theme that lends itself to social growth is that of friendship. This has particular appeal during February, when the meaning of friendship is enhanced by the celebration of Valentine's Day. At other times, relay races and noncompetitive games (those in which everyone is a winner) promote working with friends to achieve a goal. Teachers who encourage children to help each other read, tie shoes, pour milk, fasten a smock, or sponge a table reinforce what friendship can

be in the early years. Many books and songs can be found that emphasize friendship. Group discussions can help children define what is a friend.

Children can observe friendships that cross age group, race, gender, and ability. Figure 14.22 illustrates how a unit on friendship can be developed for a setting with children as young as 3 and as old as third grade. Other themes can be generated from the children. "Make It Fair" in a first grade classroom was started from a child's complaint about the raisins in her cereal ("not enough," she said). Teachers wanting to create more prosocial and global awareness can develop themes around community service; for example, second graders can make monthly visits to a nearby retirement home for sing-a-longs and readings. A third grade class can hold bake sales to buy rainforest acreage. Figure 14.23 shows a "Family" unit for the early primary (K–1) level.

● UNIT 14-2 Checkpoint

Early in life children become aware of their social nature. The socialization process begins under the guidance of parents and family members. When children enter group settings, they are further exposed to behavior, social rules, and attitudes that foster social development. Much of a child's social repertoire is learned by playing with other children.

Children learn a great many social skills in these early years. They learn to enjoy and trust adults other than their parents. In their relationships with others, children learn ways to cooperate, disagree, share, communicate, and assert themselves effectively.

Children also learn how to be a member of a group—to take part in group activities, to adapt to school expectations, and to respect the rights and feelings of others. The young child also learns to express feelings in appropriate ways and to begin self-care tasks.

Teachers plan and arrange the early childhood environment in ways that will promote social growth and interaction. The adults help children understand

OUR DIVERSE WORLD OUR DIVERSE WORLD OUR DIVERSE WORLD OUR DIVERSE WORLD OUR DIVERSE WORLD OUR DIVERSE WORLD OUR DIVERSE WORLD OUR DIVERSE WORLD

[1] Be aware that some cultures in your classroom have a more cooperative orientation and can offer help to the teacher who is trying to expand from an individualistic focus to a more communal one.

Theme: Friendship

Concepts Children Will Learn	Activity
Everyone has a name and likes to have it used.	Friendship songs, using children's names
Each person is something special and unique.	Make a "Friend Puppet" with paper plates, tongue depressor handles. Child decorates it with felt pieces and yarn to look like a friend.
Friends are different; they do not all look the same.	Children respond to: "Tell me about your friend Alice. She . . ." (Child describes a friend as teacher writes the words.)
Having friends is fun.	Make a friendship ring: each child traces own hands on mural, making a circle.
Friends enjoy doing things together.	Go on a scavenger hunt with a friend.
Adults can be your friends.	Teacher helps child solve conflict or gives comfort when child is hurt.
Animals and pets can be your friends.	Children have an opportunity to bring small house pets to school to share with rest of class.
To have a friend is to be a friend.	Children respond to: "A Friend Is Someone Who . . ." (They describe their impressions while teacher writes down their words.)
Friends enjoy doing things for one another.	Children respond to: "Being a Friend with Someone Means . . ." (Teacher writes down children's dictation.)
Everyone can have a friend.	Teacher reads stories about friendships. *Will I Have A Friend?* (Cohen), *Corduroy* (Freeman), *Play with Me* (Ets), *Little Bear's Friend* (Minarik), *A Letter to Amy* (Keats), *Hold My Hand* (Zolotow), *Jessica* (Henkes), *Harry & Willie & Carrothead* (Caseley).
You can show someone you want to be friends.	Write a letter to a friend; invite a friend over to play.
Friends will help you.	Form a relay team and have a race.

Figure 14.22 ● A friendship unit can encourage children to express positive emotions while they use their cognitive, language, and motor skills to enhance their social development.

each other's actions and motivations by interpreting the behavior to children as they play.

Curriculum to develop social skills in young children can be spontaneous as well as planned. Much of the focus in an early childhood setting is on social interactions throughout the day. At other times, social growth is enhanced by grouptime discussions, awareness of the community and society at large, and an emphasis on specific social skills.

Ask yourself:

● What are social expectations of infants and toddlers? Preschoolers? School-aged children?

● Why is peer group experience important?

● What social skills do children develop with adults? With other children? In a group? As individuals?

● How do teachers help children develop social skills?

● How are social skills fostered in the curriculum?

● UNIT 14-3 Creative Growth

THE DEVELOPMENT OF CREATIVITY

Creativity is the ability to have new ideas, to be original and imaginative, and to make new adaptations on old ideas. Inventors, composers, and designers are creative people, as are those who paint and dance, write speeches, or create curriculum for children.[1] Thinking in a different way and changing a way of

[1] Introduce children to a diverse range of creative adults—men and women from a variety of cultural backgrounds. When we become too concerned with molding children to "fit," we miss the fact that accepting and developing the differences among children enhance creativity.

Theme: About Families

Step 1: Establish Background Knowledge
Large Group Brainstorm: What is a family?
What are they called (Dad, Mama, Hermano, Nona, etc.)?
Individual List: Your own family and their names
A picture of your family
Small Group Discussion: Feeling words for families
Family jobs in the home
Charades depicting family jobs
Think-Pair-Share: List, then draw how families have fun together
List, then draw the tough times families have

Step 2: Decide the Theme Focus (e.g., "Family Fun")

Step 3: Review Knowledge, Make a Plan
Large Group: Review how families have fun
Pairs: Cut pictures from magazines showing family fun, make collage for classroom bulletin board
Small Group Discussion: Brainstorm then list and prioritize list of a family activity the class can do as a "family"
Large Group: Small groups present ideas, class vote (e.g., campground)

Step 4: Plan
List what is needed, vote on placement of areas, make assignments for building and map-making

Step 5: Building
Create areas in classroom (e.g., campground, forest, lake, camp store, ranger station, cave, trails, etc.)

Step 6: Play!

Step 7: Review and Conclusion
Ongoing: Teacher observes and evaluates individual participation
At the end: Group discussion on what went well and didn't work; suggestions for future projects and taking down of building

Figure 14.23 ● Cooperative learning activities involve children socially in their own academic learning. An *early primary* theme that is derived from the children and executed by them increases both learning and participation. (Thanks to Amy Buras for the kindergarten unit.)

learning or seeing something are all creative acts (Adams, 1987). The more teachers realize they are a part of a creative act, the more sensitive they become in helping young children develop creatively.

The roots of creativity reach into infancy, for it is every individual's unique and creative process to explore and understand the world, searching to answer larger questions such as "Who am I? What and where am I, and where am I going?" Infants' creativity is seen in their efforts to move, feed, and dress themselves.

Toddlers begin to scribble, build, and move for the pure physical sensation of movement. Young preschoolers create as they try for more control, such as scribbling with purpose or bobbing and jumping to music. Older preschoolers enjoy their budding mastery. Their drawings take on some basic forms, and they repeat movements deliberately while making a dance. As they grow, 5- to 8-year-olds communicate to the world through artistic and expressive creation. These young children have more advanced motor control and hand–eye coordination. Their drawings are representational and pictorial; dancing can include more refined movements and structured dance steps. Their dramatic play is more cohesive; their stories have imagination and form.

Creativity is a process; as such, it is hard to define. As one becomes involved in creative activity, the process and the product merge.

> ... It is probably best to think of creativity as a continual process for which the best preparation is creativity itself. . . . there is real joy in discovery—which not only is its own reward, but provides the urge for continuing exploration and discovery (Lowenfeld & Brittain, 1975).

The young child is open to experience, exploring materials with curiosity and eagerness. For young children, developing the senses is part of acquiring creative skills. Children are also quick to question, wonder, and see things that do not quite match up. These are traits of creative children.

CREATIVE SKILLS IN EARLY CHILDHOOD

There are characteristics common to creative people. For the teacher interested in fostering creative growth in children, these are the skills they should help children learn.

Flexibility and Fluency

Flexibility and fluency are dual skills that allow for creative responses. Flexibility is the capacity to shift from one idea to another; fluency is the ability to produce many ideas. "How many ways can you move from one side of the room to another?" is a question likely to produce many different ideas, one example of fluency. Children who must think of another way to share the wagons when taking turns doesn't work learn flexibility.[1]

Figure 14.24 ● Creativity is the ability to be original and imaginative: to soar above the commonplace. (Courtesy of the city of Reggio Emilia, Italy.)

Sensitivity

Being creative involves a high degree of sensitivity to one's self and one's mental images. Creative people, from an early age, seem to be aware of the world around them; how things smell, feel, and taste. They are sensitive to mood, texture, and how they feel about someone or something. Creative people notice details; how a pine cone is attached to the branch is a detail the creative person does not overlook.

 OUR DIVERSE WORLD OUR DIVERSE WORLD OUR DIVERSE WORLD OUR DIVERSE WORLD OUR DIVERSE WORLD OUR DIVERSE WORLD OUR DIVERSE WORLD OUR DIVERSE WORLD

[1] Creative individuals defy being placed in categories because their special ability to solve problems in new ways is not measured by intelligence tests or by cultural, gender, or ability stereotyping.

Figure 14.25 ● Sensitivity to one's own mental images, such as perceiving direction and movement, are part of creativity in the young child. A 5½-year-old sketched how a pet rat looked from below after picking it up often and watching it run on its exercise wheel.

A special aspect of this skill is a sensitivity to beauty. Also known as aesthetics this sensitivity to what is beautiful is emphasized in some programs (such as Reggio Emilia) and some cultures (such as *tokonoma*, or alcove dedicated to display, in Japanese homes).[1] Growing evidence (Cohen, 1994; Spodek et al., 1996) indicates that children have an awareness and value about their natural environment and what is aesthetically pleasing.

Creative children take delight and satisfaction in making images come to life. Their creative response is in the way they paint a picture, dance with streamers, or find a solution to a problem. Figure 14.25 shows how a 5½-year-old's sensitivity to perspective and detail comes out through a drawing.

Use of Imagination

Imagination is a natural part of the creative process. Children use their imagination to develop their creativity in several ways.

Role Playing. In taking on another role, children combine their knowledge of the real world with their internal images. The child becomes a new character, and that role comes to life.

Image Making. When children create a rainbow with a hose or with paints, they are adding something of their own to their understanding of that visual image. In dance, children use their imagination as they pretend to be objects or feelings, images brought to life.

Constructing. In building and constructing activities, children seem to be re-creating an image they have about tall buildings, garages, or farms. In the process of construction, however, children do not intend that the end product resemble the building itself. Their imagination allows them to experiment with size, shape, and relationships.

A Willingness to Take Risks

People who are willing to break the ordinary mental set and push the boundaries in defining and using ordinary objects, materials, and ideas are creative people. They take risks. Being open to thinking differently or seeing things differently is essential to creativity.

Self-esteem is a factor in risk-taking because people who are tied to what others think of them are more likely to conform rather than follow their own intuitive and creative impulses. People usually do not like to make mistakes or be ridiculed; therefore, they avoid taking risks.

A teacher concerned about creative growth in children realizes that it will surface if allowed and encouraged. When a child is relaxed and not anxious about being judged by others, creativity will more likely be expressed. With support, children can be encouraged to risk themselves.

 OUR DIVERSE WORLD OUR DIVERSE WORLD OUR DIVERSE WORLD OUR DIVERSE WORLD OUR DIVERSE WORLD OUR DIVERSE WORLD OUR DIVERSE WORLD OUR DIVERSE WORLD

[1] Teachers can ask the families of children in their care about special places, objects, and rituals that celebrate beauty and help children acquire an aesthetic interest in their environment.

Using Self As a Resource

Creative people who are aware of themselves and confident in their abilities draw on their own perceptions, questions, and feelings. They know they are their own richest source of inspiration. Those who excel in creative productivity have a great deal of respect for themselves and they use the self as a resource.

Experience

Children need experience to gain skills in using materials creatively. They must learn how to hold a paint brush before they can paint a picture; once they know how to paint, they can be creative in what they paint. Teachers of young children sometimes overlook the fact that children need competence with the tools to be creative with them. A little sensitive, individual demonstration on proper use of a watercolor brush, sandpaper, or ink roller can expand a child's ability to create and eliminate needless frustration and disappointment. The teachers of Reggio Emilia, for instance, demonstrate how to use the tools so that the children can then make outstanding creations, Figure 14.26. Anecdotes from highly accomplished people in creative endeavors (pianists, mathematicians, Olympic swimmers) highlight the value of long-term systematic instruction in a sort of apprenticeship with inspiring teachers as well as parents who are committed to assist (Bloom & Sosniak, 1992). As teachers we can see how Vygotsky's theory applies in the arts and can provide the initial palette of creative activities so that children can dabble and become experienced. When the skill of the medium is mastered, the child is ready to create.

THE TEACHER'S ROLE

Considerations

The early childhood curriculum offers many rich avenues for self-expression and creativity. Beyond art and music, there is the ability to think and question, to find more than one answer to a problem. Blocks, climbing equipment, and social relationships offer risk-taking opportunities. Children use themselves as resources as they play outdoor games, experiment with science projects, and participate in dramatic play. Taruna exhibits many creative traits as she attempts to enter into play with two other children. She first asks if she can play, and when met with rejection, she

Figure 14.26 ● When children have a chance to create, with permission to use an abundance of materials, the results are creative. (Courtesy of the city of Reggio Emilia, Italy.)

demands to be one of the mommies. Taruna finally offers her doll as a prop and is accepted into the group. Her persistence is exceeded only by her creative problem-solving.

A primary consideration when developing creativity is *to provide "continuous availability, abundance, and variety"* (Gandini, 1996) *of materials*, as is done in Reggio Emilia, Italy (Gandini et al., 1992). Second, *regular creative opportunities* give children the experience and skill necessary to be creative. Children need frequent occasions to be creative to function in a highly creative manner. When children have a chance to create, their skills in perceiving the world are enhanced.

One of the teacher's most crucial considerations for supporting creative growth is *to encourage divergent thinking*. To diverge means to take a different line of thought or action, deviating from the normal. Finding ideas that branch out rather than converge and center on one answer is divergent thinking. Recent works suggest that creativity and problem-solving may stem from similar sources (Hitz, 1987). Real-life problem-solving calls for creative thinking as well as logic and concept development. The creative arts are important if only because they tend to stress this kind of thinking. Where there are no "right" or "wrong" answers, there will undoubtedly be many solutions for problems. The curriculum section of this chapter contains creativity questions as examples of divergent thinking.

Children and teachers can *discuss issues and seek solutions* to problems when divergent thinking is encouraged. In a child care center, for instance, children were fighting over the use of the two swings. The children's responses indicate their willingness to take a different line of thought:

Teacher: How do you think we could share the swings?

David: The kids who give me a turn can come to my birthday party.

Sabrina: No. We will have to make a waiting list.

Xenia: Only girls can use the swings. The boys can have all the cars.

Frederico: Buy a new swing set.

Teachers who *talk with young children about what they create*—be it their artwork, table toy creations, dramatic play sequences—help creativity considerably. Schirrmacher (1986) offers some suggestions about talking with children about art; these hints could apply to all creative endeavors. Rather than approach children's work with compliments, judgments, or even questions:

● Allow children to go about their artistic discoveries without your comparing, correcting, or projecting yourself into their art.

● Shift from searching for representation in children's art to a focus on the abstract, design qualities.

● Use reflective dialogue.

● Smile, pause, and say nothing at first.

Teachers *allow children to take the lead* in their own creative works from start to finish. Adults do not need to take over at any point, particularly at the end with questions ("What is it?") or praise ("I like it!"). If a child seems to want more response, comment on the color ("What a lot of blue you used"), texture ("I see wiggly lines all down one side"), or the child's efforts ("You really worked on this painting, huh?"). Then reflect their own ideas back to the children:

Child: The monster's gonna get you and eat you up!

Teacher: You made a monster with the wood scraps.

Child: Yes and it's for my daddy.

Teacher: Let's put in on the counter so it will dry when he picks you up.

Integrating creativity and learning in the classroom is especially valuable. Early childhood theorists from Dewey and Piaget to Montessori and Malaguzzi (see Chapter 1) have advocated multisensory learning through experimentation and discovery. Several examples come to mind. Toddlers and 2-year-olds can become better acquainted with colors through such an approach (Stone, 1997); preschoolers can be introduced to clay with careful questions and guided play experiences (Topal, 1996); and primary children can be taught and demonstrate what they've learned about volcanoes through drawing and paper-and-wire sculpture (Forman, 1996).

Teacher timing and attitudes are also important in stimulating creative development in young children. The early childhood years are probably the most crucial time to encourage creative thinking. Indeed, one study found that kindergartners gave a higher proportion of original responses to creativity tasks than did second-graders (Moran et al., 1983). "It is here that initial attitudes are established . . . and school can be a fun place where the individual's contribution is welcome and where changes can be sought and made" (Lowenfeld & Brittain, 1975).

Children need plenty of time and a relaxed atmosphere to be creative. They need encouragement and respect for the process and products of their creative nature. The teacher's attitude tells the children that what they do is important and that how they do it makes a difference. Rather than expecting a predetermined right answer, the teacher encourages creativity by valuing the answers the children give even when they appear unusual or illogical.

Curriculum Planning for Creative Growth

In the Environment

Teachers set up an environment that promotes creative expression; they choose activities and materials that can be used in many ways. These *open-ended materials* provide a continuing challenge as children use them repeatedly in new and different ways. Clay, playdough, paints, crayons and pens, blocks, water, sand and other sensory materials, and movable outdoor equipment are good examples of open-ended materials that stimulate creativity. Particularly in the area of creative art, it is important to *avoid* projects that masquerade as creative activities, such as duplicated, photocopied, or mimeographed sheets, cut-and-paste activities, tracing patterns, coloring-book pages, dot-to-dot books (Schirrmacher, 1993), and any art "project" that is based on a model for children to copy or imitate. Children are motivated to try new ways to use materials when a project is flexible and challenging.

Indoors. Every classroom has a potential for creative activity.

● *The Arts.* A wide variety of materials and opportunities to choose how they will be used is the basis of the creative process. An open table with a shelf of simple, familiar materials that can be combined in many ways will lead to inventiveness. Two-year-olds like crayons, paste, and colored paper pieces; 3- to 5-year-olds will enjoy the addition of markers, string, hole punches and scissors, and tape. Older children can manage staplers, rulers, and protractors. Plenty of paper, such as recycled computer printouts and cardboard, round out an open-ended, self-help art shelf. More structured art activities can also be offered, particularly for the preschool child, as long as the focus is on the child's process, rather than an end product or model. As they approach the primary years, children become interested in what their creations look like and then are ready for practical help and advice on getting started. *Creativity question: "What other ways can you think of to use the paint?"*

● *Blocks/Manipulatives.* Children use their imagination when blocks become castles, tunnels, corrals, and swamps. These areas encourage creativity when children have enough materials of one kind to "really" make something; one long block is just not enough for a road. Also, creations have a sense of permanence when they are noted and kept. Sketching or photographing a block structure, attaching signs (including taking dictation) for the day, even rethinking cleanup periodically shows how valuable these creations are. *Creativity question: "How can you use the blocks to make a forest? A stairway? Can you think of a design using the pegs?"*

● *Discovery/Science.* Building geoboards or making tangrams and cube art all blend math and art. Art

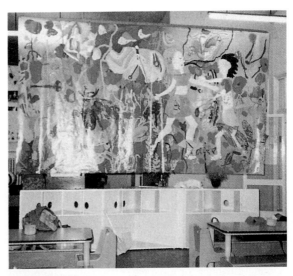

Figure 14.27 ● When children are given the materials and allowed the time, they will use their own ideas for creating masterpieces! (Courtesy of the city of Reggio Emilia, Italy.)

activities can lead children to discover scientific principles, such as color mixing, dissolving powder paint in water, and having water available with clay. Nature materials can be used for rubbings, mobiles, and prints. Collecting materials during a "litter walk" makes interesting and informative collages. *Creativity question: What do you think will happen? Now, how can you find out why it happened that way?*

● *Dramatic Play.* The dramatic arts offer opportunities for children to express themselves. Every "unit" in the dramatic play corner brings out children's own interpretations of their world, be it a house, shoestore, farmer's market, or a campout, dinosaur cave, or space shuttle. Moreover, to perform a familiar story, such as *Goldilocks and the Three Bears*, children can create costumes, props, a stage, and the musical accompaniment. *Creativity question: What could you use to help you pretend you are the grandpapa? How could this scarf be used in your house?*

● *Language/Library.* Besides a variety of books and children's literary experiences (see Chapter 13), the booknook can be a place for teachers to ask open-ended questions for fun and pondering. "What if you were a twin? What would you wear or eat? Where would you live?" is a social creation;

"If I were a hat, I would . . ." is physical creativity; "How many ways could we make triangles with these materials on the table" challenges a child to cognitive creativity. Creative responses for language development can use a familiar storyline: for instance, the book *Did You Ever See?* (Einsel) or the song "Down by the Bay" can be used to ask children to make a rhyme to end the sentence "Did you ever see a whale . . . ("flipping its tail!") *Creativity question: What do you think will happen next in the story?*

Outdoors. Creativity happens out-of-doors also. Large, hollow blocks can become a stairway, and wagons and carts become fire engines, buses, doll carriages, moving vans, or trucks. Dancing with ribbons, making a banner for a parade, rearranging equipment to make a tumbling or obstacle course all combine children's motor skills with music for creative growth. The use of these activities is limited only by the creativity of the children. Sand, water, and mud provide a place for children to dig, haul, manipulate, and control in any number of ways. *Creativity questions: How many parts of your body can you use to get the ball to your friend? How many ways can you think of to cross over on the climber? I wonder how you could get the wet sand into the bucket? What is your tricycle going to be today?*

Routines, Transitions, and Groups

Teachers can apply their own creativity to many routine situations. Children looking for a lost mitten organize a "hunt." Pretending to be vacuum cleaners, dump trucks, or robots gets the blocks picked up faster. Saying good-bye can be an exercise in creativity; the child can say "See you Later, Alligator," and the adults (parents and teacher) can make up a silly response. Another day, the child and parent can reverse roles. *Creativity question for dismissal transition: How can you use one foot and one hand in some way to go to your snack groups?*

Music is a special outlet for children's creative expression in groups. Music is a universal language that develops every aspect of affective development. It allows the expression of emotions and the opportunity to take roles as well as a delightful time to create with movement. There is a kind of developmental sequence in the creative expression of music.[1] The very young child is receptive to music, responding by listening, singing, and making noise with instruments. Preschoolers move to rhythmic music, often singing spontaneously in play and responding to repeated songs or repetitious phrasing. Their interest in musical instruments precedes their skill, and they often need instruments to be introduced and their proper use demonstrated. Older preschoolers and school-age children are more accurate in matching their pitch and tempo to the group or played music.

Music can permeate the early childhood program. It can set the tone at naptime, signal that a cleanup task is at hand, summon children to a group, and offer cultural experiences that are meaningful and enjoyable.[2] For instance, New Year is often a noisy time; it can be celebrated by making ankle bells and doing a Sri Lankan dance or making a West Indian Conga line. In Waldorf schools, music is quite important. Children are engaged daily in eurythmy exercises (developed by Steiner, see Chapter 1). Taught by a specialist, it is a kind of creative form that translates music and speech into movement.

Indoors or out, in structured or unstructured times children need the time and trusting atmosphere that encourage them to create. Figure 14.28 shows some ways that *art* can be the primary medium for learning, as in the community preschools of Reggio Emilia. Regardless of the materials, environments and teachers encourage children's creativity.

Focus on Skills

The wide range of skills necessary for creative development can be supported throughout the early

OUR DIVERSE WORLD OUR DIVERSE WORLD OUR DIVERSE WORLD OUR DIVERSE WORLD OUR DIVERSE WORLD OUR DIVERSE WORLD OUR DIVERSE WORLD OUR DIVERSE WORLD OUR DIVERSE WORLD

[1] Sharing music and dance from home is an ideal way to incorporate children's individual cultures into the classroom. Translate a simple song into another language; teach the children the song, working in the language that is "home base" for most of the children, then re-teach it. Words and phrases made familiar by melody are remembered and made valuable.

[2] Improvised music and lyrics can sustain sociodramatic play between children with developmental delays and nondelayed peers (Gunsberg, 1991).

Figure 14.28 ● When a community values creativity, it puts creative skill development high as a school priority. (Courtesy of the city of Reggio Emilia, Italy.)

THEME: GREEN AND GROWING THINGS

OUTDOOR ACTIVITIES

1. Plant a garden in a corner of the yard, in an old barrel, or in a box flat on a table. Children learn through experimentation why some things grow and other's don't. Make space for a compost heap.
2. Add wheelbarrows to the transportation toys.
3. Take a field trip to a farm, at planting time if possible.
4. Add gardening tools to the sand area. With proper supervision, children can see how trowels, hand claws, rakes, and shovels can be used to create new patterns in the sand and mud.
5. Plan group games that emphasize green and growing things. Older children could run wheelbarrow races, using one child as the wheelbarrow and another as the driver.
6. Play "musical vegetables" with large cards or chalk drawings. Dance with gourds, coconut instruments, sugar cane rhythm sticks.

INDOOR ACTIVITIES

1. Leaf rubbings, printing with surplus apples, onions, carrots, potatoes, lemons, oranges, and celery, and painting with pine boughs are ways children can create art with green and growing things, make cornhusk dolls, avocado seed porcupines.
2. Book accessories might include blue felt forms for lakes, hay for corrals and barns.
3. In the manipulative area, match a photo of familiar plants with a sample of the plant. Add sorting trays with various kinds of seeds to count, feel, mix, and match. Match pictures of eggs, bacon, milk, and cheese with the animals from which they come.
4. In the science area, grow alfalfa sprouts and mung beans. Let children mix them in salads and feed to classroom pets. As the sprouts grow, children can chart the growth. This activity can lead to charting their own development, comparing it with when they were infants.
5. The dramatic play center can be transformed into a grocery store to emphasize the food we buy to eat, how it helps us, and why good nutrition is important. Other dramatic play units are a florist shop or nursery, stocked with garden gloves, seed packets, peat pots, and sun hats.
6. The language area can be stocked with books about how plants, baby animals, and children grow. In small groups, children can respond to "When I plant a seed . . ." or "When I was a baby I . . . Now I . . ." to stimulate creative expression.
7. Songs and fingerplays can help focus on green and growing things, children's growth, and animals. "The Green Grass Grows All Around" can be sketched by a teacher so that children will have visual cues to each successive verse. A favorite fingerplay, "Way Up in the Apple Tree," can be adapted to a number of fruits and vegetables.

Figure 14.29 ● Creativity around the classroom. Creativity and problem-solving may stem from the same source. Real-life experiences, such as planning and building a garden, expand to provide creative thinking and logic in the classroom.

childhood program. The creative thinker is one who finds many ways to solve a problem, approach a situation, use materials, and interact with others. The teacher's role is one of supporting imaginative use of equipment and using a multisensory approach to deepen learning.

To encourage creative thinking, teachers also look at the ways they ask children questions. How can they prompt children to view the unusual and think of the exceptional? How can they encourage divergent thinking? What will encourage children to use their cognitive and language skills in creative ways? The *Creativity Questions* in the previous section demonstrate some of the ways teachers focus on children's creative skills through the use of questions.

Use of Themes

As teachers plan curriculum around a theme, they keep in mind what creative skills can be developed. Figure 14.29 charts the theme of "Green and Growing Things" and can bring out the child's creative nature. In addition, such a theme touches on aspects of social responsibility (see previous section) by promoting eco-logical responsibility through the arts and nurturing an environmental and social ethic (Hoot & Foster, 1993; Peters, 1994). Children can begin to respect life early in age with a curriculum that encourages a respect for oneself, cooperation with others, and a responsibility for all living things (Karmozyn et al., 1993).

A Final Note. The spiritual development of the child fits with our analogy of "heart and soul" and is con-sidered part of affective development (see Chapter 4). Not limited to religious training, this area acknowl-edges that children at early ages explore concepts of the divine and the meaning of life. In addressing this topic, we do not intend to give the impression that teachers of young children should be required to believe or teach religious precepts. However, by including this aspect of affective development we are pointing out that for many children and families, spiritual matters are of fundamental importance in family life. Coles (1991) has written *The Spiritual Life of Children*, and Hilliard has done some preliminary work in this area, but, as he notes, it is often difficult to find a common framework in which to communicate about spiritual matters (R. L. Saxton, personal com-munication, Summer, 1998). Religious diversity is perhaps the final frontier to be explored!

● UNIT 14-3 Checkpoint

Young children are open to the creative process and to creative experiences. The early years are a good time to acquire the skills of flexibility, sensitivity, imagination, risk taking, resourcefulness, and experi-ence.

The greatest challenge for adults in nurturing children's creativity is to help children find and de-velop their Creativity Intersection—the area where their talents, skills, and interests overlap (Amabile, 1989). The role of the teacher is to plan curricula that will help develop children's creativity. An atmosphere conducive to creative work is one that supports children's divergent thinking, encourages them to take risks, and provides ways they can use themselves as resources.

Ask yourself:

● What are the creative skills learned in early child-hood?

● What is the teacher's role in the development of creativity?

● What classroom area, skill, or unit promotes creative thinking

● How can I ask children to use language to pro-mote creative thinking?

Summary

Emotional, social, and creative growth develop-ment are at the center of the early childhood curricu-lum. Planning for these areas involves an understand-ing of how each develops in the young child and how they are interrelated. Children learn many skills in these three areas as they interact with each other, with adults, and in the environment.

Planning curriculum for emotional, social, and creative growth calls upon teachers to play a supportive role, facilitating children's involvement with the mate-rials and each other. Only then can children discover themselves, explore their relationships, and develop the ability to use their imagination and resources.

Review Questions

1. How are emotional, social, and creative growth related to each other?

2. How can teachers recognize children's biased remarks or social behavior? Do they need to respond? Why?

3. What are the advantages of and problems with superhero play?

4. List some of the developmental milestones and expectations for socialization of young children.

5. How can teachers support conflict resolution and problem-solving?

6. What kinds of activities masquerade as creative art?

7. Write three examples of a child's divergent thinking. How do these show the "creativity intersection"?

Learning Activities

1. Name five people you consider creative. Match their skills with those we have identified in early childhood. Where are they similar? Different?

2. How does your center promote positive self-concept? What else could be done?

3. Observe a group of 4-year-olds at play. How do they decide what roles each one takes? Are they clear in their expectations of what sex roles are appropriate for boys and girls? Is there sex-role stereotyping?

4. Taking turns and sharing equipment and materials are difficult for young children. Cite three examples you have seen where children used their social skills to negotiate a turn. Was teacher intervention necessary?

5. Make behavioral definitions of emotions you think you will see in the children you teach. Observe the children, then check the accuracy of your definitions.

6. Give three examples of children in your center trying to "break mental set." In what area of the classroom did it occur? What were the adults' responses?

7. How do teachers in your setting plan for creativity? What place does such expression take in the priority of the school philosophy?

Bibliography

General

Berk, L. E. (1999) *Infants, children, and adolescents* (3rd ed.). Boston: Allyn & Bacon.

Bredekamp, S., & Copple, F. (1997). *Developmentally appropriate practices in early childhood programs.* Washington, DC: National Association for the Education of Young Children.

Marshall, H. H. (1989, July). Research in review: The development of self-concept. *Young Children, 44*(5).

Neugebauer, B. (1992). *Alike and different: Exploring our humanity with young children* (Rev. ed.). Washington, DC: National Association for the Education of Young Children.

York, S. (1991). *Roots and wings: Affirming culture in early childhood programs.* St. Paul, MN: Redleaf Press.

Emotional Growth

Barrera, R. (1993, March). Retrato de mi familia: A portrait of my Hispanic family. *Exchange.*

Briggs, D. C. (1970). *Your child's self-esteem.* New York: Doubleday.

Burgess, R. (1993, March). African American children. *Exchange.*

Cooper, R. M. (1992, November). *The impact of child care on the socialization of African American children.* Paper presented at the National Association for the Education of Young Children, New Orleans.

Diaz, R. (1992, April). *The development of self-direction in the preschool years.* Address given to Peninsula Association of the Education of Young Children.

Greenman, J. (1991, January/February). See children: A question of perspective. *Exchange.*

Greenspan, S. I., & Salmon, J. (1993). *Playground politics: Understanding the emotional life of your school-age child.* Menlo Park, CA: Addison-Wesley.

Honig, A. S. (1986, May and July). Stress and coping in children. *Young Children, 41*(4 & 5).

Kostelnik, M., Whiren, A. P., & Stein, L. G. (1986, May). Living with he-man: Managing superhero fantasy play. *Young Children, 41*(4).

McCormick, J. (1993). Family child care. In A. Gordon & K. B. Browne (Eds.), *Beginnings and beyond* (3rd ed.). Albany, NY: Delmar.

Sample, W. (1993, March). The American Indian child. *Exchange.*

Selye, H. (1982). History and present status of the stress concept. In L. Goldberger & S. Breznitz (Ed.), *Handbook of stress.* New York: The Free Press.

Simon, T. (1994, September). Helping children make choices. *The Creative Classroom.*

Wardle, F. (1993, March). How young children build images of themselves. *Exchange.*

Social Growth

Bhavnagri, N. P., & Samuels, B. G. (1996, Summer). Making and keeping friends. *Childhood Education.*

Bergen, D. (1993, Summer). Facilitating friendship development in inclusion classrooms. *Childhood Education.*

Bullock, J. R. (1993). Lonely children. *Young Children, 48*(6).

Buras, A. (1991, Spring). Social settings in the classroom. *ACEI Focus, 3*(3).

Burk, D. I. (1996). Understanding friendship and social interaction. *Childhood Education.* Annual Theme.

Buzzelli, C. A. & File, N. (1989, March). Building trust in friends. *Young Children.*

Carlsson-Paige, N., & Levin, D. E. (1987). *The war play dilemma.* New York: Teacher's College.

Carlsson-Paige, N., et al. (1992, March). Beginnings workshop: Conflict resolution. *Exchange.*

Derman-Sparks, L. (1989). *The anti-bias curriculum.* Washington, DC: National Association for the Education of Young Children.

Derman-Sparks, L. (1993/94, Winter), Empowering children to create a caring culture in a world of differences. *Childhood Education.*

DeVries, R., & Kohlberg, L. (1987). *Programs of early education.* New York: Longman Books.

Dick, Kelly. (1991, Spring). "Cooperative learning" mastering the bundle of sticks. *Childhood Education, 67*(3).

Dodge, R. P. (1991). *The communication lab: A classroom-based collaboration program for the speech-language pathologist.* Menlo Park, CA: The Pritchard Group.

Gilligan, C. (1982). *In a different voice.* Cambridge, MA: Harvard University Press.

Gordon, A. M., & Browne, K. W. (1996). *Guiding young children in a diverse society.* Needham Heights, MA: Allyn & Bacon.

Greenman, J., et al. (1995, January) Beginnings workshop: Building a classroom culture. *Exchange.*

Kemple, K. M. (1991, July). Research in review: Preschool children's peer acceptance and social interaction. *Young Children, 46*(5).

Lally, J. R., Provence, S., Szanton, E., & Weissbourd, B. (1987). Developmentally appropriate care for children from birth to age 3. In S. Bredekamp (Ed.), *Developmentally appropriate practice in early childhood programs serving children from birth through age 8.* Washington, DC: National Association for the Education of Young Children.

Lawhon, T. (1997, Summer). Encouraging friendships among children. *Childhood Education.*

Lowenthal, B. (1996, Spring). Teaching social skills to preschoolers with special needs. *Childhood Education.*

Maniates, H., & Heath, M. (1998, Spring). Creating a climate for learning. *Early Childhood Resources.*

Mecca, M. (1995–96, Winter). Classrooms where children learn to care. *Childhood Education.*

Miller, F. (1998, Summer). Helping the overly aggressive child develop pro-social behavior. *ACEI Newsletter, 10*(4).

Noddings, N. (1992). *The challenge to care in schools.* New York: Teachers College Press.

Noddings, N. (1994). Learning to engage in moral dialogue. *Holistic Educational Review. 7*(2).

Nowicki, S., & Duke, M. P. (1992). *Helping the child who doesn't fit in.* Atlanta, GA: Peachtree Publishers.

Nurss, S. (1990, December). Learning to share. *Ladybug Magazine.*

Paley, V. G. (1992). *You can't say you can't play.* Cambridge, MA: Harvard University Press.

Porro, B. (1996). *Talk it out: Conflict resolution in the elementary classroom.* Alexandria, VA: Association for Supervision and Curriculum Development.

Schickedanz, J. A., et al. (1993). *Understanding children* (2nd ed.). Mountain View, CA: Mayfield Publishing.

Smith, C. A. (1982). *Promoting the social development of young children.* Palo Alto, CA: Mayfield Publishing.

Stephens K., et al. (1996, May). Beginnings workshop: Circle time. *Exchange.*

Creative Growth

Adams, J. (1987). *The care and feeding of ideas.* Reading, MA: Addison-Wesley.

Amabile, T. M. (1989). *Growing up creative.* New York: Crown.

Bloom, B. S., & Sosniak, L. A. (1992). Talent development vs. schooling. *Educational Leadership,* p. 39.

Cech, M. (1991). *Globalchild: Multicultural resources for young children.* Menlo Park, CA: Addison-Wesley.

Cohen, S. (1994). Children and the environment: Aesthetic learning. *Childhood Education.* Annual Theme.

Edwards, C., Gandini, L., & Forman, G. (1993). *The hundred languages of children.* Norwood, NJ: Ablex Press.

Forman, G. (1996, March). Negotiating with art media to deepen learning. *Exchange.*

Gandini, L. (1996, March). Teachers and children together: Constructing new learning. *Exchange.*

Gandini, L., et al. (1992, May). Beginnings workshop: Creativity and learning. *Exchange.*

Gunsberg, A. (1991, Summer). Improvised musical play with delayed and nondelayed children. *Childhood Education*.

Hitz, R. (1987, January). Creative problem solving through music activities. *Young Children, 42*(2).

Hoot, J. L., & Foster, M. L., (1993, Spring). Promoting ecological responsibility . . . through the arts. *Childhood Education*.

Karmozyn, P., et al. (1993, Summer). A better earth—Let it begin with me. *Childhood Education*.

Lowenfeld, V., & Brittain, W. L. (1975). *Creative and mental growth*. New York: Macmillan.

Moran, J. D., Milgram, R. M., Sawyers, J. K., & Fu, V. R. (1983). Original thinking in preschool children. *Child Development*. 921–926, p. 54.

Peters, R. (1993/1994, Winter). Nurturing an environmental and social ethic. *Childhood Education*.

Pirtle, s. (1997, Spring). Music in the peaceable classroom: Linking up. *Forum Newsletter of Educators for Social Responsibility, 14*(2).

Schirrmacher, R. (1986, July). Talking with young children about their art. *Young Children, 41*(5).

Schirrmacher. (1993). *Art and creative development for young children* (2nd ed.). Albany, NY: Delmar.

Spodek, B. S., et al. (1996, March). Beginnings workshop: Art experiences. *Exchange*.

Stone, S. J. (1997, Summer). What does purple smell like? *Childhood Education*.

Topal, C. W. (1996, March). Fostering experiences between young children and clay. *Exchange*.

Whitson, A. (1994, Fall). The creative minority in our schools. *Childhood Education*.

Spiritual Growth

Coles, R. (1991). *The spiritual life of children*. New York: Houghton-Mifflin.

Acknowledgment

Special thanks to Chris Asaro for children's social conversations.

How Do We Teach for Tomorrow?

Guest Editorial   TAKE A STAND FOR CHILDREN

Jonah Edelman

You have chosen to enter the nation's most powerful profession. You will be the caretakers, educators, and teachers of our nation's future: our children.

Every day early childhood educators take responsibility for the health and well-being of three-fifths of the nation's young children, some 13 million preschoolers including 6 million infants and toddlers. These children will be the leaders of the 21st century—the teachers, the public servants, the scientists, and the artists of the future. You will be entrusted with these children's care during their earliest, most important years. What they learn from you today will determine who they will become tomorrow and their ability to be good parents and citizens and productive members of the 21st century work force.

With so much in your hands, one would think that the nation would provide you with the best possible resources to guarantee your success. Elected leaders, however, have neglected your profession and the children it serves. Last year, although the federal government spent $270 billion on defense, it spent only $9 billion on child care. The result: quality child care is scarce and generally unaffordable, and early childhood educators are paid far below what they deserve, leading to a high turnover rate.

This sad situation begs an important question: How can our leaders neglect such a vitally important profession? How can child care be such a low priority when 13 million children rely on it each day? How can it be such a low priority when the majority of mothers with children under the age of 3 are working? How can it

be such a low priority when numerous studies have shown that the earliest years are the most crucial years to a child's development? How? It's simple. Child care professionals, parents, and others who Stand For Children don't stand up together.

I applaud your career choice and appreciate the incredible work that goes into being an excellent early childhood educator. At the same time, I want to challenge you. Be not only a great teacher of young children but also a great leader for young children. Turn passivity into participation. Use your passion for and knowledge about children to energize action. Turn division into solidarity. Build relationships with additional leaders—other educators, parents, clergy, seniors—so that people overcome differences and unite to accomplish their common goals. Instill a sense of purpose and momentum. Work for recognizable victories, small and large. Build an organized constituency in your community, your state, and the nation that will force elected leaders to change their priorities.

In a democracy, which we are so lucky to live in, power springs from two sources: organized money and organized people. Those of us who Stand For Children will never have the money. But, in a time of tremendous pressures on families and children, and massive unmet needs, we *can* organize the people. It starts with you. If you who Stand For Children every day make the commitment to be the leader children need, we can truly begin to turn things around.

Thank you again for the direction you have chosen. We look forward to working with you to improve the lives of children in your community, your state, and this nation.

More on Stand For Children

Since Stand For Children began in 1996, it has recruited a diverse grassroots membership including retired persons and high school students, security guards and stay-at-home moms, roofers and corporate executives, to form Stand For Children chapters. Stand For Children chapters have completed hundreds of initiatives for children, including educating parents about the availability of free or low-cost health insurance for their children, conducting immunization campaigns and basic needs and book drives, and organizing campaigns to improve after-school options. For more information about how to form a Stand For Children chapter, visit *www.stand.org*, e-mail *Chapters@stand.org*, or call 202–234–0095.

Jonah Edelman is Executive Director of Stand For Children.

Issues and Trends in Early Childhood Education

CHAPTER 15

Questions for Thought

What are the major issues facing early childhood educators today?

How are the major themes of early childhood education reflected in the issues facing children, families, and teachers today?

What are the challenges children and their families face, and what can we do to help them?

How are the role and structure of the family changing, and how do these changes affect the children we teach?

What is the impact of the education reform movement on early childhood?

What is the role of television and other media in children's lives?

How do we become advocates for a quality life for children?

How does the history of the field suggest the agenda for the future?

Figure 15.1 ● How do we prepare our children to live successfully in the future?

INTRODUCTION

Early childhood education has undergone remarkable changes in the past 30 years. It has evolved from being an option for middle-class preschool children to a necessity for millions of families with children from infancy through the primary years.[1] These changes have signaled a new level of professionalism and training for teachers and family child care providers. Such transformations are a reflection of the economic, social, and political climate of the times, as well as research in child development and early education. Changes in education historically have been linked to societal reform and upheaval. Issues of today and trends for tomorrow grow out of the problems and solutions of the past.

In the 1960s, social action and the War on Poverty captured the American interest and spirit. Head Start programs opened around the country and were the symbols of social action of that era. The 1970s brought changes related to economic crisis. Social services were scrutinized to determine their worth and value. The family unit was affected by the job market, the end of the Vietnam War, an energy crisis, inflation, rising divorce rates, and the feminist movement. All of these factors led more women toward work in the marketplace rather than in the home. One of the expansions in public funding at this time was in the services to the handicapped and bilingual populations.

The 1980s meant further budget cuts, reduced services for children and families, and an altered state of childhood. Computers were being installed at all grade levels. Children were often in group care for

OUR DIVERSE WORLD OUR DIVERSE WORLD OUR DIVERSE WORLD OUR DIVERSE WORLD OUR DIVERSE WORLD OUR DIVERSE WORLD OUR DIVERSE WORLD OUR DIVERSE WORLD

[1] Early childhood education and care continues to be on the forefront in dealing with the outcomes of immense social change in American society.

most of their waking hours. They grew up with change, rather than stability, as a constant in their lives. Child abuse became a national cause for alarm. The need for early child care and educational services was well established and will be here for the next several decades. To ignore this need is to deny the reality of family life today.

The reforms in general education that began in the early 1980s brought about some rethinking in early childhood education by the early 1990s. As people became aware of the shortcomings of education at higher levels, they could view the early years as a starting point for improvements. Interest in young children flourished along with reforms at other grade levels.

As the 1990s ended, there was an expanded acceptance of child care for children under 5 and an increasing awareness of the needs of the whole child in the early primary years. At the same time, a wide range of global and sociopolitical issues emerged that affected both the nation and the family, thus having a major impact on children and teachers.

Looking ahead, it seems especially appropriate to discuss current questions in light of the history of the early childhood profession. Take another look at Chapter 1 of this book. For all its diverse and varied pasts, early childhood education has had a consistent commitment to three major themes: the ethic of social reform, the importance of childhood, and transmitting values. These three themes are reflected in the major issues facing early childhood educators today and tomorrow:

● *Ethic of Social Reform*

1. What programs and services are needed for young children and families? Who will pay for and provide them?

2. What education reforms are in place that speak to the quality of life for all children? What is developmentally appropriate teaching? What else is needed to improve education for children under 8 years of age?

● *Importance of Childhood*

1. What are the crises children face today, and what can be done to help them?

2. What is the value of childhood? How is the commitment to children demonstrated?

3. What is the role of family and community in children's lives?[1]

● *Transmitting Values*

1. What is the role of television and other media in children's lives? How are concerns about media violence best addressed?

2. How do we teach children the value of peace?

3. What are the challenges and opportunities presented by diversity in schools, neighborhoods, and families?

4. What are the basic values children should be taught in schools?

ETHIC OF SOCIAL REFORM

Changing our expectations of what poor and disadvantaged children can achieve is central to helping them learn their way out of poverty.

Richard W. Riley
U.S. Secretary of Education, 1996

The ethic of social reform, first mentioned in Chapter 1, refers to an expectation that education and schooling for young children have the potential for significant social change and improvement. There is also the clear implication that educating the mind and teaching the skills are intertwined with a person's ability to get a job and provide for one's future well-being. This relationship is dramatically demonstrated in the discussion of the two major issues of child care and educational reform. How will young children be affected by these two forces—the need for child care and the growing call for excellence in education? The realities of cost and quality create a tension that has not yet been resolved and is only now being aggressively pursued within the early childhood field.

In this section, we look at these two issues of child care and educational reform separately as they relate to the ethic of social reform.

OUR DIVERSE WORLD OUR DIVERSE WORLD OUR DIVERSE WORLD OUR DIVERSE WORLD OUR DIVERSE WORLD OUR DIVERSE WORLD OUR DIVERSE WORLD OUR DIVERSE WORLD

[1] Remember the ongoing theme that school-home partnerships strengthen a child's position for success in school and life.

Child Care

Between the mid-1970s and the mid-1990s,

- The percentage of children under age 6 whose mothers were in the work force more than doubled.

- Enrollment of children ages 3 to 5 in preschool increased from 38% to 61%.

- The proportion of families with children under 18 who were headed by single parents more than doubled (U.S. Department of Education, 1996).

Without question the need for child care has been firmly established. The significant increase in enrollment in child care centers over the last 20 years, underscored by the demographic facts, has had a profound impact on this country: in 1990 Congress passed the first comprehensive child care legislation in nearly 20 years; a year later Head Start funding was increased significantly (see Chapter 2).

It is obvious that child care has public support. Quality child care programs have earned the respect of parents and legislators and demonstrated to society that children can thrive in good early childhood programs. (See discussion on child care in Chapter 2.)

Quality and Cost

The key word, however, is *quality*—the terms "good quality" and "high quality" identify specific features in early childhood programs (see Chapter 2).

Two recent broad-based studies, one conducted in child care centers and the other in family day care settings, examined the critical relationship between quality and cost and present a disturbing picture.

Inadequate child care was found to be rampant in the first study, which was conducted in hundreds of centers in California, Colorado, Connecticut, and North Carolina (Costs, Quality and Child Outcomes Study Team, 1995). In a dramatic conclusion, the study found that most child care centers provided mediocre services and that some were of such poor quality that they threatened children's emotional and intellectual development.[1] Infants and toddlers were most likely to be at risk for poor care in these centers; nearly half of their settings failed to meet basic health and safety needs. Yet 90% of the parents rated the care as "good."

The report was the first of its kind to examine the relationship between the costs of child care and the nature of children's experiences in child care settings (quality). In centers in which researchers found high-quality care, the center staffs were paid higher wages, there were more personnel, and more of them were trained in early childhood education. They were also programs that were subsidized in some way, by the government, a university, or employers of families using these services. The states that had more demanding licensing requirements had few poor-quality programs. According to this report, these factors, along with teachers' salaries and administrators' prior experience are strong determinants of quality.

The results of the first major study of family day care in a decade are similarly distressing, highlighting uneven and poorly regulated conditions. Conducted by Galinsky and coworkers. (1994), the study concluded that only 9% of the homes they observed were of good quality and that over one third of the providers were so indifferent in their caregiving as to be harmful to children's development.[2] More than 40% of the providers planned no activities for children in their care, and only half the children showed signs of trust or attachment to the caregiver. The more a provider was paid, the better the care; the licensed or regulated providers were more likely to be warm and attentive to children, communicate with parents, and provide a safe home. Look at the 10 "Indicators of Quality" as defined by NAEYC, which are cited in Chapter 2, to see where there is a relationship with the findings of these two studies.[3]

The two forms of child care—child care centers and family day care—are equally popular; they are the programs of choice by America's working families,

 OUR DIVERSE WORLD OUR DIVERSE WORLD OUR DIVERSE WORLD OUR DIVERSE WORLD OUR DIVERSE WORLD OUR DIVERSE WORLD OUR DIVERSE WORLD OUR DIVERSE WORLD OUR DIVERSE WORLD OUR DIVERSE WORLD

1,2 Hundreds of thousands of children are spending their critical years in environments that compromise their optimal growth and development.

3 The National Academy of Early Childhood Programs—the accreditation department of NAEYC—base their criteria for quality on the knowledge and experience of thousands of early childhood professionals.

Figure 15.2 ● The quality of a child care program is directly related to the experience and training of the teachers.

who, according to this research, either do not recognize what makes a quality program or who think they cannot demand it. Quality is a function of group size, low teacher-child ratios, trained and experienced staff, adequate compensation, and safe and stimulating environments. Yet these are not the first things parents look for. The family child care study found that parents rate safety as the most important factor in choosing a provider, communications with parents second, and warm attention to children as third. Adult-child ratios, professional training, and licensing rank much lower. Geographical distance and price have been cited by others as the primary criteria for choosing a child care setting (Hofferth, 1994).

To improve the quality of family child care, the reports call on government and business to increase their support in a number of ways: help parents pay for good care, establish training programs for providers, bring providers into regulation, and educate parents about high-quality care. All of the studies share a com-

mon concern that parents must be able to distinguish good from poor quality centers and demand higher quality care before the centers will increase their fees to cover the costs of providing better care.

A National Crisis

Quality care and education of young children has a cost that must be addressed. The cost of quality is directly related to the needs of the families served by the specific program. In some programs, securing the basic needs of food, housing, and health care is an important obligation. The added cost of helping families connect with the right resources and providing the necessary comprehensive services will contribute to a higher cost for quality in that program. Fee reductions and financial aid for low-income families also add to the costs for a quality program.

Quality is significantly related to staff: how many adults there are compared with the number of children in a class; whether the salaries and benefits provide incentive for teachers to be retained for a number of years; the level of the staff's education and training and their years of experience. These factors have created a staffing crisis of major proportion in the country today.

The crisis refers to the difficulties of recruiting and retaining qualified staff for good early childhood programs. The programs center around the costs of providing for quality teachers and staff. Salaries for early childhood employees are disgracefully low, and pension plans and health care benefits are nonexistent for many.

In 1998, entry-level positions for child care workers paid $10,500 per year, a rate that keeps many of them below the federal poverty line. The highest paid child care teacher, with college training in early childhood, earned $19,000, less than the average salary of a working woman with a high school diploma (Lewin, 1998). It is no wonder that employee turnover rate is 31%, as indicated in a study by the Center for the Child Care Work Force (1997), which also found that only 14% of center teachers have remained in their positions over a 10-year period. The researchers also found that 80% of for-profit child care center chains employ welfare recipients. With such low salaries, it would seem their prospects for economic self-sufficiency are limited.

These cost factors are the reason people leave early childhood to find employment in other fields and new people are not attracted to working with young children. At the same time, there is currently an unprecedented demand for child care services. The increased recognition of the need for high-quality child care, however, does not solve the problem of how to keep fees low enough to provide the necessary services yet compensate child care employees what they are worth to attract and retain them. The challenge is before all of us—the child care professionals, the parents, the leaders of business and industry, and the legislators on the local, state, and national scene. National efforts called "Worthy Wage Campaign" and "Full Cost of Quality in Early Childhood Education Programs Campaign" are leading the charge in mobilizing the early childhood field to advocacy and in bringing the issues of the child care crisis to national attention.

Quality 2000: Advancing Early Child Care and Education is an initiative whose goal is to provide high-quality early care and education to all children from birth to age 5, by 2010 (Kagan & Neuman, 1997). In a report entitled, *Not by Chance: Creating an Early Care and Education System for America's Children*, a comprehensive vision is set forth that includes:

● Promoting cultural sensitivity and cultural pluralism

● Increasing the number of accredited programs

● Linking programs to support services and other community resources

● Creating three separate types of licenses for early childhood care and education workers and developing national licensing guidelines

● Focusing staff training and preparation on children and families, with respect to cultural and linguistic diversity

● Funding that is commensurate with per-child levels for elementary school children

● Establishing governance and accountability structures in every state and locality

The depth and breadth of some of the recommendations will help ensure that families have equal access to good programs where consistent standards at a national and local level guarantees equality and excellence for all children.

Education Reform

The ethic of social reform can be strongly felt in the current education reform movement. One of the primary functions of the public school system in the United States is to prepare students for productive roles in society—to produce skilled workers who will enter the job market and contribute to a healthy, competitive economy worldwide.

In the spring of 1983, the National Commission on Excellence in Education issued a report on American schools that precipitated the current reform movement. *A Nation at Risk*, as the report was called, was soon followed by a number of other significant publications that defined the educational crisis at hand and offered a variety of solutions. Early childhood education; vocational education; elementary and secondary schooling; urban schools; teacher education, preparation, and recruitment; character development; literacy; dropouts; and disadvantaged children all came under scrutiny by blue-ribbon panels.

By the 1980s, education emerged as a dominant issue in the presidential campaign. American public schools faced a crisis of quality; a national education problem was identified and a sense of urgency instilled in the public mind. In the first wave of reform, virtually every state enacted reform measures of some kind. The focus was on higher standards of student performance through the upgrading of curricula, increased requirements for homework, and firmer disciplinary methods. Reform of teacher education and restructuring of schools to strengthen the role of the teacher were included as well.

The trend in the 1990s has been toward a national agenda.[1] In 1989, a national summit on the future of American education resulted in the creation of eight national goals, the first of which is that by 2000, every child will start school ready to learn. It is the first time in history that we have had a national consensus on a vision of public education. The first goal has received widespread attention, for it is pivotal in ensuring the success of the remaining goals.

OUR DIVERSE WORLD OUR DIVERSE WORLD OUR DIVERSE WORLD OUR DIVERSE WORLD OUR DIVERSE WORLD OUR DIVERSE WORLD OUR DIVERSE WORLD OUR DIVERSE WORLD

[1] This agenda speaks aggressively to parent involvement and participation in their child's schooling.

Ready to Learn

Goal number one of America 2000 states that by the year 2000, all children in America will start school ready to learn and that the following objectives will be met:

● All children will have access to high-quality and developmentally appropriate preschool programs that help prepare children for school.

● Every parent in America will be a child's first teacher and devote time each day to helping his or her preschool child learn; parents will have access to the training and support they need.

● Children will receive the nutrition, physical activity experiences, and health care needed to arrive at school with healthy minds and bodies and to maintain the mental alertness necessary to be prepared to learn, and the number of low-birthweight babies will be significantly reduced through enhanced prenatal health systems (U.S. Department of Education, 1998a).

By 1996, performance in two areas had improved significantly. The proportion of infants born with one or more health risks decreased, and more families reported that they were reading and telling stories to their children on a regular basis. There were no discernible changes in reducing the gap in preschool participation between high- and low-income families[1] (National Education Goals Panel, 1996). Immunization rates for 2-year-olds increased by 23% between 1992 and 1996 (U.S. Department of Health and Human Services, 1996). Although infant mortality declined among white, African American, and Hispanic infants in 1995, a disproportionate number of African American babies died at a rate twice that for whites[2] (Children's Defense Fund, 1998).

The National Education Goals Panel suggests that setting high standards and developing new and appropriate assessments are the first steps in meeting the objectives of Goals 2000. Acknowledging the difficulty in testing young children, the panel recommended a variety of strategies including informal observations, parental input, and age-appropriate measures to monitor children's progress. The panel

Figure 15.3 ● How do we know that all children will start school ready to learn? How can good-quality early childhood programs help America 2000 reach its first goal?

also raised the idea that preparing schools for children should be as much of a goal as preparing children for schools, suggesting that schools that are "ready" plan for smooth transitions for incoming students, address individual needs, and promote staff development. The report states that efforts to improve school readiness begin with "efforts to support families, educate parents, expand access to health care, and raise the quality of early care and education" (National Education Goals Panel, 1996).

As education policymakers go about the task of defining the issue of readiness and discuss ways to measure it, other noteworthy reform efforts related to America 2000's first goal have emerged.

Reform Issues and Strategies

Some of the most important issues to come out of the school reform movement are:

● *Professionalization of teaching.* To place teaching on a par with other professions, such as law and medicine; looking at the ways in which teachers are educated and trained in 4-year institutions.

 OUR DIVERSE WORLD OUR DIVERSE WORLD OUR DIVERSE WORLD OUR DIVERSE WORLD OUR DIVERSE WORLD OUR DIVERSE WORLD OUR DIVERSE WORLD OUR DIVERSE WORLD

1,2 Eliminating inequalities such as these requires a national agenda for children.

School governance. The need for more on-site autonomy, involving teachers as well as administrators.

 Promoting parent partnerships. Encouraging a range of programs that respond to the varying needs of parents, home, and school, including greater parental involvement, shared decision-making, and accountability.[1]

Teacher recruitment. Providing professionally competitive salaries to attract good teachers; using merit pay schedules and master teacher roles to keep qualified teachers in the classroom.

Experimental programs. The use of smaller school settings, smaller classes, and magnet and charter schools.

Involvement of the larger community. To support schools in new ways; to provide more child care functions wherever necessary. Involving the private sector through business leaders promoting school improvements.

 Equal access. To ensure that disadvantaged students, minority students, students with disabilities, and others at risk have their needs addressed and, specifically, more comprehensive programs to prepare them as adequately as middle-class students.[2]

 Seeing the child in context. Taking into account the context of family, culture, and community, with respect for cultural and linguistic diversity.[3]

Common factors in the reform agenda that early childhood educators share with other educational professionals are those related to the professionalization of teaching, parental choice, program quality, and serving all children equitably.

A growing band of national organizations (led by Children's Defense Fund) calling for reforms has stressed that unless more is done to meet the early health, social, and developmental needs of young children, school reform will fail. According to the Children's Defense Fund (1998), kindergarten teachers estimate that one third of children entering kindergarten are unprepared to meet the challenges of school.

To meet the needs of working parents and ensure that children are ready to learn, reform strategies should be enlarged to include the following. These six reform issues predict the agenda for the early childhood profession for the remainder of this decade.

1. *Link education and child care.* The existing separation between early childhood programs is counterproductive to the reform effort. The early childhood profession includes both the caregiving and educating aspects of teaching; in recent years the distinction between the two has blurred within the profession and the two have been intentionally linked. There is a greater acknowledgment that caretaking and educational factors are involved in all programs that serve very young children. However, the general public, as well as government agencies, tend to be unaware of the critical relationships between these two factors and perpetuate the division. This dichotomy between care and education must be eliminated.

2. *Establish continuity between early childhood programs and kindergartens.* Good early childhood education is more than getting children ready to start school. It is a comprehensive vision that supports child development principles, appropriate teaching practices, active parent involvement, family support, and health services. Until there is a restructuring of the present early elementary system, many of the advantages of the preschool years and early intervention programs will be negated. Providing continuity requires clarity on how preschool and child care programs should differ from standard elementary school classes and how elementary school curricula can support good preschool practices. The Task Force on Early Childhood Education of the National Association of State Boards of Education calls for a restructuring of the early elementary grades to include upgraded early childhood units serving children ages 4 to 8.

3. *Address children's nonacademic needs.* Unless more is done to meet the early health and social needs of children, school reform is likely to fail.

 OUR DIVERSE WORLD OUR DIVERSE WORLD OUR DIVERSE WORLD OUR DIVERSE WORLD OUR DIVERSE WORLD OUR DIVERSE WORLD OUR DIVERSE WORLD OUR DIVERSE WORLD OUR DIVERSE WORLD

1 Through these efforts, the values and needs of all parents can be represented.

2,3 Equal access and cultural sensitivity will influence what children learn about the variety of people in the world around them.

The societal problems that lie outside traditional education must be met if children are to be ready to learn. Child health and nutrition services and pre-natal care will help ensure that children will enter school ready to learn. Meeting the needs of poor families also includes making high-quality pre-school programs available to children of all income levels and abilities. We must not choose between quality and equality (Ravitch, 1990).

4. *Promote developmental learning.* Educational policymakers must alter their perspective of readiness. When there is a mismatch between the expectations of the school and the children's abilities to meet those demands, the schools need to change. The programs must adapt to meet the developmental needs of children rather than the other way around. Get *schools* ready for young children as opposed to having children be pressured and pushed to get ready for school. Ensure that schools respect the unique way children under 8 learn and allow for their differing timetable of learning. Discourage the use of standardized testing for screening, tracking, and retaining young children. Avoid labeling young children or linking student readiness evaluations to school entry. Teaching practices in the elementary school years should be based on child development principles and modeled after successful preschool programs. Although some progress is being made through Goals 2000, developmentally appropriate practices must be continually addressed in all areas of school reform.

5. *Initiate programs and policies that strengthen the family.* Develop programs that help to increase parents' abilities to help their children become learners and that involve the family in the educational endeavor. Education and learning are profoundly affected by what happens to children outside of schools. The family support for learning should be addressed by focusing on parental attitudes and involvement at home as well as at school and on the parents' responsibility for meeting the basic care and needs of their children.[1]

6. *Develop partnerships with the community and with business.* Coordinating the efforts of the many providers of child care services and collaborating with

Figure 15.4 ● Good early childhood programs do not distinguish between education and care but understand that both are vital to the growing child.

other community agencies that service young children and their families serve more children, make better use of public funds, and improve the quality of all programs. A comprehensive system of early childhood services would include parent education and family support programs, child care, and health and social services. The effort should involve programs that are public and private, profit and nonprofit, church and government sponsored, and home based as well as center based. Under such a partnership, the community as a whole could build and improve services to children and parents through joint planning and advocacy and information and resource sharing (National Association of State Boards of Education, 1988).

Solutions

Changes in education are historically linked to social reform. Nowhere is this link more obvious than in the current reform movement. The link between poverty and school failure has been recognized and

[1] Children's programs should reflect the attitude that diversity is an opportunity for learning—not a problem.

clearly demonstrated. Poor children are twice as likely to drop out of school than middle-income youths (Children's Defense Fund, 1998). Poor health affects a child's ability to succeed in school. *Poverty Matters*, a Children's Defense Fund report (1998), cites studies of homeless children showing that they have lower math and reading scores, are less likely to finish high school on time, and often develop respiratory illness from poor housing conditions that results in missing school. The reform itself was spurred in part by one of the most powerful social and economic changes in this century: the employed mother.

The reforms that have been suggested cannot be solved by any single agency or institution. We must look beyond individual programs to the trend toward a diversity of services provided by an equally diverse coalition of state and federal government, business and industry, research and education. Together, a common agenda to enhance school success in the context of the child's family, community, and culture can be established.

THE IMPORTANCE OF CHILDHOOD

Endangered Childhood

Children and childhood have changed. Gone are the days when the majority of children arrived home from school to be greeted by mom in the kitchen, serving milk and homemade cookies. Today's child spends the bulk of time in child care centers or with a neighbor while the parent is at work. Too many arrive at empty homes and spend the next few hours alone or caring for younger siblings. As often as not, the child of today lives with just one parent at best.[1]

Emphasis on Survival

A decade or two ago children seemed to be more protected than they are today; they seemed more innocent. Today's parents are concerned that their children learn to survive, to cope with problems at an early age. They believe the best way to teach children survival skills is to expose them to adult experiences and "reality" early.

Figure 15.5 ● Every child has the right to a full and wondrous childhood.

The impact of social changes in the last 20 years has been hardest felt by the children of the nation. The breakdown of the nuclear family unit, the sexual and feminist revolutions, television, drugs, and worldwide violence have thrust children into adult situations with adult troubles. Dual-parent careers and single working parents, together with the lack of extended families, have meant that children's behavior is not as closely monitored as it once was.

Stress and Changing Parent–Child Relations

Childhood has been misplaced. The boundaries between adults and children are hazy. Adults exert pressure on children to hurry and grow up, to achieve

 OUR DIVERSE WORLD OUR DIVERSE WORLD OUR DIVERSE WORLD OUR DIVERSE WORLD OUR DIVERSE WORLD OUR DIVERSE WORLD OUR DIVERSE WORLD OUR DIVERSE WORLD

[1] Do we as a society have a mindset of OUR DIVERSE WORLD, or an image/mythology based on middle-class family life of the mid-1940s to mid-1960s?

and succeed, to perform and to please. Children respond by doing their best, all the while sensing the pressure to mature (Gordon, 1986).

People are dealing with their children differently than did their parents. They are opening up to their children, telling them of (rather than protecting them from) their own fears and anxieties. Children have been enlisted as coparents in their own upbringing, collaborating with their parents on child-rearing practices, dress codes, and behavior expectations. Although this is obviously more democratic and less authoritarian, the results have been that the boundaries between children and adults have become increasingly hazy. It would appear that we are asking young children of today to assume a mantle of maturity before they are capable. We are requiring them to respond to life as adults, not as children. We no longer assure children that the adult is in charge and that their needs will be met. Instead, we ask children to share that burden with us.

Another type of parent emerged in the 1980s, the creator of the "superbaby" (Langway et al., 1983). These children began life enrolled in a series of classes by parents who hoped to give them as many stimulating experiences as they could absorb. Infant gymnastic workouts, alphabet flashcards in the nursery, and violin or acting lessons to supplement preschool signaled parental expectations for these children. These wonderkids, children of the post–World War II "baby-boom" children (who are now affluent, knowledgeable, and generally over 30), had to fulfill every conceivable potential as early as possible. They were being pushed toward success by parents who themselves were more successful than their parents had been. "The more, the better" sometimes seemed the motto of the day.

The focus for these parents was and is often on infant academics and superior physical achievement. This focus raises concerns about the welfare of the child. When the emphasis is on performance and not on unconditional acceptance or feelings, the development of the child may be focused on only one or a few areas of the child's growth. It raises questions as to whether all the basics are being met—social and emotional needs as well as creative, intellectual, and physical ones.

Figure 15.6 ● How do we help children cope with stress?

Today's children are expected to cope with changing family structures. Only a small percentage of U.S. households are traditional, nuclear families.[1] Instead, children face divorce, single parenthood, sexuality issues, dual-career parents, poverty, homelessness, and other late-20th-century phenomena that produce stress. Adult coping skills are expected of 2-, 4-, and 7-year-olds, rather than allowing children to respond to life as children (Gordon, 1986).

For many children, the result has been a hurried childhood (Elkind, 1988). Parents push their children through the early years, urging them to grow up fast, succeed, achieve. Designer clothes are just the outward trappings these parents use to encourage adult attitudes and behaviors. The loss of childhood seems to have brought with it new problems for children. Clinicians are seeing more children with stress-related problems: headaches, abdominal pains, and even ulcers are occurring in children 3- and 4-years-old.

OUR DIVERSE WORLD OUR DIVERSE WORLD OUR DIVERSE WORLD OUR DIVERSE WORLD OUR DIVERSE WORLD OUR DIVERSE WORLD OUR DIVERSE WORLD OUR DIVERSE WORLD

[1] Some myths die hard. The early childhood educator must be aware of the demographics on family patterns.

Many common experiences that produce stress in young children are family related. Most adults would identify divorce, a move to a new home, prolonged visits from a relative, and a new sibling as classic stress situations for children. Yet there are homlier and less dramatic sources of stress, the simple everyday occurrences that children face: being told not to do something, not having a friend, being ignored by a parent, experiencing changes in the routine, not being able to read or zip a zipper or put a puzzle together. Stress may also occur in families where both parents pursue high-powered careers and children feel the need to live up to exceptional standards in academic achievement or sports proficiency. Apathetic parents, parents who ignore their children or have no time for them, and parents who push children into frantic schedules of activity also cause stress in their children. Stress can result from happy occasions as well—holidays, vacation, or a new puppy may be overanticipated, overstructured, and overstimulating to a child.

Children respond to stress in many ways. In adults, and sometimes in older children, depression, substance abuse, underachievement, and obsession with financial success are common responses to stress. In children, signs of stress include sleeping problems (such as nightmares or sleepwalking), depression, regression to the behavior of an earlier stage, aches and pains, acting out, eating problems, and overreactions, as well as medical problems (such as headaches, upset stomach, and bleeding ulcers) (Reed, 1986).

Stress is a natural part of life and is a factor in every child's development. Review Chapter 14 for the stages of stress children go through and for ways to help them cope with their responses.

Child Abuse and Neglect

The Crisis

In 1997, over 3 million children were reported for child abuse and neglect to child protective services, representing an increase of 41% since 1988 (National Committee to Prevent Child Abuse, 1998). Respect for children and childhood is seriously eroded when adults violate the trust of and responsibility for children

through neglect and abuse. Social change over the last few decades has put many of our children at risk. The changes in the family unit, unemployment, loss of funding for programs and subsidies for families, and rising divorce rates have put parents under stress and are having a negative effect on children's well-being. When children are cared for improperly, the results are often child neglect and abuse.

A neglected child may be one whose waking hours are mostly unsupervised by adults, in front of the television or simply unconnected with—and unnoticed by—parents or an important caregiver. **Child neglect** takes other, more hazardous, forms, however. When the basic needs of adequate food, clothing, shelter, and health are unmet, parents are being neglectful. Failure to exercise the care that children need shows an inattention to and lack of concern for children.

Child abuse is the most severe form of disrespect for children. Violence in the form of physical maltreatment and sexual abuse is an improper treatment of children, regardless of their behavior. Abusive language and harsh physical aggression are other forms of child abuse that occur in families and, unfortunately, some settings for child care.

Publicized investigations into sexual abuse of children in child care centers, preschools, and family situations have brought national attention to this hideous violence. Yet reports of abuse in day care, foster care, or other institutional care settings represents only about 3% of all confirmed cases in 1997 (Wang & Daro, 1998).[1] Whether or not its increased incidence is due to a change in reporting practices, it is clear that the abuse of children knows no social, racial, or economic barriers. It is happening to children at all levels of the social spectrum.

Standards of Care

For child care workers, the heart of the issue lies in the regulation and licensing of early childhood programs. In light of recent disclosures concerning incidents in centers, we need to take a long, hard look at who is caring for children. In what physical, emotional, and interpersonal environments are our children living? Licensing regulations for schools and teacher

OUR DIVERSE WORLD OUR DIVERSE WORLD OUR DIVERSE WORLD OUR DIVERSE WORLD OUR DIVERSE WORLD OUR DIVERSE WORLD OUR DIVERSE WORLD OUR DIVERSE WORLD

[1] These cases often become sensationalized in the press. Low numbers of incidence, however, do not eliminate the need for clear policies and procedures in all early childhood programs.

certification vary greatly throughout the country. Primarily they ensure only minimum health and safety standards of the physical environment. The great number of unlicensed child care facilities and the quality of children's programs are urgent issues. Governing and regulatory agencies in most states are inadequately staffed and insufficiently budgeted to handle the monitoring of child care settings.

A national call to action to increase public awareness and understanding of child abuse is under way. Standardized licensing procedures, upgrading of the certification of child care workers, and national accreditation of all preschools are some of the most frequently mentioned solutions to the problem. Helping parents identify what qualities to look for when placing their children in someone else's care is another way to prevent child abuse in centers.

Role of the Teacher

Teachers have a role to play. Reporting suspected child abuse is mandated by law in *all* states. Educators must assume the responsibility to inform the proper authorities if they suspect that a child in their care is being abused by adults. Figure 15.8 lists the signs a teacher should look for if child abuse is suspected.[1]

The mandate to report suspected child abuse applies to teachers, principals, counselors, school nurses, and staff members of child care centers and summer camps. Certain knowledge that abuse took place is not required; reports are legally required if there is reasonable cause to suspect a child has been mistreated. For the protection of anyone reporting abuse or neglect, the person filing the report is held immune from civil or criminal liability if the report was made in good faith.

What to Do If You Suspect Child Abuse

● Make notes of child's appearance—any bruises, marks, or behaviors that cause you concern.

● Inform the director of the program and/or your immediate supervisor; plan together who will

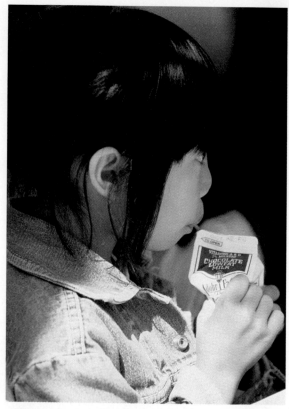

Figure 15.7 ● When basic needs such as food and shelter are met, children are free to develop interests in other people and other things.

inform the proper authorities and how to contact the parent(s).

● Discuss ways to support the staff members who make the report, the parent(s), and the child.

● Call the locally designated agency for child abuse. A written report may be required within 24 to 48 hours.

● Support the parent(s) throughout the investigation. Be available to the parent(s) and the child as they deal with the other agencies who are trained and equipped to handle this problem.

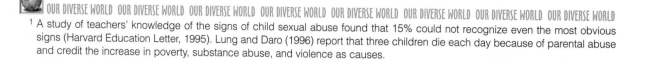

OUR DIVERSE WORLD OUR DIVERSE WORLD OUR DIVERSE WORLD OUR DIVERSE WORLD OUR DIVERSE WORLD OUR DIVERSE WORLD OUR DIVERSE WORLD OUR DIVERSE WORLD

[1] A study of teachers' knowledge of the signs of child sexual abuse found that 15% could not recognize even the most obvious signs (Harvard Education Letter, 1995). Lung and Daro (1996) report that three children die each day because of parental abuse and credit the increase in poverty, substance abuse, and violence as causes.

● Follow through with assistance or support if requested to do so by the child-protective services agency. Help the family by working with others who are counseling them and performing parent support services.

What to Do If a Child Tells You He or She Has Been Abused

● Believe the child; children rarely lie about sexual abuse.

● Commend the child for telling you what happened.

● Convey your support for the child. Children's greatest fear is that they are at fault and responsible for the incident. It is important to help children avoid blaming themselves.

● Temper your own reactions, recognizing that your perspective and acceptance are critical signals to the child. Do not convey your own feelings about the abuse.

● Report the suspected abuse to the child's parent(s), the designated social service agency, and/or the police.

● Find specialized agencies that evaluate sexual abuse victims and a physician with the experience and training to detect and recognize sexual abuse.

Source of Information. *Child Sexual Abuse Prevention.* Washington, DC: U.S. Department of Health and Human Services, 1998.

In some early childhood programs, teachers and other specialists have started programs for young children that will help them recognize and avoid abuse. Perhaps most important, teachers must stay in close touch with the parents of all their children. By knowing parents personally and being in contact with them regularly, an early childhood professional may be able to detect early signs of impending problems of both abuse and neglect. The perceptive teacher can then support parents through their difficulties, offering them help by informing them of a parental stress hotline, suggesting strategies to avoid stress and violence, and recommending professional help.

In 1996, NAEYC adopted a "Position Statement on the Prevention of Child Abuse in Early Childhood Programs and the Responsibilities of Early Childhood Professionals to Prevent Child Abuse" urging that early

Child abuse should be suspected if a child:
● Is constantly late, stays away from school for long periods of time, or arrives early and stays late, avoiding going home
● Is withdrawn passive, and uncommunicative or aggressive, destructive, and nervous
● Has unexplained injuries, too many "explained" ones, or has an injury that is inadequately explained
● Complains of numerous beatings, of someone "doing things," whether or not the parents are home
● Goes to the bathroom with difficulty; has burns, lumps, or bruises, patches of hair missing, bad teeth
● Wears clothing that is too small, soiled, or inappropriate for the weather, or uses clothing to cover injuries
● Is dirty, smells, is too thin or constantly tired; exhibits dehydration or malnutrition
● Is usually fearful of other children or adults
● Has been fed inappropriate food, drink, or drugs
● Is often tired or listless or sleeps in class
● Is often hungry
● Has torn, stained, or bloody underclothing; has bruises or bleeding in genital areas
● Has unattended physical problems or lacks routine medical care
● May seem unduly afraid of parents, may take on the protective role with parent(s), and/or lack parental supervision at home
● Has learning problems that cannot be diagnosed

Figure 15.8 ● A child who exhibits several of these signs should be investigated as a possible victim of child abuse. (Adapted from *Child Abuse: Betraying a Trust*, 1995.)

childhood programs in homes, centers, and schools adopt a set of policies based on guidelines such as employing adequate staff and adequate supervision of staff; environments that reduce possibility of hidden places; orientation and training on child abuse detection, prevention, and reporting; defined and articulated policies for a safe environment; avoidance of creating "no-touch" policies by the caregivers and staff. In regard to staff recruitment, NAEYC recommends that early childhood programs in the home, center, or school initiate policies that require personal interviews, verification of references and education background and qualifications, criminal record checks, and disclosure of previous convictions. New employees should serve a probationary period, and programs should have policies that provide for the removal of anyone whose performance is unacceptable. Procedures must also be in place for responding to an accusation of child abuse and provide due process for the accused (NAEYC, 1997). All those involved in early childhood care and education would be well advised to secure a copy of the statement and use it to reflect on the effectiveness of their own program's policies and procedures.

Children and AIDS

Gretchen Buchenholz's Focus Box is an example of confronting prejudice with a group of children who are often treated unfairly because of their disability. The story sets the tone to discuss the critical issue of children and AIDS.

Acquired immunodeficiency syndrome (AIDS) is a communicable disease that breaks down the body's immune system, leaving it unable to fend off harmful bacteria, viruses, and the like. Illnesses that are not usually life-threatening to a healthy person can result in death for someone who has AIDS. When reading this section, the student is reminded that statistics and information on AIDS are constantly changing; the reader is strongly urged to consult the most recent research data.

AIDS is caused by the human immunodeficiency virus (HIV), which is primarily sexually transmitted, although it can pass from one person to another by contact with blood, blood products, or through bodily secretions that mix with a person's blood. The AIDS virus may be present in the blood even though the full AIDS syndrome does not develop. The infection, however, can be transmitted to someone else even if the person carrying it has no symptoms.

AIDS is thought to have first occurred in the 1970s, although documentation of AIDS patients did not begin until 1979. In the United States the disease is prevalent among males (85% of the AIDS victims are men) and occurs primarily in homosexuals, in intravenous drug users, and in hemophiliacs and other persons who receive contaminated blood transfusions.

Children, too, are AIDS victims. Those at greatest risk are:

● Infants born to mothers who have AIDS

● Infants who are breast-fed by mothers with AIDS

● Infants and children who receive blood transfusions (blood screening programs may have reduced this risk)

● Sexually abused children

The highest incidence of pediatric AIDS is found in metropolitan areas, in large cities that also have a high rate of intravenous drug use. African American children account for 52% of reported pediatric AIDS cases; Latino children make up 25% of the cases; the remaining 23% are Euro-American children. Approximately 80% of the diagnosed children were infected by their mothers before or at birth. Between 1992 and 1996, however, the number of U.S. newborns contracting AIDS dropped 43%. This decline is credited to the use of the drug known as AZT, which is given to infected mothers as part of their prenatal care (Children's Defense Fund, 1998). Children around the world, however, do not fare as well. UNAIDS, a program of the United Nations, estimates that by the end of 1997, a million children under the age of 15 were living with AIDS, over 90% of them in developing countries (Centers for Disease Control and Prevention, 1998).

Along racial and ethnic lines, the proportion of AIDS cases in the United States for 1996 breaks down like this:

	By Total Population	In Children Under 13
White, non-Hispanic	72%	64%
Black, non-Hispanic	12%	15%
Hispanic	12%	16%
Asian/Pacific Islanders	3%	4%
Native Americans	1%	1%

(Centers for Disease Control and Prevention, 1998)

The greatest fears—and misconceptions—about AIDS are how contagious is the disease and how is it transmitted. Sexual contacts and mingling of blood are the two known routes of infection, and not one case is known to have been transmitted any other way, even to close family members of AIDS patients. No children have contracted AIDS from ordinary contact with other children. None of the cases of AIDS in the United States has been transmitted in a school or child care setting or through hugging, sharing a glass or a plate, sharing bathrooms, or in kissing that is not mouth to mouth kissing (Centers for Disease Control and Prevention, 1998).

Cody House

Gretchen Buchenholz

Mikey has AIDS. He has learned to ride a tricycle with breathtaking abandon. He is able to eat his Cheerios with a spoon. He pulls off his own shoes and socks often. He's full of himself and full of joy. There's enough warmth in him to melt the hardest heart, enough radiance to light up the darkest hour, and enough life in him each day of his life for a whole lifetime.

Mikey attends Cody House, a preschool program on New York City's East Side. It is one of six programs under the auspices of the Association to Benefit Children (ABC). There, his sunny classroom is further brightened by red, yellow, and blue mats and the smiles of the sickest children in the world. There is a secret garden out back, a beautiful and serene oasis. Doves and hollyhocks are painted on the garden wall. Each dove flies skyward. Some carry the name of a child who has died—Wilfredo 9/15/91, Tenay 6/30/91, Sean 4/9/94, Franklin 9/24/94, James 1/29/94, Laurie 10/17/92, Lisa 12/23/93, and Jacqueline 1/30/95. Others wait. Eric is there splashing in the pool. Laughter rings out from Tunisha,, who's playing.

Cody House is warm and nurturing and provides the close attention and special therapies essential for optimizing the mental physical, emotional, social, and spiritual development of each child. Because Cody House serves children who have life-threatening illnesses, the program is specifically designed for managing children's medical needs while simultaneously meeting their educational, social, and emotional needs.

Children who require daily infusions are given their treatments during the school day by medically trained staff members. Along with the debilitating emotional and physical stresses of the disease itself, families of young children with terminal illness frequently have their lives disrupted by medical treatments. Hospitalizations make it difficult for families to maintain the relatively stable routine so critical to the emotional health of any young child. Children who would have been faced with these routine but disruptive overnight hospital stays in sterile and frightening settings are now able to receive that same treatment in the stimulating, more "normal" environment of the classroom. Lives are normalized; life spans are increased.

Cody House makes family support services an integral part of the educational program. It provides the array of services necessary to meet each family member's needs and includes educational, medical pediatric, nutritional, rehabilitative, psychological, and language therapy services. ABC has created with Cody House a safe haven and place of hope for many families who face the devastating combination of terminal illness and poverty. Cody House is a place where parents will find sustenance and where children will find quiet tenderness, the time to wash a doll's hair or put jelly on toast.

ABC's other preschools are for homeless, handicapped, and medically fragile children as well as children from the neighborhoods in which they are located. Because vulnerable children are brought

567

together with normally developing kids, each child's experience makes its own unique contribution to the collective experience of all. Children are more alike than different because they care about the same things. They care about transforming Play-Doh into snakes and birthday cakes, singing silly songs, and rolling in the sweet grass. All children need to be part of the mainstream of life. At ABC they are. They're known and loved for their strengths, not for their limitations. And everyone gains infinitely in patience and tenderness and understanding. When children are allowed to learn and play and laugh together, respect and an appreciation for diversity become a part of their lives forever.

Gretchen Buchenholz is the executive director of the Association to Benefit Children, New York, N.Y.

Role of the Teacher

The number of AIDS victims multiplies rapidly. The Centers for Disease Control and Prevention predict a continued increase in the heterosexual population and in babies. Early childhood professionals clearly have a role to play regarding this misunderstood disease:

- Be an informed resource to parents and other teachers. Keep abreast of current data and educate others about the *facts* of AIDS.

- Know how to answer the questions a preschooler will ask. Begin to educate children.

- Examine your own attitudes about sexually transmitted diseases, homosexuality, and drug usage.

- Keep up to date on research about AIDS; information changes rapidly and is released frequently.

- Take appropriate precautions—careful handwashing and use of plastic gloves when contact with blood may occur.

- Be prepared to counsel children and their families through long illness and death in the same way as with other fatal diseases.

- Develop school policies that reflect the current knowledge and recommendations of medical experts.

At Risk: Children in Need

Of major concern to educators for the 21st century is a group of Americans who are destined for limited participation in the social, political, and economic mainstream of national life. The children who are at risk of academic failure are likely to be: those who live in poverty, members of minority groups in racial isolation, children with various physical and mental disabilities, children with limited English proficiency, children from single-parent families, or children attending schools with a high concentration of students who live in poverty (National Study Panel on Education Indicators, 1991).

Millions of children are poverty-bound and are at risk to repeat the cycles that keep them poor and disadvantaged. As Edelman (1993) reports,

> Young children are the poorest Americans. Almost one in four American children younger than six lived in a family with income below the poverty line in 1990, and more than one in 10 in a family with income less than one-half of the poverty line. Living in dire poverty means that children's nutrition and health care too often are traded against paying the rent or the heat; after paying the rent, a typical poor family with children has an average of $3.49 per day left to spend on all other needs.

These children and youth are undereducated, marginally literate, and lacking the necessary skill for employment. They are high risks for dropping out of school and becoming teenaged parents who will perpetuate the cycle. Although the number of children under 6 increased by less than 10% between 1971 and 1991, the number of poor children under 6 increased by more than 60% (Carnegie Foundation, 1995). The population of children living in working poor families has jumped from 3.4 million to 5.6 million in the past 20 years (Casey Foundation, 1995). And, though the feminization of poverty is still a reality (in 1989, 51% of children in female-headed families lived in poverty), by 1994 only 14% of all children in working poor families were born to teenage mothers, and half the children lived in two-parent, married families.

The face of child poverty is, indeed, diverse. There is a striking correlation between poverty and school failure. Children who start out at a disadvantage fall farther behind in academic achievement throughout their school years.[1]

The changing school population suggests that these problems will only increase as the proportion of minority groups expands (because they are overrepresented among the poor), as a larger and larger percentage of children fall below the poverty line, and as traditional patterns of child-rearing and marriage change so that fewer children will have the emotional and educational advantages of a two-parent family.

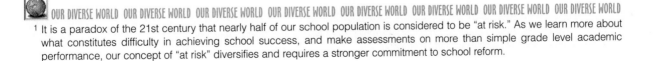

[1] It is a paradox of the 21st century that nearly half of our school population is considered to be "at risk." As we learn more about what constitutes difficulty in achieving school success, and make assessments on more than simple grade level academic performance, our concept of "at risk" diversifies and requires a stronger commitment to school reform.

A dramatic and intensive reform effort is needed for at-risk children, and a number of solutions are being considered. With 20.5% of America's children in poverty—the range running from 16.3% to 40.3% by race or ethnicity (Children's Defense Fund, 1998)—committment and action are urgent. As the National Commission on Children (1991) states:

> ...Too many of today's children and adolescents will reach adulthood unhealthy, illiterate, unemployable, lacking moral direction and a vision of a secure future. This is a personal tragedy for the young people involved and a staggering loss for the nation as a whole. We must begin today to place children and their families at the top of the national agenda.

Families and Communities

The family of today has many shapes, sizes, and styles. A family can be:

- A dual-career family, with two parents working outside the home and children in child care

- A single parent supporting children, with little or no help—either financial or personal—from the absent parent

- Older parents raising their grandchildren

- Teen parents living with, or without, family support

- A blended family—adults with children remarried to form a new structure, with children living full- or part-time in residence

- An extended family (or several families) living together in a small dwelling

- A gay or lesbian couple raising children

- An unmarried person living either alone or with others who do not have children

In fact, the American family has evolved so extensively over the last few decades that the Children's Defense Fund (1998) reports:

- One in two preschoolers has a mother in the labor force.

- Two thirds of mothers of young children [6 and under] work outside the home; 55% of working women provide half or more of the family's income.

- One in two children will live in a single-parent family at some point in childhood.

- Families with children accounted for more than a third of the homeless Americans in urban areas who sought shelter in 1997.

- One in three children will be poor at some point in childhood.

- The United States ranks first among industrialized countries in gross domestic product, but 18th in the income gap between rich and poor children.

The changing family structure and circumstances affect early childhood professionals in several ways. Teachers should understand the nature of these changes and their effects on families and children. What new child-rearing guidelines will be needed for families? What is the role of educators with the new American family?

Divorce and Family Structures

Perhaps no one single change has affected children as much as the *divorce* rate. The trend toward more divorce is significant. Nearly 50% of marriages end in divorce, and five of ten children born in the 1990s will spend part of their growing years in a single-parent home (Osborn, 1991; Children's Defense Fund, 1998).[1] One school child in three has parents who are divorced; 30% of these are children in stepfamilies and the other 70% live with their mothers or fathers alone (Clarke-Stewart, 1989). The issues for teachers are (1) dealing with the effects of divorce on children and (2) supporting the recovery process and resumption of family life. The effects of divorce are felt for years. Getting over divorce and onto a productive life is critical for both child and parent; teachers can help.

 OUR DIVERSE WORLD OUR DIVERSE WORLD OUR DIVERSE WORLD OUR DIVERSE WORLD OUR DIVERSE WORLD OUR DIVERSE WORLD OUR DIVERSE WORLD OUR DIVERSE WORLD

[1] Consider the stories read to young children. Is this reality reflected? Is this reality reflected in messages sent from program to home? When scheduling parent-program meetings?

The effects of divorce are felt by children well before the event itself. Children exhibit "predivorce family stress" by increased impulsive or aggressive behavior, and parents show the stress with headaches, fatigue, mood swings, or depression. Children's initial reaction to their parents' separation is traumatic— shock and distress (the "stage 1" responses to stress as described in Chapter 14). Even if parents are not in violent conflict with each other, no child is happy about divorce (Clarke-Stewart, 1989). After divorce, many parents become overworked and overwhelmed. Children are often neglected or left with less than what both parents could provide, including emotional and financial support. Studies indicate that after a divorce women suffer a drastic drop in income (Galinsky, 1986). Because 90% of children in divorced families live with their mothers, economic disaster is felt by most children of divorce.

Adjustment to divorce is difficult, and the psychological effects of divorce on children are often felt well into adulthood. "Divorce is a cumulative experience for the child. Its impact increases over time," writes Wallerstein (1997), reporting on a 25-year research project initiated in the early 1970s. For instance, of the people who were 2½- to 6-years-old when their parents divorced, one third did not pursue any education beyond high school, though 40% of them did graduate from college.

Growing up in a divorced home does not mean children cannot live happy lives. Fortunately, children are amazingly resilient. The age and sex of the children involved seem to have some bearing on their adjustment. Very young children recover more easily than older ones, and boys react more intensely than girls to the loss of their fathers from the home (Carlisle, 1991). The parents' ability to be caring and available makes a difference, as does the parents' relationship with each other and the quality of the children's relationship with both parents.

What can teachers do? For one, teachers should be informed about what to expect from children in the divorce cycle. They can help parents get access to outside help, such as a parent support group, community welfare services, or a parental stress hotline. Particularly with parents involved in a divorce, teachers must plan strategies for family involvement that takes into account the work demands, resources, and expertise of parents themselves. With children, teachers are open and forthcoming about the reality of different kinds of families (see "Community and School

Support" section). Moreover, they must realize that divorce "does superimpose a series of special and difficult tasks on top of the normative tasks of growing up" (Wallerstein, 1997). Teachers help children and parents understand and cope with the challenges and responsibilities of marriage and family life. Providing a place and time to heal makes a program or family child care home a safe haven to begin to heal and become whole again. Suggestions (Carlisle, 1991) include:

- *Know your children.* Confer with families as often as possible and be aware of family stresses and crises.

- *Talk about feelings.* Anger and sadness are predominant, along with guilt, loss, helplessness, and loneliness; an understanding teacher can go a long way to help a child feel less alone and can offer appropriate opportunities—through intimate moments, puppets and dolls, unstructured drawings, role playing and creative drawing— for expression.

- *Use bibliotherapy.* Books are powerful tools to connect with children, with understanding and kindness. They are also wonderful resources to families.

- *Keep aware of family diversity.* Be sure to include many family structures in the curriculum, during informal discussions, with any correspondence to home.

- *Include open communication with parents and family members.* Divorce tends to complicate communication between teachers and parents. Make adjustments in conferences, newsletters, and notes about the child so both the primary and noncustodial parents are included as much as possible.

Work, Economics, and Public Policy: The Working Parent

Two thirds of all preschool children under 6 have mothers in the work force (Children's Defense Fund, 1998), and the percentage rises when considering school-aged children as well. Mothers at work affect the family and the teacher.

The implications for families are considerable. For women, the double roles of job or career and family nurturer can be overwhelming, creating great conflict and the stress of chronic fatigue. Men are looking at their role in a different light; many are learning about greater involvement in child-rearing and how to adjust to a new financial provider role.[1] For both parents, three issues loom large: the concern for good child care, the struggle to provide "quality time" with children and as a family unit, and the financial burden. Without parental leave, parents are forced to return to work during the critical early months of infancy or lose income and even their job. The Children's Defense Fund (1998) reports a study that found that the annual earnings of women without job-protected leave dropped 29% the first year after having a baby, compared with an 18% drop with a job-protected leave.

For educators, working families have special new issues. As more parents are fully occupied with work during the school day, they are less available for direct participation in a classroom or on a constant basis. Teachers plan *flexible* opportunities for them to become involved in their children's education. "Just as societal changes have brought about the increased need for early childhood services, so will the ingenuity and creativity of professionals lead to the development of services adapted to new family realities" (Caldwell, 1989).

In the public sector, several proposals gained momentum in the 1990s. The most successful so far, the ABC Bill of 1990, allotted federal dollars to the states to provide support for centers, improving the quality of children's services available. The National Commission on Children, in 1990, recommended a child tax credit ($1000 per child) as part of a comprehensive blueprint for supporting children and families. In 1991, legislation was introduced to establish regular monies in the federal budget, a kind of "children's investment trust fund." Leading pediatrician T. Berry Brazelton's Washington-based lobby group, Parent Action, is garnering support for a family medical leave that would enable parents of newborns several months of unpaid leave from their jobs to be at home and establish an attachment bond and family setting, so critical to infants' well-being and survival.

The value of children is demonstrated in the support given to parents through employment-based or household-based plans. Such support is essential for children's health and education and for their future prospects as people and workers. Most European countries fund public programs for children and support services for parents at a much higher rate than in this country. Public policy is a reflection of the attitude and values we as a nation hold toward children and families, and the inequities are glaring. We look toward a future trend of clearer and more supportive public policies. Policies and attitudes must change to make it more attractive for adults to spend time with children, for, in the words of Colorado Representative Pat Schroeder (1991), "I have seen the future and it is wearing diapers."

Community and School Support

The relationship between schools and the community at large and the families they serve dictates the role schools play in the lives of families. Yet, as the Children's Defense Fund (1998) points out,

> Our communities, our work places, and our nation offer little support for parents engaged in the extraordinarily difficult task of caring for young children. Unlike virtually all of our Western European competitors, the United States has no parental leave policy (paid or unpaid) to allow parents to stay home with an infant without jeopardizing their jobs and income. Unlike those same nations, we have failed to ensure the availability of high-quality, affordable child care.

At the same time, the history of education in the United States is the story of the "progressive assumption" (Elkind, 1991). This means that the trend over time is for educational institutions to assume functions once performed by the family. There are difficulties in this progression, however, as schools are reluctant to assume some of these responsibilities and parents are wary of giving them up.

In colonial times, schools were primarily private, church-based programs for boys. After the Revolution the government began a forming a national public

[1] The sweeping changes in social behavior have resulted in changing attitudes about adults. However, there are vast differences among the various cultural groups and individual adults about the value of and care for children. Do not assume that a change in what you consider a "traditional" family pattern equals an inferior commitment to children.

school system, based on the belief that a democracy demands literate participants. This trend continued as the "public" came to include women and people of color. In modern times, the government provides subsidies to schools to provide free or low-cost meals, medical and dental services, and physical education programs, although many of these are in jeopardy at the time of this book's printing.

In the last 25 years, schools have continued to take on more child-rearing functions. The concept of school has changed as has the concept of family. In the past, educational duties were divided into two complementary tasks, occupational (by the schools) and personal (by the parents). The reduced time available for parenting today, paired with street issues, drugs, violence, sex, and so on, calls for a renewed definition and sense of mission for schools.

Schools have a key role to play in nurturing parental involvement in education and family life. Coleman (1991) describes this role as rebuilding the "social capital" both within the family and in the community. Drawing on an economic model, social capital refers to the richness and resources that social relationships provide for a child. The strength of these social relations helps shape a child's habits, establish norms of acceptable behavior, and encourage the development of children's character, long-range goals, and even educational attainment.

One example of the school as a reflection of community life is the Reggio Emilia system, as described throughout this text (see Chapters 2, 5, 8, 9, and 11 through 14). Founder Malaguzzi understood that the child cannot be thought of in the abstract, but as tightly connected to the world of relationships and experiences. Both Vygotsky (see Chapters 4 and 13) and Bronfenbrenner (see Chapter 2) emphasize these ties, and the Reggio system implements it in several ways. Parents are elected to local school boards and thus influence (and are influenced by) a close connection with the decision-making process around educational priorities. Besides "field trips," children are expected and anticipated in public places, rather than being simply tolerated, as they are in much of the United States.

The issue today in the United States is to define a new role for schools. One that many early childhood programs already do well is to provide avenues to strengthen children's resources in the family. Some specific ways include a comprehensive approach to families, so that the early childhood program is fully integrated into the families it serves. School systems

Figure 15.9 ● What responsibility does the community have to young children and their families? How do families with young children influence the community in which they reside? They join forces to advocate for important early childhood issues. (Courtesy of Stand For Children.)

can help parents get needed medical, dental, mental, job-related, and social services by collaborating with other agencies and individuals. Teachers who understand the powerful role of family and child-rearing styles in children's developing values will make special efforts to include parents in the "how-tos" of discipline, self-help, problem-solving, or homework. By offering parents meaningful and personal ways to be involved, educators promote parents' involvement with their own children. Thus children's "social capital" is rich and deep, giving children ample resources to call upon as they grow.

"It takes a village to raise a child." This old adage has new significance in today's society. But what is today's village community? John Gardner (1990) provides a stirring definition:

It is in community that the attributes that distinguish humans as social creatures are nourished.

Families and communities are the ground-level generators and preservers of values and ethical systems. . . . [Values] are generated chiefly in the family, school, church, and other intimate settings in which people deal with one another face to face. . . . We know that where community exists it confers upon its members identity, a sense of belonging, and a measure of security. . . . [F]rom the culture of their native place, the things, the customs, the honored deeds of their elders . . . humans [learn] a sense of community.

We see a future trend toward education's being part of that "village," forming partnerships among parents, teachers, school boards, and community groups, working in concert so children's needs are met. As part of this effort, early childhood professionals provide the knowledge and understanding of child development, but also the ability to relate to all children, parents, and coworkers with compassion, empathy, and understanding. Early childhood programs can help articulate the *shared values* of the community and the support for *diversity* of the whole community. *Trust* and *teamwork* go together to care for community members of all ages and to encourage *full participation* in decision-making as well as services. Children depend on healthy "villages" second only to their own families to develop into members of a world community (Young-Holt, personal communication, 1991).

For the Children

What, then, do children need from a family? Three areas have been identified that greatly affect children's development: role models, family values, and the **"ecology" of the family.**

Role Models. How people look at themselves and their roles in life is undergoing considerable transformation. Women who are heads of households and men who are serious participants in parenting are likely to deal with their children differently than did those in the traditional nuclear family. They have new ideas and habits of how parents and children treat each other, what they do and talk about together, and who is responsible for the children's upbringing. Blended families will have yet again another set of parenting issues to decide together. All these changes will affect the kinds of parents children experience. Power and custom must make way for the needs of children.

Family and Its Values. The major changes in family structure call for new ways to preserve the family and it values. To deal with the changes taking place in society, we must consider a number of possibilities, from economic issues to gender-role differentiation. Adults must question and clarify their values about children, caretaking, and child-rearing. Families with young children are increasingly dependent on agencies outside their informal social networks for emotional, informational, and material support, as demonstrated by the increasing use of information-and-referral services. Early childhood care and the education community have a central responsibility with respect to this task. How we help the family is the issue most important to the future of our society.

Ecology of the Family. Bronfenbrenner (see Chapter 2) uses the phrase "ecology of development" to describe the system or network of family and cultural relationships that significantly influence how children develop (see also the discussion of Vygotsky in Chapters 4 and 13). Just as important, this network is one in which children themselves have a significant influence. This principle suggests looking beyond the ages and stages of child development to a larger context in which the child grows (see discussions of the anti-bias approach, Chapters 9 and 11 through 14).

It makes good sense to look at ways parents and children affect one another's growth. Galinsky (see Chapter 8) sets out stages of parent development that affect the ways parents look at themselves in the life cycle of a family. Parents are growing, changing human beings and are influenced by their children's personalities, demands, and ages. Parents' original family and friends, society, culture, and religion all influence their thinking. In turn, parents influence their children by the way they discipline, the way they show affection or withhold it, the materials they provide, and the expectations they have for their children at varying ages.

The Role of the Teacher. The role of the teacher and the school system is to accept children and families for who they are and to invite them into the process of education and care for children. Therefore, teachers' first role is as a *resource for children.* Teachers organize space and develop materials that encourage broad participation. They clarify roles for children and interpret others' behavior to children so that they learn to understand and are able to act for themselves in a socially responsible way. Teachers attempt to bring in

Figure 15.10 ● When both parents work outside the home, new roles for fathers emerge.

children to the exciting world of learning. This is done best with choices that invite a freedom of response. Rather than offering a classroom where restrictions abound, teachers invite children (and their parents) to share their own family customs in an atmosphere of trust. Children can bring who they are in their family into school. When teachers model curiosity and acceptance of children and their families and cultures, children feel that they belong and have a second "family," the family of their classroom.

A second and more involving role for teachers is that of a *support for parents*. Parents need sources of support outside kin networks, developing relationships with caregivers that allow parents to talk about themselves and their lives at home. Teachers are more helpful when they can be available to listen to and confer with parents about their child's behavior, but also about the parents' own hopes and dreams for themselves and their children, their feelings as parents, and getting along as adults.

Parents learn from role models, too, particularly in the changing family structures so evident today.

Many experts, from Dr. Spock to Mr. Rogers, try to tell parents to trust themselves and listen to their own inner voices of what is good and healthy for themselves and their children. Early childhood professionals can help parents stay focused on what is important, to help them distinguish between the distracting noise of a busy society and the words of wisdom that do exist. The trend now, and certainly into the 21st century, is for the role of the teacher to become greater with families. Teachers will all come to accept the idea of teaching as a two-client job: a teacher of the child and a resource for the parent. It is complicated work, but one with internal integrity, building relationships that will endure for the child.

TRANSMITTING VALUES

As with the other themes in early childhood education, the issue of transmitting values is not for the teacher or school alone. A deep and primary source of values is that of the family and culture. The school must work with the family to provide a sense of shared values; nonetheless, both parents and teachers must acknowledge other sources that shape children's values and behavior. Three other critical sources are television and other media, war and violence, and social diversity.

Television and Other Media

In many homes, the television set has replaced the adult supervision of the past. Ninety-eight percent of the homes in the United States have televisions, and the average set is on for more than 6 hours each day. The average kindergarten graduate has already seen more hours of television than the time it takes to get a bachelor's degree from college (Trelease, 1984). "The average American child watches about 3½ hours of TV each day," reports Chen (1994). "That means by the time children graduate from high school, they've logged some 18,000 hours in front of a TV set— compared to about 13,000 hours in a classroom. Now consider what these kids are seeing: 20,000 commercials each year, and about 100,000 acts of TV violence—including 8,000 murders—by the time they reach sixth grade."

The issue for educators revolves around the influence of television on young children. There are four basic concerns that parents and teachers express about children's viewing of television and videos:

1. Television violence can lead to aggression and desensitization to violence.

2. Television promotes passivity, slowing intellectual development and stifling imagination.

3. Television promotes racist and sexist attitudes.

4. Television promotes materialistic consumism.

Research from the 1960s and 1970s expanded our knowledge of the powerful effects on children of the models they see, whether they be of children, adults, or fantasy characters. Bandura's social learning theory reinforced this notion (see Chapter 4), and it is generally accepted that media images can have similar influences. Knowing this, early childhood professionals are particularly concerned as the amount of violent television programming increases dramatically (Carlsson-Paige & Levin, 1987; Levin, 1998). Many claim that children who watch violent programs become more aggressive than those who do not (David, 1988; ERIC, 1990; Solter, 1986). With television so available to children, the effects of film-mediated aggression are important in determining the content of children's media programs. The Center for Media Literacy (1993) documents four effects of viewing media violence:

1. Increased aggressiveness and antisocial behavior. *"There is absolutely no doubt that higher levels of viewing violence on television are correlated with increased acceptance of aggressive attitudes and increased aggressive behavior."*

2. Increased fear of becoming a victim. *"Viewing violence increases the fear of becoming a victim of violence, with a resultant increase in self-protective behaviors and increase mistrust of others."* In other words, the brain engages in "downshifting" (see Chapters 4 and 13) that is detrimental to learning.

3. Increased densensitization to violence and victims of violence. *"Viewing violence increases densensitization to violence, resulting in a calloused attitude towards violence directed at others and a decreased likelihood to take action on behalf of the victim when violence occurs."*

4. Increased appetite for more violence in entertainment and real life. *"Viewing violence increases viewers' appetite for becoming involved with violence or exposing themselves to violence."*

As to the passivity argument, one need only see the enthralled look on children's faces to know that the screen images are engaging. Children do spend large amounts of time with television, but the research available seems to indicate that children actually do many other activities while the set is on and that their attention to TV is variable. Preschool children seem to attend to minute details of a show that interests them; most parents report very young children learning advertising jingles or details of slogans. Research about the cognitive effects of television viewing reveals that TV viewing seems to be a fairly complex cognitive activity. Still, there is little consistent evidence concerning television's influence on imagination and creativity. More research is critical, as well as an analysis of the content of the shows that children watch.

In the area of bias and stereotyping, children's television is an arena "where boys are king" (Carter, 1991). Networks generally assert that boys will not watch female-lead shows, but girls will watch shows with a male lead, and that the viewer audience is male majority (estimates are around 53% boys, 47% girls as child viewers). The pattern of "boy" dominance extends beyond the networks into public and cable broadcasting. Minority groups are also inadequately represented on TV, although there has been some improvement. Thus, with children's television shows, the Euro-American and male attitudes and behaviors are reinforced.[1]

Does television promote consumerism? As Bob Keeshan, affectionately known as Captain Kangaroo, once put it, "In America, television is not a tool for nurturing. It is a tool for selling" (Minow, 1991). After the deregulation of the television industry in 1985, the amount of commercial time in children's shows increased, and the "program-length commercial" was introduced, whereby a show was developed based on a line of consumer toys and products aimed at the children's market. Proponents of deregulation had reasoned that a free market and competition would improve the quality of television. "Competition, it is

OUR DIVERSE WORLD OUR DIVERSE WORLD OUR DIVERSE WORLD OUR DIVERSE WORLD OUR DIVERSE WORLD OUR DIVERSE WORLD OUR DIVERSE WORLD OUR DIVERSE WORLD

[1] An important task of early childhood educators is to actively counteract gender and ethnic group stereotypes.

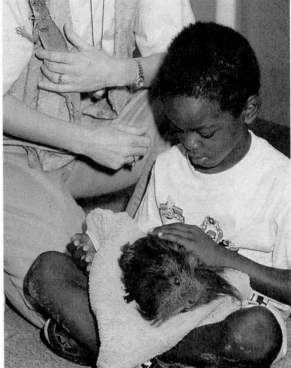

Figure 15.11 ● Antidotes to television.

said, brings out the best in products and the worst in people. In children's television, competition seems to bring out the worst in programs and the worst in children" (Minow, 1991). Therefore, in 1990 the Children's Television Act became law, requiring that stations submit an assessment of children's television offerings when they apply for license renewal with the Federal Communications Commission (FCC). The FCC also adopted rules that encourage broadcasters to air more educational programming for children and limit the amount of advertising during children's shows.

Television and the lessons it teachers are and will be a part of children's lives. Research needs to continue about the effects of media viewing. The studies available today do indicate clear modifiers of those effects, namely, parent coviewing and teaching of critical television viewing skills. The regulation of children's television advertising is a positive step. Another is the 1996 ruling by the FCC requiring broadcasters to provide 3 hours of educational programs for children each week. But these steps are small and not enough. Families and teachers need guidelines for television viewing and for dealing with the hazards of media culture (video games, computer games, assorted toys and games, etc.). Several professionals and organizations (ERIC, 1990; Klemm, 1995; Levin, 1998; Levin & Carlsson-Paige, 1984; NAEYC, 1990) make some of these suggestions:

1. *Set limits*. Know how many hours of TV children watch, and set limits. The American Academy of Pediatrics suggests a maximum of 1 to 2 hours daily. Keep the TV turned off unless someone is actively viewing; TV can easily become more of a habit than a choice. Involve your children in discussions about video-game systems or computer games; consider establishing rules (for instance, "Game-playing counts as 'screen time'" and "I can't play when a friend comes over.")

2. *Plan and participate*. Work together with children to decide what to watch. Help children choose shows with an age-appropriate viewing length, bias-free content, and peaceful action. Consider watching shows together, pointing out parts that are prosocial and asking about those parts you wonder about or disagree with. Uses the "pause," "rewind," and "mute" buttons as part of the process. Watch carefully what children are doing with video and computer games.

3. *Resist commercials*. Children do not distinguish easily between the sales-pitch commercial and the ordinary show. Help them become "critical consumers" by pointing out the exaggerated claims. Even 3-year-olds can answer the question "What are they trying to sell us?"

4. *Express your views*. Call a station that airs a show or commercial you find offensive, or write a letter to the Children's Advertising Review unit of the Better Business Bureau. Action for Children's Television in Cambridge, Mass., has been a leading public interest group for more than 20 years and has valuable suggestions for how adults can influence children's television programming.

Violence

The Situation

The trend of children's increasing exposure to violence is alarming. What is offered on television and other media, the kinds and choices of toys, and the interpersonal situations in children's homes, neighborhoods, and the world all contribute to an increased awareness of and exposure to violence. Parents report tensions in the relationships between themselves and their children. Increased violence on television along with a rising tide of war toys (abundantly advertised on television) contribute to a sense of being out of control in limiting or influencing children's behavior. Teachers see similar tensions with children in school and child care and notice changes in children's play. Many teachers report that the weapon and war play in classrooms is so single-purpose and intense that it is difficult to redirect; rule-setting and controlling overzealous play take an inordinate amount of teachers' energy.

Tragically, there is an alarming rash of unexplainable attacks *in school* of children wounding and killing other children and teachers. Access to real guns, as well as to TV and video images of violence, has fueled this deadly phenomenon. Community terrorism is becoming a particularly "American" interpretation of "war play." It is no wonder that Dr. Jocelyn Elders, when Surgeon General, declared that the primary health concern of our society is violence (Hoot & Roberson, 1994).

The increasing violence of American society has so alarmed educators and parents alike (Levin, 1994) that programs are being developed for children and for teachers. Organizations such as the Educators for Social Responsibility and the National Association for Mediation Educators serve as both clearinghouses for information and material and as training institutes for teachers. Additionally, California is piloting a "Safe Start" program for teachers-in-training and those already in the field to work more effectively with both children and families living in a violent world (Eyer, personal communication, 1995).

The Dilemma

Thoughtful adults find themselves in a dilemma. Should they allow war and violence play to continue (unchecked? with limits? with intervention?)? Or ought this kind of play be altered (redirected? contained? banned?)? This dilemma illustrates children's play from two different viewpoints, a developmental one and a sociopolitical one. The *developmental viewpoint* states that play, including war play, is the primary vehicle through which children work on developmental issues. Because children need to develop a sense of how the world works, of fantasy and reality, of good and bad, war play is an extension of "superhero" play (see Chapter 14), and is, therefore, a necessary part of children's play. The *sociopolitical view* assumes that children learn basic social and political behavior at an early age and, therefore, will learn militaristic concepts and values through war play. This viewpoint contends that children learn about conflict and resolution, the use of fighting, and the meaning of friends and enemies in their play, and that allowing war play endorses the use of force (Carlsson-Paige & Levin, 1987).

These two ideas give teachers the basic building blocks for how to deal with the issue of developing shared values and for engaging in a dialogue with fellow teachers and parents. Every viewpoint encourages a way of understanding and explaining war and violence to and with children.

Children's Needs

What children need most is reassurance, to know they will be safe and that caring grown-ups will still take care of them. Constancy and predictability, in the form of a consistent routine and continued habits of behavior and tradition, will help children feel anchored in their lives. Listening carefully, answering children's questions in simple ways, asking questions to elicit their thoughts all encourage communication and a dialogue about their feelings. Most educators and counselors also remind adults to monitor children's media exposure to war. Teachers help children find peaceful resolutions to their everyday conflicts, ensuring that, in their daily school life, war will not break out and take over (see Chapters 7 and 14 for suggestions).

This last suggestion may take several paths. A family child care provider of infants and toddlers may spend extra time giving hugs and helping children share toys. One class of preschoolers may choose a cross-town child care center to exchange drawings and visits with, to increase their knowledge of their city neighbors and of ideas they could create to solve each others' problems. In a first grade class, children were so concerned that they chose to write letters to the President ("I don't like it when you make war. My big sister says to use words when I have a problem and you should too.")

What to Do

As for the larger issues of war and violence, teachers can look at several courses of action. It is helpful to consider the options teachers have in these situations.

● Talk about and decide on your viewpoint and values with parents and the school board.

● Develop guidelines that address your values and the needs of the children.

● Talk with parents about toys and the role of the media in the development of children's interests and the role of parents in helping children decide and choose what and how to play.

● Investigate peace education, building peaceable classrooms that have conflict resolution teaching as part of the curriculum (see Chapters 7 and 14).

Creating safer environments for children in school will help children cope with violence (Groves & Mazur, 1995). Listening to children's own dilemmas both at school and from home allows teachers to provide opportunities for problem-solving and for vehicles for safe self-expression (Carter, 1995; Hopkins & Peppers, 1995).

Although peace is a complex issues, children know instinctively about peace and war, because they feel these contradictory emotions in themselves. By starting with what each individual child knows and feels, teachers can begin to build a foundation that emphasizes the positive steps toward peaceful negotiation, toward a balance of self and others, in terms children can understand and use.

A few general guidelines hold for children of all ages. Teachers work on their own personal feelings about war and seek out supportive resources. A teacher must prepare for controversy; differences in opinions about war and peace will be as common as those of the daily social interactions of children in the classroom. Recognizing children's need to discuss their feelings, teachers help parents to be a source of information and support for their children (Wallinga, Boyd, Skeen, & Paguio, 1991). A thorough and thoughtful approach to the issues of war and violence will help teachers and parents work together.

Diversity

Facing Reality

America as "melting pot," where all racial and cultural differences are smoothly mixed into one single blend, is a myth. Unfortunately, much of America's history can be characterized as racist, classist, sexist, and ethnocentric in nature by one group or another. The discrepancy between our ideals of equal opportunity and freedom and the daily reality can be altered only if we recognize the problems and then set specific goals for change.

Today's demographics point to a trend of an increasingly diverse society. In 1991 California became a "minority majority" state: that is a majority of public school students are members of minority groups. By the year 2000, Hispanic students may be almost as numerous as whites, and other groups are expected to account for a total of 22.2% of all students (*Education Week*, 1991). It is predicted that 46% of the nation's school children will be children of color by the year 2000 (Viadero, 1990). Review the data in Chapter 3.

The issue is that attitudes have not yet responded to reality. A University of Chicago survey on racial attitudes found that, although support for racial equality has grown, "negative images of members of other racial and ethnic groups are widespread among whites, and most groups have at least one prejudice against all the other groups" (Armstrong, 1991). In a comprehensive study entitled *A Common Destiny:*

Black and American Society, the National Research Council concluded that, despite gains in recent decades, "blacks still face formidable barriers on their path to educational parity with whites. . . . our findings imply several negative developments for blacks in the near future, developments that in turn do not bode well for American society" (Schmidt, 1989).

Moreover, school reform efforts have done little to meet the educational needs of America's demographic profile. The Center for Demographic Policy (1989) concludes that, despite reforms, neither high school dropout rates nor poverty among the young have decreased. Standardized test scores for the lowest academic groups have not gone up, and resources have not been increased.

Not Whether, But What Kind. We know that children exhibit an awareness of racial and gender differences by age 3 (Derman-Sparks, 1989) and are formulating rudimentary concepts about the meaning of those differences in the preschool years. It is logical to conclude that, by the end of the early childhood years, children have consolidated their attitudes about race, ethnicity, gender, and (dis)ability, and are far along the path of attitude crystallization. Unless the social environment changes, children will recreate the prejudices of the current adult society.

New concepts of society are needed, concepts that educators translate into programs for children. Children, their teachers and parents begin by forming an awareness of difference and learn with sensitivity the meaning of diversity.

Multicultural Education

Multicultural education is the system of teaching and learning that includes the contributions of all ethnic and racial groups. In other words, it is a comprehensive educational approach that reflects more minority perspectives, providing all children with a fuller, more balanced truth about themselves, their own history, and culture. This means a responsiveness to the child's origins, habits at home, ways of self-expression.

At higher levels of education there is a great debate about how to deal with diversity. Two views dominate. One is a "separatist" education in which education is taught from a particular viewpoint, be it European, Afro-centrist, or the like. The other is a more traditional, "pluralist," approach in which education stresses the commonalities of varying peoples. Janice E. Hale (1993) offers her ideas:

We can get our message across more effectively if we use a culturally salient vehicle. . . . [For instance], culturally appropriate pedagogy would expose African-American children to Anglo-centric and Afro-centric literature at each grade level. Exposure to Anglo-centric literature would provide them with the vocabulary, history, and information about the cultural orientation of mainstream America. This exposure is essential for African-American children to be able to negotiate the mainstream. Exposure to Afro-centric literature would broaden their vocabulary, provide them with information about African-American cultural values, enhance their self-esteem, and provide motivation and inspiration. . . . to educate African-American children in a culturally appropriate manner, there is a kind of dual educational process that is required.

What underlies the debate is how we see ourselves as a common culture. Our country and our schools are struggling. When we change the metaphor of "melting pot" to one of "mosaic" or "mixed salad," we encourage a new way of thinking that might be termed cultural pluralism—the idea that "Yes, we are all one people, but we do not necessarily divest ourselves of our ethnic origin" (Sobol in Viadero, 1990).

In early childhood education, teachers know that the basis of an authentic curriculum for children is with the individual child. Therefore, the program that responds most genuinely to diversity is one in which the child is accepted, the child's total personal diversity is respected, and the child's family and cultural traditions are part of the classroom. The section titled "Schools For Human Values: In the Classroom" and Chapters 9 through 14 have specific suggestions. Based on developmental principles, responsive to the individual, and proactive in its embrace of societal realities, a good early childhood program represents the best of multicultural education.

Bilingual Education

The 1980s left unresolved basic questions concerning bilingual education, and the 1990s were an explosive and exploratory time for the issues of language and learning. The goals and purposes of bilingual education remain controversial, for there are still disagreements over how to define bilingualism, how to determine who needs it, and who is to provide the services. Chapter 13 discusses bilingual education in light of language learning and curriculum development. This section highlights the broader issues and implications.

Bilingual education has been part of the American experience since before the Revolutionary War, when school was taught in any one of the more than 18 languages that were spoken by the colonists. Nonetheless, numerous cultures have been suppressed with regularity in the United States. Both Native American and immigrant groups have categorically faced discrimination. Speaking English is only part of bilingual education: at issue are the civil and educational rights of people who speak limited English, the respect or assimilation of their culture, and their participation and acceptance in society.

Changing populations and the influx of immigrants from Asia as well as from the Hispanic nations have brought with them today new challenges of bilingual education. Bilingual programs serve primarily Spanish-speaking students. States that do not have bilingual programs still need to meet the needs of limited-English-proficient (LEP) students in schools through other means. In 1998, a California state initiative effectively ended publicly funded bilingual programs, to be replaced by shorter-term, intensive English-immersion programs at the elementary and secondary levels. Because it is estimated that the number of school-age Spanish-speaking children in the country will increase by 50% by the year 2000, early childhood teaching will be affected.

The School-Age Child. The questions about bilingualism for the school-age child are different from those for the young child. In elementary school, teachers and children are forced to deal with issues beyond those of receptive and expressive language. Learning graphic language (reading and writing), acquiring concepts in other subject areas through listening, and dealing with the more complex social patterns and interpersonal issues are just a few of these issues. Moreover, the age at which children should be taught a second language is highly controversial. Research shows that children *can* acquire native-like mastery of a second language if they learn to speak the language before the age of 5. Others will argue that a child should learn all the fine points of the first language before being exposed to a second one and that this exposure should not occur before the age of 6.

Much research is centered on how children achieve second-language competence and performance. We do know that by age 5 children know most of the sounds and grammatical structure of their native tongue and appear to learn a second language in a similar way. With a bilingual child, the level of competence in both languages may be low while gaining mastery in the second language.

The two government actions that have most influenced the bilingual issue in our time are the passing of the 1968 Bilingual Education Act and the 1974 *Lau v. Nichols* Supreme Court decision. In 1974, the Supreme Court determined that a lack of instruction in one's first language is a violation of children's civil rights.

Since 1968, Title VII programs (the Elementary and Secondary Education Act, also known as the Bilingual Education Act) addressed the needs of students with limited proficiency in English. State bilingual education laws followed, requiring special instruction for children who lack competence in English.

The result is that children are taught, in public kindergarten and elementary schools, by using both the primary language and English. For instance, children may be taught to read in their primary language first; once they have learned the reading process in their own language, they are then taught to decode in English. Yet bilingual programs are so varied that it is difficult to assess them. Some work to mainstream children into regular classrooms as quickly as possible; others try to maintain the child's native language. A more recent program, the *dual* or *bilingual immersion method*, attempts a blending of language instruction by putting both English speakers and those with limited English into classes together and teaching "two-way" bilingual education. By bringing together both groups for language instruction, this method also indicates respect for both languages as assets. It shows promise as a truly multicultural tool for desegregation.

Still, the controversy continues. Another political backlash occurred in the late 1980s against non-English speakers. The U.S. Office Education claimed that bilingual education programs have not helped children learn English. California voters declared English as the official state language, and in 1998 publicly funded bilingual programs were voted down. Without consensus on the effectiveness and goals of bilingual education, educators must press for continuing research and clarity.

The Young Child. In preschools and child care centers, children are still taught in regular class settings, usually with little extra instruction. This type of instruction is known as the *English immersion system*. Recent research has generated controversy about what is best for children under age 5. In a survey for the National Association for Bilingual Education conducted in 1990, professor of education Lily Wong Fillmore of the University of California, Berkeley, found striking differences between families who participated in English-based programs and those whose children received native-language instruction. Her data indicate that language-minority children in English-speaking schools experience a substantial erosion of their native-language ability and have difficulty communicating with their parents.

The Plight of the Immigrant

Another serious challenge for schools is posed by the educational and socioeconomic needs of immigrant children. Attempting to immerse new children into an "American way" and to teach basic skills needed to succeed in the new country have been central functions of schools throughout U.S. history (see Chapter 1). Nationwide, there are more than 2.5 million school-age immigrants and at least as many children under 5; one in six children in the United States has a foreign-born mother (Children's Defense Fund, 1998). There are probably of children of undocumented adults. Immigrant enrollment in schools varies among the states and can reach as high as 95% in some schools.

The eroding financial and social supports for legal immigrant children are a critical problem. For instance, the 1996 federal welfare law denied supplemental Social Security income and food stamps to most legal immigrants until they become citizens and prohibited Medicaid and Temporary Assistance for Needy Families (TANF) for 5 years to immigrants who entered the country after August 1996. Although every state except Alabama has voted to continue TANF to some degree, only 12 states are providing aid in some form to families without food stamps. Estimates (Children's Defense Fund, 1998) are that 70% to 75% of the legal immigrants in this country are unaided by food stamps; the actual need is difficult to calculate.

The language barrier is the most immediate problem, followed by that of acceptance of the immigrants' native culture. Further, many newcomers arrive from countries racked with war, violence, and poverty. These children and families are under tremendous pressures and need help coping with the overwhelming stress and dislocation (see Chapters 14 and 15). The way schools place and monitor these immigrant children—both their educational progress and their general well-being—challenges educators and all American citizens to clarify the responsibilities our society has toward its newcomers.

Class Differences

By the year 2000, more than one third of the school population will be minority and poor (Haycock, 1991). These are the very children we have been the least successful in educating (Vukelich, 1991). Although these children enter kindergarten only slightly behind (thanks, in part, to quality early child-hood education such as a Head Start, High/Scope, and thousands of nursery schools and child care programs), by third grade, the average African American and Latino student is already 6 months behind (Haycock, 1991). In the 1990s the ethnic gap in academic achievement was either staying the same or widening, depending on grade and subject area (Children's Defense Fund, 1998). A 1997 report from the Department of Education found that

> schools with the highest proportion of poor children have markedly fewer resources than schools serving affluent students. . . . Schools serving large numbers of poor children have fewer books and supplies and teachers with less training. . . . Many schools are in disrepair, but those in the poorest communities are in the most dire shape (Children's Defense Fund, 1998).

Writing about the children of South Bronx, New York, Kozol (1997) noted that "America's enduring sin of racial segregation in our cities is even worse now than when I started out 30 years ago." Although no one likes to talk about it, the class differences cause many children, particularly children of poor and minority families, to get less:

● Less in the way of experienced and well-trained teachers

● Less in the way of a rich and well-balanced cur-riculum

● Less actual instructional time

● Less in the way of well-equipped and well-stocked laboratories and libraries

● Less of what undoubtedly is most important of all—a belief that they can really learn (Haycock, 1991)

So what can teachers do? First, we will have to deal with the "lesses." All of us know what makes good schools work, and our work on developmentally appro-priate practices, though still needing continual refine-ment, helps us articulate what makes good teaching and improved educational experiences for all children. We will have to join with other community efforts in building support systems so families can thrive and help their children succeed. In speaking out about chil-dren's needs and pushing for adequate teaching condi-tions, we in early childhood education can do our part.

Implications for Early Education

The issues of diversity in early childhood edu-cation are substantial. Although many have been addressed throughout the book, new issues develop every day that we need to keep in mind. Certainly we must welcome each child who enters our care and stay aware of issues and responsibilities.

One can conclude that, particularly for young children under 5, the primary language of language-minority children should be used in schools and centers. This is not a unanimous conclusion and it may not be practical in areas where there are small numbers and many language groups. Nonetheless, Wong Fillmore sheds important light on our thinking about educating language-minority children. We need to take into consideration what we know of the development of cognition and primary language. Are young children vulnerable in this area? Do we disrupt their developing thinking skills as well as their sense of self and the parent–child relationship to require English-language proficiency so young? Educating language-minority children can be made developmentally appropriate, by making school meaningful and welcoming of whole children, whatever languages they bring.

Clearly, one of the biggest challenges facing educators today is preparing children—and preparing the teachers to teach them—to live and work within an increasingly diverse population. A multifaceted approach is necessary to address diversity. Teachers will need special training that prepares them to be effective educators, addressing such topics as prejudice reduction training, bicultural expectations, physical and interpersonal environmental factors, varied teaching strategies, inclusive curriculum, and "culturally *responsible*, not just *responsive*, curriculum and conduct" (Association for Childhood Education International, 1996).

There are several guidelines teachers can follow (Bowman, 1991, with our own interpretations):

1. *"Teachers need to learn to recognize developmentally equivalent patterns of behavior. Before children come to school, they have all learned many of the same things, such as a primary language and communication styles."* Before judging a child as difficult or problematic, assume he or she is normal and look again. Your own vision may be clouded with "cultural myopia."

2. *"It is essential not to value some ways of achieving developmental milestones more highly than others."* When children find that the way they talk is not understood or appreciated in school, they are apt to become confused or disengaged. Remember, different is not deficient.

3. *"Teachers need to begin instruction with interactive styles and content that is familiar to the children. . . . [Teachers] can become more adept at planning and implementing a culturally sensitive curriculum."* You may not be fluent in a child's primary language, but you can learn key words and phrases that help a child feel a sense of belonging.

4. *"School learning is most likely to occur when family values reinforce school expectations."* Parent involvement is more than just a phrase; when parents and teachers are partners in education, children are the winners.

5. *"When differences exist between the cultural patterns of the home and community and those of the school, the teacher must deal with those discrepancies directly."* Teachers ask questions and create shared understandings between themselves and children, inviting children to be interested in creating a common culture of the classroom.

Equal Play and Gender Issues

There is ample research to confirm the widespread occurrence of gender segregation in childhood

(American Association of University Women, 1992; Grossman & Grossman, 1994; Hoyenga & Hoyenga, 1993; Maccoby & Jacklin, 1985). Although adults may not always directly contribute to biased development, teachers and parents are indirectly responsible for the inequity between the sexes in their children. For instance, in unstructured play situations, the free-play backbone of early education programs and most at-home play, children will choose playmates and play situations that are comfortable to them. They will not, typically, choose those activities with which they have had little or no experience, nor will they ordinarily choose cross-sex playmates (particularly as peer pressure increases with age). Further, boys still get more attention than girls do at most grade levels and in most subject areas (Sadker & Sadker, 1994). Sexist treatment in the classroom encourages the formation of patterns of power and dominance that occur very early (Maccoby & Jacklin, 1985), though it is inappropriate to our current culture.

Teachers and parents must take an assertive role in recognizing this sexist bias and replacing it with more equitable experiences for all children. Summaries of wide-ranging research (Grossman & Grossman, 1994; Hoyenga & Hoyenga, 1993) indicate that both our homes and schools are "gendered environments" that spell different expectations and conduct for children on the basis of their gender. If we are committed to an anti-bias education and environment (see Chapters 9 to 14), we must attempt to reduce gender-stereotypical behavior.

What are teachers to do? Educators Schlank and Metzger (1997) suggest that these guidelines be followed when trying to teach for change:

● *Begin with yourself.* Just as in other issues of diversity and anti-bias, it all begins with self-awareness and reflection on one's own behavior, responses, and attitudes.

● *What you say and do can make a difference.* Whenever possible, be gender inclusive or neutral, acknowledging positive behaviors and milestones by describing what you see and avoiding using gender designations (such as "all boys get your jackets", or "all girls go to the snack tables.")

● *Watch your language.* Avoid descriptions of children such as "pretty/handsome" and treat the class as a group ("friends" rather than "boys and girls"); be careful of word choices that reflect gender bias (such as "He is confident/She is full of herself").

● *Establish rules and conduct for cooperation and gender equity.* Everybody may play everywhere with any toy; blocks are not just for boys and the house corner is not for girls only; no child may be kept from playing because of something she or he cannot change—skin color, disability, or gender.

● *Be ready to intervene and support.* If you hear a "No boys allowed," or "Girls can't do that," be ready to intervene in a supportive way, finding out why children think that, and what you think or what the class rule is.

● *Think about how to cope with superheroes and Barbie dolls.* As we were thinking about the dilemmas described earlier about violence, it occured to us that weapon and doll play can also be seen in this developmental versus sociocultural light. Teachers need to think of ways to handle superhero and doll play that supports children and the values teachers and families hold dear.

Teachers will work to eliminate personal biased perceptions and behavior and to correct children's stereotypical behavior and attitudes about gender roles. Exposing children to nonsexist roles, books, and materials is a good start. Expanding children's learning styles is helpful. Girls need more experiences with spatial exploration and gross-motor coordination as well as quality attention from—without dependence on—adults. Boys in particular need experiences in flexibility, nurturance, and learning from modeling.

Eliminating stereotypical relationships is also important. Be sure that all members of a group have the opportunity to participate equally. For instance, try to reduce male dominance of females in mixed-gender situations. Keep a watchful eye in the environment to see that areas do not get labeled "off limits" by one gender, such as the blocks and trikes that become "boy places" or the house corner and art "for girls only." Encourage cross-gender interaction, and use cooperative learning activities. Whereas there is little research about the long-term effects of these strategies, a combination of these techniques has been found effective to increase mixed-gender interactions, helping behavior and friendships (Lockheed & Klein, 1985).

Finally, if we are talking about gender inequity, we can't just talk about girls. "Gender bias goes both ways. There are some areas where the advantage seems to go to boys, but there are also areas where girls perform better" (Lee in Zernike, 1997). A prudent course to follow would be to develop strategies for all

children, including:

● Providing activities that all children may use, that are sex fair and sex affirmative in content.

● Developing verbal and physical interactive patterns that make all children equal participants.

● Using strategies such as teacher proximity and structured playtime to involve children in activities they may otherwise avoid (Greenberg, 1985).

Sexuality

As we move into the 21st century in the United States, teachers and citizens alike are learning to address many issues of diversity. One of the most complicated issues that touches the lives of early childhood educators is homosexuality. Although human sexuality is not likely to be among typical early childhood curriculum topics, teachers are increasingly more likely to encounter issues of homosexuality in the following ways: working with gay or lesbian families or coworkers, dealing with aspects of femininity and masculinity in children's sex role identity, and having multicultural children's books about gay families. Some experts estimate that approximately 10% of the children in our classes will grow up to be gay or lesbian adults (Corbett, 1993). Although critics judge these numbers to be inflated, it is important to separate the facts from the myths and distortions about homosexuality. Whether or not the estimates are accurate, gay issues are controversial and anxiety producing for many; it is difficult and risky and often seems easier to ignore the whole issue and conclude that it is an "adult problem."

A number of studies suggest a possible genetic basis for homosexual behavior (McGuire, 1995). "It is difficult, however, to conclusively establish genetic origins for any human behavior, and the study of homosexuality presents some unique problems" (Friemann, O'Hara, & Settel, 1996). Little direct research has been done with young children, and it is likely that, "while a handful may show early indications of seeming 'different' in some way, the vast majority will offer no clue to even the most observant eye" (Corbett, 1993).

If teachers are relinquishing ethnic, ability, and gender stereotypes, they must also consider avoiding the rejection of a family for its choice of life-style or the criticism of a child on the basis of some notion of "femininity"or "masculinity." The homophobia at the root of such biased behavior, either subtle on the part of teachers or overt by other children, can be hurtful and harassing. Friemann et al. (1996) offer steps for teachers to take that will sound familiar because they are similar to those dealing with other forms of bias:

> Teachers should examine their own feelings about homosexuality. . . . [They] must honestly recognize any biases that they may have about children who are stigmatized as sissies [or tomboys], and keep those biases out of the classroom. . . . Second, teachers should immediately handle any instances of students-to-student abuse and harassment, no matter how slight. . . . [Third] teachers should challenge negative remarks about gay people and other minority groups. . . . Classroom meetings are a good tool to deal with harassment cases. Start with a "stem" phrase for the children to complete, such as "When I am teased it makes me feel..." and help children focus on how people feel when they are harassed.

Our attitude ought to be one that no child should feel ashamed about her family, her teachers, or herself.

Schools for Human Values

The complexities of modern life can complicate the development of values in children. In a society so diverse, it is sometimes difficult to determine what values are "basic." With changing family structures, shifting political and religious viewpoints, and a multitude of cultures to consider, the teacher can, understandably, feel confused and reluctant to "teach" any particular values at all.

Teaching, however, is not a "value-neutral" endeavor. Whenever something is taught, the choice of what and how to teach it implies the teacher's values. When a teacher prevents a child from hitting another, she states the value of peaceful conflict resolution. When a caregiver puts a crying child into his lap, he shows the value of responsive comforting. When children are taught reading, given free play choices, asked to sing, they are being given a sense of what is important.

Children who leave childhood without experience in making decisions and paying attention to what matters, finding out what is fair or kind or "right," miss a critical part of human development. Developing

Figure 15.12 ● The program that responds to diversity is one in which the individual child is accepted and respected.

moral and ethical values is an important part of growing up, giving children a basis for choice about how to behave and what conduct to follow. Teaching children our belief system is part of their education. The issue is how.

In response to growing concerns such as drugs, violence, and lack of continuity through family or neighborhood, schools are beginning to respond by providing some guidance about what is right and wrong. The school of the past could be concerned with simply academic and vocational, leaving the moral and personal responsibilities to the parents. The school of the present and future can not afford that luxury.

Several states are now taking steps to encourage the teaching of values. School districts often set up councils or task forces to poll their communities about what values to teach and how to teach them. In programs for children under age 5, parents and teachers have historically been more involved with teaching children right and wrong. Church-related schools in particular are selected by parents because of the values, including religious values, that are taught. Discussions of discipline can go beyond technique to the values that underlie those techniques. Teachers in a center can start the dialogue about what is important to teach.

Teaching values starts with knowing your own belief system and its place in your career. Ask yourself:

● Why am I teaching? Why young children? Why children at all?

● What made me choose early childhood education as my career?

● What do stand for? Why?

● How did I come to have my beliefs?

● Do I allow others their beliefs?

● How do I state my values to children? To parents?

● How do I keep my values and integrity while allowing myself to grow and change?

Other educators are clear about their own values, and are engaged in dialogue with parents, there remains the issue of how to generate values in young children. Riley (1984) puts it this way:

> When you give boys and girls the freedom to evaluate, decide, create, and re-create their world, they usually construct a happy place, a place with meaning that expresses truths and dreams that are very real to them. When children interpret those meanings and truths, and select priorities, and finally make efforts to change— freely and frequently—what does not satisfy them, they generate within themselves an inspiring force that they feel in the form of confidence and a positive attitude about their lives which any parent or teacher can see as the children work and play.

Integrity, honesty, individuality, self-confidence, responsibility can all be taught in an authentic way to young children. We prepare children to live successfully by embracing the willingness to change while at the same time holding to our beliefs of personal choice, equality, and opportunity.

Implications for Educators

Some Strategies. There are several, more global strategies about multicultural, bilingual, and values education that all educators can use. First *education must promote minority involvement in school reform.* The end of the 20th century marks the beginning of an awareness of including all constituencies in real decision- and policy-making. From minority businesses to parents to minority policymakers, it is critical that the populations served by education become involved.

Second, *we need an adult understanding of development.* In particular, teachers and parents must know how children develop racial, cultural, sex, and ability awareness and how children come to an understanding of what differences mean and how children develop a sense of fairness and morality. Moreover, teachers' expectations about how and when children learn skills will be influenced by their knowledge of culture. Adults who know child development and how attitudes are formed will be more effective in developing positive concepts and in countering stereotypes.

Third, *teachers need more training and education about multicultural education and about various diverse cultures.* Teachers must take the time, and be supported in their efforts, to learn about both the various groups they have in their classrooms and the diversity of our culture at large. Teachers can provide an anti-bias classroom only if they are educated resources themselves.

Finally, *it is time educators examined their own attitudes and policies about diversity, difference, and inclusion.* Most early childhood centers want their programs to represent a pluralistic society, but how do their organizational structures stack up? Staff meetings that evaluate both the children's environments and the school as a whole are useful.

In the Classroom. How do we implement a multicultural, anti-bias approach to teaching? Staff and families work cooperatively to provide each child with something familiar and comfortable in the environment. Teachers base their programs on sharing of self, culture, ability, and experiences that encourages a healthy acceptance of themselves and a positive awareness and tolerance of others. Differences are noticed, discussed openly, even celebrated. At the same time, it is the fabric of custom, language, values, music, food, life-styles, and celebrations that is shared, not a minor or dramatic detail that trivializes a group or child. Teachers can analyze their environments, plan with parents, and set goals for curriculum enhancement or change. Understanding children from other cultures (DiMartino, 1989) can be an outgrowth of this process, but the program itself begins with the children's own culture (Head Start, 1986).

In summary, the future dictates that we equip children to live in the United States of the 21st century, where a diversity of races, cultures, and life-styles will be the norm. As teachers of young children, we teach the values of a pluralistic society as well as what these diverse cultures hold in common. No one culture, religion, or child should be made to feel less valuable than another. We must be certain that we respect and celebrate the uniqueness of each child and the values of others.

TEACHING FOR THE 21ST CENTURY

Every day, teachers and caregivers open their doors to young children by the thousands. As they do so, they are influencing the course of our nation in the next century. If this statement seems exaggerated, consider this: the child born in 1992 will be a fourth grader in the 21st century and a voting adult by 2010. We are teaching the children of the future.

Issues

Early childhood education is a broad field that encompasses children, parents, communities, and a staggering variety of programs. The issues of the day have changed over the last 40 years. A review of these gives teachers a perspective on what has been and may become important in our profession:

● *The 1960s*: How important are the early years for the field of formal education? Can education in those years compensate for inadequate childhood experiences? What kind of schooling makes a difference?

● *The 1970s*: What kind of early childhood program is best? Which ones are financially efficient?

● *The 1980s*: What are the effects of child care on children's development? What is the best match between programs and their participants? How do the family and children interact?

● *The 1990s*: How can cultural diversity be preserved while equal opportunity for all children is ensured? What will be the effect of such diversity on curriculum content? Will family-oriented policies and practices by business and government be far-reaching enough to support parents in their child-rearing roles? Can education reform be radical enough to alter the course of students who now seem destined to fail?

● *2000*: Will schools become social institutions that support academics as well as social services? How will the nation face its responsibility to see that all of its children start school ready to learn? What

Figure 15.13 ● Young children need programs in which they can learn to trust each other as they work and play together.

new partnerships will need to be created to continue public education reform? How will the role of parents continue to be underscored? Will "parental choice" become a viable reform vehicle for public education? Will parent demands raise the quality of child care and therefore the wage and benefit structure for early childhood professionals?

The issues of the new century are evolving out of those of previous decades. The need for child care and education for young children is an accepted fact: the issue is no longer "whether," but "what kind." Families, too, have changed in their outward appearance, as have the many faces of American society. How we accept such diversity and still maintain the notions of family and society is important. The nature of the job of teacher will depend, in part, on working conditions for teachers so that they may provide a high-quality experience for children and support for families. Our challenge for the new century is before us.

Child Advocacy

Teachers are, by definition, advocates for children as they are dedicated to providing a better future for America's children.

With the issues of money and educational reform of such immediate concern, teachers need to understand the forces that affect how these issues are resolved. Teachers will have to educate themselves

What a Wonderful Career It Is!

Carol Sharpe

The care and education of young children has become a key issue in our country, and more and more people are realizing that the quality of care in child development centers is linked to the training and education of the staff. Consequently, it is imperative that we attract and recruit to the field of early childhood individuals who not only are dedicated to working with young children but also are skilled and competent in doing this important work. We need to help people realize that this is not a stop-gap job that they do while they prepare for a "real" career, but that working in early childhood is an enriching career in itself.

Currently, in an effort to address this and other issues, people in many states are working on developing a career lattice and professional development plan for early childhood staff. Consideration must be given to developing a coordinated system that (1) welcomes people into the field from a variety of points, (2) offers clear career pathways with articulated training and credentialing systems, and (3) provides a variety of incentives to stay in the field.

In California the professional development and career lattice plan has been spearheaded by Pacific Oaks College and the Advancing Careers in Child Development Project. A group of dedicated individuals representing a diversity of early childhood programs and agencies worked together for several years to develop a new Child Development Permit Matrix and accompanying professional growth plan. This statewide certification program is housed in the Commission on Teacher Credentialing in Sacramento. The permit matrix consists of the following six levels:

Level	Education Requirement	Experience Requirement
Assistant	6 units of ECE or CD	None
Associate Teacher	12 units ECE/CD including core courses	50 days of 3+ hr/day within 4 yr
Teacher	24 units ECE/CD, including core courses + 16 GE units	175 days of 3+ hr/day within 4 yr
Master Teacher	24 units ECE/CD including 16 GE units + 6 specialization units + 2 adult supervision units	350 days of 3+ hr/day within 4 yr
Site Supervisor	AA (or 60 units) with 24 ECE/CD units, including core + 6 units administration, + 2 units adult supervision	350 days of 4+ hr/day including at least 100 days of supervising adults
Program Director	BA with 24 ECE/CD units including core + 6 units administration + 2 units adult supervision	Site supervisor status and one program year of site supervisor experience

Each level of the permit matrix has alternative qualifications for meeting the requirements, and the concept of lifelong learning has been incorporated into the structure by requiring that all permit holders become part of a 5-year renewal, professional growth plan. Each permit holder links up with a professional growth adviser to plan career goals, objectives, and activities.

The Child Development Permit Matrix was designed with multiple levels for a variety of reasons: (1) it offers a better opportunity for linking compensation to training; (2) it gives people coming into the field the sense that there really is a career in early care and education; and (3) it provides the opportunity for individuals to come into the field through various entry points.

It is so very exciting to be part of this long-term professional/career development project where over 100 individuals have worked together in various committees to improve the system for preparing and licensing center staff while striving to maintain high-quality, affordable early care and education programs. What a wonderful career early childhood is, and how crucial it is that we have a well-trained and stable work force working with our children and families.

Carol Sharpe is the project director of Advancing Careers in Child Development, at Pacific Oaks College.

about the political process. They will need to know the rules and regulations regarding public funding sources. It is important to know how monies are allocated and whom to work with to affect the decisions regarding education. By being acquainted with legislation, teachers can rally support for bills that will help children, families, and schools.

Teachers have long kept out of the political process. But they have not been immune from its effects. As teachers we must become informed to increase our power in the political and financial arenas of daily life. Just as we encourage children to help themselves, we must support each other in taking the initiative for our own profession's well-being. It was just such a coalition and coordinated effort among many people in child advocacy that secured the passage of the Child Care and Development Block Grants in 1990, the first such legislation to pass Congress in 20 years. Large-scale cooperation increased significantly the political success of that bill on behalf of all children.

Every teacher can become a child advocate. By working for children and children's services, teachers advocate for themselves as well. Effective legislative involvement proceeds through these steps:

1. Make a personal commitment.

2. Keep informed.

3. Know the process.

4. Express your views.

5. Let others know.

6. Be visible.

7. Show appreciation.

8. Watch the implementation.

9. Build rapport and trust.

10. Educate your legislators.

Jonah Edelman's Guest Editorial at the beginning of this section raises the challenge to us to become effective advocates for all children and suggests actions to take. Stand For Children, begun in 1996 by the Children's Defense Fund, can be found in many localities.

The teacher who works to ensure high quality programs and services for children and their families also increases the likelihood of achieving the improved working conditions, professional opportunities, and

Figure 15.14 ● How do adults become advocates to ensure a fulfilling life for children in the 21st century?

public recognition that the field of early childhood education so richly deserves.

The Past Suggests the Future

History suggests how we might approach the future as we start a new century. By reflecting on our past, we are reminded of several important factors that illuminate today's issues:

1. We remind ourselves of what the pioneers of early education did to bring about reform. We look at their successes for inspiration, models, and ideas; we examine their failures to avoid the same mistakes.

2. Out of the past, we create a vision or the future. A backward glance along the timeline shows us that today we have a living, viable organism: a growing comprehensive vision of the field of early childhood; a growing definition of what early childhood means; a growing collaboration of early childhood professionals from all walks of life; a growing involvement in the education reform movement; a growing system of early childhood programs to serve the families of the 21st century; and a growing sense of our own effectiveness as advocates.

Figure 15.15 ● What is our vision of the future for these children?

3. The ultimate goal seems timeless but bears frequent repetition. Our aim is to help all children learn so that they can live full and satisfying lives, to help them develop their talents and capabilities so that they are prepared for the challenges and responsibilities of adult life. Today's children will be learning in a new century and in a different economic and technological age.

There is one unique aspect of the present that, when blended with the past, defines the future even more directly. The growing cultural diversity that now makes up the United States provides a richness of resources from which to learn. Learning about the values and attributes of other cultures through meaningful and accurate experience becomes an imperative agenda for the children and families of the 21st century.

Summary

Early childhood educators are facing issues today that challenge the very definition of childhood. How society handles these issues will help determine where we are headed—as teachers, children, families, a nation.

Some of the issues presented here may seem somewhat personal and even political. Our choice of issues was deliberate: as caretakers of the future—our children—we have serious and far-reaching questions that we must ask ourselves now. This book is dedicated to the quest for knowledge and action concerning a most important endeavor: teaching young children. We can hardly do anything less than address those topics that are critical to the success of this task and of our profession.

1. Why do you think child care workers have low salaries? How can you work to change these conditions?

2. Is it possible for child care centers to provide quality programs at the same time they pay fair wages and work benefits? How?

3. What can you say to parents who ask what you teach their child? How can you respond to their insistence on teaching children to read and print before kindergarten?

4. What would you do if you suspected that a child in your center was being seriously neglected or abused?

5. What can you say to help children handle separation and divorce? How will you deal with *both* parents?

6. What does the phrase "It takes a village to raise a child" mean in your program? How could that adage be applied in your community?

7. What can you do to support diversity while building a classroom community of common goals?

8. What do you do when children say "No boys (girls) allowed"? How will you include a new child with little English proficiency into your program? How do you respond when someone is called a "sissy"?

9. How will you prepare yourself for the 21st century?

10. How do you think the education reform movement will affect your community? An early childhood program you know or work in?

11. What changes in AIDS statistics and research have occurred since this text was published?

12. Select one of the pioneers discussed in this book, and describe how that person had an impact on the reform movements of the times; compare the issue and its resolution with today's reform movement. What issues do you see repeated over time?

Bibliography

Ethic of Social Reform and Child Care

General
Center for the Child Care Work Force. (1997). *Worthy work, unlivable wages: The National Child Care Staffing Study, 1996–1997.* Washington, DC: Author.
Costs, Quality and Child Outcomes Study Team. (1995). *Cost, quality and child outcomes in child care centers, executive summary.* Denver: Economics Department, University of Colorado at Denver.

Galinsky, E., Howe, C., Cantos, S., & Schinn, M. (1994). *The study of children in family child care and relative care: Highlight of findings.* New York: Families and Work Institute.

Hofferth, S. (1994). Bringing parents and employers back. In *The implications of new findings for child care policy.* Washington, DC: Urban Institute.

Lewin, T. (1998, April 29). From welfare roll to child care worker. *New York Times,* p. A14.

National Education Goals Panel (1996). *National education goals report. Building a nation of learners.* Washington, DC: Author

Riley, R. W. (1996, August 21). Investing in America's future. In *Back to school: special report: The baby boom echo.*

U.S. Department of Education, National Center for Education Statistics. (1996, September). *Youth indicators, 1996: Trends in the well-being of American youth.* Washington, DC: Author.

Education Reform

Children's Defense Fund. (1998). *The state of America's children: Yearbook 1998.* Washington, DC: Author.

Kagan, S. L., & Neuman, M. J. (1997, September). Highlights of the Quality 2000 Initiative: Not by chance. *Young Children,* pp. 54–62.

National Association of State Boards of Education. (1988). *Right from the start.* Alexandria, VA: The report of the NABE Task Force on Early Childhood Education

Ravitch, D. (1990, January 10). Education in the 1980s: A concern for quality. *Education Week,* p. 48.

U.S. Department of Education, National Education Goals Panel. (1998a). *Ready schools.* Washington, DC: Author.

U.S. Department of Education, National Education Goals Panel (1998b). *Principles and recommendations for early childhood assessments.* Washington, DC: Author

U.S. Department of Health and Human Services. (1996). *National immunization survey.* Washington, DC: Author.

The Importance of Childhood

General

Elkind, D. (1988). *The hurried child: Growing up too fast too soon.* Reading, MA: Addision-Wesley.

Gordon, A.M. (1986, Winter). Ministries to childhood. *National Association of Episcopal Schools Journal,* pp. 22–26.

Langway, L., et al. (1983, March 28). Bringing up superbaby. *Newsweek,* pp. 62–63.

National Commission on Children. (1991). *Beyond rhetoric: A new American agenda for children and families.* Washington, DC: Author.

Reed, M. S. (1986, March 2). Stress at an early age. *San Francisco Chronicle and Examiner,* Sunday supplement *This World,* p. 13.

Child Abuse and Neglect and AIDS

Centers for Disease Control and Prevention. (1998). *AIDS surveillance by race/ethnicity.* Atlanta, GA: Author.

Child abuse: Betraying a trust. (1995). Wylie, TX: Information Plus.

Children's Defense Fund. (1998). *The State of America's children: Yearbook 1998.* Washington, DC: Author.

Lung, C., & Daro, D. (1996). *Current trends in child abuse reporting and fatalities: The results of the 1995 annual fifty state survey.* Chicago: National Committee to Prevent Child Abuse.

National Association for the Education of Young Children. (1997, March). *Position statement on the prevention of child abuse in early childhood programs and the responsibilities of early childhood professionals to prevent child abuse* (pp. 42–46). Washington, DC: Author.

National Committee to Prevent Child Abuse (1998). *Child abuse and neglect statistics.* Chicago: Author.

U.S. Department of Health and Human Services. (1998). *Child sexual abuse prevention—Tips to parents.* Washington, DC: Author.

Wang, C. T., & Daro, D. (1998). *Current trends in child abuse reporting and fatalities: The results of the 1997 annual fifty state survey*. Chicago: National Committee to Prevent Child Abuse.

At Risk: Children in Need

Carnegie Foundation. (1995). *Starting points*. Washington, DC: Author.

Casey Foundation. (1995). *Kids count data book*. Baltimore: Author.

Children's Defense Fund. (1998). *The state of America's children: Yearbook 1998*. Washington, DC: Author.

Edelman, M. W. (1993). Young children and school readiness. In A. Gordon & K. B. Browne (Eds.), *Beginnings and beyond* (3rd ed.). Albany, NY: Delmar.

National Study Panel on Education Indicators. (1991). *Education counts*. Washington, DC: National Center for Education Statistics, U.S. Department of Education.

Families and Communities

Carlisle, C. (1991, Summer). Children of divorce. *Childhood Education*.

Chandler, L. A. (1996). Changing children in a changing society. *Childhood Education*. Annual Theme.

Clarke-Stewart, K. A. (1989, January). Single-parent families: How bad for the children? *NEA Today*.

Galinsky, E. (1986, November). *Investing in quality child care*. AT&T Report.

Osborn, D. K. (1991). *Early childhood education in historical perspective* (3rd ed.). Athens, GA: Daye Press.

Wallerstein, J., in Jacobson, L. (1997, June 11). Emotional damage from divorce found to linger. *Education Week*.

Work, Economics, and Public Policy: The Working Parent

Brazelton, T. B. (1989, February 13). Working parents. *Newsweek*.

Caldwell, B. (1989). *The state of the ECE field*. Address to the annual conference of the National Association for the Education of Young Children.

Fuchs, V., & Reklis, D. (1990, October). *Children, economics, and public policy*. Unpublished report.

Schroeder, P. (1991, March). *Children in America today*. Address to the California Association for the Education of Young Children, Los Angeles.

Community and School Support

Coleman, J. S. (1991). *Parental involvement in education*. Washington, DC: Office of Educational Research and Improvement, U.S. Department of Education.

Elkind, D. (1991, September). The family and education in the postmodern world. *Momentum*.

Gardner, J. W. (1990, January). *Community*. Palo Alto, CA: Graduate School of Business, Stanford University.

Transmitting Values

Television and Other Media

Carter, B. (1991, May 1). Children's TV, where boys are king. *New York Times*.

David, J. (1988, September). When to turn it on—and off. *Good Housekeeping*.

ERIC Clearinghouse on Elementary and Early Childhood Education. (1990, Fall). *Guidelines for family television viewing* (Vol. 2, No. 2).

Minow, N. (1991, June 19). *Worth noting*. Address to commemorate 30th anniversary of his "vast wasteland" speech. *Education Week*.

National Association for the Education of Young Children. (1990). *Media violence and children*. Washington, DC: Author.

Solter, A. (1986, Fall). Television and children. *Mothering*.

Trelease, J. (1984). *The read-aloud handbook*. New York: Penguin Books.

Violence

Carlsson-Paige, N., & Levin, D. (1987). *The war play dilemma*. New York: Teachers College.

Carlsson-Paige, N., & Levin, D. (1990). *Helping children understand peace, war, and the nuclear threat*. Washington, DC: National Association for the Education of Young Children.

Carter, M. (1995, March). Supporting teachers to create a culture of non-violence. *Exchange*.

Center for Media Literacy. (1993, August). *Beyond blame: Challenging violence in the media: Report from the American Psychological Association's Commission on Violence and Youth in America*.

Chen, M. (1994). *The smart parents' guide to kids' TV*. San Francisco: KQED Books.

Groves, B. M., & Mazur, S. (1995, March). Shelter from the storm: Using the classroom to help children cope with violence. *Exchange*.

Hoot, J., & Roberson, G. (1994). Creating safer environments for children in the home, school and community. *Childhood Education*. Annual Theme.

Hopkins, S., & Peppers, S. (1995, March). Listening to understanding violence. The voices of youth. *Exchange*.

Klemm, B. (1995, July). Video-game violence. *Young Children*, 50(5).

Levin, D. (1994). *Teaching young children in violent times*. Cambridge, MA: Educators for Social Responsibility.

Levin, D. (1998). *Remote control children?* Washington, DC: National Association for the Education of Young Children.

Levin, D., & Carlsson-Paige, N. (1984, July). Developmentally appropriate television: Putting children first. *Young Children*, 49(5).

Wallinga, C., Boyd, B., Skeen, P., & Paguio, L. (1991, Summer). Reviews of research: Children and nuclear war. *Childhood Education*.

Diversity

Armstrong, L. S. (1991, January 16). Racial ethnic prejudice still prevalent, survey finds. *Education Week*.

Association for Childhood Education International. (1996, Spring). Professional standard: Issues of diversity in teacher education. *Childhood Education*.

Barrera, R., et al. (1993). Beginnings workshop: Considering ethnic culture. *Exchange*.

Bowman, B. T. (1991). Educating language-minority children. *ERIC Digest*, University of Illinois.

Center for Demographic Policy. (1989). *The same client: The demographics of education and service delivery system*. Washington, D C: Institute for Educational Leadership.

Chang, H. (Ed.). (1993). *Affirming children's roots: Cultural and linguistic diversity in early care and education*. San Francisco: California Tomorrow.

Children's Defense Fund. (1998). *The state of America's children: Yearbook 1998*. Washington, DC: Author.

Derman-Sparks, L. (1989). *Anti-bias curriculum*. Washington, DC: National Association for the Education of Young Children.

Dowell, C. (1996). *Looking in, looking out: Redefining child care and early education in a diverse society*. San Francisco: California Tomorrow.

Education Week. (1990, November 14). Dimensions: In California, nation's first minority majority.

Fillmore, L. W. (1991, June 19). A question for early-childhood programs: English first or families first? *Education Week*.

Hale, J. E. (1993). Culturally appropriate pedagogy and the African American child. In A. Gordon & K. B. Browne (Eds.), *Beginnings and beyond* (3rd ed.). Albany, NY: Delmar.

Haycock, K. (1991, March). Reaching for the year 2000. *Childhood Education*.

Kozol, J. (1997, January 12). Author's work among poor is experience of spirituality. (Interview by Winifred Yu). *Albany Times Union*.

Schmidt, P. (1989, August 2). Outlook is bleak for many blacks. *Education Week*.

Southern Poverty Law Center. (1995–98, Spring and Fall). *Teaching tolerance*. Montgomery, AL: Author.

Viadero, D. (1990, November 28). Battle over multicultural education rises in intensity. *Education Week*.

Vukelich, C. (1991). Are schools really ready for kids? *Childhood Education*.

Equal Play and Gender Issue

American Association of University Women. (1992). *How schools shortchange girls.* Washington, DC: Author.

Chapman, A. (1997). *The great balancing act: Equitable education.* New York: National Association of Independent Schools.

Corbett, S. (1993, March). A complicated bias. *Young Children.*

Friemann, B. B., O'Hara, H., & Settel, J. (1996, Fall). What heterosexual teachers need to know about homosexuality. *Childhood Education.*

Greenberg, S. (1985). Recommendations for creating the five Es: Educational equity in early educational environments. In S. Klein (Ed.). *Achieving sex equity through education.* Baltimore: Johns Hopkins Press.

Grossman, H., & Grossman, S. H. (1994). *Gender issues in education.* Boston: Allyn & Bacon.

Hoyenga, K. B., & Hoyenga, K. T. (1993). *Gender-related differences.* Boston: Allyn & Bacon.

Lee, V. (1997, January 12). A new advocacy forms for boys (Interview by K. Zernike). *Albany Times Union.*

Lockheed, M., & Klein, S. (1985). Sex equity in classroom organization and climate. In S. Klein (Ed.). *Handbook for achieving sex equity through education.* Baltimore: Johns Hopkins Press.

Maccoby, E., & Jacklin, C. N. (1985, April). *Gender segregation in nursery school: Predictors and outcomes.* Paper presented to to the National Convention of the Society for Research in Child Development, Toronto.

McGuire, T. R. (1995). Is homosexuality genetic? A critical review and some suggestions. *Journal of Homosexuality, 28*(1 & 2).

Sadker, M., & Sadker, D. (1994). *Failing at fairness: How our schools cheat girls.* New York: Simon & Schuster.

Schlank, C. H., & Metzger, B. (1997). *Together and equal.* Boston: Allyn & Bacon

Zernike, K. (1997, January 12). A new advocacy forms for boys. *Albany Times Union.*

Schools for Human Values

Derman–Sparks, L. (1989). *The anti-bias curriculum.* Washington, DC: National Association for the Education of Young Children.

DiMartino, E. D. (1989, Fall). Understanding children from other cultures. *Childhood Education, 66*(1).

Head Start. (1986, November/December). Bringing our world together. In *Pre-K today.* From the Head Start manual: *Multi-cultural education for Head Start children: An introduction for parents and teachers.* Washington, DC: Author.

Neugebauer, B. (1987, March). Evaluating program resources for attitudes about diversity. *Exchange.*

Riley, S. S. (1984). *How to generate values in young children.* Washington, DC: National Association for the Education of Young Children.

APPENDIX A

Timeline for Early Childhood Education

Authors' Note: A debt of gratitude is owed to D. Keith Osborn for his outstanding historical research and to James L. Hymes, Jr., for his generous time and perspective.

5th–3rd centuries BC to AD 1400s Few records exist concerning child-rearing practices; the development of cities gives rise to schooling on a larger scale.

1423 & 1439 The invention of printing and movable type allows knowledge to spread rapidly; ideas and techniques become available to large numbers of people; printing is credited with bringing about the end of the Middle Ages and the beginning of the Renaissance.

1592–1670 Johann Amos Comenius

1657 *Orbis Pictus*, by Comenius, is the first children's book with pictures.

1632–1714 John Locke
English philosopher, considered the founder of educational philosophy, who postulated that children are born with a *tabula rasa*, or clean slate, on which all experiences are written.

1712–1788 Jean Jacques Rousseau

1762 *Emile*, by Rousseau, proclaims the child's natural goodness.

1746–1826 Johann Heinrich Pestalozzi

1801 *How Gertrude Teaches Her Children*, by Pestalozzi, emphasizes home education.

1740–1860s Sabbath Schools and Clandestine Schools are established as facilities to educate African Americans in the United States.

1782–1852 Friedrich Wilhelm Froebel

1826 *Education of Man*, by Froebel, describes the first system of kindergarten education as a "child's garden," with activities known as "gifts from God."

1837 Froebel opens the first kindergarten in Blankenburgh, Germany.

1861 Robert Owen sets up infant school in New Lanark, England, as an instrument of social reform for children of parent workers in his mills.

1873 The Butler School at Hampton Institute is opened as a free school for black children, including kindergarten curriculum for 5-year-olds.

1837 Horace Mann, known as the "Father of the Common Schools" because of his contributions in setting up the U.S. elementary school system, becomes Secretary of Massachusetts State Board of Education.

1856 Margarethe Schurz opens the first American kindergarten, a German-speaking class in her home in Watertown, Wisconsin.

1804–1894 Elizabeth Peabody

1860 Elizabeth Peabody opens the first English-speaking kindergarten in Boston.

1843–1916 Susan Blow

1873 First public school kindergarten, supported by Superintendent William Harris, is directed by Susan Blow in St. Louis, Missouri, who becomes the leading proponent of Froebel in America. The first public kindergarten in North America opens in 1871 in Ontario, Canada.

1856–1939 Sigmund Freud (see Chapter 4)

1892 Freud cites the importance of early experiences to later mental illness, ushering in the beginning of psychoanalysis and the emphasis on the importance of the first 5 years.

1858–1952 John Dewey

1896 John Dewey establishes a laboratory school at the University of Chicago and develops a pragmatic approach to education, becoming the father of the Progressive Movement in American education.

1897 *My Pedagogic Creed* is published, detailing the opposition to rote learning and the philosophy of educating "the whole child."

1860–1931 Margaret McMillan

1911 Deptford School, an open-air school in the slums of London, is opened by Margaret McMillan. The school emphasizes health and play, thus coining the phrase "nursery school."

1868–1946 Patty Smith Hill

1893 Patty Smith Hill becomes director of the Louisville Free Kindergarten Society, augmenting her original Froebelian training with her work in scientific psychology (G. Stanley Hall) and progressive education (John Dewey). She goes on to found the National Association of Nursery Education (now known as NAEYC) in 1926.

1870–1952 Maria Montessori (see Chapters 1 and 2)

1907 Casa di Bambini (Children's House) is opened by Maria Montessori in a slum district in Rome, Italy. She later develops an educational philosophy and program to guide children's growth through the senses and practical life experiences.

1874–1949 Edward Thorndike, behavioral psychologist (see Chapter 4)

1878–1958 John B. Watson, behavioral psychologist (see Chapter 4)

1878–1967 Lucy Sprague Mitchell

1916 The Bureau of Educational Experiments, which becomes Bank Street College of Education (and laboratory school) in 1922, is founded by L. S. Mitchell, who is a leading proponent of progressive education at the early childhood level.

1879 The first psychological laboratory is established in Germany to train psychologists in the systematic study of human beings.

1880 First teacher-training program for kindergarteners, Oshkosh Normal School, Pennsylvania.

1880–1961 Arnold Gesell (see Chapter 4)

1923 Gesell, originally a student of G. Stanley Hall, publishes *The Preschool Child*, which emphasizes the importance of the early years.

1926 Gesell establishes the Clinic of Child Development at Yale University and studies norms of child growth and behavior, founding the maturation theory of development (see Chapters 1 and 4)

1885–1948 Susan Isaacs

1929 Susan Isaacs publishes *The Nursery Years*, which contradicts the more scientific psychological view of behavior shaping and emphasizes the child's viewpoint and the value of play.

1892–1992 Abigail Eliot

1922 Dr. Eliot opens Ruggles Street Nursery School and Training Center.

1892 International Kindergarten Union founded.

1895 G. Stanley Hall runs a child development seminar with kindergarten teachers, explaining the "scientific/new psychology" approach to education. While most leave, Anny Bryan and Patty Smith Hill go on to incorporate such techniques and to see early childhood education as a more multidisciplinary effort.

1896–1980 Jean Jacques Piaget (see Chapter 4)

1926 *The Language and Thought of the Child*, one of a multitude of writings on the development of children's thought, is published by Jean Piaget, who becomes one of the largest forces in child development in the twentieth century.

1952 Piaget's *Origins of Intelligence* in children is published in English.

1896–1934 Lev Vygotsky (see Chapter 4). 1978 *Mind in Society: The Development of Higher Psychological Processes*, the seminal work of Vygotsky's sociocultural theory, is first published in English.

1897–1905 Alfred Binet develops a test for the French government to determine feeblemindedness in children. Known as the Binet-Simon test (and tested by Jean Piaget, among others), it is now known as the Stanford-Binet IQ test.

1902–1994 Erik Erikson (see Chapter 4)

1950 *Childhood and Society*, which details Erikson's Eight Stages of Man, is published, thus adding a psychoanalytic influence to early childhood education.

1903–1998 Benjamin Spock

1946 Dr. Spock's *Baby and Child Care* is published. It advocates a more permissive attitude toward children's behavior and encourages exploratory behavior.

1903 The Committee of Nineteen, a splinter group of the International Kindergarten Union, forms to report various philosophical concepts. Members include Patty Smith Hill, Lucy Wheelock, and Susan Blow.

1904–1988 B. F. Skinner (see Chapter 4)

1938 *The Behavior of Organisms*, by B. F. Skinner, is published, advocating the concepts of "radical behaviorism" in psychology.

1906 Josephine Yates publishes an article in the *Colored American Magazine*, which advocates play in the kindergarten and helps translate Froebel's concepts into Black kindergartens of the day.

1908–1984 Sylvia Ashton Warner

1963 *Teacher*, published by this New Zealand kindergarten teacher, develops the concepts of "organic vocabulary" and "key vocabulary."

1909 First White House Conference on Children by Theodore Roosevelt, is held, leading to the establishment of the Children's Bureau in 1912.

1915 First U.S. Montessori school opens in New York City.

1916 First Cooperative Nursery School opens at the University of Chicago.

1918 First public nursery schools are opened in England.

1918– T. Berry Brazelton

1969 *Infants and Mothers*, along with several other books and numerous articles, is published by this pediatrician, advocating a sensible and intimate relationship between parents and children.

1980s Dr. Brazelton is one of the founders of "Parent Action," a federal lobby to advocate for the needs of parents and children, particularly for a national policy granting parental leave from work to care for newborns or newly adopted children.

1919 Harriet Johnson starts the Nursery School of the Bureau of Educational Experiments, which later becomes Bank Street School.

1920–1994 Loris Malaguzzi theorizes about good programs and relationships for children, emphasizing the child's individual creative expression; starts school of Reggio Emilia, Italy, in 1946.

1921 Patty Smith Hill opens Columbia Teacher's College Laboratory School.

1921 A. S. Neill founds Summerhill school in England, which becomes a model for the "free school" movement (the book entitled *Summerhill* is published in 1960).

1922 Edna Nobel White directs the Merrill-Palmer School of Motherhood and Home Training, which later becomes the Merrill-Palmer Institute Nursery School.

1925–1926 The National Committee on Nursery Schools is founded by Patty Smith Hill; it becomes NANE and eventually NAEYC.

1925– Albert Bandura, psychologist in social learning theory (see Chapter 4)

1926–1927 Research facilities are founded at several American universities and colleges (e.g., Smith College, Vassar College, Yale University, Mills College).

1927 Dorothy Howard establishes the first Black Nursery School in Washington, DC, and operates it for over 50 years.

1928 John B. Watson publishes *Psychological Care of Infant and Child*, applying his theories of conditioning to child-rearing (see Chapter 4).

1929 Lois Meeks Stolz (1891–1984) becomes the first President of the National Association for Nursery Education (later to become National Association for the Education of Young Children) and joins the Teachers College (Columbia University) faculty to start the laboratory school and Child Development Institute. Stolz later becomes the Director of the Kaiser Child Service Centers during World War II.

1929–1931 Hampton Institute, Spellman College, and Bennett College open Black laboratory nursery schools, emphasizing child development principles as in other lab schools and serving as training centers.

1930 International Kindergarten Union, founded in 1892, becomes the Association for Childhood Education, increasing its scope to include elementary education.

1933 WPA (Works Projects Association) opens emergency nurseries for Depression relief of unemployed teachers. Enrolling over 4000 teachers in 3000 schools, they also help children of unemployed parents and operate under the guidance of people such as Edna Noble White, Abigail Eliot, and Lois Meeks Stolz until World War II.

1935 First toy lending library, Toy Loan, begins in Los Angeles.

1936 The first commercial telecast is shown in New York City, starring Felix the Cat. The pervasiveness of television sets and children's viewing habits become a source of concern for educators and parents in the latter half of the twentieth century.

1943–1945 Kaiser Shipyard Child Care Center, run by Lois Meeks Stolz, James Hymes, and Edith Dowley, operates 24-hour care in Portland, Oregon.

1944 *Young Children* is first published.

1946 Stanford University laboratory school is founded by Edith Dowley.

1948 USNC OMEP, the United States National Committee of the World Organization for Early Childhood Education, is founded to promote the education of children internationally and begins to consult with UNICEF and UNESCO in the United Nations. It starts publishing a journal, *The International Journal of Early Childhood*, in 1969.

1956 *La Leche League* is established to provide mothers with information on breast-feeding, childbirth, infants, and child care.

1957 *Sputnik*, a Soviet satellite, is successfully launched, sparking a renewed interest in—and criticism of—American education.

1960 Katherine Whiteside Taylor founds the American Council of Parent Cooperatives, which later becomes the Parent Cooperative Pre-schools International.

1960 Nancy McCormick Rambusch (1927–1994) founds the American Montessori movement, splitting from her European counterparts to try to shape Montessori education as a viable American public school alternative and to establish teacher taining programs at both early childhood and elementary levels.

1962 Perry Preschool Project, directed by David Weikart, opens in Ypsilanti, Michigan, and conducts longitudinal study to measure the effects of preschool education on later school and life (see Chapter 2).

1963 & 1966 Lawrence Kohlberg publishes child development works on the development of gender and sex roles and on moral development (see Chapter 4).

1964–1965 The Economic Opportunity Act of 1964 passes, becoming the foundation of Head Start Programs in the United States, as part of a federal "War on Poverty."

1966 The Bureau of Education for the Handicapped is established.

1966 NANE becomes National Association for the Education of Young Children (NAEYC).

1967 Plowden Report from England details the British Infant School system.

The Follow Through Program extends Head Start into the primary grades of the elementary system.

1969 John Bowlby publishes the first of his major works on *Attachment* (see Chapter 4).

The Ford Foundation, Carnegie Corporation, and Department of Health, Education, and Welfare subsidize the Children's Television Workshop, which develops *Sesame Street*.

1971 Stride-Rite Corporation of Boston opens a children's program on site, becoming a vanguard for employer-supported child care.

1972 The Child Development Associate Consortium, headed by Dr. Edward Ziegler, is established to develop a professional training program. Now known as CDA, its administration moves to NAEYC in 1985.

1974 Eleanor Maccoby publishes *The Development of Sex Differences* (see Chapter 4).

1975 P.L. 94-142, the Education for All Handicapped Children bill, passes, mandating appropriate education for special needs children in the "least restrictive environment" possible, thus defining the concepts of "mainstreaming" and "full inclusion."

1975 Mary Ainsworth publishes developmental research on mother–child interaction and follows up with work on patterns of attachment (see Chapter 4).

1979 Nancy Eisenberg publishes the theory of the development of prosocial development in children (see Chapter 4).

The United Nations declares an International Year of the Child.

1980 The Department of Health, Education, and Welfare is changed to that of Health and Human Services, and a separate Department of Education is established.

1982   Carol Gilligan publishes *In a Different Voice*, challenging accepted psychological theory on moral development (see Chapter 4).

1982–   Marion Wright Edelman establishes the Children's Defense Fund, a Washington-based lobby on behalf of children, and particularly children of poverty and color.

1983   Howard Gardner publishes *Frames of Mind*, which outlines the concept of multiple intelligences (see Chapters 4 and 13).

1984   NAEYC publishes a report entitled "Developmentally Appropriate Practices," which outlines what is meant by "quality" work with young children from infancy through age 8.

1985   NAEYC establishes a National Academy and a voluntary accreditation system for centers, in an effort to improve the quality of children's lives, and confers its first accreditation the next year.

1986   U.S. Department of Education declares the Year of the Elementary School.
        P.L. 99-457, amending 94-142, establishes a national policy on early intervention for children as young as infants.

1988–1990 The Alliance for Better Child Care, a coalition of groups advocating on behalf of young children, sponsors the ABC bill in an effort to get federal support for children and families. It fails to be signed in 1989, but is passed in 1990 and establishes the Child Care Development Block Grant to improve the quality, availability, and affordability of child care programs.

1988   The National Association of State Boards of Education issues *Right from the Start*, a report that calls for a new vision of early childhood education with the establishment of separate public school early childhood units.

1988   The National Education Goals are adopted by President Bush and the nation's governors. Goal One states that all children will come to school ready to learn.

1990   U.N. Children's World Summit includes the following goals to be reached by the year 2000: (1) to reduce child mortality below age 5 by one third; (2) to provide universal access to basic education; and (3) to protect children in dangerous situations.
        The Americans with Disabilities Act (ADA) is passed, requiring programs of all sizes to care for and accommodate the needs of children with disabilities whenever they are reasonably able to do so.

1991   "Ready to Learn/America 2000" Part of the U.S. government's educational strategy for reforming American public schools is published.

1991   The first Worthy Wage Day, organized by the Child Care Employee Project, is held on April 9, drawing attention to the inadequate compensation of early childhood workers and how this affects the retention of a skilled and stable work force.

1993   The Family and Medical Leave Act (FMLA) is passed, providing new parents with 12 weeks of unpaid, job-protected leave.

1996   The first "Stand For Children" demonstration is held in Washington, DC, drawing 200,000 participants.
        Rethinking the Brain, published by the Family and Work Institute, summarizes the new research on children's brain development, shows the decisive impact of early experiences, and considers policy and program implications of these findings.

1997   The Child Development Permit Matrix is adopted by the California Commission on Teacher Credentialing, introducing the career ladder concept into early childhood public education.

1998   The 100,000th CDA Credential is awarded by Carol Brunson Phillips, Executive Director of the Council for Early Childhood Professional Recognition, at NAEYC Annual Conference in Toronto, Ontario, Canada.

APPENDIX B

NAEYC Statement of Commitment

As an individual who works with young children, I commit myself to furthering the values of early childhood education as they are reflected in the NAEYC Code of Ethical Conduct. To the best of my ability I will

- Ensure that programs for young children are based on current knowledge of child development and early childhood education.

- Respect and support families in their task of nurturing children.

- Respect colleagues in early childhood education and support them in maintaining the NAEYC Code of Ethical Conduct.

- Serve as an advocate for children, their families, and their teachers in community and society.

- Maintain high standards of professional conduct.

- Recognize how personal values, opinions, and biases can affect professional judgment.

- Be open to new ideas and be willing to learn from the suggestions of others.

- Continue to learn, grow, and contribute as a professional.

- Honor the ideals and principles of the NAEYC Code of Ethical Conduct.

The Statement of Commitment expresses those basic personal commitments that individuals must make in order to align themselves with the profession's responsibilities as set forth in the NAEYC Code of Ethical Conduct.

APPENDIX C

NAEYC Position Statement: Responding to Linguistic and Cultural Diversity— Recommendations for Effective Early Childhood Education

Authors' Note: The Position Statement was adopted by NAEYC in November, 1995. The following passage was excerpted by the authors (November 1998) to give readers a sense of the position statement. It is strongly recommended that the Statement be read in its entirety. It is published in the January 1996 edition of Young Children.

INTRODUCTION

The children and families in early childhood programs reflect the ethnic, cultural, and linguistic diversity of the nation. The nation's children all deserve an early childhood education that is responsive to their families, communities, and racial, ethnic, and cultural backgrounds. For young children to develop and learn optimally, the early childhood professional must be prepared to meet their diverse developmental, cultural, linguistic, and educational needs. Early childhood educators face the challenge of how best to respond to those needs. . . .

Linguistic and culturally diverse is an educational term used by the U.S. Department of Education to define children enrolled in educational programs who are either non-English-proficient (NEP) or limited-English-proficient (LEP). Educators use this phrase, linguistically and culturally diverse, to identify children from homes and communities where English is not the primary language of communication. For the

purposes of this statement, the phrase will be used in a similar manner. . . .

NAEYC's position. NAEYC's goal is to build support for equal access to high-quality educational programs that recognize and promote all aspects of children's development and learning, establish all children to become competent, successful, and socially responsible adults. . . . For the optimal development and learning of all children, educators must accept the legitimacy of children's home language, respect (hold in high regard) and value (esteem, appreciate) the home culture, and promote and encourage the active involvement and support of all families, including extended and nontraditional family units. . . .

The challenges. Historically, our nation has tended to regard differences, especially language differences, as cultural handicaps rather than cultural resources. "Although most Americans are reluctant to say it publicly, many are anxious about the changing racial and ethnic composition of the country." As the early childhood profession transforms its thinking,

603

The challenge for early childhood educators is to become more knowledgeable about how to relate to children and families whose linguistic or cultural background is different from their own.

RECOMMENDATIONS FOR A RESPONSIVE LEARNING ENVIRONMENT

The issue of home language and its importance to young children is also relevant for children who speak English but come from different cultural backgrounds, for example, speakers of English who have dialects, such as people from Appalachia or other regions having distinct patterns of speech, speakers of Black English, or second- and third-generation speakers of English who maintain the dominant accent of their heritage language. Although this position statement basically responds to children who are from homes in which English is not the dominant language, the recommendations provided may be helpful when working with children who come from diverse cultural backgrounds, even when they speak only English. The overall goal for early childhood professionals, however, is to provide every child, including children who are linguistically and culturally diverse, with a responsive learning environment. The following recommendations help achieve this goal:

A. Recommendations for working with children

- Recognize that all children are cognitively, linguistically and emotionally connected to the language and culture of their home.

- Acknowledge that children can demonstrate their knowledge and capabilities in many ways.

- Understand that without comprehensive input, second-language learning can be difficult.

B. Recommendations for working with families

- Actively involve parents and families in the early learning program and setting.

- Encourage and assist all parents in becoming knowledgeable about the cognitive value for children of knowing more than one language, and provide them with strategies to support, maintain, and preserve home-language learning.

- Recognize that parents and families must rely on caregivers and educators to honor and support their children in the cultural values and norms of the home.

C. Recommendations for professional preparation

- Provide early childhood educators with professional preparation and development in the areas of culture, language, and diversity.

- Recruit and support early childhood educators who are trained in languages other than English.

D. Recommendations for programs and practice

- Recognize that children can and will acquire the use of English even when their home language is used and respected.

- Support and preserve home language usage.

- Develop and provide alternative and creative strategies for young children's learning.

SUMMARY

Early childhood educators can best help linguistic and culturally diverse children and their families by acknowledging and responding to the importance of the child's home language and culture. Administrative support for bilingualism as a goal is necessary within the educational setting. Educational practices should focus on "school culture" while preserving and respecting the diversity of the home language and culture that each child brings to the early learning setting. Early childhood professionals and families must work together to achieve high-quality care and education for *all* children.

APPENDIX D

Early Childhood Organizations

ACEI
Association for Childhood Education International
11501 Georgia Avenue, Suite 315
Wheaton, MD 20902
1-800-423-3563

ACT
Action for Children's Television
46 Austin Street
Newtonville, MA 02160

American Academy of Pediatrics
PO Box 747
Elk Grove Village, IL 60009–0747
1–800–433–9016

AMS
American Montessori Society
175 Fifth Avenue
New York, NY 10010

Canadian Association for Young Children
252 Bloor Street, W, Suite 12-155
Toronto, Ontario M5S 1V5
Canada

CDF
Children's Defense Fund
25 E Street NW
Washington, DC 20001
1-800-424-2460
www.childrensdefense.org

Center for Child Care Workforce
733 15th Street NW, Suite 1037
Washington, DC 20005-2112
202-737-7700
www.ccw.org

Child Care Action Campaign
330 Seventh Avenue, 17th Floor
New York, NY 10001-5010

Council for Early Childhood Professional Recognition
2460 16th Street, NW
Washington, DC 20009-3575

CWLA
Child Welfare League of America, Inc.
440 First Street NW, Suite 310
Washington DC 20001-2085

DEC/CEC
Division for Early Childhood
Council for Exceptional Children
1920 Association Drive
Reston, VA 22091

Ecumenical Child Care Network
1580 North Northwest Hwy
Park Ridge, IL 60068
708-298-1612

Educational (Gender) Equity Concepts
1114 East 32nd Street
New York, NY 10017

Educators for Social Responsibility
23 Garden Street
Cambridge, MA 02138

ERIC/ECE
Educational Clearinghouse on Elementary and Early
Childhood Education
805 West Pennsylvania Avenue
Urbana, IL 61801
217-333-1386
www.ericps.ed.uiuc.edu/ericeece.html

Families and Work Institute
330 Seventh Avenue, 14th Floor
New York, NY
www.familiesandwork.org

Head Start Bureau
Department of Health and Human Services
330 C Street, SW
Washington, DC 20013
www.head-start.lane

High/Scope Educational Resource Foundation
600 North River Street
Ypsilanti, MI 48197

NAEYC
National Association for the Education of Young
Children
National Academy of Early Childhood Programs
National Institute for Early Childhood Professional
Development
1509 16th Street, NW
Washington, DC 20036-1426
1-800-424-8777
www.naeyc.org/naeyc

National Association for Family Child Care
206 6th Avenue, Suite 900
Des Moines, IA 50209-4018
515-181-8192
www.nafcc.org

National Association of Nannies
7413 Six Forks Road, Suite 317
Raleigh, NC 27615

National Black Child Development Institute
1023 15th Street NW, Suite 600
Washington, DC 20005
www.nbcdi.org/aboutb.html

National Committee to Prevent Child Abuse
332 South Michigan Avenue, Suite 1600
Chicago, IL 60604
312-663-3520
www.childabuse.org

National Head Start Association
201 North Union Street, Suite 320
Alexandria, VA 22314
703-739-0875

NIOST
National Institute on Out-Of-School Time
Wellesley College
106 Central Street
Wellesley, MA 02181
781-283-2547
www.wellesley.edu/WCW/CRW/SAC

OMEP
Organisation Mondiale pour l'Education Prescolaire
School of Education
Indiana State University
Terre Haute, IN 47809

Reggio Children USA
1341 G Street NW, Suite 400
Washington, DC 20005
202-265-9090

Stand For Children
1834 Connecticut Avenue, NW
Washington, DC 20009–5732
202-234-0095
www.stand.org/

SRCD
Society for Research in Child Development
100 North Carolina Avenue SE, Suite 1
Washington, DC 20003

SECA
Southern Early Childhood Association
PO Box 5403
Brady Station
Little Rock, AR 72215

Zero to Three/National Center for Infants, Toddlers,
and Families
734 15th Street NW, Suite 1000
Washington, DC 20005
202-638-1144

WestEd Laboratory for Educational Research and
Development
Center for Child and Family Studies
180 Harbour Drive, Suite 112
Sausalito, CA 94965

Glossary

Aberrant. Deviating from the usual or natural type; abnormal, atypical.

Accommodation. A concept in Piaget's cognitive theory as one of two processes people use to learn and incorporate new information; the person adjusts what is already known to "accommodate" new learning. Children usually will change their way of thinking into a "schema," once they see that their usual ways do not take new information into account; they then will add new thought patterns to handle the new knowledge.

Accountability. The quality or state of being answerable to someone or of being responsible for explaining exact conditions; schools often must give specific account of their actions to a funding agency to assure the group that the funds and operation of the school are being handled properly.

Accreditation. A system of voluntary evaluation for early childhood centers. The goal is to improve the quality of care and education provided for young children. Accreditation is administered by the National Academy, a branch of the National Association for the Education of Young Children.

Active Listening. A child guidance technique of reflecting back to the speaker what the listener thinks has been said.

Activity Centers. Similar to learning centers and interest areas; areas in a classroom or yard that are designed and arranged for various activities to take place. An early childhood setting will offer several centers, or stations, that are based on both children's interests and what the staff hopes for them to learn in class.

Advocate. One who maintains, defends, or pleads the cause of another; in early childhood terms, an advocate is someone who furthers the principles and issues of the field by speaking to others about such issues.

Aesthetics. Sensitivity to what is beautiful; the study of beauty.

After-School Care. Programs designed to care for children after the regular academic school day.

Age-Level Characteristics. Those features of children's development and behavior that are most common among a given age group.

Androgynous. Having to do with either sex; associated with both the male and the female identity, behavior, etc.

Anti-bias. A phrase describing the development of curriculum that emphasizes an inclusive look at people and problems, extending the tenets of multicultural education and pluralism.

Arbitrary. A decision based on individual judgment or on a whim.

Articulation. The manner in which sounds and words are actually spoken.

Assess. To make an evaluation or determine the importance, disposition, or state of something or someone, such as in evaluating a child's skills, a classroom environment, or a teacher's effectiveness.

Assimilation. A concept in Piaget's cognitive theory as one of two processes people use to learn and incorporate new information; the person takes new information and puts it together with what is already known in order to "assimilate" the new information intellectually, such as when a toddler shakes a toy magnet first, as with all other toys, in order to get to know this new object. Children usually first try to put new experiences into the "schema," or categories, they already know and use.

Atelerista. A person trained in the arts who acts as a resource and teaches techniques and skills to children in the schools of Reggio Emilia, Italy.

Attachment/Attachment Behaviors. The relational bond that connects a child to another important person; feelings and behaviors of devotion or positive connection.

Attitude Crystallization. To assume a definite, concrete form in one's attitudes; refers to the formation of a firm set of attitudes and behaviors about others' race, ethnicity, gender, and ability that may be prejudicial and difficult to change.

Authentic Assessment. The quantitative and qualitative study of a child's work, activity, and interactions that focuses on the whole child within the context of family, school, and community. Such assessment occurs in a child's natural settings in which the child is performing real tasks. Viewed as a process rather than an end, authentic assessment includes collecting and organizing information over time, from multiple sources, and using a variety of methods.

Autonomy. The state of being able to exist and operate independently, of being self-sufficient rather than dependent on others.

Baby Biographies. One of the first methods of child study, these narratives were written accounts by parents of what their babies did and said, usually in the form of a diary or log.

Back to Basics. A movement of the 1970s and 1980s prompted by a desire for schools to return to teaching the "basic" skills usually associated with academic learning, such as reading, writing, and arithmetic.

Baseline. A picture of the status of a child, teacher, or environment that serves as the basis for evaluation and later comparison.

Basic Emotions. Those emotions that are present and observable in the newborn or within the first few months of life; they include happiness, interest, surprise, disgust, distress, fear, anger, and sadness.

Basic Needs. Conditions, described by Abraham Maslow and other humanists, that are necessary for growth; these needs, such as physiologic conditions and safety and security, are critical for a person's survival.

Behavior Swings. Shifts from one behavior to another, usually by a sharp change in what one is doing; e.g., from highly active to motionless or from gregarious to shy.

Behaviorist Theory. A psychological theory developed in the United States in the 20th century, which states that all important aspects of behavior and people are learned and can be modified or changed by varying external conditions.

Bicognitive Development. A term coined by Ramirez and Casteneda (see Chapter 4) to describe a set of experiences and environments that promote children's ability to use more than one mode of thinking or linguistic system. Each of us grows up with a preferred cognitive style, such as global or analytic, field dependent or field independent, seeing the parts vs. seeing the whole, as well as a linguistic style. For true cultural democracy to take place, we need to develop a flexibility to switch learning styles or cognitive modes (i.e., develop bicognitive abilities) and have an awareness of and respect for differing cognitive styles.

Bilingualism. The acquisition of two languages during the first years of life; using or being able to use two languages.

Brainstorming. The process of thinking that involves bringing up as many ideas as possible about a subject, person, event, etc.

Cephalocaudal. In the direction from head (cephalic) to toe (caudal, of the tail or hind part of the body), as in how children develop physically.

Cerebral Palsy. A disorder that is the result of damage to a certain part of the brain (motor cortex); CP, as it is commonly called, is a nonprogressive disorder (does not get worse as the child grows older); usually movement dysfunction is paired with some intellectual and perceptual impairment.

Checklist. A modified child study technique that uses a list of items for comparison, such as a "yes/no" checklist for the demonstration of a task.

Child Abuse. Violence in the form of physical maltreatment, abusive language, and sexual harassment or misuse of children.

Child Care Center. A place for care of children for a large portion of their waking day; includes basic caretaking activities of eating, dressing, resting, toileting, as well as playing and learning time.

Child-Centered Approach. The manner of establishing educational experiences that takes into consideration children's ways of perceiving and learning; manner of organizing a classroom, schedule, and teaching methods with an eye toward the child's viewpoint.

Child Neglect. The act or situation of parents' or other adults' inattention to a child's basic health needs of adequate food, clothing, shelter, and health care; child neglect may also include not noticing a child or not paying enough attention in general.

Church-Related Schools. Educational programs affiliated with a church or religious organization; they may have a direct relationship with the church by including religious education, by employing church members as teachers, or by being housed in a church building and using the facilities for a fee.

Classical Conditioning. The most common and basic category of learning in behaviorist theory, involving an association between a stimulus and a response so that a reflex response (eye-blinking, salivating, etc.) occurs *whenever* a neutral and new stimulus is activated (a bell for a light, food, etc.); conditioned-response experiments conforming to the pattern of Pavlov's experiment, sometimes known as "stimulus substitution."

Classist. A biased or discriminating attitude based on distinctions made between social or economic classes.

Clinical Method. An information-gathering technique, derived from therapy and counseling fields, in which the adult observes and then interacts with the client (in this case, children) by asking questions and posing ideas to the person or group being observed.

Cognition. The act or process of knowing, thinking, and perceiving. Cognition involves perceptual, intellectual, and emotional skills that begin as a child makes connections among objects and people and later extends to formulating mental representations.

Cognitive Confusion. State of being unsure or forgetful about what is already known, such as becoming perplexed about things or facts already learned.

Cognitive Theory. The psychological theory developed by Jean Piaget and others; the theory focuses on thought processes and how they change with age and experience; this point of view contrasts with the stimulus-response aspects of behaviorist theory.

Collaborated/Assisted Learning. A type of teaching-learning experience in which a child is helped by another, usually more skilled, person, often an older child or adult; this kind of learning is highly regarded in Vygotsky's theory of child development.

Compensatory Education. Education designed to supply what is thought to be lacking or missing in children's experiences or ordinary environments.

Competency-Based Assessment. Evaluation in which a teacher is judged or rated in comparison with a predetermined set of skills, or competencies, related to the job.

Complex Emotions. Those emotions that emerge in the child after infancy; these include shame, guilt, envy, and pride.

Comprehensive. Inclusive, covering completely, such as a program for children that concerns itself with the physical, intellectual, social, emotional, creative, and health needs of the children.

Concrete. Concerning the immediate experience of actual things or events; specific and particular rather than general or symbolic.

Connected Knowledge. That kind of knowledge and information that is connected to the child in ways that are real and relevant to that individual; also known as meaningful knowledge in Piagetian terms, it is elaborated by Gilligan (see Chapter 4) and others.

Constructivism. A theory of learning, developed from the principles of children's thinking by Piaget and implemented in programs as those in Reggio Emilia, Italy, which states that individuals learn through adaptation. The "constructivist" model of learning posits that children are not passive receptacles into which knowledge is poured but rather are active at making meaning, testing out theories, and trying to make sense of the world and themselves. Knowledge is subjective as each person creates personal meaning out of experiences and integrates new ideas into existing knowledge structures.

Continuing Education. The commitment of teachers to learning new approaches and ideas and to continuing to challenge themselves to higher levels of learning and competence.

Continuum. Something that is continuous; an uninterrupted, ordered sequence.

Core Values. The basic purposes or issues a professional group acknowledges as common concerns to all its members.

Cultural Pluralism. A state or society in which members of diverse ethnic, racial, or cultural groups maintain participation in and development of their traditional culture within the common society.

Custodial. Those tasks relating to guardianship of a child's basic needs for food, clothing, and shelter; they include providing for eating, dressing, toileting, resting, and appropriate protection from physical hardships such as weather, danger, etc.

Decoding. Converting from code into ordinary language; in terms of language development, decoding is the process of making sense out of printed letters or words.

Deficiency Needs. In Maslow's theory, those needs without which a person will have insufficient resources to survive.

Demographics. The statistical graphics of a population, especially showing average age, income, etc.

Developmentally Appropriate Practice (DAP). That which is suitable or fitting to the development of the child; refers to those teaching practices that are based on the observation and responsiveness to children as learners with developing abilities who differ from one another by rate of growth and individual differences, rather than of differing amounts of abilities. It also refers to learning experiences that are relevant to and respectful of the social and cultural aspects of the children and their families.

Developmental Schedule. Arrangement of a daily plan for children that is based on both individual and group levels of development.

Development Tasks. Those functions or work to be done by children at a particular point in their development.

Dialect. A variation of a language, sufficiently different from the original to become a separate entity but not different enough to be considered as a separate language.

Diary Descriptions. A form of observation technique that involves making a comprehensive narrative record of behavior, in diary form.

Disability. A measurable impairment or incapacity that may be moderate to severe. The Individuals with Disabilities Act defines 13 categories that identify specific limitations or challenges, such as hearing, speech, visual, or orthopedic impairments. Individuals who are classified with one or more impairments may be eligible for early intervention and special education classes.

Discipline. Ability to follow an example or to follow rules; the development of self-control or control in general, such as by imposing order on a group. In early childhood terms, discipline means everything adults do and say to influence children's behavior.

Disequilibrium. Loss of balance, or a period of change.

Divergent Thinking. The processes of thought and perception that involve taking a line of thought or action different from what is the norm or common; finding ideas that branch out rather than converge and center on one answer.

Downshifting. A process by which the brain reacts to perceived threat. The brain/mind learns optimally when appropriately challenged; however, should the person sense a threat or danger (either physical or emotional), the brain will become less flexible and revert to primitive attitudes and procedures (downshift).

Down Syndrome. A genetic abnormality that results in mongolism, one of the most common and easily identified forms of mental retardation.

Dramatic Play. Also known as imaginative play, this is a common form of spontaneous play in which children use their imagination and fantasy as part of the setting and activity.

Dynamic. Having energy or effective action; a basic skill is one with consequences that will motivate the child, affecting development or stability.

Early Childhood Education. Education in the early years of life; the field of study that deals mainly with the learning and experiences of children from infancy through the primary years (up to approximately 8 years of age).

Ebonics. Term used to describe "black English" and the center of a controversy in the late 1990s over whether such language is a dialect of standard English or a separate language altogether.

Eclectic. Choosing what appears to be best in various doctrines, methods, styles; comprising elements drawn from various sources.

Ecology of the Family. The concept of viewing the child in the context of his or her impact on the family and the family's impact on the child; stresses the interrelationship of the various family members with one another.

Educaring. A concept of teaching as both educating and care giving; coined by Magda Gerber in referring to people working with infants and toddlers.

Egocentric. Self-centered; regarding the self as the center of all things; in Piaget's theory, young children think using themselves as the center of the universe or as the entire universe.

Elaboration. The act of expanding language; developing language by building complex structures from simple ones and adding details.

Emergent Curriculum. A process for curriculum planning that draws on teachers' observations and children's interests. Plans emerge from daily life interests and issues. This approach takes advantage of children's spontaneity and teachers' planning.

Emergent Literacy. The process of building upon pre-reading skills in a child-centered fashion, so that the ability to read evolves from children's direct experiences.

Emotional Framework. The basic "feeling" structure of a classroom that determines the tone and underlying sensibilities that affect how people feel and behave while in class.

Employer-Sponsored Child Care. Child care supported in some way by the parents' employers. Support may be financial (as an employee benefit or subsidy) or physical (offering on-site care).

Entry Level. The level of development or behavior that a child shows on beginning a program or group experience; usually an observation-based informal assessment after the first few weeks of school.

Environment. All those conditions that affect children's surroundings and the people in them; the physical, interpersonal, and temporal aspects of an early childhood setting.

Environmental. Forces that are not innate or hereditary aspects of development; in early childhood terms, environmental aspects of growth are all those influences of physical conditions, interpersonal relationships, and world experiences that interact with a person to change the way he or she behaves, feels, and lives.

Equilibration. To balance equally; in Piaget's theory, the thinking process by which a person "makes sense" and puts into balance new information with what is already known.

Ethics. A theory or system of oral principles and standards; what is "right and wrong"; one's values; the principles of conduct governing both an individual teacher and the teaching profession.

Ethnocentric. Having one's race as a central interest, or regarding one's race or cultural group as superior to others.

Evaluation. A study to determine or set significance or quality.

Event Sampling. An observation technique that involves defining the event to be observed and coding the event to record what is important to remember about it.

Experimental Procedure. An observation technique that gathers information by establishing a hypothesis, controlling the variables that might influence behavior, and testing the hypothesis.

Expressive Language. Those aspects of language development and skill that deal with expression: pronunciation, vocabulary, and grammar, as well as speaking and articulation.

Extrinsic. Originating from or on the outside; external, not derived from one's essential nature.

Family Child Care. Care for children in a small, homelike setting; usually six or fewer children in a family residence.

Feedback Loop. In terms of evaluation, *feedback loop* is used to describe the process whereby an evaluator gives information to a teacher, who in turn uses this information to improve teaching skills.

Fine Motor. Having to do with the smaller muscles of the body and the extremities, such as those in the fingers, toes, and face.

Flexibility. Capable of modification or change; willing or easily moved from one idea to another.

Fluency. The ability to produce many ideas; an easy and ready flow of ideas.

Formal Tests. Evaluation instruments that are administered in a conventional, "testlike" atmosphere for use with groups of children and that may or may not be developed commercially.

Four "I"s. The four components (I, Initiative, Independence, and Interaction) of early childhood curriculum for building self-esteem.

Frames of Mind. A theory of intelligence developed by Gardner that refers to intelligence as a host of different skills and abilities.

Full Inclusion. Providing the "least restrictive environment" for children with physical limitations.

Genes. The biological elements that transmit hereditary characteristics.

Gifted Children. Children who have unusually high intelligence, as characterized by: learning to read spontaneously; being able to solve problems and communicate at a level far advanced from their chronological age; excellent memory; extensive vocabulary; and unusual approaches to ideas, tasks, people.

Gross Motor. Having to do with the entire body or the large muscles of the body, such as the legs, arms, and trunk.

Group Times. Those parts of the program in which the whole class or group is together during one activity, such as music, movement, fingerplays, or stories.

Growth Needs. Conditions, as described by Abraham Maslow and other humanists, that are important to a person's well-being; these needs, such as love and belonging, self-esteem and respect for others, playfulness, truth, beauty, etc., while not critical to a person's survival, are necessary for growth.

Holistic. A viewpoint that takes into account several conceptions of a child or situation to form a wider, more rounded description; in early childhood terms, this view includes a child's history, present status, relationships with others, and the interrelationships of development to arrive at a picture of the child; in medicine, this view includes dealing with a person's mental and emotional state, relationships, etc., as well as body signs.

Humanist Theory. The psychological theory of Abraham Maslow and others; it involves principles of motivation and wellness, centering on people's needs, goals, and successes.

Hypothesis. A tentative theory or assumption made to draw inferences or test conclusions; an interpretation of a practical situation that is then taken as the ground for action.

IEP. An individualized education plan is a process of planning for the education of children with special needs that involves joint efforts of specialists, teachers, and parents.

Inadequacy. The state of being or feeling insufficient, of not being or having "enough"; if feeling discouraged, children will display their feelings of inadequacy by misbehaving.

Inclusion. When a child with a disability is a full-time member of a regular classroom with children who are developing normally as well as with children with special needs.

Independent. Not controlled or influenced by others; thinking for oneself and autonomous.

Individualized Curriculum. A course of study developed and tailored to meet the needs and interests of an individual, rather than those of a group without regard for the individual child.

Inductive Guidance. A guidance process in which children are held accountable for their actions and are called on to think about the impact of their behavior on others. Reasoning and problem-solving skills are stressed.

Inference. A conclusion reached by reasoning from evidence or after gathering information, whether direct or indirect.

Informal Assessment. Evaluation based on methods and instruments that are not administered formally, as in paper-and-pencil tests, but rather are done while the subjects are at work or play in their natural environments.

Infusion. The integration of multicultural awareness into the current learning environment. It allows for the integration of many diverse perspectives while maintaining the existing curriculum.

Initiative. An introductory step; in early childhood terms, the energy, capacity, and will to begin taking action.

Integrated Curriculum. A set of courses designed to form a whole; coordination of the various areas of study, making for continuous and harmonious learning.

Integrated Day. A school schedule with no prescribed time periods for subject matter, but rather an environment organized around various interest centers among which children choose in organizing their own learning experiences.

Integrated Development. Growth that occurs in a continuous, interrelated manner; a child's progress as a whole, rather than in separate areas.

Intelligence. The cluster of capabilities that involves thinking (see Chapter 13 for details.)

Interaction. Acting on one another, as in the interplay or reciprocal effect of one child upon another.

Interdependence. Dependence on one another, as in the relationship between teachers' experience in the areas of discipline and their competence at knowing and using appropriate language for discipline.

Interdisciplinary Approach. A method of teaching/ learning that draws from sources in more than one field of study: e.g., a course in education that uses background from the fields of medicine, psychology, and social work as well as education itself.

Interest Areas. Similar to learning centers and activity areas; one way to design physical space in a classroom or yard, dividing the space into separate centers among which children move about, rather than assigning them desks.

Interpersonal. Relating to, or involving relationships with, other people; those parts of the environment that have to do with the people in a school setting.

Intervention. Entering into a situation between two or more persons or between a person and an object; to interpose oneself into another's affairs, such as when teachers enter into children's interactions when their behavior calls for some action on the part of an adult.

Intrinsic. Belonging to the essential nature of or originating from within a person or body, such as intrinsic motivation, whereby one needs no external reward in order to do something.

Intuition. The direct perception of a fact or truth without any reasoning process; immediate insight.

Invented Spelling. Children's first attempts at spelling words the way they sound to them, based on their current knowledge of letters and sounds. Far from

"correct" ("scnd" for second, "grrn" for green, or "relly" for really), invented spelling becomes more conventional over time.

Job Burnout. Exhaustion and stress from one's job, characterized by a wearing down of body and attitude.

Kindergarten. A school or class for children 4 to 6 years old; in the United States, kindergarten is either the first year of formal, public school or the year of schooling before first grade.

Kindergartners. (1) A modern term to describe the children who are attending kindergarten programs; (2) a term used in 19th-century America to describe early childhood practitioners who worked in kindergartens patterned after Froebelian models.

Laboratory Schools. Educational settings whose purposes include experimental study; schools for testing and analysis of educational and/or psychological theory and practice, with an opportunity for experimentation, observation, and practice.

Latchkey Children. Children who are left home after school unattended or unsupervised by an adult; children who are responsible after school for themselves and perhaps younger siblings while their parents/guardians are not at home, usually working; such children have a "latchkey" (housekey) to let themselves into an empty home. Also referred to as "self-care."

Laterality. Of or relating to the side, as in children having an awareness of what is situated on, directed toward, or coming from either side of themselves.

Learning Centers. Similar to interest areas and activity areas; hubs or areas in a classroom designed to promote learning; the classroom is arranged in discrete areas for activity, and children move from one area to another rather than stay at an assigned desk or seat.

Licensing. The process of fulfilling legal requirements, standards and regulations for operating child care facilities.

Limits. The boundaries of acceptable behavior beyond which actions are considered misbehavior and unacceptable conduct; the absolute controls an adult puts on children's behavior.

Linchpin. Something that serves to hold together the elements of a situation.

Logical Mathematical Knowledge. One of three types of knowledge in Piagetian theory; the component of intelligence that uses thinking derived from logic.

Log/Journal. A form of observation technique that involves making a page of notes about children's behavior in a cumulative journal.

Mainstreaming. The process of integrating handicapped children into classrooms with the nonhandicapped.

Maturation. The process of growth whereby a body matures regardless of, and relatively independent of, intervention such as exercise, experience, or environment.

Maturation Theory. A set of ideas based on the notion that the sequence of behavior and the emergence of personal characteristics develop more through predetermined growth processes than through learning and interaction with the environment; the theory of growth and development proposed and supported by Dr. Arnold Gesell and associates.

Meaningful Knowledge. The form of knowing that is learned within the context of what is already known; that knowledge that has meaning because it has particular significance of value to an individual.

Merit Pay. A system for teachers that gives pay bonuses for excellent teaching.

Methode Clinique. A kind of information-gathering technique, first used extensively by Jean Piaget, that involves observing children and asking questions as the situation unfolds. The purpose of this technique is to elicit information about how children are thinking as they behave naturally.

Misbehavior. Improper behavior or conduct.

Miseducation. David Elkind's term describing the end result of contemporary parents rushing their children into formal instruction too early.

Mixed-Age Groups. The practice of placing children of several levels, generally one year apart, into the same classroom. Also referred to as family grouping, heterogeneous grouping, multiage grouping, vertical grouping, and ungraded classes.

Modeling. A part of behavior theory, modeling is a way of learning social behavior that involves observing a model (either real, filmed, or animated) and mimicking its behavior, thus acquiring new behavior.

Multiple Intelligences. A theory of intelligence, proposed by Howard Gardner, that outlines several different kinds of intelligence, rather than the notion of intelligence as measured by standardized testing, such as the IQ (see Frames of Mind).

Myelination. The forming of the myelin sheath, the material in the membrane of certain cells in the brain; the development of the myelination of the brain seems to parallel Piagetian stages of cognitive development.

Narratives. A major observation technique that involves attempting to record nearly everything that happens, in as much detail as possible, as it happens. Narratives include several subtypes such as baby biographies, specimen descriptions, diary descriptions, and logs or journals.

Nature/Nurture Controversy. The argument regarding human development that centers around two opposing viewpoints; *nature* refers to the belief that it is a person's genetic, inherent character that determines development; *nurture* applies to the notion that it is the sum total of experiences and the environment that determine development.

Negative Reinforcement. Response to a behavior that decreases the likelihood that the behavior will recur; for instance, a teacher's glare might stop a child from whispering at group time, and from then on, the anticipation of such an angry look could reinforce not whispering in the future.

Networking. Making connections with others who can further career and professional opportunities.

Nonpunitive. Methods that do not involve or aim at punishment; for instance, letting a child be hungry later when he refuses to eat at snack time is a nonpunitive method of enforcing the need to snack with the group; hunger is a natural and logical consequence of the child's behavior rather than a punishment meted out by the teacher (such as scolding or threatening).

Norm. An average or general standard of development or achievement, usually derived from the average or median of a large group; a pattern or trait taken to be typical of the behavior, skills, or interests of a group.

Objectivity. The quality or state of being able to see what is real and realistic, as distinguished from subjective and personal opinion or bias.

Open-ended. Activities or statements that allow a variety of responses, as opposed to those that allow only one response; anything organized to allow for variation.

Open School. A style of education, developed in progressive American schools and in the British infant schools, that is organized to encourage freedom of choice and that does not use predetermined roles and structure as the basis of education; an educational setting whose ultimate goal and base for curriculum is the development of the individual child, rather than of programmed academic experiences.

Operant Conditioning. A category of learning in behavior theory that involves a relation between a stimulus and a response. The response is learned, rather than reflexive, and is gradually and carefully developed through reinforcement of the desired behavior as it occurs in response to the stimulus; behavior leading to a reward.

Organic Reading. A system of learning to read, popularized by Sylvia Ashton-Warner, that lets children build their own vocabulary with the words they choose.

Out-of-School Time Care. Programs for school-age children that take place before and after their regular school day.

Parent Cooperative Schools. An educational setting organized by parents for their young children, often with parental control and/or support in the operation of the program itself.

Pedagogista. A person trained in early childhood education who meets weekly with the teachers in the schools of Reggio Emilia, Italy.

Pediatrician. A medical specialist in pediatrics, the branch of medicine dealing with children, their development, care, and diseases.

Peer Interactions. Associations with people of the same age group or with those one considers equals.

Perceptual-Motor Development. The growth of a person's ability to move (motor) and perceive (perceptual) together; perceptual-motor activity involves the body and the mind together, to coordinate movement.

Performance-Based Assessment. Evaluation based on observable, specific information on what a teacher actually does (performance while on the job).

Philosophy. Concepts expressing one's fundamental beliefs; in early childhood educational terms, the beliefs, ideas, and attitudes of our profession.

Phobia. A strong, exaggerated, and illogical fear of an object or class of things, people, etc.; one of several reactions children often have to divorce.

Phonemes. Language sounds; the smallest units of meaningful speech; two examples of phonemes are /a/ (as in hat) and /p/ (as in sip).

Physical Environment. Having to do with equipment and material, room arrangement, the outdoor space, and facilities available.

Physical Knowledge. One of three types of knowledge in Piagetian theory; that knowledge that is learned through external, sensory experiences.

Pluralism. (1) A theory that holds to the notion that there is more than one kind of reality or correct way of perceiving and acting upon the world; (2) a state in which members of diverse ethnic, racial, religious, or social groups participate in their traditional cultures while still belonging to the common society.

Positive Reinforcement. A response to a behavior that increases the likelihood that the behavior will be repeated or increased; for instance, if a child gets attention and praise for crawling, it is likely that the crawling will increase — thus, the attention and praise were positive reinforcers for crawling.

Positive Stress. Refers to an amount of strain or tension that encourages a person to be active and challenged rather than overwhelmed or discouraged.

Power Assertive Discipline. Harsh, punitive discipline methods that rely on children's fear of punishment rather than on the use of reason and understanding. Hitting and spanking are examples of power assertion.

Practice Teaching. The period of "internship" that students experience when working in a classroom with supervision, as opposed to having a role as a regular working staff member.

Precedent. Something done or said that serves as an example or rule to authorize or justify other acts of the same or similar kind; an earlier occurrence of something similar.

Precursor. What precedes and indicates the approach of another; predecessor or forerunner.

Prejudices. Ideas and attitudes that are already formed about other people, situations, ideas, etc., before hearing or experiencing full or sufficient information; in teaching terms, those attitudes or biases that may be based less on mature thought and reasoning than on incomplete or nonexistent personal experiences.

Prepared Environment. The physical and interpersonal surroundings of an educational setting that are planned and arranged in advance with the group of children in mind.

Prerequisite. Something necessary or essential to carrying out an objective or performing an activity; when early childhood teachers determine what skills children will need in order to successfully engage in an activity, they are clarifying the prerequisites for that activity.

Private (Inner) Speech. The language children use for self-guidance and self-direction, as well as for helping them think about their behavior and plan for action; once known as "egocentric speech," it is used for self-regulation.

Professional. One engaged and participating in a profession and accepting the technical and ethical standards of that profession; in early childhood terms, one who has accumulated methods, course work, and teaching experience with young children along with attitudes of competency, flexibility, and continual learning.

Professional Confidentiality. Spoken, written, or acted on in strict privacy, such as keeping the names of children or schools in confidence when discussing observations.

Professional Organizations. Those associations developed for the purpose of extending knowledge and teaching/learning opportunities in the field of education.

Project Approach. An in-depth study of a particular subject or theme by one or more children. Exploration of themes and topics over a period of days or weeks. Working in small groups, children are able to accommodate various levels of complexity and understanding

to meet the needs of all the children working on the project.

Prosocial. Behaviors that are considered positive and social in nature, such as sharing, inviting, including, offering help or friendship.

Proximal to Distal. In the direction from the center of the body (proximal) toward the outer part (distal, far from the center), as in the way children's bodies develop.

Psychodynamic Theory. The psychological theory of Dr. Sigmund Freud and others; it asserts that the individual develops a basic personality core in childhood and that responses stem from personality organization and emotional problems as a result of environmental experiences.

Psychometric. Having to do with measurement of mental traits, abilities, and processes; usually a formal assessment using a standardized test.

Psychosocial. Those psychological issues that deal with how people relate to others and the problems that arise on a social level; a modification by Erikson of the psychodynamic theories of Freud with attention to social and environmental problems of life.

Punishment. The act of inflicting a penalty for an offense or behavior.

Racist. Attitudes, behavior, or policies that imply either a hatred or intolerance of other race(s) or involving the idea that one's own race is superior and has the right to rule or dominate others.

Rating Scale. A modified child study technique similar to a checklist that classifies behavior according to grade or rank, such as using the descriptors "always, sometimes, never" to describe the frequency of a certain behavior.

Readiness. The condition of being ready, such as being in the state or stage of development so that the child has the capacity to understand, be taught, or engage in a particular activity.

Receptive Language. Those aspects of language development and skill that deal with the ability to receive messages: listening, understanding, and responding.

Reciprocal. The stage of children's friendship in which friendship is given or felt by each toward the other; a kind of give-and-take or two-way relationship, this is the stage most often seen in the latter part of the early childhood years.

Reinforcement. A procedure, such as reward or punishment, that changes a response to a stimulus; the act of encouraging a behavior to increase in frequency.

Reinforcers. Rewards in response to a specific behavior, thus increasing the likelihood that that behavior will recur; reinforcers may be either social (praise) or nonsocial (food) in nature and may or may not be deliberately controlled.

Rote Knowledge. A form of knowing that is learned by routine or habit and without thought of the meaning.

Roughhousing. Rough and disorderly, but playful, behavior.

Routines. Regular procedures; habitual, repeated or regular parts of the school day; in early childhood programs, routines are those parts of the program schedule that remain constant, such as indoor time followed by cleanup and snack, regardless of what activities are being offered within those time slots.

Running Record. The narrative form of recording behavior; this kind of descriptive record of one's observations involves writing down all behavior as it occurs.

Schemas. A plan, scheme, or framework that helps make an organizational pattern from which to operate; in Piaget's theory, cognitive schemas are used for thinking.

Screening. Evaluations to determine a child's readiness for a particular class, grade, or experience.

Self-Actualization. The set of principles set forth by Abraham Maslow for a person's wellness or ability to be the most that a person can be; the state of being that results from having met all the basic and growth needs.

Self-Awareness. An awareness of one's own personality or individuality; in teaching terms, an ability to understand one's self and assess personal strengths and weaknesses.

Self-Care. A current description for latchkey children (see Latchkey Children).

Self-Concept. A person's view and opinion of self; in young children, the concept of self develops as they interact with the environment (objects, people, etc.); self-concept can be inferred in how children carry themselves, approach situations, use expressive materials such as art, etc.

Self-Correcting. Materials or experiences that are built or arranged so that the person using them can act automatically to correct errors, without needing another person to check or point out mistakes.

Self-Esteem. The value we place on ourselves; how much we like or dislike who we are; self-respect.

Self-Help. The act of helping or providing for oneself without dependence on others; in early childhood terms, activities that a child can do alone, without adult assistance.

Self-Regulation. The term used to describe a child's capacity to plan and guide the self. A disposition or part of the personality (rather than a skill or behavior such as self-control), self-regulation is a way of monitoring one's own activity flexibly over changing circumstances.

Sensorimotor. Relating to or functioning in both sensory and motor aspects of body activity.

Sensory. Having to do with the senses or sensation, as in an awareness of the world as it looks, sounds, feels, smells, tastes.

Separation Process. The act and procedure that occur when parents leave a child at school.

Sequential Learning. Learning based on a method of consecutive steps; an arrangement of concepts or ideas in a succession of related steps so that what is learned results in continuous development.

Seriation. The process of sequencing from beginning to end or in a particular series or succession.

Sexist. Attitudes or behavior based on the traditional stereotype of sexual roles that includes a devaluation or discrimination based on a person's sex.

Sex-Role Stereotyping. A standardized mental picture or set of attitudes that represents an oversimplified opinion of people's abilities or behavior according to their sex; overgeneralizing a person's skills or behavior on the basis of an inequitable standard of sex differences.

Shadow Study. A modified child study technique that profiles an individual at a given moment in time; similar to diary description, the shadow study is a narrative recorded as the behavior happens.

Social Action. Individual or group behavior that involves interaction with other individuals or groups, especially organized action toward social reform.

Social Cognition. The application of thinking to personal and social behavior; giving meaning to social experience.

Socialization. The process of learning the skills, appropriate behaviors, and expectations of being part of a group, particularly society at large.

Social Knowledge. One of three types of knowledge in Piagetian theory; that knowledge that is learned about and from people, such as family and ethnic culture, group behavior, social mores, etc.

Social Learning. Any acquired skills or knowledge having to do with interacting with others; in Bandura's theory, social learning happens when children watch other people directly or in books and film.

Social Mores. Standards of conduct and behavior that are determined by society, as opposed to those established by family or personal preference.

Social Referencing. The process used to gauge one's own response to a situation by relying on another person's emotional reaction, such as a child who looks to a teacher after falling down before crying or getting up.

Social Skills. Strategies children learn to enable them to respond appropriately in many environments.

Sociocentric. Oriented toward or focused on one's social group rather than on oneself.

Sociocultural. Aspects of theory or development that refer to the social and cultural issues; key descriptor of Vygotsky's theory of development.

Spatial. Having to do with the nature of space, as in the awareness of the space around a person's body.

Special-Needs Children. Children whose development and/or behavior require help or intervention beyond the scope of the ordinary classroom or adult interactions.

Specific Development. Area of a person's growth and maturation that can be defined distinctly, such as physical, social, emotional, intellectual, and creative growth.

Specimen Description. A form of narrative observations technique that involves taking on-the-spot notes about a child (the "specimen") to describe behavior.

Spontaneous Play. The unplanned, self-selected activity in which a child freely participates.

Standardized Testing. Formal assessment techniques whose results have been tabulated for many children and thus have predetermined standards, or norms, for evaluating the child being tested.

Stewardship. Responsibility for judicious management of resources; the obligation assumed by an individual or agency to act responsibly in the use of both personal and natural resources.

Stimulus–Response. The kind of psychological learning, first characterized in behavior theory, that makes a connection between a response and a stimulus; that is, the kind of learning that takes place when pairing something that rouses or incites an activity with the activity itself in such a way that the stimulus (such as a bell) will trigger a response (such as salivating).

Stress. The physical and emotional reactions and behaviors that come from having to cope with difficult situations beyond one's capabilities.

Superhero. Those characters who embody a higher nature and powers beyond ordinary human abilities, such as Superman, Wonder Woman, etc.

Support System. A network of people who support each other in their work and advancement.

Surrogate. Substitute, such as a teacher acting in the place of the parent, a school toy taking the place of a blanket from home, a thumb taking the place of a pacifier.

Tabula Rasa. A mind not affected yet by experiences, sensations, and the like. In John Locke's theory, a child was born with this "clean slate" upon which all experiences were written.

Tactile. Perceptible or able to be learned through the sense of touch.

Teaching Objectives. A set of goals teachers set for themselves as they plan activities for children; these goals remind teachers what they will do to help children learn.

Temporal. Having to do with time and time sequence; in the early childhood setting, refers to scheduling and how time is sequenced and spent, both at home and in school.

Theory. A group of general principles, ideas, or proposed explanations for explaining some kind of phenomenon; in this case, child development.

Time Sampling. A form of observational technique that involves observing certain behavior and settings within a prescribed time frame.

Traditional Nursery School. The core of early childhood educational theory and practice; program designed for children aged 2½ to 5 years of age, which may be a part- or an all-day program.

Transactional Model. A model of education that describes the interaction of an individual with one or more persons, especially as influenced by their assumed roles. This model implies that the role of parent, child, or teacher has an effect on what and how information is taught and learned.

Transcurricular. Able to be used or applied in a variety of situations or activities.

Transitions. Changes from one state or activity to another; in early childhood terms, transitions are those times of change in the daily schedule (whether planned or not), such as from being with a parent to being alone in school, from playing with one toy to choosing another, from being outside to being inside, etc.

Transmission Model. A model of education describing the transference of information directly from one person to another, such as in the sense of passing on knowledge directly from teacher to child.

Unconscious. Not conscious, without awareness, occurring below the level of conscious thought.

Undifferentiated. The stage of children's friendships in which children do not distinguish between "friend" and "person I'm playing with," considered the first stage, usually from infancy into the preschool years.

Unilateral. The stage of children's friendships in which children think of friendship as involving one side only; that is, a one-way situation in that a "friend" is "someone who does what I want him to do," usually spanning the preschool years and into early primary.

Unobtrusive. Being inconspicuous, as in remaining in the background while observing children.

Upward Evaluation. Assessment procedure in which employees evaluate their superiors.

Vicariously. Experienced or realized through the imagination or the participation of another, rather than from doing it oneself, as in learning vicariously about something by listening to a story.

Volatile. Easily aroused; tending to erupt into violent action or explosive speech or behavior.

Webbing. A process through which teachers create a diagram based on a topic or theme. It is a planning tool for curriculum and includes as many resources as teachers can name.

Whole Language. The area of graphic language development that refers to a particular way in which language, particularly reading and writing, is learned; whole language refers to that movement within primary education that emphasizes an integrated and literary-based approach rather than a phonics, decoding-skills approach.

Word Pictures. Descriptions of children that depict, in words, norms of development; in this text, these are age-level charts that describe common behaviors and characteristics, particularly those that have implications for teaching children (in groups, for curriculum planning, with discipline and guidance).

Zone of Proximal Development. The term in Vygotsky's sociocultural theory that defines which children can learn. Interpersonal and dynamic, the zone refers to the area a child can master (skill, information, etc.) with the assistance of another skilled person; below that, children can learn on their own; above the limit are areas beyond the child's capacity to learn, even with help.

Subject Index

Note: Page numbers in bold type reference non-text material.

Name Index